PARADIGMS OF ARTIFICIAL INTELLIGENCE PROGRAMMING: CASE STUDIES IN COMMON LISP

Paradigms of Artificial Intelligence Programming:

CASE STUDIES IN COMMON LISP

Peter Norvig

An Imprint of Elsevier

MORGAN KAUFMANN PUBLISHERS ◇ SAN FRANCISCO, CALIFORNIA

Sponsoring Editor   *Michael B. Morgan*
Production Manager   *Yonie Overton*
Cover Designer   *Sandra Popovich*
Text Design/Composition   *SuperScript Typography*
Copyeditor   *Barbara Beidler Kendrick*
Proofreaders   *Lynn Meinhardt, Sharilyn Hovind, Gary Morris*
Printer   *Malloy Lithographing*

Morgan Kaufmann Publishers, Inc.
Editorial and Sales Office:
340 Pine Street, Sixth Floor
San Francisco, CA 94104-3205
USA
Telephone   415/392-2665
Facsimile   415/982-2665
Internet   mkp@mkp.com
Web site   http://mkp.com

Library of Congress Cataloging-in-Publication Data

Norvig, Peter.
        Paradigms of artificial intelligence programming : case studies in
    common Lisp / Peter Norvig.
            p.   cm.
        Includes bibliographical references and index.
        ISBN 1-55860-191-0 :
        1. Electronic digital computers–Programming. 2. COMMON LISP
    (Computer program language)   3. Artificial intelligence.   I. Title.
    QA76.6.N687 1991
    006.3–dc20   91-39187
                                                                CIP

To my family...

Preface

paradigm *n* **1** an example or pattern; *esp* an outstandingly clear or typical example.
—Longman's Dictionary of the English Language, 1984

This book is concerned with three related topics: the field of artificial intelligence, or AI; the skill of computer programming; and the programming language Common Lisp. Careful readers of this book can expect to come away with an appreciation of the major questions and techniques of AI, an understanding of some important AI programs, and an ability to read, modify, and create programs using Common Lisp. The examples in this book are designed to be clear examples of good programming style—paradigms of programming. They are also paradigms of AI research—historically significant programs that use widely applicable techniques to solve important problems.

Just as a liberal arts education includes a course in "the great books" of a culture, so this book is, at one level, a course in "the great programs" that define the AI culture.[1]

At another level, this book is a highly technical compendium of the knowledge you will need to progress from being an intermediate Lisp programmer to being an expert. Parts I and II are designed to help the novice get up to speed, but the complete beginner may have a hard time even with this material. Fortunately, there are at least five good texts available for the beginner; see page xiii for my recommendations.

---

[1] This does not imply that the programs chosen are the best of all AI programs—just that they are representative.

All too often, the teaching of computer programming consists of explaining the syntax of the chosen language, showing the student a 10-line program, and then asking the student to write programs. In this book, we take the approach that the best way to learn to write is to read (and conversely, a good way to improve reading skills is to write). After the briefest of introductions to Lisp, we start right off with complex programs and ask the reader to understand and make small modifications to these programs.

The premise of this book is that you can only write something useful and interesting when you both understand what makes good writing and have something interesting to say. This holds for writing programs as well as for writing prose. As Kernighan and Plauger put it on the cover of *Software Tools in Pascal*:

> *Good programming is not learned from generalities, but by seeing how significant programs can be made clean, easy to read, easy to maintain and modify, human-engineered, efficient, and reliable, by the application of common sense and good programming practices. Careful study and imitation of good programs leads to better writing.*

The proud craftsman is often tempted to display only the finished work, without any indication of the false starts and mistakes that are an unfortunate but unavoidable part of the creative process. Unfortunately, this reluctance to unveil the process is a barrier to learning; a student of mathematics who sees a beautiful 10-line proof in a textbook can marvel at its conciseness but does not learn how to construct such a proof. This book attempts to show the complete programming process, "warts and all." Each chapter starts with a simple version of a program, one that works on some examples but fails on others. Each chapter shows how these failures can be analyzed to build increasingly sophisticated versions of the basic program. Thus, the reader can not only appreciate the final result but also see how to learn from mistakes and refine an initially incomplete design. Furthermore, the reader who finds a particular chapter is becoming too difficult can skip to the next chapter, having gained some appreciation of the problem area, and without being overwhelmed by the details.

This book presents a body of knowledge loosely known as "AI programming techniques," but it must be recognized that there are no clear-cut boundaries on this body of knowledge. To be sure, no one can be a good AI programmer without first being a good programmer. Thus, this book presents topics (especially in parts III and V) that are not AI per se, but are essential background for any AI practitioner.

Why Lisp? Why Common Lisp?

Lisp is one of the oldest programming languages still in widespread use today. There have been many versions of Lisp, each sharing basic features but differing in detail. In this book we use the version called Common Lisp, which is the most widely accepted standard. Lisp has been chosen for three reasons.

First, Lisp is the most popular language for AI programming, particularly in the United States. If you're going to learn a language, it might as well be one with a growing literature, rather than a dead tongue.

Second, Lisp makes it easy to capture relevant generalizations in defining new objects. In particular, Lisp makes it easy to define new languages especially targeted to the problem at hand. This is especially handy in AI applications, which often manipulate complex information that is most easily represented in some novel form. Lisp is one of the few languages that allows full flexibility in defining and manipulating programs as well as data. All programming languages, by definition, provide a means of defining programs, but many other languages limit the ways in which a program can be used, or limit the range of programs that can be defined, or require the programmer to explicitly state irrelevant details.

Third, Lisp makes it very easy to develop a working program fast. Lisp programs are concise and are uncluttered by low-level detail. Common Lisp offers an unusually large number of useful predefined objects, including over 700 functions. The programming environment (such as debugging tools, incremental compilers, integrated editors, and interfaces to window systems) that surround Lisp systems are usually very good. And the dynamic, interactive nature of Lisp makes it easy to experiment and change a program while it is being developed.

It must be mentioned that in Europe and Japan, Prolog has been as popular as Lisp for AI work. Prolog shares most of Lisp's advantages in terms of flexibility and conciseness. Recently, Lisp has gained popularity worldwide, and Prolog is becoming more well known in the United States. As a result, the average AI worker today is likely to be bilingual. This book presents the key ideas behind Prolog in chapters 11 and 12, and uses these ideas in subsequent chapters, particularly 20 and 21.

The dialect of Lisp known as Scheme is also gaining in popularity, but primarily for teaching and experimenting with programming language design and techniques, and not so much for writing large AI programs. Scheme is presented in chapters 22 and 23. Other dialects of Lisp such as Franz Lisp, MacLisp, InterLisp, ZetaLisp, and Standard Lisp are now considered obsolete. The only new dialect of Lisp to be proposed recently is EuLisp, the European Lisp. A few dialects of Lisp live on as embedded extension languages. For example, the Gnu Emacs text editor uses elisp, and the AutoCad computer-aided design package uses AutoLisp, a derivative of Xlisp. In the future, it is likely that Scheme will become a popular extension language, since it is small but powerful and has an officially sanctioned standard definition.

There is a myth that Lisp (and Prolog) are "special-purpose" languages, while languages like Pascal and C are "general purpose." Actually, just the reverse is true. Pascal and C are special-purpose languages for manipulating the registers and memory of a von Neumann-style computer. The majority of their syntax is devoted to arithmetic and Boolean expressions, and while they provide some facilities for forming data structures, they have poor mechanisms for procedural abstraction or control abstraction. In addition, they are designed for the state-oriented style of programming: computing a result by changing the value of variables through assignment statements.

Lisp, on the other hand, has no special syntax for arithmetic. Addition and multiplication are no more or less basic than list operations like appending, or string operations like converting to upper case. But Lisp provides all you will need for programming in general: defining data structures, functions, and the means for combining them.

The assignment-dominated, state-oriented style of programming is possible in Lisp, but in addition object-oriented, rule-based, and functional styles are all supported within Lisp. This flexibility derives from two key features of Lisp: First, Lisp has a powerful *macro* facility, which can be used to extend the basic language. When new styles of programming were invented, other languages died out; Lisp simply incorporated the new styles by defining some new macros. The macro facility is possible because Lisp programs are composed of a simple data structure: the list. In the early days, when Lisp was interpreted, most manipulation of programs was done through this data structure. Nowadays, Lisp is more often compiled than interpreted, and programmers rely more on Lisp's second great flexible feature: the *function*. Of course, other languages have functions, but Lisp is rare in allowing the creation of new functions while a program is running.

Lisp's flexibility allows it to adapt as programming styles change, but more importantly, Lisp can adapt to your particular programming problem. In other languages you fit your problem to the language; with Lisp you extend the language to fit your problem.

Because of its flexibility, Lisp has been succesful as a high-level language for rapid prototyping in areas such as AI, graphics, and user interfaces. Lisp has also been the dominant language for exploratory programming, where the problems are so complex that no clear solution is available at the start of the project. Much of AI falls under this heading.

The size of Common Lisp can be either an advantage or a disadvantage, depending on your outlook. In David Touretzky's (1989) fine book for beginning programmers, the emphasis is on simplicity. He chooses to write some programs slightly less concisely, rather than introduce an esoteric new feature (he cites pushnew as an example). That approach is entirely appropriate for beginners, but this book goes well past the level of beginner. This means exposing the reader to new features of the language whenever they are appropriate. Most of the time, new features are described as they are introduced, but sometimes explaining the details of a low-level function would detract from the explanation of the workings of a program. In accepting the privilege of being treated as an "adult," the reader also accepts a responsibility—to look up unfamiliar terms in an appropriate reference source.

Outline of the Book

This book is organized into five parts.

Part I introduces the Common Lisp programming language.

Chapter 1 gives a quick introduction by way of small examples that demonstrate the novel features of Lisp. It can be safely skipped or skimmed by the experienced programmer.

Chapter 2 is a more extended example showing how the Lisp primitives can be put together to form a program. It should be studied carefully by the novice, and even the experienced programmer will want to look through it to get a feel for my programming style.

Chapter 3 provides an overview of the Lisp primitives. It can be skimmed on first reading and used as a reference whenever an unfamiliar function is mentioned in the text.

Part I has been kept intentionally brief, so that there is more room for presenting actual AI programs. Unfortunately, that means that another text or reference book (or online help) may be needed to clarify some of the more esoteric features of the language. My recommendations for texts are on page xiii.

The reader may also want to refer to chapter 25, which offers some debugging and troubleshooting hints.

Part II covers four early AI programs that all use rule-based pattern-matching techniques. By starting with relatively simple versions of the programs and then improving them and moving on to more complex programs, the reader is able to gradually acquire increasingly advanced programming skills.

Chapter 4 presents a reconstruction of GPS, the General Problem Solver. The implementation follows the STRIPS approach.

Chapter 5 describes ELIZA, a program that mimics human dialogue. This is followed by a chapter that generalizes some of the techniques used in GPS and ELIZA and makes them available as tools for use in subsequent programs.

Chapter 7 covers STUDENT, a program that solves high-school-level algebra word problems.

Chapter 8 develops a small subset of the MACSYMA program for doing symbolic algebra, including differential and integral calculus. It may be skipped by those who shy away from heavy mathematics.

Part III detours from AI for a moment to present some general tools for more efficient programming. The reader who masters the material in this part can be considered an advanced Lisp programmer.

Chapter 9 is a detailed study of efficiency techniques, concentrating on caching, indexing, compilation, and delaying computation. Chapter 10 covers lower-level efficiency issues such as using declarations, avoiding garbage generation, and choosing the right data structure.

Chapter 11 presents the Prolog language. The aim is two-fold: to show how to write an interpreter for another language, and to introduce the important features of Prolog, so that they can be used where appropriate. Chapter 12 shows how a compiler for Prolog can be 20 to 200 times faster than the interpreter.

Chapter 13 introduces object-oriented programming in general, then explores the Common Lisp Object System (CLOS).

Chapter 14 discusses the advantages and limitations of both logic-oriented and object-oriented programming, and develops a knowledge representation formalism using all the techniques of part III.

Part IV covers some advanced AI programs.

Chapter 15 uses the techniques of part III to come up with a much more efficient implementation of MACSYMA. It uses the idea of a canonical form, and replaces the very general rewrite rule approach with a series of more specific functions.

Chapter 16 covers the EMYCIN expert system shell, a backward chaining rule-based system based on certainty factors. The MYCIN medical expert system is also covered briefly.

Chapter 17 covers the Waltz line-labeling algorithm for polyhedra (using Huffman-Clowes labels). Different approaches to constraint propagation and backtracking are discussed.

Chapter 18 presents a program that plays an excellent game of Othello. The technique used, alpha-beta searching, is appropriate to a wide variety of two-person games.

Chapter 19 is an introduction to natural language processing. It covers context-free grammar, top-down and bottom-up parsing, chart parsing, and some semantic interpretation and preferences.

Chapter 20 extends the linguistic coverage of the previous chapter and introduces logic grammars, using the Prolog compiler developed in chapter 11.

Chapter 21 is a fairly comprehensive grammar of English using the logic grammar formalism. The problems of going from a simple idea to a realistic, comprehensive program are discussed.

Part V includes material that is peripheral to AI but important for any serious Lisp programmer.

Chapter 22 presents the Scheme dialect of Lisp. A simple Scheme interpreter is developed, then a properly tail-recursive interpreter, then an interpreter that explicitly manipulates continuations and supports `call/cc`. Chapter 23 presents a Scheme compiler.

Chapter 24 presents the features that are unique to American National Standards Institute (ANSI) Common Lisp. This includes the `loop` macro, as well as error handling, pretty printing, series and sequences, and the package facility.

Chapter 25 is a guide to troubleshooting and debugging Lisp programs.

The bibliography lists over 200 sources, and there is a comprehensive index. In addition, the appendix provides a directory of publicly available Lisp programs.

How to Use This Book

The intended audience for this book is broad: anyone who wants to become an advanced Lisp programmer, and anyone who wants to be an advanced AI practitioner. There are several recommended paths through the book:

- *In an Introductory AI Course:* Concentrate on parts I and II, and at least one example from part IV.

- *In an Advanced AI Programming Course:* Concentrate on parts I, II and IV, skipping chapters that are of less interest and adding as much of part III as time permits.

- *In an Advanced Programming Languages Course:* Concentrate on parts I and V, with selections from part III. Cover chapters 11 and 13 if similar material is not presented with another text.

- *For the Professional Lisp Programmer:* Read as much of the book as possible, and refer back to it often. Part III and chapter 25 are particularly important.

Supplementary Texts and Reference Books

The definitive reference source is Steele's *Common Lisp the Language.* From 1984 to 1990, this unambiguously defined the language Common Lisp. However, in 1990 the picture became more complicated by the publication of *Common Lisp the Language*, 2d edition. This book, also by Steele, contains the recommendations of ANSI subcommittee X3J13, whose charter is to define a standard for Lisp. These recommendations include many minor changes and clarifications, as well as brand new material on object-oriented programming, error condition handling, and the loop macro. The new material doubles the size of the book from 465 to 1029 pages.

Until the ANSI recommendations are formally accepted, Common Lisp users are in the unfortunate situation of having two distinct and incompatible standards: "original" Common Lisp and ANSI Common Lisp. Most of the code in this book is compliant with both standards. The most significant use of an ANSI function is the `loop` macro. The ANSI `map-into`, `complement`, and `reduce` functions are also used, although rarely. Definitions for all these functions are included, so even those using an "original" Common Lisp system can still run all the code in the book.

While *Common Lisp the Language* is the definitive standard, it is sometimes terse and can be difficult for a beginner. *Common Lisp: the Reference*, published by Franz Inc., offers complete coverage of the language with many helpful examples. *Common LISPcraft*, by Robert Wilensky, and *Artificial Intelligence Programming*, by Charniak et al., also include brief summaries of the Common Lisp functions. They are not as comprehensive, but that can be a blessing, because it can lead the reader more directly to the functions that are important (at least in the eyes of the author).

It is a good idea to read this book with a computer at hand, to try out the examples and experiment with examples of your own. A computer is also handy because Lisp is self-documenting, through the functions `apropos`, `describe`, and `documentation`. Many implementations also provide more extensive documentation through some kind of 'help' command or menu.

The five introductory Lisp textbooks I recommend are listed below. The first is more elementary than the others.

- *Common Lisp: A Gentle Introduction to Symbolic Computation* by David Touretzky. Most appropriate for beginners, including those who are not computer scientists.

- *A Programmer's Guide to Common Lisp* by Deborah G. Tatar. Appropriate for those with experience in another programming language, but none in Lisp.

- *Common LISPcraft* by Robert Wilensky. More comprehensive and faster paced, but still useful as an introduction as well as a reference.

- *Common Lisp* by Wade L. Hennessey. Somewhat hit-and-miss in terms of the topics it covers, but with an enlightened discussion of implementation and efficiency issues that do not appear in the other texts.

- *LISP* (3d edition) by Patrick H. Winston and Bertold Horn. Covers the most ground in terms of programming advice, but not as comprehensive as a reference. May be difficult for beginners. Includes some AI examples.

While it may be distracting for the beginner to be continually looking at some reference source, the alternative—to have this book explain every new function in complete detail as it is introduced—would be even more distracting. It would interrupt the description of the AI programs, which is what this book is all about.

There are a few texts that show how to write AI programs and tools, but none that go into the depth of this book. Nevertheless, the expert AI programmer will want to be familiar with all the following texts, listed in rough order of increasing sophistication:

- *LISP* (3d edition). (See above.)

- *Programming Paradigms in Lisp* by Rajeev Sangal. Presents the different styles of programming that Lisp accommodates, illustrating them with some useful AI tools.

- *Programming for Artificial Intelligence* by Wolfgang Kreutzer and Bruce McKenzie. Covers some of the basics of rule-based and pattern-matching systems well, but covers Lisp, Prolog, and Smalltalk, and thus has no time left for details in any of the languages.

- *Artificial Intelligence Programming* (2d edition) by Eugene Charniak, Christopher Riesbeck, Drew McDermott, and James Meehan. Contains 150 pages of Lisp overview, followed by an advanced discussion of AI tools, but no actual AI programs.

- *AI in Practice: Examples in Pop-11* by Allan Ramsey and Rosalind Barrett. Advanced, high-quality implementations of five AI programs, unfortunately using a language that has not gained popularity.

The current text combines the virtues of the last two entries: it presents both actual AI programs and the tools necessary to build them. Furthermore, the presentation is in an incremental fashion, with simple versions presented first for clarity, followed by more sophisticated versions for completeness.

A Note on Exercises

Sample exercises are provided throughout. Readers can test their level of understanding by faithfully doing the exercises. The exercises are graded on the scale [s], [m], [h], [d], which can be interpreted either as a level of difficulty or as an expected time it will take to do the exercise:

Code	Difficulty	Time to Do
[s]	Simple	Seconds
[m]	Medium	Minutes
[h]	Hard	Hours
[d]	Difficult	Days

The time to do the exercise is measured from the point that the concepts have been well understood. If the reader is unclear on the underlying concepts, it might take hours of review to understand a [m] problem. Answers to the exercises can be found in a separate section at the end of each chapter.

Acknowledgments

A great many people contributed to this book. First of all I would like to thank my students at USC and Berkeley, as well as James Martin's students at Colorado and Michael Pazzani's students at Irvine, who course-tested earlier versions of this book. Useful suggestions, corrections, and additions were made by:

Nina Amenta (Berkeley), Ray S. Babcock and John Paxton (Montana State), Bryan A. Bentz (BBN), Mary P. Boelk (Johnson Controls), Michael Braverman (Berkeley), R. Chandrasekar and M. Sasikumar (National Centre for Software Technology, Bombay), Mike Clancy (Berkeley), Michael Covington (Georgia), Bruce D'Ambrosio (Oregon State), Piew Datta (Irvine), Shawn Dettrey (USC), J. A. Durieux (AI Engineering BV, Amsterdam), Joseph Faletti (ETS), Paul Fuqua (Texas Instruments), Robert Goldman (Tulane), Marty Hall (Johns Hopkins), Marti Hearst (Berkeley), Jim Hendler (Maryland), Phil Laird (NASA), Raymond Lang (Tulane), David D. Loeffler (MCC), George Luger (New Mexico), Rob MacLachlan (CMU), Barry Margolin (Thinking Machines), James Mayfield (UMBC), Sanjay Manchandi (Arizona), Robert McCartney (Connecticut), James Meehan (DEC), Andrew L. Ressler, Robert S. Rist (University of Technology, Sydney), Paul Snively (Apple), Peter Van Roy (Berkeley), David Gumby Wallace (Cygnus), and Jeff Wu (Colorado).

Sam Dooley and Eric Wefald both wrote Othello-playing programs without which I would not have written chapter 18. Eric also showed me Aristotle's quotes on means-ends analysis. Tragically, Eric died in August 1989. He is sorely missed by his friends and colleagues. Richard Fateman made suggestions for chapter 8, convinced me to write chapter 15, and, with help from Peter Klier, wrote a substantial program from which I adapted some code for that chapter. Charley Cox (Franz Inc.), Jamie Zawinski (Lucid Inc.), and Paul Fuqua (Texas Instruments) explained the inner workings of their respective companies' compilers. Mike Harrison, Paul Hilfinger, Marc Luria, Ethan Munson, and Stephan Slade helped with LaTeX. Narciso Jarimillo tested all the code and separated it into the files that are available to the reader (see page 897).

During the writing of this book I was supported by a grant from the Defense Advanced Research Projects Agency (DoD), Arpa Order No. 4871, monitored by Space and Naval Warfare Systems Command under Contract N00039-84-C-0089. Special thanks to DARPA and to Robert Wilensky and the rest of my colleagues and students at Berkeley for providing a stimulating environment for research, programming, and writing.

Finally, thanks to Mike Morgan and Yonie Overton for overseeing the production of the book and encouraging me to finish on time.

Contents

PART I

INTRODUCTION TO COMMON LISP

CHAPTER 1

Introduction to Lisp

*You think you know when you learn, are more sure
when you can write, even more when you can teach,
but certain when you can program.*

—Alan Perlis
Yale University computer scientist

This chapter is for people with little or no experience in Lisp. Readers who feel confident in their Lisp programming ability can quickly skim the chapter or skip it entirely. This chapter necessarily moves quickly, so those with little programming experience, or any reader who finds this chapter tough going, should seek out a supplementary introductory text. My recommendations are in the preface.

Computers allow one to carry out computations. A word processing program deals with words while a calculator deals with numbers, but the principles are the same. In both cases, you provide the input (words or numbers) and specify the operations (such as deleting a word or adding two numbers) to yield a result (a completed document or calculation).

We will refer to anything that can be represented in the memory of a computer as a *computational object*, or just an *object*. So, words, paragraphs, and numbers can be objects. And because the operations (deleting and adding) must be represented somewhere in the computer's memory, they are objects, too.

Normally, the distinction between a computer "user" and a computer "programmer" is that the user provides new input, or data (words or numbers), while the programmer defines new *operations*, or programs, as well as new *types* of data. Every new object, be it datum or operation, must be defined in terms of previously defined objects. The bad news is that it can be quite tedious to get these definitions right. The good news is that each new object can in turn be used in the definition of future objects. Thus, even complex programs can be built out of smaller, simpler objects. This book covers a number of typical AI problems, showing how each problem can be broken down into manageable pieces, and also how each piece can be described in the programming language Common Lisp. Ideally, readers will learn enough through studying these examples to attack new AI problems with style, grace, and success.

Let's consider a simple example of a computation: finding the sum of two numbers, let's say 2 and 2. If we had a calculator handy, we would type "2 + 2 =" and see the answer displayed. On a calculator using reverse Polish notation, we would have to type " 2 2 +" to see the same answer. In Lisp, as with the calculator, the user carries out an interactive dialog with the computer by typing in an expression and seeing the computer print the value of that expression. This interactive mode is different from many other programming languages that only offer a batch mode, wherein an entire program is compiled and run before any output can be seen.

We start up a pocket calculator by flipping the on/off switch. The Lisp program must also be started, but the details vary from one computer to another, so I can't explain how your Lisp will work. Assuming we have managed to start up Lisp, we are likely to see a *prompt* of some kind. On my computer, Lisp types ">" to indicate it is ready to accept the next computation. So we are faced with a screen that looks like this:

```
>
```

We may now type in our computation and see the result displayed. It turns out that the Lisp convention for arithemtic expressions is slightly different: a computation consists of a parenthesized list with the operation name first, followed by any number of operands, or arguments. This is called *prefix notation*.

```
> (+ 2 2)
4
>
```

We see that Lisp has printed the answer, 4, and then another prompt, >, to indicate it is ready for the next computation. Throughout this book, all Lisp expressions will be displayed in typewriter font. Text on the same line as the ">" prompt is input typed by the user, and text following it is output printed by the computer. Usually, input that is typed by the programmer will be in lowercase letters, while output that is printed back by the computer will be in UPPERCASE letters. Of course, with symbols like + and 4 there is no difference.

To save space on the page, the output will sometimes be shown on the same line as the input, separated by an arrow ($\Rightarrow$), which can be read as "evaluates to," and can also be thought of as standing for the return or enter key that the user presses to complete the input:

```
> (+ 2 2) ⇒ 4
```

One advantage of parenthesized prefix notation is that the parentheses clearly mark the beginning and end of an expression. If we want, we can give + more than two arguments, and it will still add them all:

```
> (+ 1 2 3 4 5 6 7 8 9 10) ⇒ 55
```

This time we try $(9000 + 900 + 90 + 9) - (5000 + 500 + 50 + 5)$:

```
> (- (+ 9000 900 90 9) (+ 5000 500 50 5)) ⇒ 4444
```

This example shows that expressions can be nested. The arguments to the - function are parenthesized lists, while the arguments to each + are atoms. The Lisp notation may look unusual compared to standard mathematical notation, but there are advantages to this notation; since Lisp expressions can consist of a function followed by any number of arguments, we don't have to keep repeating the "+." More important than the notation is the rule for evaluation. In Lisp, lists are evaluated by first evaluating all the arguments, then applying the function to the arguments, thereby computing the result. This rule is much simpler than the rule for evaluating normal mathematical expressions, where there are many conventions to remember, such as doing multiplications and divisions before sums and differences. We will see below that the actual Lisp evaluation rule is a little more complicated, but not much.

Sometimes programmers who are familiar with other languages have preconceptions that make it difficult for them to learn Lisp. For them, three points are worth stressing here. First, many other languages make a distinction between statements and expressions. An expression, like 2 + 2, has a value, but a statement, like x = 2 + 2, does not. Statements have effects, but they do not return values. In Lisp, there is no such distinction: every expression returns a value. It is true that some expressions have effects, but even those expressions also return values.

Second, the lexical rules for Lisp are much simpler than the rules for other languages. In particular, there are fewer punctuation characters: only parentheses, quote marks (single, double, and backward), spaces, and the comma serve to separate symbols from each other. Thus, while the statement y=a*x+3 is analyzed as seven separate tokens in other languages, in Lisp it would be treated as a single symbol. To get a list of tokens, we would have to insert spaces: (y = a * x + 3).[1]

Third, while many languages use semicolons to delimit statements, Lisp has no need of semicolons, since expressions are delimited by parentheses. Lisp chooses to use semicolons for another purpose—to mark the beginning of a comment, which lasts until the end of the line:

```
> (+ 2 2) ; this is a comment
4
```

1.1   Symbolic Computation

All we've done so far is manipulate numbers in the same way a simple pocket calculator would. Lisp is more useful than a calculator for two main reasons. First, it allows us to manipulate objects other than numbers, and second, it allows us to define new objects that might be useful in subsequent computations. We will examine these two important properties in turn.

Besides numbers, Lisp can represent characters (letters), strings of characters, and arbitrary symbols, where we are free to interpret these symbols as referring to things outside the world of mathematics. Lisp can also build nonatomic objects by combining several objects into a list. This capability is fundamental and well supported in the language; in fact, the name Lisp is short for LISt Processing.

Here's an example of a computation on lists:

```
> (append '(Pat Kim) '(Robin Sandy)) ⇒ (PAT KIM ROBIN SANDY)
```

This expression appends together two lists of names. The rule for evaluating this expression is the same as the rule for numeric calculations: apply the function (in this case append) to the value of the arguments.

The unusual part is the quote mark ('), which serves to block the evaluation of the following expression, returning it literally. If we just had the expression (Pat Kim), it would be evaluated by considering Pat as a function and applying it to the value of the expression Kim. This is not what we had in mind. The quote mark instructs Lisp to treat the list as a piece of data rather than as a function call:

```
> '(Pat Kim) ⇒ (PAT KIM)
```

In other computer languages (and in English), quotes usually come in pairs: one to mark the beginning, and one to mark the end. In Lisp, a single quote is used to mark

---

[1]This list of symbols is not a legal Lisp assignment statement, but it is a Lisp data object.

the beginning of an expression. Since we always know how long a single expression is—either to the end of an atom or to the matching parenthesis of a list—we don't need an explicit punctuation mark to tell us where the expression ends. Quotes can be used on lists, as in '(Pat Kim), on symbols as in 'Robin, and in fact on anything else. Here are some examples:

```
> 'John ⇒ JOHN

> '(John Q Public) ⇒ (JOHN Q PUBLIC)

> '2 ⇒ 2

> 2 ⇒ 2

> '(+ 2 2) ⇒ (+ 2 2)

> (+ 2 2) ⇒ 4

> John ⇒ Error: JOHN is not a bound variable

> (John Q Public) ⇒ Error: JOHN is not a function
```

Note that '2 evaluates to 2 because it is a quoted expression, and 2 evaluates to 2 because numbers evaluate to themselves. Same result, different reason. In contrast, 'John evaluates to John because it is a quoted expression, but evaluating John leads to an error, because evaluating a symbol means getting the value of the symbol, and no value has been assigned to John.

Symbolic computations can be nested and even mixed with numeric computations. The following expression builds a list of names in a slightly different way than we saw before, using the built-in function list. We then see how to find the number of elements in the list, using the built-in function length:

```
> (append '(Pat Kim) (list '(John Q Public) 'Sandy))
(PAT KIM (JOHN Q PUBLIC) SANDY)

> (length (append '(Pat Kim) (list '(John Q Public) 'Sandy)))
4
```

There are four important points to make about symbols:

- First, it is important to remember that Lisp does not attach any external significance to the objects it manipulates. For example, we naturally think of (Robin Sandy) as a list of two first names, and (John Q Public) as a list of one person's first name, middle initial, and last name. Lisp has no such preconceptions. To Lisp, both Robin and xyzzy are perfectly good symbols.

- Second, to do the computations above, we had to know that append, length, and + are defined functions in Common Lisp. Learning a language involves remembering vocabulary items (or knowing where to look them up) as well as learning the basic rules for forming expressions and determining what they mean. Common Lisp provides over 700 built-in functions. At some point the reader should flip through a reference text to see what's there, but most of the important functions are presented in part I of this book.

- Third, note that symbols in Common Lisp are not case sensitive. By that I mean that the inputs John, john, and jOhN all refer to the same symbol, which is normally printed as JOHN.[2]

- Fourth, note that a wide variety of characters are allowed in symbols: numbers, letters, and other punctuation marks like '+' or '!'. The exact rules for what constitutes a symbol are a little complicated, but the normal convention is to use symbols consisting mostly of letters, with words separated by a dash (-), and perhaps with a number at the end. Some programmers are more liberal in naming variables, and include characters like '?!$/<=>'. For example, a function to convert dollars to yen might be named with the symbol $-to-yen or $->yen in Lisp, while one would use something like DollarsToYen, dollars_to_yen or dol2yen in Pascal or C. There are a few exceptions to these naming conventions, which will be dealt with as they come up.

1.2 Variables

We have seen some of the basics of symbolic computation. Now we move on to perhaps the most important characteristic of a programming language: the ability to define new objects in terms of others, and to name these objects for future use. Here symbols again play an important role—they are used to name variables. A variable can take on a value, which can be any Lisp object. One way to give a value to a variable is with setf:

```
> (setf p '(John Q Public)) ⇒ (JOHN Q PUBLIC)
> p ⇒ (JOHN Q PUBLIC)
> (setf x 10) ⇒ 10
> (+ x x) ⇒ 20
> (+ x (length p)) ⇒ 13
```

After assigning the value (John Q Public) to the variable named p, we can refer to the value with the name p. Similarly, after assigning a value to the variable named x, we can refer to both x and p.

---

[2]The variable *print-case* controls how symbols will be printed. By default, the value of this variable is :upcase, but it can be changed to :downcase or :capitalize.

Symbols are also used to name functions in Common Lisp. Every symbol can be used as the name of a variable or a function, or both, although it is rare (and potentially confusing) to have symbols name both. For example, append and length are symbols that name functions but have no values as variables, and pi does not name a function but is a variable whose value is 3.1415926535897936 (or thereabout).

1.3   Special Forms

The careful reader will note that setf violates the evaluation rule. We said earlier that functions like +, - and append work by first evaluating all their arguments and then applying the function to the result. But setf doesn't follow that rule, because setf is not a function at all. Rather, it is part of the basic syntax of Lisp. Besides the syntax of atoms and function calls, Lisp has a small number of syntactic expressions. They are known as *special forms*. They serve the same purpose as statements in other programming languages, and indeed have some of the same syntactic markers, such as if and loop. There are two main differences between Lisp's syntax and other languages. First, Lisp's syntactic forms are always lists in which the first element is one of a small number of privileged symbols. setf is one of these symbols, so (setf x 10) is a special form. Second, special forms are expressions that return a value. This is in contrast to statements in most languages, which have an effect but do not return a value.

In evaluating an to expression like (setf x (+ 1 2)), we set the variable named by the symbol x to the value of (+ 1 2), which is 3. If setf were a normal function, we would evaluate both the symbol x and the expression (+ 1 2) and do something with these two values, which is not what we want at all. setf is called a special form because it does something special: if it did not exist, it would be impossible to write a function that assigns a value to a variable. The philosophy of Lisp is to provide a small number of special forms to do the things that could not otherwise be done, and then to expect the user to write everthing else as functions.

The term *special form* is used confusingly to refer both to symbols like setf and expressions that start with them, like (setf x 3). In the book *Common LISPcraft*, Wilensky resolves the ambiguity by calling setf a *special function,* and reserving the term *special form* for (setf x 3). This terminology implies that setf is just another function, but a special one in that its first argument is not evaluated. Such a view made sense in the days when Lisp was primarily an interpreted language. The modern view is that setf should not be considered some kind of abnormal function but rather a marker of special syntax that will be handled specially by the compiler. Thus, the special form (setf x (+ 2 1)) should be considered the equivalent of x = 2 + 1 in C. When there is risk of confusion, we will call setf a *special form operator* and (setf x 3) a *special form expression*.

It turns out that the quote mark is just an abbreviation for another special form. The expression 'x is equivalent to (quote x), a special form expression that evaluates to x. The special form operators used in this chapter are:

defun	define function
defparameter	define special variable
setf	set variable or field to new value
let	bind local variable(s)
case	choose one of several alternatives
if	do one thing or another, depending on a test
function (#')	refer to a function
quote (')	introduce constant data

1.4   Lists

So far we have seen two functions that operate on lists: append and length. Since lists are important, let's look at some more list processing functions:

```
> p ⇒ (JOHN Q PUBLIC)

> (first p) ⇒ JOHN

> (rest p) ⇒ (Q PUBLIC)

> (second p) ⇒ Q

> (third p) ⇒ PUBLIC

> (fourth p) ⇒ NIL

> (length p) ⇒ 3
```

The functions first, second, third, and fourth are aptly named: first returns the first element of a list, second gives you the second element, and so on. The function rest is not as obvious; its name stands for "the rest of the list after the first element." The symbol nil and the form () are completely synonymous; they are both representations of the empty list. nil is also used to denote the "false" value in Lisp. Thus, (fourth p) is nil because there is no fourth element of p. Note that lists need not be composed only of atoms, but can contain sublists as elements:

```
> (setf x '((1st element) 2 (element 3) ((4)) 5))
((1ST ELEMENT) 2 (ELEMENT 3) ((4)) 5)

> (length x) ⇒ 5

> (first x) ⇒ (1ST ELEMENT)
```

```
> (second x)  ⇒ 2

> (third x)  ⇒ (ELEMENT 3)

> (fourth x)  ⇒ ((4))

> (first (fourth x))  ⇒ (4)

> (first (first (fourth x)))  ⇒ 4

> (fifth x)  ⇒ 5

> (first x)  ⇒ (1ST ELEMENT)

> (second (first x))  ⇒ ELEMENT
```

So far we have seen how to access parts of lists. It is also possible to build up new lists, as these examples show:

```
> p  ⇒ (JOHN Q PUBLIC)

> (cons 'Mr p)  ⇒ (MR JOHN Q PUBLIC)

> (cons (first p) (rest p))  ⇒ (JOHN Q PUBLIC)

> (setf town (list 'Anytown 'USA))  ⇒ (ANYTOWN USA)

> (list p 'of town 'may 'have 'already 'won!)  ⇒
((JOHN Q PUBLIC) OF (ANYTOWN USA) MAY HAVE ALREADY WON!)

> (append p '(of) town '(may have already won!))  ⇒
(JOHN Q PUBLIC OF ANYTOWN USA MAY HAVE ALREADY WON!)

> p  ⇒ (JOHN Q PUBLIC)
```

The function cons stands for "construct." It takes as arguments an element and a list,[3] and constructs a new list whose first is the element and whose rest is the original list. list takes any number of elements as arguments and returns a new list containing those elements in order. We've already seen append, which is similar to list; it takes as arguments any number of lists and appends them all together, forming one big list. Thus, the arguments to append must be lists, while the arguments to list may be lists or atoms. It is important to note that these functions create new lists; they don't modify old ones. When we say (append p q), the effect is to create a brand new list that starts with the same elements that were in p. p itself remains unchanged.

Now let's move away from abstract functions on lists, and consider a simple problem: given a person's name in the form of a list, how might we extract the family name? For (JOHN Q PUBLIC) we could just use the function third, but that wouldn't

---

[3]Later we will see what happens when the second argument is not a list.

work for someone with no middle name. There is a function called last in Common Lisp; perhaps that would work. We can experiment:

```
> (last p) ⇒ (PUBLIC)

> (first (last p)) ⇒ PUBLIC
```

It turns out that last perversely returns a list of the last element, rather than the last element itself.[4] Thus we need to combine first and last to pick out the actual last element. We would like to be able to save the work we've done, and give it a proper description, like last-name. We could use setf to save the last name of p, but that wouldn't help determine any other last name. Instead we want to define a new function that computes the last name of *any* name that is represented as a list. The next section does just that.

1.5 Defining New Functions

The special form defun stands for "define function." It is used here to define a new function called last-name:

```
(defun last-name (name)
  "Select the last name from a name represented as a list."
  (first (last name)))
```

We give our new function the name last-name. It has a *parameter list* consisting of a single parameter: (name). This means that the function takes one argument, which we will refer to as name. It also has a *documentation string* that states what the function does. This is not used in any computation, but documentation strings are crucial tools for debugging and understanding large systems. The body of the definition is (first (last name)), which is what we used before to pick out the last name of p. The difference is that here we want to pick out the last name of any name, not just of the particular name p.

   In general, a function definition takes the following form (where the documentation string is optional, and all other parts are required):

---

[4]In ANSI Common Lisp, last is defined to return a list of the last n elements, where n defaults to 1. Thus (last p) ≡ (last p 1) = (PUBLIC), and (last p 2) = (Q PUBLIC). This may make the definition of last seem less perverse.

```
(defun function-name (parameter...)
  "documentation string"
  function-body...)
```

The function name must be a symbol, the parameters are usually symbols (with some complications to be explained later), and the function body consists of one or more expressions that are evaluated when the function is called. The last expression is returned as the value of the function call.

Once we have defined last-name, we can use it just like any other Lisp function:

```
> (last-name p) ⇒ PUBLIC

> (last-name '(Rear Admiral Grace Murray Hopper)) ⇒ HOPPER

> (last-name '(Rex Morgan MD)) ⇒ MD

> (last-name '(Spot)) ⇒ SPOT

> (last-name '(Aristotle)) ⇒ ARISTOTLE
```

The last three examples point out an inherent limitation of the programming enterprise. When we say (defun last-name...) we are not really defining what it means for a person to have a last name; we are just defining an operation on a representation of names in terms of lists. Our intuitions—that MD is a title, Spot is the first name of a dog, and Aristotle lived before the concept of last name was invented—are not represented in this operation. However, we could always change the definition of last-name to incorporate these problematic cases.

We can also define the function first-name. Even though the definition is trivial (it is the same as the function first), it is still good practice to define first-name explicitly. Then we can use the function first-name when we are dealing with names, and first when we are dealing with arbitrary lists. The computer will perform the same operation in each case, but we as programmers (and readers of programs) will be less confused. Another advanatge of defining specific functions like first-name is that if we decide to change the representation of names we will only have to change the definition of first-name. This is a much easier task than hunting through a large program and changing the uses of first that refer to names, while leaving other uses alone.

```
(defun first-name (name)
  "Select the first name from a name represented as a list."
  (first name))

> p ⇒ (JOHN Q PUBLIC)

> (first-name p) ⇒ JOHN

> (first-name '(Wilma Flintstone)) ⇒ WILMA
```

```
> (setf names '((John Q Public) (Malcolm X)
                (Admiral Grace Murray Hopper)(Spot)
                (Aristotle) (A A Milne) (Z Z Top)
                (Sir Larry Olivier) (Miss Scarlet))) ⇒
((JOHN Q PUBLIC) (MALCOLM X) (ADMIRAL GRACE MURRAY HOPPER)
 (SPOT) (ARISTOTLE) (A A MILNE) (Z Z TOP) (SIR LARRY OLIVIER)
 (MISS SCARLET))

> (first-name (first names)) ⇒ JOHN
```

In the last expression we used the function first to pick out the first element in a list of names, and then the function first-name to pick out the first name of that element. We could also have said (first (first names)) or even (first (first-name names)) and still have gotten JOHN, but we would not be accurately representing what is being considered a name and what is being considered a list of names.

1.6   Using Functions

One good thing about defining a list of names, as we did above, is that it makes it easier to test our functions. Consider the following expression, which can be used to test the last-name function:

```
> (mapcar #'last-name names)
(PUBLIC X HOPPER SPOT ARISTOTLE MILNE TOP OLIVIER SCARLET)
```

The funny #' notation maps from the name of a function to the function itself. This is analogous to 'x notation. The built-in function mapcar is passed two arguments, a function and a list. It returns a list built by calling the function on every element of the input list. In other words, the mapcar call above is equivalent to:

```
(list (last-name (first names))
      (last-name (second names))
      (last-name (third names))
      ...)
```

mapcar's name comes from the fact that it "maps" the function across each of the arguments. The car part of the name refers to the Lisp function car, an old name for first. cdr is the old name for rest. The names stand for "contents of the address register" and "contents of the decrement register," the instructions that were used in the first implementation of Lisp on the IBM 704. I'm sure you'll agree that first and rest are much better names, and they will be used instead of car and cdr whenever we are talking about lists. However, we will continue to use car and cdr on occasion when we are considering a pair of values that are not considered as a list. Beware that some programmers still use car and cdr for lists as well.

Here are some more examples of mapcar:

```
> (mapcar #'- '(1 2 3 4)) ⇒ (-1 -2 -3 -4)
> (mapcar #'+ '(1 2 3 4) '(10 20 30 40)) ⇒ (11 22 33 44)
```

This last example shows that mapcar can be passed three arguments, in which case the first argument should be a binary function, which will be applied to corresponding elements of the other two lists. In general, mapcar expects an n-ary function as its first argument, followed by n lists. It first applies the function to the argument list obtained by collecting the first element of each list. Then it applies the function to the second element of each list, and so on, until one of the lists is exhausted. It returns a list of all the function values it has computed.

Now that we understand mapcar, let's use it to test the first-name function:

```
> (mapcar #'first-name names)
(JOHN MALCOLM ADMIRAL SPOT ARISTOTLE A Z SIR MISS)
```

We might be disappointed with these results. Suppose we wanted a version of first-name which ignored titles like Admiral and Miss, and got to the "real" first name. We could proceed as follows:

```
(defparameter *titles*
  '(Mr Mrs Miss Ms Sir Madam Dr Admiral Major General)
  "A list of titles that can appear at the start of a name.")
```

We've introduced another new special form, defparameter, which defines a parameter—a variable that does not change over the course of a computation, but that might change when we think of new things to add (like the French Mme or the military Lt.). The defparameter form both gives a value to the variable and makes it possible to use the variable in subsequent function definitions. In this example we have exercised the option of providing a documentation string that describes the variable. It is a widely used convention among Lisp programmers to mark special variables by spelling their names with asterisks on either end. This is just a convention; in Lisp, the asterisk is just another character that has no particular meaning.

We next give a new definition for first-name, which supersedes the previous definition.[5] This definition says that if the first word of the name is a member of the

---

[5] Just as we can change the value of a variable, we can also change the value of a function

list of titles, then we want to ignore that word and return the first-name of the rest of the words in the name. Otherwise, we use the first word, just as before. Another built-in function, member, tests to see if its first argument is an element of the list passed as the second argument.

The special form if has the form (if *test then-part else-part*). There are many special forms for performing conditional tests in Lisp; if is the most appropriate for this example. An if form is evaluated by first evaluating the *test* expression. If it is true, the *then-part* is evaluated and returned as the value of the if form; otherwise the *else-part* is evaluated and returned. While some languages insist that the value of a conditional test must be either true or false, Lisp is much more forgiving. The test may legally evaluate to any value at all. Only the value nil is considered false; all other values are considered true. In the definition of first-name below, the function member will return a non-nil (hence true) value if the first element of the name is in the list of titles, and will return nil (hence false) if it is not. Although all non-nil values are considered true, by convention the constant t is usually used to represent truth.

```
(defun first-name (name)
  "Select the first name from a name represented as a list."
  (if (member (first name) *titles*)
      (first-name (rest name))
      (first name)))
```

When we map the new first-name over the list of names, the results are more encouraging. In addition, the function gets the "right" result for '(Madam Major General Paula Jones) by dropping off titles one at a time.

```
> (mapcar #'first-name names)
(JOHN MALCOLM GRACE SPOT ARISTOTLE A Z LARRY SCARLET)

> (first-name '(Madam Major General Paula Jones))
PAULA
```

We can see how this works by *tracing* the execution of first-name, and seeing the values passed to and returned from the function. The special forms trace and untrace are used for this purpose.

```
> (trace first-name)
(FIRST-NAME)
```

---

in Lisp. It is not necessary to recompile everything when a change is made, as it would be in other languages.

```
> (first-name '(John Q Public))
(1 ENTER FIRST-NAME: (JOHN Q PUBLIC))
(1 EXIT FIRST-NAME: JOHN)
JOHN
```

When first-name is called, the definition is entered with the single argument, name, taking on the value (JOHN Q PUBLIC). The value returned is JOHN. Trace prints two lines indicating entry and exit from the function, and then Lisp, as usual, prints the final result, JOHN.

The next example is more complicated. The function first-name is used four times. First, it is entered with name bound to (Madam Major General Paula Jones). The first element of this list is Madam, and since this is a member of the list of titles, the result is computed by calling first-name again on the rest of the name—(Major General Paula Jones). This process repeats two more times, and we finally enter first-name with name bound to (Paula Jones). Since Paula is not a title, it becomes the result of this call to first-name, and thus the result of all four calls, as trace shows. Once we are happy with the workings of first-name, the special form untrace turns off tracing.

```
> (first-name '(Madam Major General Paula Jones)) ⇒
(1 ENTER FIRST-NAME: (MADAM MAJOR GENERAL PAULA JONES))
  (2 ENTER FIRST-NAME: (MAJOR GENERAL PAULA JONES))
    (3 ENTER FIRST-NAME: (GENERAL PAULA JONES))
      (4 ENTER FIRST-NAME: (PAULA JONES))
      (4 EXIT FIRST-NAME: PAULA)
    (3 EXIT FIRST-NAME: PAULA)
  (2 EXIT FIRST-NAME: PAULA)
(1 EXIT FIRST-NAME: PAULA)
PAULA

> (untrace first-name) ⇒ (FIRST-NAME)

> (first-name '(Mr Blue Jeans)) ⇒ BLUE
```

The function first-name is said to be *recursive* because its definition includes a call to itself. Programmers who are new to the concept of recursion sometimes find it mysterious. But recursive functions are really no different from nonrecursive ones. Any function is required to return the correct value for the given input(s). Another way to look at this requirement is to break it into two parts: a function must return a value, and it must not return any incorrect values. This two-part requirement is equivalent to the first one, but it makes it easier to think about and design function definitions.

Next I show an abstract description of the first-name problem, to emphasize the design of the function and the fact that recursive solutions are not tied to Lisp in any way:

```
function first-name(name):
    if the first element of name is a title
        then do something complicated to get the first-name
        else return the first element of the name
```

This breaks up the problem into two cases. In the second case, we return an answer, and it is in fact the correct answer. We have not yet specified what to do in the first case. But we do know that it has something to do with the rest of the name after the first element, and that what we want is to extract the first name out of those elements. The leap of faith is to go ahead and use first-name, even though it has not been fully defined yet:

```
function first-name(name):
    if the first element of name is a title
        then return the first-name of the rest of the name
        else return the first element of the name
```

Now the first case in first-name is recursive, and the second case remains unchanged. We already agreed that the second case returns the correct answer, and the first case only returns what first-name returns. So first-name as a whole can only return correct answers. Thus, we're halfway to showing that the function is correct; the other half is to show that it eventually returns some answer. But every recursive call chops off the first element and looks at the rest, so for an n-element list there can be at most n recursive calls. This completes the demonstration that the function is correct. Programmers who learn to think this way find recursion to be a valuable tool rather than a confusing mystery.

1.7   Higher-Order Functions

Functions in Lisp can not only be "called," or applied to arguments, they can also be manipulated just like any other kind of object. A function that takes another function as an argument is called a *higher-order function*. mapcar is an example. To demonstrate the higher-order-function style of programming, we will define a new function called mappend. It takes two arguments, a function and a list. mappend maps the function over each element of the list and appends together all the results. The first definition follows immediately from the description and the fact that the function apply can be used to apply a function to a list of arguments.

```
(defun mappend (fn the-list)
  "Apply fn to each element of list and append the results."
  (apply #'append (mapcar fn the-list)))
```

Now we experiment a little to see how apply and mappend work. The first example applies the addition function to a list of four numbers.

```
> (apply #'+ '(1 2 3 4)) ⇒ 10
```

The next example applies append to a list of two arguments, where each argument is a list. If the arguments were not lists, it would be an error.

```
> (apply #'append '((1 2 3) (a b c))) ⇒ (1 2 3 A B C)
```

Now we define a new function, self-and-double, and apply it to a variety of arguments.

```
> (defun self-and-double (x) (list x (+ x x)))
> (self-and-double 3) ⇒ (3 6)
> (apply #'self-and-double '(3)) ⇒ (3 6)
```

If we had tried to apply self-and-double to a list of more than one argument, or to a list that did not contain a number, it would be an error, just as it would be an error to evaluate (self-and-double 3 4) or (self-and-double 'Kim). Now let's return to the mapping functions:

```
> (mapcar #'self-and-double '(1 10 300)) ⇒ ((1 2) (10 20) (300 600))
> (mappend #'self-and-double '(1 10 300)) ⇒ (1 2 10 20 300 600)
```

When mapcar is passed a function and a list of three arguments, it always returns a list of three values. Each value is the result of calling the function on the respective argument. In contrast, when mappend is called, it returns one big list, which is equal to all the values that mapcar would generate appended together. It would be an error to call mappend with a function that didn't return lists, because append expects to see lists as its arguments.

Now consider the following problem: given a list of elements, return a list consisting of all the numbers in the original list and the negation of those numbers. For example, given the list (testing 1 2 3 test), return (1 -1 2 -2 3 -3). This problem can be solved very easily using mappend as a component:

```
(defun numbers-and-negations (input)
  "Given a list, return only the numbers and their negations."
  (mappend #'number-and-negation input))

(defun number-and-negation (x)
  "If x is a number, return a list of x and -x."
  (if (numberp x)
      (list x (- x))
      nil))

> (numbers-and-negations '(testing 1 2 3 test)) ⇒ (1 -1 2 -2 3 -3)
```

The alternate definition of mappend shown in the following doesn't make use of
mapcar; instead it builds up the list one element at a time:

```
(defun mappend (fn the-list)
  "Apply fn to each element of list and append the results."
  (if (null the-list)
      nil
      (append (funcall fn (first the-list))
              (mappend fn (rest the-list)))))
```

funcall is similar to apply; it too takes a function as its first argument and applies the
function to a list of arguments, but in the case of funcall, the arguments are listed
separately:

```
> (funcall #'+ 2 3) ⇒ 5

> (apply #'+ '(2 3)) ⇒ 5

> (funcall #'+ '(2 3)) ⇒ Error: (2 3) is not a number.
```

These are equivalent to (+ 2 3), (+ 2 3), and (+ '(2 3)), respectively.

So far, every function we have used has been either predefined in Common Lisp
or introduced with a defun, which pairs a function with a name. It is also possible to
introduce a function without giving it a name, using the special syntax lambda.

The name *lambda* comes from the mathematician Alonzo Church's notation for
functions (Church 1941). Lisp usually prefers expressive names over terse Greek
letters, but lambda is an exception. A better name would be make-function. Lambda
derives from the notation in Russell and Whitehead's *Principia Mathematica*, which
used a caret over bound variables: $\hat{x}(x + x)$. Church wanted a one-dimensional
string, so he moved the caret in front: $\char94 x(x + x)$. The caret looked funny with nothing
below it, so Church switched to the closest thing, an uppercase lambda, $\Lambda x(x + x)$.
The Λ was easily confused with other symbols, so eventually the lowercase lambda
was substituted: $\lambda x(x + x)$. John McCarthy was a student of Church's at Princeton,
so when McCarthy invented Lisp in 1958, he adopted the lambda notation. There

were no Greek letters on the keypunches of that era, so McCarthy used (lambda (x) (+ x x)), and it has survived to this day. In general, the form of a lambda expression is

(lambda *(parameters...) body...*)

A lambda expression is just a nonatomic *name* for a function, just as append is an atomic name for a built-in function. As such, it is appropriate for use in the first position of a function call, but if we want to get at the actual function, rather than its name, we still have to use the #' notation. For example:

```
> ((lambda (x) (+ x 2)) 4) ⇒ 6
> (funcall #'(lambda (x) (+ x 2)) 4) ⇒ 6
```

To understand the distinction we have to be clear on how expressions are evaluated in Lisp. The normal rule for evaluation states that symbols are evaluated by looking up the value of the variable that the symbol refers to. So the x in (+ x 2) is evaluated by looking up the value of the variable named x. A list is evaluated in one of two ways. If the first element of the list is a special form operator, then the list is evaluated according to the syntax rule for that special form. Otherwise, the list represents a function call. The first element is evaluated in a unique way, as a function. This means it can either be a symbol or a lambda expression. In either case, the function named by the first element is applied to the values of the remaining elements in the list. These values are determined by the normal evaluation rules. If we want to refer to a function in a position other than the first element of a function call, we have to use the #' notation. Otherwise, the expressions will be evaluated by the normal evaluation rule, and will not be treated as functions. For example:

```
> append ⇒ Error: APPEND is not a bound variable
> (lambda (x) (+ x 2)) ⇒ Error: LAMBDA is not a function
```

Here are some more examples of the correct use of functions:

```
> (mapcar #'(lambda (x) (+ x x))
          '(1 2 3 4 5)) ⇒
(2 4 6 8 10)
> (mappend #'(lambda (l) (list l (reverse l)))
           '((1 2 3) (a b c))) ⇒
((1 2 3) (3 2 1) (A B C) (C B A))
```

Programmers who are used to other languages sometimes fail to see the point of lambda expressions. There are two reasons why lambda expressions are very useful.

First, it can be messy to clutter up a program with superfluous names. Just as it is clearer to write (a+b)*(c+d) rather than to invent variable names like temp1 and temp2 to hold a+b and c+d, so it can be clearer to define a function as a lambda expression rather than inventing a name for it.

Second, and more importantly, lambda expressions make it possible to create new functions at run time. This is a powerful technique that is not possible in most programming languages. These run-time functions, known as *closures*, will be covered in section 3.16.

1.8   Other Data Types

So far we have seen just four kinds of Lisp objects: numbers, symbols, lists, and functions. Lisp actually defines about 25 different types of objects: vectors, arrays, structures, characters, streams, hash tables, and others. At this point we will introduce one more, the string. As you can see in the following, strings, like numbers, evaluate to themselves. Strings are used mainly for printing out messages, while symbols are used for their relationships to other objects, and to name variables. The printed representation of a string has a double quote mark (") at each end.

```
> "a string" ⇒ "a string"
> (length "a string") ⇒ 8
> (length "") ⇒ 0
```

1.9   Summary: The Lisp Evaluation Rule

We can now summarize the evaluation rule for Lisp.

- Every expression is either a *list* or an *atom*.

- Every list to be evaluated is either a *special form expression* or a *function application*.

- A *special form expression* is defined to be a list whose first element is a special form operator. The expression is evaluated according to the operator's idiosyncratic evaluation rule. For example, the evaluation rule for setf is to evaluate the second argument according to the normal evaluation rule, set the first argument to that value, and return the value as the result. The rule for defun is to define a new function, and return the name of the function. The rule for quote is to return the first argument unevaluated. The notation 'x is actually an abbreviation for the special form expression (quote x). Similarly, the notation #'f is an abbreviation for the special form expression (function f).

```
'John ≡ (quote John) ⇒ JOHN
(setf p 'John) ⇒ JOHN
(defun twice (x) (+ x x)) ⇒ TWICE
(if (= 2 3) (error) (+ 5 6)) ⇒ 11
```

- A *function application* is evaluated by first evaluating the arguments (the rest of the list) and then finding the function named by the first element of the list and applying it to the list of evaluated arguments.

```
(+ 2 3)  ⇒ 5
(- (+ 90 9) (+ 50 5 (length '(Pat Kim))))  ⇒  42
```

Note that if '(Pat Kim) did not have the quote, it would be treated as a function application of the function pat to the value of the variable kim.

- Every atom is either a *symbol* or a *nonsymbol*.

- A *symbol* evaluates to the most recent value that has been assigned to the variable named by that symbol. Symbols are composed of letters, and possibly digits and, rarely, punctuation characters. To avoid confusion, we will use symbols composed mostly of the letters a-z and the '-' character, with a few exceptions.[6]

```
names

p

*print-pretty*
```

- A *nonsymbol atom* evaluates to itself. For now, numbers and strings are the only such non-symbol atoms we know of. Numbers are composed of digits, and possibly a decimal point and sign. There are also provisions for scientific notation, rational and complex numbers, and numbers with different bases, but we won't describe the details here. Strings are delimited by double quote marks on both sides.

---

[6]For example, symbols that denote so-called *special* variables usually begin and end in asterisks. Also, note that I did not hesitate to use the symbol won! on page 11.

```
42  ⇒  42

-273.15  ⇒  -273.15

"a string"  ⇒  "a string"
```

There are some minor details of Common Lisp that complicate the evaluation rules, but this definition will suffice for now.

One complication that causes confusion for beginning Lispers is the difference between *reading* and *evaluating* an expression. Beginners often imagine that when they type an expression, such as

```
> (+ (* 3 4) (* 5 6))
```

the Lisp system first reads the (+, then fetches the addition function, then reads (* 3 4) and computes 12, then reads (* 5 6) and computes 30, and finally computes 42. In fact, what actually happens is that the system first reads the entire expression, the list (+ (* 3 4) (* 5 6)). Only after it has been read does the system begin to evaluate it. This evaluation can be done by an interpreter that looks at the list directly, or it can be done by a compiler that translates the list into machine language instructions and then executes those instructions.

We can see now that it was a little imprecise to say, "Numbers are composed of digits, and possibly a decimal point and sign." It would be more precise to say that the printed representation of a number, as expected by the function read and as produced by the function print, is composed of digits, and possibly a decimal point and sign. The internal representation of a number varies from one computer to another, but you can be sure that it will be a bit pattern in a particular memory location, and it will no longer contain the original characters used to represent the number in decimal notation. Similarly, it is the printed representation of a string that is surrounded by double quote marks; the internal representation is a memory location marking the beginning of a vector of characters.

Beginners who fail to grasp the distinction between reading and evaluating may have a good model of what expressions evaluate to, but they usually have a terrible model of the efficiency of evaluating expressions. One student used only one-letter variable names, because he felt that it would be faster for the computer to look up a one-letter name than a multiletter name. While it may be true that shorter names can save a microsecond at read time, this makes no difference at all at evaluation time. Every variable, regardless of its name, is just a memory location, and the time to access the location does not depend on the name of the variable.

1.10   What Makes Lisp Different?

What is it that sets Lisp apart from other languages? Why is it a good language for AI applications? There are at least eight important factors:

- Built-in Support for Lists

- Automatic Storage Management

- Dynamic Typing

- First-Class Functions

- Uniform Syntax

- Interactive Environment

- Extensibility

- History

In sum, these factors allow a programmer to delay making decisions. In the example dealing with names, we were able to use the built-in list functions to construct and manipulate names without making a lot of explicit decisions about their representation. If we decided to change the representation, it would be easy to go back and alter parts of the program, leaving other parts unchanged.

This ability to delay decisions—or more accurately, to make temporary, nonbinding decisions—is usually a good thing, because it means that irrelevant details can be ignored. There are also some negative points of delaying decisions. First, the less we tell the compiler, the greater the chance that it may have to produce inefficient code. Second, the less we tell the compiler, the less chance it has of noticing inconsistencies and warning us. Errors may not be detected until the program is run. Let's consider each factor in more depth, weighing the advantages and disadvantages:

- *Built-in Support for Lists.* The list is a very versatile data structure, and while lists can be implemented in any language, Lisp makes it easy to use them. Many AI applications involve lists of constantly changing size, making fixed-length data structures like vectors harder to use.

  Early versions of Lisp used lists as their only aggregate data structure. Common Lisp provides other types as well, because lists are not always the most efficient choice.

- *Automatic Storage Management.* The Lisp programmer needn't keep track of memory allocation; it is all done automatically. This frees the programmer of a lot of effort, and makes it easy to use the functional style of programming. Other

languages present programmers with a choice. Variables can be allocated on
the stack, meaning that they are created when a procedure is entered, and
disappear when the procedure is done. This is an efficient use of storage, but
it rules out functions that return complex values. The other choice is for the
programmer to explicitly allocate and free storage. This makes the functional
style possible but can lead to errors.

For example, consider the trivial problem of computing the expression $a \times (b + c)$, where a, b, and c are numbers. The code is trivial in any language; here it is
in Pascal and in Lisp:

```
/* Pascal */                    ;;; Lisp

a * (b + c)                     (* a (+ b c))
```

The only difference is that Pascal uses infix notation and Lisp uses prefix. Now
consider computing $a \times (b + c)$ when a, b, and c are matrices. Assume we have
procedures for matrix multiplication and addition. In Lisp the form is exactly
the same; only the names of the functions are changed. In Pascal we have the
choice of approaches mentioned before. We could declare temporary variables
to hold intermediate results on the stack, and replace the functional expression
with a series of procedure calls:

```
/* Pascal */                    ;;; Lisp

var temp, result: matrix;


add(b,c,temp);                  (mult a (add b c))

mult(a,temp,result);

return(result);
```

The other choice is to write Pascal functions that allocate new matrices on the
heap. Then one can write nice functional expressions like `mult(a,add(b,c))`
even in Pascal. However, in practice it rarely works this nicely, because of the
need to manage storage explicitly:

```
/* Pascal */                    ;;; Lisp

var a,b,c,x,y: matrix;
```

```
x := add(b,c);                              (mult a (add b c))
y := mult(a,x);
free(x);
return(y);
```

In general, deciding which structures to free is a difficult task for the Pascal programmer. If the programmer misses some, then the program may run out of memory. Worse, if the programmer frees a structure that is still being used, then strange errors can occur when that piece of memory is reallocated. Lisp automatically allocates and frees structures, so these two types of errors can *never* occur.

- *Dynamic Typing.* Lisp programmers don't have to provide type declarations, because the language keeps track of the type of each object at run time, rather than figuring out all types at compile time. This makes Lisp programs shorter and hence faster to develop, and it also means that functions can often be extended to work for objects to which they were not originally intended to apply. In Pascal, we can write a procedure to sort an array of 100 integers, but we can't use that same procedure to sort 200 integers, or 100 strings. In Lisp, one sort fits all.

  One way to appreciate this kind of flexibility is to see how hard it is to achieve in other languages. It is impossible in Pascal; in fact, the language Modula was invented primarily to fix this problem in Pascal. The language Ada was designed to allow flexible generic functions, and a book by Musser and Stepanov (1989) describes an Ada package that gives some of the functionality of Common Lisp's sequence functions. But the Ada solution is less than ideal: it takes a 264-page book to duplicate only part of the functionality of the 20-page chapter 14 from Steele (1990), and Musser and Stepanov went through five Ada compilers before they found one that would correctly compile their package. Also, their package is considerably less powerful, since it does not handle vectors or optional keyword parameters. In Common Lisp, all this functionality comes for free, and it is easy to add more.

  On the other hand, dynamic typing means that some errors will go undetected until run time. The great advantage of strongly typed languages is that they are able to give error messages at compile time. The great frustration with strongly typed languages is that they are only able to warn about a small class of errors. They can tell you that you are mistakenly passing a string to a function that expects an integer, but they can't tell you that you are passing an odd number to a function that expects an even number.

- *First-Class Functions.* A *first-class* object is one that can be used anywhere and can be manipulated in the same ways as any other kind of object. In Pascal or C, for example, functions can be passed as arguments to other functions, but they are not first-class, because it is not possible to create new functions while the program is running, nor is it possible to create an anonymous function without giving it a name. In Lisp we can do both those things using lambda. This is explained in section 3.16, page 92.

- *Uniform Syntax.* The syntax of Lisp programs is simple. This makes the language easy to learn, and very little time is wasted correcting typos. In addition, it is easy to write programs that manipulate other programs or define whole new languages—a very powerful technique. The simple syntax also makes it easy for text editing programs to parse Lisp. Your editor program should be able to indent expressions automatically and to show matching parentheses. This is harder to do for languages with complex syntax.

  On the other hand, some people object to all the parentheses. There are two answers to this objection. First, consider the alternative: in a language with "conventional" syntax, Lisp's parentheses pairs would be replaced either by an implicit operator precedence rule (in the case of arithmetic and logical expressions) or by a begin/end pair (in the case of control structures). But neither of these is necessarily an advantage. Implicit precedence is notoriously error-prone, and begin/end pairs clutter up the page without adding any content. Many languages are moving away from begin/end: C uses { and }, which are equivalent to parentheses, and several modern functional languages (such as Haskell) use horizontal blank space, with no explicit grouping at all.

  Second, many Lisp programmers *have* considered the alternative. There have been a number of preprocessors that translate from "conventional" syntax into Lisp. None of these has caught on. It is not that Lisp programmers find it *tolerable* to use all those parentheses, rather, they find it *advantageous*. With a little experience, you may too.

  It is also important that the syntax of Lisp data is the same as the syntax of programs. Obviously, this makes it easy to convert data to program. Less obvious is the time saved by having universal functions to handle input and output. The Lisp functions read and print will automatically handle any list, structure, string, or number. This makes it trivial to test individual functions while developing your program. In a traditional language like C or Pascal, you would have to write special-purpose functions to read and print each data type you wanted to debug, as well as a special-purpose driver to call the routines. Because this is time-consuming and error-prone, the temptation is to avoid testing altogether. Thus, Lisp encourages better-tested programs, and makes it easier to develop them faster.

- *Interactive Environment.* Traditionally, a programmer would write a complete program, compile it, correct any errors detected by the compiler, and then run and debug it. This is known as the *batch* mode of interaction. For long programs, waiting for the compiler occupied a large portion of the debugging time. In Lisp one normally writes a few small functions at a time, getting feedback from the Lisp system after evaluating each one. This is known as an *interactive* environment. When it comes time to make a change, only the changed functions need to be recompiled, so the wait is much shorter. In addition, the Lisp programmer can debug by typing in arbitrary expressions at any time. This is a big improvement over editing the program to introduce print statements and recompiling.

Notice that the distinction between *interactive* and a *batch* languages is separate from the distinction between *interpreted* and *compiled* languages. It has often been stated, incorrectly, that Lisp has an advantage by virtue of being an interpreted language. Actually, experienced Common Lisp programmers tend to use the compiler almost exclusively. The important point is interaction, not interpretation.

The idea of an interactive environment is such a good one that even traditional languages like C and Pascal are starting to offer interactive versions, so this is not an exclusive advantage of Lisp. However, Lisp still provides much better access to the interactive features. A C interpreter may allow the programmer to type in an expression and have it evaluated immediately, but it will not allow the programmer to write a program that, say, goes through the symbol table and finds all the user-defined functions and prints information on them. In C—even interpreted C—the symbol table is just a Cheshire-cat-like invention of the interpreter's imagination that disappears when the program is run. In Lisp, the symbol table is a first-class object[7] that can be accessed and modified with functions like read, intern and do-symbols.

Common Lisp offers an unusually rich set of useful tools, including over 700 built-in functions (ANSI Common Lisp has over 900). Thus, writing a new program involves more gathering of existing pieces of code and less writing of new code from scratch. In addition to the standard functions, Common Lisp implementations usually provide extensions for interacting with the editor, debugger, and window system.

- *Extensibility.* When Lisp was invented in 1958, nobody could have foreseen the advances in programming theory and language design that have taken place in the last thirty years. Other early languages have been discarded, replaced by ones based on newer ideas. However, Lisp has been able to survive, because it has been able to adapt. Because Lisp is extensible, it has been changed to incorporate the newest features as they become popular.

---

[7]Actually, there can be several symbol tables. They are known as *packages* in Common Lisp.

The easiest way to extend the language is with macros. When so-called structured programming constructs such as *case* and *if-then-else* arose, they were incorporated into Lisp as macros. But the flexibility of Lisp goes beyond adding individual constructs. Brand new styles of programming can easily be implemented. Many AI applications are based on the idea of *rule-based* programming. Another new style is *object-oriented* programming, which has been incorporated with the Common Lisp Object System (CLOS),[8] a set of macros, functions, and data types that have been integrated into ANSI Common Lisp.

To show how far Lisp has come, here's the only sample program given in the *Lisp/MTS Programmer's Guide* (Hafner and Wilcox 1974):

```
(PROG (LIST DEPTH TEMP RESTLIST)
(SETQ RESTLIST (LIST (CONS (READ) 0)) )
A (COND
((NOT RESTLIST) (RETURN 'DONE))
(T (SETQ LIST (UNCONS (UNCONS RESTLIST
    RESTLIST ) DEPTH))
(COND ((ATOM LIST)
(MAPC 'PRIN1 (LIST '"ATOM:" LIST '"," 'DEPTH DEPTH))
(TERPRI))
(T (SETQ TEMP (UNCONS LIST LIST))
(COND (LIST
(SETQ RESTLIST (CONS(CONS LIST DEPTH) RESTLIST))))
(SETQ RESTLIST (CONS (CONS TEMP
    (ADD1 DEPTH)) RESTLIST))
))))
(GO A))
```

Note the use of the now-deprecated goto (GO) statement, and the lack of consistent indentation conventions. The manual also gives a recursive version of the same program:

```
(PROG NIL (
(LABEL ATOMPRINT (LAMBDA (RESTLIST)
(COND ((NOT RESTLIST) (RETURN 'DONE))
((ATOM (CAAR RESTLIST)) (MAPC 'PRIN1
    (LIST '"ATOM:" (CAAR RESTLIST)
        '"," 'DEPTH (CDAR RESTLIST)))
(TERPRI)
(ATOMPRINT (CDR RESTLIST)))
( T (ATOMPRINT (GRAFT
(LIST (CONS (CAAAR RESTLIST) (ADD1 (CDAR RESTLIST))))
(AND (CDAAR RESTLIST) (LIST (CONS (CDAAR RESTLIST)
```

---

[8]Pronounced "see-loss." An alternate pronunciation, "klaus," seems to be losing favor.

```
            (CDAR RESTLIST))))
                (CDR RESTLIST))))))))
      (LIST (CONS (READ) 0))))
```

Both versions are very difficult to read. With our modern insight (and text editors that automatically indent), a much simpler program is possible:

```
(defun atomprint (exp &optional (depth 0))
  "Print each atom in exp, along with its depth of nesting."
  (if (atom exp)
      (format t "~&ATOM: ~a, DEPTH ~d" exp depth)
      (dolist (element exp)
        (atomprint element (+ depth 1)))))
```

1.11   Exercises

Exercise 1.1 [m]   Define a version of last-name that handles "Rex Morgan MD," "Morton Downey, Jr.," and whatever other cases you can think of.

Exercise 1.2 [m]   Write a function to exponentiate, or raise a number to an integer power. For example: (power 3 2) $= 3^2 = 9$.

Exercise 1.3 [m]   Write a function that counts the number of atoms in an expression. For example: (count-atoms '(a (b) c)) = 3. Notice that there is something of an ambiguity in this: should (a nil c) count as three atoms, or as two, because it is equivalent to (a () c)?

Exercise 1.4 [m]   Write a function that counts the number of times an expression occurs anywhere within another expression. Example: (count-anywhere 'a '(a ((a) b) a)) $\Rightarrow$ 3.

Exercise 1.5 [m]   Write a function to compute the dot product of two sequences of numbers, represented as lists. The dot product is computed by multiplying corresponding elements and then adding up the resulting products. Example:

(dot-product '(10 20) '(3 4)) $= 10 \times 3 + 20 \times 4 = 110$

1.12   Answers

Answer 1.2

```lisp
(defun power (x n)
  "Power raises x to the nth power.  N must be an integer >= 0.
   This executes in log n time, because of the check for even n."
  (cond ((= n 0) 1)
        ((evenp n) (expt (power x (/ n 2)) 2))
        (t (* x (power x (- n 1)))))))
```

Answer 1.3

```lisp
(defun count-atoms (exp)
  "Return the total number of non-nil atoms in the expression."
  (cond ((null exp) 0)
        ((atom exp) 1)
        (t (+ (count-atoms (first exp))
              (count-atoms (rest exp))))))

(defun count-all-atoms (exp &optional (if-null 1))
  "Return the total number of atoms in the expression,
   counting nil as an atom only in non-tail position."
  (cond ((null exp) if-null)
        ((atom exp) 1)
        (t (+ (count-all-atoms (first exp) 1)
              (count-all-atoms (rest exp) 0)))))
```

Answer 1.4

```lisp
(defun count-anywhere (item tree)
  "Count the times item appears anywhere within tree."
  (cond ((eql item tree) 1)
        ((atom tree) 0)
        (t (+ (count-anywhere item (first tree))
              (count-anywhere item (rest tree))))))
```

Answer 1.5   Here are three versions:

```
(defun dot-product (a b)
  "Compute the mathematical dot product of two vectors."
  (if (or (null a) (null b))
      0
      (+ (* (first a) (first b))
         (dot-product (rest a) (rest b)))))

(defun dot-product (a b)
  "Compute the mathematical dot product of two vectors."
  (let ((sum 0))
    (dotimes (i (length a))
      (incf sum (* (elt a i) (elt b i))))
    sum))

(defun dot-product (a b)
  "Compute the mathematical dot product of two vectors."
  (apply #'+ (mapcar #'* a b)))
```

CHAPTER 2

A Simple Lisp Program

Certum quod factum.
(One is certain of only what one builds.)
—Giovanni Battista Vico (1668–1744)
Italian royal historiographer

Y ou will never become proficient in a foreign language by studying vocabulary lists. Rather, you must hear and speak (or read and write) the language to gain proficiency. The same is true for learning computer languages.

This chapter shows how to combine the basic functions and special forms of Lisp into a complete program. If you can learn how to do that, then acquiring the remaining vocabulary of Lisp (as outlined in chapter 3) will be easy.

2.1 A Grammar for a Subset of English

The program we will develop in this chapter generates random English sentences. Here is a simple grammar for a tiny portion of English:

> *Sentence* ⇒ *Noun-Phrase + Verb-Phrase*
> *Noun-Phrase* ⇒ *Article + Noun*
> *Verb-Phrase* ⇒ *Verb + Noun-Phrase*
> *Article* ⇒ *the, a, . . .*
> *Noun* ⇒ *man, ball, woman, table . . .*
> *Verb* ⇒ *hit, took, saw, liked . . .*

To be technical, this description is called a *context-free phrase-structure grammar*, and the underlying paradigm is called *generative syntax*. The idea is that anywhere we want a sentence, we can generate a noun phrase followed by a verb phrase. Anywhere a noun phrase has been specified, we generate instead an article followed by a noun. Anywhere an article has been specified, we generate either "the," "a," or some other article. The formalism is "context-free" because the rules apply anywhere regardless of the surrounding words, and the approach is "generative" because the rules as a whole define the complete set of sentences in a language (and by contrast the set of nonsentences as well). In the following we show the derivation of a single sentence using the rules:

> To get a *Sentence*, append a *Noun-Phrase* and a *Verb-Phrase*
>   To get a *Noun-Phrase*, append an *Article* and a *Noun*
>   Choose "*the*" for the *Article*
>   Choose "*man*" for the *Noun*
>   The resulting *Noun-Phrase* is "*the man*"
>   To get a *Verb-Phrase*, append a *Verb* and a *Noun-Phrase*
>   Choose "*hit*" for the *Verb*
>   To get a *Noun-Phrase*, append an *Article* and a *Noun*
>   Choose "*the*" for the *Article*
>   Choose "*ball*" for the *Noun*
>   The resulting *Noun-Phrase* is "*the ball*"
>   The resulting *Verb-Phrase* is "*hit the ball*"
> The resulting *Sentence* is "*The man hit the ball*"

2.2 A Straightforward Solution

We will develop a program that generates random sentences from a phrase-structure grammar. The most straightforward approach is to represent each grammar rule by a separate Lisp function:

```
(defun sentence ()     (append (noun-phrase) (verb-phrase)))
(defun noun-phrase () (append (Article) (Noun)))
(defun verb-phrase () (append (Verb) (noun-phrase)))
(defun Article ()      (one-of '(the a)))
(defun Noun ()         (one-of '(man ball woman table)))
(defun Verb ()         (one-of '(hit took saw liked)))
```

Each of these function definitions has an empty parameter list, (). That means the functions take no arguments. This is unusual because, strictly speaking, a function with no arguments would always return the same thing, so we would use a constant instead. However, these functions make use of the random function (as we will see shortly), and thus can return different results even with no arguments. Thus, they are not functions in the mathematical sense, but they are still called functions in Lisp, because they return a value.

All that remains now is to define the function one-of. It takes a list of possible choices as an argument, chooses one of these at random, and returns a one-element list of the element chosen. This last part is so that all functions in the grammar will return a list of words. That way, we can freely apply append to any category.

```
(defun one-of (set)
  "Pick one element of set, and make a list of it."
  (list (random-elt set)))

(defun random-elt (choices)
  "Choose an element from a list at random."
  (elt choices (random (length choices))))
```

There are two new functions here, elt and random. elt picks an element out of a list. The first argument is the list, and the second is the position in the list. The confusing part is that the positions start at 0, so (elt choices 0) is the first element of the list, and (elt choices 1) is the second. Think of the position numbers as telling you how far away you are from the front. The expression (random n) returns an integer from 0 to n-1, so that (random 4) would return either 0,1,2, or 3.

Now we can test the program by generating a few random sentences, along with a noun phrase and a verb phrase:

```
> (sentence) ⇒ (THE WOMAN HIT THE BALL)

> (sentence) ⇒ (THE WOMAN HIT THE MAN)

> (sentence) ⇒ (THE BALL SAW THE WOMAN)

> (sentence) ⇒ (THE BALL SAW THE TABLE)

> (noun-phrase) ⇒ (THE MAN)

> (verb-phrase) ⇒ (LIKED THE WOMAN)
```

```
> (trace sentence noun-phrase verb-phrase article noun verb) ⇒
(SENTENCE NOUN-PHRASE VERB-PHRASE ARTICLE NOUN VERB)

> (sentence) ⇒
(1 ENTER SENTENCE)
  (1 ENTER NOUN-PHRASE)
    (1 ENTER ARTICLE)
    (1 EXIT ARTICLE: (THE))
    (1 ENTER NOUN)
    (1 EXIT NOUN: (MAN))
  (1 EXIT NOUN-PHRASE: (THE MAN))
  (1 ENTER VERB-PHRASE)
    (1 ENTER VERB)
    (1 EXIT VERB: (HIT))
    (1 ENTER NOUN-PHRASE)
      (1 ENTER ARTICLE)
      (1 EXIT ARTICLE: (THE))
      (1 ENTER NOUN)
      (1 EXIT NOUN: (BALL))
    (1 EXIT NOUN-PHRASE: (THE BALL))
  (1 EXIT VERB-PHRASE: (HIT THE BALL))
(1 EXIT SENTENCE: (THE MAN HIT THE BALL))
(THE MAN HIT THE BALL)
```

The program works fine, and the trace looks just like the sample derivation above, but the Lisp definitions are a bit harder to read than the original grammar rules. This problem will be compounded as we consider more complex rules. Suppose we wanted to allow noun phrases to be modified by an indefinite number of adjectives and an indefinite number of prepositional phrases. In grammatical notation, we might have the following rules:

Noun-Phrase ⇒ *Article* + *Adj** + *Noun* + *PP**
*Adj** ⇒ ∅, *Adj* + *Adj**
*PP** ⇒ ∅, *PP* + *PP**
PP ⇒ *Prep* + *Noun-Phrase*
Adj ⇒ *big, little, blue, green, . . .*
Prep ⇒ *to, in, by, with, . . .*

In this notation, ∅ indicates a choice of nothing at all, a comma indicates a choice of several alternatives, and the asterisk is nothing special—as in Lisp, it's just part of the name of a symbol. However, the convention used here is that names ending in an asterisk denote zero or more repetitions of the underlying name. That is, *PP** denotes zero or more repetitions of *PP*. This is known as "Kleene star" notation (pronounced "clean-E") after the mathematician Stephen Cole Kleene.[1]

The problem is that the rules for *Adj** and *PP** contain choices that we would have to represent as some kind of conditional in Lisp. For example:

```lisp
(defun Adj* ()
  (if (= (random 2) 0)
      nil
      (append (Adj) (Adj*))))

(defun PP* ()
  (if (random-elt '(t nil))
      (append (PP) (PP*))
      nil))

(defun noun-phrase () (append (Article) (Adj*) (Noun) (PP*)))
(defun PP () (append (Prep) (noun-phrase)))
(defun Adj () (one-of '(big little blue green adiabatic)))
(defun Prep () (one-of '(to in by with on)))
```

I've chosen two different implementations for Adj* and PP*; either approach would work in either function. We have to be careful, though; here are two approaches that would not work:

```lisp
(defun Adj* ()
  "Warning - incorrect definition of Adjectives."
  (one-of '(nil (append (Adj) (Adj*)))))

(defun Adj* ()
  "Warning - incorrect definition of Adjectives."
  (one-of (list nil (append (Adj) (Adj*)))))
```

The first definition is wrong because it could return the literal expression ((append (Adj) (Adj*))) rather than a list of words as expected. The second definition would cause infinite recursion, because computing the value of (Adj*) always involves a recursive call to (Adj*). The point is that what started out as simple functions are now becoming quite complex. To understand them, we need to know many Lisp conventions—defun, (), case, if, quote, and the rules for order of evaluation—when ideally the implementation of a grammar rule should use only *linguistic* conventions. If we wanted to develop a larger grammar, the problem could get worse, because the rule-writer might have to depend more and more on Lisp.

---

[1]We will soon see "Kleene plus" notation, wherein *PP+* denotes one or more repetition of *PP*.

2.3   A Rule-Based Solution

An alternative implementation of this program would concentrate on making it easy to write grammar rules and would worry later about how they will be processed. Let's look again at the original grammar rules:

Sentence ⇒ *Noun-Phrase + Verb-Phrase*
Noun-Phrase ⇒ *Article + Noun*
Verb-Phrase ⇒ *Verb + Noun-Phrase*
Article ⇒ *the, a, . . .*
Noun ⇒ *man, ball, woman, table . . .*
Verb ⇒ *hit, took, saw, liked . . .*

Each rule consists of an arrow with a symbol on the left-hand side and something on the right-hand side. The complication is that there can be two kinds of right-hand sides: a concatenated list of symbols, as in *"Noun-Phrase ⇒ Article + Noun,"* or a list of alternate words, as in *"Noun ⇒ man, ball, . . ."* We can account for these possibilities by deciding that every rule will have a list of possibilities on the right-hand side, and that a concatenated list, *for example "Article + Noun,"* will be represented as a Lisp list, *for example "*(Article Noun)*"*. The list of rules can then be represented as follows:

```
(defparameter *simple-grammar*
  '((sentence -> (noun-phrase verb-phrase))
    (noun-phrase -> (Article Noun))
    (verb-phrase -> (Verb noun-phrase))
    (Article -> the a)
    (Noun -> man ball woman table)
    (Verb -> hit took saw liked))
  "A grammar for a trivial subset of English.")

(defvar *grammar* *simple-grammar*
  "The grammar used by generate.  Initially, this is
  *simple-grammar*, but we can switch to other grammars.")
```

Note that the Lisp version of the rules closely mimics the original version. In particular, I include the symbol "->", even though it serves no real purpose; it is purely decorative.

The special forms defvar and defparameter both introduce special variables and assign a value to them; the difference is that a *variable*, like *grammar*, is routinely changed during the course of running the program. A *parameter*, like *simple-grammar*, on the other hand, will normally stay constant. A change to a parameter is considered a change *to* the program, not a change *by* the program.

Once the list of rules has been defined, it can be used to find the possible rewrites of a given category symbol. The function assoc is designed for just this sort of task.

It takes two arguments, a "key" and a list of lists, and returns the first element of the list of lists that starts with the key. If there is none, it returns `nil`. Here is an example:

```
> (assoc 'noun *grammar*) ⇒ (NOUN -> MAN BALL WOMAN TABLE)
```

Although rules are quite simply implemented as lists, it is a good idea to impose a layer of abstraction by defining functions to operate on the rules. We will need three functions: one to get the right-hand side of a rule, one for the left-hand side, and one to look up all the possible rewrites (right-hand sides) for a category.

```
(defun rule-lhs (rule)
  "The left-hand side of a rule."
  (first rule))

(defun rule-rhs (rule)
  "The right-hand side of a rule."
  (rest (rest rule)))

(defun rewrites (category)
  "Return a list of the possible rewrites for this category."
  (rule-rhs (assoc category *grammar*)))
```

Defining these functions will make it easier to read the programs that use them, and it also makes changing the representation of rules easier, should we ever decide to do so.

We are now ready to address the main problem: defining a function that will generate sentences (or noun phrases, or any other category). We will call this function generate. It will have to contend with three cases: (1) In the simplest case, generate is passed a symbol that has a set of rewrite rules associated with it. We choose one of those at random, and then generate from that. (2) If the symbol has no possible rewrite rules, it must be a terminal symbol—a word, rather than a grammatical category—and we want to leave it alone. Actually, we return the list of the input word, because, as in the previous program, we want all results to be lists of words. (3) In some cases, when the symbol has rewrites, we will pick one that is a list of symbols, and try to generate from that. Thus, generate must also accept a list as input, in which case it should generate each element of the list, and then append them all together. In the following, the first clause in generate handles this case, while the second clause handles (1) and the third handles (2). Note that we used the mappend function from section 1.7 (page 18).

```
(defun generate (phrase)
  "Generate a random sentence or phrase"
  (cond ((listp phrase)
         (mappend #'generate phrase))
```

```
((rewrites phrase)
 (generate (random-elt (rewrites phrase))))
(t (list phrase))))
```

Like many of the programs in this book, this function is short, but dense with information: the craft of programming includes knowing what *not* to write, as well as what to write.

This style of programming is called *data-driven* programming, because the data (the list of rewrites associated with a category) drives what the program does next. It is a natural and easy-to-use style in Lisp, leading to concise and extensible programs, because it is always possible to add a new piece of data with a new association without having to modify the original program.

Here are some examples of generate in use:

```
> (generate 'sentence) ⇒ (THE TABLE SAW THE BALL)

> (generate 'sentence) ⇒ (THE WOMAN HIT A TABLE)

> (generate 'noun-phrase) ⇒ (THE MAN)

> (generate 'verb-phrase) ⇒ (TOOK A TABLE)
```

There are many possible ways to write generate. The following version uses if instead of cond:

```
(defun generate (phrase)
  "Generate a random sentence or phrase"
  (if (listp phrase)
      (mappend #'generate phrase)
      (let ((choices (rewrites phrase)))
        (if (null choices)
            (list phrase)
            (generate (random-elt choices)))))))
```

This version uses the special form let, which introduces a new variable (in this case, choices) and also binds the variable to a value. In this case, introducing the variable saves us from calling the function rewrites twice, as was done in the cond version of generate. The general form of a let form is:

```
(let ((var value)...)
  body-containing-vars)
```

let is the most common way of introducing variables that are not parameters of functions. One must resist the temptation to use a variable without introducing it:

```
(defun generate (phrase)
  (setf choices ...)          ;; wrong!
  ... choices ...)
```

This is wrong because the symbol choices now refers to a special or global variable, one that may be shared or changed by other functions. Thus, the function generate is not reliable, because there is no guarantee that choices will retain the same value from the time it is set to the time it is referenced again. With let we introduce a brand new variable that nobody else can access; therefore it is guaranteed to maintain the proper value.

Exercise 2.1 [m]   Write a version of generate that uses cond but avoids calling rewrites twice.

Exercise 2.2 [m]   Write a version of generate that explicitly differentiates between terminal symbols (those with no rewrite rules) and nonterminal symbols.

2.4   Two Paths to Follow

The two versions of the preceding program represent two alternate approaches that come up time and time again in developing programs: (1) Use the most straightforward mapping of the problem description directly into Lisp code. (2) Use the most natural notation available to solve the problem, and then worry about writing an interpreter for that notation.

Approach (2) involves an extra step, and thus is more work for small problems. However, programs that use this approach are often easier to modify and expand. This is especially true in a domain where there is a lot of data to account for. The grammar of natural language is one such domain—in fact, most AI problems fit this description. The idea behind approach (2) is to work with the problem as much as possible in its own terms, and to minimize the part of the solution that is written directly in Lisp.

Fortunately, it is very easy in Lisp to design new notations—in effect, new programming languages. Thus, Lisp encourages the construction of more robust programs. Throughout this book, we will be aware of the two approaches. The reader may notice that in most cases, we choose the second.

2.5 Changing the Grammar without Changing the Program

We show the utility of approach (2) by defining a new grammar that includes adjectives, prepositional phrases, proper names, and pronouns. We can then apply the generate function without modification to this new grammar.

```
(defparameter *bigger-grammar*
  '((sentence -> (noun-phrase verb-phrase))
    (noun-phrase -> (Article Adj* Noun PP*) (Name) (Pronoun))
    (verb-phrase -> (Verb noun-phrase PP*))
    (PP* -> () (PP PP*))
    (Adj* -> () (Adj Adj*))
    (PP -> (Prep noun-phrase))
    (Prep -> to in by with on)
    (Adj -> big little blue green adiabatic)
    (Article -> the a)
    (Name -> Pat Kim Lee Terry Robin)
    (Noun -> man ball woman table)
    (Verb -> hit took saw liked)
    (Pronoun -> he she it these those that)))

(setf *grammar* *bigger-grammar*)

> (generate 'sentence)
(A TABLE ON A TABLE IN THE BLUE ADIABATIC MAN SAW ROBIN
 WITH A LITTLE WOMAN)

> (generate 'sentence)
(TERRY SAW A ADIABATIC TABLE ON THE GREEN BALL BY THAT WITH KIM
 IN THESE BY A GREEN WOMAN BY A LITTLE ADIABATIC TABLE IN ROBIN
 ON LEE)

> (generate 'sentence)
(THE GREEN TABLE HIT IT WITH HE)
```

Notice the problem with case agreement for pronouns: the program generated "with he," although "with him" is the proper grammatical form. Also, it is clear that the program does not distinguish sensible from silly output.

2.6 Using the Same Data for Several Programs

Another advantage of representing information in a declarative form—as rules or facts rather than as Lisp functions—is that it can be easier to use the information for multiple purposes. Suppose we wanted a function that would generate not just the list of words in a sentence but a representation of the complete syntax of a sentence. For example, instead of the list (a woman took a ball), we want to get the nested list:

```
(SENTENCE (NOUN-PHRASE (ARTICLE A) (NOUN WOMAN))
          (VERB-PHRASE (VERB TOOK)
                       (NOUN-PHRASE (ARTICLE A) (NOUN BALL))))
```

This corresponds to the tree that linguists draw as in figure 2.1.

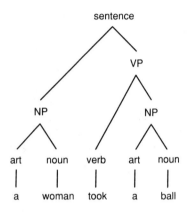

Figure 2.1: Sentence Parse Tree

Using the "straightforward functions" approach we would be stuck; we'd have to rewrite every function to generate the additional structure. With the "new notation" approach we could keep the grammar as it is and just write one new function: a version of generate that produces nested lists. The two changes are to cons the category onto the front of each rewrite, and then not to append together the results but rather just list them with mapcar:

```
(defun generate-tree (phrase)
  "Generate a random sentence or phrase,
  with a complete parse tree."
  (cond ((listp phrase)
         (mapcar #'generate-tree phrase))
        ((rewrites phrase)
         (cons phrase
               (generate-tree (random-elt (rewrites phrase)))))
        (t (list phrase))))
```

Here are some examples:

```
> (generate-tree 'Sentence)
(SENTENCE (NOUN-PHRASE (ARTICLE A)
                       (ADJ*)
                       (NOUN WOMAN)
                       (PP*))
         (VERB-PHRASE (VERB HIT)
                      (NOUN-PHRASE (PRONOUN HE))
                      (PP*)))

> (generate-tree 'Sentence)
(SENTENCE (NOUN-PHRASE (ARTICLE A)
                       (NOUN WOMAN))
          (VERB-PHRASE (VERB TOOK)
                       (NOUN-PHRASE (ARTICLE A) (NOUN BALL))))
```

As another example of the one-data/multiple-program approach, we can develop a function to generate all possible rewrites of a phrase. The function generate-all returns a list of phrases rather than just one, and we define an auxiliary function, combine-all, to manage the combination of results. Also, there are four cases instead of three, because we have to check for nil explicitly. Still, the complete program is quite simple:

```
(defun generate-all (phrase)
  "Generate a list of all possible expansions of this phrase."
  (cond ((null phrase) (list nil))
        ((listp phrase)
         (combine-all (generate-all (first phrase))
                      (generate-all (rest phrase))))
        ((rewrites phrase)
         (mappend #'generate-all (rewrites phrase)))
        (t (list (list phrase)))))

(defun combine-all (xlist ylist)
  "Return a list of lists formed by appending a y to an x.
  E.g., (combine-all '((a) (b)) '((1) (2)))
  -> ((A 1) (B 1) (A 2) (B 2))."
  (mappend #'(lambda (y)
               (mapcar #'(lambda (x) (append x y)) xlist))
           ylist))
```

We can now use generate-all to test our original little grammar. Note that a serious drawback of generate-all is that it can't deal with recursive grammar rules like 'Adj* $\Rightarrow$ Adj + Adj*' that appear in *bigger-grammar*, since these lead to an infinite number of outputs. But it works fine for finite languages, like the language generated by *simple-grammar*:

```
> (generate-all 'Article)
((THE) (A))

> (generate-all 'Noun)
((MAN) (BALL) (WOMAN) (TABLE))

> (generate-all 'noun-phrase)
((A MAN) (A BALL) (A WOMAN) (A TABLE)
 (THE MAN) (THE BALL) (THE WOMAN) (THE TABLE))

> (length (generate-all 'sentence))
256
```

There are 256 sentences because every sentence in this language has the form Article-Noun-Verb-Article-Noun, and there are two articles, four nouns and four verbs $(2 \times 4 \times 4 \times 2 \times 4 = 256)$.

2.7   Exercises

Exercise 2.3 [h]   Write a trivial grammar for some other language. This can be a natural language other than English, or perhaps a subset of a computer language.

Exercise 2.4 [m]   One way of describing combine-all is that it calculates the cross-product of the function append on the argument lists. Write the higher-order function cross-product, and define combine-all in terms of it.

The moral is to make your code as general as possible, because you never know what you may want to do with it next.

2.8   Answers

Answer 2.1

```
(defun generate (phrase)
  "Generate a random sentence or phrase"
  (let ((choices nil))
    (cond ((listp phrase)
           (mappend #'generate phrase))
          ((setf choices (rewrites phrase))
           (generate (random-elt choices)))
          (t (list phrase)))))
```

Answer 2.2

```
(defun generate (phrase)
  "Generate a random sentence or phrase"
  (cond ((listp phrase)
         (mappend #'generate phrase))
        ((non-terminal-p phrase)
         (generate (random-elt (rewrites phrase))))
        (t (list phrase))))

(defun non-terminal-p (category)
  "True if this is a category in the grammar."
  (not (null (rewrites category))))
```

Answer 2.4

```
(defun cross-product (fn xlist ylist)
  "Return a list of all (fn x y) values."
  (mappend #'(lambda (y)
               (mapcar #'(lambda (x) (funcall fn x y))
                       xlist))
           ylist))

(defun combine-all (xlist ylist)
  "Return a list of lists formed by appending a y to an x"
  (cross-product #'append xlist ylist))
```

Now we can use the cross-product in other ways as well:

```
> (cross-product #'+ '(1 2 3) '(10 20 30))
(11 12 13
 21 22 23
 31 32 33)

> (cross-product #'list '(a b c d e f g h)
                        '(1 2 3 4 5 6 7 8))
((A 1) (B 1) (C 1) (D 1) (E 1) (F 1) (G 1) (H 1)
 (A 2) (B 2) (C 2) (D 2) (E 2) (F 2) (G 2) (H 2)
 (A 3) (B 3) (C 3) (D 3) (E 3) (F 3) (G 3) (H 3)
 (A 4) (B 4) (C 4) (D 4) (E 4) (F 4) (G 4) (H 4)
 (A 5) (B 5) (C 5) (D 5) (E 5) (F 5) (G 5) (H 5)
 (A 6) (B 6) (C 6) (D 6) (E 6) (F 6) (G 6) (H 6)
 (A 7) (B 7) (C 7) (D 7) (E 7) (F 7) (G 7) (H 7)
 (A 8) (B 8) (C 8) (D 8) (E 8) (F 8) (G 8) (H 8))
```

CHAPTER 3

Overview of Lisp

No doubt about it. Common Lisp is a big *language.*

—Guy L. Steele, Jr.
Foreword to Koschman 1990

This chapter briefly covers the most important special forms and functions in Lisp. It can be safely skipped or skimmed by the experienced Common Lisp programmer but is required reading for the novice Lisp programmer, or one who is new to the Common Lisp dialect.

This chapter can be used as a reference source, but the definitive reference is Steele's *Common Lisp the Language,* 2d edition, which should be consulted whenever there is any confusion. Since that book is 25 times longer than this chapter, it is clear that we can only touch on the important highlights here. More detailed coverage is given later in this book as each feature is used in a real program.

3.1 A Guide to Lisp Style

The beginning Common Lisp programmer is often overwhelmed by the number of options that the language provides. In this chapter we show fourteen different ways to find the length of a list. How is the programmer to choose between them? One answer is by reading examples of good programs—as illustrated in this book—and copying that style. In general, there are six maxims that every programmer should follow:

- Be specific.

- Use abstractions.

- Be concise.

- Use the provided tools.

- Don't be obscure.

- Be consistent.

These require some explanation.

Using the most specific form possible makes it easier for your reader to understand your intent. For example, the conditional special form when is more specific than if. The reader who sees a when knows to look for only one thing: the clause to consider when the test is true. The reader who sees an if can rightfully expect two clauses: one for when the test is true, and one for when it is false. Even though it is possible to use if when there is only one clause, it is preferable to use when, because when is more specific.

One important way of being specific is using abstractions. Lisp provides very general data structures, such as lists and arrays. These can be used to implement specific data structures that your program will use, but you should not make the mistake of invoking primitive functions directly. If you define a list of names:

```
(defvar *names* '((Robert E. Lee) ...))
```

then you should also define functions to get at the components of each name. To get at Lee, use (last-name (first *names*)), not (caddar *names*).

Often the maxims are in concord. For example, if your code is trying to find an element in a list, you should use find (or maybe find-if), not loop or do. find is more specific than the general constructs loop or do, it is an abstraction, it is more concise, it is a built-in tool, and it is simple to understand.

Sometimes, however, the maxims are in conflict, and experience will tell you which one to prefer. Consider the following two ways of placing a new key/value pair on an association list:[1]

```
(push (cons key val) a-list)
(setf a-list (acons key val a-list))
```

The first is more concise. But the second is more specific, as it uses the `acons` function, which is designed specifically for association lists. The decision between them probably hinges on obscurity: those who find `acons` to be a familiar function would prefer the second, and those who find it obscure would prefer the first.

A similar choice arises in the question of setting a variable to a value. Some prefer (`setq x val`) because it is most specific; others use (`setf x val`), feeling that it is more consistent to use a single form, `setf`, for all updating. Whichever choice you make on such issues, remember the sixth maxim: be consistent.

3.2   Special Forms

As noted in chapter 1, "special form" is the term used to refer both to Common Lisp's syntactic constructs and the reserved words that mark these constructs. The most commonly used special forms are:

definitions	conditional	variables	iteration	other
defun	and	let	do	declare
defstruct	case	let*	do*	function
defvar	cond	pop	dolist	progn
defparameter	if	push	dotimes	quote
defconstant	or	setf	loop	return
defmacro	unless	incf		trace
labels	when	decf		untrace

To be precise, only `declare`, `function`, `if`, `labels`, `let`, `let*`, `progn` and `quote` are true special forms. The others are actually defined as macros that expand into calls to more primitive special forms and functions. There is no real difference to the programmer, and Common Lisp implementations are free to implement macros as special forms and vice versa, so for simplicity we will continue to use "special form" as a blanket term for both true special forms and built-in macros.

---

[1] Association lists are covered in section 3.6.

Special Forms for Definitions

In this section we survey the special forms that can be used to introduce new global functions, macros, variables, and structures. We have already seen the defun form for defining functions; the defmacro form is similar and is covered on page 66.

> (defun *function-name* (*parameter...*) *"optional documentation" body...*)
> (defmacro *macro-name* (*parameter...*) *"optional documentation" body...*)

There are three forms for introducing special variables. defvar defines a special variable and can optionally be used to supply an initial value and a documentation string. The initial value is evaluated and assigned only if the variable does not yet have any value. defparameter is similar, except that the value is required, and it will be used to change any existing value. defconstant is used to declare that a symbol will always stand for a particular value.

> (defvar *variable-name initial-value* "optional documentation")
> (defparameter *variable-name value* "optional documentation")
> (defconstant *variable-name value* "optional documentation")

All the def- forms define global objects. It is also possible to define local variables with let, and to define local functions with labels, as we shall see.

Most programming languages provide a way to group related data together into a structure. Common Lisp is no exception. The defstruct special form defines a structure type (known as a *record* type in Pascal) and automatically defines functions to get at components of the structure. The general syntax is:

> (defstruct *structure-name "optional documentation" slot...*)

As an example, we could define a structure for names:

```
(defstruct name
  first
  (middle nil)
  last)
```

This automatically defines the constructor function make-name, the recognizer predicate name-p, and the accessor functions name-first, name-middle and name-last. The (middle nil) means that each new name built by make-name will have a middle name of nil by default. Here we create, access, and modify a structure:

```
> (setf b (make-name :first 'Barney :last 'Rubble)) ⇒
#S(NAME :FIRST BARNEY :LAST RUBBLE)

> (name-first b) ⇒ BARNEY

> (name-middle b) ⇒ NIL

> (name-last b) ⇒ RUBBLE

> (name-p b) ⇒ T

> (name-p 'Barney) ⇒ NIL      ; only the results of make-name are names

> (setf (name-middle b) 'Q) ⇒ Q

> b ⇒ #S(NAME :FIRST BARNEY :MIDDLE Q :LAST RUBBLE)
```

The printed representation of a structure starts with a #S and is followed by a list consisting of the type of the structure and alternating pairs of slot names and values. Do not let this representation fool you: it is a convenient way of printing the structure, but it is not an accurate picture of the way structures are represented internally. Structures are actually implemented much like vectors. For the name structure, the type would be in the zero element of the vector, the first name in the first element, middle in the second, and last in the third. This means structures are more efficient than lists: they take up less space, and any element can be accessed in a single step. In a list, it takes n steps to access the nth element.

There are options that give more control over the structure itself and the individual slots. They will be covered later as they come up.

Special Forms for Conditionals

We have seen the special form if, which has the form (if *test then-part else-part*), where either the *then-part* or the *else-part* is the value, depending on the success of the *test*. Remember that only nil counts as false; all other values are considered true for the purpose of conditionals. However, the constant t is the conventional value used to denote truth (unless there is a good reason for using some other value).

There are actually quite a few special forms for doing conditional evaluation. Technically, if is defined as a special form, while the other conditionals are macros, so in some sense if is supposed to be the most basic. Some programmers prefer to use if for most of their conditionals; others prefer cond because it has been around the longest and is versatile (if not particularly pretty). Finally, some programmers opt for a style more like English prose, and freely use when, unless, if, and all the others.

The following table shows how each conditional can be expressed in terms of if and cond. Actually, these translations are not quite right, because or, case, and cond take care not to evaluate any expression more than once, while the translations with if can lead to multiple evaluation of some expressions. The table also has translations to cond. The syntax of cond is a series of *cond-clauses*, each consisting of a test expression followed by any number of *result* expressions:

```
(cond (test result...)
      (test result...)
      ...)
```

cond goes through the cond-clauses one at a time, evaluating each test expression. As soon as a test expression evaluates non-nil, the result expressions for that clause are each evaluated, and the last expression in the clause is the value of the whole cond. In particular, if a cond-clause consists of just a test and no result expressions, then the value of the cond is the test expression itself, if it is non-nil. If all of the test expressions evaluate to nil, then nil is returned as the value of the cond. A common idiom is to make the last cond-clause be (t *result...*).

The forms when and unless operate like a single cond clause. Both forms consist of a test followed by any number of consequents, which are evaluated if the test is satisfied—that is, if the test is true for when or false for unless.

The and form tests whether every one of a list of conditions is true, and or tests whether any one is true. Both evaluate the arguments left to right, and stop as soon as the final result can be determined. Here is a table of equivalences:

conditional	if **form**	cond **form**
(when *test a b c*)	(if *test* (progn *a b c*))	(cond (*test a b c*))
(unless *test x y*)	(if (not *test*) (progn *x y*))	(cond ((not *test*) *x y*))
(and *a b c*)	(if *a* (if *b c*))	(cond (*a* (cond (*b c*))))
(or *a b c*)	(if *a a* (if *b b c*))	(cond (*a*) (*b*) (*c*))
(case *a* (*b c*) (t *x*))	(if (eql *a* '*b*) *c x*)	(cond ((eql *a* '*b*) *c*) (t *x*))

It is considered poor style to use and and or for anything other than testing a logical condition. when, unless, and if can all be used for taking conditional action. For example:

```
(and (> n 100)
     (princ "N is large."))    ; Bad style!

(or (<= n 100)
    (princ "N is large."))     ; Even worse style!

(cond ((> n 100)               ; OK, but not MY preference
       (princ "N is large."))

(when (> n 100)
  (princ "N is large."))       ; Good style.
```

When the main purpose is to return a value rather than take action, cond and if (with explicit nil in the else case) are preferred over when and unless, which implicitly return nil in the else case. when and unless are preferred when there is only one possibility, if (or, for some people, cond) when there are two, and cond when there are more than two:

```
(defun tax-bracket (income)
  "Determine what percent tax should be paid for this income."
  (cond ((< income 10000.00) 0.00)
        ((< income 30000.00) 0.20)
        ((< income 50000.00) 0.25)
        ((< income 70000.00) 0.30)
        (t                   0.35)))
```

If there are several tests comparing an expression to constants, then case is appropriate. A case form looks like:

```
(case expression
  (match result...)...)
```

The *expression* is evaluated and compared to each successive *match*. As soon as one is eql, the *result* expressions are evaluated and the last one is returned. Note that the *match* expressions are *not* evaluated. If a *match* expression is a list, then case tests if the *expression* is eql to any member of the list. If a *match* expression is the symbol otherwise (or the symbol t), then it matches anything. (It only makes sense for this otherwise clause to be the last one.)

There is also another special form, typecase, which compares the type of an expression against several possibilities and, like case, chooses the first clause that matches. In addition, the special forms ecase and etypecase are just like case and typecase except that they signal an error if there is no match. You can think of the e as standing for either "exhaustive" or "error." The forms ccase and ctypecase also signal errors, but they can be continuable errors (as opposed to fatal errors): the user is offered the chance to change the expression to something that satisfies one of the matches. Here are some examples of case forms and their cond equivalents:

```
(case x                        (cond
  (1 10)                         ((eql x 1) 10)
  (2 20))                        ((eql x 2) 20))

(typecase x                    (cond
  (number (abs x))               ((typep x 'number) (abs x))
  (list (length x)))             ((typep x 'list) (length x)))

(ecase x                       (cond
  (1 10)                         ((eql x 1) 10)
  (2 20))                        ((eql x 2) 20)
                                 (t (error "no valid case")))
```

```
(etypecase x                    (cond
  (number (abs x))                ((typep x 'number) (abs x))
  (list (length x)))              ((typep x 'list) (length x))
                                  (t (error "no valid typecase")))
```

Special Forms for Dealing with Variables and Places

The special form setf is used to assign a new value to a variable or *place*, much as an assignment statement with = or := is used in other languages. A place, or *generalized variable* is a name for a location that can have a value stored in it. Here is a table of corresponding assignment forms in Lisp and Pascal:

```
;; Lisp                         /* Pascal */
(setf x 0)                      x := 0;
(setf (aref A i j) 0)           A[i,j] := 0;
(setf (rest list) nil)          list^.rest := nil;
(setf (name-middle b) 'Q)       b^.middle := "Q";
```

setf can be used to set a component of a structure as well as to set a variable. In languages like Pascal, the expressions that can appear on the left-hand side of an assignment statement are limited by the syntax of the language. In Lisp, the user can extend the expressions that are allowed in a setf form using the special forms defsetf or define-setf-method. These are introduced on pages 514 and 884 respectively.

There are also some built-in functions that modify places. For example, (rplacd list nil) has the same effect as (setf (rest list) nil), except that it returns list instead of nil. Most Common Lisp programmers prefer to use the setf forms rather than the specialized functions.

If you only want to set a variable, the special form setq can be used instead. In this book I choose to use setf throughout, opting for consistency over specificity.

The discussion in this section makes it seem that variables (and slots of structures) are assigned new values all the time. Actually, many Lisp programs do no assignments whatsoever. It is very common to use Lisp in a functional style where new variables may be introduced, but once a new variable is established, it never changes. One way to introduce a new variable is as a parameter of a function. It is also possible to introduce local variables using the special form let. Following are the general let form, along with an example. Each variable is bound to the corresponding value, and then the body is evaluated:

```
(let ((variable value)...)        (let ((x 40)
    body...)                            (y (+ 1 1)))
                                    (+ x y)) ⇒ 42
```

Defining a local variable with a let form is really no different from defining parameters to an anonymous function. The former is equivalent to:

```
((lambda (variable...)            ((lambda (x y)
     body...)                          (+ x y))
   value...)                       40
                                   (+ 1 1))
```

First, all the values are evaluated. Then they are bound to the variables (the parameters of the lambda expression), and finally the body is evaluated, using those bindings.

The special form let* is appropriate when you want to use one of the newly introduced variables in a subsequent *value* computation. For example:

```
(let* ((x 6)
       (y (* x x)))
    (+ x y)) ⇒ 42
```

We could not have used let here, because then the variable x would be unbound during the computation of y's value.

Exercise 3.1 [m] Show a lambda expression that is equivalent to the above let* expression. You may need more than one lambda.

Because lists are so important to Lisp, there are special forms for adding and deleting elements from the front of a list—in other words, for treating a list as a stack. If list is the name of a location that holds a list, then (push x list) will change list to have *x* as its first element, and (pop list) will return the first element and, as a side-effect, change list to no longer contain the first element. push and pop are equivalent to the following expressions:

```
(push x list) ≡ (setf list (cons x list))
(pop list)    ≡ (let ((result (first list)))
                   (setf list (rest list))
                   result)
```

Just as a list can be used to accumulate elements, a running sum can be used to accumulate numbers. Lisp provides two more special forms, incf and decf, that can be used to increment or decrement a sum. For both forms the first argument must be a location (a variable or other `setf`-able form) and the second argument, which is optional, is the number to increment or decrement by. For those who know C, (`incf x`) is equivalent to ++x, and (`incf x 2`) is equivalent to x+=2. In Lisp the equivalence is:

```
(incf x) ≡ (incf x 1) ≡ (setf x (+ x 1))
(decf x) ≡ (decf x 1) ≡ (setf x (- x 1))
```

When the location is a complex form rather than a variable, Lisp is careful to expand into code that does not evaluate any subform more than once. This holds for `push`, `pop`, `incf`, and `decf`. In the following example, we have a list of players and want to decide which player has the highest score, and thus has won the game. The structure `player` has slots for the player's score and number of wins, and the function `determine-winner` increments the winning player's `wins` field. The expansion of the `incf` form binds a temporary variable so that the sort is not done twice.

```
(defstruct player (score 0) (wins 0))

(defun determine-winner (players)
  "Increment the WINS for the player with highest score."
  (incf (player-wins (first (sort players #'>
                                  :key #'player-score)))))
≡
(defun determine-winner (players)
  "Increment the WINS for the player with highest score."
  (let ((temp (first (sort players #'> :key #'player-score))))
    (setf (player-wins temp) (+ (player-wins temp) 1))))
```

Functions and Special Forms for Repetition

Many languages have a small number of reserved words for forming iterative loops. For example, Pascal has `while`, `repeat`, and `for` statements. In contrast, Common Lisp has an almost bewildering range of possibilities, as summarized below:

`dolist`	loop over elements of a list
`dotimes`	loop over successive integers
`do, do*`	general loop, sparse syntax
`loop`	general loop, verbose syntax
`mapc, mapcar`	loop over elements of lists(s)
`some, every`	loop over list until condition
`find, reduce,` *etc.*	more specific looping functions
recursion	general repetition

To explain each possibility, we will present versions of the function length, which returns the number of elements in a list. First, the special form dolist can be used to iterate over the elements of a list. The syntax is:

(dolist (*variable list optional-result*) *body...*)

This means that the body is executed once for each element of the list, with *variable* bound to the first element, then the second element, and so on. At the end, dolist evaluates and returns the *optional-result* expression, or nil if there is no result expression.

Below is a version of length using dolist. The let form introduces a new variable, len, which is initially bound to zero. The dolist form then executes the body once for each element of the list, with the body incrementing len by one each time. This use is unusual in that the loop iteration variable, element, is not used in the body.

```
(defun length1 (list)
  (let ((len 0))           ; start with LEN=0
    (dolist (element list)  ; and on each iteration
      (incf len))           ;  increment LEN by 1
    len))                   ; and return LEN
```

It is also possible to use the optional result of dolist, as shown below. While many programmers use this style, I find that it is too easy to lose track of the result, and so I prefer to place the result last explictly.

```
(defun length1.1 (list)    ; alternate version:
  (let ((len 0))           ; (not my preference)
    (dolist (element list len)  ; uses len as result here
      (incf len))))
```

The function mapc performs much the same operation as the special form dolist. In the simplest case, mapc takes two arguments, the first a function, the second a list. It applies the function to each element of the list. Here is length using mapc:

```
(defun length2 (list)
  (let ((len 0))           ; start with LEN=0
    (mapc #'(lambda (element)  ; and on each iteration
              (incf len))       ;  increment LEN by 1
          list)
    len))                   ; and return LEN
```

There are seven different mapping functions, of which the most useful are mapc and mapcar. mapcar executes the same function calls as mapc, but then returns the results in a list.

There is also a dotimes form, which has the syntax:

(dotimes (*variable number optional-result*) *body...*)

and executes the body with *variable* bound first to zero, then one, all the way up to *number*−1 (for a total of *number* times). Of course, dotimes is not appropriate for implementing length, since we don't know the number of iterations ahead of time.

There are two very general looping forms, do and loop. The syntax of do is as follows:

```
(do  ((variable initial next)...)
     (exit-test  result)
   body...)
```

Each *variable* is initially bound to the *initial* value. If *exit-test* is true, then *result* is returned. Otherwise, the body is executed and each *variable* is set to the corresponding *next* value and *exit-test* is tried again. The loop repeats until *exit-test* is true. If a *next* value is omitted, then the corresponding variable is not updated each time through the loop. Rather, it is treated as if it had been bound with a let form.

Here is length implemented with do, using two variables, len to count the number of elements, and l to go down the list. This is often referred to as *cdr-ing down a list,* because on each operation we apply the function cdr to the list. (Actually, here we have used the more mnemonic name rest instead of cdr.) Note that the do loop has no body! All the computation is done in the variable initialization and stepping, and in the end test.

```
(defun length3 (list)
  (do ((len 0 (+ len 1))    ; start with LEN=0, increment
       (l list (rest l)))   ; ... on each iteration
      ((null l) len)))      ; (until the end of the list)
```

I find the do form a little confusing, because it does not clearly say that we are looping through a list. To see that it is indeed iterating over the list requires looking at both the variable l and the end test. Worse, there is no variable that stands for the current element of the list; we would need to say (first l) to get at it. Both dolist and mapc take care of stepping, end testing, and variable naming automatically. They are examples of the "be specific" principle. Because it is so unspecific, do will not be used much in this book. However, many good programmers use it, so it is important to know how to read do loops, even if you decide never to write one.

The syntax of loop is an entire language by itself, and a decidedly non-Lisp-like language it is. Rather than list all the possibilities for loop, we will just give examples here, and refer the reader to *Common Lisp the Language,* 2d edition, or chapter 24.5 for more details. Here are three versions of length using loop:

```lisp
(defun length4 (list)
    (loop for element in list      ; go through each element
          count t))                ;    counting each one

(defun length5 (list)
    (loop for element in list      ; go through each element
          summing 1))              ;    adding 1 each time

(defun length6 (list)
    (loop with len = 0             ; start with LEN=0
          until (null list)        ; and (until end of list)
          for element = (pop list) ; on each iteration
          do (incf len)            ;    increment LEN by 1
          finally (return len)))   ; and return LEN
```

Every programmer learns that there are certain kinds of loops that are used again and again. These are often called *programming idioms* or *cliches.* An example is going through the elements of a list or array and doing some operation to each element. In most languages, these idioms do not have an explicit syntactic marker. Instead, they are implemented with a general loop construct, and it is up to the reader of the program to recognize what the programmer is doing.

Lisp is unusual in that it provides ways to explicitly encapsulate such idioms, and refer to them with explicit syntactic and functional forms. dolist and dotimes are two examples of this—they both follow the "be specific" principle. Most programmers prefer to use a dolist rather than an equivalent do, because it cries out "this loop iterates over the elements of a list." Of course, the corresponding do form also says the same thing—but it takes more work for the reader to discover this.

In addition to special forms like dolist and dotimes, there are quite a few functions that are designed to handle common idioms. Two examples are count-if, which counts the number of elements of a sequence that satisfy a predicate, and position-if, which returns the index of an element satisfying a predicate. Both can be used to implement length. In length7 below, count-if gives the number of elements in list that satisfy the predicate true. Since true is defined to be always true, this gives the length of the list.

```lisp
(defun length7 (list)
    (count-if #'true list))

(defun true (x) t)
```

In length8, the function position-if finds the position of an element that satisfies the predicate true, starting from the end of the list. This will be the very last element of the list, and since indexing is zero-based, we add one to get the length. Admittedly, this is not the most straightforward implementation of length.

```
(defun length8 (list)
  (if (null list)
      0
      (+ 1 (position-if #'true list :from-end t))))
```

A partial table of functions that implement looping idioms is given below. These functions are designed to be flexible enough to handle almost all operations on sequences. The flexibility comes in three forms. First, functions like mapcar can apply to an arbitrary number of lists, not just one:

```
> (mapcar #'- '(1 2 3)) ⇒ (-1 -2 -3)
> (mapcar #'+ '(1 2) '(10 20)) ⇒ (11 22)
> (mapcar #'+ '(1 2) '(10 20) '(100 200)) ⇒ (111 222)
```

Second, many of the functions accept keywords that allow the user to vary the test for comparing elements, or to only consider part of the sequence.

```
> (remove 1 '(1 2 3 2 1 0 -1)) ⇒ (2 3 2 0 -1)

> (remove 1 '(1 2 3 2 1 0 -1) :key #'abs) ⇒ (2 3 2 0)

> (remove 1 '(1 2 3 2 1 0 -1) :test #'<) ⇒ (1 1 0 -1)

> (remove 1 '(1 2 3 2 1 0 -1) :start 4) ⇒ (1 2 3 2 0 -1)
```

Third, some have corresponding functions ending in -if or -if-not that take a predicate rather than an element to match against:

```
> (remove-if #'oddp '(1 2 3 2 1 0 -1)) ⇒ (2 2 0)

> (remove-if-not #'oddp '(1 2 3 2 1 0 -1)) ⇒ (1 3 1 -1)

> (find-if #'evenp '(1 2 3 2 1 0 -1)) ⇒ 2
```

The following two tables assume these two values:

```
(setf x '(a b c))
(setf y '(1 2 3))
```

The first table lists functions that work on any number of lists but do not accept keywords:

(every #'oddp y)	⇒ nil	test if every element satisfies a predicate
(some #'oddp y)	⇒ t	test if some element satisfies predicate
(mapcar #'- y)	⇒ (-1 -2 -3)	apply function to each element and return result
(mapc #'print y)	*prints* 1 2 3	perform operation on each element

The second table lists functions that have -if and -if-not versions and also accept keyword arguments:

(member 2 y)	⇒ (2 3)	see if element is in list
(count 'b x)	⇒ 1	count the number of matching elements
(delete 1 y)	⇒ (2 3)	omit matching elements
(find 2 y)	⇒ 2	find first element that matches
(position 'a x)	⇒ 0	find index of element in sequence
(reduce #'+ y)	⇒ 6	apply function to succesive elements
(remove 2 y)	⇒ (1 3)	like delete, but makes a new copy
(substitute 4 2 y)	⇒ (1 4 3)	replace elements with new ones

Repetition through Recursion

Lisp has gained a reputation as a "recursive" language, meaning that Lisp encourages programmers to write functions that call themselves. As we have seen above, there is a dizzying number of functions and special forms for writing loops in Common Lisp, but it is also true that many programs handle repetition through recursion rather than with a syntactic loop.

One simple definition of length is "the empty list has length 0, and any other list has a length which is one more than the length of the rest of the list (after the first element)." This translates directly into a recursive function:

```
(defun length9 (list)
  (if (null list)
      0
      (+ 1 (length9 (rest list))))))
```

This version of length arises naturally from the recursive definition of a list: "a list is either the empty list or an element consed onto another list." In general, most recursive functions derive from the recursive nature of the data they are operating on. Some kinds of data, like binary trees, are hard to deal with in anything but a recursive fashion. Others, like lists and integers, can be defined either recursively (leading to recursive functions) or as a sequence (leading to iterative functions). In this book, I tend to use the "list-as-sequence" view rather than the "list-as-first-and-rest" view. The reason is that defining a list as a first and a rest is an arbitrary and artificial distinction that is based on the implementation of lists that Lisp happens to use. But there are many other ways to decompose a list. We could break it into the last element and all-but-the-last elements, for example, or the first half and the second half. The "list-as-sequence" view makes no such artificial distinction. It treats all elements identically.

One objection to the use of recursive functions is that they are inefficient, because the compiler has to allocate memory for each recursive call. This may be true for the function length9, but it is not necessarily true for all recursive calls. Consider the following definition:

```
(defun length10 (list)
  (length10-aux list 0))

(defun length10-aux (sublist len-so-far)
  (if (null sublist)
      len-so-far
      (length10-aux (rest sublist) (+ 1 len-so-far))))
```

length10 uses length10-aux as an auxiliary function, passing it 0 as the length of the list so far. length10-aux then goes down the list to the end, adding 1 for each element. The invariant relation is that the length of the sublist plus len-so-far always equals the length of the original list. Thus, when the sublist is nil, then len-so-far is the length of the original list. Variables like len-so-far that keep track of partial results are called *accumulators*. Other examples of functions that use accumulators include flatten-all on page 329; one-unknown on page 237; the Prolog predicates discussed on page 686; and anonymous-variables-in on pages 400 and 433, which uses two accumulators.

The important difference between length9 and length10 is *when* the addition is done. In length9, the function calls itself, then returns, and then adds 1. In length10-aux, the function adds 1, then calls itself, then returns. There are no pending operations to do after the recursive call returns, so the compiler is free to release any memory allocated for the original call before making the recursive call. length10-aux is called a *tail-recursive* function, because the recursive call appears as the last thing the function does (the tail). Many compilers will optimize tail-recursive calls, although not all do. (Chapter 22 treats tail-recursion in more detail, and points out that Scheme compilers guarantee that tail-recursive calls will be optimized.)

Some find it ugly to introduce length10-aux. For them, there are two alternatives. First, we could combine length10 and length10-aux into a single function with an optional parameter:

```
(defun length11 (list &optional (len-so-far 0))
  (if (null list)
      len-so-far
      (length11 (rest list) (+ 1 len-so-far))))
```

Second, we could introduce a *local* function inside the definition of the main function. This is done with the special form labels:

```lisp
(defun length12 (the-list)
  (labels
    ((length13 (list len-so-far)
       (if (null list)
           len-so-far
           (length13 (rest list) (+ 1 len-so-far)))))
    (length13 the-list 0)))
```

In general, a labels form (or the similar flet form) can be used to introduce one or more local functions. It has the following syntax:

```lisp
(labels
  ((function-name (parameter...) function-body)...)
  body-of-labels)
```

Other Special Forms

A few more special forms do not fit neatly into any category. We have already seen the two special forms for creating constants and functions, quote and function. These are so common that they have abbreviations: 'x for (quote x) and #'f for (function f).

The special form progn can be used to evaluate a sequence of forms and return the value of the last one:

```lisp
(progn (setf x 0) (setf x (+ x 1)) x) ⇒ 1
```

progn is the equivalent of a begin...end block in other languages, but it is used very infrequently in Lisp. There are two reasons for this. First, programs written in a functional style never need a sequence of actions, because they don't have side effects. Second, even when side effects are used, many special forms allow for a body which is a sequence—an implicit progn. I can only think of three places where a progn is justified. First, to implement side effects in a branch of a two-branched conditional, one could use either an if with a progn, or a cond:

```lisp
(if (> x 100)                    (cond ((> x 100)
    (progn (print "too big")            (print "too big")
           (setf x 100))                (setf x 100))
    x)                                 (t x))
```

If the conditional had only one branch, then when or unless should be used, since they allow an implicit progn. If there are more than two branches, then cond should be used.

Second, progn is sometimes needed in macros that expand into more than one top-level form, as in the defun* macro on page 326, section 10.3. Third, a progn is sometimes needed in an unwind-protect, an advanced macro. An example of this is the with-resource macro on page 338, section 10.4.

The forms trace and untrace are used to control debugging information about entry and exit to a function:

```
> (trace length9) ⇒ (LENGTH9)

> (length9 '(a b c)) ⇒
(1 ENTER LENGTH9: (A B C))
  (2 ENTER LENGTH9: (B C))
    (3 ENTER LENGTH9: (C))
      (4 ENTER LENGTH9: NIL)
      (4 EXIT LENGTH9: 0)
    (3 EXIT LENGTH9: 1)
  (2 EXIT LENGTH9: 2)
(1 EXIT LENGTH9: 3)
3

> (untrace length9) ⇒ (LENGTH9)

> (length9 '(a b c)) ⇒ 3
```

Finally, the special form return can be used to break out of a block of code. Blocks are set up by the special form block, or by the looping forms (do, do*, dolist, dotimes, or loop). For example, the following function computes the product of a list of numbers, but if any number is zero, then the whole product must be zero, so we immediately return zero from the dolist loop. Note that this returns from the dolist only, not from the function itself (although in this case, the value returned by dolist becomes the value returned by the function, because it is the last expression in the function). I have used uppercase letters in RETURN to emphasize the fact that it is an unusual step to exit from a loop.

```
(defun product (numbers)
  "Multiply all the numbers together to compute their product."
  (let ((prod 1))
    (dolist (n numbers prod)
      (if (= n 0)
          (RETURN 0)
          (setf prod (* n prod)))))))
```

Macros

The preceding discussion has been somewhat cavalier with the term "special form." Actually, some of these special forms are really *macros*, forms that the compiler expands into some other code. Common Lisp provides a number of built-in macros and allows the user to extend the language by defining new macros. (There is no way for the user to define new special forms, however.)

Macros are defined with the special form `defmacro`. Suppose we wanted to define a macro, `while`, that would act like the `while` loop statement of Pascal. Writing a macro is a four-step process:

- Decide if the macro is really necessary.

- Write down the syntax of the macro.

- Figure out what the macro should expand into.

- Use `defmacro` to implement the syntax/expansion correspondence.

The first step in writing a macro is to recognize that every time you write one, you are defining a new language that is just like Lisp except for your new macro. The programmer who thinks that way will rightfully be extremely frugal in defining macros. (Besides, when someone asks, "What did you get done today?" it sounds more impressive to say "I defined a new language and wrote a compiler for it" than to say "I just hacked up a couple of macros.") Introducing a macro puts much more memory strain on the reader of your program than does introducing a function, variable or data type, so it should not be taken lightly. Introduce macros only when there is a clear need, and when the macro fits in well with your existing system. As C.A.R. Hoare put it, "One thing the language designer should not do is to include untried ideas of his own."

The next step is to decide what code the macro should expand into. It is a good idea to follow established Lisp conventions for macro syntax whenever possible. Look at the looping macros (`dolist`, `dotimes`, `do-symbols`), the defining macros (`defun`, `defvar`, `defparameter`, `defstruct`), or the the I/O macros (`with-open-file`, `with-open-stream`, `with-input-from-string`), for example. If you follow the naming and syntax conventions for one of these instead of inventing your own conventions, you'll be doing the reader of your program a favor. For `while`, a good syntax is:

```
(while test body...)
```

The third step is to write the code that you want a macro call to expand into:

```
(loop
  (unless test (return nil))
  body)
```

The final step is to write the definition of the macro, using defmacro. A defmacro form is similar to a defun in that it has a parameter list, optional documentation string, and body. There are a few differences in what is allowed in the parameter list, which will be covered later. Here is a definition of the macro while, which takes a test and a body, and builds up the loop code shown previously:

```
(defmacro while (test &rest body)
  "Repeat body while test is true."
  (list* 'loop
         (list 'unless test '(return nil))
         body))
```

(The function list* is like list, except that the last argument is appended onto the end of the list of the other arguments.) We can see what this macro expands into by using macroexpand, and see how it runs by typing in an example:

```
> (macroexpand-1 '(while (< i 10)
                    (print (* i i))
                    (setf i (+ i 1)))) ⇒
(LOOP (UNLESS (< I 10) (RETURN NIL))
      (PRINT (* I I))
      (SETF I (+ I 1)))

> (setf i 7) ⇒ 7

> (while (< i 10)
    (print (* i i))
    (setf i (+ i 1))) ⇒
49
64
81
NIL
```

Section 24.6 (page 853) describes a more complicated macro and some details on the pitfalls of writing complicated macros (page 855).

Backquote Notation

The hardest part about defining while is building the code that is the expansion of the macro. It would be nice if there was a more immediate way of building code. The following version of while following attempts to do just that. It defines the local variable code to be a template for the code we want, and then substitutes the real values of the variables test and body for the placeholders in the code. This is done with the function subst; (subst *new old tree*) substitutes *new* for each occurrence of *old* anywhere within *tree*.

```
(defmacro while (test &rest body)
  "Repeat body while test is true."
  (let ((code '(loop (unless test (return nil)) . body)))
    (subst test 'test (subst body 'body code))))
```

The need to build up code (and noncode data) from components is so frequent that there is a special notation for it, the *backquote* notation. The backquote character "`" is similar to the quote character "'". A backquote indicates that what follows is *mostly* a literal expression but may contain some components that are to be evaluated. Anything marked by a leading comma "," is evaluated and inserted into the structure, and anything marked with a leading ",@" must evaluate to a list that is spliced into the structure: each element of the list is inserted, without the top-level parentheses. The notation is covered in more detail in section 23.5. Here we use the combination of backquote and comma to rewrite while:

```
(defmacro while (test &rest body)
  "Repeat body while test is true."
  `(loop (unless ,test (return nil))
         ,@body))
```

Here are some more examples of backquote. Note that at the end of a list, ",@" has the same effect as "." followed by ",". In the middle of a list, only ",@" is a possibility.

```
> (setf test1 '(a test)) ⇒ (A TEST)

> `(this is ,test1) ⇒ (THIS IS (A TEST))

> `(this is ,@test1) ⇒ (THIS IS A TEST)

> `(this is . ,test1) ⇒ (THIS IS A TEST)

> `(this is ,@test1 -- this is only ,@test1) ⇒
(THIS IS A TEST -- THIS IS ONLY A TEST)
```

This completes the section on special forms and macros. The remaining sections of this chapter give an overview of the important built-in functions in Common Lisp.

3.3   Functions on Lists

For the sake of example, assume we have the following assignments:

```
(setf x '(a b c))
(setf y '(1 2 3))
```

The most important functions on lists are summarized here. The more complicated ones are explained more thoroughly when they are used.

(first x)	⇒ a	first element of a list
(second x)	⇒ b	second element of a list
(third x)	⇒ c	third element of a list
(nth 0 x)	⇒ a	nth element of a list, 0-based
(rest x)	⇒ (b c)	all but the first element
(car x)	⇒ a	another name for the first element of a list
(cdr x)	⇒ (b c)	another name for all but the first element
(last x)	⇒ (c)	last cons cell in a list
(length x)	⇒ 3	number of elements in a list
(reverse x)	⇒ (c b a)	puts list in reverse order
(cons 0 y)	⇒ (0 1 2 3)	add to front of list
(append x y)	⇒ (a b c 1 2 3)	append together elements
(list x y)	⇒ ((a b c) (1 2 3))	make a new list
(list* 1 2 x)	⇒ (1 2 a b c)	append last argument to others
(null nil)	⇒ T	predicate is true of the empty list
(null x)	⇒ nil	...and false for everything else
(listp x)	⇒ T	predicate is true of any list, including nil
(listp 3)	⇒ nil	...and is false for nonlists
(consp x)	⇒ t	predicate is true of non-nil lists
(consp nil)	⇒ nil	...and false for atoms, including nil
(equal x x)	⇒ t	true for lists that look the same
(equal x y)	⇒ nil	...and false for lists that look different
(sort y #'>)	⇒ (3 2 1)	sort a list according to a comparison function
(subseq x 1 2)	⇒ (B)	subsequence with given start and end points

We said that (cons *a b*) builds a longer list by adding element *a* to the front of list *b*, but what if *b* is not a list? This is not an error; the result is an object *x* such that (first *x*) ⇒ *a*, (rest *x*) ⇒ *b*, and where *x* prints as (*a* . *b*). This is known as *dotted pair* notation. If *b* is a list, then the usual list notation is used for output rather than the dotted pair notation. But either notation can be used for input.

So far we have been thinking of lists as sequences, using phrases like "a list of three elements." The list is a convenient abstraction, but the actual implementation of lists relies on lower-level building blocks called *cons cells*. A cons cell is a data structure with two fields: a first and a rest. What we have been calling "a list of three elements" can also be seen as a single cons cell, whose first field points to the first element and whose rest field points to another cons cell that is a cons cell representing a list of two elements. This second cons cell has a rest field that is a third cons cell, one whose rest field is nil. All proper lists have a last cons cell whose rest field is nil. Figure 3.1 shows the cons cell notation for the three-element list (one two three), as well as for the result of (cons 'one 'two).

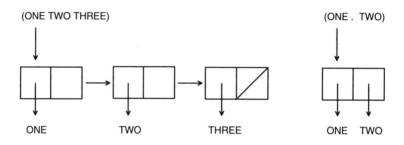

Figure 3.1: Cons Cell Diagrams

Exercise 3.2 [s]   The function cons can be seen as a special case of one of the other functions listed previously. Which one?

Exercise 3.3 [m]   Write a function that will print an expression in dotted pair notation. Use the built-in function princ to print each component of the expression.

Exercise 3.4 [m]   Write a function that, like the regular print function, will print an expression in dotted pair notation when necessary but will use normal list notation when possible.

3.4   Equality and Internal Representation

In Lisp there are five major equality predicates, because not all objects are created equally equal. The numeric equality predicate, =, tests if two numbers are the same. It is an error to apply = to non-numbers. The other equality predicates operate on any kind of object, but to understand the difference between them, we need to understand some of the internals of Lisp.

When Lisp reads a symbol in two different places, the result is guaranteed to be the exact same symbol. The Lisp system maintains a symbol table that the function read uses to map between characters and symbols. But when a list is read (or built) in two different places, the results are *not* identically the same, even though the corresponding elements may be. This is because read calls cons to build up the list, and each call to cons returns a new cons cell. Figure 3.2 shows two lists, x and y, which are both equal to (one two), but which are composed of different cons cells, and hence are not identical. Figure 3.3 shows that the expression (rest x) does not generate new cons cells, but rather shares structure with x, and that the expression (cons 'zero x) generates exactly one new cons cell, whose rest is x.

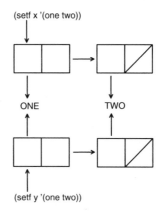

Figure 3.2: Equal But Nonidentical Lists

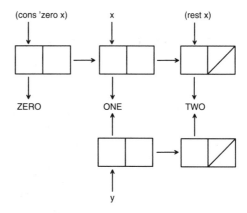

Figure 3.3: Parts of Lists

When two mathematically equal numbers are read (or computed) in two places, they may or may not be the same, depending on what the designers of your implementation felt was more efficient. In most systems, two equal fixnums will be identical, but equal numbers of other types will not (except possibly short floats). Common Lisp provides four equality predicates of increasing generality. All four begin with the letters eq, with more letters meaning the predicate considers more objects to be equal. The simplest predicate is eq, which tests for the exact same object. Next, eql tests for objects that are either eq or are equivalent numbers. equal tests for objects that are either eql or are lists or strings with eql elements. Finally, equalp is like equal except it also matches upper- and lowercase characters and numbers of different types. The following table summarizes the results of applying each of the four predicates to various values of x and y. The ? value means that the result depends on your implementation: two integers that are eql may or may not be eq.

x	y	eq	eql	equal	equalp
'x	'x	T	T	T	T
'0	'0	?	T	T	T
'(x)	'(x)	nil	nil	T	T
'"xy"	'"xy"	nil	nil	T	T
'"Xy"	'"xY"	nil	nil	nil	T
'0	'0.0	nil	nil	nil	T
'0	'1	nil	nil	nil	nil

In addition, there are specialized equality predicates such as =, tree-equal, char-equal, and string-equal, which compare numbers, trees, characters, and strings, respectively.

3.5   Functions on Sequences

Common Lisp is in a transitional position halfway between the Lisps of the past and the Lisps of the future. Nowhere is that more apparent than in the sequence functions. The earliest Lisps dealt only with symbols, numbers, and lists, and provided list functions like append and length. More modern Lisps added support for vectors, strings, and other data types, and introduced the term *sequence* to refer to both vectors and lists. (A vector is a one-dimensional array. It can be represented more compactly than a list, because there is no need to store the rest pointers. It is also more efficient to get at the nth element of a vector, because there is no need to follow a chain of pointers.) Modern Lisps also support strings that are vectors of characters, and hence also a subtype of sequence.

With the new data types came the problem of naming functions that operated on them. In some cases, Common Lisp chose to extend an old function: length can apply to vectors as well as lists. In other cases, the old names were reserved for the list functions, and new names were invented for generic sequence functions. For example, append and mapcar only work on lists, but concatenate and map work on any kind of sequence. In still other cases, new functions were invented for specific data types. For example, there are seven functions to pick the *n*th element out of a sequence. The most general is elt, which works on any kind of sequence, but there are specific functions for lists, arrays, strings, bit vectors, simple bit vectors, and simple vectors. Confusingly, nth is the only one that takes the index as the first argument:

```
(nth n list)
(elt sequence n)
(aref array n)
(char string n)
(bit bit vector n)
(sbit simple-bit vector n)
(svref simple-vector n)
```

The most important sequence functions are listed elsewhere in this chapter, depending on their particular purpose.

3.6 Functions for Maintaining Tables

Lisp lists can be used to represent a one-dimensional sequence of objects. Because they are so versatile, they have been put to other purposes, such as representing tables of information. The *association list* is a type of list used to implement tables. An association list is a list of dotted pairs, where each pair consists of a *key* and a *value*. Together, the list of pairs form a table: given a key, we can retrieve the corresponding value from the table, or verify that there is no such key stored in the table. Here's an example for looking up the names of states by their two-letter abbreviation. The function assoc is used. It returns the key/value pair (if there is one). To get the value, we just take the cdr of the result returned by assoc.

```
(setf state-table
  '((AL . Alabama) (AK . Alaska) (AZ . Arizona) (AR . Arkansas)))
> (assoc 'AK state-table) ⇒ (AK . ALASKA)
> (cdr (assoc 'AK state-table)) ⇒ ALASKA
> (assoc 'TX state-table) ⇒ NIL
```

If we want to search the table by value rather than by key, we can use rassoc:

```
> (rassoc 'Arizona table) ⇒ (AZ . ARIZONA)
```

```
> (car (rassoc 'Arizona table)) ⇒ AZ
```

Managing a table with assoc is simple, but there is one drawback: we have to search through the whole list one element at a time. If the list is very long, this may take a while.

Another way to manage tables is with *hash tables*. These are designed to handle large amounts of data efficiently but have a degree of overhead that can make them inappropriate for small tables. The function gethash works much like get—it takes two arguments, a key and a table. The table itself is initialized with a call to make-hash-table and modified with a setf of gethash:

```
(setf table (make-hash-table))

(setf (gethash 'AL table) 'Alabama)
(setf (gethash 'AK table) 'Alaska)
(setf (gethash 'AZ table) 'Arizona)
(setf (gethash 'AR table) 'Arkansas)
```

Here we retrieve values from the table:

```
> (gethash 'AK table) ⇒ ALASKA
> (gethash 'TX table) ⇒ NIL
```

The function remhash removes a key/value pair from a hash table, clrhash removes all pairs, and maphash can be used to map over the key/value pairs. The keys to hash tables are not restricted; they can be any Lisp object. There are many more details on the implementation of hash tables in Common Lisp, and an extensive literature on their theory.

A third way to represent table is with *property lists*. A property list is a list of alternating key/value pairs. Property lists (sometimes called p-lists or plists) and association lists (sometimes called a-lists or alists) are similar:

```
a-list: ((key₁ . val₁) (key₂ . val₂) ... (keyₙ . valₙ))
p-list: (key₁ val₁ key₂ val₂ ... keyₙ valₙ)
```

Given this representation, there is little to choose between a-lists and p-lists. They are slightly different permutations of the same information. The difference is in how they are normally used. Every symbol has a property list associated with it. That means we can associate a property/value pair directly with a symbol. Most programs use only a few different properties but have many instances of property/value pairs for each property. Thus, each symbol's p-list will likely be short. In our example, we are only interested in one property: the state associated with each abbreviation.

That means that the property lists will be very short indeed: one property for each abbreviation, instead of a list of 50 pairs in the association list implementation.

Property values are retrieved with the function get, which takes two arguments: the first is a symbol for which we are seeking information, and the second is the property of that symbol that we are interested in. get returns the value of that property, if one has been stored. Property/value pairs can be stored under a symbol with a setf form. A table would be built as follows:

```
(setf (get 'AL 'state) 'Alabama)
(setf (get 'AK 'state) 'Alaska)
(setf (get 'AZ 'state) 'Arizona)
(setf (get 'AR 'state) 'Arkansas)
```

Now we can retrieve values with get:

```
> (get 'AK 'state) ⇒ ALASKA
> (get 'TX 'state) ⇒ NIL
```

This will be faster because we can go immediately from a symbol to its lone property value, regardless of the number of symbols that have properties. However, if a given symbol has more than one property, then we still have to search linearly through the property list. As Abraham Lincoln might have said, you can make some of the table lookups faster some of the time, but you can't make all the table lookups faster all of the time. Notice that there is no equivalent of rassoc using property lists; if you want to get from a state to its abbreviation, you could store the abbreviation under a property of the state, but that would be a separate setf form, as in:

```
(setf (get 'Arizona 'abbrev) 'AZ)
```

In fact, when source, property, and value are all symbols, there are quite a few possibilities for how to use properties. We could have mimicked the a-list approach, and listed all the properties under a single symbol, using setf on the function symbol-plist (which gives a symbol's complete property list):

```
(setf (symbol-plist 'state-table)
      '(AL Alabama AK Alaska AZ Arizona AR Arkansas))
> (get 'state-table 'AL) ⇒ ALASKA
> (get 'state-table 'Alaska) ⇒ NIL
```

Property lists have a long history in Lisp, but they are falling out of favor as new alternatives such as hash tables are introduced. There are two main reasons why property lists are avoided. First, because symbols and their property lists are global, it is easy to get conflicts when trying to put together two programs that use property lists. If two programs use the same property for different purposes, they cannot be used together. Even if two programs use *different* properties on the same symbols, they will slow each other down. Second, property lists are messy. There is no way to remove quickly every element of a table implemented with property lists. In contrast, this can be done trivially with clrhash on hash tables, or by setting an association list to nil.

3.7   Functions on Trees

Many Common Lisp functions treat the expression ((a b) ((c)) (d e)) as a sequence of three elements, but there are a few functions that treat it as a tree with five non-null leaves. The function copy-tree creates a copy of a tree, and tree-equal tests if two trees are equal by traversing cons cells, but not other complex data like vectors or strings. In that respect, tree-equal is similar to equal, but tree-equal is more powerful because it allows a :test keyword:

```
> (setf tree '((a b) ((c)) (d e)))

> (tree-equal tree (copy-tree tree)) ⇒ T

(defun same-shape-tree (a b)
  "Are two trees the same except for the leaves?"
  (tree-equal a b :test #'true))

(defun true (&rest ignore) t)

> (same-shape-tree tree '((1 2) ((3)) (4 5))) ⇒ T

> (same-shape-tree tree '((1 2) (3) (4 5))) ⇒ NIL
```

Figure 3.4 shows the tree ((a b) ((c)) (d e)) as a cons cell diagram.

There are also two functions for substituting a new expression for an old one anywhere within a tree. subst substitutes a single value for another, while sublis takes a list of substitutions in the form of an association list of (*old . new*) pairs. Note that the order of old and new in the a-list for sublis is reversed from the order of arguments to subst. The name sublis is uncharacteristically short and confusing; a better name would be subst-list.

```
> (subst 'new 'old '(old ((very old)))) ⇒ (NEW ((VERY NEW)))

> (sublis '((old . new)) '(old ((very old)))) ⇒ (NEW ((VERY NEW)))

> (subst 'new 'old 'old) ⇒ 'NEW
```

```
(defun english->french (words)
  (sublis '((are . va) (book . libre) (friend . ami)
            (hello . bonjour) (how . comment) (my . mon)
            (red . rouge) (you . tu))
          words))
```

```
> (english->french '(hello my friend - how are you today?)) ⇒
(BONJOUR MON AMI - COMMENT VA TU TODAY?)
```

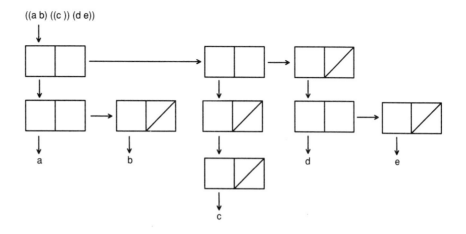

Figure 3.4: Cons Cell Diagram of a Tree

3.8   Functions on Numbers

The most commonly used functions on numbers are listed here. There are quite a few other numeric functions that have been omitted.

`(+ 4 2)`	$\Rightarrow 6$	add
`(- 4 2)`	$\Rightarrow 2$	subtract
`(* 4 2)`	$\Rightarrow 8$	multiply
`(/ 4 2)`	$\Rightarrow 2$	divide
`(> 100 99)`	$\Rightarrow$ t	greater than (also >=, greater than or equal to)
`(= 100 100)`	$\Rightarrow$ t	equal (also /=, not equal)
`(< 99 100)`	$\Rightarrow$ t	less than (also <=, less than or equal to)
`(random 100)`	$\Rightarrow 42$	random integer from 0 to 99
`(expt 4 2)`	$\Rightarrow 16$	exponentiation (also exp, e^x and `log`)
`(sin pi)`	$\Rightarrow 0.0$	sine function (also `cos`, `tan`, etc.)
`(asin 0)`	$\Rightarrow 0.0$	arcsine or $\sin^{-1}$ function (also `acos`, `atan`, etc.)
`(min 2 3 4)`	$\Rightarrow 2$	minimum (also `max`)
`(abs -3)`	$\Rightarrow 3$	absolute value
`(sqrt 4)`	$\Rightarrow 2$	square root
`(round 4.1)`	$\Rightarrow 4$	round off (also `truncate`, `floor`, `ceiling`)
`(rem 11 5)`	$\Rightarrow 1$	remainder (also `mod`)

3.9   Functions on Sets

One of the important uses of lists is to represent sets. Common Lisp provides functions that treat lists in just that way. For example, to see what elements the sets $r = \{a, b, c, d\}$ and $s = \{c, d, e\}$ have in common, we could use:

```
> (setf r '(a b c d)) ⇒ (A B C D)
> (setf s '(c d e)) ⇒ (C D E)
> (intersection r s) ⇒ (C D)
```

This implementation returned (C D) as the answer, but another might return (D C). They are equivalent sets, so either is valid, and your program should not depend on the order of elements in the result. Here are the main functions on sets:

`(intersection r s)`	$\Rightarrow$ (c d)	find common elements of two sets
`(union r s)`	$\Rightarrow$ (a b c d e)	find all elements in either of two sets
`(set-difference r s)`	$\Rightarrow$ (a b)	find elements in one but not other set
`(member 'd r)`	$\Rightarrow$ (d)	check if an element is a member of a set
`(subsetp s r)`	$\Rightarrow$ nil	see if all elements of one set are in another
`(adjoin 'b s)`	$\Rightarrow$ (b c d e)	add an element to a set
`(adjoin 'c s)`	$\Rightarrow$ (c d e)	... but don't add duplicates

It is also possible to represent a set with a sequence of bits, given a particular universe of discourse. For example, if every set we are interested in must be a subset of (a b c d e), then we can use the bit sequence 11110 to represent (a b c d), 00000 to represent the empty set, and 11001 to represent (a b e). The bit sequence can be represented in Common Lisp as a bit vector, or as an integer in binary notation. For example, (a b e) would be the bit vector #*11001 or the integer 25, which can also be written as #b11001.

The advantage of using bit sequences is that it takes less space to encode a set, assuming a small universe. Computation will be faster, because the computer's underlying instruction set will typically process 32 elements at a time.

Common Lisp provides a full complement of functions on both bit vectors and integers. The following table lists some, their correspondence to the list functions.

lists	integers	bit vectors
intersection	logand	bit-and
union	logior	bit-ior
set-difference	logandc2	bit-andc2
member	logbitp	bit
length	logcount	

For example,

```
(intersection '(a b c d) '(a b e)) ⇒ (A B)
(bit-and        #*11110    #*11001) ⇒ #*11000
(logand         #b11110    #b11001) ⇒ 24 ≡ #b11000
```

3.10 Destructive Functions

In mathematics, a function is something that computes an output value given some input arguments. Functions do not "do" anything, they just compute results. For example, if I tell you that $x = 4$ and $y = 5$ and ask you to apply the function "plus" to x and y, I expect you to tell me 9. If I then ask, "Now what is the value of x?" it would be surprising if x had changed. In mathematics, applying an operator to x can have no effect on the value of x.

In Lisp, some functions *are* able to take effect beyond just computing the result. These "functions" are not functions in the mathematical sense,[2] and in other languages they are known as "procedures." Of course, most of the Lisp functions *are* true mathematical functions, but the few that are not can cause great problems. They can

---

[2] In mathematics, a function must associate a unique output value with each input value.

also be quite useful in certain situations. For both reasons, they are worth knowing about.

Consider the following:

```
> (setf x '(a b c)) ⇒ (A B C)
> (setf y '(1 2 3)) ⇒ (1 2 3)
> (append x y) ⇒ (A B C 1 2 3)
```

append is a pure function, so after evaluating the call to append, we can rightfully expect that x and y retain their values. Now consider this:

```
> (nconc x y) ⇒ (A B C 1 2 3)
> x ⇒ (A B C 1 2 3)
> y ⇒ (1 2 3)
```

The function nconc computes the same result as append, but it has the side effect of altering its first argument. It is called a *destructive* function, because it destroys existing structures, replacing them with new ones. This means that there is quite a conceptual load on the programmer who dares to use nconc. He or she must be aware that the first argument may be altered, and plan accordingly. This is far more complicated than the case with nondestructive functions, where the programmer need worry only about the results of a function call.

The advantage of nconc is that it doesn't use any storage. While append must make a complete copy of x and then have that copy end with y, nconc does not need to copy anything. Instead, it just changes the rest field of the last element of x to point to y. So use destructive functions when you need to conserve storage, but be aware of the consequences.

Besides nconc, many of the destructive functions have names that start with n, including nreverse, nintersection, nunion, nset-difference, and nsubst. An important exception is delete, which is the name used for the destructive version of remove. Of course, the setf special form can also be used to alter structures, but it is the destructive functions that are most dangerous, because it is easier to overlook their effects.

Exercise 3.5 [h]   (Exercise in altering structure.) Write a program that will play the role of the guesser in the game Twenty Questions. The user of the program will have in mind any type of thing. The program will ask questions of the user, which must be answered yes or no, or "it" when the program has guessed it. If the program runs out of guesses, it gives up and asks the user what "it" was. At first the program will not play well, but each time it plays, it will remember the user's replies and use them for subsequent guesses.

3.11 Overview of Data Types

This chapter has been organized around functions, with similar functions grouped together. But there is another way of organizing the Common Lisp world: by considering the different data types. This is useful for two reasons. First, it gives an alternative way of seeing the variety of available functionality. Second, the data types themselves are objects in the Common Lisp language, and as we shall see, there are functions that manipulate data types. These are useful mainly for testing objects (as with the typecase macro) and for making declarations.

Here is a table of the most commonly used data types:

Type	Example	Explanation
character	#\c	A single letter, number, or punctuation mark.
number	42	The most common numbers are floats and integers.
float	3.14159	A number with a decimal point.
integer	42	A whole number, of either fixed or indefinite size:
fixnum	123	An integer that fits in a single word of storage.
bignum	123456789	An integer of unbounded size.
function	#'sin	A function can be applied to an argument list.
symbol	sin	Symbols can name fns and vars, and are themselves objects.
null	nil	The object nil is the only object of type null.
keyword	:key	Keywords are a subtype of symbol.
sequence	(a b c)	Sequences include lists and vectors.
list	(a b c)	A list is either a cons or null.
vector	#(a b c)	A vector is a subtype of sequence.
cons	(a b c)	A cons is a non-nil list.
atom	t	An atom is anything that is not a cons.
string	"abc"	A string is a type of vector of characters.
array	#1A(a b c)	Arrays include vectors and higher-dimensional arrays.
structure	#S(type ...)	Structures are defined by defstruct.
hash-table	...	Hash tables are created by make-hash-table.

Almost every data type has a *recognizer predicate*—a function that returns true for only elements of that type. In general, a predicate is a function that always returns one of two values: true or false. In Lisp, the false value is nil, and every other value is considered true, although the most common true value is t. In most cases, the recognizer predicate's name is composed of the type name followed by p: characterp recognizes characters, numberp recognizes numbers, and so on. For example, (numberp 3) returns t because 3 is a number, but (numberp "x") returns nil because "x" is a string, not a number.

Unfortunately, Common Lisp is not completely regular. There are no recognizers for fixnums, bignums, sequences, and structures. Two recognizers, null and atom, do not end in p. Also note that there is a hyphen before the p in hash-table-p, because the type has a hyphen in it. In addition, all the recognizers generated by defstruct have a hyphen before the p.

The function `type-of` returns the type of its argument, and `typep` tests if an object is of a specified type. The function `subtypep` tests if one type can be determined to be a subtype of another. For example:

> `(type-of 123)` ⇒ `FIXNUM`

> `(typep 123 'fixnum)` ⇒ `T`

> `(typep 123 'number)` ⇒ `T`

> `(typep 123 'integer)` ⇒ `T`

> `(typep 123.0 'integer)` ⇒ `NIL`

> `(subtypep 'fixnum 'number)` ⇒ `T`

The hierarchy of types is rather complicated in Common Lisp. As the prior example shows, there are many different numeric types, and a number like 123 is considered to be of type `fixnum`, `integer`, and `number`. We will see later that it is also of type `rational` and `t`.

The type hierarchy forms a graph, not just a tree. For example, a vector is both a sequence and an array, although neither array nor sequence are subtypes of each other. Similarly, `null` is a subtype of both `symbol` and `list`.

The following table shows a number of more specialized data types that are not used as often:

Type	Example	Explanation
t	42	Every object is of type t.
nil		No object is of type nil.
complex	#C(0 1)	Imaginary numbers.
bit	0	Zero or one.
rational	2/3	Rationals include integers and ratios.
ratio	2/3	Exact fractional numbers.
simple-array	#1A(x y)	An array that is not displaced or adjustable.
readtable	...	A mapping from characters to their meanings to read.
package	...	A collection of symbols that form a module.
pathname	#P"/usr/spool/mail"	A file or directory name.
stream	...	A pointer to an open file; used for reading or printing.
random-state	...	A state used as a seed by random.

In addition, there are even more specialized types, such as `short-float`, `compiled-function`, and `bit-vector`. It is also possible to construct more exact types, such as `(vector (integer 0 3) 100)`, which represents a vector of 100 elements, each of which is an integer from 0 to 3, inclusive. Section 10.1 gives more information on types and their use.

While almost every type has a predicate, it is also true that there are predicates that are not type recognizers but rather recognize some more general condition. For example, `oddp` is true only of odd integers, and `string-greaterp` is true if one string is alphabetically greater than another.

3.12   Input/Output

Input in Lisp is incredibly easy because a complete lexical and syntactic parser is available to the user. The parser is called `read`. It is used to read and return a single Lisp expression. If you can design your application so that it reads Lisp expressions, then your input worries are over. Note that the expression parsed by `read` need not be a legal *evaluable* Lisp expression. That is, you can read `("hello" cons zzz)` just as well as `(+ 2 2)`. In cases where Lisp expressions are not adequate, the function `read-char` reads a single character, and `read-line` reads everything up to the next newline and returns it as a string.

To read from the terminal, the functions `read`, `read-char`, or `read-line` (with no arguments) return an expression, a character, and a string up to the end of line, respectively. It is also possible to read from a file. The function `open` or the macro `with-open-stream` can be used to open a file and associate it with a *stream*, Lisp's name for a descriptor of an input/output source. All three read functions take three optional arguments. The first is the stream to read from. The second, if true, causes an error to be signaled at end of file. If the second argument is nil, then the third argument indicates the value to return at end of file.

Output in Lisp is similar to output in other languages, such as C. There are a few low-level functions to do specific kinds of output, and there is a very general function to do formatted output. The function `print` prints any object on a new line, with a space following it. `prin1` will print any object without the new line and space. For both functions, the object is printed in a form that could be processed by `read`. For example, the string `"hello there"` would print as `"hello there"`. The function `princ` is used to print in a human-readable format. The string in question would print as `hello there` with `princ`—the quote marks are not printed. This means that `read` cannot recover the original form; `read` would interpret it as two symbols, not one string. The function `write` accepts eleven different keyword arguments that control whether it acts like `prin1` or `princ`, among other things.

The output functions also take a stream as an optional argument. In the following, we create the file `"test.text"` and print two expressions to it. Then we open the file for reading, and try to read back the first expression, a single character, and then two more expressions. Note that the `read-char` returns the character `#\G`, so the following `read` reads the characters `OODBYE` and turns them into a symbol. The final `read` hits the end of file, and so returns the specified value, `eof`.

```
> (with-open-file (stream "test.text" :direction :output)
    (print '(hello there) stream)
    (princ 'goodbye stream)) ⇒
GOODBYE          ; and creates the file test.text

> (with-open-file (stream "test.text" :direction :input)
    (list (read stream) (read-char stream) (read stream)
          (read stream nil 'eof))) ⇒
((HELLO THERE) #\G OODBYE EOF)
```

The function `terpri` stands for "terminate print line," and it skips to the next line. The function `fresh-line` also skips to the next line, unless it can be determined that the output is already at the start of a line.

Common Lisp also provides a very general function for doing formatted output, called `format`. The first argument to `format` is always the stream to print to; use t to print to the terminal. The second argument is the format string. It is printed out verbatim, except for *format directives*, which begin with the character "~". These directives tell how to print out the remaining arguments. Users of C's `printf` function or FORTRAN's `format` statement should be familiar with this idea. Here's an example:

```
> (format t "hello, world")
hello, world
NIL
```

Things get interesting when we put in additional arguments and include format directives:

```
> (format t "~&~a plus ~s is ~f" "two" "two" 4)
two plus "two" is 4.0
NIL
```

The directive "`~&`" moves to a fresh line, "`~a`" prints the next argument as `princ` would, "`~s`" prints the next argument as `prin1` would, and "`~f`" prints a number in floating-point format. If the argument is not a number, then `princ` is used. `format` always returns nil. There are 26 different format directives. Here's a more complex example:

```
> (let ((numbers '(1 2 3 4 5)))
    (format t "~&~{~r~^ plus ~} is ~@r"
            numbers (apply #'+ numbers)))
one plus two plus three plus four plus five is XV
NIL
```

The directive "`~r`" prints the next argument, which should be a number, in English, and "~@r" prints a number as a roman numeral. The compound directive "~{...~}" takes the next argument, which must be a list, and formats each element of the list according to the format string inside the braces. Finally, the directive "~^" exits from the enclosing "~{...~}" loop if there are no more arguments. You can see that format, like loop, comprises almost an entire programming language, which, also like loop, is not a very Lisplike language.

3.13   Debugging Tools

In many languages, there are two strategies for debugging: (1) edit the program to insert print statements, recompile, and try again, or (2) use a debugging program to investigate (and perhaps alter) the internal state of the running program.

Common Lisp admits both these strategies, but it also offers a third: (3) add annotations that are not part of the program but have the effect of automatically altering the running program. The advantage of the third strategy is that once you are done you don't have to go back and undo the changes you would have introduced in the first strategy. In addition, Common Lisp provides functions that display information about the program. You need not rely solely on looking at the source code.

We have already seen how trace and untrace can be used to provide debugging information (page 65). Another useful tool is step, which can be used to halt execution before each subform is evaluated. The form (step *expression*) will evaluate and return *expression*, but pauses at certain points to allow the user to inspect the computation, and possibly change things before proceeding to the next step. The commands available to the user are implementation-dependent, but typing a ? should give you a list of commands. As an example, here we step through an expression twice, the first time giving commands to stop at each subevaluation, and the second time giving commands to skip to the next function call. In this implementation, the commands are control characters, so they do not show up in the output. All output, including the symbols ⇐ and ⇒ are printed by the stepper itself; I have added no annotation.

```
> (step (+ 3 4 (* 5 6 (/ 7 8))))
⇐ (+ 3 4 (* 5 6 (/ 7 8)))
  ⇐ 3 ⇒ 3
  ⇐ 4 ⇒ 4
  ⇐ (* 5 6 (/ 7 8))
    ⇐ 5 ⇒ 5
    ⇐ 6 ⇒ 6
    ⇐ (/ 7 8)
      ⇐ 7 ⇒ 7
      ⇐ 8 ⇒ 8
    ⇐ (/ 7 8) ⇒ 7/8
```

```
  ⇐ (* 5 6 (/ 7 8)) ⇒ 105/4
 ⇐ (+ 3 4 (* 5 6 (/ 7 8))) ⇒ 133/4
 133/4

 > (step (+ 3 4 (* 5 6 (/ 7 8))))
 ⇐ (+ 3 4 (* 5 6 (/ 7 8)))
   /: 7 8  ⇒ 7/8
   *: 5 6 7/8  ⇒ 105/4
   +: 3 4 105/4  ⇒ 133/4
 ⇐ (+ 3 4 (* 5 6 (/ 7 8))) ⇒ 133/4
 133/4
```

The functions describe, inspect, documentation, and apropos provide information about the state of the current program. apropos prints information about all symbols whose name matches the argument:

```
> (apropos 'string)
MAKE-STRING            function (LENGTH &KEY INITIAL-ELEMENT)
PRIN1-TO-STRING        function (OBJECT)
PRINC-TO-STRING        function (OBJECT)
STRING                 function (X)
 . . .
```

Once you know what object you are interested in, describe can give more information on it:

```
> (describe 'make-string)
Symbol MAKE-STRING is in LISP package.
The function definition is #<FUNCTION MAKE-STRING -42524322>:
  NAME:         MAKE-STRING
  ARGLIST:      (LENGTH &KEY INITIAL-ELEMENT)
  DOCUMENTATION: "Creates and returns a string of LENGTH elements,
all set to INITIAL-ELEMENT."
  DEFINITION:   (LAMBDA (LENGTH &KEY INITIAL-ELEMENT)
                   (MAKE-ARRAY LENGTH :ELEMENT-TYPE 'CHARACTER
                               :INITIAL-ELEMENT (OR INITIAL-ELEMENT
                                                    #\SPACE)))
MAKE-STRING has property INLINE: INLINE
MAKE-STRING has property :SOURCE-FILE: #P"SYS:KERNEL; STRINGS"

> (describe 1234.56)
1234.56 is a single-precision floating-point number.
  Sign 0, exponent #o211, 23-bit fraction #o6450754
```

If all you want is a symbol's documentation string, the function documentation will do the trick:

```
> (documentation 'first 'function) ⇒ "Return the first element of LIST."
> (documentation 'pi 'variable) ⇒ "pi"
```

If you want to look at and possibly alter components of a complex structure, then inspect is the tool. In some implementations it invokes a fancy, window-based browser.

Common Lisp also provides a debugger that is entered automatically when an error is signalled, either by an inadvertent error or by deliberate action on the part of the program. The details of the debugger vary between implementations, but there are standard ways of entering it. The function break enters the debugger after printing an optional message. It is intended as the primary method for setting debugging break points. break is intended only for debugging purposes; when a program is deemed to be working, all calls to break should be removed. However, it is still a good idea to check for unusual conditions with error, cerror, assert, or check-type, which will be described in the following section.

3.14 Antibugging Tools

It is a good idea to include *antibugging* checks in your code, in addition to doing normal debugging. Antibugging code checks for errors and possibly takes corrective action.

The functions error and cerror are used to signal an error condition. These are intended to remain in the program even after it has been debugged. The function error takes a format string and optional arguments. It signals a fatal error; that is, it stops the program and does not offer the user any way of restarting it. For example:

```
(defun average (numbers)
  (if (null numbers)
      (error "Average of the empty list is undefined.")
      (/ (reduce #'+ numbers)
         (length numbers))))
```

In many cases, a fatal error is a little drastic. The function cerror stands for continuable error. cerror takes two format strings; the first prints a message indicating what happens if we continue, and the second prints the error message itself. cerror does not actually take any action to repair the error, it just allows the user to signal that continuing is alright. In the following implementation, the user continues by typing :continue. In ANSI Common Lisp, there are additional ways of specifying options for continuing.

```
(defun average (numbers)
  (if (null numbers)
      (progn
        (cerror "Use 0 as the average."
                "Average of the empty list is undefined.")
        0)
      (/ (reduce #'+ numbers)
         (length numbers)))))
> (average '())
Error: Average of the empty list is undefined.
Error signaled by function AVERAGE.
If continued: Use 0 as the average.
>> :continue
0
```

In this example, adding error checking nearly doubled the length of the code. This is not unusual; there is a big difference between code that works on the expected input and code that covers all possible errors. Common Lisp tries to make it easier to do error checking by providing a few special forms. The form ecase stands for "exhaustive case" or "error case." It is like a normal case form, except that if none of the cases are satisfied, an error message is generated. The form ccase stands for "continuable case." It is like ecase, except that the error is continuable. The system will ask for a new value for the test object until the user supplies one that matches one of the programmed cases.

To make it easier to include error checks without inflating the length of the code too much, Common Lisp provides the special forms check-type and assert. As the name implies, check-type is used to check the type of an argument. It signals a continuable error if the argument has the wrong type. For example:

```
(defun sqr (x)
  "Multiply x by itself."
  (check-type x number)
  (* x x))
```

If sqr is called with a non-number argument, an appropriate error message is printed:

```
> (sqr "hello")
Error: the argument X was "hello", which is not a NUMBER.
If continued: replace X with new value
>> :continue 4
16
```

assert is more general than check-type. In the simplest form, assert tests an expression and signals an error if it is false. For example:

```
(defun sqr (x)
  "Multiply x by itself."
  (assert (numberp x))
  (* x x))
```

There is no possibility of continuing from this kind of assertion. It is also possible to give assert a list of places that can be modified in an attempt to make the assertion true. In this example, the variable x is the only thing that can be changed:

```
(defun sqr (x)
  "Multiply x by itself."
  (assert (numberp x) (x))
  (* x x))
```

If the assertion is violated, an error message will be printed and the user will be given the option of continuing by altering x. If x is given a value that satisfies the assertion, then the program continues. assert always returns nil.

Finally, the user who wants more control over the error message can provide a format control string and optional arguments. So the most complex syntax for assert is:

```
(assert test-form (place...) format-ctl-string format-arg...)
```

Here is another example. The assertion tests that the temperature of the bear's porridge is neither too hot nor too cold.

```
(defun eat-porridge (bear)
  (assert (< too-cold (temperature (bear-porridge bear)) too-hot)
          (bear (bear-porridge bear))
          "~a's porridge is not just right: ~a"
          bear (hotness (bear-porridge bear)))
  (eat (bear-porridge bear)))
```

In the interaction below, the assertion failed, and the programmer's error message was printed, along with two possibilities for continuing. The user selected one, typed in a call to make-porridge for the new value, and the function succesfully continued.

```
> (eat-porridge momma-bear)
Error: #<MOMMA BEAR>'s porridge is not just right: 39
Restart actions (select using :continue):
 0: Supply a new value for BEAR
 1: Supply a new value for (BEAR-PORRIDGE BEAR)
>> :continue 1
Form to evaluate and use to replace (BEAR-PORRIDGE BEAR):
(make-porridge :temperature just-right)
nil
```

It may seem like wasted effort to spend time writing assertions that (if all goes well) will never be used. However, for all but the perfect programmer, bugs do occur, and the time spent antibugging will more than pay for itself in saving debugging time.

Whenever you develop a complex data structure, such as some kind of data base, it is a good idea to develop a corresponding consistency checker. A consistency checker is a function that will look over a data structure and test for all possible errors. When a new error is discovered, a check for it should be incorporated into the consistency checker. Calling the consistency checker is the fastest way to help isolate bugs in the data structure.

In addition, it is a good idea to keep a list of difficult test cases on hand. That way, when the program is changed, it will be easy to see if the change reintroduces a bug that had been previously removed. This is called *regression testing*, and Waters (1991) presents an interesting tool for maintaining a suite of regression tests. But it is simple enough to maintain an informal test suite with a function that calls assert on a series of examples:

```
(defun test-ex ()
  "Test the program EX on a series of examples."
  (init-ex) ; Initialize the EX program first.
  (assert (equal (ex 3 4)   5))
  (assert (equal (ex 5 0)   0))
  (assert (equal (ex 'x 0)  0)))
```

Timing Tools

A program is not complete just because it gives the right output. It must also deliver the output in a timely fashion. The form (time *expression*) can be used to see how long it takes to execute *expression*. Some implementations also print statistics on the amount of storage required. For example:

```
> (defun f (n) (dotimes (i n) nil)) ⇒ F
```

```
> (time (f 10000)) ⇒ NIL
Evaluation of (F 10000) took 4.347272 Seconds of elapsed time,
including 0.0 seconds of paging time for 0 faults. Consed 27 words.

> (compile 'f) ⇒ F

> (time (f 10000)) ⇒ NIL
Evaluation of (F 10000) took 0.011518 Seconds of elapsed time,
including 0.0 seconds of paging time for 0 faults. Consed 0 words.
```

This shows that the compiled version is over 300 times faster and uses less storage to boot. Most serious Common Lisp programmers work exclusively with compiled functions. However, it is usually a bad idea to worry too much about efficiency details while starting to develop a program. It is better to design a flexible program, get it to work, and then modify the most frequently used parts to be more efficient. In other words, separate the development stage from the fine-tuning stage. Chapters 9 and 10 give more details on efficiency consideration, and chapter 25 gives more advice on debugging and antibugging techniques.

3.15   Evaluation

There are three functions for doing evaluation in Lisp: funcall, apply, and eval. funcall is used to apply a function to individual arguments, while apply is used to apply a function to a list of arguments. Actually, apply can be given one or more individual arguments before the final argument, which is always a list. eval is passed a single argument, which should be an entire form—a function or special form followed by its arguments, or perhaps an atom. The following five forms are equivalent:

```
> (+ 1 2 3 4)              ⇒ 10
> (funcall #'+ 1 2 3 4)   ⇒ 10
> (apply #'+ '(1 2 3 4))  ⇒ 10
> (apply #'+ 1 2 '(3 4))  ⇒ 10
> (eval '(+ 1 2 3 4))     ⇒ 10
```

In the past, eval was seen as the key to Lisp's flexibility. In modern Lisps with lexical scoping, such as Common Lisp, eval is used less often (in fact, in Scheme there is no eval at all). Instead, programmers are expected to use lambda to create a new function, and then apply or funcall the function. In general, if you find yourself using eval, you are probably doing the wrong thing.

3.16   Closures

What does it mean to create a new function? Certainly every time a `function` (or `#'`) special form is evaluated, a function is returned. But in the examples we have seen and in the following one, it is always the *same* function that is returned.

```
> (mapcar #'(lambda (x) (+ x x)) '(1 3 10))  ⇒ (2 6 20)
```

Every time we evaluate the `#'(lambda ...)` form, it returns the function that doubles its argument. However, in the general case, a function consists of the body of the function coupled with any *free lexical variables* that the function references. Such a pairing is called a *lexical closure*, or just a *closure*, because the lexical variables are enclosed within the function. Consider this example:

```
(defun adder (c)
  "Return a function that adds c to its argument."
  #'(lambda (x) (+ x c)))
> (mapcar (adder 3) '(1 3 10))  ⇒ (4 6 13)
> (mapcar (adder 10) '(1 3 10))  ⇒ (11 13 20)
```

Each time we call `adder` with a different value for `c`, it creates a different function, the function that adds `c` to its argument. Since each call to `adder` creates a new local variable named `c`, each function returned by `adder` is a unique function.

Here is another example. The function `bank-account` returns a closure that can be used as a representation of a bank account. The closure captures the local variable `balance`. The body of the closure provides code to access and modify the local variable.

```
(defun bank-account (balance)
  "Open a bank account starting with the given balance."
  #'(lambda (action amount)
      (case action
        (deposit (setf balance (+ balance amount)))
        (withdraw (setf balance (- balance amount))))))
```

In the following, two calls to `bank-account` create two different closures, each with a separate value for the lexical variable `balance`. The subsequent calls to the two closures change their respective balances, but there is no confusion between the two accounts.

```
> (setf my-account (bank-account 500.00))  ⇒ #<CLOSURE 52330407>
```

```
> (setf your-account (bank-account 250.00))  ⇒  #<CLOSURE 52331203>

> (funcall my-account 'withdraw 75.00)  ⇒  425.0

> (funcall your-account 'deposit 250.00)  ⇒  500.0

> (funcall your-account 'withdraw 100.00)  ⇒  400.0

> (funcall my-account 'withdraw 25.00)  ⇒  400.0
```

This style of programming will be considered in more detail in chapter 13.

3.17   Special Variables

Common Lisp provides for two kinds of variables: *lexical* and *special* variables. For the beginner, it is tempting to equate the special variables in Common Lisp with global variables in other languages. Unfortunately, this is not quite correct and can lead to problems. It is best to understand Common Lisp variables on their own terms.

By default, Common Lisp variables are *lexical variables*. Lexical variables are introduced by some syntactic construct like let or defun and get their name from the fact that they may only be referred to by code that appears lexically within the body of the syntactic construct. The body is called the *scope* of the variable.

So far, there is no difference between Common Lisp and other languages. The interesting part is when we consider the *extent,* or lifetime, of a variable. In other languages, the extent is the same as the scope: a new local variable is created when a block is entered, and the variable goes away when the block is exited. But because it is possible to create new functions—closures—in Lisp, it is therefore possible for code that references a variable to live on after the scope of the variable has been exited. Consider again the bank-account function, which creates a closure representing a bank account:

```
(defun bank-account (balance)
  "Open a bank account starting with the given balance."
  #'(lambda (action amount)
      (case action
        (deposit  (setf balance (+ balance amount)))
        (withdraw (setf balance (- balance amount)))))))
```

The function introduces the lexical variable balance. The scope of balance is the body of the function, and therefore references to balance can occur only within this scope. What happens when bank-account is called and exited? Once the body of the function has been left, no other code can refer to that instance of balance. The scope has been exited, but the extent of balance lives on. We can call the closure, and it can reference balance, because the code that created the closure appeared lexically within the scope of balance.

In summary, Common Lisp lexical variables are different because they can be captured inside closures and referred to even after the flow of control has left their scope.

Now we will consider special variables. A variable is made special by a defvar or defparameter form. For example, if we say

```
(defvar *counter* 0)
```

then we can refer to the special variable *counter* anywhere in our program. This is just like a familiar global variable. The tricky part is that the global binding of *counter* can be shadowed by a local binding for that variable. In most languages, the local binding would introduce a local lexical variable, but in Common Lisp, special variables can be bound both locally and globally. Here is an example:

```
(defun report ()
  (format t "Counter = ~d " *counter*))
> (report)
Counter = 0
NIL
> (let ((*counter* 100))
    (report))
Counter = 100
NIL
> (report)
Counter = 0
NIL
```

There are three calls to report here. In the first and third, report prints the global value of the special variable *counter*. In the second call, the let form introduces a new binding for the special variable *counter*, which is again printed by report. Once the scope of the let is exited, the new binding is disestablished, so the final call to report uses the global value again.

In summary, Common Lisp special variables are different because they have global scope but admit the possibility of local (dynamic) shadowing. Remember: A lexical variable has lexical scope and indefinite extent. A special variable has indefinite scope and dynamic extent.

The function call (symbol-value *var*), where *var* evaluates to a symbol, can be used to get at the current value of a special variable. To set a special variable, the following two forms are completely equivalent:

```
(setf (symbol-value var) value)
(set var value)
```

where both *var* and *value* are evaluated. There are no corresponding forms for accessing and setting lexical variables. Special variables set up a mapping between symbols and values that is accessible to the running program. This is unlike lexical variables (and all variables in traditional languages) where symbols (identifiers) have significance only while the program is being compiled. Once the program is running, the identifiers have been compiled away and cannot be used to access the variables; only code that appears within the scope of a lexical variable can reference that variable.

Exercise 3.6 [s] Given the following initialization for the lexical variable a and the special variable *b*, what will be the value of the let form?

```
(setf a 'global-a)
(defvar *b* 'global-b)

(defun fn () *b*)

(let ((a 'local-a)
      (*b* 'local-b))
  (list a *b* (fn) (symbol-value 'a) (symbol-value '*b*)))
```

3.18 Multiple Values

Throughout this book we have spoken of "the value returned by a function." Historically, Lisp was designed so that every function returns a value, even those functions that are more like procedures than like functions. But sometimes we want a single function to return more than one piece of information. Of course, we can do that by making up a list or structure to hold the information, but then we have to go to the trouble of defining the structure, building an instance each time, and then taking that instance apart to look at the pieces. Consider the function round. One way it can be used is to round off a floating-point number to the nearest integer. So (round 5.1) is 5. Sometimes, though not always, the programmer is also interested in the fractional part. The function round serves both interested and disinterested programmers by returning two values: the rounded integer and the remaining fraction:

```
> (round 5.1) ⇒ 5 .1
```

There are two values after the ⇒ because round returns two values. Most of the time, multiple values are ignored, and only the first value is used. So (* 2 (round 5.1)) is 10, just as if round had only returned a single value. If you want to get at multiple values, you have to use a special form, such as multiple-value-bind:

```
(defun show-both (x)
  (multiple-value-bind (int rem)
      (round x)
    (format t "~f = ~d + ~f" x int rem)))

> (show-both 5.1)
5.1 = 5 + 0.1
```

You can write functions of your own that return multiple values using the function values, which returns its arguments as multiple values:

```
> (values 1 2 3) ⇒ 1 2 3
```

Multiple values are a good solution because they are unobtrusive until they are needed. Most of the time when we are using round, we are only interested in the integer value. If round did not use multiple values, if it packaged the two values up into a list or structure, then it would be harder to use in the normal cases.

It is also possible to return no values from a function with (values). This is sometimes used by procedures that are called for effect, such as printing. For example, describe is defined to print information and then return no values:

```
> (describe 'x)
Symbol X is in the USER package.
It has no value, definition or properties.
```

However, when (values) or any other expression returning no values is nested in a context where a value is expected, it still obeys the Lisp rule of one-value-per-expression and returns nil. In the following example, describe returns no values, but then list in effect asks for the first value and gets nil.

```
> (list (describe 'x))
Symbol X is in AILP package.
It has no value, definition or properties.
(NIL)
```

3.19   More about Parameters

Common Lisp provides the user with a lot of flexibility in specifying the parameters to a function, and hence the arguments that the function accepts. Following is a program that gives practice in arithmetic. It asks the user a series of n problems, where each problem tests the arithmetic operator op (which can be +, -, *, or /, or perhaps another binary operator). The arguments to the operator will be random integers from 0 to range. Here is the program:

```
(defun math-quiz (op range n)
  "Ask the user a series of math problems."
  (dotimes (i n)
    (problem (random range) op (random range))))

(defun problem (x op y)
  "Ask a math problem, read a reply, and say if it is correct."
  (format t "~&How much is ~d ~a ~d?" x op y)
  (if (eql (read) (funcall op x y))
      (princ "Correct!")
      (princ "Sorry, that's not right.")))
```

and here is an example of its use:

```
> (math-quiz '+ 100 2)
How much is 32 + 60? 92
Correct!
How much is 91 + 19? 100
Sorry, that's not right.
```

One problem with the function math-quiz is that it requires the user to type three arguments: the operator, a range, and the number of iterations. The user must remember the order of the arguments, and remember to quote the operator. This is quite a lot to expect from a user who presumably is just learning to add!

Common Lisp provides two ways of dealing with this problem. First, a programmer can specify that certain arguments are *optional*, and provide default values for those arguments. For example, in math-quiz we can arrange to make + be the default operator, 100 be the default number range, and 10 be the default number of examples with the following definition:

```
(defun math-quiz (&optional (op '+) (range 100) (n 10))
  "Ask the user a series of math problems."
  (dotimes (i n)
    (problem (random range) op (random range))))
```

Now (math-quiz) means the same as (math-quiz '+ 100 10). If an optional
parameter appears alone without a default value, then the default is nil. Optional
parameters are handy; however, what if the user is happy with the operator and
range but wants to change the number of iterations? Optional parameters are still
position-dependent, so the only solution is to type in all three arguments: (math-quiz
'+ 100 5).

Common Lisp also allows for parameters that are position-independent. These
keyword parameters are explicitly named in the function call. They are useful when
there are a number of parameters that normally take default values but occasionally
need specific values. For example, we could have defined math-quiz as:

```
(defun math-quiz (&key (op '+) (range 100) (n 10))
  "Ask the user a series of math problems."
  (dotimes (i n)
    (problem (random range) op (random range))))
```

Now (math-quiz :n 5) and (math-quiz :op '+ :n 5 :range 100) mean the same.
Keyword arguments are specified by the parameter name preceded by a colon, and
followed by the value. The keyword/value pairs can come in any order.

A symbol starting with a colon is called a *keyword*, and can be used anywhere,
not just in argument lists. The term *keyword* is used differently in Lisp than in many
other languages. For example, in Pascal, keywords (or *reserved* words) are syntactic
symbols, like if, else, begin, and end. In Lisp we call such symbols *special form
operators* or just *special forms*. Lisp keywords are symbols that happen to reside in
the keyword package.[3] They have no special syntactic meaning, although they do
have the unusual property of being self-evaluating: they are constants that evaluate
to themselves, unlike other symbols, which evaluate to whatever value was stored in
the variable named by the symbol. Keywords also happen to be used in specifying
&key argument lists, but that is by virtue of their value, not by virtue of some syntax
rule. It is important to remember that keywords are used in the function call, but
normal nonkeyword symbols are used as parameters in the function definition.

Just to make things a little more confusing, the symbols &optional, &rest, and
&key are called *lambda-list keywords*, for historical reasons. Unlike the colon in real
keywords, the & in lambda-list keywords has no special significance. Consider these
annotated examples:

---

[3]A *package* is a symbol table: a mapping between strings and the symbols they name.

```
> :xyz  ⇒  :XYZ                          ; keywords are self-evaluating

> &optional  ⇒                           ; lambda-list keywords are normal symbols
Error: the symbol &optional has no value

> '&optional  ⇒  &OPTIONAL

> (defun f (&xyz) (+ &xyz &xyz))  ⇒  F ; & has no significance

> (f 3)  ⇒  6

> (defun f (:xyz) (+ :xyz :xyz))  ⇒
Error: the keyword :xyz appears in a variable list.
Keywords are constants, and so cannot be used as names of variables.

> (defun g (&key x y) (list x y))  ⇒  G

> (let ((keys '(:x :y :z)))              ; keyword args can be computed
    (g (second keys) 1 (first keys) 2))  ⇒  (2 1)
```

Many of the functions presented in this chapter take keyword arguments that make them more versatile. For example, remember the function find, which can be used to look for a particular element in a sequence:

```
> (find 3 '(1 2 3 4 -5 6.0))  ⇒  3
```

It turns out that find takes several optional keyword arguments. For example, suppose we tried to find 6 in this sequence:

```
> (find 6 '(1 2 3 4 -5 6.0))  ⇒  nil
```

This fails because find tests for equality with eql, and 6 is not eql to 6.0. However, 6 is equalp to 6.0, so we could use the :test keyword:

```
> (find 6 '(1 2 3 4 -5 6.0) :test #'equalp)  ⇒  6.0
```

In fact, we can specify any binary predicate for the :test keyword; it doesn't have to be an equality predicate. For example, we could find the first number that 4 is less than:

```
> (find 4 '(1 2 3 4 -5 6.0) :test #'<)  ⇒  6.0
```

Now suppose we don't care about the sign of the numbers; if we look for 5, we want to find the -5. We can handle this with the key keyword to take the absolute value of each element of the list with the abs function:

```
> (find 5 '(1 2 3 4 -5 6.0) :key #'abs) ⇒ -5
```

Keyword parameters significantly extend the usefulness of built-in functions, and they can do the same for functions you define. Among the built-in functions, the most common keywords fall into two main groups: :test, :test-not and :key, which are used for matching functions, and :start, :end, and :from-end, which are used on sequence functions. Some functions accept both sets of keywords. (*Common Lisp the Language,* 2d edition, discourages the use of :test-not keywords, although they are still a part of the language.)

The matching functions include sublis, position, subst, union, intersection, set-difference, remove, remove-if, subsetp, assoc, find, and member. By default, each tests if some item is eql to one or more of a series of other objects. This test can be changed by supplying some other predicate as the argument to :test, or it can be reversed by specifying :test-not. In addition, the comparison can be made against some part of the object rather than the whole object by specifying a selector function as the :key argument.

The sequence functions include remove, remove-if, position, and find. The most common type of sequence is the list, but strings and vectors can also be used as sequences. A sequence function performs some action repeatedly for some elements of a sequence. The default is to go through the sequence from beginning to end, but the reverse order can be specified with :from-end t, and a subsequence can be specifed by supplying a number for the :start or :end keyword. The first element of a sequence is numbered 0, not 1, so be careful.

As an example of keyword parameters, suppose we wanted to write sequence functions that are similar to find and find-if, except that they return a list of all matching elements rather than just the first matching element. We will call the new functions find-all and find-all-if. Another way to look at these functions is as variations of remove. Instead of removing items that match, they keep all the items that match, and remove the ones that don't. Viewed this way, we can see that the function find-all-if is actually the same function as remove-if-not. It is sometimes useful to have two names for the same function viewed in different ways (like not and null). The new name could be defined with a defun, but it is easier to just copy over the definition:

```
(setf (symbol-function 'find-all-if) #'remove-if-not)
```

Unfortunately, there is no built-in function that corresponds exactly to find-all, so we will have to define it. Fortunately, remove can do most of the work. All we have to do is arrange to pass remove the complement of the :test predicate. For example, finding all elements that are equal to 1 in a list is equivalent to removing elements that are not equal to 1:

```
> (setf nums '(1 2 3 2 1)) ⇒ (1 2 3 2 1)

> (find-all 1 nums :test #'=) ≡ (remove 1 nums :test #'/=) ⇒ (1 1)
```

Now what we need is a higher-order function that returns the complement of a function. In other words, given =, we want to return /=. This function is called complement in ANSI Common Lisp, but it was not defined in earlier versions, so it is given here:

```
(defun complement (fn)
  "If FN returns y, then (complement FN) returns (not y)."
  ;; This function is built-in in ANSI Common Lisp,
  ;; but is defined here for those with non-ANSI compilers.
  #'(lambda (&rest args) (not (apply fn args)))))
```

When find-all is called with a given :test predicate, all we have to do is call remove with the complement as the :test predicate. This is true even when the :test function is not specified, and therefore defaults to eql. We should also test for when the user specifies the :test-not predicate, which is used to specify that the match succeeds when the predicate is false. It is an error to specify both a :test and :test-not argument to the same call, so we need not test for that case. The definition is:

```
(defun find-all (item sequence &rest keyword-args
                 &key (test #'eql) test-not &allow-other-keys)
  "Find all those elements of sequence that match item,
  according to the keywords.  Doesn't alter sequence."
  (if test-not
      (apply #'remove item sequence
             :test-not (complement test-not) keyword-args)
      (apply #'remove item sequence
             :test (complement test) keyword-args)))
```

The only hard part about this definition is understanding the parameter list. The &rest accumulates all the keyword/value pairs in the variable keyword-args. In addition to the &rest parameter, two specific keyword parameters, :test and :test-not, are specified. Any time you put a &key in a parameter list, you need an &allow-other-keys if, in fact, other keywords are allowed. In this case we want to accept keywords like :start and :key and pass them on to remove.

All the keyword/value pairs will be accumulated in the list keyword-args, including the :test or :test-not values. So we will have:

```
(find-all 1 nums :test #'= :key #'abs)
  ≡ (remove 1 nums :test (complement #'=) :test #'= :key #'abs)
  ⇒ (1 1)
```

Note that the call to remove will contain two :test keywords. This is not an error; Common Lisp declares that the leftmost value is the one that counts.

Exercise 3.7 [s] Why do you think the leftmost of two keys is the one that counts, rather than the rightmost?

Exercise 3.8 [m] Some versions of Kyoto Common Lisp (KCL) have a bug wherein they use the rightmost value when more than one keyword/value pair is specified for the same keyword. Change the definition of find-all so that it works in KCL.

There are two more lambda-list keywords that are sometimes used by advanced programmers. First, within a macro definition (but not a function definition), the symbol &body can be used as a synonym for &rest. The difference is that &body instructs certain formatting programs to indent the rest as a body. Thus, if we defined the macro:

```
(defmacro while2 (test &body body)
  "Repeat body while test is true."
  '(loop (if (not ,test) (return nil))
        . ,body))
```

Then the automatic indentation of while2 (on certain systems) is prettier than while:

```
(while (< i 10)                    (while2 (< i 10)
       (print (* i i))                (print (* i i))
       (setf i (+ i 1)))              (setf i (+ i 1)))
```

Finally, an &aux can be used to bind a new local variable or variables, as if bound with let*. Personally, I consider this an abomination, because &aux variables are not parameters at all and thus have no place in a parameter list. I think they should be clearly distinguished as local variables with a let. But some good programmers do use &aux, presumably to save space on the page or screen. Against my better judgement, I show an example:

```
(defun length14 (list &aux (len 0))
  (dolist (element list len)
    (incf len)))
```

3.20   The Rest of Lisp

There is a lot more to Common Lisp than what we have seen here, but this overview should be enough for the reader to comprehend the programs in the chapters to come. The serious Lisp programmer will further his or her education by continuing to consult reference books and online documentation. You may also find part V of this book to be helpful, particularly chapter 24, which covers advanced features of Common Lisp (such as packages and error handling) and chapter 25, which is a collection of troubleshooting hints for the perplexed Lisper.

While it may be distracting for the beginner to be continually looking at some reference source, the alternative—to explain every new function in complete detail as it is introduced—would be even more distracting. It would interrupt the description of the AI programs, which is what this book is all about.

3.21   Exercises

Exercise 3.9 [m]   Write a version of length using the function reduce.

Exercise 3.10 [m]   Use a reference manual or describe to figure out what the functions lcm and nreconc do.

Exercise 3.11 [m]   There is a built-in Common Lisp function that, given a key, a value, and an association list, returns a new association list that is extended to include the key/value pair. What is the name of this function?

Exercise 3.12 [m]   Write a single expression using format that will take a list of words and print them as a sentence, with the first word capitalized and a period after the last word. You will have to consult a reference to learn new format directives.

3.22   Answers

Answer 3.2   (cons $a\,b$) ≡ (list* $a\,b$)

Answer 3.3

```
(defun dprint (x)
  "Print an expression in dotted pair notation."
  (cond ((atom x) (princ x))
        (t (princ "(")
           (dprint (first x))
           (pr-rest (rest x))
           (princ ")")
           x)))

(defun pr-rest (x)
  (princ " . ")
  (dprint x))
```

Answer 3.4   Use the same dprint function defined in the last exercise, but change pr-rest.

```
(defun pr-rest (x)
  (cond ((null x))
        ((atom x) (princ " . ") (princ x))
        (t (princ " ") (dprint (first x)) (pr-rest (rest x)))))
```

Answer 3.5   We will keep a data base called *db*. The data base is organized into a tree structure of nodes. Each node has three fields: the name of the object it represents, a node to go to if the answer is yes, and a node for when the answer is no. We traverse the nodes until we either get an "it" reply or have to give up. In the latter case, we destructively modify the data base to contain the new information.

```
(defstruct node
  name
  (yes nil)
  (no nil))

(defvar *db*
  (make-node :name 'animal
             :yes (make-node :name 'mammal)
             :no (make-node
                   :name 'vegetable
                   :no (make-node :name 'mineral))))
```

```
(defun questions (&optional (node *db*))
  (format t "~&Is it a ~a? " (node-name node))
  (case (read)
    ((y yes) (if (not (null (node-yes node)))
                 (questions (node-yes node))
                 (setf (node-yes node) (give-up))))
    ((n no)  (if (not (null (node-no node)))
                 (questions (node-no node))
                 (setf (node-no node) (give-up))))
    (it 'aha!)
    (t (format t "Reply with YES, NO, or IT if I have guessed it.")
       (questions node))))

(defun give-up ()
  (format t "~&I give up - what is it? ")
  (make-node :name (read)))
```

Here it is used:

```
> (questions)
Is it a ANIMAL? yes
Is it a MAMMAL? yes
I give up - what is it? bear
#S(NODE :NAME BEAR)

> (questions)
Is it a ANIMAL? yes
Is it a MAMMAL? no
I give up - what is it? penguin
#S(NODE :NAME PENGUIN)

> (questions)
Is it a ANIMAL? yes
Is it a MAMMAL? yes
Is it a BEAR? it
AHA!
```

Answer 3.6 The value is (LOCAL-A LOCAL-B LOCAL-B GLOBAL-A LOCAL-B).
  The let form binds a lexically and *b* dynamically, so the references to a and *b* (including the reference to *b* within fn) all get the local values. The function symbol-value always treats its argument as a special variable, so it ignores the lexical binding for a and returns the global binding instead. However, the symbol-value of *b* is the local dynamic value.

Answer 3.7 There are two good reasons: First, it makes it faster to search through the argument list: just search until you find the key, not all the way to the end. Second, in the case where you want to override an existing keyword and pass the argument list on to another function, it is cheaper to cons the new keyword/value pair on the front of a list than to append it to the end of a list.

Answer 3.9

```
(defun length-r (list)
  (reduce #'+ (mapcar #'(lambda (x) 1) list)))
```

or more efficiently:

```
(defun length-r (list)
  (reduce #'(lambda (x y) (+ x 1)) list
          :initial-value 0))
```

or, with an ANSI-compliant Common Lisp, you can specify a :key

```
(defun length-r (list)
  (reduce #'+ list :key #'(lambda (x) 1)))
```

Answer 3.12 `(format t "~@(~{~a~^ ~}.~)" '(this is a test))`

PART   II

EARLY AI PROGRAMS

CHAPTER 4

GPS: The General Problem Solver

There are now in the world machines that think.

—Herbert Simon
Nobel Prize-winning AI researcher

T he General Problem Solver, developed in 1957 by Alan Newell and Herbert Simon, embodied a grandiose vision: a single computer program that could solve *any* problem,
given a suitable description of the problem. GPS caused quite a stir when it was introduced, and some people in AI felt it would sweep in a grand new era of intelligent machines.
Simon went so far as to make this statement about his creation:

> *It is not my aim to surprise or shock you. ... But the simplest way I can summarize is to say
> that there are now in the world machines that think, that learn and create. Moreover, their
> ability to do these things is going to increase rapidly until—in a visible future—the range of
> problems they can handle will be coextensive with the range to which the human mind has
> been applied.*

Although GPS never lived up to these exaggerated claims, it was still an important program for historical reasons. It was the first program to separate its problem-solving strategy from its knowledge of particular problems, and it spurred much further research in problem solving. For all these reasons, it is a fitting object of study.

The original GPS program had a number of minor features that made it quite complex. In addition, it was written in an obsolete low-level language, IPL, that added gratuitous complexity. In fact, the confusing nature of IPL was probably an important reason for the grand claims about GPS. If the program was that complicated, it *must* do something important. We will be ignoring some of the subtleties of the original program, and we will use Common Lisp, a much more perspicuous language than IPL. The result will be a version of GPS that is quite simple, yet illustrates some important points about AI.

On one level, this chapter is about GPS. But on another level, it is about the process of developing an AI computer program. We distinguish five stages in the development of a program. First is the problem description, which is a rough idea—usually written in English prose—of what we want to do. Second is the program specification, where we redescribe the problem in terms that are closer to a computable procedure. The third stage is the implementation of the program in a programming language such as Common Lisp, the fourth is testing, and the fifth is debugging and analysis. The boundaries between these stages are fluid, and the stages need not be completed in the order stated. Problems at any stage can lead to a change in the previous stage, or even to complete redesign or abandonment of the project. A programmer may prefer to complete only a partial description or specification, proceed directly to implementation and testing, and then return to complete the specification based on a better understanding.

We follow all five stages in the development of our versions of GPS, with the hope that the reader will understand GPS better and will also come to understand better how to write a program of his or her own. To summarize, the five stages of an AI programming project are:

1. **Describe** the problem in vague terms

2. **Specify** the problem in algorithmic terms

3. **Implement** the problem in a programming language

4. **Test** the program on representative examples

5. **Debug** and **analyze** the resulting program, and repeat the process

4.1   Stage 1: Description

As our problem description, we will start with a quote from Newell and Simon's 1972 book, *Human Problem Solving*:

> *The main methods of GPS jointly embody the heuristic of means-ends analysis. Means-ends analysis is typified by the following kind of common-sense argument:*
>
> > *I want to take my son to nursery school. What's the difference between what I have and what I want? One of distance. What changes distance? My automobile. My automobile won't work. What is needed to make it work? A new battery. What has new batteries? An auto repair shop. I want the repair shop to put in a new battery; but the shop doesn't know I need one. What is the difficulty? One of communication. What allows communication? A telephone . . . and so on.*
>
> *The kind of analysis—classifying things in terms of the functions they serve and oscillating among ends, functions required, and means that perform them—forms the basic system of heuristic of GPS.*

Of course, this kind of analysis is not exactly new. The theory of means-ends analysis was laid down quite elegantly by Aristotle 2300 years earlier in the chapter entitled "The nature of deliberation and its objects" of the *Nicomachean Ethics* (Book III. 3, 1112b):

> *We deliberate not about ends, but about means. For a doctor does not deliberate whether he shall heal, nor an orator whether he shall persuade, nor a statesman whether he shall produce law and order, nor does any one else deliberate about his end. They assume the end and consider how and by what means it is attained; and if it seems to be produced by several means they consider by which it is most easily and best produced, while if it is achieved by one only they consider how it will be achieved by this and by what means this will be achieved, till they come to the first cause, which in the order of discovery is last . . . and what is last in the order of analysis seems to be first in the order of becoming. And if we come on an impossibility, we give up the search, e.g., if we need money and this cannot be got; but if a thing appears possible we try to do it.*

Given this description of a theory of problem solving, how should we go about writing a program? First, we try to understand more fully the procedure outlined in the quotes. The main idea is to solve a problem using a process called means-ends analysis, where the problem is stated in terms of what we want to happen. In Newell and Simon's example, the problem is to get the kid to school, but in general we would like the program to be able to solve a broad class of problems. We can solve a problem if we can find some way to eliminate "the difference between what I have and what I want." For example, if what I have is a child at home, and what I want is a child at school, then driving may be a solution, because we know that driving leads to a change in location. We should be aware that using means-ends analysis is a choice: it is also possible to start from the current situation and search forward to the goal, or to employ a mixture of different search strategies.

Some actions require the solving of *preconditions* as subproblems. Before we can drive the car, we need to solve the subproblem of getting the car in working condition. It may be that the car is already working, in which case we need do nothing to solve the subproblem. So a problem is solved either by taking appropriate action directly, or by first solving for the preconditions of an appropriate action and then taking the action. It is clear we will need some description of allowable actions, along with their preconditions and effects. We will also need to develop a definition of appropriateness. However, if we can define these notions better, it seems we won't need any new notions. Thus, we will arbitrarily decide that the problem description is complete, and move on to the problem specification.

4.2   Stage 2: Specification

At this point we have an idea—admittedly vague—of what it means to solve a problem in GPS. We can refine these notions into representations that are closer to Lisp as follows:

- We can represent the current state of the world—"what I have"—or the goal state—"what I want"—as sets of conditions. Common Lisp doesn't have a data type for sets, but it does have lists, which can be used to implement sets. Each condition can be represented by a symbol. Thus, a typical goal might be the list of two conditions (rich famous), and a typical current state might be (unknown poor).

- We need a list of allowable operators. This list will be constant over the course of a problem, or even a series of problems, but we want to be able to change it and tackle a new problem domain.

- An operator can be represented as a structure composed of an action, a list of preconditions, and a list of effects. We can place limits on the kinds of possible effects by saying that an effect either adds or deletes a condition from the current state. Thus, the list of effects can be split into an add-list and a delete-list. This was the approach taken by the STRIPS[1] implementation of

---

[1] STRIPS is the Stanford Research Institute Problem Solver, designed by Richard Fikes and Nils Nilsson (1971).

GPS, which we will be in effect reconstructing in this chapter. The original GPS allowed more flexibility in the specification of effects, but flexibility leads to inefficiency.

- A complete problem is described to GPS in terms of a starting state, a goal state, and a set of known operators. Thus, GPS will be a function of three arguments. For example, a sample call might be:

```
(GPS '(unknown poor) '(rich famous) list-of-ops)
```

In other words, starting from the state of being poor and unknown, achieve the state of being rich and famous, using any combination of the known operators. GPS should return a true value only if it solves the problem, and it should print a record of the actions taken. The simplest approach is to go through the conditions in the goal state one at a time and try to achieve each one. If they can all be achieved, then the problem is solved.

- A single goal condition can be achieved in two ways. If it is already in the current state, the goal is trivially achieved with no effort. Otherwise, we have to find some appropriate operator and try to apply it.

- An operator is appropriate if one of the effects of the operator is to add the goal in question to the current state; in other words, if the goal is in the operator's add-list.

- We can apply an operator if we can achieve all the preconditions. But this is easy, because we just defined the notion of achieving a goal in the previous paragraph. Once the preconditions have been achieved, applying an operator means executing the action and updating the current state in term of the operator's add-list and delete-list. Since our program is just a simulation—it won't be actually driving a car or dialing a telephone—we must be content simply to print out the action, rather than taking any real action.

4.3   Stage 3: Implementation

The specification is complete enough to lead directly to a complete Common Lisp program. Figure 4.1 summarizes the variables, data types, and functions that make up the GPS program, along with some of the Common Lisp functions used to implement it.

	Top-Level Function
GPS	Solve a goal from a state using a list of operators.
	Special Variables
state	The current state: a list of conditions.
ops	A list of available operators.
	Data Types
op	An operation with preconds, add-list and del-list.
	Functions
achieve	Achieve an individual goal.
appropriate-p	Decide if an operator is appropriate for a goal.
apply-op	Apply operator to current state.
	Selected Common Lisp Functions
member	Test if an element is a member of a list. (p. 78)
set-difference	All elements in one set but not the other.
union	All elements in either of two sets.
every	Test if every element of a list passes a test. (p. 62)
some	Test if any element of a list passes a test.
	Previously Defined Functions
find-all	A list of all matching elements. (p. 101)

Figure 4.1: Glossary for the GPS Program

Here is the complete GPS program itself:

```lisp
(defvar *state* nil "The current state: a list of conditions.")

(defvar *ops* nil "A list of available operators.")

(defstruct op "An operation"
  (action nil) (preconds nil) (add-list nil) (del-list nil))

(defun GPS (*state* goals *ops*)
  "General Problem Solver: achieve all goals using *ops*."
  (if (every #'achieve goals) 'solved))

(defun achieve (goal)
  "A goal is achieved if it already holds,
  or if there is an appropriate op for it that is applicable."
  (or (member goal *state*)
      (some #'apply-op
            (find-all goal *ops* :test #'appropriate-p))))

(defun appropriate-p (goal op)
  "An op is appropriate to a goal if it is in its add list."
  (member goal (op-add-list op)))
```

```
(defun apply-op (op)
  "Print a message and update *state* if op is applicable."
  (when (every #'achieve (op-preconds op))
    (print (list 'executing (op-action op)))
    (setf *state* (set-difference *state* (op-del-list op)))
    (setf *state* (union *state* (op-add-list op)))
    t))
```

We can see the program is made up of seven definitions. These correspond to the seven items in the specification above. In general, you shouldn't expect such a perfect fit between specification and implementation. There are two defvar forms, one defstruct, and four defun forms. These are the Common Lisp forms for defining variables, structures, and functions, respectively. They are the most common top-level forms in Lisp, but there is nothing magic about them; they are just special forms that have the side effect of adding new definitions to the Lisp environment.

The two defvar forms, repeated below, declare special variables named *state* and *ops*, which can then be accessed from anywhere in the program.

```
(defvar *state* nil "The current state: a list of conditions.")

(defvar *ops* nil "A list of available operators.")
```

The defstruct form defines a structure called an op, which has slots called action, preconds, add-list, and del-list. Structures in Common Lisp are similar to structures in C, or records in Pascal. The defstruct automatically defines a constructor function, which is called make-op, and an access function for each slot of the structure. The access functions are called op-action, op-preconds, op-add-list, and op-del-list. The defstruct also defines a copier function, copy-op, a predicate, op-p, and setf definitions for changing each slot. None of those are used in the GPS program. Roughly speaking, it is as if the defstruct form

```
(defstruct op "An operation"
  (action nil) (preconds nil) (add-list nil) (del-list nil))
```

expanded into the following definitions:

```
(defun make-op (&key action preconds add-list del-list)
  (vector 'op action preconds add-list del-list))

(defun op-action   (op) (elt op 1))
(defun op-preconds (op) (elt op 2))
(defun op-add-list (op) (elt op 3))
(defun op-del-list (op) (elt op 4))

(defun copy-op (op) (copy-seq op))
```

```
(defun op-p (op)
  (and (vectorp op) (eq (elt op 0) 'op)))

(setf (documentation 'op 'structure) "An operation")
```

Next in the GPS program are four function definitions. The main function, GPS, is passed three arguments. The first is the current state of the world, the second the goal state, and the third a list of allowable operators. The body of the function says simply that if we can achieve every one of the goals we have been given, then the problem is solved. The unstated alternative is that otherwise, the problem is not solved.

The function achieve is given as an argument a single goal. The function succeeds if that goal is already true in the current state (in which case we don't have to do anything) or if we can apply an appropriate operator. This is accomplished by first building the list of appropriate operators and then testing each in turn until one can be applied. achieve calls find-all, which we defined on page 101. In this use, find-all returns a list of operators that match the current goal, according to the predicate appropriate-p.

The function appropriate-p tests if an operator is appropriate for achieving a goal. (It follows the Lisp naming convention that predicates end in -p.)

Finally, the function apply-op says that if we can achieve all the preconditions for an appropriate operator, then we can apply the operator. This involves printing a message to that effect and changing the state of the world by deleting what was in the delete-list and adding what was in the add-list. apply-op is also a predicate; it returns t only when the operator can be applied.

4.4   Stage 4: Test

This section will define a list of operators applicable to the "driving to nursery school" domain and will show how to pose and solve some problems in that domain. First, we need to construct the list of operators for the domain. The defstruct form for the type op automatically defines the function make-op, which can be used as follows:

```
(make-op :action 'drive-son-to-school
        :preconds '(son-at-home car-works)
        :add-list '(son-at-school)
        :del-list '(son-at-home))
```

This expression returns an operator whose action is the symbol drive-son-to-school and whose preconditions, add-list and delete-list are the specified lists. The intent of this operator is that whenever the son is at home and the car works, drive-son-to-school can be applied, changing the state by deleting the fact that the son is at home, and adding the fact that he is at school.

It should be noted that using long hyphenated atoms like son-at-home is a useful approach only for very simple examples like this one. A better representation would break the atom into its components: perhaps (at son home). The problem with the atom-based approach is one of combinatorics. If there are 10 predicates (such as at) and 10 people or objects, then there will be $10 \times 10 \times 10 = 1000$ possible hyphenated atoms, but only 20 components. Clearly, it would be easier to describe the components. In this chapter we stick with the hyphenated atoms because it is simpler, and we do not need to describe the whole world. Subsequent chapters take knowledge representation more seriously.

With this operator as a model, we can define other operators corresponding to Newell and Simon's quote on page 109. There will be an operator for installing a battery, telling the repair shop the problem, and telephoning the shop. We can fill in the "and so on" by adding operators for looking up the shop's phone number and for giving the shop money:

```
(defparameter *school-ops*
  (list
    (make-op :action 'drive-son-to-school
        :preconds '(son-at-home car-works)
        :add-list '(son-at-school)
        :del-list '(son-at-home))
    (make-op :action 'shop-installs-battery
        :preconds '(car-needs-battery shop-knows-problem shop-has-money)
        :add-list '(car-works))
    (make-op :action 'tell-shop-problem
        :preconds '(in-communication-with-shop)
        :add-list '(shop-knows-problem))
    (make-op :action 'telephone-shop
        :preconds '(know-phone-number)
        :add-list '(in-communication-with-shop))
    (make-op :action 'look-up-number
        :preconds '(have-phone-book)
        :add-list '(know-phone-number))
    (make-op :action 'give-shop-money
        :preconds '(have-money)
        :add-list '(shop-has-money)
        :del-list '(have-money))))
```

The next step is to pose some problems to GPS and examine the solutions. Following are three sample problems. In each case, the goal is the same: to achieve the single condition son-at-school. The list of available operators is also the same in each problem; the difference is in the initial state. Each of the three examples consists of the prompt, ">", which is printed by the Lisp system, followed by a call to GPS, "(gps ...)", which is typed by the user, then the output from the program, "(EXECUTING ...)", and finally the result of the function call, which can be either SOLVED or NIL.

```
> (gps '(son-at-home car-needs-battery have-money have-phone-book)
        '(son-at-school)
        *school-ops*)
(EXECUTING LOOK-UP-NUMBER)
(EXECUTING TELEPHONE-SHOP)
(EXECUTING TELL-SHOP-PROBLEM)
(EXECUTING GIVE-SHOP-MONEY)
(EXECUTING SHOP-INSTALLS-BATTERY)
(EXECUTING DRIVE-SON-TO-SCHOOL)
SOLVED

> (gps '(son-at-home car-needs-battery have-money)
        '(son-at-school)
        *school-ops*)
NIL

> (gps '(son-at-home car-works)
        '(son-at-school)
        *school-ops*)
(EXECUTING DRIVE-SON-TO-SCHOOL)
SOLVED
```

In all three examples the goal is to have the son at school. The only operator that has son-at-school in its add-list is drive-son-to-school, so GPS selects that operator initially. Before it can execute the operator, GPS has to solve for the preconditions. In the first example, the program ends up working backward through the operators shop-installs-battery, give-shop-money, tell-shop-problem, and telephone-shop to look-up-number, which has no outstanding preconditions. Thus, the look-up-number action can be executed, and the program moves on to the other actions. As Aristotle said, "What is the last in the order of analysis seems to be first in the order of becoming."

The second example starts out exactly the same, but the look-up-number operator fails because its precondition, have-phone-book, cannot be achieved. Knowing the phone number is a precondition, directly or indirectly, of all the operators, so no action is taken and GPS returns NIL.

Finally, the third example is much more direct; the initial state specifies that the car works, so the driving operator can be applied immediately.

4.5 Stage 5: Analysis, or "We Lied about the G"

In the sections that follow, we examine the question of just how general this General Problem Solver is. The next four sections point out limitations of our version of GPS, and we will show how to correct these limitations in a second version of the program.

One might ask if "limitations" is just a euphemism for "bugs." Are we "enhancing" the program, or are we "correcting" it? There are no clear answers on this point, because we never insisted on an unambiguous problem description or specification. AI programming is largely exploratory programming; the aim is often to discover more about the problem area rather than to meet a clearly defined specification. This is in contrast to a more traditional notion of programming, where the problem is completely specified before the first line of code is written.

4.6 The Running Around the Block Problem

Representing the operator "driving from home to school" is easy: the precondition and delete-list includes being at home, and the add-list includes being at school. But suppose we wanted to represent "running around the block." There would be no net change of location, so does that mean there would be no add- or delete-list? If so, there would be no reason ever to apply the operator. Perhaps the add-list should contain something like "got some exercise" or "feel tired," or something more general like "experience running around the block." We will return to this question later.

4.7 The Clobbered Sibling Goal Problem

Consider the problem of not only getting the child to school but also having some money left over to use for the rest of the day. GPS can easily solve this problem from the following initial condition:

```
> (gps '(son-at-home have-money car-works)
        '(have-money son-at-school)
        *school-ops*)
(EXECUTING DRIVE-SON-TO-SCHOOL)
SOLVED
```

However, in the next example GPS incorrectly reports success, when in fact it has spent the money on the battery.

```
> (gps '(son-at-home car-needs-battery have-money have-phone-book)
       '(have-money son-at-school)
       *school-ops*)
(EXECUTING LOOK-UP-NUMBER)
(EXECUTING TELEPHONE-SHOP)
(EXECUTING TELL-SHOP-PROBLEM)
(EXECUTING GIVE-SHOP-MONEY)
(EXECUTING SHOP-INSTALLS-BATTERY)
(EXECUTING DRIVE-SON-TO-SCHOOL)
SOLVED
```

The "bug" is that GPS uses the expression (every #'achieve goals) to achieve a set of goals. If this expression returns true, it means that every one of the goals has been achieved in sequence, but it doesn't mean they are all still true at the end. In other words, the goal (have-money son-at-school), which we intended to mean "end up in a state where both have-money and son-at-school are true," was interpreted by GPS to mean "first achieve have-money, and then achieve son-at-school." Sometimes achieving one goal can undo another, previously achieved goal. We will call this the "prerequisite clobbers sibling goal" problem.[2] That is, have-money and son-at-school are sibling goals, one of the prerequisites for the plan for son-at-school is car-works, and achieving that goal clobbers the have-money goal.

Modifying the program to recognize the "prerequisite clobbers sibling goal" problem is straightforward. First note that we call (every #'achieve *something*) twice within the program, so let's replace those two forms with (achieve-all *something*). We can then define achieve-all as follows:

```
(defun achieve-all (goals)
  "Try to achieve each goal, then make sure they still hold."
  (and (every #'achieve goals) (subsetp goals *state*)))
```

The Common Lisp function subsetp returns true if its first argument is a subset of its second. In achieve-all, it returns true if every one of the goals is still in the current state after achieving all the goals. This is just what we wanted to test.

The introduction of achieve-all prevents GPS from returning true when one of the goals gets clobbered, but it doesn't force GPS to replan and try to recover from a clobbered goal. We won't consider that possibility now, but we will take it up again in the section on the blocks world domain, which was Sussman's primary example.

---

[2]Gerald Sussman, in his book *A Computer Model of Skill Acquisition*, uses the term "prerequisite clobbers brother goal" or PCBG. I prefer to be gender neutral, even at the risk of being labeled a historical revisionist.

4.8   The Leaping before You Look Problem

Another way to address the "prerequisite clobbers sibling goal" problem is just to be more careful about the order of goals in a goal list. If we want to get the kid to school and still have some money left, why not just specify the goal as (son-at-school have-money) rather than (have-money son-at-school)? Let's see what happens when we try that:

```
> (gps '(son-at-home car-needs-battery have-money have-phone-book)
       '(son-at-school have-money)
       *school-ops*)
(EXECUTING LOOK-UP-NUMBER)
(EXECUTING TELEPHONE-SHOP)
(EXECUTING TELL-SHOP-PROBLEM)
(EXECUTING GIVE-SHOP-MONEY)
(EXECUTING SHOP-INSTALLS-BATTERY)
(EXECUTING DRIVE-SON-TO-SCHOOL)
NIL
```

GPS returns nil, reflecting the fact that the goal cannot be achieved, but only after executing all actions up to and including driving to school. I call this the "leaping before you look" problem, because if you asked the program to solve for the two goals (jump-off-cliff land-safely) it would happily jump first, only to discover that it had no operator to land safely. This is less than prudent behavior.

The problem arises because planning and execution are interleaved. Once the preconditions for an operator are achieved, the action is taken—and *state* is irrevocably changed—even if this action may eventually lead to a dead end. An alternative would be to replace the single global *state* with distinct local state variables, such that a new variable is created for each new state. This alternative is a good one for another, independent reason, as we shall see in the next section.

4.9   The Recursive Subgoal Problem

In our simulated nursery school world there is only one way to find out a phone number: to look it up in the phone book. Suppose we want to add an operator for finding out a phone number by asking someone. Of course, in order to ask someone something, you need to be in communication with him or her. The asking-for-a-phone-number operator could be implemented as follows:

```
(push (make-op :action 'ask-phone-number
               :preconds '(in-communication-with-shop)
               :add-list '(know-phone-number))
      *school-ops*)
```

(The special form (push *item list*) puts the item on the front of the list; it is equivalent to (setf *list* (cons *item list*)) in the simple case.) Unfortunately, something
unexpected happens when we attempt to solve seemingly simple problems with this
new set of operators. Consider the following:

```
> (gps '(son-at-home car-needs-battery have-money)
       '(son-at-school)
       *school-ops*)
```

```
>>TRAP 14877 (SYSTEM:PDL-OVERFLOW EH::REGULAR)
The regular push-down list has overflown.
While in the function ACHIEVE <- EVERY <- REMOVE
```

The error message (which will vary from one implementation of Common Lisp to
another) means that too many recursively nested function calls were made. This
indicates either a very complex problem or, more commonly, a bug in the program
leading to infinite recursion. One way to try to see the cause of the bug is to trace a
relevant function, such as achieve:

```
> (trace achieve) ⇒ (ACHIEVE)
```

```
> (gps '(son-at-home car-needs-battery have-money)
       '(son-at-school)
       *school-ops*)
(1 ENTER ACHIEVE: SON-AT-SCHOOL)
  (2 ENTER ACHIEVE: SON-AT-HOME)
  (2 EXIT ACHIEVE: (SON-AT-HOME CAR-NEEDS-BATTERY HAVE-MONEY))
  (2 ENTER ACHIEVE: CAR-WORKS)
    (3 ENTER ACHIEVE: CAR-NEEDS-BATTERY)
    (3 EXIT ACHIEVE: (CAR-NEEDS-BATTERY HAVE-MONEY))
    (3 ENTER ACHIEVE: SHOP-KNOWS-PROBLEM)
      (4 ENTER ACHIEVE: IN-COMMUNICATION-WITH-SHOP)
        (5 ENTER ACHIEVE: KNOW-PHONE-NUMBER)
          (6 ENTER ACHIEVE: IN-COMMUNICATION-WITH-SHOP)
            (7 ENTER ACHIEVE: KNOW-PHONE-NUMBER)
              (8 ENTER ACHIEVE: IN-COMMUNICATION-WITH-SHOP)
                (9 ENTER ACHIEVE: KNOW-PHONE-NUMBER)
                    .
                   .
                  .
```

The output from trace gives us the necessary clues. Newell and Simon talk of "oscillating among ends, functions required, and means that perform them." Here it seems we have an infinite oscillation between being in communication with the shop (levels 4, 6, 8, . . .) and knowing the shop's phone number (levels 5, 7, 9, . . .). The reasoning is as follows: we want the shop to know about the problem with the battery, and this requires being in communication with him or her. One way to get in communication is to phone, but we don't have a phone book to look up the number. We could ask them their phone number, but this requires being in communication with them. As Aristotle put it, "If we are to be always deliberating, we shall have to go on to infinity." We will call this the "recursive subgoal" problem: trying to solve a problem in terms of itself. One way to avoid the problem is to have achieve keep track of all the goals that are being worked on and give up if it sees a loop in the goal stack.

4.10   The Lack of Intermediate Information Problem

When GPS fails to find a solution, it just returns nil. This is annoying in cases where the user expected a solution to be found, because it gives no information about the cause of failure. The user could always trace some function, as we traced achieve above, but the output from trace is rarely exactly the information desired. It would be nice to have a general debugging output tool where the programmer could insert print statements into his code and have them selectively printed, depending on the information desired.

The function dbg provides this capability. dbg prints output in the same way as format, but it will only print when debugging output is desired. Each call to dbg is accompanied by an identifer that is used to specify a class of debugging messages. The functions debug and undebug are used to add or remove message classes to the list of classes that should be printed. In this chapter, all the debugging output will use the identifier :gps. Other programs will use other identifiers, and a complex program will use many identifiers.

A call to dbg will result in output if the first argument to dbg, the identifier, is one that was specified in a call to debug. The other arguments to dbg are a format string followed by a list of arguments to be printed according to the format string. In other words, we will write functions that include calls to dbg like:

```
(dbg :gps "The current goal is: ~a" goal)
```

If we have turned on debugging with (debug :gps), then calls to dbg with the identifier :gps will print output. The output is turned off with (undebug :gps).

debug and undebug are designed to be similar to trace and untrace, in that they turn diagnostic output on and off. They also follow the convention that debug with no arguments returns the current list of identifiers, and that undebug with no arguments turns all debugging off. However, they differ from trace and untrace in that they are functions, not macros. If you use only keywords and integers for identifiers, then you won't notice the difference.

Two new built-in features are introduced here. First, *debug-io* is the stream normally used for debugging input/output. In all previous calls to format we have used t as the stream argument, which causes output to go to the *standard-output* stream. Sending different types of output to different streams allows the user some flexibility. For example, debugging output could be directed to a separate window, or it could be copied to a file. Second, the function fresh-line advances to the next line of output, unless the output stream is already at the start of the line.

```lisp
(defvar *dbg-ids* nil "Identifiers used by dbg")

(defun dbg (id format-string &rest args)
  "Print debugging info if (DEBUG ID) has been specified."
  (when (member id *dbg-ids*)
    (fresh-line *debug-io*)
    (apply #'format *debug-io* format-string args)))

(defun debug (&rest ids)
  "Start dbg output on the given ids."
  (setf *dbg-ids* (union ids *dbg-ids*)))

(defun undebug (&rest ids)
  "Stop dbg on the ids.  With no ids, stop dbg altogether."
  (setf *dbg-ids* (if (null ids) nil
                      (set-difference *dbg-ids* ids))))
```

Sometimes it is easier to view debugging output if it is indented according to some pattern, such as the depth of nested calls to a function. To generate indented output, the function dbg-indent is defined:

```lisp
(defun dbg-indent (id indent format-string &rest args)
  "Print indented debugging info if (DEBUG ID) has been specified."
  (when (member id *dbg-ids*)
    (fresh-line *debug-io*)
    (dotimes (i indent) (princ "  " *debug-io*))
    (apply #'format *debug-io* format-string args)))
```

4.11 GPS Version 2: A More General Problem Solver

At this point we are ready to put together a new version of GPS with solutions for the "running around the block," "prerequisite clobbers sibling goal," "leaping before you look," and "recursive subgoal" problems. The glossary for the new version is in figure 4.2.

	Top-Level Function
GPS	Solve a goal from a state using a list of operators.
	Special Variables
ops	A list of available operators.
	Data Types
op	An operation with preconds, add-list and del-list.
	Major Functions
achieve-all	Achieve a list of goals.
achieve	Achieve an individual goal.
appropriate-p	Decide if an operator is appropriate for a goal.
apply-op	Apply operator to current state.
	Auxiliary Functions
executing-p	Is a condition an executing form?
starts-with	Is the argument a list that starts with a given atom?
convert-op	Convert an operator to use the executing convention.
op	Create an operator.
use	Use a list of operators.
member-equal	Test if an element is equal to a member of a list.
	Selected Common Lisp Functions
member	Test if an element is a member of a list. (p. 78)
set-difference	All elements in one set but not the other.
subsetp	Is one set wholly contained in another?
union	All elements in either of two sets.
every	Test if every element of a list passes a test. (p. 62)
some	Test if any element of a list passes a test.
remove-if	Remove all items satisfying a test.
	Previously Defined Functions
find-all	A list of all matching elements. (p. 101)
find-all-if	A list of all elements satisfying a predicate.

Figure 4.2: Glossary for Version 2 of GPS

The most important change is that, instead of printing a message when each operator is applied, we will instead have GPS return the resulting state. A list of "messages" in each state indicates what actions have been taken. Each message is actually a condition, a list of the form (executing *operator*). This solves the "running around the block" problem: we could call GPS with an initial goal of ((executing run-around-block)), and it would execute the run-around-block operator, thereby satisfying the goal. The following code defines a new function, op, which builds operators that include the message in their add-list.

```
(defun executing-p (x)
  "Is x of the form: (executing ...) ?"
  (starts-with x 'executing))

(defun starts-with (list x)
  "Is this a list whose first element is x?"
  (and (consp list) (eql (first list) x)))

(defun convert-op (op)
  "Make op conform to the (EXECUTING op) convention."
  (unless (some #'executing-p (op-add-list op))
    (push (list 'executing (op-action op)) (op-add-list op)))
  op)

(defun op (action &key preconds add-list del-list)
  "Make a new operator that obeys the (EXECUTING op) convention."
  (convert-op
    (make-op :action action :preconds preconds
             :add-list add-list :del-list del-list)))
```

Operators built by op will be correct, but we can convert existing operators using convert-op directly:

```
(mapc #'convert-op *school-ops*)
```

This is an example of exploratory programming: instead of starting all over when we discover a limitation of the first version, we can use Lisp to alter existing data structures for the new version of the program.

The definition of the variable *ops* and the structure op are exactly the same as before, and the rest of the program consists of five functions we have already seen: GPS, achieve-all, achieve, appropriate-p, and apply-op. At the top level, the function GPS calls achieve-all, which returns either nil or a valid state. From this we remove all the atoms, which leaves only the elements of the final state that are lists—in other words, the actions of the form (executing *operator*). Thus, the value of GPS itself is the list of actions taken to arrive at the final state. GPS no longer returns SOLVED when it finds a solution, but it still obeys the convention of returning nil for failure, and non-nil for success. In general, it is a good idea to have a program return a meaningful value rather than print that value, if there is the possibility that some other program might ever want to use the value.

```
(defvar *ops* nil "A list of available operators.")

(defstruct op "An operation"
  (action nil) (preconds nil) (add-list nil) (del-list nil))

(defun GPS (state goals &optional (*ops* *ops*))
  "General Problem Solver: from state, achieve goals using *ops*."
  (remove-if #'atom (achieve-all (cons '(start) state) goals nil)))
```

The first major change in version 2 is evident from the first line of the program: there is no *state* variable. Instead, the program keeps track of local state variables. This is to solve the "leaping before you look" problem, as outlined before. The functions achieve, achieve-all, and apply-op all take an extra argument which is the current state, and all return a new state as their value. They also must still obey the convention of returning nil when they fail.

Thus we have a potential ambiguity: does nil represent failure, or does it represent a valid state that happens to have no conditions? We resolve the ambiguity by adopting the convention that all states must have at least one condition. This convention is enforced by the function GPS. Instead of calling (achieve-all state goals nil), GPS calls (achieve-all (cons '(start) state) goals nil). So even if the user passes GPS a null initial state, it will pass on a state containing (start) to achieve-all. From then on, we are guaranteed that no state will ever become nil, because the only function that builds a new state is apply-op, and we can see by looking at the last line of apply-op that it always appends something onto the state it is returning. (An add-list can never be nil, because if it were, the operator would not be appropriate. Besides, every operator includes the (executing ...) condition.)

Note that the final value we return from GPS has all the atoms removed, so we end up reporting only the actions performed, since they are represented by conditions of the form (executing *action*). Adding the (start) condition at the beginning also serves to differentiate between a problem that cannot be solved and one that is solved without executing any actions. Failure returns nil, while a solution with no steps will at least include the (start) condition, if nothing else.

Functions that return nil as an indication of failure and return some useful value otherwise are known as *semipredicates*. They are error prone in just these cases where nil might be construed as a useful value. Be careful when defining and using semipredicates: (1) Decide if nil could ever be a meaningful value. (2) Insure that the *user* can't corrupt the program by supplying nil as a value. In this program, GPS is the only function the user should call, so once we have accounted for it, we're covered. (3) Insure that the *program* can't supply nil as a value. We did this by seeing that there was only one place in the program where new states were constructed, and that this new state was formed by appending a one-element list onto another state. By following this three-step procedure, we have an informal proof that the semipredicates involving states will function properly. This kind of informal proof procedure is a common element of good program design.

The other big change in version 2 is the introduction of a goal stack to solve the recursive subgoal problem. The program keeps track of the goals it is working on and immediately fails if a goal appears as a subgoal of itself. This test is made in the second clause of achieve.

The function achieve-all tries to achieve each one of the goals in turn, setting the variable state2 to be the value returned from each successive call to achieve. If all goals are achieved in turn, and if all the goals still hold at the end (as subsetp checks for), then the final state is returned; otherwise the function fails, returning nil.

Most of the work is done by achieve, which gets passed a state, a single goal condition, and the stack of goals worked on so far. If the condition is already in the state, then achieve succeeds and returns the state. On the other hand, if the goal condition is already in the goal stack, then there is no sense continuing—we will be stuck in an endless loop—so achieve returns nil. Otherwise, achieve looks through the list of operators, trying to find one appropriate to apply.

```
(defun achieve-all (state goals goal-stack)
  "Achieve each goal, and make sure they still hold at the end."
  (let ((current-state state))
    (if (and (every #'(lambda (g)
                        (setf current-state
                              (achieve current-state g goal-stack)))
                    goals)
             (subsetp goals current-state :test #'equal))
        current-state)))

(defun achieve (state goal goal-stack)
  "A goal is achieved if it already holds,
  or if there is an appropriate op for it that is applicable."
  (dbg-indent :gps (length goal-stack) "Goal: ~a" goal)
  (cond ((member-equal goal state) state)
        ((member-equal goal goal-stack) nil)
        (t (some #'(lambda (op) (apply-op state goal op goal-stack))
                 (find-all goal *ops* :test #'appropriate-p)))))
```

The goal ((executing run-around-block)) is a list of one condition, where the condition happens to be a two-element list. Allowing lists as conditions gives us more flexibility, but we also have to be careful. The problem is that not all lists that look alike actually are the same. The predicate equal essentially tests to see if its two arguments look alike, while the predicate eql tests to see if its two arguments actually are identical. Since functions like member use eql by default, we have to specify with a :test keyword that we want equal instead. Since this is done several times, we introduce the function `member-equal`. In fact, we could have carried the abstraction one step further and defined `member-situation`, a function to test if a condition is true in a situation. This would allow the user to change the matching function from `eql` to `equal`, and to anything else that might be useful.

```
(defun member-equal (item list)
  (member item list :test #'equal))
```

The function `apply-op`, which used to change the state irrevocably and print a message reflecting this, now returns the new state instead of printing anything. It first computes the state that would result from achieving all the preconditions of the operator. If it is possible to arrive at such a state, then `apply-op` returns a new state derived from this state by adding what's in the add-list and removing everything in the delete-list.

```
(defun apply-op (state goal op goal-stack)
  "Return a new, transformed state if op is applicable."
  (dbg-indent :gps (length goal-stack) "Consider: ~a" (op-action op))
  (let ((state2 (achieve-all state (op-preconds op)
                             (cons goal goal-stack))))
    (unless (null state2)
      ;; Return an updated state
      (dbg-indent :gps (length goal-stack) "Action: ~a" (op-action op))
      (append (remove-if #'(lambda (x)
                             (member-equal x (op-del-list op)))
                         state2)
              (op-add-list op)))))
```

```
(defun appropriate-p (goal op)
  "An op is appropriate to a goal if it is in its add-list."
  (member-equal goal (op-add-list op)))
```

There is one last complication in the way we compute the new state. In version 1 of GPS, states were (conceptually) unordered sets of conditions, so we could use `union` and `set-difference` to operate on them. In version 2, states become ordered lists, because we need to preserve the ordering of actions. Thus, we have to use the functions `append` and `remove-if`, since these are defined to preserve order, while `union` and `set-difference` are not.

Finally, the last difference in version 2 is that it introduces a new function: `use`. This function is intended to be used as a sort of declaration that a given list of operators is to be used for a series of problems.

```
(defun use (oplist)
  "Use oplist as the default list of operators."
  ;; Return something useful, but not too verbose:
  ;; the number of operators.
  (length (setf *ops* oplist)))
```

Calling use sets the parameter *ops*, so that it need not be specified on each call to GPS. Accordingly, in the definition of GPS itself the third argument, *ops*, is now optional; if it is not supplied, a default will be used. The default value for *ops* is given as *ops*. This may seem redundant or superfluous—how could a variable be its own default? The answer is that the two occurrences of *ops* look alike, but they actually refer to two completely separate bindings of the special variable *ops*. Most of the time, variables in parameter lists are local variables, but there is no rule against binding a special variable as a parameter. Remember that the effect of binding a special variable is that all references to the special variable that occur anywhere in the program—even outside the lexical scope of the function—refer to the new binding of the special variable. So after a sequence of calls we eventually reach achieve, which references *ops*, and it will see the newly bound value of *ops*.

The definition of GPS is repeated here, along with an alternate version that binds a local variable and explicitly sets and resets the special variable *ops*. Clearly, the idiom of binding a special variable is more concise, and while it can be initially confusing, it is useful once understood.

```
(defun GPS (state goals &optional (*ops* *ops*))
  "General Problem Solver: from state, achieve goals using *ops*."
  (remove-if #'atom (achieve-all (cons '(start) state) goals nil)))

(defun GPS (state goals &optional (ops *ops*))
  "General Problem Solver: from state, achieve goals using *ops*."
  (let ((old-ops *ops*))
    (setf *ops* ops)
    (let ((result (remove-if #'atom (achieve-all
                                      (cons '(start) state)
                                      goals nil))))
      (setf *ops* old-ops)
      result)))
```

Now let's see how version 2 performs. We use the list of operators that includes the "asking the shop their phone number" operator. First we make sure it will still do the examples version 1 did:

```
> (use *school-ops*) ⇒ 7
```

```
> (gps '(son-at-home car-needs-battery have-money have-phone-book)
        '(son-at-school))
((START)
 (EXECUTING LOOK-UP-NUMBER)
 (EXECUTING TELEPHONE-SHOP)
 (EXECUTING TELL-SHOP-PROBLEM)
 (EXECUTING GIVE-SHOP-MONEY)
 (EXECUTING SHOP-INSTALLS-BATTERY)
 (EXECUTING DRIVE-SON-TO-SCHOOL))

> (debug :gps) ⇒ (:GPS)

> (gps '(son-at-home car-needs-battery have-money have-phone-book)
        '(son-at-school))
Goal: SON-AT-SCHOOL
Consider: DRIVE-SON-TO-SCHOOL
  Goal: SON-AT-HOME
  Goal: CAR-WORKS
  Consider: SHOP-INSTALLS-BATTERY
    Goal: CAR-NEEDS-BATTERY
    Goal: SHOP-KNOWS-PROBLEM
    Consider: TELL-SHOP-PROBLEM
      Goal: IN-COMMUNICATION-WITH-SHOP
      Consider: TELEPHONE-SHOP
        Goal: KNOW-PHONE-NUMBER
        Consider: ASK-PHONE-NUMBER
          Goal: IN-COMMUNICATION-WITH-SHOP
        Consider: LOOK-UP-NUMBER
          Goal: HAVE-PHONE-BOOK
        Action: LOOK-UP-NUMBER
      Action: TELEPHONE-SHOP
    Action: TELL-SHOP-PROBLEM
    Goal: SHOP-HAS-MONEY
    Consider: GIVE-SHOP-MONEY
      Goal: HAVE-MONEY
    Action: GIVE-SHOP-MONEY
  Action: SHOP-INSTALLS-BATTERY
Action: DRIVE-SON-TO-SCHOOL
((START)
 (EXECUTING LOOK-UP-NUMBER)
 (EXECUTING TELEPHONE-SHOP)
 (EXECUTING TELL-SHOP-PROBLEM)
 (EXECUTING GIVE-SHOP-MONEY)
 (EXECUTING SHOP-INSTALLS-BATTERY)
 (EXECUTING DRIVE-SON-TO-SCHOOL))

> (undebug) ⇒ NIL
```

```
> (gps '(son-at-home car-works)
        '(son-at-school))
((START)
 (EXECUTING DRIVE-SON-TO-SCHOOL))
```

Now we see that version 2 can also handle the three cases that version 1 got wrong. In each case, the program avoids an infinite loop, and also avoids leaping before it looks.

```
> (gps '(son-at-home car-needs-battery have-money have-phone-book)
        '(have-money son-at-school))
NIL

> (gps '(son-at-home car-needs-battery have-money have-phone-book)
        '(son-at-school have-money))
NIL

> (gps '(son-at-home car-needs-battery have-money)
        '(son-at-school))
NIL
```

Finally, we see that this version of GPS also works on trivial problems requiring no action:

```
> (gps '(son-at-home) '(son-at-home)) ⇒ ((START))
```

4.12   The New Domain Problem: Monkey and Bananas

To show that GPS is at all general, we have to make it work in different domains. We will start with a "classic" AI problem.[3] Imagine the following scenario: a hungry monkey is standing at the doorway to a room. In the middle of the room is a bunch of bananas suspended from the ceiling by a rope, well out of the monkey's reach. There is a chair near the door, which is light enough for the monkey to push and tall enough to reach almost to the bananas. Just to make things complicated, assume the monkey is holding a toy ball and can only hold one thing at a time.

In trying to represent this scenario, we have some flexibility in choosing what to put in the current state and what to put in with the operators. For now, assume we define the operators as follows:

---

[3]Originally posed by Saul Amarel (1968).

```
(defparameter *banana-ops*
  (list
    (op 'climb-on-chair
        :preconds '(chair-at-middle-room at-middle-room on-floor)
        :add-list '(at-bananas on-chair)
        :del-list '(at-middle-room on-floor))
    (op 'push-chair-from-door-to-middle-room
        :preconds '(chair-at-door at-door)
        :add-list '(chair-at-middle-room at-middle-room)
        :del-list '(chair-at-door at-door))
    (op 'walk-from-door-to-middle-room
        :preconds '(at-door on-floor)
        :add-list '(at-middle-room)
        :del-list '(at-door))
    (op 'grasp-bananas
        :preconds '(at-bananas empty-handed)
        :add-list '(has-bananas)
        :del-list '(empty-handed))
    (op 'drop-ball
        :preconds '(has-ball)
        :add-list '(empty-handed)
        :del-list '(has-ball))
    (op 'eat-bananas
        :preconds '(has-bananas)
        :add-list '(empty-handed not-hungry)
        :del-list '(has-bananas hungry))))
```

Using these operators, we could pose the problem of becoming not-hungry, given
the initial state of being at the door, standing on the floor, holding the ball, hungry,
and with the chair at the door. GPS can find a solution to this problem:

```
> (use *banana-ops*)  ⇒ 6

> (GPS '(at-door on-floor has-ball hungry chair-at-door)
       '(not-hungry))
((START)
 (EXECUTING PUSH-CHAIR-FROM-DOOR-TO-MIDDLE-ROOM)
 (EXECUTING CLIMB-ON-CHAIR)
 (EXECUTING DROP-BALL)
 (EXECUTING GRASP-BANANAS)
 (EXECUTING EAT-BANANAS))
```

Notice we did not need to make any changes at all to the GPS program. We just used
a different set of operators.

4.13   The Maze Searching Domain

Now we will consider another "classic" problem, maze searching. We will assume a particular maze, diagrammed here.

1	2	3	4	5
6	7	8	9	10
11	12	13	14	15
16	17	18	19	20
21	22	23	24	25

It is much easier to define some functions to help build the operators for this domain than it would be to type in all the operators directly. The following code defines a set of operators for mazes in general, and for this maze in particular:

```
(defun make-maze-ops (pair)
  "Make maze ops in both directions"
  (list (make-maze-op (first pair) (second pair))
        (make-maze-op (second pair) (first pair))))

(defun make-maze-op (here there)
  "Make an operator to move between two places"
  (op '(move from ,here to ,there)
      :preconds '((at ,here))
      :add-list '((at ,there))
      :del-list '((at ,here))))

(defparameter *maze-ops*
  (mappend #'make-maze-ops
      '((1 2) (2 3) (3 4) (4 9) (9 14) (9 8) (8 7) (7 12) (12 13)
        (12 11) (11 6) (11 16) (16 17) (17 22) (21 22) (22 23)
        (23 18) (23 24) (24 19) (19 20) (20 15) (15 10) (10 5) (20 25))))
```

Note the backquote notation, ('). It is covered in section 3.2, page 67.

We can now use this list of operators to solve several problems with this maze. And we could easily create another maze by giving another list of connections. Note that there is nothing that says the places in the maze are arranged in a five-by-five layout—that is just one way of visualizing the connectivity.

```
> (use *maze-ops*) ⇒ 48
```

```
> (gps '((at 1)) '((at 25)))
((START)
 (EXECUTING (MOVE FROM 1 TO 2))
 (EXECUTING (MOVE FROM 2 TO 3))
 (EXECUTING (MOVE FROM 3 TO 4))
 (EXECUTING (MOVE FROM 4 TO 9))
 (EXECUTING (MOVE FROM 9 TO 8))
 (EXECUTING (MOVE FROM 8 TO 7))
 (EXECUTING (MOVE FROM 7 TO 12))
 (EXECUTING (MOVE FROM 12 TO 11))
 (EXECUTING (MOVE FROM 11 TO 16))
 (EXECUTING (MOVE FROM 16 TO 17))
 (EXECUTING (MOVE FROM 17 TO 22))
 (EXECUTING (MOVE FROM 22 TO 23))
 (EXECUTING (MOVE FROM 23 TO 24))
 (EXECUTING (MOVE FROM 24 TO 19))
 (EXECUTING (MOVE FROM 19 TO 20))
 (EXECUTING (MOVE FROM 20 TO 25))
 (AT 25))
```

There is one subtle bug that the maze domain points out. We wanted GPS to return a list of the actions executed. However, in order to account for the case where the goal can be achieved with no action, I included (START) in the value returned by GPS. These examples include the START and EXECUTING forms but also a list of the form (AT *n*), for some *n*. This is the bug. If we go back and look at the function GPS, we find that it reports the result by removing all atoms from the state returned by achieve-all. This is a "pun"—we said remove atoms, when we really meant to remove all conditions except the (START) and (EXECUTING *action*) forms. Up to now, all these conditions were atoms, so this approach worked. The maze domain introduced conditions of the form (AT *n*), so for the first time there was a problem. The moral is that when a programmer uses puns—saying what's convenient instead of what's really happening—there's bound to be trouble. What we really want to do is not to remove atoms but to find all elements that denote actions. The code below says what we mean:

```
(defun GPS (state goals &optional (*ops* *ops*))
  "General Problem Solver: from state, achieve goals using *ops*."
  (find-all-if #'action-p
               (achieve-all (cons '(start) state) goals nil)))
```

```
(defun action-p (x)
  "Is x something that is (start) or (executing ...)?"
  (or (equal x '(start)) (executing-p x)))
```

The domain of maze solving also points out an advantage of version 2: that it returns a representation of the actions taken rather than just printing them out. The reason this is an advantage is that we may want to use the results for something, rather than just look at them. Suppose we wanted a function that gives us a path through a maze as a list of locations to visit in turn. We could do this by calling GPS as a subfunction and then manipulating the results:

```
(defun find-path (start end)
  "Search a maze for a path from start to end."
  (let ((results (GPS '((at ,start)) '((at ,end)))))
    (unless (null results)
      (cons start (mapcar #'destination
                          (remove '(start) results
                                  :test #'equal))))))

(defun destination (action)
  "Find the Y in (executing (move from X to Y))"
  (fifth (second action)))
```

The function find-path calls GPS to get the results. If this is nil, there is no answer, but if it is not, then take the rest of results (in other words, ignore the (START) part). Pick out the destination, y, from each (EXECUTING (MOVE FROM x TO y)) form, and remember to include the starting point.

```
> (use *maze-ops*) ⇒ 48

> (find-path 1 25) ⇒
(1 2 3 4 9 8 7 12 11 16 17 22 23 24 19 20 25)

> (find-path 1 1) ⇒ (1)

> (equal (find-path 1 25) (reverse (find-path 25 1))) ⇒ T
```

4.14   The Blocks World Domain

Another domain that has attracted more than its share of attention in AI circles is the blocks world domain. Imagine a child's set of building blocks on a table top. The problem is to move the blocks from their starting configuration into some goal configuration. We will assume that each block can have only one other block directly on top of it, although they can be stacked to arbitrary height. The only action that can be taken in this world is to move a single block that has nothing on top of it either to the top of another block or onto the table that represents the block world. We will create an operator for each possible block move.

```lisp
(defun make-block-ops (blocks)
  (let ((ops nil))
    (dolist (a blocks)
      (dolist (b blocks)
        (unless (equal a b)
          (dolist (c blocks)
            (unless (or (equal c a) (equal c b))
              (push (move-op a b c) ops)))
          (push (move-op a 'table b) ops)
          (push (move-op a b 'table) ops))))
    ops))

(defun move-op (a b c)
  "Make an operator to move A from B to C."
  (op '(move ,a from ,b to ,c)
      :preconds '((space on ,a) (space on ,c) (,a on ,b))
      :add-list (move-ons a b c)
      :del-list (move-ons a c b)))

(defun move-ons (a b c)
  (if (eq b 'table)
      '((,a on ,c))
      '((,a on ,c) (space on ,b))))
```

Now we try these operators out on some problems. The simplest possible problem is stacking one block on another:

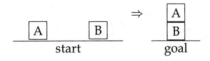

```lisp
> (use (make-block-ops '(a b))) ⇒ 4

> (gps '((a on table) (b on table) (space on a) (space on b)
         (space on table))
       '((a on b) (b on table)))
((START)
 (EXECUTING (MOVE A FROM TABLE TO B)))
```

Here is a slightly more complex problem: inverting a stack of two blocks. This time we show the debugging output.

```
┌───┐        ┌───┐
│ A │   ⇒    │ B │
├───┤        ├───┤
│ B │        │ A │
┴───┴──      ┴───┴──
 start        goal
```

```
> (debug :gps) ⇒ (:GPS)

> (gps '((a on b) (b on table) (space on a) (space on table))
        '((b on a)))
Goal: (B ON A)
Consider: (MOVE B FROM TABLE TO A)
  Goal: (SPACE ON B)
  Consider: (MOVE A FROM B TO TABLE)
    Goal: (SPACE ON A)
    Goal: (SPACE ON TABLE)
    Goal: (A ON B)
  Action: (MOVE A FROM B TO TABLE)
  Goal: (SPACE ON A)
  Goal: (B ON TABLE)
Action: (MOVE B FROM TABLE TO A)
((START)
 (EXECUTING (MOVE A FROM B TO TABLE))
 (EXECUTING (MOVE B FROM TABLE TO A)))

> (undebug) ⇒ NIL
```

Sometimes it matters what order you try the conjuncts in. For example, you can't have your cake and eat it too, but you can take a picture of your cake and eat it too, as long as you take the picture *before* eating it. In the blocks world, we have:

```
┌───┐        ┌───┐
│ A │        │ C │
├───┤        ├───┤
│ B │   ⇒    │ B │
├───┤        ├───┤
│ C │        │ A │
┴───┴──      ┴───┴──
 start        goal
```

```
> (use (make-block-ops '(a b c))) ⇒ 18

> (gps '((a on b) (b on c) (c on table) (space on a) (space on table))
        '((b on a) (c on b)))
((START)
 (EXECUTING (MOVE A FROM B TO TABLE))
 (EXECUTING (MOVE B FROM C TO A))
 (EXECUTING (MOVE C FROM TABLE TO B)))
```

```
> (gps '((a on b) (b on c) (c on table) (space on a) (space on table))
        '((c on b) (b on a)))
NIL
```

In the first case, the tower was built by putting B on A first, and then C on B. In the second case, the program gets C on B first, but clobbers that goal while getting B on A. The "prerequisite clobbers sibling goal" situation is recognized, but the program doesn't do anything about it. One thing we could do is try to vary the order of the conjunct goals. That is, we could change achieve-all as follows:

```
(defun achieve-all (state goals goal-stack)
  "Achieve each goal, trying several orderings."
  (some #'(lambda (goals) (achieve-each state goals goal-stack))
        (orderings goals)))

(defun achieve-each (state goals goal-stack)
  "Achieve each goal, and make sure they still hold at the end."
  (let ((current-state state))
    (if (and (every #'(lambda (g)
                        (setf current-state
                              (achieve current-state g goal-stack)))
                    goals)
             (subsetp goals current-state :test #'equal))
        current-state)))

(defun orderings (l)
  (if (> (length l) 1)
      (list l (reverse l))
      (list l)))
```

Now we can represent the goal either way, and we'll still get an answer. Notice that we only consider two orderings: the order given and the reversed order. Obviously, for goal sets of one or two conjuncts this is all the orderings. In general, if there is only one interaction per goal set, then one of these two orders will work. Thus, we are assuming that "prerequisite clobbers sibling goal" interactions are rare, and that there will seldom be more than one interaction per goal set. Another possibility would be to consider all possible permutations of the goals, but that could take a long time with large goal sets.

Another consideration is the efficiency of solutions. Consider the simple task of getting block C on the table in the following diagram:

```
> (gps '((c on a) (a on table) (b on table)
         (space on c) (space on b) (space on table))
       '((c on table)))
((START)
 (EXECUTING (MOVE C FROM A TO B))
 (EXECUTING (MOVE C FROM B TO TABLE)))
```

The solution is correct, but there is an easier solution that moves C directly to the table. The simpler solution was not found because of an accident: it happens that make-block-ops defines the operators so that moving C from B to the table comes before moving C from A to the table. So the first operator is tried, and it succeeds provided C is on B. Thus, the two-step solution is found before the one-step solution is ever considered. The following example takes four steps when it could be done in two:

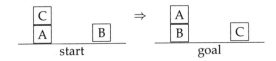

```
> (gps '((c on a) (a on table) (b on table)
         (space on c) (space on b) (space on table))
       '((c on table) (a on b)))
((START)
 (EXECUTING (MOVE C FROM A TO B))
 (EXECUTING (MOVE C FROM B TO TABLE))
 (EXECUTING (MOVE A FROM TABLE TO C))
 (EXECUTING (MOVE A FROM C TO B)))
```

How could we find shorter solutions? One way would be to do a full-fledged search: shorter solutions are tried first, temporarily abandoned when something else looks more promising, and then reconsidered later on. This approach is taken up in chapter 6, using a general searching function. A less drastic solution is to do a limited rearrangement of the order in which operators are searched: the ones with fewer unfulfilled preconditions are tried first. In particular, this means that operators with all preconditions filled would always be tried before other operators. To implement this approach, we change achieve:

```
(defun achieve (state goal goal-stack)
  "A goal is achieved if it already holds,
  or if there is an appropriate op for it that is applicable."
  (dbg-indent :gps (length goal-stack) "Goal: ~a" goal)
  (cond ((member-equal goal state) state)
        ((member-equal goal goal-stack) nil)
```

```
              (t (some #'(lambda (op) (apply-op state goal op goal-stack))
                    (appropriate-ops goal state)))))) ;***
  (defun appropriate-ops (goal state)
    "Return a list of appropriate operators,
    sorted by the number of unfulfilled preconditions."
    (sort (copy-list (find-all goal *ops* :test #'appropriate-p)) #'<
        :key #'(lambda (op)
                 (count-if #'(lambda (precond)
                              (not (member-equal precond state)))
                    (op-preconds op)))))
```

Now we get the solutions we wanted:

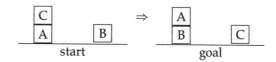

```
> (gps '((c on a) (a on table) (b on table)
         (space on c) (space on b) (space on table))
        '((c on table) (a on b)))
((START)
 (EXECUTING (MOVE C FROM A TO TABLE))
 (EXECUTING (MOVE A FROM TABLE TO B)))
```

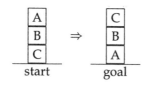

```
> (gps '((a on b) (b on c) (c on table) (space on a) (space on table))
        '((b on a) (c on b)))
((START)
 (EXECUTING (MOVE A FROM B TO TABLE))
 (EXECUTING (MOVE B FROM C TO A))
 (EXECUTING (MOVE C FROM TABLE TO B)))
> (gps '((a on b) (b on c) (c on table) (space on a) (space on table))
        '((c on b) (b on a)))
((START)
 (EXECUTING (MOVE A FROM B TO TABLE))
 (EXECUTING (MOVE B FROM C TO A))
 (EXECUTING (MOVE C FROM TABLE TO B)))
```

The Sussman Anomaly

Surprisingly, there are problems that can't be solved by *any* reordering of goals. Consider:

This doesn't look too hard, so let's see how our GPS handles it:

```
> (setf start '((c on a) (a on table) (b on table) (space on c)
                (space on b) (space on table)))
((C ON A) (A ON TABLE) (B ON TABLE) (SPACE ON C)
 (SPACE ON B) (SPACE ON TABLE))

> (gps start '((a on b) (b on c)))  ⇒ NIL

> (gps start '((b on c) (a on b)))  ⇒ NIL
```

There is a "prerequisite clobbers sibling goal" problem regardless of which way we order the conjuncts! In other words, no combination of plans for the two individual goals can solve the conjunction of the two goals. This is a surprising fact, and the example has come to be known as "the Sussman anomaly."[4] We will return to this problem in chapter 6.

4.15   Stage 5 Repeated: Analysis of Version 2

We have shown that GPS is extensible to multiple domains. The main point is that we didn't need to change the program itself to get the new domains to work; we just changed the list of operators passed to GPS. Experience in different domains did suggest changes that could be made, and we showed how to incorporate a few changes. Although version 2 is a big improvement over version 1, it still leaves much to be desired. Now we will discover a few of the most troubling problems.

---

[4] A footnote in Waldinger 1977 says, "This problem was proposed by Allen Brown. Perhaps many children thought of it earlier but did not recognize that it was hard." The problem is named after Gerald Sussman because he popularized it in Sussman 1973.

4.16   The Not Looking after You Don't Leap Problem

We solved the "leaping before you look" problem by introducing variables to hold a representation of possible future states, rather than just a single variable representing the current state. This prevents GPS from taking an ill-advised action, but we shall see that even with all the repair strategies introduced in the last section, it doesn't guarantee that a solution will be found whenever one is possible.

To see the problem, add another operator to the front of the *school-ops* list and turn the debugging output back on:

```
(use (push (op 'taxi-son-to-school
              :preconds '(son-at-home have-money)
              :add-list '(son-at-school)
              :del-list '(son-at-home have-money))
           *school-ops*))

(debug :gps)
```

Now, consider the problem of getting the child to school without using any money:

```
> (gps '(son-at-home have-money car-works)
       '(son-at-school have-money))
Goal: SON-AT-SCHOOL
Consider: TAXI-SON-TO-SCHOOL
  Goal: SON-AT-HOME
  Goal: HAVE-MONEY
Action: TAXI-SON-TO-SCHOOL
Goal: HAVE-MONEY
Goal: HAVE-MONEY
Goal: SON-AT-SCHOOL
Consider: TAXI-SON-TO-SCHOOL
  Goal: SON-AT-HOME
  Goal: HAVE-MONEY
Action: TAXI-SON-TO-SCHOOL
NIL
```

The first five lines of output succesfully solve the son-at-school goal with the TAXI-SON-TO-SCHOOL action. The next line shows an unsuccessful attempt to solve the have-money goal. The next step is to try the other ordering. This time, the have-money goal is tried first, and succeeds. Then, the son-at-school goal is achieved again by the TAXI-SON-TO-SCHOOL action. But the check for consistency in achieve-each fails, and there are no repairs available. The goal fails, even though there is a valid solution: driving to school.

The problem is that `achieve` uses `some` to look at the `appropriate-ops`. Thus, if there is some appropriate operator, `achieve` succeeds. If there is only one goal, this will yield a correct solution. However, if there are multiple goals, as in this case, `achieve` will still only find one way to fulfill the first goal. If the first solution is a bad one, the only recourse is to try to repair it. In domains like the block world and maze world, repair often works, because all steps are reversible. But in the taxi example, no amount of plan repair can get the money back once it is spent, so the whole plan fails.

There are two ways around this problem. The first approach is to examine all possible solutions, not just the first solution that achieves each subgoal. The language Prolog, to be discussed in chapter 11, does just that. The second approach is to have `achieve` and `achieve-all` keep track of a list of goals that must be *protected*. In the taxi example, we would trivially achieve the `have-money` goal and then try to achieve `son-at-school`, while protecting the goal `have-money`. An operator would only be appropriate if it didn't delete any protected goals. This approach still requires some kind of repair or search through multiple solution paths. If we tried only one ordering—achieving `son-at-school` and then trying to protect it while achieving `have-money`—then we would not find the solution. David Warren's WARPLAN planner makes good use of the idea of protected goals.

4.17   The Lack of Descriptive Power Problem

It would be a lot more economical, in the maze domain, to have one operator that says we can move from here to there if we are at "here," and if there is a connection from "here" to "there." Then the input to a particular problem could list the valid connections, and we could solve any maze with this single operator. Similarly, we have defined an operator where the monkey pushes the chair from the door to the middle of the room, but it would be better to have an operator where the monkey can push the chair from wherever it is to any other nearby location, or better yet, an operator to push any "pushable" object from one location to a nearby one, as long as there is no intervening obstacle. The conclusion is that we would like to have variables in the operators, so we could say something like:

```
(op '(push X from A to B)
  :preconds '((monkey at A) (X at A) (pushable X) (path A B))
  :add-list '((monkey at B) (X at B))
  :del-list '((monkey at A) (X at A)))
```

Often we want to characterize a state in terms of something more abstract than a list of conditions. For example, in solving a chess problem, the goal is to have the opponent in checkmate, a situation that cannot be economically described in terms of primitives like (`black king on A 4`), so we need to be able to state some kind of constraint on the goal state, rather than just listing its components. We might want to be able to achieve a disjunction or negation of conditions, where the current formalism allows only a conjunction.

It also is important, in many domains, to be able to state problems dealing with time: we want to achieve X before time T_0, and then achieve Y before time T_2, but not before T_1. Scheduling work on a factory floor or building a house are examples of planning where time plays an important role.

Often there are costs associated with actions, and we want to find a solution with minimal, or near-minimal costs. The cost might be as simple as the number of operators required for a solution—we saw in the blocks world domain that sometimes an operator that could be applied immediately was ignored, and an operator that needed several preconditions satisfied was chosen instead. Or we may be satisfied with a partial solution, if a complete solution is impossible or too expensive. We may also want to take the cost (and time) of computation into account.

4.18   The Perfect Information Problem

All the operators we have seen so far have unambiguous results; they add or delete certain things from the current state, and GPS always knows exactly what they are going to do. In the real world, things are rarely so cut and dried. Going back to the problem of becoming rich, one relevant operator would be playing the lottery. This operator has the effect of consuming a few dollars, and once in a while paying off a large sum. But we have no way to represent a payoff "once in a while." Similarly, we have no way to represent unexpected difficulties of any kind. In the nursery school problem, we could represent the problem with the car battery by having GPS explicitly check to see if the car was working, or if it needed a battery, every time the program considered the driving operator. In the real world, we are seldom this careful; we get in the car, and only when it doesn't start do we consider the possibility of a dead battery.

4.19   The Interacting Goals Problem

People tend to have multiple goals, rather than working on one at a time. Not only do I want to get the kid to nursery school, but I want to avoid getting hit by another car, get to my job on time, get my work done, meet my friends, have some fun, continue breathing, and so on. I also have to discover goals on my own, rather than work on a set of predefined goals passed to me by someone else. Some goals I can keep in the background for years, and then work on them when the opportunity presents itself. There is never a notion of satisfying all possible goals. Rather, there is a continual process of achieving some goals, partially achieving others, and deferring or abandoning still others.

In addition to having active goals, people also are aware of undesirable situations that they are trying to avoid. For example, suppose I have a goal of visiting a friend in the hospital. This requires being at the hospital. One applicable operator might be to walk to the hospital, while another would be to severly injure myself and wait for the ambulance to take me there. The second operator achieves the goal just as well (perhaps faster), but it has an undesirable side effect. This could be addressed either with a notion of solution cost, as outlined in the last section, or with a list of background goals that every solution attempts to protect.

Herb Simon coined the term "satisficing" to describe the strategy of satisfying a reasonable number of goals to a reasonable degree, while abandoning or postponing other goals. GPS only knows success and failure, and thus has no way of maximizing partial success.

4.20   The End of GPS

These last four sections give a hint as to the scope of the limitations of GPS. In fact, it is not a very general problem solver at all. It *is* general in the sense that the algorithm is not tied to a particular domain; we can change domain by changing the operators. But GPS fails to be general in that it can't solve many interesting problems. It is confined to small tricks and games.

There is an important yet subtle reason why GPS was destined to fail, a reason that was not widely appreciated in 1957 but now is at the core of computer science. It is now recognized that there are problems that computers can't solve—not because a theoretically correct program can't be written, but because the execution of the program will take too long. A large number of problems can be shown to fall into the class of "NP-hard" problems. Computing a solution to these problems takes time that grows exponentially as the size of the problem grows. This is a property of the problems themselves, and holds no matter how clever the programmer is. Exponential growth means that problems that can be solved in seconds for, say, a five-input case may take trillions of years when there are 100 inputs. Buying a faster computer won't help much. After all, if a problem would take a trillion years to solve on your computer, it won't help much to buy 1000 computers each 1000 times faster than the one you have: you're still left with a million years wait. For a theoretical computer scientist, discovering that a problem is NP-hard is an end in itself. But for an AI worker, it means that the wrong question is being asked. Many problems are NP-hard when we insist on the optimal solution but are much easier when we accept a solution that might not be the best.

The input to GPS is essentially a program, and the execution of GPS is the execution of that program. If GPS's input language is general enough to express any program, then there will be problems that can't be solved, either because they take too long to execute or because they have no solution. Modern problem-solving programs recognize this fundamental limitation, and either limit the class of problems they try to solve or consider ways of finding approximate or partial solutions. Some problem solvers also monitor their own execution time and know enough to give up when a problem is too hard.

The following quote from Drew McDermott's article "Artificial Intelligence Meets Natural Stupidity" sums up the current feeling about GPS. Keep it in mind the next time you have to name a program.

> *Remember GPS? By now, "GPS" is a colorless term denoting a particularly stupid program to solve puzzles. But it originally meant "General Problem Solver," which caused everybody a lot of needless excitement and distraction. It should have been called LFGNS—"Local Feature-Guided Network Searcher."*

Nonetheless, GPS has been a useful vehicle for exploring programming in general, and AI programming in particular. More importantly, it has been a useful vehicle for exploring "the nature of deliberation." Surely we'll admit that Aristotle was a smarter person than you or me, yet with the aid of the computational model of mind as a guiding metaphor, and the further aid of a working computer program to help explore the metaphor, we have been led to a more thorough appreciation of means-ends analysis—at least within the computational model. We must resist the temptation to believe that all thinking follows this model.

The appeal of AI can be seen as a split between means and ends. The end of a successful AI project can be a program that accomplishes some useful task better, faster, or cheaper than it could be before. By that measure, GPS is a mostly a failure, as it doesn't solve many problems particularly well. But the means toward that end involved an investigation and formalization of the problem-solving process. By that measure, our reconstruction of GPS is a success to the degree in which it leads the reader to a better understanding of the issues.

4.21 History and References

The original GPS is documented in Newell and Simon's 1963 paper and in their 1972 book, *Human Problem Solving*, as well as in Ernst and Newell 1969. The implementation in this chapter is based on the STRIPS program (Fikes and Nilsson 1971).

There are other important planning programs. Earl Sacerdoti's ABSTRIPS program was a modification of STRIPS that allowed for hierarchical planning. The idea was to sketch out a skeletal plan that solved the entire program at an abstract level, and then fill in the details. David Warren's WARPLAN planner is covered in Warren 1974a,b and in a section of Coelho and Cotta 1988. Austin Tate's NONLIN system (Tate 1977) achieved greater efficiency by considering a plan as a partially ordered sequence of operations rather than as a strictly ordered sequence of situations. David Chapman's TWEAK synthesizes and formalizes the state of the art in planning as of 1987.

All of these papers—and quite a few other important planning papers—are reprinted in Allen, Hendler, and Tate 1990.

4.22   Exercises

Exercise 4.1 [m]   It is possible to implement dbg using a single call to format. Can you figure out the format directives to do this?

Exercise 4.2 [m]   Write a function that generates all permutations of its input.

Exercise 4.3 [h]   GPS does not recognize the situation where a goal is accidentally solved as part of achieving another goal. Consider the goal of eating dessert. Assume that there are two operators available: eating ice cream (which requires having the ice cream) and eating cake (which requires having the cake). Assume that we can buy a cake, and that the bakery has a deal where it gives out free ice cream to each customer who purchases and eats a cake. (1) Design a list of operators to represent this situation. (2) Give gps the goal of eating dessert. Show that, with the right list of operators, gps will decide to eat ice cream, then decide to buy and eat the cake in order to get the free ice cream, and then go ahead and eat the ice cream, even though the goal of eating dessert has already been achieved by eating the cake. (3) Fix gps so that it does not manifest this problem.

The following exercises address the problems in version 2 of the program.

Exercise 4.4 [h]   *The Not Looking after You Don't Leap Problem.* Write a program that keeps track of the remaining goals so that it does not get stuck considering only one possible operation when others will eventually lead to the goal. Hint: have achieve take an extra argument indicating the goals that remain to be achieved after the current goal is achieved. achieve should succeed only if it can achieve the current goal and also achieve-all the remaining goals.

Exercise 4.5 [d]   Write a planning program that, like Warren's WARPLAN, keeps track of the list of goals that remain to be done as well as the list of goals that have been achieved and should not be undone. The program should never undo a goal that has been achieved, but it should allow for the possibility of reordering steps that have already been taken. In this way, the program will solve the Sussman anomaly and similar problems.

Exercise 4.6 [d] *The Lack of Descriptive Power Problem.* Read chapters 5 and 6 to learn about pattern matching. Write a version of GPS that uses the pattern matching tools, and thus allows variables in the operators. Apply it to the maze and blocks world domains. Your program will be more efficient if, like Chapman's TWEAK program, you allow for the possibility of variables that remain unbound as long as possible.

Exercise 4.7 [d] Speculate on the design of a planner that can address the *Perfect Information* and *Interacting Goals* problems.

4.23 Answers

Answer 4.1 In this version, the format string `"~&~V@T~?"` breaks down as follows: `"~&"` means go to a fresh line; `"~V@T"` means insert spaces (@T) but use the next argument (V) to get the number of spaces. The `"~?"` is the indirection operator: use the next argument as a format string, and the argument following that as the list of arguments for the format string.

```
(defun dbg-indent (id indent format-string &rest args)
  "Print indented debugging info if (DEBUG ID) has been specified."
  (when (member id *dbg-ids*)
    (format *debug-io* "~&~V@T~?" (* 2 indent) format-string args)))
```

Answer 4.2 Here is one solution. The sophisticated Lisp programmer should also see the exercise on page 680.

```lisp
(defun permutations (bag)
  "Return a list of all the permutations of the input."
  ;; If the input is nil, there is only one permutation:
  ;; nil itself
  (if (null bag)
      '(())
      ;; Otherwise, take an element, e, out of the bag.
      ;; Generate all permutations of the remaining elements,
      ;; And add e to the front of each of these.
      ;; Do this for all possible e to generate all permutations.
      (mapcan #'(lambda (e)
                  (mapcar #'(lambda (p) (cons e p))
                          (permutations
                            (remove e bag :count 1 :test #'eq))))
              bag)))
```

CHAPTER 5

ELIZA: Dialog with a Machine

It is said that to explain is to explain away.
—Joseph Weizenbaum
MIT computer scientist

This chapter and the rest of part I will examine three more well-known AI programs of the 1960s. ELIZA held a conversation with the user in which it simulated a psychotherapist. STUDENT solved word problems of the kind found in high school algebra books, and MACSYMA solved a variety of symbolic mathematical problems, including differential and integral calculus. We will develop versions of the first two programs that duplicate most of the essential features, but for the third we will implement only a tiny fraction of the original program's capabilities.

All three programs make heavy use of a technique called pattern matching. Part I serves to show the versatility—and also the limitations—of this technique.

Of the three programs, the first two process input in plain English, and the last two solve nontrivial problems in mathematics, so there is some basis for describing them as being "intelligent." On the other hand, we shall see that this intelligence is largely an illusion, and that ELIZA in particular was actually designed to demonstrate this illusion, not to be a "serious" AI program.

ELIZA was one of the first programs to feature English output as well as input. The program was named after the heroine of *Pygmalion,* who was taught to speak proper English by a dedicated teacher. ELIZA's principal developer, MIT professor Joseph Weizenbaum, published a paper on ELIZA in the January 1966 issue of the *Communications of the Association for Computing Machinery.* The introduction to that paper is reproduced in its entirety here:

> *It is said that to explain is to explain away. This maxim is nowhere so well fulfilled as in the area of computer programming, especially in what is called heuristic programming and artificial intelligence. For in those realms machines are made to behave in wondrous ways, often sufficient to dazzle even the most experienced observer. But once a particular program is unmasked, once its inner workings are explained in language sufficiently plain to induce understanding, its magic crumbles away; it stands revealed as a mere collection of procedures, each quite comprehensible. The observer says to himself, "I could have written that." With that thought he moves the program in question from the shelf marked "intelligent," to that reserved for curios, fit to be discussed only with people less enlightened than he.*
>
> *The object of this paper is to cause just such a re-evaluation of the program about to be "explained." Few programs ever needed it more.*

Let me point out in passing that the main object of this book is to cause the reader to say to him or herself, "I could have written that." It is hoped that in some cases this will be because the reader has gained something, and not solely because the programs in question have lost their ability to dazzle.

Let's start our investigation of ELIZA by looking at a sample dialog from the Weizenbaum article. ELIZA was designed to be instructed by a variety of scripts, or patterns of interaction. In fact it had several scripts, including ones in German and Welsh. But the only script that was used to any extent was in English, and it made ELIZA emulate a Rogerian psychoanalyst. Rogerians are "nondirective"—they try to let the patient reveal himself. This is an easy script for ELIZA to follow, because it involves being passive and reacting, rather than volunteering new information. In the listing that follows, the user's input is in mixed case, and ELIZA's response is in capitals:

```
Men are all alike.
IN WHAT WAY
They're always bugging us about something or another.
CAN YOU BE MORE SPECIFIC
Well, my boyfriend made me come here.
YOUR BOYFRIEND MADE YOU COME HERE
He says I'm depressed much of the time.
I AM SORRY TO HEAR YOU ARE DEPRESSED
```

```
It's true.  I am unhappy.
DO YOU THINK COMING HERE WILL HELP YOU NOT TO BE UNHAPPY
I need some help, that much seems certain.
WHAT WOULD IT MEAN TO YOU IF YOU GOT SOME HELP
Perhaps I could learn to get along with my mother.
TELL ME MORE ABOUT YOUR FAMILY
```

This seems quite impressive; the program is responding reasonably to a variety of inputs and appears to be exhibiting true "understanding." But, as Weizenbaum explains, this appearance is an illusion, and the program has finessed the difficult task of understanding by carefully recognizing, transforming, and echoing pieces of the input. The procedure is to look for specific patterns, based on a key word or words in the input. For example, whenever the program sees the words "alike" or "same," it prints a message asking about similarity, in this case, "IN WHAT WAY." Other patterns are more complicated. In the next to last exchange, ELIZA first throws away everything after the comma, and then uses a pattern that looks for input of the form "I need X" and transforms it to the output "What would it mean to you if you got X," where X is the phrase "some help" in this case. The great advantage of this approach is that the response will make sense for a variety of inputs: "I need a vacation" will elicit "What would it mean to you if you got a vacation." This will work automatically, without having to tell the program the difference between "some help" and "a vacation." The disadvantage is that the program will sometimes make silly responses: "I need this like a hole in the head" will be answered with "What would it mean to you if you got this like a hole in the head." In fact, the program only makes any sense at all if it is receiving input from someone who makes sense—and someone who interprets its answers charitably. When given "I need gibble plix zzq," ELIZA would reply "What would it mean to you if you got gibble plix zzq," without any inkling that something is wrong. Another example of the original ELIZA program has it communicating with another program, PARRY, which was written by Dr. Kenneth Colby to mimic paranoid behavior. Part of the conversation follows, with ELIZA again in capitals and PARRY in mixed case:

```
I don't understand your motives.
WHY DON'T YOU UNDERSTAND MY MOTIVES?
Shouldn't I be?
WHY DO YOU SAY THAT JUST NOW?
That's just the way it is.
SUPPOSE THAT'S JUST THE WAY IT WERE NOT.
So?
I AM NOT SURE I UNDERSTAND YOU FULLY.
You harp on the same questions too much.
WHAT DOES THAT SIMILARITY SUGGEST TO YOU?
I don't get you.
DO YOU WISH THAT YOU DID GET I?
```

This suggests that neither ELIZA nor PARRY had a deep understanding of the dialog. When there is a human to take on most of the burden of carrying forth the conversation, these programs can be convincing, but when the human is taken out of the conversation, the weaknesses of the programs are revealed.

5.1   Describing and Specifying ELIZA

Now that we have an idea of what ELIZA is like, we can begin the description and specification of the program, and eventually move to the implementation and debugging.

The ELIZA algorithm can be described simply as: (1) read an input, (2) find a pattern that matches the input, (3) transform the input into a response, and (4) print the response. These four steps are repeated for each input.

The specification and implementation of steps (1) and (4) are trivial: for (1), use the built-in `read` function to read a list of words, and for (4) use `print` to print the list of words in the response.

Of course, there are some drawbacks to this specification. The user will have to type a real list—using parentheses—and the user can't use characters that are special to `read`, like quotation marks, commas, and periods. So our input won't be as unconstrained as in the sample dialog, but that's a small price to pay for the convenience of having half of the problem neatly solved.

5.2   Pattern Matching

The hard part comes with steps (2) and (3)—this notion of pattern matching and transformation. There are four things to be concerned with: a general pattern and response, and a specific input and transformation of that input. Since we have agreed to represent the input as a list, it makes sense for the other components to be lists too. For example, we might have:

```
Pattern: (i need a X)
Response: (what would it mean to you if you got a X ?)

Input: (i need a vacation)
Transformation: (what would it mean to you if you got a vacation ?)
```

The pattern matcher must match the literals i with i, need with need, and a with a, as well as match the variable X with vacation. This presupposes that there is some way of deciding that X is a variable and that need is not. We must then arrange to substitute vacation for X within the response, in order to get the final transformation.

Ignoring for a moment the problem of transforming the pattern into the response, we can see that this notion of pattern matching is just a generalization of the Lisp function equal. Below we show the function simple-equal, which is like the built-in function equal,[1] and the function pat-match, which is extended to handle pattern-matching variables:

```
(defun simple-equal (x y)
  "Are x and y equal?  (Don't check inside strings.)"
  (if (or (atom x) (atom y))
      (eql x y)
      (and (simple-equal (first x) (first y))
           (simple-equal (rest x) (rest y)))))

(defun pat-match (pattern input)
  "Does pattern match input?  Any variable can match anything."
  (if (variable-p pattern)
      t
      (if (or (atom pattern) (atom input))
          (eql pattern input)
          (and (pat-match (first pattern) (first input))
               (pat-match (rest pattern) (rest input))))))
```

Exercise 5.1 [s]   Would it be a good idea to replace the complex and form in pat-match with the simpler (every #'pat-match pattern input)?

Before we can go on, we need to decide on an implementation for pattern-matching variables. We could, for instance, say that only a certain set of symbols, such as {X,Y,Z}, are variables. Alternately, we could define a structure of type variable, but then we'd have to type something verbose like (make-variable :name 'X) every time we wanted one. Another choice would be to use symbols, but to distinguish variables from constants by the name of the symbol. For example, in Prolog, variables start with capital letters and constants with lowercase. But Common Lisp is case-insensitive, so that won't work. Instead, there is a tradition in Lisp-based AI programs to have variables be symbols that start with the question mark character.

So far we have dealt with symbols as atoms—objects with no internal structure. But things are always more complicated than they first appear and, as in Lisp as in physics, it turns out that even atoms have components. In particular, symbols have names, which are strings and are accessible through the symbol-name function. Strings in turn have elements that are characters, accessible through the function char. The character '?' is denoted by the self-evaluating escape sequence #\?. So the predicate variable-p can be defined as follows, and we now have a complete pattern matcher:

---

[1]The difference is that simple-equal does not handle strings.

```
(defun variable-p (x)
  "Is x a variable (a symbol beginning with '?')?"
  (and (symbolp x) (equal (char (symbol-name x) 0) #\?)))

> (pat-match '(I need a ?X) '(I need a vacation))
T

> (pat-match '(I need a ?X) '(I really need a vacation))
NIL
```

In each case we get the right answer, but we don't get any indication of what ?X is, so we couldn't substitute it into the response. We need to modify pat-match to return some kind of table of variables and corresponding values. In making this choice, the experienced Common Lisp programmer can save some time by being opportunistic: recognizing when there is an existing function that will do a large part of the task at hand. What we want is to substitute values for variables throughout the response. The alert programmer could refer to the index of this book or the Common Lisp reference manual and find the functions substitute, subst, and sublis. All of these substitute some new expression for an old one within an expression. It turns out that sublis is most appropriate because it is the only one that allows us to make several substitutions all at once. sublis takes two arguments, the first a list of old-new pairs, and the second an expression in which to make the substitutions. For each one of the pairs, the car is replaced by the cdr. In other words, we would form each pair with something like (cons old new). (Such a list of pairs is known as an *association list*, or *a-list*, because it associates keys with values. See section 3.6.) In terms of the example above, we would use:

```
> (sublis '((?X . vacation))
          '(what would it mean to you if you got a ?X ?))
(WHAT WOULD IT MEAN TO YOU IF YOU GOT A VACATION ?)
```

Now we need to arrange for pat-match to return an a-list, rather than just T for success. Here's a first attempt:

```
(defun pat-match (pattern input)
  "Does pattern match input? WARNING: buggy version."
  (if (variable-p pattern)
      (list (cons pattern input))
      (if (or (atom pattern) (atom input))
          (eql pattern input)
          (append (pat-match (first pattern) (first input))
                  (pat-match (rest pattern) (rest input))))))
```

This implementation looks reasonable: it returns an a-list of one element if the pattern is a variable, and it appends alists if the pattern and input are both lists. However, there are several problems. First, the test (eql pattern input) may return T, which is not a list, so append will complain. Second, the same test might return nil, which should indicate failure, but it will just be treated as a list, and will be appended to the rest of the answer. Third, we haven't distinguished between the case where the match fails—and returns nil—versus the case where everything matches, but there are no variables, so it returns the null a-list. (This is the semipredicate problem discussed on page 127.) Fourth, we want the bindings of variables to agree—if ?X is used twice in the pattern, we don't want it to match two different values in the input. Finally, it is inefficient for pat-match to check both the first and rest of lists, even when the corresponding first parts fail to match. (Isn't it amazing that there could be five bugs in a seven-line function?)

We can resolve these problems by agreeing on two major conventions. First, it is very convenient to make pat-match a true predicate, so we will agree that it returns nil only to indicate failure. That means that we will need a non-nil value to represent the empty binding list. Second, if we are going to be consistent about the values of variables, then the first will have to know what the rest is doing. We can accomplish this by passing the binding list as a third argument to pat-match. We make it an optional argument, because we want to be able to say simply (pat-match *a b*).

To abstract away from these implementation decisions, we define the constants fail and no-bindings to represent the two problematic return values. The special form defconstant is used to indicate that these values will not change. (It is customary to give special variables names beginning and ending with asterisks, but this convention usually is not followed for constants. The reasoning is that asterisks shout out, "Careful! I may be changed by something outside of this lexical scope." Constants, of course, will not be changed.)

```
(defconstant fail nil "Indicates pat-match failure")

(defconstant no-bindings '((t . t))
  "Indicates pat-match success, with no variables.")
```

Next, we abstract away from assoc by introducing the following four functions:

```
(defun get-binding (var bindings)
  "Find a (variable . value) pair in a binding list."
  (assoc var bindings))

(defun binding-val (binding)
  "Get the value part of a single binding."
  (cdr binding))

(defun lookup (var bindings)
  "Get the value part (for var) from a binding list."
  (binding-val (get-binding var bindings)))
```

```
(defun extend-bindings (var val bindings)
  "Add a (var . value) pair to a binding list."
  (cons (cons var val) bindings))
```

Now that variables and bindings are defined, pat-match is easy. It consists of five cases. First, if the binding list is fail, then the match fails (because some previous match must have failed). If the pattern is a single variable, then the match returns whatever match-variable returns; either the existing binding list, an extended one, or fail. Next, if both pattern and input are lists, we first call pat-match recursively on the first element of each list. This returns a binding list (or fail), which we use to match the rest of the lists. This is the only case that invokes a nontrivial function, so it is a good idea to informally prove that the function will terminate: each of the two recursive calls reduces the size of both pattern and input, and pat-match checks the case of atomic patterns and inputs, so the function as a whole must eventually return an answer (unless both pattern and input are of infinite size). If none of these four cases succeeds, then the match fails.

```
(defun pat-match (pattern input &optional (bindings no-bindings))
  "Match pattern against input in the context of the bindings"
  (cond ((eq bindings fail) fail)
        ((variable-p pattern)
         (match-variable pattern input bindings))
        ((eql pattern input) bindings)
        ((and (consp pattern) (consp input))
         (pat-match (rest pattern) (rest input)
                    (pat-match (first pattern) (first input)
                               bindings)))
        (t fail)))

(defun match-variable (var input bindings)
  "Does VAR match input?  Uses (or updates) and returns bindings."
  (let ((binding (get-binding var bindings)))
    (cond ((not binding) (extend-bindings var input bindings))
          ((equal input (binding-val binding)) bindings)
          (t fail))))
```

We can now test pat-match and see how it works:

```
> (pat-match '(i need a ?X) '(i need a vacation))
((?X . VACATION) (T . T))
```

The answer is a list of variable bindings in dotted pair notation; each element of the list is a (*variable . value*) pair. The (T . T) is a remnant from no-bindings. It does no real harm, but we can eliminate it by making extend-bindings a little more complicated:

```
(defun extend-bindings (var val bindings)
  "Add a (var . value) pair to a binding list."
  (cons (cons var val)
        ;; Once we add a "real" binding,
        ;; we can get rid of the dummy no-bindings
        (if (eq bindings no-bindings)
            nil
            bindings)
```

```
> (sublis (pat-match '(i need a ?X) '(i need a vacation))
          '(what would it mean to you if you got a ?X ?))
(WHAT WOULD IT MEAN TO YOU IF YOU GOT A VACATION ?)

> (pat-match '(i need a ?X) '(i really need a vacation))
NIL

> (pat-match '(this is easy) '(this is easy))
((T . T))

> (pat-match '(?X is ?X) '((2 + 2) is 4))
NIL

> (pat-match '(?X is ?X) '((2 + 2) is (2 + 2)))
((?X 2 + 2))

> (pat-match '(?P need . ?X) '(i need a long vacation))
((?X A LONG VACATION) (?P . I))
```

Notice the distinction between NIL and ((T . T)). The latter means that the match succeeded, but there were no bindings to return. Also, remember that (?X 2 + 2) means the same as (?X . (2 + 2)).

A more powerful implementation of pat-match is given in chapter 6. Yet another implementation is given in section 10.4. It is more efficient but more cumbersome to use.

5.3   Segment Pattern Matching

In the pattern (?P need .   ?X), the variable ?X matches the rest of the input list, regardless of its length. This is in contrast to ?P, which can only match a single element, namely, the first element of the input. For many applications of pattern matching, this is fine; we only want to match corresponding elements. However, ELIZA is somewhat different in that we need to account for variables in any position that match a sequence of items in the input. We will call such variables *segment variables.* We will need a notation to differentiate segment variables from normal variables. The possibilities fall into two classes: either we use atoms to represent segment variables and distinguish them by some spelling convention (as we did to distinguish variables from constants) or we use a nonatomic construct. We will choose the latter, using a list of the form (?* *variable*) to denote segment variables. The symbol ?* is chosen because it combines the notion of variable with the Kleene-star notation. So, the behavior we want from pat-match is now:

```
> (pat-match '((?* ?p) need (?* ?x))
             '(Mr Hulot and I need a vacation))
((?P MR HULOT AND I) (?X A VACATION))
```

In other words, when both pattern and input are lists and the first element of the pattern is a segment variable, then the variable will match some initial part of the input, and the rest of the pattern will attempt to match the rest. We can update pat-match to account for this by adding a single cond-clause. Defining the predicate to test for segment variables is also easy:

```
(defun pat-match (pattern input &optional (bindings no-bindings))
  "Match pattern against input in the context of the bindings"
  (cond ((eq bindings fail) fail)
        ((variable-p pattern)
         (match-variable pattern input bindings))
        ((eql pattern input) bindings)
        ((segment-pattern-p pattern)                ; ***
         (segment-match pattern input bindings))    ; ***
        ((and (consp pattern) (consp input))
         (pat-match (rest pattern) (rest input)
                    (pat-match (first pattern) (first input)
                               bindings)))
        (t fail)))

(defun segment-pattern-p (pattern)
  "Is this a segment matching pattern: ((?* var) . pat)"
  (and (consp pattern)
       (starts-with (first pattern) '?*)))
```

In writing segment-match, the important question is how much of the input the segment variable should match. One answer is to look at the next element of the pattern (the one after the segment variable) and see at what position it occurs in the input. If it doesn't occur, the total pattern can never match, and we should fail. If it does occur, call its position pos. We will want to match the variable against the initial part of the input, up to pos. But first we have to see if the rest of the pattern matches the rest of the input. This is done by a recursive call to pat-match. Let the result of this recursive call be named b2. If b2 succeeds, then we go ahead and match the segment variable against the initial subsequence.

The tricky part is when b2 fails. We don't want to give up completely, because it may be that if the segment variable matched a longer subsequence of the input, then the rest of the pattern would match the rest of the input. So what we want is to try segment-match again, but forcing it to consider a longer match for the variable. This is done by introducing an optional parameter, start, which is initially 0 and is increased with each failure. Notice that this policy rules out the possibility of any kind of variable following a segment variable. (Later we will remove this constraint.)

```lisp
(defun segment-match (pattern input bindings &optional (start 0))
  "Match the segment pattern ((?* var) . pat) against input."
  (let ((var (second (first pattern)))
        (pat (rest pattern)))
    (if (null pat)
        (match-variable var input bindings)
        ;; We assume that pat starts with a constant
        ;; In other words, a pattern can't have 2 consecutive vars
        (let ((pos (position (first pat) input
                             :start start :test #'equal)))
          (if (null pos)
              fail
              (let ((b2 (pat-match pat (subseq input pos) bindings)))
                ;; If this match failed, try another longer one
                ;; If it worked, check that the variables match
                (if (eq b2 fail)
                    (segment-match pattern input bindings (+ pos 1))
                    (match-variable var (subseq input 0 pos) b2))))))))
```

Some examples of segment matching follow:

```lisp
> (pat-match '((?* ?p) need (?* ?x))
             '(Mr Hulot and I need a vacation))
((?P MR HULOT AND I) (?X A VACATION))

> (pat-match '((?* ?x) is a (?* ?y)) '(what he is is a fool))
((?X WHAT HE IS) (?Y FOOL))
```

The first of these examples shows a fairly simple case: ?p matches everything up to need, and ?x matches the rest. The next example involves the more complicated backup case. First ?x matches everything up to the first is (this is position 2, since counting starts at 0 in Common Lisp). But then the pattern a fails to match the input is, so segment-match tries again with starting position 3. This time everything works; is matches is, a matches a, and (?* ?y) matches fool.

Unfortunately, this version of segment-match does not match as much as it should. Consider the following example:

```
> (pat-match '((?* ?x) a b (?* ?x)) '(1 2 a b a b 1 2 a b)) ⇒ NIL
```

This fails because ?x is matched against the subsequence (1 2), and then the remaining pattern succesfully matches the remaining input, but the final call to match-variable fails, because ?x has two different values. The fix is to call match-variable before testing whether the b2 fails, so that we will be sure to try segment-match again with a longer match no matter what the cause of the failure.

```
(defun segment-match (pattern input bindings &optional (start 0))
  "Match the segment pattern ((?* var) . pat) against input."
  (let ((var (second (first pattern)))
        (pat (rest pattern)))
    (if (null pat)
        (match-variable var input bindings)
        ;; We assume that pat starts with a constant
        ;; In other words, a pattern can't have 2 consecutive vars
        (let ((pos (position (first pat) input
                             :start start :test #'equal)))
          (if (null pos)
              fail
              (let ((b2 (pat-match
                          pat (subseq input pos)
                          (match-variable var (subseq input 0 pos)
                                          bindings))))
                ;; If this match failed, try another longer one
                (if (eq b2 fail)
                    (segment-match pattern input bindings (+ pos 1))
                    b2)))))))
```

Now we see that the match goes through:

```
> (pat-match '((?* ?x) a b (?* ?x)) '(1 2 a b a b 1 2 a b))
((?X 1 2 A B))
```

Note that this version of segment-match tries the shortest possible match first. It would also be possible to try the longest match first.

5.4 The ELIZA Program: A Rule-Based Translator

Now that we have a working pattern matcher, we need some patterns to match. What's more, we want the patterns to be associated with responses. We can do this by inventing a data structure called a rule, which consists of a pattern and one or more associated responses. These are rules in the sense that they assert, "If you see A, then respond with B or C, chosen at random." We will choose the simplest possible implementation for rules: as lists, where the first element is the pattern and the rest is a list of responses:

```
(defun rule-pattern (rule) (first rule))
(defun rule-responses (rule) (rest rule))
```

Here's an example of a rule:

```
((((?* ?x) I want (?* ?y))
 (What would it mean if you got ?y)
 (Why do you want ?y)
 (Suppose you got ?y soon))
```

When applied to the input (I want to test this program), this rule (when interpreted by the ELIZA program) would pick a response at random, substitute in the value of ?y, and respond with, say, (why do you want to test this program).

Now that we know what an individual rule will do, we need to decide how to handle a set of rules. If ELIZA is to be of any interest, it will have to have a variety of responses. So several rules may all be applicable to the same input. One possibility would be to choose a rule at random from among the rules having patterns that match the input.

Another possibility is just to accept the first rule that matches. This implies that the rules form an ordered list, rather than an unordered set. The clever ELIZA rule writer can take advantage of this ordering and arrange for the most specific rules to come first, while more vague rules are near the end of the list.

The original ELIZA had a system where each rule had a priority number associated with it. The matching rule with the highest priority was chosen. Note that putting the rules in order achieves the same effect as having a priority number on each rule: the first rule implicitly has the highest priority, the second rule is next highest, and so on.

Here is a short list of rules, selected from Weizenbaum's original article, but with the form of the rules updated to the form we are using. The answer to exercise 5.19 contains a longer list of rules.

```lisp
(defparameter *eliza-rules*
 '((((?* ?x) hello (?* ?y))
    (How do you do.  Please state your problem.))
   (((?* ?x) I want (?* ?y))
    (What would it mean if you got ?y)
    (Why do you want ?y) (Suppose you got ?y soon))
   (((?* ?x) if (?* ?y))
    (Do you really think its likely that ?y) (Do you wish that ?y)
    (What do you think about ?y) (Really-- if ?y))
   (((?* ?x) no (?* ?y))
    (Why not?) (You are being a bit negative)
    (Are you saying "NO" just to be negative?))
   (((?* ?x) I was (?* ?y))
    (Were you really?) (Perhaps I already knew you were ?y)
    (Why do you tell me you were ?y now?))
   (((?* ?x) I feel (?* ?y))
    (Do you often feel ?y ?))
   (((?* ?x) I felt (?* ?y))
    (What other feelings do you have?))))
```

Finally we are ready to define ELIZA proper. As we said earlier, the main program should be a loop that reads input, transforms it, and prints the result. Transformation is done primarily by finding some rule such that its pattern matches the input, and then substituting the variables into the rule's response. The program is summarized in figure 5.1.

There are a few minor complications. We print a prompt to tell the user to input something. We use the function flatten to insure that the output won't have imbedded lists after variable substitution. An important trick is to alter the input by swapping "you" for "me" and so on, since these terms are relative to the speaker. Here is the complete program:

```lisp
(defun eliza ()
  "Respond to user input using pattern matching rules."
  (loop
    (print 'eliza>)
    (write (flatten (use-eliza-rules (read))) :pretty t)))

(defun use-eliza-rules (input)
  "Find some rule with which to transform the input."
  (some #'(lambda (rule)
            (let ((result (pat-match (rule-pattern rule) input)))
              (if (not (eq result fail))
                  (sublis (switch-viewpoint result)
                          (random-elt (rule-responses rule))))))
        *eliza-rules*))
```

	Top-Level Function
eliza	Respond to user input using pattern matching rules.
	Special Variables
eliza-rules	A list of transformation rules.
	Data Types
rule	An association of a pattern with a list of responses.
	Functions
eliza	Respond to user input using pattern matching rules.
use-eliza-rules	Find some rule with which to transform the input.
switch-viewpoint	Change I to you and vice versa, and so on.
flatten	Append together elements of a list.
	Selected Common Lisp Functions
sublis	Substitute elements into a tree.
	Previously Defined Functions
random-elt	Pick a random element from a list. (p. 36)
pat-match	Match a pattern against an input. (p. 160)
mappend	Append together the results of a mapcar.

Figure 5.1: Glossary for the ELIZA Program

```lisp
(defun switch-viewpoint (words)
  "Change I to you and vice versa, and so on."
  (sublis '((I . you) (you . I) (me . you) (am . are))
          words))
```

Note the use of write with the :pretty keyword true. This will give better formatted output in some cases. The program makes use of the previously defined random-elt, and flatten, which is defined here using mappend and mklist, a function that is defined in the InterLisp dialect but not in Common Lisp.

```lisp
(defun flatten (the-list)
  "Append together elements (or lists) in the list."
  (mappend #'mklist the-list))

(defun mklist (x)
  "Return x if it is a list, otherwise (x)."
  (if (listp x)
      x
      (list x)))

(defun mappend (fn the-list)
  "Apply fn to each element of list and append the results."
  (apply #'append (mapcar fn the-list)))
```

```
(defun random-elt (choices)
  "Choose an element from a list at random."
  (elt choices (random (length choices))))
```

The actual ELIZA program had a few complications that don't show up in this version. First, there was an alias method for associating several words with the same pattern; both "mother" and "father" could be associated with the "family" pattern. There was also a synonym mechanism that would treat "don't" and "do not" or "everybody" and "everyone" the same. In the case of input with several comma-separated phrases, each phrase was processed separately, and the response with the highest priority was selected. In addition, the original ELIZA had a "memory" mechanism. When no pattern matched the input, it said something like "Tell me more about X," where X is some input given earlier. Finally, our version has fewer rules. Despite the shortcomings of our version, it can occasionally hold up its end of a conversation, as shown below:

```
> (eliza)
ELIZA> (hello there)
(HOW DO YOU DO. PLEASE STATE YOUR PROBLEM.)
ELIZA> (i want to test this program)
(WHAT WOULD IT MEAN IF YOU GOT TO TEST THIS PROGRAM)
ELIZA> (i could see if it works)
(DO YOU REALLY THINK ITS LIKELY THAT IT WORKS)
ELIZA> (no not really)
(ARE YOU SAYING "NO" JUST TO BE NEGATIVE?)
ELIZA> (no)
(ARE YOU SAYING "NO" JUST TO BE NEGATIVE?)
ELIZA> (forget it-- i was wondering how general the program is)
(WHY DO YOU TELL ME YOU WERE WONDERING HOW GENERAL THE PROGRAM IS NOW?)
ELIZA> (i felt like it)
(WHAT OTHER FEELINGS DO YOU HAVE?)
ELIZA> (i feel this is enough)
(DO YOU OFTEN FEEL THIS IS ENOUGH ?)
ELIZA> [Abort]
>
```

In the end, it is the technique that is important—not the program. ELIZA has been "explained away" and should rightfully be moved to the curio shelf. Pattern matching in general remains important technique, and we will see it again in subsequent chapters. The notion of a rule-based translator is also important. The problem of understanding English (and other languages) remains an important part of AI. Clearly, the problem of understanding English is not solved by ELIZA. In part V, we will address the problem again, using more sophisticated techniques.

5.5   History and References

As mentioned above, the original article describing ELIZA is Weizenbaum 1966. Another dialog system using similar pattern-matching techniques is Kenneth Colby's (1975) PARRY. This program simulated the conversation of a paranoid person well enough to fool several professional psychologists. Although the pattern matching techniques were simple, the model of belief maintained by the system was much more sophisticated than ELIZA. Colby has suggested that dialog programs like ELIZA, augmented with some sort of belief model like PARRY, could be useful tools in treating mentally disturbed people. According to Colby, it would be inexpensive and effective to have patients converse with a specially designed program, one that could handle simple cases and alert doctors to patients that needed more help. Weizenbaum's book *Computer Power and Human Reason* (1976) discusses ELIZA and PARRY and takes a very critical view toward Colby's suggestion. Other interesting early work on dialog systems that model belief is reported by Allan Collins (1978) and Jamie Carbonell (1981).

5.6   Exercises

Exercise 5.2 [m]   Experiment with this version of ELIZA. Show some exchanges where it performs well, and some where it fails. Try to characterize the difference. Which failures could be fixed by changing the rule set, which by changing the pat-match function (and the pattern language it defines), and which require a change to the eliza program itself?

Exercise 5.3 [h]   Define a new set of rules that make ELIZA give stereotypical responses to some situation other than the doctor–patient relationship. Or, write a set of rules in a language other than English. Test and debug your new rule set.

Exercise 5.4 [s]   We mentioned that our version of ELIZA cannot handle commas or double quote marks in the input. However, it seems to handle the apostrophe in both input and patterns. Explain.

Exercise 5.5 [h]   Alter the input mechanism to handle commas and other punctuation characters. Also arrange so that the user doesn't have to type parentheses around the whole input expression. (Hint: this can only be done using some Lisp functions we have not seen yet. Look at read-line and read-from-string.)

Exercise 5.6 [m]   Modify ELIZA to have an explicit exit. Also arrange so that the output is not printed in parentheses either.

Exercise 5.7 [m]   Add the "memory mechanism" discussed previously to ELIZA. Also add some way of definining synonyms like "everyone" and "everybody."

Exercise 5.8 [h]   It turns out that none of the rules in the given script uses a variable more than once—there is no rule of the form (?x ... ?x). Write a pattern matcher that only adds bindings, never checks variables against previous bindings. Use the time special form to compare your function against the current version.

Exercise 5.9 [h]   Winston and Horn's book *Lisp* presents a good pattern-matching program. Compare their implementation with this one. One difference is that they handle the case where the first element of the pattern is a segment variable with the following code (translated into our notation):

```
(or (pat-match (rest pattern) (rest input) bindings)
    (pat-match pattern (rest input) bindings))
```

This says that a segment variable matches either by matching the first element of the input, or by matching more than the first element. It is much simpler than our approach using position, partly because they don't update the binding list. Can you change their code to handle bindings, and incorporate it into our version of pat-match? Is it still simpler? Is it more or less efficient?

Exercise 5.10   What is wrong with the following definition of simple-equal?

```
(defun simple-equal (x y)
  "Test if two lists or atoms are equal."
  ;; Warning - incorrect
  (or (eql x y)
      (and (listp x) (listp y)
           (simple-equal (first x) (first y))
           (simple-equal (rest x) (rest y)))))
```

Exercise 5.11 [m]   Weigh the advantages of changing no-bindings to nil, and fail to something else.

⌨️ Exercise 5.12 [m]   Weigh the advantages of making `pat-match` return multiple values: the first would be true for a match and false for failure, and the second would be the binding list.

⌨️ Exercise 5.13 [m]   Suppose that there is a call to `segment-match` where the variable already has a binding. The current definition will keep making recursive calls to `segment-match`, one for each possible matching position. But this is silly—if the variable is already bound, there is only one sequence that it can possibly match against. Change the definition so that it looks only for this one sequence.

⌨️ Exercise 5.14 [m]   Define a version of `mappend` that, like `mapcar`, accepts any number of argument lists.

⌨️ Exercise 5.15 [m]   Give an informal proof that `segment-match` always terminates.

⌨️ Exercise 5.16 [s]   Trick question: There is an object in Lisp which, when passed to `variable-p`, results in an error. What is that object?

⌨️ Exercise 5.17 [m]   The current version of ELIZA takes an input, transforms it according to the first applicable rule, and outputs the result. One can also imagine a system where the input might be transformed several times before the final output is printed. Would such a system be more powerful? If so, in what way?

⌨️ Exercise 5.18 [h]   Read Weizenbaum's original article on ELIZA and transpose his list of rules into the notation used in this chapter.

5.7 Answers

Answer 5.1 No. If either the pattern or the input were shorter, but matched every existing element, the every expression would incorrectly return true.

```
(every #'pat-match '(a b c) '(a)) ⇒ T
```

Furthermore, if either the pattern or the input were a dotted list, then the result of the every would be undefined—some implementations might signal an error, and others might just ignore the expression after the dot.

```
(every #'pat-match '(a b . c) '(a b . d)) ⇒ T, NIL, or error.
```

Answer 5.4 The expression don't may look like a single word, but to the Lisp reader it is composed of the two elements don and 't, or (quote t). If these elements are used consistently, they will match correctly, but they won't print quite right—there will be a space before the quote mark. In fact the :pretty t argument to write is specified primarily to make (quote t) print as 't (See page 559 of Steele's *Common Lisp the Language,* 2d edition.)

Answer 5.5 One way to do this is to read a whole line of text with read-line rather than read. Then, substitute spaces for any punctuation character in that string. Finally, wrap the string in parentheses, and read it back in as a list:

```
(defun read-line-no-punct ()
  "Read an input line, ignoring punctuation."
  (read-from-string
    (concatenate 'string "(" (substitute-if #\space #'punctuation-p
                                            (read-line))
             ")")))

(defun punctuation-p (char) (find char ".,;:`!?#-()\\\""))
```

This could also be done by altering the readtable, as in section 23.5, page 821.

Answer 5.6

```
(defun eliza ()
  "Respond to user input using pattern matching rules."
  (loop
    (print 'eliza>)
    (let* ((input (read-line-no-punct))
           (response (flatten (use-eliza-rules input))))
      (print-with-spaces response)
      (if (equal response '(good bye)) (RETURN)))))

(defun print-with-spaces (list)
  (mapc #'(lambda (x) (prin1 x) (princ " ")) list))
```
or
```
(defun print-with-spaces (list)
  (format t "~{~a ~}" list))
```

Answer 5.10   Hint: consider `(simple-equal '() '(nil . nil))`.

Answer 5.14

```
(defun mappend (fn &rest list)
  "Apply fn to each element of lists and append the results."
  (apply #'append (apply #'mapcar fn lists)))
```

Answer 5.16   It must be a symbol, because for nonsymbols, `variable-p` just returns nil. Getting the `symbol-name` of a symbol is just accessing a slot, so that can't cause an error. The only thing left is `elt`; if the symbol name is the empty string, then accessing element zero of the empty string is an error. Indeed, there is a symbol whose name is the empty string: the symbol .

Answer 5.17   Among other things, a recursive transformation system could be used to handle abbreviations. That is, a form like "don't" could be transformed into "do not" and then processed again. That way, the other rules need only work on inputs matching "do not."

Answer 5.19   The following includes most of Weizenbaum's rules:

```
(defparameter *eliza-rules*
 '((((?* ?x) hello (?* ?y))
    (How do you do.  Please state your problem.))
   (((?* ?x) computer (?* ?y))
    (Do computers worry you?) (What do you think about machines?)
    (Why do you mention computers?)
    (What do you think machines have to do with your problem?))
   (((?* ?x) name (?* ?y))
    (I am not interested in names))
   (((?* ?x) sorry (?* ?y))
    (Please don't apologize) (Apologies are not necessary)
    (What feelings do you have when you apologize))
   (((?* ?x) I remember (?* ?y))
    (Do you often think of ?y)
    (Does thinking of ?y bring anything else to mind?)
    (What else do you remember) (Why do you recall ?y right now?)
    (What in the present situation reminds you of ?y)
    (What is the connection between me and ?y))
   (((?* ?x) do you remember (?* ?y))
    (Did you think I would forget ?y ?)
    (Why do you think I should recall ?y now)
    (What about ?y) (You mentioned ?y))
   (((?* ?x) if (?* ?y))
    (Do you really think its likely that ?y) (Do you wish that ?y)
    (What do you think about ?y) (Really-- if ?y))

   (((?* ?x) I dreamt (?* ?y))
    (Really-- ?y) (Have you ever fantasized ?y while you were awake?)
    (Have you dreamt ?y before?))
   (((?* ?x) dream about (?* ?y))
    (How do you feel about ?y in reality?))
   (((?* ?x) dream (?* ?y))
    (What does this dream suggest to you?) (Do you dream often?)
    (What persons appear in your dreams?)
    (Don't you believe that dream has to do with your problem?))
   (((?* ?x) my mother (?* ?y))
    (Who else in your family ?y) (Tell me more about your family))
   (((?* ?x) my father (?* ?y))
    (Your father) (Does he influence you strongly?)
    (What else comes to mind when you think of your father?))
```

```
(((?* ?x) I want (?* ?y))
 (What would it mean if you got ?y)
 (Why do you want ?y) (Suppose you got ?y soon))
(((?* ?x) I am glad (?* ?y))
 (How have I helped you to be ?y) (What makes you happy just now)
 (Can you explain why you are suddenly ?y))
(((?* ?x) I am sad (?* ?y))
 (I am sorry to hear you are depressed)
 (I'm sure it's not pleasant to be sad))
(((?* ?x) are like (?* ?y))
 (What resemblance do you see between ?x and ?y))
(((?* ?x) is like (?* ?y))
 (In what way is it that ?x is like ?y)
 (What resemblance do you see?)
 (Could there really be some connection?) (How?))
(((?* ?x) alike (?* ?y))
 (In what way?) (What similarities are there?))
(((?* ?x) same (?* ?y))
 (What other connections do you see?))

(((?* ?x) I was (?* ?y))
 (Were you really?) (Perhaps I already knew you were ?y)
 (Why do you tell me you were ?y now?))
(((?* ?x) was I (?* ?y))
 (What if you were ?y ?) (Do you think you were ?y)
 (What would it mean if you were ?y))
(((?* ?x) I am (?* ?y))
 (In what way are you ?y) (Do you want to be ?y ?))
(((?* ?x) am I (?* ?y))
 (Do you believe you are ?y) (Would you want to be ?y)
 (You wish I would tell you you are ?y)
 (What would it mean if you were ?y))
(((?* ?x) am (?* ?y))
 (Why do you say "AM?") (I don't understand that))
(((?* ?x) are you (?* ?y))
 (Why are you interested in whether I am ?y or not?)
 (Would you prefer if I weren't ?y)
 (Perhaps I am ?y in your fantasies))
(((?* ?x) you are (?* ?y))
 (What makes you think I am ?y ?))
```

```
((((?* ?x) because (?* ?y))
 (Is that the real reason?) (What other reasons might there be?)
 (Does that reason seem to explain anything else?))
(((?* ?x) were you (?* ?y))
 (Perhaps I was ?y) (What do you think?) (What if I had been ?y))
(((?* ?x) I can't (?* ?y))
 (Maybe you could ?y now) (What if you could ?y ?))
(((?* ?x) I feel (?* ?y))
 (Do you often feel ?y ?))
(((?* ?x) I felt (?* ?y))
 (What other feelings do you have?))
(((?* ?x) I (?* ?y) you (?* ?z))
 (Perhaps in your fantasy we ?y each other))
(((?* ?x) why don't you (?* ?y))
 (Should you ?y yourself?)
 (Do you believe I don't ?y) (Perhaps I will ?y in good time))
(((?* ?x) yes (?* ?y))
 (You seem quite positive) (You are sure) (I understand))
(((?* ?x) no (?* ?y))
 (Why not?) (You are being a bit negative)
 (Are you saying "NO" just to be negative?))

(((?* ?x) someone (?* ?y))
 (Can you be more specific?))
(((?* ?x) everyone (?* ?y))
 (surely not everyone) (Can you think of anyone in particular?)
 (Who for example?) (You are thinking of a special person))
(((?* ?x) always (?* ?y))
 (Can you think of a specific example) (When?)
 (What incident are you thinking of?) (Really-- always))
(((?* ?x) what (?* ?y))
 (Why do you ask?) (Does that question interest you?)
 (What is it you really want to know?) (What do you think?)
 (What comes to your mind when you ask that?))
(((?* ?x) perhaps (?* ?y))
 (You do not seem quite certain))
(((?* ?x) are (?* ?y))
 (Did you think they might not be ?y)
 (Possibly they are ?y))
(((?* ?x))
 (Very interesting) (I am not sure I understand you fully)
 (What does that suggest to you?) (Please continue) (Go on)
 (Do you feel strongly about discussing such things?))))
```

CHAPTER 6

Building Software Tools

Man is a tool-using animal. . . .
Without tools he is nothing,
with tools he is all.

—Thomas Carlyle (1795–1881)

I n chapters 4 and 5 we were concerned with building two particular programs, GPS and ELIZA. In this chapter, we will reexamine those two programs to discover some common patterns. Those patterns will be abstracted out to form reusable software tools that will prove helpful in subsequent chapters.

6.1   An Interactive Interpreter Tool

The structure of the function `eliza` is a common one. It is repeated below:

```
(defun eliza ()
  "Respond to user input using pattern matching rules."
  (loop
    (print 'eliza>)
    (print (flatten (use-eliza-rules (read))))))
```

Many other applications use this pattern, including Lisp itself. The top level of Lisp could be defined as:

```
(defun lisp ()
  (loop
    (print '>)
    (print (eval (read)))))
```

The top level of a Lisp system has historically been called the "read-eval-print loop." Most modern Lisps print a prompt before reading input, so it should really be called the "prompt-read-eval-print loop," but there was no prompt in some early systems like MacLisp, so the shorter name stuck. If we left out the prompt, we could write a complete Lisp interpreter using just four symbols:

```
(loop (print (eval (read))))
```

It may seem facetious to say those four symbols and eight parentheses constitute a Lisp interpreter. When we write that line, have we really accomplished anything? One answer to that question is to consider what we would have to do to write a Lisp (or Pascal) interpreter in Pascal. We would need a lexical analyzer and a symbol table manager. This is a considerable amount of work, but it is all handled by read. We would need a syntactic parser to assemble the lexical tokens into statements. read also handles this, but only because Lisp statements have trivial syntax: the syntax of lists and atoms. Thus read serves fine as a syntactic parser for Lisp, but would fail for Pascal. Next, we need the evaluation or interpretation part of the interpreter; eval does this nicely, and could handle Pascal just as well if we parsed Pascal syntax into Lisp expressions. print does much less work than read or eval, but is still quite handy.

The important point is not whether one line of code can be considered an implementation of Lisp; it is to recognize common patterns of computation. Both eliza and lisp can be seen as interactive interpreters that read some input, transform or evaluate the input in some way, print the result, and then go back for more input. We can extract the following common pattern:

```
(defun program ()
  (loop
    (print prompt)
    (print (transform (read)))))
```

There are two ways to make use of recurring patterns like this: formally and informally. The informal alternative is to treat the pattern as a cliche or idiom that will occur frequently in our writing of programs but will vary from use to use. When we want to write a new program, we remember writing or reading a similar one, go back and look at the first program, copy the relevant sections, and then modify them for the new program. If the borrowing is extensive, it would be good practice to insert a comment in the new program citing the original, but there would be no "official" connection between the original and the derived program.

The formal alternative is to create an abstraction, in the form of functions and perhaps data structures, and refer explicitly to that abstraction in each new application— in other words, to capture the abstraction in the form of a useable software tool. The interpreter pattern could be abstracted into a function as follows:

```
(defun interactive-interpreter (prompt transformer)
  "Read an expression, transform it, and print the result."
  (loop
    (print prompt)
    (print (funcall transformer (read)))))
```

This function could then be used in writing each new interpreter:

```
(defun lisp ()
  (interactive-interpreter '> #'eval))

(defun eliza ()
  (interactive-interpreter 'eliza>
    #'(lambda (x) (flatten (use-eliza-rules x)))))
```

Or, with the help of the higher-order function compose:

```
(defun compose (f g)
  "Return the function that computes (f (g x))."
  #'(lambda (x) (funcall f (funcall g x))))

(defun eliza ()
  (interactive-interpreter 'eliza>
    (compose #'flatten #'use-eliza-rules)))
```

There are two differences between the formal and informal approaches. First, they look different. If the abstraction is a simple one, as this one is, then it is probably easier to read an expression that has the loop explicitly written out than to read one that calls interactive-interpreter, since that requires finding the definition of interactive-interpreter and understanding it as well.

The other difference shows up in what's called *maintenance*. Suppose we find a missing feature in the definition of the interactive interpreter. One such omission is that the loop has no exit. I have been assuming that the user can terminate the loop by hitting some interrupt (or break, or abort) key. A cleaner implementation would allow the user to give the interpreter an explicit termination command. Another useful feature would be to handle errors within the interpreter. If we use the informal approach, then adding such a feature to one program would have no effect on the others. But if we use the formal approach, then improving interactive-interpreter would automatically bring the new features to all the programs that use it.

The following version of interactive-interpreter adds two new features. First, it uses the macro handler-case[1] to handle errors. This macro evaluates its first argument, and normally just returns that value. However, if an error occurs, the subsequent arguments are checked for an error condition that matches the error that occurred. In this use, the case error matches all errors, and the action taken is to print the error condition and continue.

This version also allows the prompt to be either a string or a function of no arguments that will be called to print the prompt. The function prompt-generator, for example, returns a function that will print prompts of the form [1], [2], and so forth.

```
(defun interactive-interpreter (prompt transformer)
  "Read an expression, transform it, and print the result."
  (loop
    (handler-case
      (progn
        (if (stringp prompt)
            (print prompt)
            (funcall prompt))
        (print (funcall transformer (read))))
      ;; In case of error, do this:
      (error (condition)
        (format t "~&;; Error ~a ignored, back to top level."
                condition)))))

(defun prompt-generator (&optional (num 0) (ctl-string "[~d] "))
  "Return a function that prints prompts like [1], [2], etc."
  #'(lambda () (format t ctl-string (incf num))))
```

6.2   A Pattern-Matching Tool

The pat-match function was a pattern matcher defined specifically for the ELIZA program. Subsequent programs will need pattern matchers too, and rather than write specialized matchers for each new program, it is easier to define one general

---

[1]The macro handler-case is only in ANSI Common Lisp.

pattern matcher that can serve most needs, and is extensible in case novel needs come up.

The problem in designing a "general" tool is deciding what features to provide. We can try to define features that might be useful, but it is also a good idea to make the list of features open-ended, so that new ones can be easily added when needed.

Features can be added by generalizing or specializing existing ones. For example, we provide segment variables that match zero or more input elements. We can specialize this by providing for a kind of segment variable that matches one or more elements, or for an optional variable that matches zero or one element. Another possibility is to generalize segment variables to specify a match of m to n elements, for any specified m and n. These ideas come from experience with notations for writing regular expressions, as well as from very general heuristics for generalization, such as "consider important special cases" and "zero and one are likely to be important special cases."

Another useful feature is to allow the user to specify an arbitrary predicate that a match must satisfy. The notation (?is ?n numberp) could be used to match any expression that is a number and bind it to the variable ?n. This would look like:

```
> (pat-match '(x = (?is ?n numberp)) '(x = 34)) ⇒ ((?n . 34))
> (pat-match '(x = (?is ?n numberp)) '(x = x)) ⇒ NIL
```

Since patterns are like boolean expressions, it makes sense to allow boolean operators on them. Following the question-mark convention, we will use ?and, ?or and ?not for the operators.[2] Here is a pattern to match a relational expression with one of three relations. It succeeds because the < matches one of the three possibilities specified by (?or <=>).

```
> (pat-match '(?x (?or < = >) ?y) '(3 < 4)) ⇒ ((?Y . 4) (?X . 3))
```

Here is an example of an ?and pattern that checks if an expression is both a number and odd:

```
> (pat-match '(x = (?and (?is ?n numberp) (?is ?n oddp)))
             '(x = 3))
((?N . 3))
```

---

[2]An alternative would be to reserve the question mark for variables only and use another notation for these match operators. Keywords would be a good choice, such as :and, :or, :is, etc.

The next pattern uses ?not to insure that two parts are not equal:

```
> (pat-match '(?x /= (?not ?x)) '(3 /= 4)) ⇒ ((?X . 3))
```

The segment matching notation we have seen before. It is augmented to allow for three possibilities: zero or more expressions; one or more expressions; and zero or one expressions. Finally, the notation (?if *exp*) can be used to test a relationship between several variables. It has to be listed as a segment pattern rather than a single pattern because it does not consume any of the input at all:

```
> (pat-match '(?x > ?y (?if (> ?x ?y))) '(4 > 3)) ⇒
((?Y . 3) (?X . 4))
```

When the description of a problem gets this complicated, it is a good idea to attempt a more formal specification. The following table describes a grammar of patterns, using the same grammar rule format described in chapter 2.

pat ⇒	*var*	match any one expression
	constant	match just this atom
	segment-pat	match something against a sequence
	single-pat	match something against one expression
	(*pat* . *pat*)	match the first and the rest
single-pat ⇒	(?is *var predicate*)	test predicate on one expression
	(?or *pat...*)	match any pattern on one expression
	(?and *pat...*)	match every pattern on one expression
	(?not *pat...*)	succeed if pattern(s) do not match
segment-pat ⇒	((?* *var*) ...)	match zero or more expressions
	((?+ *var*) ...)	match one or more expressions
	((?? *var*) ...)	match zero or one expression
	((?if *exp*) ...)	test if exp (which may contain variables) is true
var ⇒	?*chars*	a symbol starting with ?
constant ⇒	*atom*	any nonvariable atom

Despite the added complexity, all patterns can still be classified into five cases. The pattern must be either a variable, constant, a (generalized) segment pattern, a (generalized) single-element pattern, or a cons of two patterns. The following definition of pat-match reflects the five cases (along with two checks for failure):

```lisp
(defun pat-match (pattern input &optional (bindings no-bindings))
  "Match pattern against input in the context of the bindings"
  (cond ((eq bindings fail) fail)
        ((variable-p pattern)
         (match-variable pattern input bindings))
        ((eql pattern input) bindings)
        ((segment-pattern-p pattern)
         (segment-matcher pattern input bindings))
        ((single-pattern-p pattern)                    ; ***
         (single-matcher pattern input bindings))      ; ***
        ((and (consp pattern) (consp input))
         (pat-match (rest pattern) (rest input)
                    (pat-match (first pattern) (first input)
                               bindings)))
        (t fail)))
```

For completeness, we repeat here the necessary constants and low-level functions from ELIZA:

```lisp
(defconstant fail nil "Indicates pat-match failure")

(defconstant no-bindings '((t . t))
  "Indicates pat-match success, with no variables.")

(defun variable-p (x)
  "Is x a variable (a symbol beginning with '?')?"
  (and (symbolp x) (equal (char (symbol-name x) 0) #\?)))

(defun get-binding (var bindings)
  "Find a (variable . value) pair in a binding list."
  (assoc var bindings))

(defun binding-var (binding)
  "Get the variable part of a single binding."
  (car binding))

(defun binding-val (binding)
  "Get the value part of a single binding."
  (cdr binding))

(defun make-binding (var val) (cons var val))

(defun lookup (var bindings)
  "Get the value part (for var) from a binding list."
  (binding-val (get-binding var bindings)))
```

```
(defun extend-bindings (var val bindings)
  "Add a (var . value) pair to a binding list."
  (cons (make-binding var val)
        ;; Once we add a "real" binding,
        ;; we can get rid of the dummy no-bindings
        (if (eq bindings no-bindings)
            nil
            bindings)

(defun match-variable (var input bindings)
  "Does VAR match input?  Uses (or updates) and returns bindings."
  (let ((binding (get-binding var bindings)))
    (cond ((not binding) (extend-bindings var input bindings))
          ((equal input (binding-val binding)) bindings)
          (t fail))))
```

The next step is to define the predicates that recognize generalized segment and single-element patterns, and the matching functions that operate on them. We could implement segment-matcher and single-matcher with case statements that consider all possible cases. However, that would make it difficult to extend the matcher. A programmer who wanted to add a new kind of segment pattern would have to edit the definitions of both segment-pattern-p and segment-matcher to install the new feature. This by itself may not be too bad, but consider what happens when two programmers each add independent features. If you want to use both, then neither version of segment-matcher (or segment-pattern-p) will do. You'll have to edit the functions again, just to merge the two extensions.

The solution to this dilemma is to write one version of segment-pattern-p and segment-matcher, once and for all, but to have these functions refer to a table of pattern/action pairs. The table would say "if you see ?* in the pattern, then use the function segment-match," and so on. Then programmers who want to extend the matcher just add entries to the table, and it is trivial to merge different extensions (unless of course two programmers have chosen the same symbol to mark different actions).

This style of programming, where pattern/action pairs are stored in a table, is called *data-driven programming*. It is a very flexible style that is appropriate for writing extensible systems.

There are many ways to implement tables in Common Lisp, as discussed in section 3.6, page 73. In this case, the keys to the table will be symbols (like ?*), and it is fine if the representation of the table is distributed across memory. Thus, property lists are an appropriate choice. We will have two tables, represented by the segment-match property and the single-match property of symbols like ?*. The value of each property will be the name of a function that implements the match. Here are the table entries to implement the grammar listed previously:

```
(setf (get '?is  'single-match) 'match-is)
(setf (get '?or  'single-match) 'match-or)
(setf (get '?and 'single-match) 'match-and)
(setf (get '?not 'single-match) 'match-not)

(setf (get '?*  'segment-match) 'segment-match)
(setf (get '?+  'segment-match) 'segment-match+)
(setf (get '??  'segment-match) 'segment-match?)
(setf (get '?if 'segment-match) 'match-if)
```

With the table defined, we need to do two things. First, define the "glue" that holds the table together: the predicates and action-taking functions. A function that looks up a data-driven function and calls it (such as segment-matcher and single-matcher) is called a *dispatch function*.

```
(defun segment-pattern-p (pattern)
  "Is this a segment-matching pattern like ((?* var) . pat)?"
  (and (consp pattern) (consp (first pattern))
       (symbolp (first (first pattern)))
       (segment-match-fn (first (first pattern)))))

(defun single-pattern-p (pattern)
  "Is this a single-matching pattern?
  E.g. (?is x predicate) (?and . patterns) (?or . patterns)."
  (and (consp pattern)
       (single-match-fn (first pattern))))

(defun segment-matcher (pattern input bindings)
  "Call the right function for this kind of segment pattern."
  (funcall (segment-match-fn (first (first pattern)))
           pattern input bindings))

(defun single-matcher (pattern input bindings)
  "Call the right function for this kind of single pattern."
  (funcall (single-match-fn (first pattern))
           (rest pattern) input bindings))

(defun segment-match-fn (x)
  "Get the segment-match function for x,
  if it is a symbol that has one."
  (when (symbolp x) (get x 'segment-match)))

(defun single-match-fn (x)
  "Get the single-match function for x,
  if it is a symbol that has one."
  (when (symbolp x) (get x 'single-match)))
```

The last thing to do is define the individual matching functions. First, the single-pattern matching functions:

```
(defun match-is (var-and-pred input bindings)
  "Succeed and bind var if the input satisfies pred,
  where var-and-pred is the list (var pred)."
  (let* ((var (first var-and-pred))
         (pred (second var-and-pred))
         (new-bindings (pat-match var input bindings)))
    (if (or (eq new-bindings fail)
            (not (funcall pred input)))
        fail
        new-bindings)))

(defun match-and (patterns input bindings)
  "Succeed if all the patterns match the input."
  (cond ((eq bindings fail) fail)
        ((null patterns) bindings)
        (t (match-and (rest patterns) input
                      (pat-match (first patterns) input
                                 bindings)))))

(defun match-or (patterns input bindings)
  "Succeed if any one of the patterns match the input."
  (if (null patterns)
      fail
      (let ((new-bindings (pat-match (first patterns)
                                     input bindings)))
        (if (eq new-bindings fail)
            (match-or (rest patterns) input bindings)
            new-bindings))))

(defun match-not (patterns input bindings)
  "Succeed if none of the patterns match the input.
  This will never bind any variables."
  (if (match-or patterns input bindings)
      fail
      bindings))
```

Now the segment-pattern matching functions. segment-match is similar to the version presented as part of ELIZA. The difference is in how we determine pos, the position of the first element of the input that could match the next element of the pattern after the segment variable. In ELIZA, we assumed that the segment variable was either the last element of the pattern or was followed by a constant. In the following version, we allow nonconstant patterns to follow segment variables. The function first-match-pos is added to handle this. If the following element is in fact a constant, the same calculation is done using position. If it is not a constant, then we just return the first possible starting position—unless that would put us past the end of the input, in which case we return nil to indicate failure:

```lisp
(defun segment-match (pattern input bindings &optional (start 0))
  "Match the segment pattern ((?* var) . pat) against input."
  (let ((var (second (first pattern)))
        (pat (rest pattern)))
    (if (null pat)
        (match-variable var input bindings)
        (let ((pos (first-match-pos (first pat) input start)))
          (if (null pos)
              fail
              (let ((b2 (pat-match
                          pat (subseq input pos)
                          (match-variable var (subseq input 0 pos)
                                          bindings))))
                ;; If this match failed, try another longer one
                (if (eq b2 fail)
                    (segment-match pattern input bindings (+ pos 1))
                    b2)))))))

(defun first-match-pos (pat1 input start)
  "Find the first position that pat1 could possibly match input,
  starting at position start.  If pat1 is non-constant, then just
  return start."
  (cond ((and (atom pat1) (not (variable-p pat1)))
         (position pat1 input :start start :test #'equal))
        ((< start (length input)) start)
        (t nil)))
```

In the first example below, the segment variable ?x matches the sequence (b c). In the second example, there are two segment variables in a row. The first successful match is achieved with the first variable, ?x, matching the empty sequence, and the second one, ?y, matching (b c).

```lisp
> (pat-match '(a (?* ?x) d) '(a b c d)) ⇒ ((?X B C))

> (pat-match '(a (?* ?x) (?* ?y) d) '(a b c d)) ⇒ ((?Y B C) (?X))
```

In the next example, ?x is first matched against nil and ?y against (b c d), but that fails, so we try matching ?x against a segment of length one. That fails too, but finally the match succeeds with ?x matching the two-element segment (b c), and ?y matching (d).

```
> (pat-match '(a (?* ?x) (?* ?y) ?x ?y)
             '(a b c d (b c) (d))) ⇒ ((?Y D) (?X B C))
```

Given segment-match, it is easy to define the function to match one-or-more elements and the function to match zero-or-one element:

```
(defun segment-match+ (pattern input bindings)
  "Match one or more elements of input."
  (segment-match pattern input bindings 1))

(defun segment-match? (pattern input bindings)
  "Match zero or one element of input."
  (let ((var (second (first pattern)))
        (pat (rest pattern)))
    (or (pat-match (cons var pat) input bindings)
        (pat-match pat input bindings))))
```

Finally, we supply the function to test an arbitrary piece of Lisp code. It does this by evaluating the code with the bindings implied by the binding list. This is one of the few cases where it is appropriate to call eval: when we want to give the user unrestricted access to the Lisp interpreter.

```
(defun match-if (pattern input bindings)
  "Test an arbitrary expression involving variables.
  The pattern looks like ((?if code) . rest)."
  (and (progv (mapcar #'car bindings)
              (mapcar #'cdr bindings)
         (eval (second (first pattern))))
       (pat-match (rest pattern) input bindings)))
```

Here are two examples using ?if. The first succeeds because (+ 3 4) is indeed 7, and the second fails because (> 3 4) is false.

```
> (pat-match '(?x ?op ?y is ?z (?if (eql (?op ?x ?y) ?z)))
             '(3 + 4 is 7))
((?Z . 7) (?Y . 4) (?OP . +) (?X . 3))
> (pat-match '(?x ?op ?y (?if (?op ?x ?y)))
             '(3 > 4))
NIL
```

The syntax we have defined for patterns has two virtues: first, the syntax is very general, so it is easy to extend. Second, the syntax can be easily manipulated by pat-match. However, there is one drawback: the syntax is a little verbose, and some may find it ugly. Compare the following two patterns:

```
(a (?* ?x) (?* ?y) d)
(a ?x* ?y* d)
```

Many readers find the second pattern easier to understand at a glance. We could change pat-match to allow for patterns of the form ?x*, but that would mean pat-match would have a lot more work to do on every match. An alternative is to leave pat-match as is, but define another level of syntax for use by human readers only. That is, a programmer could type the second expression above, and have it translated into the first, which would then be processed by pat-match.

In other words, we will define a facility to define a kind of pattern-matching macro that will be expanded the first time the pattern is seen. It is better to do this expansion once than to complicate pat-match and in effect do the expansion every time a pattern is used. (Of course, if a pattern is only used once, then there is no advantage. But in most programs, each pattern will be used again and again.)

We need to define two functions: one to define pattern-matching macros, and another to expand patterns that may contain these macros. We will only allow symbols to be macros, so it is reasonable to store the expansions on each symbol's property list:

```
(defun pat-match-abbrev (symbol expansion)
  "Define symbol as a macro standing for a pat-match pattern."
  (setf (get symbol 'expand-pat-match-abbrev)
    (expand-pat-match-abbrev expansion)))

(defun expand-pat-match-abbrev (pat)
  "Expand out all pattern matching abbreviations in pat."
  (cond ((and (symbolp pat) (get pat 'expand-pat-match-abbrev)))
    ((atom pat) pat)
    (t (cons (expand-pat-match-abbrev (first pat))
         (expand-pat-match-abbrev (rest pat))))))
```

We would use this facility as follows:

```
> (pat-match-abbrev '?x* '(?* ?x)) ⇒ (?* ?X)

> (pat-match-abbrev '?y* '(?* ?y)) ⇒ (?* ?Y)

> (setf axyd (expand-pat-match-abbrev '(a ?x* ?y* d))) ⇒
(A (?* ?X) (?* ?Y) D)

> (pat-match axyd '(a b c d)) ⇒ ((?Y B C) (?X))
```

📟 **Exercise 6.1 [m]** Go back and change the ELIZA rules to use the abbreviation facility. Does this make the rules easier to read?

Exercise 6.2 [h]   In the few prior examples, every time there was a binding of pattern variables that satisfied the input, that binding was found. Informally, show that pat-match will always find such a binding, or show a counterexample where it fails to find one.

6.3   A Rule-Based Translator Tool

As we have defined it, the pattern matcher matches one input against one pattern. In eliza, we need to match each input against a number of patterns, and then return a result based on the rule that contains the first pattern that matches. To refresh your memory, here is the function use-eliza-rules:

```
(defun use-eliza-rules (input)
  "Find some rule with which to transform the input."
  (some #'(lambda (rule)
            (let ((result (pat-match (rule-pattern rule) input)))
              (if (not (eq result fail))
                  (sublis (switch-viewpoint result)
                          (random-elt (rule-responses rule))))))
        *eliza-rules*))
```

It turns out that this will be a quite common thing to do: search through a list of rules for one that matches, and take action according to that rule. To turn the structure of use-eliza-rules into a software tool, we will allow the user to specify each of the following:

- What kind of rule to use. Every rule will be characterized by an if-part and a then-part, but the ways of getting at those two parts may vary.

- What list of rules to use. In general, each application will have its own list of rules.

- How to see if a rule matches. By default, we will use pat-match, but it should be possible to use other matchers.

- What to do when a rule matches. Once we have determined which rule to use, we have to determine what it means to use it. The default is just to substitute the bindings of the match into the then-part of the rule.

The rule-based translator tool now looks like this:

```
(defun rule-based-translator
        (input rules &key (matcher #'pat-match)
        (rule-if #'first) (rule-then #'rest) (action #'sublis))
  "Find the first rule in rules that matches input,
  and apply the action to that rule."
  (some
    #'(lambda (rule)
        (let ((result (funcall matcher (funcall rule-if rule)
                                input)))
          (if (not (eq result fail))
              (funcall action result (funcall rule-then rule)))))
    rules))


(defun use-eliza-rules (input)
  "Find some rule with which to transform the input."
  (rule-based-translator input *eliza-rules*
    :action #'(lambda (bindings responses)
                (sublis (switch-viewpoint bindings)
                        (random-elt responses)))))
```

6.4   A Set of Searching Tools

The GPS program can be seen as a problem in *search*. In general, a search problem involves exploring from some starting state and investigating neighboring states until a solution is reached. As in GPS, *state* means a description of any situation or state of affairs. Each state may have several neighbors, so there will be a choice of how to search. We can travel down one path until we see it is a dead end, or we can consider lots of different paths at the same time, expanding each path step by step. Search problems are called *nondeterministic* because there is no way to determine what is the best step to take next. AI problems, by their very nature, tend to be nondeterministic. This can be a source of confusion for programmers who are used to deterministic problems. In this section we will try to clear up that confusion. This section also serves as an example of how higher-order functions can be used to implement general tools that can be specified by passing in specific functions.

Abstractly, a search problem can be characterized by four features:

- The *start* state.

- The *goal* state (or states).

- The *successors,* or states that can be reached from any other state.

- The *strategy* that determines the *order* in which we search.

The first three features are part of the problem, while the fourth is part of the solution. In GPS, the starting state was given, along with a description of the goal states. The successors of a state were determined by consulting the operators. The search strategy was means-ends analysis. This was never spelled out explicitly but was implicit in the structure of the whole program. In this section we will formulate a general searching tool, show how it can be used to implement several different search strategies, and then show how GPS could be implemented with this tool.

The first notion we have to define is the *state space,* or set of all possible states. We can view the states as nodes and the successor relation as links in a graph. Some state space graphs will have a small number of states, while others have an infinite number, but they can still be solved if we search cleverly. Some graphs will have a regular structure, while others will appear random. We will start by considering only trees—that is, graphs where a state can be reached by only one unique sequence of successor links. Here is a tree:

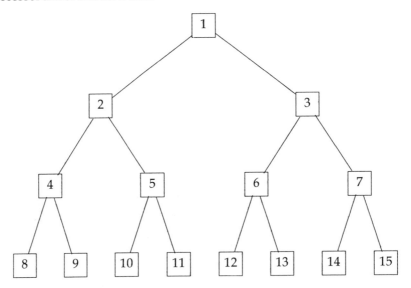

Searching Trees

We will call our first searching tool tree-search, because it is designed to search state spaces that are in the form of trees. It takes four arguments: (1) a list of valid starting states, (2) a predicate to decide if we have reached a goal state, (3) a function to generate the successors of a state, and (4) a function that decides in what order to search. The first argument is a list rather than a single state so that tree-search can recursively call itself after it has explored several paths through the state space. Think of the first argument not as a starting state but as a list of possible states from which the goal may be reached. This lists represents the fringe of the tree that has been explored so far. tree-search has three cases: If there are no more states to consider, then give up and return fail. If the first possible state is a goal state, then return the succeful state. Otherwise, generate the successors of the first state and combine them with the other states. Order this combined list according to the particular search strategy and continue searching. Note that tree-search itself does not specify any particular searching strategy.

```lisp
(defun tree-search (states goal-p successors combiner)
  "Find a state that satisfies goal-p.  Start with states,
  and search according to successors and combiner."
  (dbg :search "~&;; Search: ~a" states)
  (cond ((null states) fail)
        ((funcall goal-p (first states)) (first states))
        (t (tree-search
             (funcall combiner
                      (funcall successors (first states))
                      (rest states))
           goal-p successors combiner))))
```

The first strategy we will consider is called *depth-first search.* In depth-first search, the longest paths are considered first. In other words, we generate the successors of a state, and then work on the first successor first. We only return to one of the subsequent successors if we arrive at a state that has no successors at all. This strategy can be implemented by simply appending the previous states to the end of the list of new successors on each iteration. The function depth-first-search takes a single starting state, a goal predicate, and a successor function. It packages the starting state into a list as expected by tree-search, and specifies append as the combining function:

```lisp
(defun depth-first-search (start goal-p successors)
  "Search new states first until goal is reached."
  (tree-search (list start) goal-p successors #'append))
```

Let's see how we can search through the binary tree defined previously. First, we define the successor function binary-tree. It returns a list of two states, the two numbers that are twice the input state and one more than twice the input state. So the successors of 1 will be 2 and 3, and the successors of 2 will be 4 and 5. The binary-tree function generates an infinite tree of which the first 15 nodes are diagrammed in our example.

```
(defun binary-tree (x) (list (* 2 x) (+ 1 (* 2 x))))
```

To make it easier to specify a goal, we define the function is as a function that returns a predicate that tests for a particular value. Note that is does not do the test itself. Rather, it returns a function that can be called to perform tests:

```
(defun is (value) #'(lambda (x) (eql x value)))
```

Now we can turn on the debugging output and search through the binary tree, starting at 1, and looking for, say, 12, as the goal state. Each line of debugging output shows the list of states that have been generated as successors but not yet examined:

```
> (debug :search)  ⇒  (SEARCH)

> (depth-first-search 1 (is 12) #'binary-tree)
;; Search: (1)
;; Search: (2 3)
;; Search: (4 5 3)
;; Search: (8 9 5 3)
;; Search: (16 17 9 5 3)
;; Search: (32 33 17 9 5 3)
;; Search: (64 65 33 17 9 5 3)
;; Search: (128 129 65 33 17 9 5 3)
;; Search: (256 257 129 65 33 17 9 5 3)
;; Search: (512 513 257 129 65 33 17 9 5 3)
;; Search: (1024 1025 513 257 129 65 33 17 9 5 3)
;; Search: (2048 2049 1025 513 257 129 65 33 17 9 5 3)
[Abort]
```

The problem is that we are searching an infinite tree, and the depth-first search strategy just dives down the left-hand branch at every step. The only way to stop the doomed search is to type an interrupt character.

An alternative strategy is *breadth-first search*, where the shortest path is extended first at each step. It can be implemented simply by appending the new successor states to the end of the existing states:

```
(defun prepend (x y) "Prepend y to start of x" (append y x))

(defun breadth-first-search (start goal-p successors)
  "Search old states first until goal is reached."
  (tree-search (list start) goal-p successors #'prepend))
```

The only difference between depth-first and breadth-first search is the difference between append and prepend. Here we see breadth-first-search in action:

```
> (breadth-first-search 1 (is 12) 'binary-tree)
;; Search: (1)
;; Search: (2 3)
;; Search: (3 4 5)
;; Search: (4 5 6 7)
;; Search: (5 6 7 8 9)
;; Search: (6 7 8 9 10 11)
;; Search: (7 8 9 10 11 12 13)
;; Search: (8 9 10 11 12 13 14 15)
;; Search: (9 10 11 12 13 14 15 16 17)
;; Search: (10 11 12 13 14 15 16 17 18 19)
;; Search: (11 12 13 14 15 16 17 18 19 20 21)
;; Search: (12 13 14 15 16 17 18 19 20 21 22 23)
12
```

Breadth-first search ends up searching each node in numerical order, and so it will eventually find any goal. It is methodical, but therefore plodding. Depth-first search will be much faster—if it happens to find the goal at all. For example, if we were looking for 2048, depth-first search would find it in 12 steps, while breadth-first would take 2048 steps. Breadth-first search also requires more storage, because it saves more intermediate states.

If the search tree is finite, then either breadth-first or depth-first will eventually find the goal. Both methods search the entire state space, but in a different order. We will now show a depth-first search of the 15-node binary tree diagrammed previously. It takes about the same amount of time to find the goal (12) as it did with breadth-first search. It would have taken more time to find 15; less to find 8. The big difference is in the number of states considered at one time. At most, depth-first search considers four at a time; in general it will need to store only $\log_2 n$ states to search a n-node tree, while breadth-first search needs to store $n/2$ states.

```
(defun finite-binary-tree (n)
   "Return a successor function that generates a binary tree
   with n nodes."
   #'(lambda (x)
       (remove-if #'(lambda (child) (> child n))
                  (binary-tree x))))

> (depth-first-search 1 (is 12) (finite-binary-tree 15))
;; Search: (1)
;; Search: (2 3)
;; Search: (4 5 3)
;; Search: (8 9 5 3)
;; Search: (9 5 3)
;; Search: (5 3)
;; Search: (10 11 3)
;; Search: (11 3)
```

```
;; Search: (3)
;; Search: (6 7)
;; Search: (12 13 7)
12
```

Guiding the Search

While breadth-first search is more methodical, neither strategy is able to take advantage of any knowledge about the state space. They both search blindly. In most real applications we will have some estimate of how far a state is from the solution. In such cases, we can implement a *best-first search*. The name is not quite accurate; if we could really search best first, that would not be a search at all. The name refers to the fact that the state that *appears* to be best is searched first.

To implement best-first search we need to add one more piece of information: a cost function that gives an estimate of how far a given state is from the goal.

For the binary tree example, we will use as a cost estimate the numeric difference from the goal. So if we are looking for 12, then 12 has cost 0, 8 has cost 4 and 2048 has cost 2036. The higher-order function diff, shown in the following, returns a cost function that computes the difference from a goal. The higher-order function sorter takes a cost function as an argument and returns a combiner function that takes the lists of old and new states, appends them together, and sorts the result based on the cost function, lowest cost first. (The built-in function sort sorts a list according to a comparison function. In this case the smaller numbers come first. sort takes an optional :key argument that says how to compute the score for each element. Be careful—sort is a destructive function.)

```
(defun diff (num)
  "Return the function that finds the difference from num."
  #'(lambda (x) (abs (- x num))))

(defun sorter (cost-fn)
  "Return a combiner function that sorts according to cost-fn."
  #'(lambda (new old)
      (sort (append new old) #'< :key cost-fn)))


(defun best-first-search (start goal-p successors cost-fn)
  "Search lowest cost states first until goal is reached."
  (tree-search (list start) goal-p successors (sorter cost-fn)))
```

Now, using the difference from the goal as the cost function, we can search using best-first search:

```
> (best-first-search 1 (is 12) #'binary-tree (diff 12))
;; Search: (1)
;; Search: (3 2)
;; Search: (7 6 2)
;; Search: (14 15 6 2)
;; Search: (15 6 2 28 29)
;; Search: (6 2 28 29 30 31)
;; Search: (12 13 2 28 29 30 31)
12
```

The more we know about the state space, the better we can search. For example, if we know that all successors are greater than the states they come from, then we can use a cost function that gives a very high cost for numbers above the goal. The function price-is-right is like diff, except that it gives a high penalty for going over the goal.[3] Using this cost function leads to a near-optimal search on this example. It makes the "mistake" of searching 7 before 6 (because 7 is closer to 12), but does not waste time searching 14 and 15:

```
(defun price-is-right (price)
  "Return a function that measures the difference from price,
  but gives a big penalty for going over price."
  #'(lambda (x) (if (> x price)
                    most-positive-fixnum
                    (- price x))))
> (best-first-search 1 (is 12) #'binary-tree (price-is-right 12))
;; Search: (1)
;; Search: (3 2)
;; Search: (7 6 2)
;; Search: (6 2 14 15)
;; Search: (12 2 13 14 15)
12
```

All the searching methods we have seen so far consider ever-increasing lists of states as they search. For problems where there is only one solution, or a small number of solutions, this is unavoidable. To find a needle in a haystack, you need to look at a lot of hay. But for problems with many solutions, it may be worthwhile to discard unpromising paths. This runs the risk of failing to find a solution at all, but it can save enough space and time to offset the risk. A best-first search that keeps only a fixed number of alternative states at any one time is known as a *beam search*. Think of searching as shining a light through the dark of the state space. In other search

---

[3]The built-in constant most-positive-fixnum is a large integer, the largest that can be expressed without using bignums. Its value depends on the implementation, but in most Lisps it is over 16 million.

strategies the light spreads out as we search deeper, but in beam search the light remains tightly focused. Beam search is a variant of best-first search, but it is also similar to depth-first search. The difference is that beam search looks down several paths at once, instead of just one, and chooses the best one to look at next. But it gives up the ability to backtrack indefinitely. The function beam-search is just like best-first-search, except that after we sort the states, we then take only the first beam-width states. This is done with subseq; (subseq *list start end*) returns the sublist that starts at position *start* and ends just before position *end*.

```
(defun beam-search (start goal-p successors cost-fn beam-width)
  "Search highest scoring states first until goal is reached,
  but never consider more than beam-width states at a time."
  (tree-search (list start) goal-p successors
            #'(lambda (old new)
                (let ((sorted (funcall (sorter cost-fn) old new)))
                  (if (> beam-width (length sorted))
                      sorted
                      (subseq sorted 0 beam-width)))))))
```

We can successfully search for 12 in the binary tree using a beam width of only 2:

```
> (beam-search 1 (is 12) #'binary-tree (price-is-right 12) 2)
;; Search: (1)
;; Search: (3 2)
;; Search: (7 6)
;; Search: (6 14)
;; Search: (12 13)
12
```

However, if we go back to the scoring function that just takes the difference from 12, then beam search fails. When it generates 14 and 15, it throws away 6, and thus loses its only chance to find the goal:

```
> (beam-search 1 (is 12) #'binary-tree (diff 12) 2)
;; Search: (1)
;; Search: (3 2)
;; Search: (7 6)
;; Search: (14 15)
;; Search: (15 28)
;; Search: (28 30)
;; Search: (30 56)
;; Search: (56 60)
;; Search: (60 112)
;; Search: (112 120)
;; Search: (120 224)
```

[Abort]

This search would succeed if we gave a beam width of 3. This illustrates a general principle: we can find a goal either by looking at more states, or by being smarter about the states we look at. That means having a better ordering function.

Notice that with a beam width of infinity we get best-first search. With a beam width of 1, we get depth-first search with no backup. This could be called "depth-only search," but it is more commonly known as *hill-climbing*. Think of a mountaineer trying to reach a peak in a heavy fog. One strategy would be for the mountaineer to look at adjacent locations, climb to the highest one, and look again. This strategy may eventually hit the peak, but it may also get stuck at the top of a foothill, or *local maximum*. Another strategy would be for the mountaineer to turn back and try again when the fog lifts, but in AI, unfortunately, the fog rarely lifts.[4]

As a concrete example of a problem that can be solved by search, consider the task of planning a flight across the North American continent in a small airplane, one whose range is limited to 1000 kilometers. Suppose we have a list of selected cities with airports, along with their position in longitude and latitude:

```
(defstruct (city (:type list)) name long lat)

(defparameter *cities*
  '((Atlanta       84.23 33.45) (Los-Angeles   118.15 34.03)
    (Boston        71.05 42.21) (Memphis        90.03 35.09)
    (Chicago       87.37 41.50) (New-York       73.58 40.47)
    (Denver       105.00 39.45) (Oklahoma-City  97.28 35.26)
    (Eugene       123.05 44.03) (Pittsburgh     79.57 40.27)
    (Flagstaff    111.41 35.13) (Quebec         71.11 46.49)
    (Grand-Jct    108.37 39.05) (Reno          119.49 39.30)
    (Houston      105.00 34.00) (San-Francisco 122.26 37.47)
    (Indianapolis  86.10 39.46) (Tampa          82.27 27.57)
    (Jacksonville  81.40 30.22) (Victoria      123.21 48.25)
    (Kansas-City   94.35 39.06) (Wilmington     77.57 34.14))))
```

This example introduces a new option to defstruct. Instead of just giving the name of the structure, it is also possible to use:

```
(defstruct (structure-name (option value)...) "optional doc" slot...)
```

For city, the option :type is specified as list. This means that cities will be implemented as lists of three elements, as they are in the initial value for *cities*.

---

[4]In chapter 8 we will see an example where the fog did lift: symbolic integration was once handled as a problem in search, but new mathematical results now make it possible to solve the same class of integration problems without search.

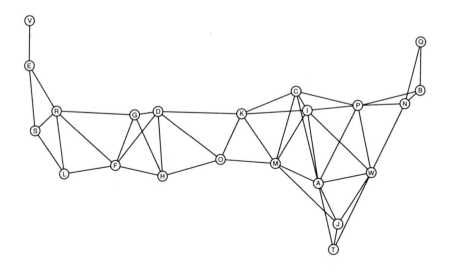

Figure 6.1: A Map of Some Cities

The cities are shown on the map in figure 6.1, which has connections between all cities within the 1000 kilometer range of each other.[5] This map was drawn with the help of air-distance, a function that returns the distance in kilometers between two cities "as the crow flies." It will be defined later. Two other useful functions are neighbors, which finds all the cities within 1000 kilometers, and city, which maps from a name to a city. The former uses find-all-if, which was defined on page 101 as a synonym for remove-if-not.

```
(defun neighbors (city)
  "Find all cities within 1000 kilometers."
  (find-all-if #'(lambda (c)
                   (and (not (eq c city))
                        (< (air-distance c city) 1000.0)))
               *cities*))

(defun city (name)
  "Find the city with this name."
  (assoc name *cities*))
```

We are now ready to plan a trip. The function trip takes the name of a starting and destination city and does a beam search of width one, considering all neighbors as

_____

[5]The astute reader will recognize that this graph is not a tree. The difference between trees and graphs and the implications for searching will be covered later.

successors to a state. The cost for a state is the air distance to the destination city:

```
(defun trip (start dest)
  "Search for a way from the start to dest."
  (beam-search start (is dest) #'neighbors
               #'(lambda (c) (air-distance c dest))
               1))
```

Here we plan a trip from San Francisco to Boston. The result seems to be the best possible path:

```
> (trip (city 'san-francisco) (city 'boston))
;; Search: ((SAN-FRANCISCO 122.26 37.47))
;; Search: ((RENO 119.49 39.3))
;; Search: ((GRAND-JCT 108.37 39.05))
;; Search: ((DENVER 105.0 39.45))
;; Search: ((KANSAS-CITY 94.35 39.06))
;; Search: ((INDIANAPOLIS 86.1 39.46))
;; Search: ((PITTSBURGH 79.57 40.27))
;; Search: ((BOSTON 71.05 42.21))
(BOSTON 71.05 42.21)
```

But look what happens when we plan the return trip. There are two detours, to Chicago and Flagstaff:

```
> (trip (city 'boston) (city 'san-francisco))
;; Search: ((BOSTON 71.05 42.21))
;; Search: ((PITTSBURGH 79.57 40.27))
;; Search: ((CHICAGO 87.37 41.5))
;; Search: ((KANSAS-CITY 94.35 39.06))
;; Search: ((DENVER 105.0 39.45))
;; Search: ((FLAGSTAFF 111.41 35.13))
;; Search: ((RENO 119.49 39.3))
;; Search: ((SAN-FRANCISCO 122.26 37.47))
(SAN-FRANCISCO 122.26 37.47)
```

Why did `trip` go from Denver to San Francisco via Flagstaff? Because Flagstaff is closer to the destination than Grand Junction. The problem is that we are minimizing the distance to the destination at each step, when we should be minimizing the sum of the distance to the destination plus the distance already traveled.

Search Paths

To minimize the total distance, we need some way to talk about the *path* that leads to the goal. But the functions we have defined so far only deal with individual states along the way. Representing paths would lead to another advantage: we could return the path as the solution, rather than just return the goal state. As it is, trip only returns the goal state, not the path to it. So there is no way to determine what trip has done, except by reading the debugging output.

The data structure path is designed to solve both these problems. A path has four fields: the current state, the previous partial path that this path is extending, the cost of the path so far, and an estimate of the total cost to reach the goal. Here is the structure definition for path. It uses the :print-function option to say that all paths are to be printed with the function print-path, which will be defined below.

```
(defstruct (path (:print-function print-path))
  state (previous nil) (cost-so-far 0) (total-cost 0))
```

The next question is how to integrate paths into the searching routines with the least amount of disruption. Clearly, it would be better to make one change to tree-search rather than to change depth-first-search, breadth-first-search, and beam-search. However, looking back at the definition of tree-search, we see that it makes no assumptions about the structure of states, other than the fact that they can be manipulated by the goal predicate, successor, and combiner functions. This suggests that we can use tree-search unchanged if we pass it paths instead of states, and give it functions that can process paths.

In the following redefinition of trip, the beam-search function is called with five arguments. Instead of passing it a city as the start state, we pass a path that has the city as its state field. The goal predicate should test whether its argument is a path whose state is the destination; we assume (and later define) a version of is that accommodates this. The successor function is the most difficult. Instead of just generating a list of neighbors, we want to first generate the neighbors, then make each one into a path that extends the current path, but with an updated cost so far and total estimated cost. The function path-saver returns a function that will do just that. Finally, the cost function we are trying to minimize is path-total-cost, and we provide a beam width, which is now an optional argument to trip that defaults to one:

```
(defun trip (start dest &optional (beam-width 1))
  "Search for the best path from the start to dest."
  (beam-search
    (make-path :state start)
    (is dest :key #'path-state)
    (path-saver #'neighbors #'air-distance
```

```
                              #'(lambda (c) (air-distance c dest)))
              #'path-total-cost
              beam-width))
```

The calculation of air-distance involves some complicated conversion of longitude and latitude to x-y-z coordinates. Since this is a problem in solid geometry, not AI, the code is presented without further comment:

```
(defconstant earth-diameter 12765.0
  "Diameter of planet earth in kilometers.")

(defun air-distance (city1 city2)
  "The great circle distance between two cities."
  (let ((d (distance (xyz-coords city1) (xyz-coords city2))))
    ;; d is the straight-line chord between the two cities,
    ;; The length of the subtending arc is given by:
    (* earth-diameter (asin (/ d 2)))))

(defun xyz-coords (city)
  "Returns the x,y,z coordinates of a point on a sphere.
  The center is (0 0 0) and the north pole is (0 0 1)."
  (let ((psi (deg->radians (city-lat city)))
        (phi (deg->radians (city-long city))))
    (list (* (cos psi) (cos phi))
          (* (cos psi) (sin phi))
          (sin psi))))

(defun distance (point1 point2)
  "The Euclidean distance between two points.
  The points are coordinates in n-dimensional space."
  (sqrt (reduce #'+ (mapcar #'(lambda (a b) (expt (- a b) 2))
                            point1 point2))))

(defun deg->radians (deg)
  "Convert degrees and minutes to radians."
  (* (+ (truncate deg) (* (rem deg 1) 100/60)) pi 1/180))
```

Before showing the auxiliary functions that implement this, here are some examples that show what it can do. With a beam width of 1, the detour to Flagstaff is eliminated, but the one to Chicago remains. With a beam width of 3, the correct optimal path is found. In the following examples, each call to the new version of trip returns a path, which is printed by show-city-path:

```
> (show-city-path (trip (city 'san-francisco) (city 'boston) 1))
#<Path 4514.8 km: San-Francisco - Reno - Grand-Jct - Denver -
  Kansas-City - Indianapolis - Pittsburgh - Boston>
```

```
> (show-city-path (trip (city 'boston) (city 'san-francisco) 1))
#<Path 4577.3 km: Boston - Pittsburgh - Chicago - Kansas-City -
  Denver - Grand-Jct - Reno - San-Francisco>

> (show-city-path (trip (city 'boston) (city 'san-francisco) 3))
#<Path 4514.8 km: Boston - Pittsburgh - Indianapolis -
  Kansas-City - Denver - Grand-Jct - Reno - San-Francisco>
```

This example shows how search is susceptible to irregularities in the search space. It was easy to find the correct path from west to east, but the return trip required more search, because Flagstaff is a falsely promising step. In general, there may be even worse dead ends lurking in the search space. Look what happens when we limit the airplane's range to 700 kilometers. The map is shown in figure 6.2.

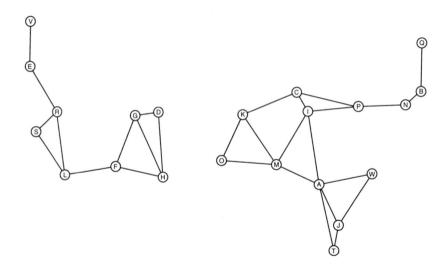

Figure 6.2: A Map of Cities within 700km

If we try to plan a trip from Tampa to Quebec, we can run into problems with the dead end at Wilmington, North Carolina. With a beam width of 1, the path to Jacksonville and then Wilmington will be tried first. From there, each step of the path alternates between Atlanta and Wilmington. The search never gets any closer to the goal. But with a beam width of 2, the path from Tampa to Atlanta is not discarded, and it is eventually continued on to Indianapolis and eventually to Quebec. So the capability to back up is essential in avoiding dead ends.

Now for the implementation details. The function is still returns a predicate that tests for a value, but now it accepts :key and :test keywords:

```
(defun is (value &key (key #'identity) (test #'eql))
  "Returns a predicate that tests for a given value."
  #'(lambda (path) (funcall test value (funcall key path))))
```

The path-saver function returns a function that will take a path as an argument and generate successors paths. path-saver takes as an argument a successor function that operates on bare states. It calls this function and, for each state returned, builds up a path that extends the existing path and stores the cost of the path so far as well as the estimated total cost:

```
(defun path-saver (successors cost-fn cost-left-fn)
  #'(lambda (old-path)
      (let ((old-state (path-state old-path)))
        (mapcar
          #'(lambda (new-state)
              (let ((old-cost
                      (+ (path-cost-so-far old-path)
                         (funcall cost-fn old-state new-state))))
                (make-path
                  :state new-state
                  :previous old-path
                  :cost-so-far old-cost
                  :total-cost (+ old-cost (funcall cost-left-fn
                                                   new-state)))))
          (funcall successors old-state)))))
```

By default a path structure would be printed as #S(PATH ...). But because each path has a previous field that is filled by another path, this output would get quite verbose. That is why we installed print-path as the print function for paths when we defined the structure. It uses the notation #<...>, which is a Common Lisp convention for printing output that can not be reconstructed by read. The function show-city-path prints a more complete representation of a path. We also define map-path to iterate over a path, collecting values:

```
(defun print-path (path &optional (stream t) depth)
  (declare (ignore depth))
  (format stream "#<Path to ~a cost ~,1f>"
          (path-state path) (path-total-cost path)))

(defun show-city-path (path &optional (stream t))
  "Show the length of a path, and the cities along it."
  (format stream "#<Path ~,1f km: ~{~:(~a~)~^ - ~}>"
          (path-total-cost path)
          (reverse (map-path #'city-name path)))
  (values))
```

```
(defun map-path (fn path)
  "Call fn on each state in the path, collecting results."
  (if (null path)
      nil
      (cons (funcall fn (path-state path))
            (map-path fn (path-previous path)))))
```

Guessing versus Guaranteeing a Good Solution

Elementary AI textbooks place a great emphasis on search algorithms that are guaranteed to find the best solution. However, in practice these algorithms are hardly ever used. The problem is that guaranteeing the best solution requires looking at a lot of other solutions in order to rule them out. For problems with large search spaces, this usually takes too much time. The alternative is to use an algorithm that will probably return a solution that is close to the best solution, but gives no guarantee. Such algorithms, traditionally known as *non-admissible heuristic search* algorithms, can be much faster.

Of the algorithms we have seen so far, best-first search almost, but not quite, guarantees the best solution. The problem is that it terminates a little too early. Suppose it has calculated three paths, of cost 90, 95 and 110. It will expand the 90 path next. Suppose this leads to a solution of total cost 100. Best-first search will then return that solution. But it is possible that the 95 path could lead to a solution with a total cost less than 100. Perhaps the 95 path is only one unit away from the goal, so it could result in a complete path of length 96. This means that an optimal search should examine the 95 path (but not the 110 path) before exiting.

Depth-first search and beam search, on the other hand, are definitely heuristic algorithms. Depth-first search finds a solution without any regard to its cost. With beam search, picking a good value for the beam width can lead to a good, quick solution, while picking the wrong value can lead to failure, or to a poor solution. One way out of this dilemma is to start with a narrow beam width, and if that does not lead to an acceptable solution, widen the beam and try again. We will call this *iterative widening*, although that is not a standard term. There are many variations on this theme, but here is a simple one:

```
(defun iter-wide-search (start goal-p successors cost-fn
                         &key (width 1) (max 100))
  "Search, increasing beam width from width to max.
  Return the first solution found at any width."
  (dbg :search "; Width: ~d" width)
  (unless (> width max)
    (or (beam-search start goal-p successors cost-fn width)
        (iter-wide-search start goal-p successors cost-fn
```

```
                         :width (+ width 1) :max max))))
```

Here `iter-wide-search` is used to search through a binary tree, failing with beam
width 1 and 2, and eventually succeeding with beam width 3:

```
> (iter-wide-search 1 (is 12) (finite-binary-tree 15) (diff 12))
; Width: 1
;; Search: (1)
;; Search: (3)
;; Search: (7)
;; Search: (14)
;; Search: NIL
; Width: 2
;; Search: (1)
;; Search: (3 2)
;; Search: (7 6)
;; Search: (14 15)
;; Search: (15)
;; Search: NIL
; Width: 3
;; Search: (1)
;; Search: (3 2)
;; Search: (7 6 2)
;; Search: (14 15 6)
;; Search: (15 6)
;; Search: (6)
;; Search: (12 13)
12
```

The name iterative widening is derived from the established term *iterative deepening*.
Iterative deepening is used to control depth-first search when we don't know the
depth of the desired solution. The idea is first to limit the search to a depth of 1,
then 2, and so on. That way we are guaranteed to find a solution at the minimum
depth, just as in breadth-first search, but without wasting as much storage space. Of
course, iterative deepening does waste some time because at each increasing depth
it repeats all the work it did at the previous depth. But suppose that the average
state has ten successors. That means that increasing the depth by one results in ten
times more search, so only 10% of the time is wasted on repeated work. So iterative
deepening uses only slightly more time and much less space. We will see it again in
chapters 11 and 18.

Searching Graphs

So far, tree-search has been the workhorse behind all the searching routines. This is curious, when we consider that the city problem involves a graph that is not a tree at all. The reason tree-search works is that any graph can be treated as a tree, if we ignore the fact that certain nodes are identical. For example, the graph in figure 6.3 can be rendered as a tree. Figure 6.4 shows only the top four levels of the tree; each of the bottom nodes (except the 6s) needs to be expanded further.

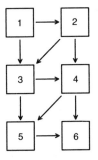

Figure 6.3: A Graph with Six Nodes

In searching for paths through the graph of cities, we were implicitly turning the graph into a tree. That is, if tree-search found two paths from Pittsburgh to Kansas City (via Chicago or Indianapolis), then it would treat them as two independent paths, just as if there were two distinct Kansas Cities. This made the algorithms simpler, but it also doubles the number of paths left to examine. If the destination is San Francisco, we will have to search for a path from Kansas City to San Francisco twice instead of once. In fact, even though the graph has only 22 cities, the tree is infinite, because we can go back and forth between adjacent cities any number of times. So, while it is possible to treat the graph as a tree, there are potential savings in treating it as a true graph.

The function graph-search does just that. It is similar to tree-search, but accepts two additional arguments: a comparison function that tests if two states are equal, and a list of states that are no longer being considered, but were examined in the past. The difference between graph-search and tree-search is in the call to new-states, which generates successors but eliminates states that are in either the list of states currently being considered or the list of old states considered in the past.

```
(defun graph-search (states goal-p successors combiner
                    &optional (state= #'eql) old-states)
  "Find a state that satisfies goal-p.  Start with states,
```

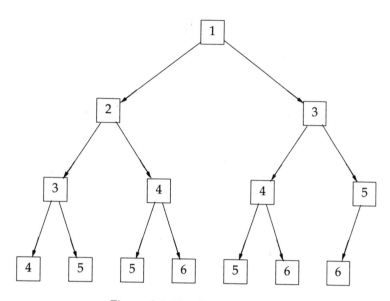

Figure 6.4: The Corresponding Tree

```
and search according to successors and combiner.
Don't try the same state twice."
(dbg :search "~&;; Search: ~a" states)
(cond ((null states) fail)
      ((funcall goal-p (first states)) (first states))
      (t (graph-search
           (funcall
             combiner
             (new-states states successors state= old-states)
             (rest states))
           goal-p successors combiner state=
           (adjoin (first states) old-states
                   :test state=)))))

(defun new-states (states successors state= old-states)
  "Generate successor states that have not been seen before."
  (remove-if
    #'(lambda (state)
        (or (member state states :test state=)
            (member state old-states :test state=)))
    (funcall successors (first states))))
```

Using the successor function next2, we can search the graph shown here either as a tree or as a graph. If we search it as a graph, it takes fewer iterations and less storage space to find the goal. Of course, there is additional overhead to test for identical states, but on graphs like this one we get an exponential speed-up for a constant amount of overhead.

```
(defun next2 (x) (list (+ x 1) (+ x 2)))

> (tree-search '(1) (is 6) #'next2 #'prepend)
;; Search: (1)
;; Search: (2 3)
;; Search: (3 3 4)
;; Search: (3 4 4 5)
;; Search: (4 4 5 4 5)
;; Search: (4 5 4 5 5 6)
;; Search: (5 4 5 5 6 5 6)
;; Search: (4 5 5 6 5 6 6 7)
;; Search: (5 5 6 5 6 6 7 5 6)
;; Search: (5 6 5 6 6 7 5 6 6 7)
;; Search: (6 5 6 6 7 5 6 6 7 6 7)
6

> (graph-search '(1) (is 6) #'next2 #'prepend)
;; Search: (1)
;; Search: (2 3)
;; Search: (3 4)
;; Search: (4 5)
;; Search: (5 6)
;; Search: (6 7)
6
```

The next step is to extend the graph-search algorithm to handle paths. The complication is in deciding which path to keep when two paths reach the same state. If we have a cost function, then the answer is easy: keep the path with the cheaper cost. Best-first search of a graph removing duplicate states is called *A* search*.

A* search is more complicated than graph-search because of the need both to add and to delete paths to the lists of current and old paths. For each new successor state, there are three possibilities. The new state may be in the list of current paths, in the list of old paths, or in neither. Within the first two cases, there are two subcases. If the new path is more expensive than the old one, then ignore the new path—it can not lead to a better solution. If the new path is cheaper than a corresponding path in the list of current paths, then replace it with the new path. If it is cheaper than a corresponding path in the list of the old paths, then remove that old path, and put the new path in the list of current paths.

Also, rather than sort the paths by total cost on each iteration, they are kept sorted, and new paths are inserted into the proper place one at a time using insert-path. Two more functions, better-path and find-path, are used to compare paths and see if a state has already appeared.

```
(defun a*-search (paths goal-p successors cost-fn cost-left-fn
                 &optional (state= #'eql) old-paths)
  "Find a path whose state satisfies goal-p.  Start with paths,
  and expand successors, exploring least cost first.
  When there are duplicate states, keep the one with the
  lower cost and discard the other."
  (dbg :search ";; Search: ~a" paths)
  (cond
    ((null paths) fail)
    ((funcall goal-p (path-state (first paths)))
     (values (first paths) paths))
    (t (let* ((path (pop paths))
              (state (path-state path)))
         ;; Update PATHS and OLD-PATHS to reflect
         ;; the new successors of STATE:
         (setf old-paths (insert-path path old-paths))
         (dolist (state2 (funcall successors state))
           (let* ((cost (+ (path-cost-so-far path)
                           (funcall cost-fn state state2)))
                  (cost2 (funcall cost-left-fn state2))
                  (path2 (make-path
                           :state state2 :previous path
                           :cost-so-far cost
                           :total-cost (+ cost cost2)))
                  (old nil))
             ;; Place the new path, path2, in the right list:
             (cond
               ((setf old (find-path state2 paths state=))
                (when (better-path path2 old)
                  (setf paths (insert-path
                                path2 (delete old paths)))))
               ((setf old (find-path state2 old-paths state=))
                (when (better-path path2 old)
                  (setf paths (insert-path path2 paths))
                  (setf old-paths (delete old old-paths))))
               (t (setf paths (insert-path path2 paths))))))
         ;; Finally, call A* again with the updated path lists:
         (a*-search paths goal-p successors cost-fn cost-left-fn
                    state= old-paths)))))
```

Here are the three auxiliary functions:

```lisp
(defun find-path (state paths state=)
  "Find the path with this state among a list of paths."
  (find state paths :key #'path-state :test state=))

(defun better-path (path1 path2)
  "Is path1 cheaper than path2?"
  (< (path-total-cost path1) (path-total-cost path2)))

(defun insert-path (path paths)
  "Put path into the right position, sorted by total cost."
  ;; MERGE is a built-in function
  (merge 'list (list path) paths #'< :key #'path-total-cost))

(defun path-states (path)
  "Collect the states along this path."
  (if (null path)
      nil
      (cons (path-state path)
            (path-states (path-previous path)))))
```

Below we use a*-search to search for 6 in the graph previously shown in figure 6.3. The cost function is a constant 1 for each step. In other words, the total cost is the length of the path. The heuristic evaluation function is just the difference from the goal. The A* algorithm needs just three search steps to come up with the optimal solution. Contrast that to the graph search algorithm, which needed five steps, and the tree search algorithm, which needed ten steps—and neither of them found the optimal solution.

```lisp
> (path-states
    (a*-search (list (make-path :state 1)) (is 6)
               #'next2 #'(lambda (x y) 1) (diff 6)))
;; Search: (#<Path to 1 cost 0.0>)
;; Search: (#<Path to 3 cost 4.0> #<Path to 2 cost 5.0>)
;; Search: (#<Path to 5 cost 3.0> #<Path to 4 cost 4.0>
            #<Path to 2 cost 5.0>)
;; Search: (#<Path to 6 cost 3.0> #<Path to 7 cost 4.0>
            #<Path to 4 cost 4.0> #<Path to 2 cost 5.0>)
(6 5 3 1)
```

It may seem limiting that these search functions all return a single answer. In some applications, we may want to look at several solutions, or at all possible solutions. Other applications are more naturally seen as optimization problems, where we don't know ahead of time what counts as achieving the goal but are just trying to find some action with a low cost.

It turns out that the functions we have defined are not limiting at all in this respect. They can be used to serve both these new purposes—provided we carefully specify the goal predicate. To find all solutions to a problem, all we have to do is pass in a goal predicate that always fails, but saves all the solutions in a list. The goal predicate will see all possible solutions and save away just the ones that are real solutions. Of course, if the search space is infinite this will never terminate, so the user has to be careful in applying this technique. It would also be possible to write a goal predicate that stopped the search after finding a certain number of solutions, or after looking at a certain number of states. Here is a function that finds all solutions, using beam search:

```
(defun search-all (start goal-p successors cost-fn beam-width)
  "Find all solutions to a search problem, using beam search."
  ;; Be careful: this can lead to an infinite loop.
  (let ((solutions nil))
    (beam-search
      start #'(lambda (x)
                (when (funcall goal-p x) (push x solutions))
                nil)
      successors cost-fn beam-width)
    solutions))
```

6.5   GPS as Search

The GPS program can be seen as a problem in search. For example, in the three-block blocks world, there are only 13 different states. They could be arranged in a graph and searched just as we searched for a route between cities. Figure 6.5 shows this graph.

The function search-gps does just that. Like the gps function on page 135, it computes a final state and then picks out the actions that lead to that state. But it computes the state with a beam search. The goal predicate tests if the current state satisfies every condition in the goal, the successor function finds all applicable operators and applies them, and the cost function simply sums the number of actions taken so far, plus the number of conditions that are not yet satisfied:

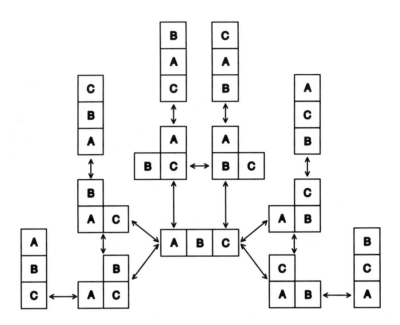

Figure 6.5: The Blocks World as a Graph

```
(defun search-gps (start goal &optional (beam-width 10))
  "Search for a sequence of operators leading to goal."
  (find-all-if
    #'action-p
    (beam-search
      (cons '(start) start)
      #'(lambda (state) (subsetp goal state :test #'equal))
      #'gps-successors
      #'(lambda (state)
          (+ (count-if #'action-p state)
             (count-if #'(lambda (con)
                           (not (member-equal con state)))
                       goal)))
      beam-width)))
```

Here is the successor function:

```
(defun gps-successors (state)
  "Return a list of states reachable from this one using ops."
  (mapcar
    #'(lambda (op)
```

```
              (append
                (remove-if #'(lambda (x)
                                (member-equal x (op-del-list op)))
                           state)
                (op-add-list op)))
          (applicable-ops state)))
(defun applicable-ops (state)
  "Return a list of all ops that are applicable now."
  (find-all-if
    #'(lambda (op)
        (subsetp (op-preconds op) state :test #'equal))
    *ops*))
```

The search technique finds good solutions quickly for a variety of problems. Here we see the solution to the Sussman anomaly in the three-block blocks world:

```
(setf start '((c on a) (a on table) (b on table) (space on c)
              (space on b) (space on table)))

> (search-gps start '((a on b) (b on c)))
((START)
 (EXECUTING (MOVE C FROM A TO TABLE))
 (EXECUTING (MOVE B FROM TABLE TO C))
 (EXECUTING (MOVE A FROM TABLE TO B)))

> (search-gps start '((b on c) (a on b)))
((START)
 (EXECUTING (MOVE C FROM A TO TABLE))
 (EXECUTING (MOVE B FROM TABLE TO C))
 (EXECUTING (MOVE A FROM TABLE TO B)))
```

In these solutions we search forward from the start to the goal; this is quite different from the means-ends approach of searching backward from the goal for an appropriate operator. But we could formulate means-ends analysis as forward search simply by reversing start and goal: GPS's goal state is the search's start state, and the search's goal predicate tests to see if a state matches GPS's start state. This is left as an exercise.

6.6   History and References

Pattern matching is one of the most important tools for AI. As such, it is covered in most textbooks on Lisp. Good treatments include Abelson and Sussman (1984), Wilensky (1986), Winston and Horn (1988), and Kreutzer and McKenzie (1990). An overview is presented in the "pattern-matching" entry in *Encyclopedia of AI* (Shapiro 1990).

Nilsson's *Problem-Solving Methods in Artificial Intelligence* (1971) was an early textbook that emphasized search as the most important defining characteristic of AI. More recent texts give less importance to search; Winston's *Artificial Intelligence* (1984) gives a balanced overview, and his *Lisp* (1988) provides implementations of some of the algorithms. They are at a lower level of abstraction than the ones in this chapter. Iterative deepening was first presented by Korf (1985), and iterative broadening by Ginsberg and Harvey (1990).

6.7 Exercises

Exercise 6.3 [m]   Write a version of `interactive-interpreter` that is more general than the one defined in this chapter. Decide what features can be specified, and provide defaults for them.

Exercise 6.4 [m]   Define a version of `compose` that allows any number of arguments, not just two. Hint: You may want to use the function `reduce`.

Exercise 6.5 [m]   Define a version of `compose` that allows any number of arguments but is more efficient than the answer to the previous exercise. Hint: try to make decisions when `compose` is called to build the resulting function, rather than making the same decisions over and over each time the resulting function is called.

Exercise 6.6 [m]   One problem with `pat-match` is that it gives special significance to symbols starting with ?, which means that they can not be used to match a literal pattern. Define a pattern that matches the input literally, so that such symbols can be matched.

Exercise 6.7 [m]   Discuss the pros and cons of data-driven programming compared to the conventional approach.

Exercise 6.8 [m]   Write a version of `tree-search` using an explicit loop rather than recursion.

Exercise 6.9 [m]   The `sorter` function is inefficient for two reasons: it calls `append`, which has to make a copy of the first argument, and it sorts the entire result, rather than just inserting the new states into the already sorted old states. Write a more efficient `sorter`.

☐ **Exercise 6.10 [m]**   Write versions of graph-search and a*-search that use hash tables rather than lists to test whether a state has been seen before.

☐ **Exercise 6.11 [m]**   Write a function that calls beam-search to find the first n solutions to a problem and returns them in a list.

☐ **Exercise 6.12 [m]**   On personal computers without floating-point hardware, the air-distance calculation will be rather slow. If this is a problem for you, arrange to compute the xyz-coords of each city only once and then store them, or store a complete table of air distances between cities. Also precompute and store the neighbors of each city.

☐ **Exercise 6.13 [d]**   Write a version of GPS that uses A* search instead of beam search. Compare the two versions in a variety of domains.

☐ **Exercise 6.14 [d]**   Write a version of GPS that allows costs for each operator. For example, driving the child to school might have a cost of 2, but calling a limousine to transport the child might have a cost of 100. Use these costs instead of a constant cost of 1 for each operation.

☐ **Exercise 6.15 [d]**   Write a version of GPS that uses the searching tools but does means-ends analysis.

6.8   Answers

Answer 6.2   Unfortunately, pat-match does not always find the answer. The problem is that it will only rebind a segment variable based on a failure to match the rest of the pattern after the segment variable. In all the examples above, the "rest of the pattern after the segment variable" was the whole pattern, so pat-match always worked properly. But if a segment variable appears nested inside a list, then the rest of the segment variable's sublist is only a part of the rest of the whole pattern, as the following example shows:

```
> (pat-match '(((?* ?x) (?* ?y))  ?x    ?y)
             '(( a   b   c   d )  (a b) (c d))) ⇒ NIL
```

The correct answer with ?x bound to (a b) and ?y bound to (c d) is not found because the inner segment match succeeds with ?x bound to ( ) and ?y bound to (a b c d), and once we leave the inner match and return to the top level, there is no going back for alternative bindings.

Answer 6.3   The following version lets the user specify all four components of the prompt-read-eval-print loop, as well as the streams to use for input and output. Defaults are set up as for a Lisp interpreter.

```
(defun interactive-interpreter
       (&key (read #'read) (eval #'eval) (print #'print)
        (prompt "> ") (input t) (output t))
  "Read an expression, evaluate it, and print the result."
  (loop
    (fresh-line output)
    (princ prompt output)
    (funcall print (funcall eval (funcall read input))
             output)))
```

Here is another version that does all of the above and also handles multiple values and binds the various "history variables" that the Lisp top-level binds.

```
(defun interactive-interpreter
       (&key (read #'read) (eval #'eval) (print #'print)
        (prompt "> ") (input t) (output t))
  "Read an expression, evaluate it, and print the result(s).
  Does multiple values and binds: * ** *** - + ++ +++ / // ///"
  (let (* ** *** - + ++ +++ / // /// vals)
    ;; The above variables are all special, except VALS
    ;; The variable - holds the current input
    ;; * ** *** are the 3 most recent values
    ;; + ++ +++ are the 3 most recent inputs
    ;; / // /// are the 3 most recent lists of multiple-values
    (loop
      (fresh-line output)
      (princ prompt output)
      ;; First read and evaluate an expression
      (setf -   (funcall read input)
            vals (multiple-value-list (funcall eval -)))
      ;; Now update the history variables
      (setf +++ ++       /// //        *** (first ///)
            ++  +        //  /         **  (first //)
            +   -        /   vals      *   (first /))
      ;; Finally print the computed value(s)
      (dolist (value vals)
        (funcall print value output)))))
```

Answer 6.4

```
(defun compose (&rest functions)
  "Return the function that is the composition of all the args.
  i.e. (compose f g h) = (lambda (x) (f (g (h x))))."
  #'(lambda (x)
      (reduce #'funcall functions :from-end t :initial-value x)))
```

Answer 6.5

```
(defun compose (&rest functions)
  "Return the function that is the composition of all the args.
  i.e. (compose f g h) = (lambda (x) (f (g (h x))))."
  (case (length functions)
    (0 #'identity)
    (1 (first functions))
    (2 (let ((f (first functions))
             (g (second functions)))
         #'(lambda (x) (funcall f (funcall g x)))))
    (t #'(lambda (x)
           (reduce #'funcall functions :from-end t
                   :initial-value x)))))
```

Answer 6.8

```
(defun tree-search (states goal-p successors combiner)
  "Find a state that satisfies goal-p.  Start with states,
  and search according to successors and combiner."
  (loop
    (cond ((null states) (RETURN fail))
          ((funcall goal-p (first states))
           (RETURN (first states)))
          (t (setf states
                   (funcall combiner
                            (funcall successors (first states))
                            (rest states)))))))
```

Answer 6.9

```
(defun sorter (cost-fn)
  "Return a combiner function that sorts according to cost-fn."
  #'(lambda (new old)
      (merge 'list (sort new #'> :key cost-fn)
             old #'> :key cost-fn)))
```

Answer 6.11

```
(defun search-n (start n goal-p successors cost-fn beam-width)
  "Find n solutions to a search problem, using beam search."
  (let ((solutions nil))
    (beam-search
      start #'(lambda (x)
                (cond ((not (funcall goal-p x)) nil)
                      ((= n 0) x)
                      (t (decf n)
                         (push x solutions)
                         nil)))
      successors cost-fn beam-width)
    solutions))
```

CHAPTER 7

STUDENT: Solving Algebra Word Problems

> *[This] is an example par excellence* of the power of
> using meaning to solve linguistic problems.
>
> —Marvin Minsky (1968)
> MIT computer scientist

S TUDENT was another early language understanding program, written by Daniel Bobrow as his Ph.D. research project in 1964. It was designed to read and solve the kind of word problems found in high school algebra books. An example is:

If the number of customers Tom gets is twice the square of 20% of the number of advertisements he runs, and the number of advertisements is 45, then what is the number of customers Tom gets?

STUDENT could correctly reply that the number of customers is 162. To do this, STUDENT must be far more sophisticated than ELIZA; it must process and "understand" a great deal of the input, rather than just concentrate on a few key words. And it must compute a response, rather than just fill in blanks. However, we shall see that the STUDENT program uses little more than the pattern-matching techniques of ELIZA to translate the input into a set of algebraic equations. From there, it must know enough algebra to solve the equations, but that is not very difficult.

The version of STUDENT we develop here is nearly a full implementation of the original. However, remember that while the original was state-of-the-art as of 1964, AI has made some progress in a quarter century, as subsequent chapters will attempt to show.

7.1   Translating English into Equations

The description of STUDENT is:

1. Break the input into phrases that will represent equations.

2. Break each phrase into a pair of phrases on either side of the = sign.

3. Break these phrases down further into sums and products, and so on, until finally we bottom out with numbers and variables. (By "variable" here, I mean "mathematical variable," which is distinct from the idea of a "pattern-matching variable" as used in pat-match in chapter 6).

4. Translate each English phrase into a mathematical expression. We use the idea of a rule-based translator as developed for ELIZA.

5. Solve the resulting mathematical equations, coming up with a value for each unknown variable.

6. Print the values of all the variables.

For example, we might have a pattern of the form (If ?x then ?y), with an associated response that says that ?x and ?y will each be equations or lists of equations. Applying the pattern to the input above, ?y would have the value (what is the number of customers Tom gets). Another pattern of the form (?x is ?y) could have a response corresponding to an equation where ?x and ?y are the two sides of the equation. We could then make up a mathematical variable for (what) and another for (the number of customers Tom gets). We would recognize this later phrase as a variable because there are no patterns to break it down further. In contrast, the phrase (twice the square of 20 per cent of the number of advertisements he runs) could match a pattern of the form (twice ?x) and transform to (* 2 (the square of 20 per cent of the number of advertisements he runs)), and by further applying patterns of the form (the square of ?x) and (?x per cent of ?y) we could arrive at a final response of (* 2 (expt (* (/ 20 100) n) 2)), where n is the variable generated by (the number of advertisements he runs).

Thus, we need to represent variables, expressions, equations, and sets of equations. The easiest thing to do is to use something we know: represent them just as Lisp itself does. Variables will be symbols, expressions and equations will be nested lists with prefix operators, and sets of equations will be lists of equations. With that in mind, we can define a list of pattern-response rules corresponding to the type of statements found in algebra word problems. The structure definition for a rule is repeated here, and the structure exp, an expression, is added. lhs and rhs stand for left- and right-hand side, respectively. Note that the constructor mkexp is defined as a constructor that builds expressions without taking keyword arguments. In general, the notation (:constructor *fn args*) creates a constructor function with the given name and argument list.[1]

```
(defstruct (rule (:type list)) pattern response)

(defstruct (exp (:type list)
                (:constructor mkexp (lhs op rhs)))
   op lhs rhs)

(defun exp-p (x) (consp x))
(defun exp-args (x) (rest x))
```

We ignored commas and periods in ELIZA, but they are crucial for STUDENT, so we must make allowances for them. The problem is that a "," in Lisp normally can be used only within a backquote construction, and a "." normally can be used only as a decimal point or in a dotted pair. The special meaning of these characters to the Lisp reader can be escaped either by preceding the character with a backslash (\,) or by surrounding the character by vertical bars (|,|).

```
(pat-match-abbrev '?x* '(?* ?x))
(pat-match-abbrev '?y* '(?* ?y))

(defparameter *student-rules* (mapcar #'expand-pat-match-abbrev
  '(((?x* |.|)                  ?x)
    ((?x* |.| ?y*)             (?x ?y))
    ((if ?x* |,| then ?y*)     (?x ?y))
    ((if ?x* then ?y*)         (?x ?y))
    ((if ?x* |,| ?y*)          (?x ?y))
    ((?x* |,| and ?y*)         (?x ?y))
    ((find ?x* and ?y*)        ((= to-find-1 ?x) (= to-find-2 ?y)))
    ((find ?x*)                (= to-find ?x))
    ((?x* equals ?y*)          (= ?x ?y))
    ((?x* same as ?y*)         (= ?x ?y))
    ((?x* = ?y*)               (= ?x ?y))
    ((?x* is equal to ?y*)     (= ?x ?y))
    ((?x* is ?y*)              (= ?x ?y))
    ((?x* - ?y*)               (- ?x ?y))
    ((?x* minus ?y*)           (- ?x ?y))
```

[1] Page 316 of *Common Lisp the Language* says, "Because a constructor of this type operates By Order of Arguments, it is sometimes known as a BOA constructor."

```
((difference between ?x* and ?y*)  (- ?y ?x))
((difference ?x* and ?y*)          (- ?y ?x))
((?x* + ?y*)            (+ ?x ?y))
((?x* plus ?y*)         (+ ?x ?y))
((sum ?x* and ?y*)      (+ ?x ?y))
((product ?x* and ?y*)  (* ?x ?y))
((?x* * ?y*)            (* ?x ?y))
((?x* times ?y*)        (* ?x ?y))
((?x* / ?y*)            (/ ?x ?y))
((?x* per ?y*)          (/ ?x ?y))
((?x* divided by ?y*)   (/ ?x ?y))
((half ?x*)             (/ ?x 2))
((one half ?x*)         (/ ?x 2))
((twice ?x*)            (* 2 ?x))
((square ?x*)           (* ?x ?x))
((?x* % less than ?y*)  (* ?y (/ (- 100 ?x) 100)))
((?x* % more than ?y*)  (* ?y (/ (+ 100 ?x) 100)))
((?x* % ?y*)            (* (/ ?x 100) ?y)))))
```

The main section of STUDENT will search through the list of rules for a response, just as ELIZA did. The first point of deviation is that before we substitute the values of the pat-match variables into the response, we must first recursively translate the value of each variable, using the same list of pattern-response rules. The other difference is that once we're done, we don't just print the response; instead we have to solve the set of equations and print the answers. The program is summarized in figure 7.1.

Before looking carefully at the program, let's try a sample problem: "If z is 3, what is twice z?" Applying the rules to the input gives the following trace:

```
Input: (If z is 3, what is twice z)
Rule: ((if ?x |,| ?y)        (?x ?y))
Binding: ((?x . (z is 3)) (?y . (what is twice z)))
 Input: (z is 3)
 Rule: ((?x is ?y)           (= ?x ?y))
 Result: (= z 3)

 Input: (what is twice z ?)
 Rule: ((?x is ?y)           (= ?x ?y))
 Binding: ((?x . what) (?y . (twice z)))
  Input: (twice z)
  Rule: ((twice ?x)          (* 2 ?x))
  Result: (* 2 z)
 Result: (= what (* 2 z))
Result: ((= z 3) (= what (* 2 z)))
```

There are two minor complications. First, we agreed to implement sets of equations as lists of equations. For this example, everything worked out, and the response

	Top-Level Function
`student`	Solve certain algebra word problems.
	Special Variables
`*student-rules*`	A list of pattern/response pairs.
	Data Types
`exp`	An operator and its arguments.
`rule`	A pattern and response.
	Major Functions
`translate-to-expression`	Translate an English phrase into an equation or expression.
`translate-pair`	Translate the value part of the pair into an equation or expression.
`create-list-of-equations`	Separate out equations embedded in nested parens.
`solve-equations`	Print the equations and their solution.
`solve`	Solve a system of equations by constraint propagation.
	Auxiliary Functions
`isolate`	Isolate the lone variable on the left-hand side of an expression.
`noise-word-p`	Is this a low-content word that can be safely ignored?
`make-variable`	Create a variable name based on the given list of words.
`print-equations`	Print a list of equations.
`inverse-op`	I.e., the inverse of $+$ is $-$.
`unknown-p`	Is the argument an unknown (variable)?
`in-exp`	True if x appears anywhere in exp.
`no-unknown`	Returns true if there are no unknowns in exp.
`one-unknown`	Returns the single unknown in exp, if there is exactly one.
`commutative-p`	Is the operator commutative?
`solve-arithmetic`	Perform arithmetic on rhs of an equation.
`binary-exp-p`	Is this a binary expression?
`prefix->infix`	Translate prefix to infix expressions.
`mkexp`	Make an expression.
	Previously Defined Functions
`pat-match`	Match pattern against an input. (p. 180)
`rule-based-translator`	Apply a set of rules. (p. 189)

Figure 7.1: Glossary for the STUDENT Program

was a list of two equations. But if nested patterns are used, the response could be something like `((= a 5) ((= b (+ a 1)) (= c (+ a b))))`, which is not a list of equations. The function `create-list-of-equations` transforms a response like this into a proper list of equations. The other complication is choosing variable names. Given a list of words like `(the number of customers Tom gets)`, we want to choose a symbol to represent it. We will see below that the symbol `customers` is chosen, but that there are other possibilities.

Here is the main function for STUDENT. It first removes words that have no content, then translates the input to one big expression with `translate-to-expression`, and breaks that into separate equations with `create-list-of-equations`. Finally, the function `solve-equations` does the mathematics and prints the solution.

```
(defun student (words)
  "Solve certain Algebra Word Problems."
  (solve-equations
    (create-list-of-equations
      (translate-to-expression (remove-if #'noise-word-p words)))))
```

The function `translate-to-expression` is a rule-based translator. It either finds some rule in `*student-rules*` to transform the input, or it assumes that the entire input represents a single variable. The function `translate-pair` takes a variable/value binding pair and translates the value by a recursive call to `translate-to-expression`.

```
(defun translate-to-expression (words)
  "Translate an English phrase into an equation or expression."
  (or (rule-based-translator
        words *student-rules*
        :rule-if #'rule-pattern :rule-then #'rule-response
        :action #'(lambda (bindings response)
                    (sublis (mapcar #'translate-pair bindings)
                            response)))
      (make-variable words)))

(defun translate-pair (pair)
  "Translate the value part of the pair into an equation or expression."
  (cons (binding-var pair)
        (translate-to-expression (binding-val pair))))
```

The function `create-list-of-equations` takes a single expression containing embedded equations and separates them into a list of equations:

```
(defun create-list-of-equations (exp)
  "Separate out equations embedded in nested parens."
  (cond ((null exp) nil)
        ((atom (first exp)) (list exp))
        (t (append (create-list-of-equations (first exp))
                   (create-list-of-equations (rest exp))))))
```

Finally, the function `make-variable` creates a variable to represent a list of words. We do that by first removing all "noise words" from the input, and then taking the first symbol that remains. So, for example, "the distance John traveled" and "the distance traveled by John" will both be represented by the same variable, distance, which is certainly the right thing to do. However, "the distance Mary traveled" will also be represented by the same variable, which is certainly a mistake. For (the number of customers Tom gets), the variable will be customers, since the, of and number are all noise words. This will match (the customers mentioned above) and (the number of customers), but not (Tom's customers). For now, we will accept the first-non-noise-word solution, but note that exercise 7.3 asks for a correction.

```lisp
(defun make-variable (words)
  "Create a variable name based on the given list of words"
  ;; The list of words will already have noise words removed
  (first words))

(defun noise-word-p (word)
  "Is this a low-content word that can be safely ignored?"
  (member word '(a an the this number of $)))
```

7.2 Solving Algebraic Equations

The next step is to write the equation-solving section of STUDENT. This is more an exercise in elementary algebra than in AI, but it is a good example of a symbol-manipulation task, and thus an interesting programming problem.

The STUDENT program mentioned the function solve-equations, passing it one argument, a list of equations to be solved. solve-equations prints the list of equations, attempts to solve them using solve, and prints the result.

```lisp
(defun solve-equations (equations)
  "Print the equations and their solution"
  (print-equations "The equations to be solved are:" equations)
  (print-equations "The solution is:" (solve equations nil)))
```

The real work is done by solve, which has the following specification: (1) Find an equation with exactly one occurrence of an unknown in it. (2) Transform that equation so that the unknown is isolated on the left-hand side. This can be done if we limit the operators to +, -, *, and /. (3) Evaluate the arithmetic on the right-hand side, yielding a numeric value for the unknown. (4) Substitute the numeric value for the unknown in all the other equations, and remember the known value. Then try to solve the resulting set of equations. (5) If step (1) fails—if there is no equation with exactly one unknown—then just return the known values and don't try to solve anything else.

The function solve is passed a system of equations, along with a list of known variable/value pairs. Initially no variables are known, so this list will be empty. solve goes through the list of equations searching for an equation with exactly one unknown. If it can find such an equation, it calls isolate to solve the equation in terms of that one unknown. solve then substitutes the value for the variable throughout the list of equations and calls itself recursively on the resulting list. Each time solve calls itself, it removes one equation from the list of equations to be solved, and adds one to the list of known variable/value pairs. Since the list of equations is always growing shorter, solve must eventually terminate.

```
(defun solve (equations known)
  "Solve a system of equations by constraint propagation."
  ;; Try to solve for one equation, and substitute its value into
  ;; the others. If that doesn't work, return what is known.
  (or (some #'(lambda (equation)
                (let ((x (one-unknown equation)))
                  (when x
                    (let ((answer (solve-arithmetic
                                    (isolate equation x))))
                      (solve (subst (exp-rhs answer) (exp-lhs answer)
                                    (remove equation equations))
                             (cons answer known))))))
            equations)
      known))
```

isolate is passed an equation guaranteed to have one unknown. It returns an equivalent equation with the unknown isolated on the left-hand side. There are five cases to consider: when the unknown is alone on the left, we're done. The second case is when the unknown is anywhere on the right-hand side. Because '=' is commutative, we can reduce the problem to solving the equivalent equation with left- and right-hand sides reversed.

Next we have to deal with the case where the unknown is in a complex expression on the left-hand side. Because we are allowing four operators and the unknown can be either on the right or the left, there are eight possibilities. Letting X stand for an expression containing the unknown and A and B stand for expressions with no unknowns, the possibilities and their solutions are as follows:

(1) X*A=B $\Rightarrow$ X=B/A   (5) A*X=B $\Rightarrow$ X=B/A

(2) X+A=B $\Rightarrow$ X=B-A   (6) A+X=B $\Rightarrow$ X=B-A

(3) X/A=B $\Rightarrow$ X=B*A   (7) A/X=B $\Rightarrow$ X=A/B

(4) X-A=B $\Rightarrow$ X=B+A   (8) A-X=B $\Rightarrow$ X=A-B

Possibilities (1) through (4) are handled by case III, (5) and (6) by case IV, and (7) and (8) by case V. In each case, the transformation does not give us the final answer, since X need not be the unknown; it might be a complex expression involving the unknown. So we have to call isolate again on the resulting equation. The reader should try to verify that transformations (1) to (8) are valid, and that cases III to V implement them properly.

```
(defun isolate (e x)
  "Isolate the lone x in e on the left-hand side of e."
  ;; This assumes there is exactly one x in e,
  ;; and that e is an equation.
  (cond ((eq (exp-lhs e) x)
         ;; Case I: X = A -> X = n
         e)
        ((in-exp x (exp-rhs e))
         ;; Case II: A = f(X) -> f(X) = A
         (isolate (mkexp (exp-rhs e) '= (exp-lhs e)) x))
        ((in-exp x (exp-lhs (exp-lhs e)))
         ;; Case III: f(X)*A = B -> f(X) = B/A
         (isolate (mkexp (exp-lhs (exp-lhs e)) '=
                         (mkexp (exp-rhs e)
                                (inverse-op (exp-op (exp-lhs e)))
                                (exp-rhs (exp-lhs e)))) x))
        ((commutative-p (exp-op (exp-lhs e)))
         ;; Case IV: A*f(X) = B -> f(X) = B/A
         (isolate (mkexp (exp-rhs (exp-lhs e)) '=
                         (mkexp (exp-rhs e)
                                (inverse-op (exp-op (exp-lhs e)))
                                (exp-lhs (exp-lhs e)))) x))
        (t ;; Case V: A/f(X) = B -> f(X) = A/B
         (isolate (mkexp (exp-rhs (exp-lhs e)) '=
                         (mkexp (exp-lhs (exp-lhs e))
                                (exp-op (exp-lhs e))
                                (exp-rhs e))) x))))
```

Recall that to prove a function is correct, we have to prove both that it gives the correct answer when it terminates and that it will eventually terminate. For a recursive function with several alternative cases, we must show that each alternative is valid, and also that each alternative gets closer to the end in some way (that any recursive calls involve 'simpler' arguments). For isolate, elementary algebra will show that each step is valid—or at least *nearly* valid. Dividing both sides of an equation by 0 does not yield an equivalent equation, and we never checked for that. It's also possible that similar errors could sneak in during the call to eval. However, if we assume the equation does have a single valid solution, then isolate performs only legal transformations.

The hard part is to prove that isolate terminates. Case I clearly terminates, and the others all contribute towards isolating the unknown on the left-hand side. For any equation, the sequence will be first a possible use of case II, followed by a number of recursive calls using cases III to V. The number of calls is bounded by the number of subexpressions in the equation, since each successive call effectively removes an expression from the left and places it on the right. Therefore, assuming the input is of finite size, we must eventually reach a recursive call to isolate that will use case I and terminate.

When isolate returns, the right-hand side must consist only of numbers and operators. We could easily write a function to evaluate such an expression. However, we don't have to go to that effort, since the function already exists. The data structure exp was carefully selected to be the same structure (lists with prefix functions) used by Lisp itself for its own expressions. So Lisp will find the right-hand side to be an acceptable expression, one that could be evaluated if typed in to the top level. Lisp evaluates expressions by calling the function eval, so we can call eval directly and have it return a number. The function solve-arithmetic returns an equation of the form (= *var number*).

Auxiliary functions for solve are shown below. Most are straightforward, but I will remark on a few of them. The function prefix->infix takes an expression in prefix notation and converts it to a fully parenthesized infix expression. Unlike isolate, it assumes the expressions will be implemented as lists. prefix->infix is used by print-equations to produce more readable output.

```
(defun print-equations (header equations)
  "Print a list of equations."
  (format t "~%~a~{~%   ~{ ~a~}~}~%" header
          (mapcar #'prefix->infix equations)))

(defconstant operators-and-inverses
  '((+ -) (- +) (* /) (/ *) (= =)))

(defun inverse-op (op)
  (second (assoc op operators-and-inverses)))

(defun unknown-p (exp)
  (symbolp exp))

(defun in-exp (x exp)
  "True if x appears anywhere in exp"
  (or (eq x exp)
      (and (exp-p exp)
           (or (in-exp x (exp-lhs exp)) (in-exp x (exp-rhs exp))))))

(defun no-unknown (exp)
  "Returns true if there are no unknowns in exp."
  (cond ((unknown-p exp) nil)
        ((atom exp) t)
        ((no-unknown (exp-lhs exp)) (no-unknown (exp-rhs exp)))
        (t nil)))
```

```
(defun one-unknown (exp)
  "Returns the single unknown in exp, if there is exactly one."
  (cond ((unknown-p exp) exp)
        ((atom exp) nil)
        ((no-unknown (exp-lhs exp)) (one-unknown (exp-rhs exp)))
        ((no-unknown (exp-rhs exp)) (one-unknown (exp-lhs exp)))
        (t nil)))

(defun commutative-p (op)
  "Is operator commutative?"
  (member op '(+ * =)))

(defun solve-arithmetic (equation)
  "Do the arithmetic for the right-hand side."
  ;; This assumes that the right-hand side is in the right form.
  (mkexp (exp-lhs equation) '= (eval (exp-rhs equation))))

(defun binary-exp-p (x)
  (and (exp-p x) (= (length (exp-args x)) 2)))

(defun prefix->infix (exp)
  "Translate prefix to infix expressions."
  (if (atom exp) exp
      (mapcar #'prefix->infix
              (if (binary-exp-p exp)
                  (list (exp-lhs exp) (exp-op exp) (exp-rhs exp))
                  exp))))
```

Here's an example of `solve-equations` in action, with a system of two equations. The reader should go through the trace, discovering which case was used at each call to `isolate`, and verifying that each step is accurate.

```
> (trace isolate solve)
(isolate solve)

> (solve-equations '((= (+ 3 4) (* (- 5 (+ 2 x)) 7))
                     (= (+ (* 3 x) y) 12)))
The equations to be solved are:
   (3 + 4) = ((5 - (2 + X)) * 7)
   ((3 * X) + Y) = 12
(1 ENTER SOLVE: ((= (+ 3 4) (* (- 5 (+ 2 X)) 7))
                (= (+ (* 3 X) Y) 12)) NIL)
  (1 ENTER ISOLATE: (= (+ 3 4) (* (- 5 (+ 2 X)) 7)) X)
    (2 ENTER ISOLATE: (= (* (- 5 (+ 2 X)) 7) (+ 3 4)) X)
      (3 ENTER ISOLATE: (= (- 5 (+ 2 X)) (/ (+ 3 4) 7)) X)
        (4 ENTER ISOLATE: (= (+ 2 X) (- 5 (/ (+ 3 4) 7))) X)
          (5 ENTER ISOLATE: (= X (- (- 5 (/ (+ 3 4) 7)) 2)) X)
          (5 EXIT ISOLATE: (= X (- (- 5 (/ (+ 3 4) 7)) 2)))
        (4 EXIT ISOLATE: (= X (- (- 5 (/ (+ 3 4) 7)) 2)))
```

```
        (3 EXIT ISOLATE: (= X (- (- 5 (/ (+ 3 4) 7)) 2)))
       (2 EXIT ISOLATE: (= X (- (- 5 (/ (+ 3 4) 7)) 2)))
      (1 EXIT ISOLATE: (= X (- (- 5 (/ (+ 3 4) 7)) 2)))
      (2 ENTER SOLVE: ((= (+ (* 3 2) Y) 12)) ((= X 2)))
        (1 ENTER ISOLATE: (= (+ (* 3 2) Y) 12) Y)
         (2 ENTER ISOLATE: (= Y (- 12 (* 3 2))) Y)
         (2 EXIT ISOLATE: (= Y (- 12 (* 3 2))))
        (1 EXIT ISOLATE: (= Y (- 12 (* 3 2))))
        (3 ENTER SOLVE: NIL ((= Y 6) (= X 2)))
        (3 EXIT SOLVE: ((= Y 6) (= X 2)))
      (2 EXIT SOLVE: ((= Y 6) (= X 2)))
    (1 EXIT SOLVE: ((= Y 6) (= X 2)))
    The solution is:
      Y = 6
      X = 2
    NIL
```

Now let's tackle the format string `"~%~a~{~% ~{ ~a~}~}~%"` in print-equations. This may look like random gibberish, but there is actually sense behind it. format processes the string by printing each character, except that `"~"` indicates some special formatting action, depending on the following character. The combination `"~%"` prints a newline, and `"~a"` prints the next argument to format that has not been used yet. Thus the first four characters of the format string, `"~%~a"`, print a newline followed by the argument header. The combination `"~{"` treats the corresponding argument as a list, and processes each element according to the specification between the `"~{"` and the next `"~}"`. In this case, equations is a list of equations, so each one gets printed with a newline (`"~%"`) followed by two spaces, followed by the processing of the equation itself as a list, where each element is printed in the `"~a"` format and preceded by a blank. The t given as the first argument to format means to print to the standard output; another output stream may be specified there.

One of the annoying minor holes in Lisp is that there is no standard convention on where to print newlines! In C, for example, the very first line of code in the reference manual is

```
printf("hello, world\n");
```

This makes it clear that newlines are printed *after* each line. This convention is so ingrained in the UNIX world that some UNIX programs will go into an infinite loop if the last line in a file is not terminated by a newline. In Lisp, however, the function print puts in a newline *before* the object to be printed, and a space after. Some Lisp programs carry the newline-before policy over to format, and others use the newline-after policy. This only becomes a problem when you want to combine two programs written under different policies. How did the two competing policies arise? In UNIX there was only one reasonable policy, because all input to the UNIX interpreter (the shell) is terminated by newlines, so there is no need for a newline-before. In some Lisp interpreters, however, input can be terminated by a matching right parenthesis. In that case, a newline-before is needed, lest the output appear on the same line as the input.

> **Exercise 7.1 [m]** Implement `print-equations` using only primitive printing functions such as `terpri` and `princ`, along with explicit loops.

7.3 Examples

Now we move on to examples, taken from Bobrow's thesis. In the first example, it is necessary to insert a "then" before the word "what" to get the right answer:

```
> (student '(If the number of customers Tom gets is twice the square of
             20 % of the number of advertisements he runs |,|
             and the number of advertisements is 45 |,|
             then what is the number of customers Tom gets ?))
The equations to be solved are:
   CUSTOMERS = (2 * (((20 / 100) * ADVERTISEMENTS) *
                     ((20 / 100) * ADVERTISEMENTS)))
   ADVERTISEMENTS = 45
   WHAT = CUSTOMERS

The solution is:
   WHAT = 162
   CUSTOMERS = 162
   ADVERTISEMENTS = 45
NIL
```

Notice that our program prints the values for all variables it can solve for, while Bobrow's program only printed the values that were explicitly asked for in the text. This is an example of "more is less"—it may look impressive to print all the answers, but it is actually easier to do so than to decide just what answers should be printed. The following example is not solved correctly:

```
> (student '(The daily cost of living for a group is the overhead cost plus
            the running cost for each person times the number of people in
            the group |.|  This cost for one group equals $ 100 |,|
            and the number of people in the group is 40 |.|
            If the overhead cost is 10 times the running cost |,|
            find the overhead and running cost for each person |.|))
The equations to be solved are:
    DAILY = (OVERHEAD + (RUNNING * PEOPLE))
    COST = 100
    PEOPLE = 40
    OVERHEAD = (10 * RUNNING)
    TO-FIND-1 = OVERHEAD
    TO-FIND-2 = RUNNING

The solution is:
    PEOPLE = 40
    COST = 100
NIL
```

This example points out two important limitations of our version of student as compared to Bobrow's. The first problem is in naming of variables. The phrases "the daily cost of living for a group" and "this cost" are meant to refer to the same quantity, but our program gives them the names daily and cost respectively. Bobrow's program handled naming by first considering phrases to be the same only if they matched perfectly. If the resulting set of equations could not be solved, he would try again, this time considering phrases with words in common to be identical. (See the following exercises.)

The other problem is in our solve function. Assuming we got the variables equated properly, solve would be able to boil the set of equations down to two:

```
100 = (OVERHEAD + (RUNNING * 40))
OVERHEAD = (10 * RUNNING)
```

This is a set of two linear equations in two unknowns and has a unique solution at RUNNING = 2, OVERHEAD = 20. But our version of solve couldn't find this solution, since it looks for equations with one unknown. Here is another example that student handles well:

```
> (student '(Fran's age divided by Robin's height is one half Kelly's IQ |.|
            Kelly's IQ minus 80 is Robin's height |.|
            If Robin is 4 feet tall |,| how old is Fran ?))
The equations to be solved are:
    (FRAN / ROBIN) = (KELLY / 2)
    (KELLY - 80) = ROBIN
    ROBIN = 4
```

```
        HOW = FRAN
The solution is:
   HOW = 168
   FRAN = 168
   KELLY = 84
   ROBIN = 4
NIL
```

But a slight variation leads to a problem:

```
> (student '(Fran's age divided by Robin's height is one half Kelly's IQ |.|
             Kelly's IQ minus 80 is Robin's height |.|
             If Robin is 0 feet tall |,| how old is Fran ?))
The equations to be solved are:
   (FRAN / ROBIN) = (KELLY / 2)
   (KELLY - 80) = ROBIN
   ROBIN = 0
   HOW = FRAN

The solution is:
   HOW = 0
   FRAN = 0
   KELLY = 80
   ROBIN = 0
NIL
```

There is no valid solution to this problem, because it involves dividing by zero (Robin's height). But student is willing to transform the first equation into:

```
FRAN = ROBIN * (KELLY / 2)
```

and then substitutes to get 0 for FRAN. Worse, dividing by zero could also come up inside eval:

```
> (student '(Fran's age times Robin's height is one half Kelly's IQ |.|
             Kelly's IQ minus 80 is Robin's height |.|
             If Robin is 0 feet tall |,| how old is Fran ?))
The equations to be solved are:
   (FRAN * ROBIN) = (KELLY / 2)
   (KELLY - 80) = ROBIN
   ROBIN = 0
   HOW = FRAN
```

```
>>Error: There was an attempt to divide a number by zero
```

However, one could claim that nasty examples with division by zero don't show up in algebra texts.

In summary, STUDENT behaves reasonably well, doing far more than the toy program ELIZA. STUDENT is also quite efficient; on my machine it takes less than one second for each of the prior examples. However, it could still be extended to have more powerful equation-solving capabilities. Its linguistic coverage is another matter. While one could add new patterns, such patterns are really just tricks, and don't capture the underlying structure of English sentences. That is why the STUDENT approach was abandoned as a research topic.

7.4 History and References

Bobrow's Ph.D. thesis contains a complete description of STUDENT. It is reprinted in Minsky 1968. Since then, there have been several systems that address the same task, with increased sophistication in both their mathematical and linguistic ability. Wong (1981) describes a system that uses its understanding of the problem to get a better linguistic analysis. Sterling et al. (1982) present a much more powerful equation solver, but it does not accept natural language input. Certainly Bobrow's language analysis techniques were not very sophisticated by today's measures. But that was largely the point: if you know that the language is describing an algebraic problem of a certain type, then you don't need to know very much linguistics to get the right answer most of the time.

7.5 Exercises

Exercise 7.2 [h] We said earlier that our program was unable to solve pairs of linear equations, such as:

```
100 = (OVERHEAD + (RUNNING * 40))
OVERHEAD = (10 * RUNNING)
```

The original STUDENT could solve these equations. Write a routine to do so. You may assume there will be only two equations in two unknowns if you wish, or if you are more ambitious, you could solve a system of n linear equations with n unknowns.

Exercise 7.3 [h] Implement a version of Bobrow's variable-naming algorithm. Instead of taking the first word of each equation, create a unique symbol, and associate with it the entire list of words. In the first pass, each nonequal list of words will be considered a distinct variable. If no solution is reached, word lists that share words in common are considered to be the same variable, and the solution is attempted again. For example, an input that contains the phrases "the rectangle's width" and "the width of the rectangle" might assign these two phrases the variables v1 and v2. If an attempt to solve the problem yields no solutions, the program should realize that v1 and v2 have the words "rectangle" and "width" in common, and add the equation (= v1 v2) and try again. Since the variables are arbitrary symbols, the printing routine should probably print the phrases associated with each variable rather than the variable itself.

Exercise 7.4 [h] The original STUDENT also had a set of "common knowledge" equations that it could use when necessary. These were mostly facts about conversion factors, such as (1 inch = 2.54 cm). Also included were equations like (distance equals rate times time), which could be used to solve problems like "If the distance from Anabru to Champaign is 10 miles and the time it takes Sandy to travel this distance is 2 hours, what is Sandy's rate of speed?" Make changes to incorporate this facility. It probably only helps in conjunction with a solution to the previous exercise.

Exercise 7.5 [h] Change student so that it prints values only for those variables that are being asked for in the problem. That is, given the problem "X is 3. Y is 4. How much is X + Y?" it should not print values for X and Y.

Exercise 7.6 [m] Try STUDENT on the following examples. Make sure you handle special characters properly:

(a) The price of a radio is 69.70 dollars. If this price is 15% less than the marked price, find the marked price.

(b) The number of soldiers the Russians have is one half of the number of guns they have. The number of guns they have is 7000. What is the number of soldiers they have?

(c) If the number of customers Tom gets is twice the square of 20% of the number of advertisements he runs, and the number of advertisements is 45, and the profit Tom receives is 10 times the number of customers he gets, then what is the profit?

(d) The average score is 73. The maximum score is 97. What is the square of the difference between the average and the maximum?

(e) Tom is twice Mary's age, and Jane's age is half the difference between Mary and Tom. If Mary is 18 years old, how old is Jane?

(f) What is $4 + 5 * 14 / 7$?

(g) $x \times b = c + d. \ b \times c = x. \ x = b + b. \ b = 5.$

Exercise 7.7 [h]   Student's infix-to-prefix rules account for the priority of operators properly, but they don't handle associativity in the standard fashion. For example, (12 - 6 - 3) translates to (- 12 (- 6 3)) or 9, when the usual convention is to interpret this as (- (- 12 6) 3) or 3. Fix student to handle this convention.

Exercise 7.8 [d]   Find a mathematically oriented domain that is sufficiently limited so that STUDENT can solve problems in it. The chemistry of solutions (calculating pH concentrations) might be an example. Write the necessary *student-rules*, and test the resulting program.

Exercise 7.9 [m]   Analyze the complexity of one-unknown and implement a more efficient version.

Exercise 7.10 [h]   Bobrow's paper on STUDENT (1968) includes an appendix that abstractly characterizes all the problems that his system can solve. Generate a similar characterization for this version of the program.

7.6   Answers

Answer 7.1

```
(defun print-equations (header equations)
  (terpri)
  (princ header)
  (dolist (equation equations)
    (terpri)
    (princ "  ")
    (dolist (x (prefix->infix equation))
      (princ " ")
      (princ x))))
```

Answer 7.9 one-unknown is very inefficient because it searches each subcomponent of an expression twice. For example, consider the equation:

```
(= (+ (+ x 2) (+ 3 4)) (+ (+ 5 6) (+ 7 8)))
```

To decide if this has one unknown, one-unknown will call no-unknown on the left-hand side, and since it fails, call it again on the right-hand side. Although there are only eight atoms to consider, it ends up calling no-unknown 17 times and one-unknown 4 times. In general, for a tree of depth n, approximately 2^n calls to no-unknown are made. This is clearly wasteful; there should be no need to look at each component more than once.

The following version uses an auxiliary function, find-one-unknown, that has an accumulator parameter, unknown. This parameter can take on three possible values: nil, indicating that no unknown has been found; or the single unknown that has been found so far; or the number 2 indicating that two unknowns have been found and therefore the final result should be nil. The function find-one-unknown has four cases: (1) If we have already found two unknowns, then return 2 to indicate this. (2) If the input expression is a nonatomic expression, then first look at its left-hand side for unknowns, and pass the result found in that side as the accumulator to a search of the right-hand side. (3) If the expression is an unknown, and if it is the second one found, return 2; otherwise return the unknown itself. (4) If the expression is an atom that is not an unknown, then just return the accumulated result.

```
(defun one-unknown (exp)
  "Returns the single unknown in exp, if there is exactly one."
  (let ((answer (find-one-unknown exp nil)))
    ;; If there were two unknowns, return nil;
    ;; otherwise return the unknown (if there was one)
    (if (eql answer 2)
        nil
        answer)))

(defun find-one-unknown (exp unknown)
  "Assuming UNKNOWN is the unknown(s) found so far, decide
  if there is exactly one unknown in the entire expression."
  (cond ((eql unknown 2) 2)
        ((exp-p exp)
         (find-one-unknown
           (exp-rhs exp)
           (find-one-unknown (exp-lhs exp) unknown)))
        ((unknown-p exp)
         (if unknown
             2
             exp))
        (t unknown)))
```

CHAPTER **8**

Symbolic Mathematics:
A Simplification Program

Our life is frittered away by detail. . . .
Simplify, simplify.

—Henry David Thoreau, *Walden* (1854)

"Symbolic mathematics" is to numerical mathematics as algebra is to arithmetic: it deals with variables and expressions rather than just numbers. Computers were first developed primarily to solve arithmetic problems: to add up large columns of numbers, to multiply many-digit numbers, to solve systems of linear equations, and to calculate the trajectories of ballistics. Encouraged by success in these areas, people hoped that computers could also be used on more complex problems; to differentiate or integrate a mathematical expression and come up with another expression as the answer, rather than just a number. Several programs were developed along these lines in the 1960s and 1970s. They were used primarily by professional mathematicians and physicists with access to large mainframe computers. Recently, programs like MATHLAB, DERIVE, and MATHEMATICA have given these capabilities to the average personal computer user.

It is interesting to look at some of the history of symbolic algebra, beginning in 1963 with SAINT, James Slagle's program to do symbolic integration. Originally, SAINT was heralded as a triumph of AI. It used general problem-solving techniques, similar in kind to GPS, to search for solutions to difficult problems. The program worked its way through an integration problem by choosing among the techniques known to it and backing up when an approach failed to pan out. SAINT's behavior on such problems was originally similar to (and eventually much better than) the performance of undergraduate calculus students.

Over time, the AI component of symbolic integration began to disappear. Joel Moses implemented a successor to SAINT called SIN. It used many of the same techniques, but instead of relying on search to find the right combination of techniques, it had additional mathematical knowledge that led it to pick the right technique at each step, without any provision for backing up and trying an alternative. SIN solved more problems and was much faster than SAINT, although it was not perfect: it still occasionally made the wrong choice and failed to solve a problem it could have.

By 1970, the mathematician R. Risch and others developed algorithms for indefinite integration of any expression involving algebraic, logarithmic, or exponential extensions of rational functions. In other words, given a "normal" function, the Risch algorithm will return either the indefinite integral of the function or an indication that no closed-form integral is possible in terms of elementary functions. Such work effectively ended the era of considering integration as a problem in search.

SIN was further refined, merged with parts of the Risch algorithm, and put into the evolving MACSYMA[1] program. For the most part, refinement of MACSYMA consisted of the incorporation of new algorithms. Few heuristics of any sort survive. Today MACSYMA is no longer considered an AI program. It is used daily by scientists and mathematicians, while ELIZA and STUDENT are now but historical footnotes.

With ELIZA and STUDENT we were able to develop miniature programs that duplicated most of the features of the original. We won't even try to develop a program worthy of the name MACSYMA; instead we will settle for a modest program to do symbolic simplification, which we will call (simply) `simplifier`. Then, we will extend `simplifier` to do differentiation, and some integration problems. The idea is that given an expression like $(2 - 1)x + 0$, we want the program to compute the simplified form x.

According to the *Mathematics Dictionary* (James and James 1949), the word "simplified" is "probably the most indefinite term used seriously in mathematics." The problem is that "simplified" is relative to what you want to use the expression for next. Which is simpler, $x^2 + 3x + 2$ or $(x + 1)(x + 2)$? The first makes it easier to

---

[1]MACSYMA is the Project MAC SYMbolic MAthematics program. Project MAC is the MIT research organization that was the precursor of MIT's Laboratory for Computer Science. MAC stood either for Machine-Aided Cognition or Multiple-Access Computer, according to one of their annual reports. The cynical have claimed that MAC really stood for Man Against Computer.

integrate or differentiate, the second easier to find roots. We will be content to limit ourselves to "obvious" simplifications. For example, x is almost always preferable to $1x + 0$.

8.1   Converting Infix to Prefix Notation

We will represent simplifications as a list of rules, much like the rules for STUDENT and ELIZA. But since each simplification rule is an algebraic equation, we will store each one as an exp rather than as a `rule`. To make things more legible, we will write each expression in infix form, but store them in the prefix form expected by exp. This requires an `infix->prefix` function to convert infix expressions into prefix notation. We have a choice as to how general we want our infix notation to be. Consider:

```
(((a * (x ^ 2)) + (b * x)) + c)
(a * x ^ 2 + b * x + c)
(a x ^ 2 + b x + c)
a x^2 + b*x+c
```

The first is fully parenthesized infix, the second makes use of operator precedence (multiplication binds tighter than addition and is thus performed first), and the third makes use of implicit multiplication as well as operator precedence. The fourth requires a lexical analyzer to break Lisp symbols into pieces.

Suppose we only wanted to handle the fully parenthesized case. To write `infix->prefix`, one might first look at `prefix->infix` (on page 228) trying to adapt it to our new purposes. In doing so, the careful reader might discover a surprise: `infix->prefix` and `prefix->infix` are in fact the exact same function! Both leave atoms unchanged, and both transform three-element lists by swapping the `exp-op` and `exp-lhs`. Both apply themselves recursively to the (possibly rearranged) input list. Once we discover this fact, it would be tempting to avoid writing `infix->prefix`, and just call `prefix->infix` instead. Avoid this temptation at all costs. Instead, define `infix->prefix` as shown below. The intent of your code will be clearer:

```
(defun infix->prefix (infix-exp)
  "Convert fully parenthesized infix-exp to a prefix expression"
  ;; Don't use this version for non-fully parenthesized exps!
  (prefix->infix infix-exp))
```

As we saw above, fully parenthesized infix can be quite ugly, with all those extra parentheses, so instead we will use operator precedence. There are a number of ways of doing this, but the easiest way for us to proceed is to use our previously defined tool `rule-based-translator` and its subtool, `pat-match`. Note that the third clause of infix->prefix, the one that calls rule-based-translator is unusual in that it consists of a single expression. Most cond-clauses have two expressions: a test and a result, but ones like this mean, "Evaluate the test, and if it is non-nil, return it. Otherwise go on to the next clause."

```lisp
(defun infix->prefix (exp)
  "Translate an infix expression into prefix notation."
  ;; Note we cannot do implicit multiplication in this system
  (cond ((atom exp) exp)
        ((= (length exp) 1) (infix->prefix (first exp)))
        ((rule-based-translator exp *infix->prefix-rules*
           :rule-if #'rule-pattern :rule-then #'rule-response
           :action
           #'(lambda (bindings response)
               (sublis (mapcar
                         #'(lambda (pair)
                             (cons (first pair)
                                   (infix->prefix (rest pair))))
                         bindings)
                       response))))
        ((symbolp (first exp))
         (list (first exp) (infix->prefix (rest exp))))
        (t (error "Illegal exp"))))
```

Because we are doing mathematics in this chapter, we adopt the mathematical convention of using certain one-letter variables, and redefine variable-p so that variables are only the symbols m through z.

```lisp
(defun variable-p (exp)
  "Variables are the symbols M through Z."
  ;; put x,y,z first to find them a little faster
  (member exp '(x y z m n o p q r s t u v w)))

(pat-match-abbrev 'x+ '(?+ x))
(pat-match-abbrev 'y+ '(?+ y))

(defun rule-pattern (rule) (first rule))
(defun rule-response (rule) (second rule))
```

```
(defparameter *infix->prefix-rules*
  (mapcar #'expand-pat-match-abbrev
    '(((x+ = y+) (= x y))
      ((- x+)    (- x))
      ((+ x+)    (+ x))
      ((x+ + y+) (+ x y))
      ((x+ - y+) (- x y))
      ((x+ * y+) (* x y))
      ((x+ / y+) (/ x y))
      ((x+ ^ y+) (^ x y))))
    "A list of rules, ordered by precedence.")
```

8.2   Simplification Rules

Now we are ready to define the simplification rules. We use the definition of the data types `rule` and `exp` (page 221) and `prefix->infix` (page 228) from STUDENT. They are repeated here:

```
(defstruct (rule (:type list)) pattern response)

(defstruct (exp (:type list)
                (:constructor mkexp (lhs op rhs)))
  op lhs rhs)

(defun exp-p (x) (consp x))
(defun exp-args (x) (rest x))

(defun prefix->infix (exp)
  "Translate prefix to infix expressions."
  (if (atom exp) exp
      (mapcar #'prefix->infix
              (if (binary-exp-p exp)
                  (list (exp-lhs exp) (exp-op exp) (exp-rhs exp))
                  exp))))

(defun binary-exp-p (x)
  (and (exp-p x) (= (length (exp-args x)) 2)))
```

We also use `rule-based-translator` (page 188) once again, this time on a list of simplification rules. A reasonable list of simplification rules is shown below. This list covers the four arithmetic operators, addition, subtraction, multiplication, and division, as well as exponentiation (raising to a power), denoted by the symbol "^".

Again, it is important to note that the rules are ordered, and that later rules will be applied only when earlier rules do not match. So, for example, 0 / 0 simplifies to undefined, and not to 1 or 0, because the rule for 0 / 0 comes before the other rules. See exercise 8.8 for a more complete treatment of this.

```
(defparameter *simplification-rules* (mapcar #'infix->prefix '(
  (x + 0   = x)
  (0 + x   = x)
  (x + x   = 2 * x)
  (x - 0   = x)
  (0 - x   = - x)
  (x - x   = 0)
  (- - x   = x)
  (x * 1   = x)
  (1 * x   = x)
  (x * 0   = 0)
  (0 * x   = 0)
  (x * x   = x ^ 2)
  (x / 0   = undefined)
  (0 / x   = 0)
  (x / 1   = x)
  (x / x   = 1)
  (0 ^ 0   = undefined)
  (x ^ 0   = 1)
  (0 ^ x   = 0)
  (1 ^ x   = 1)
  (x ^ 1   = x)
  (x ^ -1 = 1 / x)
  (x * (y / x) = y)
  ((y / x) * x = y)
  ((y * x) / x = y)
  ((x * y) / x = y)
  (x + - x = 0)
  ((- x) + x = 0)
  (x + y - x = y)
  )))

(defun ^ (x y) "Exponentiation" (expt x y))
```

We are now ready to go ahead and write the simplifier. The main function, simplifier, will repeatedly print a prompt, read an input, and print it in simplified form. Input and output is in infix and the computation is in prefix, so we need to convert accordingly; the function simp does this, and the function simplify takes care of a single prefix expression. It is summarized in figure 8.1.

Top-Level Functions	
simplifier	A read-simplify-print loop.
simp	Simplify an infix expression.
simplify	Simplify a prefix expression.
Special Variables	
infix->prefix-rules	Rules to translate from infix to prefix.
simplification-rules	Rules to simplify an expression.
Data Types	
exp	A prefix expression.
Auxiliary Functions	
simplify-exp	Simplify a non-atomic prefix expression.
infix->prefix	Convert infix to prefix notation.
variable-p	The symbols m through z are variables.
^	An alias for expt, exponentiation.
evaluable	Decide if an expression can be numerically evaluated.
simp-rule	Transform a rule into proper format.
length=1	Is the argument a list of length 1?
Previous Functions	
pat-match	Match pattern against an input. (p. 180)
rule-based-translator	Apply a set of rules. (p. 189)
pat-match-abbrev	Define an abbreviation for use in pat-match.

Figure 8.1: Glossary for the Simplifier

Here is the program:

```
(defun simplifier ()
  "Read a mathematical expression, simplify it, and print the result."
  (loop
    (print 'simplifier>)
    (print (simp (read)))))

(defun simp (inf) (prefix->infix (simplify (infix->prefix inf))))

(defun simplify (exp)
  "Simplify an expression by first simplifying its components."
  (if (atom exp) exp
      (simplify-exp (mapcar #'simplify exp))))

(defun simplify-exp (exp)
  "Simplify using a rule, or by doing arithmetic."
  (cond ((rule-based-translator exp *simplification-rules*
           :rule-if #'exp-lhs :rule-then #'exp-rhs
           :action #'(lambda (bindings response)
                       (simplify (sublis bindings response)))))
        ((evaluable exp) (eval exp))
        (t exp)))
```

```
(defun evaluable (exp)
  "Is this an arithmetic expression that can be evaluated?"
  (and (every #'numberp (exp-args exp))
       (or (member (exp-op exp) '(+ - * /))
           (and (eq (exp-op exp) '^)
                (integerp (second (exp-args exp)))))))
```

The function simplify assures that any compound expression will be simplified by first simplifying the arguments and then calling simplify-exp. This latter function searches through the simplification rules, much like use-eliza-rules and translate-to-expression. When it finds a match, simplify-exp substitutes in the proper variable values and calls simplify on the result. simplify-exp also has the ability to call eval to simplify an arithmetic expression to a number. As in STUDENT, it is for the sake of this eval that we require expressions to be represented as lists in prefix notation. Numeric evaluation is done *after* checking the rules so that the rules can intercept expressions like (/ 1 0) and simplify them to undefined. If we did the numeric evaluation first, these expressions would yield an error when passed to eval. Because Common Lisp supports arbitrary precision rational numbers (fractions), we are guaranteed there will be no round-off error, unless the input explicitly includes inexact (floating-point) numbers. Notice that we allow computations involving the four arithmetic operators, but exponentiation is only allowed if the exponent is an integer. That is because expressions like (^ 4 1/2) are not guaranteed to return 2 (the exact square root of 4); the answer might be 2.0 (an inexact number). Another problem is that −2 is also a square root of 4, and in some contexts it is the correct one to use.

The following trace shows some examples of the simplifier in action. First we show that it can be used as a calculator; then we show more advanced problems.

```
> (simplifier)
SIMPLIFIER> (2 + 2)
4
SIMPLIFIER> (5 * 20 + 30 + 7)
137
SIMPLIFIER> (5 * x - (4 + 1) * x)
0
SIMPLIFIER> (y / z * (5 * x - (4 + 1) * x))
0
SIMPLIFIER> ((4 - 3) * x + (y / y - 1) * z)
X
SIMPLIFIER> (1 * f(x) + 0)
(F X)
SIMPLIFIER> (3 * 2 * X)
(3 * (2 * X))
SIMPLIFIER> [Abort]
>
```

Here we have terminated the loop by hitting the abort key on the terminal. (The details of this mechanism varies from one implementation of Common Lisp to another.) The simplifier seems to work fairly well, although it errs on the last example: (3 * (2 * X)) should simplify to (6 * X). In the next section, we will correct that problem.

8.3　Associativity and Commutativity

We could easily add a rule to rewrite (3 * (2 * X)) as ((3 * 2) * X) and hence (6 * X). The problem is that this rule would also rewrite (X * (2 * 3)) as ((X * 2) * 3), unless we had a way to limit the rule to apply only when it would group numbers together. Fortunately, pat-match does provide just this capability, with the ?is pattern. We could write this rule:

```
(((?is n numberp) * ((?is m numberp) * x)) = ((n * m) * x))
```

This transforms (3 * (2 * x)) into ((3 * 2) * x), and hence into (6 * x). Unfortunately, the problem is not as simple as that. We also want to simplify ((2 * x) * (y * 3)) to (6 * (x * y)). We can do a better job of gathering numbers together by adopting three conventions. First, make numbers first in products: change x * 3 to 3 * x. Second, combine numbers in an outer expression with a number in an inner expression: change 3 * (5 * x) to (3 * 5) * x. Third, move numbers out of inner expressions whenever possible: change (3 * x) * y to 3 * (x * y). We adopt similar conventions for addition, except that we prefer numbers last there: x + 1 instead of 1 + x.

```
;; Define n and m as numbers; s as a non-number:
(pat-match-abbrev 'n '(?is n numberp))
(pat-match-abbrev 'm '(?is m numberp))
(pat-match-abbrev 's '(?is s not-numberp))

(defun not-numberp (x) (not (numberp x)))

(defun simp-rule (rule)
  "Transform a rule into proper format."
  (let ((exp (infix->prefix rule)))
    (mkexp (expand-pat-match-abbrev (exp-lhs exp))
           (exp-op exp) (exp-rhs exp))))
```

```
(setf *simplification-rules*
 (append *simplification-rules* (mapcar #'simp-rule
  '((s * n = n * s)
    (n * (m * x) = (n * m) * x)
    (x * (n * y) = n * (x * y))
    ((n * x) * y = n * (x * y))
    (n + s = s + n)
    ((x + m) + n = x + n + m)
    (x + (y + n) = (x + y) + n)
    ((x + n) + y = (x + y) + n)))))
```

With the new rules in place, we are ready to try again. For some problems we get just
the right answers:

```
> (simplifier)
SIMPLIFIER> (3 * 2 * x)
(6 * X)
SIMPLIFIER> (2 * x * x * 3)
(6 * (X ^ 2))
SIMPLIFIER> (2 * x * 3 * y * 4 * z * 5 * 6)
(720 * (X * (Y * Z)))
SIMPLIFIER> (3 + x + 4 + x)
((2 * X) + 7)
SIMPLIFIER> (2 * x * 3 * x * 4 * (1 / x) * 5 * 6)
(720 * X)
```

Unfortunately, there are other problems that aren't simplified properly:

```
SIMPLIFIER> (3 + x + 4 - x)
((X + (4 - X)) + 3)
SIMPLIFIER> (x + y + y + x)
(X + (Y + (Y + X)))
SIMPLIFIER> (3 * x + 4 * x)
((3 * X) + (4 * X))
```

We will return to these problems in section 8.5.

Exercise 8.1 Verify that the set of rules just prior does indeed implement the desired
conventions, and that the conventions have the proper effect, and always terminate.
As an example of a potential problem, what would happen if we used the rule (x *
n = n * x) instead of the rule (s * n = n * s)?

8.4   Logs, Trig, and Differentiation

In the previous section, we restricted ourselves to the simple arithmetic functions, so as not to intimidate those who are a little leery of complex mathematics. In this section, we add a little to the mathematical complexity, without having to alter the program itself one bit. Thus, the mathematically shy can safely skip to the next section without feeling they are missing any of the fun.

We start off by representing some elementary properties of the logarithmic and trigonometric functions. The new rules are similar to the "zero and one" rules we needed for the arithmetic operators, except here the constants e and pi ($e = 2.71828...$ and $\pi = 3.14159...$) are important in addition to 0 and 1. We also throw in some rules relating logs and exponents, and for sums and differences of logs. The rules assume that complex numbers are not allowed. If they were, $\log e^x$ (and even x^y) would have multiple values, and it would be wrong to arbitrarily choose one of these values.

```
(setf *simplification-rules*
 (append *simplification-rules* (mapcar #'simp-rule '(
 (log 1        = 0)
 (log 0        = undefined)
 (log e        = 1)
 (sin 0        = 0)
 (sin pi       = 0)
 (cos 0        = 1)
 (cos pi       = -1)
 (sin(pi / 2)  = 1)
 (cos(pi / 2)  = 0)
 (log (e ^ x)  = x)
 (e ^ (log x)  = x)
 ((x ^ y) * (x ^ z) = x ^ (y + z))
 ((x ^ y) / (x ^ z) = x ^ (y - z))
 (log x + log y = log(x * y))
 (log x - log y = log(x / y))
 ((sin x) ^ 2 + (cos x) ^ 2 = 1)
 ))))
```

Now we would like to go a step further and extend the system to handle differentiation. This is a favorite problem, and one which has historical significance: in the summer of 1958 John McCarthy decided to investigate differentiation as an interesting symbolic computation problem, which was difficult to express in the primitive programming languages of the day. This investigation led him to see the importance of functional arguments and recursive functions in the field of symbolic computation. For example, McCarthy invented what we now call mapcar to express the idea that the derivative of a sum is the sum of the derivative function applied to each argument. Further work led McCarthy to the publication in October 1958 of MIT

AI Lab Memo No. 1: "An Algebraic Language for the Manipulation of Symbolic Expressions," which defined the precursor of Lisp.

In McCarthy's work and in many subsequent texts you can see symbolic differentiation programs with a simplification routine tacked on the end to make the output more readable. Here, we take the opposite approach: the simplification routine is central, and differentiation is handled as just another operator, with its own set of simplification rules. We will require a new infix-to-prefix translation rule. While we're at it, we'll add a rule for indefinite integration as well, although we won't write simplification rules for integration yet. Here are the new notations:

math	infix	prefix
dy/dx	d y / d x	(d y x)
$\int y dx$	Int y d x	(int y x)

And here are the necessary infix-to-prefix rules:

```
(defparameter *infix->prefix-rules*
  (mapcar #'expand-pat-match-abbrev
    '(((x+ = y+) (= x y))
      ((- x+)    (- x))
      ((+ x+)    (+ x))
      ((x+ + y+) (+ x y))
      ((x+ - y+) (- x y))
      ((d y+ / d x) (d y x))      ;*** New rule
      ((Int y+ d x) (int y x))    ;*** New rule
      ((x+ * y+) (* x y))
      ((x+ / y+) (/ x y))
      ((x+ ^ y+) (^ x y)))))
```

Since the new rule for differentiation occurs before the rule for division, there won't be any confusion with a differential being interpreted as a quotient. On the other hand, there is a potential problem with integrals that contain d as a variable. The user can always avoid the problem by using (d) instead of d inside an integral.

Now we augment the simplification rules, by copying a differentiation table out of a reference book:

```
(setf *simplification-rules*
  (append *simplification-rules* (mapcar #'simp-rule '(
   (d x / d x       = 1)
   (d (u + v) / d x = (d u / d x) + (d v / d x))
   (d (u - v) / d x = (d u / d x) - (d v / d x))
   (d (- u) / d x   = - (d u / d x))
   (d (u * v) / d x = u * (d v / d x) + v * (d u / d x))
   (d (u / v) / d x = (v * (d u / d x) - u * (d v / d x))
                      / v ^ 2)
```

```
(d (u ^ n) / d x = n * u ^ (n - 1) * (d u / d x))
(d (u ^ v) / d x = v * u ^ (v - 1) * (d u / d x)
                 + u ^ v * (log u) * (d v / d x))
(d (log u) / d x = (d u / d x) / u)
(d (sin u) / d x = (cos u) * (d u / d x))
(d (cos u) / d x = - (sin u) * (d u / d x))
(d (e ^ u) / d x = (e ^ u) * (d u / d x))
(d u / d x       = 0)))))
```

We have added a default rule, (d u / d x = 0); this should only apply when the expression u is free of the variable x (that is, when u is not a function of x). We could use ?if to check this, but instead we rely on the fact that differentiation is closed over the list of operators described here—as long as we don't introduce any new operators, the answer will always be correct. Note that there are two rules for exponentiation, one for the case when the exponent is a number, and one when it is not. This was not strictly necessary, as the second rule covers both cases, but that was the way the rules were written in the table of differentials I consulted, so I left both rules in.

```
SIMPLIFIER> (d (x + x) / d x)
2
SIMPLIFIER> (d (a * x ^ 2 + b * x + c) / d x)
((2 * (A * X)) + B)
SIMPLIFIER> (d ((a * x ^ 2 + b * x + c) / x) / d x)
(((((A * (X ^ 2)) + ((B * X) + C)) - (X * ((2 * (A * X)) + B)))
 / (X ^ 2))
SIMPLIFIER> (log ((d (x + x) / d x) / 2))
0
SIMPLIFIER> (log(x + x) - log x)
(LOG 2)
SIMPLIFIER> (x ^ cos pi)
(1 / X)
SIMPLIFIER> (d (3 * x + (cos x) / x) / d x)
(((((COS X) - (X * (- (SIN X)))) / (X ^ 2)) + 3)
SIMPLIFIER> (d ((cos x) / x) / d x)
(((COS X) - (X * (- (SIN X)))) / (X ^ 2))
SIMPLIFIER> (d (3 * x ^ 2 + 2 * x + 1) / d x)
((6 * X) + 2)
SIMPLIFIER> (sin(x + x) ^ 2 + cos(d x ^ 2 / d x) ^ 2)
1
SIMPLIFIER> (sin(x + x) * sin(d x ^ 2 / d x) +
             cos(2 * x) * cos(x * d 2 * y / d y))
1
```

The program handles differentiation problems well and is seemingly clever in its use of the identity $\sin^2 x + \cos^2 x = 1$.

8.5 Limits of Rule-Based Approaches

In this section we return to some examples that pose problems for the simplifier. Here is a simple one:

```
SIMPLIFIER> (x + y + y + x) ⇒ (X + (Y + (Y + X)))
```

We would prefer 2 * (x + y). The problem is that, although we went to great trouble to group numbers together, there was no effort to group non-numbers. We could write rules of the form:

```
(y + (y + x) = (2 * y) + x)
(y + (x + y) = (2 * y) + x)
```

These would work for the example at hand, but they would not work for (x + y + z + y + x). For that we would need more rules:

```
(y + (z + (y + x)) = (2 * y) + x + z)
(y + (z + (x + y)) = (2 * y) + x + z)
(y + ((y + x) + z) = (2 * y) + x + z)
(y + ((x + y) + z) = (2 * y) + x + z)
```

To handle all the cases, we would need an infinite number of rules. The pattern-matching language is not powerful enough to express this succinctly. It might help if nested sums (and products) were unnested; that is, if we allowed + to take an arbitrary number of arguments instead of just one. Once the arguments are grouped together, we could sort them, so that, say, all the ys appear before z and after x. Then like terms could be grouped together. We have to be careful, though. Consider these examples:

```
SIMPLIFIER> (3 * x + 4 * x)
((3 * X) + (4 * X))
SIMPLIFIER> (3 * x + y + x + 4 * x)
((3 * X) + (Y + (X + (4 * X))))
```

We would want (3 * x) to sort to the same place as x and (4 * x) so that they could all be combined to (8 * x). In chapter 15, we develop a new version of the program that handles this problem.

8.6   Integration

So far, the algebraic manipulations have been straightforward. There is a direct algorithm for computing the derivative of every expression. When we consider integrals, or antiderivatives,[2] the picture is much more complicated. As you may recall from freshman calculus, there is a fine art to computing integrals. In this section, we try to see how far we can get by encoding just a few of the many tricks available to the calculus student.

The first step is to recognize that entries in the simplification table will not be enough. Instead, we will need an algorithm to evaluate or "simplify" integrals. We will add a new case to simplify-exp to check each operator to see if it has a simplification function associated with it. These simplification functions will be associated with operators through the functions set-simp-fn and simp-fn. If an operator does have a simplification function, then that function will be called instead of consulting the simplification rules. The simplification function can elect not to handle the expression after all by returning nil, in which case we continue with the other simplification methods.

```lisp
(defun simp-fn (op) (get op 'simp-fn))
(defun set-simp-fn (op fn) (setf (get op 'simp-fn) fn))

(defun simplify-exp (exp)
  "Simplify using a rule, or by doing arithmetic,
  or by using the simp function supplied for this operator."
  (cond ((simplify-by-fn exp))                              ;***
        ((rule-based-translator exp *simplification-rules*
           :rule-if #'exp-lhs :rule-then #'exp-rhs
           :action #'(lambda (bindings response)
                       (simplify (sublis bindings response)))))
        ((evaluable exp) (eval exp))
        (t exp)))

(defun simplify-by-fn (exp)
  "If there is a simplification fn for this exp,
  and if applying it gives a non-null result,
  then simplify the result and return that."
  (let* ((fn (simp-fn (exp-op exp)))
         (result (if fn (funcall fn exp))))
    (if (null result)
        nil
        (simplify result))))
```

Freshman calculus classes teach a variety of integration techniques. Fortunately, one technique—the derivative-divides technique—can be adopted to solve most of the

---

[2]The term antiderivative is more correct, because of branch point problems.

problems that come up at the freshman calculus level, perhaps 90% of the problems given on tests. The basic rule is:

$$\int f(x)\, dx = \int f(u)\frac{du}{dx}\, dx.$$

As an example, consider $\int x \sin(x^2)\, dx$. Using the substitution $u = x^2$, we can differentiate to get $du/dx = 2x$. Then by applying the basic rule, we get:

$$\int x \sin(x^2)\, dx = \frac{1}{2}\int \sin(u)\frac{du}{dx}\, dx = \frac{1}{2}\int \sin(u)\, du.$$

Assume we have a table of integrals that includes the rule $\int \sin(x)\, dx = -\cos(x)$. Then we can get the final answer:

$$-\frac{1}{2}\cos(x^2).$$

Abstracting from this example, the general algorithm for integrating an expression y with respect to x is:

1. Pick a factor of y, calling it $f(u)$.

2. Compute the derivative du/dx.

3. Divide y by $f(u) \times du/dx$, calling the quotient k.

4. If k is a constant (with respect to x), then the result is $k \int f(u)du$.

This algorithm is nondeterministic, as there may be many factors of y. In our example, $f(u) = \sin(x^2)$, $u = x^2$, and $du/dx = 2x$. So $k = \frac{1}{2}$, and the answer is $-\frac{1}{2}\cos(x^2)$.

The first step in implementing this technique is to make sure that division is done correctly. We need to be able to pick out the factors of y, divide expressions, and then determine if a quotient is free of x. The function `factorize` does this. It keeps a list of factors and a running product of constant factors, and augments them with each call to the local function `fac`.

```lisp
(defun factorize (exp)
  "Return a list of the factors of exp^n,
  where each factor is of the form (^ y n)."
  (let ((factors nil)
        (constant 1))
    (labels
      ((fac (x n)
        (cond
          ((numberp x)
           (setf constant (* constant (expt x n))))
          ((starts-with x '*)
           (fac (exp-lhs x) n)
           (fac (exp-rhs x) n))
          ((starts-with x '/)
           (fac (exp-lhs x) n)
           (fac (exp-rhs x) (- n)))
          ((and (starts-with x '-) (length=1 (exp-args x)))
           (setf constant (- constant))
           (fac (exp-lhs x) n))
          ((and (starts-with x '^) (numberp (exp-rhs x)))
           (fac (exp-lhs x) (* n (exp-rhs x))))
          (t (let ((factor (find x factors :key #'exp-lhs
                                   :test #'equal)))
               (if factor
                   (incf (exp-rhs factor) n)
                   (push '(^ ,x ,n) factors)))))))
      ;; Body of factorize:
      (fac exp 1)
      (case constant
        (0 '((^ 0 1)))
        (1 factors)
        (t '((^ ,constant 1) .,factors))))))
```

factorize maps from an expression to a list of factors, but we also need unfactorize
to turn a list back into an expression:

```lisp
(defun unfactorize (factors)
  "Convert a list of factors back into prefix form."
  (cond ((null factors) 1)
        ((length=1 factors) (first factors))
        (t '(* ,(first factors) ,(unfactorize (rest factors))))))
```

The derivative-divides method requires a way of dividing two expressions. We do this
by factoring each expression and then dividing by cancelling factors. There may be
cases where, for example, two factors in the numerator could be multiplied together

to cancel a factor in the denominator, but this possibility is not considered. It turns out that most problems from freshman calculus do not require such sophistication.

```lisp
(defun divide-factors (numer denom)
  "Divide a list of factors by another, producing a third."
  (let ((result (mapcar #'copy-list numer)))
    (dolist (d denom)
      (let ((factor (find (exp-lhs d) result :key #'exp-lhs
                          :test #'equal)))
        (if factor
            (decf (exp-rhs factor) (exp-rhs d))
            (push '(^ ,(exp-lhs d) ,(- (exp-rhs d))) result))))
    (delete 0 result :key #'exp-rhs)))
```

Finally, the predicate free-of returns true if an expression does not have any occurrences of a particular variable in it.

```lisp
(defun free-of (exp var)
  "True if expression has no occurrence of var."
  (not (find-anywhere var exp)))

(defun find-anywhere (item tree)
  "Does item occur anywhere in tree?  If so, return it."
  (cond ((eql item tree) tree)
        ((atom tree) nil)
        ((find-anywhere item (first tree)))
        ((find-anywhere item (rest tree)))))
```

In factorize we made use of the auxiliary function length=1. The function call (length=1 x) is faster than (= (length x) 1) because the latter has to compute the length of the whole list, while the former merely has to see if the list has a rest element or not.

```lisp
(defun length=1 (x)
  "Is X a list of length 1?"
  (and (consp x) (null (rest x))))
```

Given these preliminaries, the function integrate is fairly easy. We start with some simple cases for integrating sums and constant expressions. Then, we factor the expression and split the list of factors into two: a list of constant factors, and a list of factors containing x. (This is done with partition-if, a combination of remove-if and remove-if-not.) Finally, we call deriv-divides, giving it a chance with each of the factors. If none of them work, we return an expression indicating that the integral is unknown.

```
(defun integrate (exp x)
  ;; First try some trivial cases
  (cond
    ((free-of exp x) '(* ,exp x))          ; Int c dx = c*x
    ((starts-with exp '+)                  ; Int f + g  =
     '(+ ,(integrate (exp-lhs exp) x)      ;    Int f + Int g
        ,(integrate (exp-rhs exp) x)))
    ((starts-with exp '-)
     (ecase (length (exp-args exp))
       (1 (integrate (exp-lhs exp) x))     ; Int - f = - Int f
       (2 '(- ,(integrate (exp-lhs exp) x) ; Int f - g  =
             ,(integrate (exp-rhs exp) x)))))  ; Int f - Int g
    ;; Now move the constant factors to the left of the integral
    ((multiple-value-bind (const-factors x-factors)
         (partition-if #'(lambda (factor) (free-of factor x))
                       (factorize exp))
       (simplify
         '(* ,(unfactorize const-factors)
            ;; And try to integrate:
            ,(cond ((null x-factors) x)
                   ((some #'(lambda (factor)
                              (deriv-divides factor x-factors x))
                          x-factors))
                   ;; <other methods here>
                   (t '(int? ,(unfactorize x-factors) ,x)))))))))

(defun partition-if (pred list)
  "Return 2 values: elements of list that satisfy pred,
  and elements that don't."
  (let ((yes-list nil)
        (no-list nil))
    (dolist (item list)
      (if (funcall pred item)
          (push item yes-list)
          (push item no-list)))
    (values (nreverse yes-list) (nreverse no-list))))
```

Note that the place in integrate where other techniques could be added is marked. We will only implement the derivative-divides method. It turns out that the function is a little more complicated than the simple four-step algorithm outlined before:

```
(defun deriv-divides (factor factors x)
  (assert (starts-with factor '^))
  (let* ((u (exp-lhs factor))                    ; factor = u^n
         (n (exp-rhs factor))
         (k (divide-factors
              factors (factorize '(* ,factor ,(deriv u x)))))))
    (cond ((free-of k x)
           ;; Int k*u^n*du/dx dx = k*Int u^n du
           ;;                    = k*u^(n+1)/(n+1) for n /= -1
           ;;                    = k*log(u) for n = -1
           (if (= n -1)
               '(* ,(unfactorize k) (log ,u))
               '(/ (* ,(unfactorize k) (^ ,u ,(+ n 1)))
                   ,(+ n 1))))
          ((and (= n 1) (in-integral-table? u))
           ;; Int y'*f(y) dx = Int f(y) dy
           (let ((k2 (divide-factors
                       factors
                       (factorize '(* ,u ,(deriv (exp-lhs u) x))))))
             (if (free-of k2 x)
                 '(* ,(integrate-from-table (exp-op u) (exp-lhs u))
                     ,(unfactorize k2))))))))
```

There are three cases. In any case, all factors are of the form (^ u n), so we separate the factor into a base, u, and exponent, n. If u or u^n evenly divides the original expression (here represented as factors), then we have an answer. But we need to check the exponent, because $\int u^n du$ is $u^{n+1}/(n+1)$ for $n \neq -1$, but it is $\log(u)$ for $n = -1$. But there is a third case to consider. The factor may be something like (^ (sin (^ x 2)) 1), in which case we should consider $f(u) = \sin(x^2)$. This case is handled with the help of an integral table. We don't need a derivative table, because we can just use the simplifier for that.

```
(defun deriv (y x) (simplify '(d ,y ,x)))

(defun integration-table (rules)
  (dolist (i-rule rules)
    (let ((rule (infix->prefix i-rule)))
      (setf (get (exp-op (exp-lhs (exp-lhs rule))) 'int)
            rule))))
```

```
(defun in-integral-table? (exp)
  (and (exp-p exp) (get (exp-op exp) 'int)))

(defun integrate-from-table (op arg)
  (let ((rule (get op 'int)))
    (subst arg (exp-lhs (exp-lhs (exp-lhs rule))) (exp-rhs rule))))


(integration-table
  '((Int log(x) d x = x * log(x) - x)
    (Int exp(x) d x = exp(x))
    (Int sin(x) d x = - cos(x))
    (Int cos(x) d x = sin(x))
    (Int tan(x) d x = - log(cos(x)))
    (Int sinh(x) d x = cosh(x))
    (Int cosh(x) d x = sinh(x))
    (Int tanh(x) d x = log(cosh(x)))
    ))
```

The last step is to install `integrate` as the simplification function for the operator Int. The obvious way to do this is:

```
(set-simp-fn 'Int 'integrate)
```

Unfortunately, that does not quite work. The problem is that `integrate` expects two arguments, corresponding to the two arguments y and x in (Int y x). But the convention for simplification functions is to pass them a single argument, consisting of the whole expression (Int y x). We could go back and edit `simplify-exp` to change the convention, but instead I choose to make the conversion this way:

```
(set-simp-fn 'Int #'(lambda (exp)
                      (integrate (exp-lhs exp) (exp-rhs exp))))
```

Here are some examples, taken from chapters 8 and 9 of *Calculus* (Loomis 1974):

```
SIMPLIFIER> (Int x * sin(x ^ 2) d x)
(1/2 * (- (COS (X ^ 2))))
SIMPLIFIER> (Int ((3 * x ^ 3) - 1 / (3 * x ^ 3)) d x)
((3 * ((X ^ 4) / 4)) - (1/3 * ((X ^ -2) / -2)))
SIMPLIFIER> (Int (3 * x + 2) ^ -2/3 d x)
(((3 * X) + 2) ^ 1/3)
SIMPLIFIER> (Int sin(x) ^ 2 * cos(x) d x)
(((SIN X) ^ 3) / 3)
SIMPLIFIER> (Int sin(x) / (1 + cos(x)) d x)
(-1 * (LOG ((COS X) + 1)))
SIMPLIFIER> (Int (2 * x + 1) / (x ^ 2 + x - 1) d x)
```

```
(LOG ((X ^ 2) + (X - 1)))
SIMPLIFIER> (Int 8 * x ^ 2 / (x ^ 3 + 2) ^ 3 d x)
(8 * ((1/3 * (((X ^ 3) + 2) ^ -2)) / -2))
```

All the answers are correct, although the last one could be made simpler. One quick way to simplify such an expression is to factor and unfactor it, and then simplify again:

```
(set-simp-fn 'Int
  #'(lambda (exp)
      (unfactorize
       (factorize
        (integrate (exp-lhs exp) (exp-rhs exp))))))
```

With this change, we get:

```
SIMPLIFIER> (Int 8 * x ^ 2 / (x ^ 3 + 2) ^ 3 d x)
(-4/3 * (((X ^ 3) + 2) ^ -2))
```

8.7   History and References

A brief history is given in the introduction to this chapter. An interesting point is that the history of Lisp and of symbolic algebraic manipulation are deeply intertwined. It is not too gross an exaggeration to say that Lisp was invented by John McCarthy to express the symbolic differentiation algorithm. And the development of the first high-quality Lisp system, MacLisp, was driven largely by the needs of MACSYMA, one of the first large Lisp systems. See McCarthy 1958 for early Lisp history and the differentiation algorithm, and Martin and Fateman 1971 and Moses (1975) for more details on MACSYMA. A comprehensive book on computer algebra systems is Davenport 1988. It covers the MACSYMA and REDUCE systems as well as the algorithms behind those systems.

Because symbolic differentiation is historically important, it is presented in a number of text books, from the original Lisp 1.5 Primer (Weissman 1967) and Allen's influential *Anatomy of Lisp* (1978) to recent texts like Brooks 1985, Hennessey 1989, and Tanimoto 1990. Many of these books use rules or data-driven programming, but each treats differentiation as the main task, with simplification as a separate problem. None of them use the approach taken here, where differentiation is just another kind of simplification.

The symbolic integration programs SAINT and SIN are covered in Slagle 1963 and Moses 1967, respectively. The mathematical solution to the problem of integration in closed term is addressed in Risch 1969, but be warned; this paper is not for the mathematically naive, and it has no hints on programming the algorithm. A better reference is Davenport et al. 1988.

In this book, techniques for improving the efficiency of algebraic manipulation are covered in sections 9.6 and 10.4. Chapter 15 presents a reimplementation that does not use pattern-matching, and is closer to the techniques used in MACSYMA.

8.8   Exercises

Exercise 8.2 [s]   Some notations use the operator ** instead of ^ to indicate exponentiation. Fix `infix->prefix` so that either notation is allowed.

Exercise 8.3 [m]   Can the system as is deal with imaginary numbers? What are some of the difficulties?

Exercise 8.4 [h]   There are some simple expressions involving sums that are not handled by the `integrate` function. The function can integrate $a \times x^2 + b \times x + c$ but not $5 \times (a \times x^2 + b \times x + c)$. Similarly, it can integrate $x^4 + 2 \times x^3 + x^2$ but not $(x^2 + x)^2$, and it can do $x^3 + x^2 + x + 1$ but not $(x^2 + 1) \times (x + 1)$. Modify `integrate` so that it expands out products (or small exponents) of sums. You will probably want to try the usual techniques first, and do the expansion only when that fails.

Exercise 8.5 [d]   Another very general integration technique is called integration by parts. It is based on the rule:

$$\int u dv = uv - \int v du$$

So, for example, given

$$\int x \cos x dx$$

we can take $u = x, dv = \cos x dx$. Then we can determine $v = \sin x$ by integration, and come up with the solution:

$$\int x \cos x dx = x \sin x - \int \sin x \times 1 dx = x \sin x + \cos x$$

It is easy to program an integration by parts routine. The hard part is to program the control component. Integration by parts involves a recursive call to `integrate`, and of all the possible ways of breaking up the original expression into a u and a dv, few, if any, will lead to a successful integration. One simple control rule is to allow integration by parts only at the top level, not at the recursive level. Implement this approach.

Exercise 8.6 [d]   A more complicated approach is to try to decide which ways of breaking up the original expression are promising and which are not. Derive some heuristics for making this division, and reimplement `integrate` to include a search component, using the search tools of chapter 6.

Look in a calculus textbook to see how $\int \sin^2 x\, dx$ is evaluated by two integrations by parts and a division. Implement this technique as well.

Exercise 8.7 [m]   Write simplification rules for predicate calculus expressions. For example,

```
(true and x = x)
(false and x = false)
(true or x = true)
(false or x = false)
```

Exercise 8.8 [m]   The simplification rule (x / 0 = undefined) is necessary to avoid problems with division by zero, but the treatment of undefined is inadequate. For example, the expression ((0 / 0) - (0 / 0)) will simplify to zero, when it should simplify to undefined. Add rules to propagate undefined values and prevent them from being simplified away.

Exercise 8.9 [d]   Extend the method used to handle undefined to handle +infinity and -infinity as well.

PART   III

TOOLS AND TECHNIQUES

CHAPTER 9

Efficiency Issues

> *A Lisp programmer knows the value of everything,*
> *but the cost of nothing.*
> —Alan J. Perlis

> *Lisp is not inherently less efficient than other*
> *high-level languages.*
> —Richard J. Fateman

One of the reasons Lisp has enjoyed a long history is because it is an ideal language for what is now called *rapid-prototyping*—developing a program quickly, with little regards for details. That is what we have done so far in this book: concentrated on getting a working algorithm. Unfortunately, when a prototype is to be turned into a production-quality program, details can no longer be ignored. Most "real" AI programs deal with large amounts of data, and with large search spaces. Thus, efficiency considerations become very important.

However, this does not mean that writing an efficient program is fundamentaly different from writing a working program. Ideally, developing an efficient program should be a three-step process. First, develop a working program, using proper abstractions so that the program will be easy to change if necessary. Second, *instrument* the program to determine where it is spending most of the time. Third, replace the slow parts with faster versions, while maintaining the program's correctness.

The term *efficiency* will be used primarily to talk about the *speed* or run time of a program. To a lesser extent, *efficiency* is also used to refer to the *space* or amount of storage consumed by a program. We will also talk about the *cost* of a program. This is partly a use of the metaphor "time is money," and partly rooted in actual monetary costs—if a critical program runs unacceptably slowly, you may need to buy a more expensive computer.

Lisp has been saddled with a reputation as an "inefficient language." Strictly speaking, it makes no sense to call a *language* efficient or inefficient. Rather, it is only a particular *implementation* of the language executing a particular program that can be measured for efficiency. So saying Lisp is inefficient is partly a historical claim: some past implementations *have* been inefficient. It is also partly a prediction: there are some reasons why future implementations are expected to suffer from inefficiencies. These reasons mainly stem from Lisp's flexibility. Lisp allows many decisions to be delayed until run time, and that can make the run time take longer. In the past decade, the "efficiency gap" between Lisp and "conventional languages" like FORTRAN or C has narrowed. Here are the reasons—some deserved, some not—behind Lisp's reputation for inefficiency:

- Early implementations were interpreted rather than compiled, which made them inherently inefficient. Common Lisp implementations have compilers, so this is no longer a problem. While Lisp is (primarily) no longer an interpreted language, it is still an *interactive* language, so it retains its flexibility.

- Lisp has often been used to write interpreters for embedded languages, thereby compounding the problem. Consider this quote from Cooper and Wogrin's (1988) book on the rule-based programming language OPS5:

  > The efficiency of implementations that compile rules into executable code compares favorably to that of programs written in most sequential languages such as FORTRAN or Pascal. Implementations that compile rules into data structures to be interpreted, as do many Lisp-based ones, could be noticeably slower.

  Here Lisp is guilty by association. The fallacious chain of reasoning is: Lisp has been used to write interpreters; interpreters are slow; therefore Lisp is slow. While it is true that Lisp makes it very easy to write interpreters, it also makes it easy to write compilers. This book is the first that concentrates on using Lisp as both the implementation and target language for compilers.

- Lisp encourages a style with lots of function calls, particularly recursive calls. In some older systems, function calls were expensive. But it is now understood that a function call can be compiled into a simple branch instruction, and that many recursive calls can be made no more expensive than an equivalent iterative loop (see chapter 22). It is also possible to instruct a Common Lisp compiler to compile certain functions inline, so there is no calling overhead at all.

On the other hand, many Lisp systems require two fetches instead of one to find the code for a function, and thus will be slower. This extra level of indirection is the price paid for the freedom of being able to redefine functions without reloading the whole program.

- Run-time type-checking is slow. Lisp provides a repertoire of generic functions. For example, we can write (+ x y) without bothering to declare if x and y are integers, floating point, bignums, complex numbers, rationals, or some combination of the above. This is very convenient, but it means that type checks must be made at run time, so the generic + will be slower than, say, a 16-bit integer addition with no check for overflow. If efficiency is important, Common Lisp allows the programmer to include declarations that can eliminate run-time checks.

In fact, once the proper declarations are added, Lisp can be as fast or faster than conventional languages. Fateman (1973) compared the FORTRAN cube root routine on the PDP-10 to a MacLisp transliteration. The MacLisp version produced almost identical numerical code, but was 18% faster overall, due to a superior function-calling sequence.[1] The epigraph at the beginning of this chapter is from this article.

Berlin and Weise (1990) show that with a special compilation technique called *partial evaluation*, speeds 7 to 90 times faster than conventionally compiled code can be achieved. Of course, partial evaluation could be used in any language, but it is very easy to do in Lisp.

The fact remains that Lisp objects must somehow represent their type, and even with declarations, not all of this overhead can be eliminated. Most Lisp implementations optimize access to lists and fixnums but pay the price for the other, less commonly used data types.

- Lisp automatically manages storage, and so it must periodically stop and collect the unused storage, or *garbage*. In early systems, this was done by periodically sweeping through all of memory, resulting in an appreciable pause. Modern systems tend to use incremental garbage-collection techniques, so pauses are shorter and usually unnoticed by the user (although the pauses may still be too long for real-time applications such as controlling a laboratory instrument). The problem with automatic garbage collection these days is not that it is slow—in fact, the automatic systems do about as well as handcrafted storage

---

[1] One could say that the FORTRAN compiler was "broken." This underscores the problem of defining the efficiency of a language—do we judge by the most popular compiler, by the best compiler available, or by the best compiler imaginable?

allocation. The problem is that they make it convenient for the programmer to generate a lot of garbage in the first place. Programmers in conventional languages, who have to clean up their own garbage, tend to be more careful and use static rather than dynamic storage more often. If garbage becomes a problem, the Lisp programmer can just adopt these static techniques.

- Lisp systems are big and leave little room for other programs. Most Lisp systems are designed to be complete environments, within which the programmer does all program development and execution. For this kind of operation, it makes sense to have a large language like Common Lisp with a huge set of tools. However, it is becoming more common to use Lisp as just one component in a computing environment that may include UNIX, X Windows, emacs, and other interacting programs. In this kind of heterogeneous environment, it would be useful to be able to define and run small Lisp processes that do not include megabytes of unused tools. Some recent compilers support this option, but it is not widely available yet.

- Lisp is a complicated high-level language, and it can be difficult for the programmer to anticipate the costs of various operations. In general, the problem is not that an efficient encoding is impossible but that it is difficult to arrive at that efficient encoding. In a language like C, the experienced programmer has a pretty good idea how each statement will compile into assembly language instructions. But in Lisp, very similar statements can compile into widely different assembly-level instructions, depending on subtle interactions between the declarations given and the capabilities of the compiler. Page 318 gives an example where adding a declaration speeds up a trivial function by 40 times. Nonexperts do not understand when such declarations are necessary and are frustrated by the seeming inconsistencies. With experience, the expert Lisp programmer eventually develops a good "efficiency model," and the need for such declarations becomes obvious. Recent compilers such as CMU's Python provide feedback that eases this learning process.

In summary, Lisp makes it possible to write programs in a wide variety of styles, some efficient, some less so. The programmer who writes Lisp programs in the same style as C programs will probably find Lisp to be of comparable speed, perhaps slightly slower. The programmer who uses some of the more dynamic features of Lisp typically finds that it is much easier to develop a working program. Then, if the resulting program is not efficient enough, there will be more time to go back and improve critical sections. Deciding which parts of the program use the most resources is called *instrumentation*. It is foolhardy to try to improve the efficiency of a program without first checking if the improvement will make a real difference.

One route to efficiency is to use the Lisp prototype as a specification and reimplement that specification in a lower-level language, such as C or C++. Some commercial

AI vendors are taking this route. An alternative is to use Lisp as the language for both the prototype and the final implementation. By adding declarations and making minor changes to the original program, it is possible to end up with a Lisp program that is similar in efficiency to a C program.

There are four very general and language-independent techniques for speeding up an algorithm:

- *Caching* the results of computations for later reuse.

- *Compiling* so that less work is done at run time.

- *Delaying* the computation of partial results that may never be needed.

- *Indexing* a data structure for quicker retrieval.

This chapter covers each of the four techniques in order. It then addresses the important problem of *instrumentation*. The chapter concludes with a case study of the simplify program. The techniques outlined here result in a 130-fold speed-up in this program.

Chapter 10 concentrates on lower-level "tricks" for improving efficiency further.

9.1   Caching Results of Previous Computations: Memoization

We start with a simple mathematical function to demonstrate the advantages of caching techniques. Later we will demonstrate more complex examples.

The Fibonacci sequence is defined as the numbers $1, 1, 2, 3, 5, 8, \ldots$ where each number is the sum of the two previous numbers. The most straightforward function to compute the nth number in this sequence is as follows:

```
(defun fib (n)
  "Compute the nth number in the Fibonacci sequence."
  (if (<= n 1) 1
      (+ (fib (- n 1)) (fib (- n 2)))))
```

The problem with this function is that it computes the same thing over and over again. To compute (fib 5) means computing (fib 4) and (fib 3), but (fib 4) also requires (fib 3), they both require (fib 2), and so on. There are ways to rewrite the function to do less computation, but wouldn't it be nice to write the function as is, and have it automatically avoid redundant computation? Amazingly, there is a way to do just that. The idea is to use the function fib to build a new function that remembers previously computed results and uses them, rather than recompute them. This process is called *memoization*. The function memo below is a higher-order function that takes a function as input and returns a new function that will compute the same results, but not do the same computation twice.

```
(defun memo (fn)
  "Return a memo-function of fn."
  (let ((table (make-hash-table)))
    #'(lambda (x)
        (multiple-value-bind (val found-p)
            (gethash x table)
          (if found-p
              val
              (setf (gethash x table) (funcall fn x)))))))
```

The expression (memo #'fib) will produce a function that remembers its results between calls, so that, for example, if we apply it to 3 twice, the first call will do the computation of (fib 3), but the second will just look up the result in a hash table. With fib traced, it would look like this:

```
> (setf memo-fib (memo #'fib)) ⇒ #<CLOSURE -67300731>

> (funcall memo-fib 3) ⇒
(1 ENTER FIB: 3)
  (2 ENTER FIB: 2)
    (3 ENTER FIB: 1)
    (3 EXIT FIB: 1)
    (3 ENTER FIB: 0)
    (3 EXIT FIB: 1)
  (2 EXIT FIB: 2)
  (2 ENTER FIB: 1)
  (2 EXIT FIB: 1)
(1 EXIT FIB: 3)
3

> (funcall memo-fib 3) ⇒ 3
```

The second time we call memo-fib with 3 as the argument, the answer is just retrieved rather than recomputed. But the problem is that during the computation of (fib 3), we still compute (fib 2) multiple times. It would be better if even the internal, recursive calls were memoized, but they are calls to fib, which is unchanged, not to memo-fib. We can solve this problem easily enough with the function memoize:

```
(defun memoize (fn-name)
  "Replace fn-name's global definition with a memoized version."
  (setf (symbol-function fn-name) (memo (symbol-function fn-name))))
```

When passed a symbol that names a function, memoize changes the global definition of the function to a memo-function. Thus, any recursive calls will go first to the memo-function, rather than to the original function. This is just what we want. In the following, we contrast the memoized and unmemoized versions of fib. First, a call to (fib 5) with fib traced:

```
> (fib 5) ⇒
(1 ENTER FIB: 5)
  (2 ENTER FIB: 4)
    (3 ENTER FIB: 3)
      (4 ENTER FIB: 2)
        (5 ENTER FIB: 1)
        (5 EXIT FIB: 1)
        (5 ENTER FIB: 0)
        (5 EXIT FIB: 1)
      (4 EXIT FIB: 2)
      (4 ENTER FIB: 1)
      (4 EXIT FIB: 1)
    (3 EXIT FIB: 3)
    (3 ENTER FIB: 2)
      (4 ENTER FIB: 1)
      (4 EXIT FIB: 1)
      (4 ENTER FIB: 0)
      (4 EXIT FIB: 1)
    (3 EXIT FIB: 2)
  (2 EXIT FIB: 5)
  (2 ENTER FIB: 3)
    (3 ENTER FIB: 2)
      (4 ENTER FIB: 1)
      (4 EXIT FIB: 1)
      (4 ENTER FIB: 0)
      (4 EXIT FIB: 1)
    (3 EXIT FIB: 2)
    (3 ENTER FIB: 1)
    (3 EXIT FIB: 1)
  (2 EXIT FIB: 3)
(1 EXIT FIB: 8)
8
```

We see that (fib 5) and (fib 4) are each computed once, but (fib 3) is computed twice, (fib 2) three times, and (fib 1) five times. Below we call (memoize 'fib) and repeat the calculation. This time, each computation is done only once. Furthermore, when the computation of (fib 5) is repeated, the answer is returned immediately with no intermediate computation, and a further call to (fib 6) can make use of the value of (fib 5).

```
> (memoize 'fib) ⇒ #<CLOSURE 76626607>

> (fib 5) ⇒
(1 ENTER FIB: 5)
  (2 ENTER FIB: 4)
    (3 ENTER FIB: 3)
      (4 ENTER FIB: 2)
        (5 ENTER FIB: 1)
        (5 EXIT FIB: 1)
        (5 ENTER FIB: 0)
        (5 EXIT FIB: 1)
      (4 EXIT FIB: 2)
    (3 EXIT FIB: 3)
  (2 EXIT FIB: 5)
(1 EXIT FIB: 8)
8

> (fib 5) ⇒ 8

> (fib 6) ⇒
(1 ENTER FIB: 6)
(1 EXIT FIB: 13)
13
```

Understanding why this works requires a clear understanding of the distinction between functions and function names. The original (defun fib ...) form does two things: builds a function and stores it as the symbol-function value of fib. Within that function there are two references to fib; these are compiled (or interpreted) as instructions to fetch the symbol-function of fib and apply it to the argument.

What memoize does is fetch the original function and transform it with memo to a function that, when called, will first look in the table to see if the answer is already known. If not, the original function is called, and a new value is placed in the table. The trick is that memoize takes this new function and makes it the symbol-function value of the function name. This means that all the references in the original function will now go to the new function, and the table will be properly checked on each recursive call. One further complication to memo: the function gethash returns both the value found in the table and an indicator of whether the key was present or not. We use multiple-value-bind to capture both values, so that we can distinguish the case when nil is the value of the function stored in the table from the case where there is no stored value.

If you make a change to a memoized function, you need to recompile the original definition, and then redo the call to memoize. In developing your program, rather

than saying (memoize 'f), it might be easier to wrap appropriate definitions in a
memoize form as follows:

```
(memoize
 (defun f (x) ...)
 )
```

Or define a macro that combines defun and memoize:

```
(defmacro defun-memo (fn args &body body)
  "Define a memoized function."
  '(memoize (defun ,fn ,args . ,body)))

(defun-memo f (x) ...)
```

Both of these approaches rely on the fact that defun returns the name of the function
defined.

n	(fib n)	unmemoized	memoized	memoized up to
25	121393	1.1	.010	0
26	196418	1.8	.001	25
27	317811	2.9	.001	26
28	514229	4.7	.001	27
29	832040	8.2	.001	28
30	1346269	12.4	.001	29
31	2178309	20.1	.001	30
32	3524578	32.4	.001	31
33	5702887	52.5	.001	32
34	9227465	81.5	.001	33
50	2.0e10	—	.014	34
100	5.7e20	—	.031	50
200	4.5e41	—	.096	100
500	2.2e104	—	.270	200
1000	7.0e208	—	.596	500
1000	7.0e208	—	.001	1000
1000	7.0e208	—	.876	0

Now we show a table giving the values of (fib n) for certain n, and the time in
seconds to compute the value, before and after (memoize 'fib). For larger values
of n, approximations are shown in the table, although fib actually returns an exact
integer. With the unmemoized version, I stopped at $n = 34$, because the times were
getting too long. For the memoized version, even $n = 1000$ took under a second.

Note there are three entries for (fib 1000). The first entry represents the incremental computation when the table contains the memoized values up to 500, the second entry shows the time for a table lookup when (fib 1000) is already computed, and the third entry is the time for a complete computation starting with an empty table.

It should be noted that there are two general approaches to discussing the efficiency of an algorithm. One is to time the algorithm on representative inputs, as we did in this table. The other is to analyze the *asymptotic complexity* of the algorithm. For the fib problem, an asymptotic analysis considers how long it takes to compute (fib *n*) as *n* approaches infinity. The notation $O(f(n))$ is used to describe the complexity. For example, the memoized version fib is an $O(n)$ algorithm because the computation time is bounded by some constant times *n*, for any value of *n*. The unmemoized version, it turns out, is $O(1.7^n)$, meaning computing fib of n+1 can take up to 1.7 times as long as fib of *n*. In simpler terms, the memoized version has *linear* complexity, while the unmemoized version has *exponential* complexity. Exercise 9.4 (page 308) describes where the 1.7 comes from, and gives a tighter bound on the complexity.

The version of memo presented above is inflexible in several ways. First, it only works for functions of one argument. Second, it only returns a stored value for arguments that are eql, because that is how hash tables work by default. For some applications we want to retrieve the stored value for arguments that are equal. Third, there is no way to delete entries from the hash table. In many applications there are times when it would be good to clear the hash table, either because it has grown too large or because we have finished a set of related problems and are moving on to a new problem.

The versions of memo and memoize below handle these three problems. They are compatible with the previous version but add three new keywords for the extensions. The name keyword stores the hash table on the property list of that name, so it can be accessed by clear-memoize. The test keyword tells what kind of hash table to create: eq, eql, or equal. Finally, the key keyword tells which arguments of the function to index under. The default is the first argument (to be compatible with the previous version), but any combination of the arguments can be used. If you want to use all the arguments, specify identity as the key. Note that if the key is a list of arguments, then you will have to use equal hash tables.

```
(defun memo (fn name key test)
  "Return a memo-function of fn."
  (let ((table (make-hash-table :test test)))
    (setf (get name 'memo) table)
    #'(lambda (&rest args)
        (let ((k (funcall key args)))
          (multiple-value-bind (val found-p)
              (gethash k table)
            (if found-p val
```

```
                      (setf (gethash k table) (apply fn args)))))))))

(defun memoize (fn-name &key (key #'first) (test #'eql))
  "Replace fn-name's global definition with a memoized version."
  (setf (symbol-function fn-name)
        (memo (symbol-function fn-name) fn-name key test)))

(defun clear-memoize (fn-name)
  "Clear the hash table from a memo function."
  (let ((table (get fn-name 'memo)))
    (when table (clrhash table))))
```

9.2   Compiling One Language into Another

In chapter 2 we defined a new language—the language of grammar rules—which was
processed by an interpreter designed especially for that language. An *interpreter* is
a program that looks at some data structure representing a "program" or sequence
of rules of some sort and interprets or evaluates those rules. This is in contrast to a
compiler, which translates some set of rules in one language into a program in another
language.

The function generate was an interpreter for the "language" defined by the set of
grammar rules. Interpreting these rules is straightforward, but the process is somewhat inefficient, in that generate must continually search through the *grammar* to
find the appropriate rule, then count the length of the right-hand side, and so on.

A compiler for this rule-language would take each rule and translate it into a function. These functions could then call each other with no need to search through the
grammar. We implement this approach with the function compile-rule. It makes
use of the auxiliary functions one-of and rule-lhs and rule-rhs from page 40,
repeated here:

```
(defun rule-lhs (rule)
  "The left-hand side of a rule."
  (first rule))

(defun rule-rhs (rule)
  "The right-hand side of a rule."
  (rest (rest rule)))

(defun one-of (set)
  "Pick one element of set, and make a list of it."
  (list (random-elt set)))
```

```
(defun random-elt (choices)
  "Choose an element from a list at random."
  (elt choices (random (length choices))))
```

The function `compile-rule` turns a rule into a function definition by building up Lisp code that implements all the actions that `generate` would take in interpreting the rule. There are three cases. If every element of the right-hand side is an atom, then the rule is a lexical rule, which compiles into a call to `one-of` to pick a word at random. If there is only one element of the right-hand side, then `build-code` is called to generate code for it. Usually, this will be a call to append to build up a list. Finally, if there are several elements in the right-hand side, they are each turned into code by `build-code`; are given a number by `build-cases`; and then a `case` statement is constructed to choose one of the cases.

```
(defun compile-rule (rule)
  "Translate a grammar rule into a LISP function definition."
  (let ((rhs (rule-rhs rule)))
    '(defun ,(rule-lhs rule) ()
       ,(cond ((every #'atom rhs) '(one-of ',rhs))
              ((length=1 rhs) (build-code (first rhs)))
              (t '(case (random ,(length rhs))
                    ,@(build-cases 0 rhs)))))))

(defun build-cases (number choices)
  "Return a list of case-clauses"
  (when choices
    (cons (list number (build-code (first choices)))
          (build-cases (+ number 1) (rest choices)))))

(defun build-code (choice)
  "Append together multiple constituents"
  (cond ((null choice) nil)
        ((atom choice) (list choice))
        ((length=1 choice) choice)
        (t '(append ,@(mapcar #'build-code choice)))))

(defun length=1 (x)
  "Is X a list of length 1?"
  (and (consp x) (null (rest x))))
```

The Lisp code built by `compile-rule` must be compiled or interpreted to make it available to the Lisp system. We can do that with one of the following forms. Normally we would want to call `compile`, but during debugging it may be easier not to.

```
(dolist (rule *grammar*) (eval (compile-rule rule)))
(dolist (rule *grammar*) (compile (eval (compile-rule rule))))
```

One frequent way to use compilation is to define a macro that expands into the code generated by the compiler. That way, we just type in calls to the macro and don't have to worry about making sure all the latest rules have been compiled. We might implement this as follows:

```
(defmacro defrule (&rest rule)
  "Define a grammar rule"
  (compile-rule rule))

(defrule Sentence -> (NP VP))
(defrule NP -> (Art Noun))
(defrule VP -> (Verb NP))
(defrule Art -> the a)
(defrule Noun -> man ball woman table)
(defrule Verb -> hit took saw liked)
```

Actually, the choice of using one big list of rules (like *grammar*) versus using individual macros to define rules is independent of the choice of compiler versus interpreter. We could just as easily define defrule simply to push the rule onto *grammar*. Macros like defrule are useful when you want to define rules in different places, perhaps in several separate files. The defparameter method is appropriate when all the rules can be defined in one place.

We can see the Lisp code generated by compile-rule in two ways: by passing it a rule directly:

```
> (compile-rule '(Sentence -> (NP VP)))
(DEFUN SENTENCE ()
  (APPEND (NP) (VP)))

> (compile-rule '(Noun -> man ball woman table))
(DEFUN NOUN ()
  (ONE-OF '(MAN BALL WOMAN TABLE)))
```

or by macroexpanding a defrule expression. The compiler was designed to produce the same code we were writing in our first approach to the generation problem (see page 35).

```
> (macroexpand '(defrule Adj* -> () Adj (Adj Adj*)))
(DEFUN ADJ* ()
  (CASE (RANDOM 3)
    (0 NIL)
    (1 (ADJ))
    (2 (APPEND (ADJ) (ADJ*)))))
```

Interpreters are usually easier to write than compilers, although in this case, even the compiler was not too difficult. Interpreters are also inherently more flexible than compilers, because they put off making decisions until the last possible moment. For example, our compiler considers the right-hand side of a rule to be a list of words only if every element is an atom. In all other cases, the elements are treated as nonterminals. This could cause problems if we extended the definition of Noun to include the compound noun "chow chow":

```
(defrule Noun -> man ball woman table (chow chow))
```

The rule would expand into the following code:

```
(DEFUN NOUN ()
  (CASE (RANDOM 5)
    (0 (MAN))
    (1 (BALL))
    (2 (WOMAN))
    (3 (TABLE))
    (4 (APPEND (CHOW) (CHOW)))))
```

The problem is that man and ball and all the others are suddenly treated as functions, not as literal words. So we would get a run-time error notifying us of undefined functions. The equivalent rule would cause no trouble for the interpreter, which waits until it actually needs to generate a symbol to decide if it is a word or a nonterminal. Thus, the semantics of rules are different for the interpreter and the compiler, and we as program implementors have to be very careful about how we specify the actual meaning of a rule. In fact, this was probably a bug in the interpreter version, since it effectively prohibits words like "noun" and "sentence" from occurring as words if they are also the names of categories. One possible resolution of the conflict is to say that an element of a right-hand side represents a word if it is an atom, and a list of categories if it is a list. If we did indeed settle on that convention, then we could modify both the interpreter and the compiler to comply with the convention. Another possibility would be to represent words as strings, and categories as symbols.

The flip side of losing run-time flexibility is gaining compile-time diagnostics. For example, it turns out that on the Common Lisp system I am currently using, I get some useful error messages when I try to compile the buggy version of Noun:

```
> (defrule Noun -> man ball woman table (chow chow))
The following functions were referenced but don't seem defined:
 CHOW referenced by NOUN
 TABLE referenced by NOUN
 WOMAN referenced by NOUN
 BALL referenced by NOUN
 MAN referenced by NOUN
NOUN
```

Another problem with the compilation scheme outlined here is the possibility of *name clashes*. Under the interpretation scheme, the only names used were the function generate and the variable *grammar*. With compilation, every left-hand side of a rule becomes the name of a function. The grammar writer has to make sure he or she is not using the name of an existing Lisp function, and hence redefining it. Even worse, if more than one grammar is being developed at the same time, they cannot have any functions in common. If they do, the user will have to recompile with every switch from one grammar to another. This may make it difficult to compare grammars. The best away around this problem is to use the Common Lisp idea of *packages*, but for small exercises name clashes can be avoided easily enough, so we will not explore packages until section 24.1.

The major advantage of a compiler is speed of execution, when that makes a difference. For identical grammars running in one particular implementation of Common Lisp on one machine, our interpreter generates about 75 sentences per second, while the compiled approach turns out about 200. Thus, it is more than twice as fast, but the difference is negligible unless we need to generate many thousands of sentences. In section 9.6 we will see another compiler with an even greater speed-up.

The need to optimize the code produced by your macros and compilers ultimately depends on the quality of the underlying Lisp compiler. For example, consider the following code:

```
> (defun f1 (n 1)
    (let ((11 (first 1))
          (12 (second 1)))
      (expt (* 1 (+ n 0))
            (- 4 (length (list 11 12))))))
F1

> (defun f2 (n 1) (* n n)) ⇒ F2

> (disassemble 'f1)
    6 PUSH        ARG|0      ; N
    7 MOVEM       PDL-PUSH
    8 *           PDL-POP
    9 RETURN      PDL-POP
F1
```

```
> (disassemble 'f2)
   6 PUSH          ARGO      ; N
   7 MOVEM         PDL-PUSH
   8 *             PDL-POP
   9 RETURN        PDL-POP
F2
```

This particular Lisp compiler generates the exact same code for f1 and f2. Both functions square the argument n, and the four machine instructions say, "Take the 0th argument, make a copy of it, multiply those two numbers, and return the result." It's clear the compiler has some knowledge of the basic Lisp functions. In the case of f1, it was smart enough to get rid of the local variables l1 and l2 (and their initialization), as well as the calls to first, second, length, and list and most of the arithmetic. The compiler could do this because it has knowledge about the functions length and list and the arithmetic functions. Some of this knowledge might be in the form of simplification rules.

As a user of this compiler, there's no need for me to write clever macros or compilers that generate streamlined code as seen in f2; I can blindly generate code with possible inefficiencies like those in f1, and assume that the Lisp compiler will cover up for my laziness. With another compiler that didn't know about such optimizations, I would have to be more careful about the code I generate.

9.3   Delaying Computation

Back on page 45, we saw a program to generate all strings derivable from a grammar. One drawback of this program was that some grammars produce an infinite number of strings, so the program would not terminate on those grammars.

It turns out that we often want to deal with infinite sets. Of course, we can't enumerate all the elements of an infinite set, but we should be able to represent the set and pick elements out one at a time. In other words, we want to be able to specify how a set (or other object) is constructed, but delay the actual construction, perhaps doing it incrementally over time. This sounds like a job for closures: we can specify the set constructor as a function, and then call the function some time later. We will implement this approach with the syntax used in Scheme—the macro delay builds a closure to be computed later, and the function force calls that function and caches away the value. We use structures of type delay to implement this. A delay structure has two fields: the value and the function. Initially, the value field is undefined, and the function field holds the closure that will compute the value. The first time the delay is forced, the function is called, and its result is stored in the value field. The function field is then set to nil to indicate that there is no need to call the function again. The function force checks if the function needs to be called, and returns the value. If force is passed an argument that is not a delay, it just returns the argument.

```
(defstruct delay (value nil) (function nil))

(defmacro delay (&rest body)
  "A computation that can be executed later by FORCE."
  '(make-delay :function #'(lambda () . ,body)))

(defun force (x)
  "Find the value of x, by computing if it is a delay."
  (if (not (delay-p x))
      x
      (progn
        (when (delay-function x)
          (setf (delay-value x)
                (funcall (delay-function x)))
          (setf (delay-function x) nil))
        (delay-value x))))
```

Here's an example of the use of delay. The list x is constructed using a combination of normal evaluation and delayed evaluation. Thus, the 1 is printed when x is created, but the 2 is not:

```
> (setf x (list (print 1) (delay (print 2)))) ⇒
1
(1 #S(DELAY :FUNCTION (LAMBDA () (PRINT 2))))
```

The second element is evaluated (and printed) when it is forced. But then forcing it again just retrieves the cached value, rather than calling the function again:

```
> (force (second x)) ⇒
2
2

> x ⇒ (1 #S(DELAY :VALUE 2))

> (force (second x)) ⇒ 2
```

Now let's see how delays can be used to build infinite sets. An infinite set will be considered a special case of what we will call a *pipe:* a list with a first component that has been computed, and a rest component that is either a normal list or a delayed value. Pipes have also been called delayed lists, generated lists, and (most commonly) streams. We will use the term *pipe* because *stream* already has a meaning in Common Lisp. The book *Artificial Intelligence Programming* (Charniak et al. 1987) also calls these structures pipes, reserving streams for delayed structures that do not cache computed results.

To distinguish pipes from lists, we will use the accessors head and tail instead of first and rest. We will also use empty-pipe instead of nil, make-pipe instead of cons, and pipe-elt instead of elt. Note that make-pipe is a macro that delays evaluation of the tail.

```lisp
(defmacro make-pipe (head tail)
  "Create a pipe by evaluating head and delaying tail."
  '(cons ,head (delay ,tail)))

(defconstant empty-pipe nil)

(defun head (pipe) (first pipe))
(defun tail (pipe) (force (rest pipe)))

(defun pipe-elt (pipe i)
  "The i-th element of a pipe, 0-based"
  (if (= i 0)
      (head pipe)
      (pipe-elt (tail pipe) (- i 1))))
```

Here's a function that can be used to make a large or infinite sequence of integers with delayed evaluation:

```lisp
(defun integers (&optional (start 0) end)
  "A pipe of integers from START to END.
  If END is nil, this is an infinite pipe."
  (if (or (null end) (<= start end))
      (make-pipe start (integers (+ start 1) end))
      nil))
```

And here is an example of its use. The pipe c represents the numbers from 0 to infinity. When it is created, only the zeroth element, 0, is evaluated. The computation of the other elements is delayed.

```lisp
> (setf c (integers 0)) ⇒ (0 . #S(DELAY :FUNCTION #<CLOSURE -77435477>))

> (pipe-elt c 0) ⇒ 0
```

Calling pipe-elt to look at the third element causes the first through third elements to be evaluated. The numbers 0 to 3 are cached in the correct positions, and further elements remain unevaluated. Another call to pipe-elt with a larger index would force them by evaluating the delayed function.

```
> (pipe-elt c 3) ⇒ 3

> c ⇒
(0 . #S(DELAY
        :VALUE
        (1 . #S(DELAY
                :VALUE
                (2 . #S(DELAY
                        :VALUE
                        (3 . #S(DELAY
                                :FUNCTION
                                #<CLOSURE -77432724>))))))))
```

While this seems to work fine, there is a heavy price to pay. Every delayed value must be stored in a two-element structure, where one of the elements is a closure. Thus, there is some storage wasted. There is also some time wasted, as tail or pipe-elt must traverse the structures.

An alternate representation for pipes is as (*value . closure*) pairs, where the closure values are stored into the actual cons cells as they are computed. Previously we needed structures of type delay to distinguish a delayed from a nondelayed object, but in a pipe we know the rest can be only one of three things: nil, a list, or a delayed value. Thus, we can use the closures directly instead of using delay structures, if we have some way of distinguishing closures from lists. Compiled closures are atoms, so they can always be distinguished from lists. But sometimes closures are implemented as lists beginning with lambda or some other implementation-dependent symbol.[2] The built-in function functionp is defined to be true of such lists, as well as of all symbols and all objects returned by compile. But using functionp means that we can not have a pipe that includes the symbol lambda as an element, because it will be confused for a closure:

```
> (functionp (last '(theta iota kappa lambda))) ⇒ T
```

If we consistently use compiled functions, then we could eliminate the problem by testing with the built-in predicate compiled-function-p. The following definitions do not make this assumption:

```
(defmacro make-pipe (head tail)
  "Create a pipe by evaluating head and delaying tail."
  '(cons ,head #'(lambda () ,tail)))
```

---

[2]In KCL, the symbol lambda-closure is used, and in Allegro, it is excl:.lexical-closure.

```
(defun tail (pipe)
  "Return tail of pipe or list, and destructively update
  the tail if it is a function."
  (if (functionp (rest pipe))
      (setf (rest pipe) (funcall (rest pipe)))
      (rest pipe)))
```

Everything else remains the same. If we recompile `integers` (because it uses the macro `make-pipe`), we see the following behavior. First, creation of the infinite pipe `c` is similar:

```
> (setf c (integers 0)) ⇒ (0 . #<CLOSURE 77350123>)

> (pipe-elt c 0) ⇒ 0
```

Accessing an element of the pipe forces evaluation of all the intervening elements, and as before leaves subsequent elements unevaluated:

```
> (pipe-elt c 5) ⇒ 5

> c ⇒ (0 1 2 3 4 5 . #<CLOSURE 77351636>)
```

Pipes can also be used for finite lists. Here we see a pipe of length 11:

```
> (setf i (integers 0 10)) ⇒ (0 . #<CLOSURE 77375357>)

> (pipe-elt i 10) ⇒ 10

> (pipe-elt i 11) ⇒ NIL

> i ⇒ (0 1 2 3 4 5 6 7 8 9 10)
```

Clearly, this version wastes less space and is much neater about cleaning up after itself. In fact, a completely evaluated pipe turns itself into a list! This efficiency was gained at the sacrifice of a general principle of program design. Usually we strive to build more complicated abstractions, like pipes, out of simpler ones, like delays. But in this case, part of the functionality that delays were providing was duplicated by the cons cells that make up pipes, so the more efficient implementation of pipes does not use delays at all.

Here are some more utility functions on pipes:

```
(defun enumerate (pipe &key count key (result pipe))
  "Go through all (or count) elements of pipe,
  possibly applying the KEY function. (Try PRINT.)"
  ;; Returns RESULT, which defaults to the pipe itself.
  (if (or (eq pipe empty-pipe) (eql count 0))
```

```
                  result
                  (progn
                    (unless (null key) (funcall key (head pipe)))
                    (enumerate (tail pipe) :count (if count (- count 1))
                               :key key :result result)))))

(defun filter (pred pipe)
  "Keep only items in pipe satisfying pred."
  (if (funcall pred (head pipe))
      (make-pipe (head pipe)
                 (filter pred (tail pipe)))
      (filter pred (tail pipe))))
```

And here's an application of pipes: generating prime numbers using the sieve of Eratosthenes algorithm:

```
(defun sieve (pipe)
  (make-pipe (head pipe)
             (filter #'(lambda (x) (/= (mod x (head pipe)) 0))
                     (sieve (tail pipe)))))

(defvar *primes* (sieve (integers 2)))
```

```
> *primes* ⇒ (2 . #<CLOSURE 3075345>)

> (enumerate *primes* :count 10) ⇒
(2 3 5 7 11 13 17 19 23 29 31 . #<CLOSURE 5224472>)
```

Finally, let's return to the problem of generating all strings in a grammar. First we're going to need some more utility functions:

```
(defun map-pipe (fn pipe)
  "Map fn over pipe, delaying all but the first fn call."
  (if (eq pipe empty-pipe)
      empty-pipe
      (make-pipe (funcall fn (head pipe))
                 (map-pipe fn (tail pipe)))))

(defun append-pipes (x y)
  "Return a pipe that appends the elements of x and y."
  (if (eq x empty-pipe)
      y
      (make-pipe (head x)
                 (append-pipes (tail x) y))))
```

```lisp
(defun mappend-pipe (fn pipe)
  "Lazily map fn over pipe, appending results."
  (if (eq pipe empty-pipe)
      empty-pipe
      (let ((x (funcall fn (head pipe))))
        (make-pipe (head x)
                   (append-pipes (tail x)
                                 (mappend-pipe
                                   fn (tail pipe)))))))
```

Now we can rewrite `generate-all` and `combine-all` to use pipes instead of lists. Everything else is the same as on page 45.

```lisp
(defun generate-all (phrase)
  "Generate a random sentence or phrase"
  (if (listp phrase)
      (if (null phrase)
          (list nil)
          (combine-all-pipes
            (generate-all (first phrase))
            (generate-all (rest phrase))))
      (let ((choices (rule-rhs (assoc phrase *grammar*))))
        (if choices
            (mappend-pipe #'generate-all choices)
            (list (list phrase))))))

(defun combine-all-pipes (xpipe ypipe)
  "Return a pipe of pipes formed by appending a y to an x"
  ;; In other words, form the cartesian product.
  (mappend-pipe
    #'(lambda (y)
        (map-pipe #'(lambda (x) (append-pipes x y))
                  xpipe))
    ypipe))
```

With these definitions, here's the pipe of all sentences from *grammar2* (from page 43):

```lisp
> (setf ss (generate-all 'sentence)) ⇒
((THE . #<CLOSURE 27265720>) . #<CLOSURE 27266035>)
```

```
> (enumerate ss :count 5) ⇒
((THE . #<CLOSURE 27265720>)
 (A . #<CLOSURE 27273143>)
 (THE . #<CLOSURE 27402545>)
 (A . #<CLOSURE 27404344>)
 (THE . #<CLOSURE 27404527>)
 (A . #<CLOSURE 27405473>) . #<CLOSURE 27405600>)

> (enumerate ss :count 5 :key #'enumerate) ⇒
((THE MAN HIT THE MAN)
 (A MAN HIT THE MAN)
 (THE BIG MAN HIT THE MAN)
 (A BIG MAN HIT THE MAN)
 (THE LITTLE MAN HIT THE MAN)
 (THE . #<CLOSURE 27423236>) . #<CLOSURE 27423343>)

> (enumerate (pipe-elt ss 200)) ⇒
(THE ADIABATIC GREEN BLUE MAN HIT THE MAN)
```

While we were able to represent the infinite set of sentences and enumerate instances of it, we still haven't solved all the problems. For one, this enumeration will never get to a sentence that does not have "hit the man" as the verb phrase. We will see longer and longer lists of adjectives, but no other change. Another problem is that left-recursive rules will still cause infinite loops. For example, if the expansion for Adj* had been (Adj* -> (Adj* Adj) ()) instead of (Adj* -> () (Adj Adj*)), then the enumeration would never terminate, because pipes need to generate a first element.

We have used delays and pipes for two main purposes: to put off until later computations that may not be needed at all, and to have an explicit representation of large or infinite sets. It should be mentioned that the language Prolog has a different solution to the first problem (but not the second). As we shall see in chapter 11, Prolog generates solutions one at a time, automatically keeping track of possible backtrack points. Where pipes allow us to represent an infinite number of alternatives in the data, Prolog allows us to represent those alternatives in the program itself.

Exercise 9.1 [h] When given a function f and a pipe p, mappend-pipe returns a new pipe that will eventually enumerate all of (f (first p)), then all of (f (second p)), and so on. This is deemed "unfair" if (f (first p)) has an infinite number of elements. Define a function that will fairly interleave elements, so that all of them are eventually enumerated. Show that the function works by changing generate-all to work with it.

9.4   Indexing Data

Lisp makes it very easy to use lists as the universal data structure. A list can represent a set or an ordered sequence, and a list with sublists can represent a tree or graph. For rapid prototyping, it is often easiest to represent data in lists, but for efficiency this is not always the best idea. To find an element in a list of length n will take $n/2$ steps on average. This is true for a simple list, an association list, or a property list. If n can be large, it is worth looking at other data structures, such as hash tables, vectors, property lists, and trees.

Picking the right data structure and algorithm is as important in Lisp as it is in any other programming language. Even though Lisp offers a wide variety of data structures, it is often worthwhile to spend some effort on building just the right data structure for frequently used data. For example, Lisp's hash tables are very general and thus can be inefficient. You may want to build your own hash tables if, for example, you never need to delete elements, thus making open hashing an attractive possibility. We will see an example of efficient indexing in section 9.6 (page 297).

9.5   Instrumentation: Deciding What to Optimize

Because Lisp is such a good rapid-prototyping language, we can expect to get a working implementation quickly. Before we go about trying to improve the efficiency of the implementation, it is a good idea to see what parts are used most often. Improving little-used features is a waste of time.

The minimal support we need is to count the number of calls to selected functions, and then print out the totals. This is called *profiling* the functions.[3] For each function to be profiled, we change the definition so that it increments a counter and then calls the original function.

Most Lisp systems have some built-in profiling mechanism. If your system has one, by all means use it. The code in this section is provided for those who lack such a feature, and as an example of how functions can be manipulated. The following is a simple profiling facility. For each profiled function, it keeps a count of the number of times it is called under the `profile-count` property of the function's name.

---

[3]The terms *metering* and *monitoring* are sometimes used instead of profiling.

```
(defun profile1 (fn-name)
  "Make the function count how often it is called"
  ;; First save away the old, unprofiled function
  ;; Then make the name be a new function that increments
  ;; a counter and then calls the original function
  (let ((fn (symbol-function fn-name)))
    (setf (get fn-name 'unprofiled-fn) fn)
    (setf (get fn-name 'profile-count) 0)
    (setf (symbol-function fn-name)
          (profiled-fn fn-name fn))
    fn-name))

(defun unprofile1 (fn-name)
  "Make the function stop counting how often it is called."
  (setf (symbol-function fn-name) (get fn-name 'unprofiled-fn))
  fn-name)

(defun profiled-fn (fn-name fn)
  "Return a function that increments the count."
  #'(lambda (&rest args)
      (incf (get fn-name 'profile-count))
      (apply fn args)))

(defun profile-count (fn-name) (get fn-name 'profile-count))

(defun profile-report (fn-names &optional (key #'profile-count))
  "Report profiling statistics on given functions."
  (loop for name in (sort fn-names #'> :key key) do
        (format t "~&~7D ~A" (profile-count name) name)))
```

That's all we need for the bare-bones functionality. However, there are a few ways we could improve this. First, it would be nice to have macros that, like trace and untrace, allow the user to profile multiple functions at once and keep track of what has been profiled. Second, it can be helpful to see the length of time spent in each function, as well as the number of calls.

Also, it is important to avoid profiling a function twice, since that would double the number of calls reported without alerting the user of any trouble. Suppose we entered the following sequence of commands:

```
(defun f (x) (g x))
(profile1 'f)
(profile1 'f)
```

Then the definition of f would be roughly:

```
(lambda (&rest args)
  (incf (get 'f 'profile-count))
  (apply #'(lambda (&rest args)
             (incf (get 'f 'profile-count))
             (apply #'(lambda (x) (g x))
                       args))
         args))
```

The result is that any call to f will eventually call the original f, but only after incrementing the count twice.

Another consideration is what happens when a profiled function is redefined by the user. The only way we could ensure that a redefined function would continue profiling would be to change the definition of the macro defun to look for functions that should be profiled. Changing system functions like defun is a risky prospect, and in *Common Lisp the Language*, 2d edition, it is explicitly disallowed. Instead, we'll do the next best thing: ensure that the next call to profile will reprofile any functions that have been redefined. We do this by keeping track of both the original unprofiled function and the profiled function. We also keep a list of all functions that are currently profiled.

In addition, we will count the amount of time spent in each function. However, the user is cautioned not to trust the timing figures too much. First, they include the overhead cost of the profiling facility. This can be significant, particularly because the facility conses, and thus can force garbage collections that would not otherwise have been done. Second, the resolution of the system clock may not be fine enough to make accurate timings. For functions that take about 1/10 of a second or more, the figures will be reliable, but for quick functions they may not be.

Here is the basic code for profile and unprofile:

```
(defvar *profiled-functions* nil
  "Function names that are currently profiled")

(defmacro profile (&rest fn-names)
  "Profile fn-names. With no args, list profiled functions."
  '(mapcar #'profile1
           (setf *profiled-functions*
                 (union *profiled-functions* ',fn-names))))

(defmacro unprofile (&rest fn-names)
  "Stop profiling fn-names. With no args, stop all profiling."
  '(progn
     (mapcar #'unprofile1
             ,(if fn-names '',fn-names '*profiled-functions*))
     (setf *profiled-functions*
           ,(if (null fn-names)
                nil
```

```
'(set-difference *profiled-functions*
                 ',fn-names)))))
```

The idiom '',fn-names deserves comment, since it is common but can be confusing at first. It may be easier to understand when written in the equivalent form '(quote ,fn-names). As always, the backquote builds a structure with both constant and evaluated components. In this case, the quote is constant and the variable fn-names is evaluated. In MacLisp, the function kwote was defined to serve this purpose:

```
(defun kwote (x) (list 'quote x))
```

Now we need to change profile1 and unprofile1 to do the additional bookkeeping: For profile1, there are two cases. If the user does a profile1 on the same function name twice in a row, then on the second time we will notice that the current function is the same as the functioned stored under the profiled-fn property, so nothing more needs to be done. Otherwise, we create the profiled function, store it as the current definition of the name under the profiled-fn property, save the unprofiled function, and initialize the counts.

```
(defun profile1 (fn-name)
  "Make the function count how often it is called"
  ;; First save away the old, unprofiled function
  ;; Then make the name be a new function that increments
  ;; a counter and then calls the original function
  (let ((fn (symbol-function fn-name)))
    (unless (eq fn (get fn-name 'profiled-fn))
      (let ((new-fn (profiled-fn fn-name fn)))
        (setf (symbol-function fn-name) new-fn
              (get fn-name 'profiled-fn) new-fn
              (get fn-name 'unprofiled-fn) fn
              (get fn-name 'profile-time) 0
              (get fn-name 'profile-count) 0))))
  fn-name)

(defun unprofile1 (fn-name)
  "Make the function stop counting how often it is called."
  (setf (get fn-name 'profile-time) 0)
  (setf (get fn-name 'profile-count) 0)
  (when (eq (symbol-function fn-name) (get fn-name 'profiled-fn))
    ;; normal case: restore unprofiled version
    (setf (symbol-function fn-name)
          (get fn-name 'unprofiled-fn)))
  fn-name)
```

Now we look into the question of timing. There is a built-in Common Lisp function, get-internal-real-time, that returns the elapsed time since the Lisp session started. Because this can quickly become a bignum, some implementations provide another timing function that wraps around rather than increasing forever, but which may have a higher resolution than get-internal-real-time. For example, on TI Explorer Lisp Machines, get-internal-real-time measures 1/60-second intervals, while time:microsecond-time measures 1/1,000,000-second intervals, but the value returned wraps around to zero every hour or so. The function time:microsecond-time-difference is used to compare two of these numbers with compensation for wraparound, as long as no more than one wraparound has occurred.

In the code below, I use the conditional read macro characters #+ and #- to define the right behavior on both Explorer and non-Explorer machines. We have seeen that # is a special character to the reader that takes different action depending on the following character. For example, #'fn is read as (function fn). The character sequence #+ is defined so that #+*feature expression* reads as *expression* if the *feature* is defined in the current implementation, and as nothing at all if it is not. The sequence #- acts in just the opposite way. For example, on a TI Explorer, we would get the following:

```
> '(hi #+TI t #+Symbolics s #-Explorer e #-Mac m) ⇒  (HI T M)
```

The conditional read macro characters are used in the following definitions:

```
(defun get-fast-time ()
  "Return the elapsed time.  This may wrap around;
  use FAST-TIME-DIFFERENCE to compare."
  #+Explorer (time:microsecond-time)   ; do this on an Explorer
  #-Explorer (get-internal-real-time)) ; do this on a non-Explorer

(defun fast-time-difference (end start)
  "Subtract two time points."
  #+Explorer (time:microsecond-time-difference end start)
  #-Explorer (- end start))

(defun fast-time->seconds (time)
  "Convert a fast-time interval into seconds."
  #+Explorer (/ time 1000000.0)
  #-Explorer (/ time internal-time-units-per-second))
```

The next step is to update profiled-fn to keep track of the timing data. The simplest way to do this would be to set a variable, say start, to the time when a function is entered, run the function, and then increment the function's time by the difference between the current time and start. The problem with this approach is that every function in the call stack gets credit for the time of each called function. Suppose the function f calls itself recursively five times, with each call and return taking place a second apart, so that the whole computation takes nine seconds. Then f will be charged nine seconds for the outer call, seven seconds for the next call, and so on, for a total of 25 seconds, even though in reality it only took nine seconds for all of them together.

A better algorithm would be to charge each function only for the time since the last call or return. Then f would only be charged the nine seconds. The variable *profile-call-stack* is used to hold a stack of function name/entry time pairs. This stack is manipulated by profile-enter and profile-exit to get the right timings.

The functions that are used on each call to a profiled function are declared inline. In most cases, a call to a function compiles into machine instructions that set up the argument list and branch to the location of the function's definition. With an inline function, the body of the function is compiled in line at the place of the function call. Thus, there is no overhead for setting up the argument list and branching to the definition. An inline declaration can appear anywhere any other declaration can appear. In this case, the function proclaim is used to register a global declaration. Inline declarations are discussed in more depth on page 317.

```lisp
(proclaim '(inline profile-enter profile-exit inc-profile-time))

(defun profiled-fn (fn-name fn)
  "Return a function that increments the count, and times."
  #'(lambda (&rest args)
      (profile-enter fn-name)
      (multiple-value-prog1
        (apply fn args)
        (profile-exit fn-name))))

(defvar *profile-call-stack* nil)

(defun profile-enter (fn-name)
  (incf (get fn-name 'profile-count))
  (unless (null *profile-call-stack*)
    ;; Time charged against the calling function:
    (inc-profile-time (first *profile-call-stack*)
                      (car (first *profile-call-stack*))))
  ;; Put a new entry on the stack
  (push (cons fn-name (get-fast-time))
        *profile-call-stack*))

(defun profile-exit (fn-name)
  ;; Time charged against the current function:
  (inc-profile-time (pop *profile-call-stack*)
                    fn-name)
  ;; Change the top entry to reflect current time
  (unless (null *profile-call-stack*)
    (setf (cdr (first *profile-call-stack*))
          (get-fast-time))))
```

```
(defun inc-profile-time (entry fn-name)
  (incf (get fn-name 'profile-time)
        (fast-time-difference (get-fast-time) (cdr entry))))
```

Finally, we need to update `profile-report` to print the timing data as well as the counts. Note that the default `fn-names` is a copy of the global list. That is because we pass `fn-names` to `sort`, which is a destructive function. We don't want the global list to be modified as a result of this sort.

```
(defun profile-report (&optional
                        (fn-names (copy-list *profiled-functions*))
                        (key #'profile-count))
  "Report profiling statistics on given functions."
  (let ((total-time (reduce #'+ (mapcar #'profile-time fn-names))))
    (unless (null key)
      (setf fn-names (sort fn-names #'> :key key)))
    (format t "~&Total elapsed time: ~d seconds."
            (fast-time->seconds total-time))
    (format t "~& Count   Secs Time% Name")
    (loop for name in fn-names do
          (format t "~&~7D ~6,2F   ~3d% ~A"
                  (profile-count name)
                  (fast-time->seconds (profile-time name))
                  (round (/ (profile-time name) total-time) .01)
                  name))))

(defun profile-time (fn-name) (get fn-name 'profile-time))
```

These functions can be used by calling `profile`, then doing some representative computation, then calling `profile-report`, and finally `unprofile`. It can be convenient to provide a single macro for doing all of these at once:

```
(defmacro with-profiling (fn-names &rest body)
  `(progn
     (unprofile . ,fn-names)
     (profile . ,fn-names)
     (setf *profile-call-stack* nil)
     (unwind-protect
          (progn . ,body)
       (profile-report ',fn-names)
       (unprofile . ,fn-names))))
```

Note the use of `unwind-protect` to produce the report and call `unprofile` even if the computation is aborted. `unwind-protect` is a special form that takes any number of arguments. It evaluates the first argument, and if all goes well it then evaluates the other arguments and returns the first one, just like prog1. But if an error occurs during the evaluation of the first argument and computation is aborted, then the subsequent arguments (called cleanup forms) are evaluated anyway.

9.6 A Case Study in Efficiency: The SIMPLIFY Program

Suppose we wanted to speed up the simplify program of chapter 8. This section shows how a combination of general techniques—memoizing, indexing, and compiling—can be used to speed up the program by a factor of 130. Chapter 15 will show another approach: replace the algorithm with an entirely different one.

The first step to a faster program is defining a *benchmark*, a test suite representing a typical work load. The following is a short list of test problems (and their answers) that are typical of the simplify task.

```
(defvar *test-data* (mapcar #'infix->prefix
  '((d (a * x ^ 2 + b * x + c) / d x)
    (d ((a * x ^ 2 + b * x + c) / x) / d x)
    (d ((a * x ^ 3 + b * x ^ 2 + c * x + d) / x ^ 5) / d x)
    ((sin (x + x)) * (sin (2 * x)) + (cos (d (x ^ 2) / d x)) ^ 1)
    (d (3 * x + (cos x) / x) / d x))))

(defvar *answers* (mapcar #'simplify *test-data*))
```

The function test-it runs through the test data, making sure that each answer is correct and optionally printing profiling data.

```
(defun test-it (&optional (with-profiling t))
  "Time a test run, and make sure the answers are correct."
  (let ((answers
         (if with-profiling
             (with-profiling (simplify simplify-exp pat-match
                              match-variable variable-p)
               (mapcar #'simplify *test-data*))
             (time (mapcar #'simplify *test-data*)))))
    (mapc #'assert-equal answers *answers*)
    t))

(defun assert-equal (x y)
  "If x is not equal to y, complain."
  (assert (equal x y) (x y)
          "Expected ~a to be equal to ~a" x y))
```

Here are the results of (test-it) with and without profiling:

```
> (test-it nil)
Evaluation of (MAPCAR #'SIMPLIFY *TEST-DATA*) took 6.612 seconds.

> (test-it t)
Total elapsed time: 22.819614 seconds.
  Count  Secs Time% Name
  51690 11.57   51% PAT-MATCH
  37908  8.75   38% VARIABLE-P
   1393  0.32    1% MATCH-VARIABLE
    906  0.20    1% SIMPLIFY
    274  1.98    9% SIMPLIFY-EXP
```

Running the test takes 6.6 seconds normally, although the time triples when the profiling overhead is added in. It should be clear that to speed things up, we have to either speed up or cut down on the number of calls to pat-match or variable-p, since together they account for 89% of the calls (and 89% of the time as well). We will look at three methods for achieving both those goals.

Memoization

Consider the rule that transforms (x + x) into (2 * x). Once this is done, we have to simplify the result, which involves resimplifying the components. If x were some complex expression, this could be time-consuming, and it will certainly be wasteful, because x is already simplified and cannot change. We have seen this type of problem before, and the solution is memoization: make simplify remember the work it has done, rather than repeating the work. We can just say:

```
(memoize 'simplify :test #'equal)
```

Two questions are unclear: what kind of hash table to use, and whether we should clear the hash table between problems. The simplifier was timed for all four combinations of eq or equal hash tables and resetting or nonresetting between problems. The fastest result was equal hashing and nonresetting. Note that with eq hashing, the resetting version was faster, presumably because it couldn't take advantage of the common subexpressions between examples (since they aren't eq).

hashing	resetting	time
none	—	6.6
equal	yes	3.8
equal	no	3.0
eq	yes	7.0
eq	no	10.2

This approach makes the function simplify remember the work it has done, in a hash table. If the overhead of hash table maintenance becomes too large, there is an alternative: make the data remember what simplify has done. This approach was taken in MACSYMA: it represented operators as lists rather than as atoms. Thus, instead of (* 2 x), MACSYMA would use ((*) 2 x). The simplification function would destructively insert a marker into the operator list. Thus, the result of simplifying $2x$ would be ((* simp) 2 x). Then, when the simplifier was called recursively on this expression, it would notice the simp marker and return the expression as is.

The idea of associating memoization information with the data instead of with the function will be more efficient unless there are many functions that all want to place their marks on the same data. The data-oriented approach has two drawbacks: it doesn't identify structures that are equal but not eq, and, because it requires explicitly altering the data, it requires every other operation that manipulates the data to know about the markers. The beauty of the hash table approach is that it is transparent; no code needs to know that memoization is taking place.

Indexing

We currently go through the entire list of rules one at a time, checking each rule. This is inefficient because most of the rules could be trivially ruled out—if only they were indexed properly. The simplest indexing scheme would be to have a separate list of rules indexed under each operator. Instead of having simplify-exp check each member of *simplification-rules*, it could look only at the smaller list of rules for the appropriate operator. Here's how:

```
(defun simplify-exp (exp)
  "Simplify using a rule, or by doing arithmetic,
  or by using the simp function supplied for this operator.
  This version indexes simplification rules under the operator."
  (cond ((simplify-by-fn exp))
        ((rule-based-translator exp (rules-for (exp-op exp)) ;***
           :rule-if #'exp-lhs :rule-then #'exp-rhs
           :action #'(lambda (bindings response)
                       (simplify (sublis bindings response)))))
        ((evaluable exp) (eval exp))
        (t exp)))

(defvar *rules-for* (make-hash-table :test #'eq))

(defun main-op (rule) (exp-op (exp-lhs rule)))
```

```
(defun index-rules (rules)
  "Index all the rules under the main op."
  (clrhash *rules-for*)
  (dolist (rule rules)
    ;; nconc instead of push to preserve the order of rules
    (setf (gethash (main-op rule) *rules-for*)
          (nconc (gethash (main-op rule) *rules-for*)
                 (list rule)))))

(defun rules-for (op) (gethash op *rules-for*))

(index-rules *simplification-rules*)
```

Timing the memoized, indexed version gets us to .98 seconds, down from 6.6 seconds for the original code and 3 seconds for the memoized code. If this hadn't helped, we could have considered more sophisticated indexing schemes. Instead, we move on to consider other means of gaining efficiency.

Exercise 9.2 [m] The list of rules for each operator is stored in a hash table with the operator as key. An alternative would be to store the rules on the property list of each operator, assuming operators must be symbols. Implement this alternative, and time it against the hash table approach. Remember that you need some way of clearing the old rules—trivial with a hash table, but not automatic with property lists.

Compilation

You can look at simplify-exp as an interpreter for the simplification rule language. One proven technique for improving efficiency is to replace the interpreter with a compiler. For example, the rule (x + x = 2 * x) could be compiled into something like:

```
(lambda (exp)
  (if (and (eq (exp-op exp) '+) (equal (exp-lhs exp) (exp-rhs exp)))
      (make-exp :op '* :lhs 2 :rhs (exp-rhs exp))))
```

This eliminates the need for consing up and passing around variable bindings, and should be faster than the general matching procedure. When used in conjunction with indexing, the individual rules can be simpler, because we already know we have the right operator. For example, with the above rule indexed under "+", it could now be compiled as:

```
(lambda (exp)
  (if (equal (exp-lhs exp) (exp-rhs exp))
      (make-exp :op '* :lhs 2 :rhs (exp-lhs exp))))
```

It is important to note that when these functions return nil, it means that they have failed to simplify the expression, and we have to consider another means of simplification.

Another possibility is to compile a set of rules all at the same time, so that the indexing is in effect part of the compiled code. As an example, I show here a small set of rules and a possible compilation of the rule set. The generated function assumes that x is not an atom. This is appropriate because we are replacing simplify-exp, not simplify. Also, we will return nil to indicate that x is already simplified. I have chosen a slightly different format for the code; the main difference is the let to introduce variable names for subexpressions. This is useful especially for deeply nested patterns. The other difference is that I explicitly build up the answer with a call to list, rather than make-exp. This is normally considered bad style, but since this is code generated by a compiler, I wanted it to be as efficient as possible. If the representation of the exp data type changed, we could simply change the compiler; a much easier task than hunting down all the references spread throughout a human-written program. The comments following were not generated by the compiler.

```
(x * 1 = x)
(1 * x = x)
(x * 0 = 0)
(0 * x = 0)
(x * x = x ^ 2)

(lambda (x)
  (let ((xl (exp-lhs x))
        (xr (exp-rhs x)))
    (or (if (eql xr '1)          ; (x * 1 = x)
            xl)
        (if (eql xl '1)          ; (1 * x = x)
            xr)
        (if (eql xr '0)          ; (x * 0 = 0)
            '0)
        (if (eql xl '0)          ; (0 * x = 0)
            '0)
        (if (equal xr xl)        ; (x * x = x ^ 2)
            (list '^ xl '2)))))
```

I chose this format for the code because I imagined (and later show) that it would be fairly easy to write the compiler for it.

The Single-Rule Compiler

Here I show the complete single-rule compiler, to be followed by the indexed-rule-set compiler. The single-rule compiler works like this:

```
> (compile-rule '(= (+ x x) (* 2 x)))
(LAMBDA (X)
  (IF (OP? X '+)
    (LET ((XL (EXP-LHS X))
          (XR (EXP-RHS X)))
      (IF (EQUAL XR XL)
          (SIMPLIFY-EXP (LIST '* '2 XL)))))))
```

Given a rule, it generates code that first tests the pattern and then builds the right-hand side of the rule if the pattern matches. As the code is generated, correspondences are built between variables in the pattern, like x, and variables in the generated code, like xl. These are kept in the association list *bindings*. The matching can be broken down into four cases: variables that haven't been seen before, variables that have been seen before, atoms, and lists. For example, the first time we run across x in the rule above, no test is generated, since anything can match x. But the entry (x . xl) is added to the *bindings* list to mark the equivalence. When the second x is encountered, the test (equal xr xl) is generated.

Organizing the compiler is a little tricky, because we have to do three things at once: return the generated code, keep track of the *bindings*, and keep track of what to do "next"—that is, when a test succeeds, we need to generate more code, either to test further, or to build the result. This code needs to know about the bindings, so it can't be done *before* the first part of the test, but it also needs to know where it should be placed in the overall code, so it would be messy to do it *after* the first part of the test. The answer is to pass in a function that will tell us what code to generate later. This way, it gets done at the right time, and ends up in the right place as well. Such a function is often called a *continuation*, because it tells us where to continue computing. In our compiler, the variable consequent is a continuation function.

The compiler is called compile-rule. It takes a rule as an argument and returns a lambda expression that implements the rule.

```
(defvar *bindings* nil
  "A list of bindings used by the rule compiler.")

(defun compile-rule (rule)
  "Compile a single rule."
  (let ((*bindings* nil))
    '(lambda (x)
       ,(compile-exp 'x (exp-lhs rule) ; x is the lambda parameter
                     (delay (build-exp (exp-rhs rule)
```

```
                                *bindings*))))))
```

All the work is done by compile-exp, which takes three arguments: a variable that will represent the input in the generated code, a pattern that the input should be matched against, and a continuation for generating the code if the test passes. There are five cases: (1) If the pattern is a variable in the list of bindings, then we generate an equality test. (2) If the pattern is a variable that we have not seen before, then we add it to the binding list, generate no test (because anything matches a variable) and then generate the consequent code. (3) If the pattern is an atom, then the match succeeds only if the input is eql to that atom. (4) If the pattern is a conditional like (?is n numberp), then we generate the test (numberp n). Other such patterns could be included here but have not been, since they have not been used. Finally, (5) if the pattern is a list, we check that it has the right operator and arguments.

```
(defun compile-exp (var pattern consequent)
  "Compile code that tests the expression, and does consequent
  if it matches.  Assumes bindings in *bindings*."
  (cond ((get-binding pattern *bindings*)
         ;; Test a previously bound variable
         '(if (equal ,var ,(lookup pattern *bindings*))
              ,(force consequent)))
        ((variable-p pattern)
         ;; Add a new bindings; do type checking if needed.
         (push (cons pattern var) *bindings*)
         (force consequent))
        ((atom pattern)
         ;; Match a literal atom
         '(if (eql ,var ',pattern)
              ,(force consequent)))
        ((starts-with pattern '?is)
         (push (cons (second pattern) var) *bindings*)
         '(if (,(third pattern) ,var)
              ,(force consequent)))
        ;; So, far, only the ?is pattern is covered, because
        ;; it is the only one used in simplification rules.
        ;; Other patterns could be compiled by adding code here.
        ;; Or we could switch to a data-driven approach.
        (t ;; Check the operator and arguments
         '(if (op? ,var ',(exp-op pattern))
              ,(compile-args var pattern consequent)))))
```

The function compile-args is used to check the arguments to a pattern. It generates a let form binding one or two new variables (for a unary or binary expression), and then calls compile-exp to generate code that actually makes the tests. It just passes along the continuation, consequent, to compile-exp.

```lisp
(defun compile-args (var pattern consequent)
  "Compile code that checks the arg or args, and does consequent
  if the arg(s) match."
  ;; First make up variable names for the arg(s).
  (let ((L (symbol var 'L))
        (R (symbol var 'R)))
    (if (exp-rhs pattern)
        ;; two arg case
        '(let ((,L (exp-lhs ,var))
               (,R (exp-rhs ,var)))
           ,(compile-exp L (exp-lhs pattern)
                         (delay
                           (compile-exp R (exp-rhs pattern)
                                        consequent))))
        ;; one arg case
        '(let ((,L (exp-lhs ,var)))
           ,(compile-exp L (exp-lhs pattern) consequent)))))
```

The remaining functions are simpler. build-exp generates code to build the right-hand side of a rule, op? tests if its first argument is an expression with a given operator, and symbol constructs a new symbol. Also given is new-symbol, although it is not used in this program.

```lisp
(defun build-exp (exp bindings)
  "Compile code that will build the exp, given the bindings."
  (cond ((assoc exp bindings) (rest (assoc exp bindings)))
        ((variable-p exp)
         (error "Variable ~a occurred on right-hand side,~
                but not left." exp))
        ((atom exp) '',exp)
        (t (let ((new-exp (mapcar #'(lambda (x)
                                      (build-exp x bindings))
                                  exp)))
             '(simplify-exp (list .,new-exp))))))

(defun op? (exp op)
  "Does the exp have the given op as its operator?"
  (and (exp-p exp) (eq (exp-op exp) op)))

(defun symbol (&rest args)
  "Concatenate symbols or strings to form an interned symbol"
  (intern (format nil "~{~a~}" args)))

(defun new-symbol (&rest args)
  "Concatenate symbols or strings to form an uninterned symbol"
  (make-symbol (format nil "~{~a~}" args)))
```

Here are some examples of the compiler:

```
> (compile-rule '(= (log (^ e x)) x))
(LAMBDA (X)
  (IF (OP? X 'LOG)
    (LET ((XL (EXP-LHS X)))
      (IF (OP? XL '^)
          (LET ((XLL (EXP-LHS XL))
                (XLR (EXP-RHS XL)))
            (IF (EQL XLL 'E)
                XLR))))))
> (compile-rule (simp-rule '(n * (m * x) = (n * m) * x)))
(LAMBDA (X)
  (IF (OP? X '*)
    (LET ((XL (EXP-LHS X))
          (XR (EXP-RHS X)))
      (IF (NUMBERP XL)
          (IF (OP? XR '*)
              (LET ((XRL (EXP-LHS XR))
                    (XRR (EXP-RHS XR)))
                (IF (NUMBERP XRL)
                    (SIMPLIFY-EXP
                      (LIST '*
                            (SIMPLIFY-EXP (LIST '* XL XRL))
                            XRR))))))))))
```

The Rule-Set Compiler

The next step is to combine the code generated by this single-rule compiler to generate more compact code for sets of rules. We'll divide up the complete set of rules into subsets based on the main operator (as we did with the rules-for function), and generate one big function for each operator. We need to preserve the order of the rules, so only certain optimizations are possible, but if we make the assumption that no function has side effects (a safe assumption in this application), we can still do pretty well. We'll use the simp-fn facility to install the one big function for each operator.

The function compile-rule-set takes an operator, finds all the rules for that operator, and compiles each rule individually. (It uses compile-indexed-rule rather than compile-rule, because it assumes we have already done the indexing for the main operator.) After each rule has been compiled, they are combined with combine-rules, which merges similar parts of rules and concatenates the different parts. The result is wrapped in a lambda expression and compiled as the final simplification function for the operator.

```
(defun compile-rule-set (op)
  "Compile all rules indexed under a given main op,
  and make them into the simp-fn for that op."
  (set-simp-fn op
    (compile nil
      '(lambda (x)
        ,(reduce #'combine-rules
                 (mapcar #'compile-indexed-rule
                         (rules-for op)))))))

(defun compile-indexed-rule (rule)
  "Compile one rule into lambda-less code,
  assuming indexing of main op."
  (let ((*bindings* nil))
    (compile-args
      'x (exp-lhs rule)
      (delay (build-exp (exp-rhs rule) *bindings*)))))
```

Here are two examples of what `compile-indexed-rule` generates:

```
> (compile-indexed-rule '(= (log 1) 0))
(LET ((XL (EXP-LHS X)))
  (IF (EQL XL '1)
      '0))
> (compile-indexed-rule '(= (log (^ e x)) x))
(LET ((XL (EXP-LHS X)))
  (IF (OP? XL '^)
      (LET ((XLL (EXP-LHS XL))
            (XLR (EXP-RHS XL)))
        (IF (EQL XLL 'E)
            XLR))))
```

The next step is to combine several of these rules into one. The function `combine-rules` takes two rules and merges them together as much as possible.

```
(defun combine-rules (a b)
  "Combine the code for two rules into one, maintaining order."
  ;; In the default case, we generate the code (or a b),
  ;; but we try to be cleverer and share common code,
  ;; on the assumption that there are no side-effects.
  (cond ((and (listp a) (listp b)
              (= (length a) (length b) 3)
              (equal (first a) (first b))
              (equal (second a) (second b)))
         ;; a=(f x y), b=(f x z) => (f x (combine-rules y z))
         ;; This can apply when f=IF or f=LET
```

```
                    (list (first a) (second a)
                          (combine-rules (third a) (third b))))
                ((matching-ifs a b)
                 '(if ,(second a)
                      ,(combine-rules (third a) (third b))
                      ,(combine-rules (fourth a) (fourth b))))
                ((starts-with a 'or)
                 ;;   a=(or ... (if p y)), b=(if p z) =>
                 ;;        (or ... (if p (combine-rules y z)))
                 ;; else
                 ;;   a=(or ...) b => (or ... b)
                 (if (matching-ifs (last1 a) b)
                     (append (butlast a)
                             (list (combine-rules (last1 a) b)))
                     (append a (list b))))
                (t ;; a, b => (or a b)
                 '(or ,a ,b))))

(defun matching-ifs (a b)
  "Are a and b if statements with the same predicate?"
  (and (starts-with a 'if) (starts-with b 'if)
       (equal (second a) (second b))))

(defun last1 (list)
  "Return the last element (not last cons cell) of list"
  (first (last list)))
```

Here is what `combine-rules` does with the two rules generated above:

```
> (combine-rules
    '(let ((x1 (exp-lhs x))) (if (eql x1 '1) '0))
    '(let ((x1 (exp-lhs x)))
       (if (op? x1 '^)
           (let ((x11 (exp-lhs x1))
                 (x1r (exp-rhs x1)))
             (if (eql x11 'e) x1r)))))
(LET ((XL (EXP-LHS X)))
  (OR (IF (EQL XL '1) '0)
      (IF (OP? XL '^)
          (LET ((XLL (EXP-LHS XL))
                (XLR (EXP-RHS XL)))
            (IF (EQL XLL 'E) XLR)))))
```

Now we run the compiler by calling `compile-all-rules-indexed` and show the combined compiled simplification function for `log`. The comments were entered by hand to show what simplification rules are compiled where.

```
(defun compile-all-rules-indexed (rules)
  "Compile a separate fn for each operator, and store it
  as the simp-fn of the operator."
  (index-rules rules)
  (let ((all-ops (delete-duplicates (mapcar #'main-op rules))))
    (mapc #'compile-rule-set all-ops)))


> (compile-all-rules-indexed *simplification-rules*)
(SIN COS LOG ^ * / - + D)

> (simp-fn 'log)
(LAMBDA (X)
  (LET ((XL (EXP-LHS X)))
    (OR (IF (EQL XL '1)
            '0)                          ; log 1 = 0
        (IF (EQL XL '0)
            'UNDEFINED)                  ; log 0 = undefined
        (IF (EQL XL 'E)
            '1)                          ; log e = 1
        (IF (OP? XL '^)
            (LET ((XLL (EXP-LHS XL))
                  (XLR (EXP-RHS XL)))
              (IF (EQL XLL 'E)
                  XLR)))))))             ; log e^x = x
```

$; \log 1 = 0$

$; \log 0 = undefined$

$; \log e = 1$

$; \log e^{x} = x$

If we want to bypass the rule-based simplifier altogether, we can change simplify-exp once again to eliminate the check for rules:

```
(defun simplify-exp (exp)
  "Simplify by doing arithmetic, or by using the simp function
  supplied for this operator.  Do not use rules of any kind."
  (cond ((simplify-by-fn exp))
        ((evaluable exp) (eval exp))
        (t exp)))
```

At last, we are in a position to run the benchmark test on the new compiled code; the function test-it runs in about .15 seconds with memoization and .05 without. Why would memoization, which helped before, now hurt us? Probably because there is a lot of overhead in accessing the hash table, and that overhead is only worth it when there is a lot of other computation to do.

We've seen a great improvement since the original code, as the following table summarizes. Overall, the various efficiency improvements have resulted in a 130-fold speed-up—we can do now in a minute what used to take two hours. Of course, one must keep in mind that the statistics are only good for this one particular set of test data on this one machine. It is an open question what performance you will get on other problems and on other machines.

The following table summarizes the execution time and number of function calls on the test data:

	original	memo	memo+index	memo+comp	comp
run time (secs)	6.6	3.0	.98	.15	.05
speed-up	–	2	7	44	130
calls					
pat-match	51690	20003	5159	0	0
variable-p	37908	14694	4798	0	0
match-variable	1393	551	551	0	0
simplify	906	408	408	545	906
simplify-exp	274	118	118	118	274

9.7 History and References

The idea of memoization was introduced by Donald Michie 1968. He proposed using a list of values rather than a hash table, so the savings was not as great. In mathematics, the field of dynamic programming is really just the study of how to compute values in the proper order so that partial results will already be cached away when needed.

A large part of academic computer science covers compilation; Aho and Ullman 1972 is just one example. The technique of compiling embedded languages (such as the language of pattern-matching rules) is one that has achieved much more attention in the Lisp community than in the rest of computer science. See Emanuelson and Haraldsson 1980, for an example.

Choosing the right data structure, indexing it properly, and defining algorithms to operate on it is another important branch of computer science; Sedgewick 1988 is one example, but there are many worthy texts.

Delaying computation by packaging it up in a lambda expression is an idea that goes back to Algol's use of *thunks*—a mechanism to implement call-by-name parameters, essentially by passing functions of no arguments. The name *thunk* comes from the fact that these functions can be compiled: the system does not have to think about them at run time, because the compiler has already thunk about them. Peter Ingerman 1961 describes thunks in detail. Abelson and Sussman 1985 cover delays nicely. The idea of eliminating unneeded computation is so attractive that entire languages have built around the concept of *lazy evaluation*—don't evaluate an expression until its value is needed. See Hughes 1985 or Field and Harrison 1988.

9.8   Exercises

Exercise 9.3 [d]   In this chapter we presented a compiler for `simplify`. It is not too much harder to extend this compiler to handle the full power of `pat-match`. Instead of looking at expressions only, allow trees with variables in any position. Extend and generalize the definitions of `compile-rule` and `compile-rule-set` so that they can be used as a general tool for any application program that uses `pat-match` and/or `rule-based-translator`. Make sure that the compiler is data-driven, so that the programmer who adds a new kind of pattern to `pat-match` can also instruct the compiler how to deal with it. One hard part will be accounting for segment variables. It is worth spending a considerable amount of effort at compile time to make this efficient at run time.

Exercise 9.4 [m]   Define the time to compute (fib n) without memoization as T_n. Write a formula to express T_n. Given that $T_{25} \approx 1.1$ seconds, predict T_{100}.

Exercise 9.5 [m]   Consider a version of the game of Nim played as follows: there is a pile of n tokens. Two players alternate removing tokens from the pile; on each turn a player must take either one, two, or three tokens. Whoever takes the last token wins. Write a program that, given n, returns the number of tokens to take to insure a win, if possible. Analyze the execution times for your program, with and without memoization.

Exercise 9.6 [m]   A more complicated Nim-like game is known as Grundy's game. The game starts with a single pile of n tokens. Each player must choose one pile and split it into two uneven piles. The first player to be unable to move loses. Write a program to play Grundy's game, and see how memoization helps.

Exercise 9.7 [h]   This exercise describes a more challenging one-person game. In this game the player rolls a six-sided die eight times. The player forms four two-digit decimal numbers such that the total of the four numbers is as high as possible, but not higher than 170. A total of 171 or more gets scored as zero.

The game would be deterministic and completely boring if not for the requirement that after each roll the player must immediately place the digit in either the ones or tens column of one of the four numbers.

Here is a sample game. The player first rolls a 3 and places it in the ones column of the first number, then rolls a 4 and places it in the tens column, and so on. On the last roll the player rolls a 6 and ends up with a total of 180. Since this is over the limit of 170, the player's final score is 0.

roll	3	4	6	6	3	5	3	6
1st num.	-3	43	43	43	43	43	43	43
2nd num.	–	–	-6	-6	36	36	36	36
3rd num.	–	–	–	-6	-6	-6	36	36
4th num.	–	–	–	–	–	-5	-5	65
total	03	43	49	55	85	90	120	0

Write a function that allows you to play a game or a series of games. The function should take as argument a function representing a strategy for playing the game.

Exercise 9.8 [h] Define a good strategy for the dice game described above. (Hint: my strategy scores an average of 143.7.)

Exercise 9.9 [m] One problem with playing games involving random numbers is the possibility that a player can cheat by figuring out what random is going to do next. Read the definition of the function random and describe how a player could cheat. Then describe a countermeasure.

Exercise 9.10 [m] On page 292 we saw the use of the read-time conditionals, #+ and #-, where #+ is the read-time equivalent of when, and #- is the read-time equivalent of unless. Unfortunately, there is no read-time equivalent of case. Implement one.

Exercise 9.11 [h] Write a compiler for ELIZA that compiles all the rules at once into a single function. How much more efficient is the compiled version?

Exercise 9.12 [d] Write some rules to simplify Lisp code. Some of the algebraic simplification rules will still be valid, but new ones will be needed to simplify nonalgebraic functions and special forms. (Since nil is a valid expression in this domain, you will have to deal with the semipredicate problem.) Here are some example rules (using prefix notation):

```
(= (+ x 0) x)
(= 'nil nil)
(= (car (cons x y)) x)
(= (cdr (cons x y)) y)
(= (if t x y) x)
(= (if nil x y) y)
(= (length nil) 0)
(= (expt y (?if x numberp)) (expt (expt y (/ x 2)) 2))
```

Exercise 9.13 [m]   Consider the following two versions of the sieve of Eratosthenes algorithm. The second explicitly binds a local variable. Is this worth it?

```
(defun sieve (pipe)
  (make-pipe (head pipe)
             (filter #'(lambda (x) (/= (mod x (head pipe)) 0))
                     (sieve (tail pipe)))))

(defun sieve (pipe)
  (let ((first-num (head pipe)))
    (make-pipe first-num
               (filter #'(lambda (x) (/= (mod x first-num) 0))
                       (sieve (tail pipe))))))
```

9.9   Answers

Answer 9.4   Let F_n denote (fib n). Then the time to compute F_n, T_n, is a small constant for $n \le 1$, and is roughly equal to T_{n-1} plus T_{n-2} for larger n. Thus, T_n is roughly proportional to F_n:

$$T_n = F_n \frac{T_i}{F_i}$$

We could use some small value of T_i to calculate T_{100} if we knew F_{100}. Fortunately, we can use the equation:

$$F_n \propto \phi^n$$

where $\phi = (1 + \sqrt{(5)})/2 \approx 1.618$. This equation was derived by de Moivre in 1718 (see Knuth, Donald E. *Fundamental Algorithms*, pp. 78–83), but the number ϕ has a long interesting history. Euclid called it the "extreme and mean ratio," because the ratio of A to B is the ratio of $A + B$ to A if A/B is ϕ. In the Renaissance it was called the "divine proportion," and in the last century it has been known as the "golden ratio," because a rectangle with sides in this ratio can be divided into two smaller rectangles that both have the same ratio between sides. It is said to be a pleasing proportion when employed in paintings and architecture. Putting history aside, given $T_{25} \approx 1.1sec$ we can now calculate:

$$T_{100} \approx \phi^{100} \frac{1.1sec}{\phi^{25}} \approx 5 \times 10^{15} sec$$

which is roughly 150 million years. We can also see that the timing data in the table fits the equation fairly well. However, we would expect some additional time for larger numbers because it takes longer to add and garbage collect bignums than fixnums.

Answer 9.5 First we'll define the notion of a forced win. This occurs either when there are three or fewer tokens left or when you can make a move that gives your opponent a possible loss. A possible loss is any position that is not a forced win. If you play perfectly, then a possible loss for your opponent will in fact be a win for you, since there are no ties. See the functions win and loss below. Now your strategy should be to win the game outright if there are three or fewer tokens, or otherwise to choose the largest number resulting in a possible loss for your opponent. If there is no such move available to you, take only one, on the grounds that your opponent is more likely to make a mistake with a larger pile to contend with. This strategy is embodied in the function nim below.

```lisp
(defun win (n)
  "Is a pile of n tokens a win for the player to move?"
  (or (<= n 3)
      (loss (- n 1))
      (loss (- n 2))
      (loss (- n 3))))

(defun loss (n) (not (win n)))

(defun nim (n)
  "Play Nim: a player must take 1-3; taking the last one wins."
  (cond ((<= n 3) n)           ; an immediate win
        ((loss (- n 3)) 3)     ; an eventual win
        ((loss (- n 2)) 2)     ; an eventual win
        ((loss (- n 1)) 1)     ; an eventual win
        (t 1)))                ; a loss; the 1 is arbitrary

(memoize 'loss)
```

From this we are able to produce a table of execution times (in seconds), with and without memoization. Only loss need be memoized. (Why?) Do you have a good explanation of the times for the unmemoized version? What happens if you change the order of the loss clauses in win and/or nim?

Answer 9.6 We start by defining a function, moves, which generates all possible moves from a given position. This is done by considering each pile of n tokens within a set of piles s. Any pile bigger than two tokens can be split. We take care to eliminate duplicate positions by sorting each set of piles, and then removing the duplicates.

```lisp
(defun moves (s)
  "Return a list of all possible moves in Grundy's game"
  ;; S is a list of integers giving the sizes of the piles
  (remove-duplicates
    (loop for n in s append (make-moves n s))
    :test #'equal))
```

```
(defun make-moves (n s)
  (when (>= n 2)
    (let ((s/n (remove n s :count 1)))
      (loop for i from 1 to (- (ceiling n 2) 1)
            collect (sort* (list* i (- n i) s/n)
                           #'>)))))

(defun sort* (seq pred &key key)
  "Sort without altering the sequence"
  (sort (copy-seq seq) pred :key key))
```

This time a loss is defined as a position from which you have no moves, or one from which your opponent can force a win no matter what you do. A winning position is one that is not a loss, and the strategy is to pick a move that is a loss for your opponent, or if you can't, just to play anything (here we arbitrarily pick the first move generated).

```
(defun loss (s)
  (let ((choices (moves s)))
    (or (null choices)
        (every #'win choices))))

(defun win (s) (not (loss s)))

(defun grundy (s)
  (let ((choices (moves s)))
    (or (find-if #'loss choices)
        (first choices))))
```

Answer 9.7   The answer assumes that a strategy function takes four arguments: the current die roll, the score so far, the number of remaining positions in the tens column, and the number of remaining positions in the ones column. The strategy function should return 1 or 10.

```
(defun play-games (&optional (n-games 10) (player 'make-move))
  "A driver for a simple dice game.  In this game the player
  rolls a six-sided die eight times.  The player forms four
  two-digit decimal numbers such that the total of the four
  numbers is as high as possible, but not higher than 170.
  A total of 171 or more gets scored as zero.  After each die
  is rolled, the player must decide where to put it.
  This function returns the player's average score."
  (/ (loop repeat n-games summing (play-game player 0 4 4))
     (float n-games)))
```

```
(defun play-game (player &optional (total 0) (tens 4) (ones 4))
  (cond ((or (> total 170) (< tens 0) (< ones 0)) 0)
        ((and (= tens 0) (= ones 0)) total)
        (t (let ((die (roll-die)))
             (case (funcall player die total tens ones)
               (1  (play-game player (+ total die)
                               tens (- ones 1)))
               (10 (play-game player (+ total (* 10 die))
                               (- tens 1) ones))
               (t  0)))))))

(defun roll-die () (+ 1 (random 6)))
```

So, the expression (play-games 5 #'make-move) would play five games with a strategy called make-move. This returns only the average score of the games; if you want to see each move as it is played, use this function:

```
(defun show (player)
  "Return a player that prints out each move it makes."
  #'(lambda (die total tens ones)
      (when (= total 0) (fresh-line))
      (let ((move (funcall player die total tens ones)))
        (incf total (* die move))
        (format t "~2d->~3d | ~@[*~]" (* move die) total (> total 170))
        move)))
```

and call (play-games 5 (show #'make-moves)).

Answer 9.9 The expression (random 6 (make-random-state)) returns the next number that roll-die will return. To guard against this, we can make roll-die use a random state that is not accessible through a global variable:

```
(let ((state (make-random-state t)))
  (defun roll-die () (+ 1 (random 6 state))))
```

Answer 9.10 Because this has to do with read-time evaluation, it must be implemented as a macro or read macro. Here's one way to do it:

```
(defmacro read-time-case (first-case &rest other-cases)
  "Do the first case, where normally cases are
  specified with #+ or possibly #- marks."
  (declare (ignore other-cases))
  first-case)
```

A fanciful example, resurrecting a number of obsolete Lisps, follows:

```
(defun get-fast-time ()
  (read-time-case
      #+Explorer    (time:microsecond-time)
      #+Franz       (sys:time)
      #+(or PSL UCI) (time)
      #+YKT         (currenttime)
      #+MTS         (status 39)
      #+Interlisp   (clock 1)
      #+Lisp1.5     (tempus-fugit)
      ;; otherwise
                    (get-internal-real-time))))
```

Answer 9.13 Yes. Computing (head pipe) may be a trivial computation, but it will be done many times. Binding the local variable makes sure that it is only done once. In general, things that you expect to be done multiple times should be moved out of delayed functions, while things that may not be done at all should be moved inside a delay.

Low-Level Efficiency Issues

There are only two qualities in the world: efficiency and inefficiency; and only two sorts of people: the efficient and the inefficient.

—George Bernard Shaw
John Bull's Other Island (1904)

T he efficiency techniques of the previous chapter all involved fairly significant changes to an algorithm. But what happens when you already are using the best imaginable algorithms, and performance is still a problem? One answer is to find what parts of the program are used most frequently and make micro-optimizations to those parts. This chapter covers the following six optimization techniques. If your programs all run quickly enough, then feel free to skip this chapter. But if you would like your programs to run faster, the techniques described here can lead to speed-ups of 40 times or more.

- Use declarations.

- Avoid generic functions.

- Avoid complex argument lists.

- Provide compiler macros.

- Avoid unnecessary consing.

- Use the right data structure.

10.1   Use Declarations

On general-purpose computers running Lisp, much time is spent on type-checking. You can gain efficiency at the cost of robustness by declaring, or promising, that certain variables will always be of a given type. For example, consider the following function to compute the sum of the squares of a sequence of numbers:

```
(defun sum-squares (seq)
  (let ((sum 0))
    (dotimes (i (length seq))
      (incf sum (square (elt seq i))))
    sum))

(defun square (x) (* x x))
```

If this function will only be used to sum vectors of fixnums, we can make it a lot faster by adding declarations:

```
(defun sum-squares (vect)
  (declare (type (simple-array fixnum *) vect)
           (inline square) (optimize speed (safety 0)))
  (let ((sum 0))
    (declare (fixnum sum))
    (dotimes (i (length vect))
      (declare (fixnum i))
      (incf sum (the fixnum (square (svref vect i)))))
    sum))
```

The fixnum declarations let the compiler use integer arithmetic directly, rather than checking the type of each addend. The (the fixnum ...) special form is a promise that the argument is a fixnum. The (optimize speed (safety 0)) declaration tells the compiler to make the function run as fast as possible, at the possible expense of making the code less safe (by ignoring type checks and so on). Other quantities that can be optimized are compilation-speed, space and in ANSI Common Lisp only, debug (ease of debugging). Quantities can be given a number from 0 to 3 indicating how important they are; 3 is most important and is the default if the number is left out.

The (inline square) declaration allows the compiler to generate the multiplication specified by square right in the loop, without explicitly making a function call to square. The compiler will create a local variable for (svref vect i) and will not execute the reference twice—inline functions do not have any of the problems associated with macros as discussed on page 853. However, there is one drawback: when you redefine an inline function, you may need to recompile all the functions that call it.

You should declare a function inline when it is short and the function-calling overhead will thus be a significant part of the total execution time. You should not declare a function inline when the function is recursive, when its definition is likely to change, or when the function's definition is long and it is called from many places.

In the example at hand, declaring the function inline saves the overhead of a function call. In some cases, further optimizations are possible. Consider the predicate starts-with:

```
(defun starts-with (list x)
  "Is this a list whose first element is x?"
  (and (consp list) (eql (first list) x)))
```

Suppose we have a code fragment like the following:

```
(if (consp list) (starts-with list x) ...)
```

If starts-with is declared inline this will expand to:

```
(if (consp list) (and (consp list) (eql (first list) x)) ...)
```

which many compilers will simplify to:

```
(if (consp list) (eql (first list) x) ...)
```

Very few compilers do this kind of simplification across functions without the hint provided by inline.

Besides eliminating run-time type checks, declarations also allow the compiler to choose the most efficient representation of data objects. Many compilers support both *boxed* and *unboxed* representations of data objects. A boxed representation includes enough information to determine the type of the object. An unboxed representation is just the "raw bits" that the computer can deal with directly. Consider the following function, which is used to clear a 1024×1024 array of floating point numbers, setting each one to zero:

```lisp
(defun clear-m-array (array)
  (declare (optimize (speed 3) (safety 0)))
  (declare (type (simple-array single-float (1024 1024)) array))
  (dotimes (i 1024)
    (dotimes (j 1024)
      (setf (aref array i j) 0.0))))
```

In Allegro Common Lisp on a Sun SPARCstation, this compiles into quite good code, comparable to that produced by the C compiler for an equivalent C program. If the declarations are omitted, however, the performance is about 40 times worse.

The problem is that without the declarations, it is not safe to store the raw floating point representation of 0.0 in each location of the array. Instead, the program has to box the 0.0, allocating storage for a typed pointer to the raw bits. This is done inside the nested loops, so the result is that each call to the version of clear-m-array without declarations calls the floating-point-boxing function 1048567 times, allocating a megaword of storage. Needless to say, this is to be avoided.

Not all compilers heed all declarations; you should check before wasting time with declarations your compiler may ignore. The function disassemble can be used to show what a function compiles into. For example, consider the trivial function to add two numbers together. Here it is with and without declarations:

```lisp
(defun f (x y)
  (declare (fixnum x y) (optimize (safety 0) (speed 3)))
  (the fixnum (+ x y)))

(defun g (x y) (+ x y))
```

Here is the disassembled code for f from Allegro Common Lisp for a Motorola 68000-series processor:

```
> (disassemble 'f)
;; disassembling #<Function f @ #x83ef79>
;; formals: x y
;; code vector @ #x83ef44
0:      link    a6,#0
4:      move.l  a2,-(a7)
6:      move.l  a5,-(a7)
8:      move.l  7(a2),a5
12:     move.l  8(a6),d4  ; y
16:     add.l   12(a6),d4  ; x
20:     move.l  #1,d1
```

```
22:     move.l  -8(a6),a5
26:     unlk    a6
28:     rtd     #8
```

This may look intimidating at first glance, but you don't have to be an expert at 68000 assembler to gain some appreciation of what is going on here. The instructions labeled 0-8 (labels are in the leftmost column) comprise the typical function preamble for the 68000. They do subroutine linkage and store the new function object and constant vector into registers. Since f uses no constants, instructions 6, 8, and 22 are really unnecessary and could be omitted. Instructions 0, 4, and 26 could also be omitted if you don't care about seeing this function in a stack trace during debugging. More recent versions of the compiler will omit these instructions.

The heart of function f is the two-instruction sequence 12-16. Instruction 12 retrieves y, and 16 adds y to x, leaving the result in d4, which is the "result" register. Instruction 20 sets d1, the "number of values returned" register, to 1.

Contrast this to the code for g, which has no declarations and is compiled at default speed and safety settings:

```
> (disassemble 'g)
;; disassembling #<Function g @ #x83dbd1>
;; formals: x y
;; code vector @ #x83db64
0:      add.l   #8,31(a2)
4:      sub.w   #2,d1
6:      beq.s   12
8:      jmp     16(a4)  ; wnaerr
12:     link    a6,#0
16:     move.l  a2,-(a7)
18:     move.l  a5,-(a7)
20:     move.l  7(a2),a5
24:     tst.b   -208(a4)  ; signal-hit
28:     beq.s   34
30:     jsr     872(a4)  ; process-sig
34:     move.l  8(a6),d4  ; y
38:     move.l  12(a6),d0  ; x
42:     or.l    d4,d0
44:     and.b   #7,d0
48:     bne.s   62
50:     add.l   12(a6),d4  ; x
54:     bvc.s   76
56:     jsr     696(a4)  ; add-overflow
60:     bra.s   76
62:     move.l  12(a6),-(a7)  ; x
66:     move.l  d4,-(a7)
68:     move.l  #2,d1
```

```
70:     move.l   -304(a4),a0   ; +_2op
74:     jsr      (a4)
76:     move.l   #1,d1
78:     move.l   -8(a6),a5
82:     unlk     a6
84:     rtd      #8
```

See how much more work is done. The first four instructions ensure that the right number of arguments have been passed to g. If not, there is a jump to wnaerr (wrong-number-of-arguments-error). Instructions 12–20 have the argument loading code that was at 0–8 in f. At 24–30 there is a check for asynchronous signals, such as the user hitting the abort key. After x and y are loaded, there is a type check (42–48). If the arguments are not both fixnums, then the code at instructions 62–74 sets up a call to +_2op, which handles type coercion and non-fixnum addition. If all goes well, we don't have to call this routine, and do the addition at instruction 50 instead. But even then we are not done—just because the two arguments were fixnums does not mean the result will be. Instructions 54–56 check and branch to an overflow routine if needed. Finally, instructions 76–84 return the final value, just as in f.

Some low-quality compilers ignore declarations altogether. Other compilers don't need certain declarations, because they can rely on special instructions in the underlying architecture. On a Lisp Machine, both f and g compile into the same code:

```
6 PUSH        ARG|0      ; X
7 +           ARG|1      ; Y
8 RETURN      PDL-POP
```

The Lisp Machine has a microcoded + instruction that simultaneously does a fixnum add and checks for non-fixnum arguments, branching to a subroutine if either argument is not a fixnum. The hardware does the work that the compiler has to do on a conventional processor. This makes the Lisp Machine compiler simpler, so compiling a function is faster. However, on modern pipelined computers with instruction caches, there is little or no advantage to microcoding. The current trend is away from microcode toward reduced instruction set computers (RISC).

On most computers, the following declarations are most likely to be helpful:

- fixnum and float. Numbers declared as fixnums or floating-point numbers can be handled directly by the host computer's arithmetic instructions. On some systems, float by itself is not enough; you have to say single-float or double-float. Other numeric declarations will probably be ignored. For example, declaring a variable as integer does not help the compiler much, because bignums are integers. The code to add bignums is too complex to put inline, so the compiler will branch to a general-purpose routine (like +_2op in Allegro), the same routine it would use if no declarations were given.

- `list` and `array`. Many Lisp systems provide separate functions for the list- and array- versions of commonly used sequence functions. For example, (delete x (the list l)) compiles into (sys:delete-list-eql x l) on a TI Explorer Lisp Machine. Another function, sys:delete-vector, is used for arrays, and the generic function delete is used only when the compiler can't tell what type the sequence is. So if you know that the argument to a generic function is either a `list` or an `array`, then declare it as such.

- `simple-vector` and `simple-array`. Simple vectors and arrays are those that do not share structure with other arrays, do not have fill pointers, and are not adjustable. In many implementations it is faster to `aref` a `simple-vector` than a `vector`. It is certainly much faster than taking an `elt` of a sequence of unknown type. Declare your arrays to be simple (if they in fact are).

- `(array type)`. It is often important to specialize the type of array elements. For example, an `(array short-float)` may take only half the storage of a general array, and such a declaration will usually allow computations to be done using the CPU's native floating-point instructions, rather than converting into and out of Common Lisp's representation of floating points. This is very important because the conversion normally requires allocating storage, but the direct computation does not. The specifiers `(simple-array type)` and `(vector type)` should be used instead of `(array type)` when appropriate. A very common mistake is to declare `(simple-vector type)`. This is an error because Common Lisp expects `(simple-vector size)`—don't ask me why.

- `(array * dimensions)`. The full form of an `array` or `simple-array` type specifier is `(array type dimensions)`. So, for example, `(array bit (* *))` is a two-dimensional bit array, and `(array bit (1024 1024))` is a 1024×1024 bit array. It is very important to specify the number of dimensions when known, and less important to specify the exact size, although with multidimensional arrays, declaring the size is more important. The format for a `vector` type specifier is `(vector type size)`.

Note that several of these declarations can apply all at once. For example, in

```
(position #\. (the simple-string file-name))
```

the variable `filename` has been declared to be a vector, a simple array, and a sequence of type `string-char`. All three of these declarations are helpful. The type `simple-string` is an abbreviation for `(simple-array string-char)`.

This guide applies to most Common Lisp systems, but you should look in the implementation notes for your particular system for more advice on how to fine-tune your code.

10.2   Avoid Generic Functions

Common Lisp provides functions with great generality, but someone must pay the price for this generality. For example, if you write (elt x 0), different machine instruction will be executed depending on if x is a list, string, or vector. Without declarations, checks will have to be done at runtime. You can either provide declarations, as in (elt (the list x) 0), or use a more specific function, such as (first x) in the case of lists, (char x 0) for strings, (aref x 0) for vectors, and (svref x 0) for simple vectors. Of course, generic functions are useful—I wrote random-elt as shown following to work on lists, when I could have written the more efficient random-mem instead. The choice paid off when I wanted a function to choose a random character from a string—random-elt does the job unchanged, while random-mem does not.

```
(defun random-elt (s) (elt s (random (length s))))
(defun random-mem (l) (nth (random (length (the list l))) l))
```

This example was simple, but in more complicated cases you can make your sequence functions more efficient by having them explicitly check if their arguments are lists or vectors. See the definition of map-into on page 857.

10.3   Avoid Complex Argument Lists

Functions with keyword arguments suffer a large degree of overhead. This may also be true for optional and rest arguments, although usually to a lesser degree. Let's look at some simple examples:

```
(defun reg (a b c d) (list a b c d))
(defun rst (a b c &rest d) (list* a b c d))
(defun opt (&optional a b (c 1) (d (sqrt a))) (list a b c d))
(defun key (&key a b (c 1) (d (sqrt a))) (list a b c d))
```

We can see what these compile into for the TI Explorer, but remember that your compiler may be quite different.

```
> (disassemble 'reg)
  8 PUSH            ARG|0      ; A
  9 PUSH            ARG|1      ; B
 10 PUSH            ARG|2      ; C
 11 PUSH            ARG|3      ; D
 12 TAIL-REC CALL-4 FEF|3      ; #'LIST
> (disassemble 'rst)
  8 PUSH            ARG|0      ; A
  9 PUSH            ARG|1      ; B
 10 PUSH            ARG|2      ; C
 11 PUSH            LOCAL|0    ; D
 12 RETURN CALL-4   FEF|3      ; #'LIST*
```

With the regular argument list, we just push the four variables on the argument stack and branch to the list function. (Chapter 22 explains why a tail-recursive call is just a branch statement.)

With a rest argument, things are almost as easy. It turns out that on this machine, the microcode for the calling sequence automatically handles rest arguments, storing them in local variable 0. Let's compare with optional arguments:

```
(defun opt (&optional a b (c 1) (d (sqrt a))) (list a b c d))

> (disassemble 'opt)
 24 DISPATCH        FEF|5      ; [0⇒25;1⇒25;2⇒25;3⇒27;ELSE⇒30]
 25 PUSH-NUMBER     1
 26 POP             ARG|2      ; C
 27 PUSH            ARG|0      ; A
 28 PUSH CALL-1     FEF|3      ; #'SQRT
 29 POP             ARG|3      ; D
 30 PUSH            ARG|0      ; A
 31 PUSH            ARG|1      ; B
 32 PUSH            ARG|2      ; C
 33 PUSH            ARG|3      ; D
 34 TAIL-REC CALL-4 FEF|4      ; #'LIST
```

Although this assembly language may be harder to read, it turns out that optional arguments are handled very efficiently. The calling sequence stores the number of optional arguments on top of the stack, and the DISPATCH instruction uses this to index into a table stored at location FEF|5 (an offset five words from the start of the function). The result is that in one instruction the function branches to just the right place to initialize any unspecified arguments. Thus, a function with optional arguments that are all supplied takes only one more instruction (the dispatch) than the "regular" case. Unfortunately, keyword arguments don't fare as well:

```
(defun key (&key a b (c 1) (d (sqrt a))) (list a b c d))
```

```
> (disassemble 'key)
   14 PUSH-NUMBER      1
   15 POP              LOCAL|3    ; C
   16 PUSH             FEF|3      ; SYS::KEYWORD-GARBAGE
   17 POP              LOCAL|4
   18 TEST             LOCAL|0
   19 BR-NULL      24
   20 PUSH             FEF|4      ; '(:A :B :C :D)
   21 SET-NIL          PDL-PUSH
   22 PUSH-LOC         LOCAL|1    ; A
   23 (AUX) %STORE-KEY-WORD-ARGS
   24 PUSH             LOCAL|1    ; A
   25 PUSH             LOCAL|2    ; B
   26 PUSH             LOCAL|3    ; C
   27 PUSH             LOCAL|4
   28 EQ               FEF|3      ; SYS::KEYWORD-GARBAGE
   29 BR-NULL      33
   30 PUSH             LOCAL|1    ; A
   31 PUSH CALL-1      FEF|5      ; #'SQRT
   32 RETURN CALL-4    FEF|6      ; #'LIST
   33 PUSH             LOCAL|4
   34 RETURN CALL-4    FEF|6      ; #'LIST
```

It is not important to be able to read all this assembly language. The point is that there is considerable overhead, even though this architecture has a specific instruction (%STORE-KEY-WORD-ARGS) to help deal with keyword arguments.

Now let's look at the results on another system, the Allegro compiler for the 68000. First, here's the assembly code for reg, to give you an idea of the minimal calling sequence:[1]

```
> (disassemble 'reg)
;; disassembling #<Function reg @ #x83db59>
;; formals: a b c d
;; code vector @ #x83db1c
0:      link    a6,#0
4:      move.l  a2,-(a7)
6:      move.l  a5,-(a7)
8:      move.l  7(a2),a5
12:     move.l  20(a6),-(a7)    ; a
16:     move.l  16(a6),-(a7)    ; b
20:     move.l  12(a6),-(a7)    ; c
24:     move.l  8(a6),-(a7)     ; d
28:     move.l  #4,d1
30:     jsr     848(a4)         ; list
```

---

[1]These are all done with safety 0 and speed 3.

```
34:     move.l   -8(a6),a5
38:     unlk     a6
40:     rtd      #10
```

Now we see that &rest arguments take a lot more code in this system:

```
> (disassemble 'rst)
;; disassembling #<Function rst @ #x83de89>
;; formals: a b c &rest d
;; code vector @ #x83de34
0:      sub.w    #3,d1
2:      bge.s    8
4:      jmp      16(a4)           ; wnaerr
8:      move.l   (a7)+,a1
10:     move.l   d3,-(a7)         ; nil
12:     sub.w    #1,d1
14:     blt.s    38
16:     move.l   a1,-52(a4)       ; c_protected-retaddr
20:     jsr      40(a4)           ; cons
24:     move.l   d4,-(a7)
26:     dbra     d1,20
30:     move.l   -52(a4),a1       ; c_protected-retaddr
34:     clr.l    -52(a4)          ; c_protected-retaddr
38:     move.l   a1,-(a7)
40:     link     a6,#0
44:     move.l   a2,-(a7)
46:     move.l   a5,-(a7)
48:     move.l   7(a2),a5
52:     move.l   -332(a4),a0      ; list*
56:     move.l   -8(a6),a5
60:     unlk     a6
62:     move.l   #4,d1
64:     jmp      (a4)
```

The loop from 20-26 builds up the &rest list one cons at a time. Part of the difficulty is that cons could initiate a garbage collection at any time, so the list has to be built in a place that the garbage collector will know about. The function with optional arguments is even worse, taking 34 instructions (104 bytes), and keywords are worst of all, weighing in at 71 instructions (178 bytes), and including a loop. The overhead for optional arguments is proportional to the number of optional arguments, while for keywords it is proportional to the product of the number of parameters allowed and the number of arguments actually supplied.

A good guideline to follow is to use keyword arguments primarily as an interface to infrequently used functions, and to provide versions of these functions without keywords that can be used in places where efficiency is important. Consider:

```
(proclaim '(inline key))
(defun key (&key a b (c 1) (d (sqrt a))) (*no-key a b c d))
(defun *no-key (a b c d) (list a b c d))
```

Here the function key is used as an interface to the function no-key, which does the real work. The inline proclamation should allow the compiler to compile a call to key as a call to no-key with the appropriate arguments:

```
> (disassemble #'(lambda (x y) (key :b x :a y)))
   10 PUSH            ARG|1      ; Y
   11 PUSH            ARG|0      ; X
   12 PUSH-NUMBER     1
   13 PUSH            ARG|1      ; Y
   14 PUSH CALL-1     FEF|3      ; #'SQRT
   15 TAIL-REC CALL-4 FEF|4      ; #'NO-KEY
```

The overhead only comes into play when the keywords are not known at compile time. In the following example, the compiler is forced to call key, not no-key, because it doesn't know what the keyword k will be at run time:

```
> (disassemble #'(lambda (k x y) (key k x :a y)))
   10 PUSH            ARG|0      ; K
   11 PUSH            ARG|1      ; X
   12 PUSH            FEF|3      ; ':A
   13 PUSH            ARG|2      ; Y
   14 TAIL-REC CALL-4 FEF|4      ; #'KEY
```

Of course, in this simple example I could have replaced no-key with list, but in general there will be some more complex processing. If I had proclaimed no-key inline as well, then I would get the following:

```
> (disassemble #'(lambda (x y) (key :b x :a y)))
   10 PUSH            ARG|1      ; Y
   11 PUSH            ARG|0      ; X
   12 PUSH-NUMBER     1
   13 PUSH            ARG|1      ; Y
   14 PUSH CALL-1     FEF|3      ; #'SQRT
   15 TAIL-REC CALL-4 FEF|4      ; #'LIST
```

If you like, you can define a macro to automatically define the interface to the keyword-less function:

```
(defmacro defun* (fn-name arg-list &rest body)
  "Define two functions, one an interface to a &keyword-less
version.  Proclaim the interface function inline."
  (if (and (member '&key arg-list)
           (not (member '&rest arg-list)))
      (let ((no-key-fn-name (symbol fn-name '*no-key))
            (args (mapcar #'first-or-self
                          (set-difference
                            arg-list
                            lambda-list-keywords))))
        '(progn
           (proclaim '(inline ,fn-name))
           (defun ,no-key-fn-name ,args
             .,body)
           (defun ,fn-name ,arg-list
             (,no-key-fn-name .,args))))
      '(defun ,fn-name ,arg-list
         .,body)))

> (macroexpand '(defun* key (&key a b (c 1) (d (sqrt a)))
                  (list a b c d)))
(PROGN (PROCLAIM '(INLINE KEY))
       (DEFUN KEY*NO-KEY (A B C D) (LIST A B C D))
       (DEFUN KEY (&KEY A B (C 1) (D (SQRT A)))
         (KEY*NO-KEY A B C D)))

> (macroexpand '(defun* reg (a b c d) (list a b c d)))
(DEFUN REG (A B C D) (LIST A B C D))
```

There is one disadvantage to this approach: a user who wants to declare key inline or not inline does not get the expected result. The user has to know that key is implemented with key*no-key, and declare key*no-key inline.

An alternative is just to proclaim the function that uses &key to be inline. Rob MacLachlan provides an example. In CMU Lisp, the function member has the following definition, which is proclaimed inline:

```
(defun member (item list &key (key #'identity)
                         (test #'eql testp)(test-not nil notp))
  (do ((list list (cdr list)))
      ((null list) nil)
    (let ((car (car list)))
      (if (cond
            (testp
             (funcall test item
                      (funcall key car)))
            (notp
             (not
```

```
              (funcall test-not item
                       (funcall key car))))
          (t
           (funcall test item
                    (funcall key car))))
        (return list)))))
```

A call like (member ch l :key #'first-letter :test #'char=) expands into the equivalent of the following code. Unfortunately, not all compilers are this clever with inline declarations.

```
(do ((list list (cdr list)))
    ((null list) nil)
  (let ((car (car list)))
    (if (char= ch (first-letter car))
        (return list))))
```

This chapter is concerned with efficiency and so has taken a stand against the use of keyword parameters in frequently used functions. But when maintainability is considered, keyword parameters look much better. When a program is being developed, and it is not clear if a function will eventually need additional arguments, keyword parameters may be the best choice.

10.4   Avoid Unnecessary Consing

The cons function may appear to execute quite quickly, but like all functions that allocate new storage, it has a hidden cost. When large amounts of storage are used, eventually the system must spend time garbage collecting. We have not mentioned it earlier, but there are actually two relevant measures of the amount of space consumed by a program: the amount of storage allocated, and the amount of storage retained. The difference is storage that is used temporarily but eventually freed. Lisp guarantees that unused space will eventually be reclaimed by the garbage collector. This happens automatically—the programmer need not and indeed can not explicitly free storage. The problem is that the efficiency of garbage collection can vary widely. Garbage collection is particularly worrisome for real-time systems, because it can happen at any time.

The antidote to garbage woes is to avoid unnecessary copying of objects in often-used code. Try using destructive operations, like nreverse, delete, and nconc, rather than their nondestructive counterparts, (like reverse, remove, and append) whenever it is safe to do so. Or use vectors instead of lists, and reuse values rather than creating copies. As usual, this gain in efficiency may lead to errors that can be difficult to debug. However, the most common kind of unnecessary copying can be eliminated by simple reorganization of your code. Consider the following version of flatten, which returns a list of all the atoms in its input, preserving order. Unlike the version in chapter 5, this version returns a single list of atoms, with no embedded lists.

```lisp
(defun flatten (input)
  "Return a flat list of the atoms in the input.
  Ex: (flatten '((a) (b (c) d))) => (a b c d)."
  (cond ((null input) nil)
        ((atom input) (list input))
        (t (append (flatten (first input))
                   (flatten (rest input))))))
```

This definition is quite simple, and it is easy to see that it is correct. However, each call to append requires copying the first argument, so this version can cons $O(n^2)$ cells on an input with n atoms. The problem with this approach is that it computes the list of atoms in the first and rest of each subcomponent of the input. But the first sublist by itself is not part of the final answer—that's why we have to call append. We could avoid generating garbage by replacing append with nconc, but even then we would still be wasting time, because nconc would have to scan through each sublist to find its end.

The version below makes use of an *accumulator* to keep track of the atoms that have been collected in the rest, and to add the atoms in the first one at a time with cons, rather than building up unnecessary sublists and appending them. This way no garbage is generated, and no subcomponent is traversed more than once.

```lisp
(defun flatten (input &optional accumulator)
  "Return a flat list of the atoms in the input.
  Ex: (flatten '((a) (b (c) d))) => (a b c d)."
  (cond ((null input) accumulator)
        ((atom input) (cons input accumulator))
        (t (flatten (first input)
                    (flatten (rest input) accumulator)))))
```

The version with the accumulator may be a little harder to understand, but it is far more efficient than the original version. Experienced Lisp programmers become quite skilled at replacing calls to append with accumulators.

Some of the early Lisp machines had unreliable garbage-collection, so users just turned garbage collection off, used the machine for a few days, and rebooted when they ran out of space. With a large virtual memory system this is a feasible approach, because virtual memory is a cheap resource. The problem is that real memory is still an expensive resource. When each page contains mostly garbage and only a little live data, the system will spend a lot of time paging data in and out. Compacting garbage-collection algorithms can relocate live data, packing it into a minimum number of pages.

Some garbage-collection algorithms have been optimized to deal particularly well with just this case. If your system has an *ephemeral* or *generational* garbage collector, you need not be so concerned with short-lived objects. Instead, it will be the medium-aged objects that cause problems. The other problem with such systems arises when an object in an old generation is changed to point to an object in a newer generation. This is to be avoided, and it may be that reverse is actually faster than nreverse in such cases. To decide what works best on your particular system, design some test cases and time them.

As an example of efficient use of storage, here is a version of pat-match that eliminates (almost) all consing. The original version of pat-match, as used in ELIZA (page 180), used an association list of variable/value pairs to represent the binding list. This version uses two sequences: a sequence of variables and a sequence of values. The sequences are implemented as vectors instead of lists. In general, vectors take half as much space as lists to store the same information, since half of every list is just pointing to the next element.

In this case, the savings are much more substantial than just half. Instead of building up small binding lists for each partial match and adding to them when the match is extended, we will allocate a sufficiently large vector of variables and values just once, and use them over and over for each partial match, and even for each invocation of pat-match. To do this, we need to know how many variables we are currently using. We could initialize a counter variable to zero and increment it each time we found a new variable in the pattern. The only difficulty would be when the counter variable exceeds the size of the vector. We could just give up and print an error message, but there are more user-friendly alternatives. For example, we could allocate a larger vector for the variables, copy over the existing ones, and then add in the new one.

It turns out that Common Lisp has a built-in facility to do just this. When a vector is created, it can be given a *fill pointer*. This is a counter variable, but one that is conceptually stored inside the vector. Vectors with fill pointers act like a cross between a vector and a stack. You can push new elements onto the stack with the functions vector-push or vector-push-extend. The latter will automatically allocate a larger vector and copy over elements if necessary. You can remove elements with vector-pop, or you can explicitly look at the fill pointer with fill-pointer, or change it with a setf. Here are some examples (with *print-array* set to t so we can see the results):

```
> (setf a (make-array 5 :fill-pointer 0)) ⇒ #()

> (vector-push 1 a) ⇒ 0
```

```
> (vector-push 2 a) ⇒ 1

> a ⇒ #(1 2)

> (vector-pop a) ⇒ 2

> a ⇒ #(1)

> (dotimes (i 10) (vector-push-extend 'x a)) ⇒ NIL

> a ⇒ #(1 X X X X X X X X X X)

> (fill-pointer a) ⇒ 11

> (setf (fill-pointer a) 1) ⇒ 1

> a ⇒ #(1)

> (find 'x a) ⇒ NIL NIL        ; FIND can't find past the fill pointer

> (aref a 2) ⇒ X               ; But AREF can see beyond the fill pointer
```

Using vectors with fill pointers in pat-match, the total storage for binding lists is just twice the number of variables in the largest pattern. I have arbitrarily picked 10 as the maximum number of variables, but even this is not a hard limit, because vector-push-extend can increase it. In any case, the total storage is small, fixed in size, and amortized over all calls to pat-match. These are just the features that indicate a responsible use of storage.

However, there is a grave danger with this approach: the value returned must be managed carefully. The new pat-match returns the value of success when it matches. success is bound to a cons of the variable and value vectors. These can be freely manipulated by the calling routine, but only up until the next call to pat-match. At that time, the contents of the two vectors can change. Therefore, if any calling function needs to hang on to the returned value after another call to pat-match, it should make a copy of the returned value. So it is not quite right to say that this version of pat-match eliminates all consing. It will cons when vector-push-extend runs out of space, or when the user needs to make a copy of a returned value.

Here is the new definition of pat-match. It is implemented by closing the definition of pat-match and its two auxilliary functions inside a let that establishes the bindings of vars, vals, and success, but that is not crucial. Those three variables could have been implemented as global variables instead. Note that it does not support segment variables, or any of the other options implemented in the pat-match of chapter 6.

```
(let* ((vars (make-array 10 :fill-pointer 0 :adjustable t))
       (vals (make-array 10 :fill-pointer 0 :adjustable t))
       (success (cons vars vals)))
```

```
(defun efficient-pat-match (pattern input)
  "Match pattern against input."
  (setf (fill-pointer vars) 0)
  (setf (fill-pointer vals) 0)
  (pat-match-1 pattern input))

(defun pat-match-1 (pattern input)
  (cond ((variable-p pattern) (match-var pattern input))
        ((eql pattern input) success)
        ((and (consp pattern) (consp input))
         (and (pat-match-1 (first pattern) (first input))
              (pat-match-1 (rest pattern) (rest input))))
        (t fail)))

(defun match-var (var input)
  "Match a single variable against input."
  (let ((i (position var vars)))
    (cond ((null i)
           (vector-push-extend var vars)
           (vector-push-extend input vals)
           success)
          ((equal input (aref vals i)) success)
          (t fail)))))
```

An example of its use:

```
> (efficient-pat-match '(?x + ?x = ?y . ?z)
                       '(2 + 2 = (3 + 1) is true))
(#(?X ?Y ?Z) . #(2 (3 + 1) (IS TRUE)))
```

Extensible vectors with fill pointers are convenient, and much more efficient than consing up lists. However, there is some overhead involved in using them, and for those sections of code that must be most efficient, it is best to stick with simple vectors. The following version of efficient-pat-match explicitly manages the size of the vectors and explicitly replaces them with new ones when the size is exceeded:

```
(let* ((current-size 0)
       (max-size 1)
       (vars (make-array max-size))
       (vals (make-array max-size))
       (success (cons vars vals)))
  (declare (simple-vector vars vals)
           (fixnum current-size max-size))
```

```lisp
(defun efficient-pat-match (pattern input)
  "Match pattern against input."
  (setf current-size 0)
  (pat-match-1 pattern input))


;; pat-match-1 is unchanged


(defun match-var (var input)
  "Match a single variable against input."
  (let ((i (position var vars)))
    (cond
      ((null i)
       (when (= current-size max-size)
         ;; Make new vectors when we run out of space
         (setf max-size (* 2 max-size)
               vars (replace (make-array max-size) vars)
               vals (replace (make-array max-size) vals)
               success (cons vars vals)))
       ;; Store var and its value in vectors
       (setf (aref vars current-size) var)
       (setf (aref vals current-size) input)
       (incf current-size)
       success)
      ((equal input (aref vals i)) success)
      (t fail)))))
```

In conclusion, replacing lists with vectors can often save garbage. But when you must use lists, it pays to use a version of cons that avoids consing when possible. The following is such a version:

```lisp
(proclaim '(inline reuse-cons))

(defun reuse-cons (x y x-y)
  "Return (cons x y), or just x-y if it is equal to (cons x y)."
  (if (and (eql x (car x-y)) (eql y (cdr x-y)))
      x-y
      (cons x y)))
```

The trick is based on the definition of subst in Steele's *Common Lisp the Language*. Here is a definition for a version of remove that uses reuse-cons:

```
(defun remq (item list)
  "Like REMOVE, but uses EQ, and only works on lists."
  (cond ((null list) nil)
        ((eq item (first list)) (remq item (rest list)))
        (t (reuse-cons (first list)
                       (remq item (rest list))
                       list))))
```

Avoid Consing: Unique Lists

Of course, reuse-cons only works when you have candidate cons cells around. That is, (reuse-cons a b c) only saves space when c is (or might be) equal to (cons a b). For some applications, it is useful to have a version of cons that returns a unique cons cell without needing c as a hint. We will call this version ucons for "unique cons." ucons maintains a double hash table: *uniq-cons-table* is a hash table whose keys are the cars of cons cells. The value for each car is another hash table whose keys are the cdrs of cons cells. The value of each cdr in this second table is the original cons cell. So two different cons cells with the same car and cdr will retrieve the same value. Here is an implementation of ucons:

```
(defvar *uniq-cons-table* (make-hash-table :test #'eq))

(defun ucons (x y)
  "Return a cons s.t. (eq (ucons x y) (ucons x y)) is true."
  (let ((car-table (or (gethash x *uniq-cons-table*)
                       (setf (gethash x *uniq-cons-table*)
                             (make-hash-table :test #'eq)))))
    (or (gethash y car-table)
        (setf (gethash y car-table) (cons x y)))))
```

ucons, unlike cons, is a true function: it will always return the same value, given the same arguments, where "same" is measured by eq. However, if ucons is given arguments that are equal but not eq, it will not return a unique result. For that we need the function unique. It has the property that (unique x) is eq to (unique y) whenever x and y are equal. unique uses a hash table for atoms in addition to the double hash table for conses. This is necessary because strings and arrays can be equal without being eq. Besides unique, we also define ulist and uappend for convenience.

```
(defvar *uniq-atom-table* (make-hash-table :test #'equal))
```

```
(defun unique (exp)
  "Return a canonical representation that is EQUAL to exp,
  such that (equal x y) implies (eq (unique x) (unique y))."
  (typecase exp
    (symbol exp)
    (fixnum exp)  ;; Remove if fixnums are not eq in your Lisp
    (atom  (or (gethash exp *uniq-atom-table*)
               (setf (gethash exp *uniq-atom-table*) exp)))
    (cons  (unique-cons (car exp) (cdr exp)))))

(defun unique-cons (x y)
  "Return a cons s.t. (eq (ucons x y) (ucons x2 y2)) is true
  whenever (equal x x2) and (equal y y2) are true."
  (ucons (unique x) (unique y)))

(defun ulist (&rest args)
  "A uniquified list."
  (unique args))

(defun uappend (x y)
  "A unique list equal to (append x y)."
  (if (null x)
      (unique y)
      (ucons (first x) (uappend (rest x) y))))
```

The above code works, but it can be improved. The problem is that when unique is applied to a tree, it always traverses the tree all the way to the leaves. The function unique-cons is like ucons, except that unique-cons assumes its arguments are not yet unique. We can modify unique-cons so that it first checks to see if its arguments are unique, by looking in the appropriate hash tables:

```
(defun unique-cons (x y)
  "Return a cons s.t. (eq (ucons x y) (ucons x2 y2)) is true
  whenever (equal x x2) and (equal y y2) are true."
  (let ((ux) (uy))                        ; unique x and y
    (let ((car-table
            (or (gethash x *uniq-cons-table*)
                (gethash (setf ux (unique x)) *uniq-cons-table*)
                (setf (gethash ux *uniq-cons-table*)
                      (make-hash-table :test #'eq)))))
      (or (gethash y car-table)
          (gethash (setf uy (unique y)) car-table)
          (setf (gethash uy car-table)
                (cons ux uy))))))
```

Another advantage of unique is that it can help in indexing. If lists are unique, then they can be stored in an eq hash table instead of a equal hash table. This can lead to significant savings when the list structures are large. An eq hash table for lists is almost as good as a property list on symbols.

Avoid Consing: Multiple Values

Parameters and multiple values can also be used to pass around values, rather than building up lists. For example, instead of:

```
(defstruct point "A point in 3-D cartesian space." x y z)

(defun scale-point (k pt)
  "Multiply a point by a constant, K."
  (make-point :x (* k (point-x pt))
              :y (* k (point-y pt))
              :z (* k (point-z pt))))
```

one could use the following approach, which doesn't generate structures:

```
(defun scale-point (k x y z)
  "Multiply the point (x,y,z) by a constant, K."
  (values (* k x) (* k y) (* k z)))
```

Avoid Consing: Resources

Sometimes it pays to manage explicitly the storage of instances of some data type. A pool of these instances may be called a *resource.* Explicit management of a resource is appropriate when: (1) instances are frequently created, and are needed only temporarily; (2) it is easy/possible to be sure when instances are no longer needed; and (3) instances are fairly large structures or take a long time to initialize, so that it is worth reusing them instead of creating new ones. Condition (2) is the crucial one: If you deallocate an instance that is still being used, that instance will mysteriously be altered when it is reallocated. Conversely, if you fail to deallocate unneeded instances, then you are wasting valuable memory space. (The memory management scheme is said to leak in this case.)

The beauty of using Lisp's built-in memory management is that it is guaranteed never to leak and never to deallocate structures that are in use. This eliminates two potential bug sources. The penalty you pay for this guarantee is some inefficiency of the general-purpose memory management as compared to a custom user-supplied management scheme. But beware: modern garbage-collection techniques are highly optimized. In particular, the so-called *generation scavenging* or *ephemeral* garbage collectors look more often at recently allocated storage, on the grounds that recently made objects are more likely to become garbage. If you hold on to garbage in your own data structures, you may end up with worse performance.

With all these warnings in mind, here is some code to manage resources:

```
(defmacro defresource (name &key constructor (initial-copies 0)
                            (size (max initial-copies 10)))
  (let ((resource (symbol name '-resource))
        (deallocate (symbol 'deallocate- name))
        (allocate (symbol 'allocate- name)))
    `(let ((,resource (make-array ,size :fill-pointer 0)))
       (defun ,allocate ()
         "Get an element from the resource pool, or make one."
         (if (= (fill-pointer ,resource) 0)
             ,constructor
             (vector-pop ,resource)))
       (defun ,deallocate (,name)
         "Place a no-longer-needed element back in the pool."
         (vector-push-extend ,name ,resource))
       ,(if (> initial-copies 0)
            `(mapc #',deallocate (loop repeat ,initial-copies
                                       collect (,allocate))))
       ',name)))
```

Let's say we had some structure called a buffer which we were constantly making instances of and then discarding. Furthermore, suppose that buffers are fairly complex objects to build, that we know we'll need at least 10 of them at a time, and that we probably won't ever need more than 100 at a time. We might use the buffer resource as follows:

```
(defresource buffer :constructor (make-buffer)
             :size 100 :initial-copies 10)
```

This expands into the following code:

```
(let ((buffer-resource (make-array 100 :fill-pointer 0)))
  (defun allocate-buffer ()
    "Get an element from the resource pool, or make one."
    (if (= (fill-pointer buffer-resource) 0)
      (make-buffer)
      (vector-pop buffer-resource)))
  (defun deallocate-buffer (buffer)
    "Place a no-longer-needed element back in the pool."
    (vector-push-extend buffer buffer-resource))
  (mapc #'deallocate-buffer
        (loop repeat 10 collect (allocate-buffer)))
  'buffer)
```

We could then use:

```
(let ((b (allocate-buffer)))
  ...
  (process b)
  ...
  (deallocate-buffer b)))
```

The important thing to remember is that this works only if the buffer b really can be deallocated. If the function process stored away a pointer to b somewhere, then it would be a mistake to deallocate b, because a subsequent allocation could unpredictably alter the stored buffer. Of course, if process stored a *copy* of b, then everything is alright. This pattern of allocation and deallocation is so common that we can provide a macro for it:

```
(defmacro with-resource ((var resource &optional protect) &rest body)
  "Execute body with VAR bound to an instance of RESOURCE."
  (let ((allocate (symbol 'allocate- resource))
        (deallocate (symbol 'deallocate- resource)))
    (if protect
        '(let ((,var nil))
           (unwind-protect
             (progn (setf ,var (,allocate)) ,@body)
             (unless (null ,var) (,deallocate ,var))))
        '(let ((,var (,allocate)))
           ,@body
           (,deallocate ,var)))))
```

The macro allows for an optional argument that sets up an unwind-protect environment, so that the buffer gets deallocated even when the body is abnormally exited. The following expansions should make this clearer:

```
> (macroexpand '(with-resource (b buffer)
                  "..." (process b) "..."))
(let ((b (allocate-buffer)))
  "..."
  (process b)
  "..."
  (deallocate-buffer b))
> (macroexpand '(with-resource (b buffer t)
                  "..." (process b) "..."))
(let ((b nil))
  (unwind-protect
      (progn (setf b (allocate-buffer))
             "..."
```

```
                          (process b)
                          "...")
          (unless (null b)
            (deallocate-buffer b)))))
```

An alternative to full resources is to just save a single data object. Such an approach is simpler because there is no need to index into a vector of objects, but it is sufficient for some applications, such as a tail-recursive function call that only uses one object at a time.

Another possibility is to make the system slower but safer by having the deallocate function check that its argument is indeed an object of the correct type.

Keep in mind that using resources may put you at odds with the Lisp system's own storage management scheme. In particular, you should be concerned with paging performance on virtual memory systems. A common problem is to have only a few live objects on each page, thus forcing the system to do a lot of paging to get any work done. Compacting garbage collectors can collect live objects onto the same page, but using resources may interfere with this.

10.5 Use the Right Data Structures

It is important to implement key data types with the most efficient implementation. This can vary from machine to machine, but there are a few techniques that are universal. Here we consider three case studies.

The Right Data Structure: Variables

As an example, consider the implementation of pattern-matching variables. We saw from the instrumentation of simplify that variable-p was one of the most frequently used functions. In compiling the matching expressions, I did away with all calls to variable-p, but let's suppose we had an application that required run-time use of variables. The specification of the data type variable will include two operators, the recognizer variable-p, and the constructor make-variable, which gives a new, previously unused variable. (This was not needed in the pattern matchers shown so far, but will be needed for unification with backward chaining.) One implementation of variables is as symbols that begin with the character #\?:

```
(defun variable-p (x)
  "Is x a variable (a symbol beginning with '?')?"
  (and (symbolp x) (equal (elt (symbol-name x) 0) #\?)))
```

```
(defun make-variable () "Generate a new variable" (gentemp "?"))
```

We could try to speed things up by changing the implementation of variables to be keywords and making the functions inline:

```
(proclaim '(inline variable-p make-variable))
(defun variable-p (x) "Is x a variable?" (keywordp x))
(defun make-variable () (gentemp "X" #.(find-package "KEYWORD")))
```

(The reader character sequence #. means to evaluate at read time, rather than at execution time.) On my machine, this implementation is pretty fast, and I accepted it as a viable compromise. However, other implementations were also considered. One was to have variables as structures, and provide a read macro and print function:

```
(defstruct (variable (:print-function print-variable)) name)

(defvar *vars* (make-hash-table))

(set-macro-character #\?
  #'(lambda (stream char)
      ;; Find an old var, or make a new one with the given name
      (declare (ignore char))
      (let ((name (read stream t nil t)))
        (or (gethash name *vars*)
            (setf (gethash name *vars*) (make-variable :name name))))))

(defun print-variable (var stream depth)
  (declare (ignore depth))
  (format stream "?~a" (var-name var)))
```

It turned out that, on all three Lisps tested, structures were slower than keywords or symbols. Another alternative is to have the ? read macro return a cons whose first is, say, :var. This requires a special output routine to translate back to the ? notation. Yet another alternative, which turned out to be the fastest of all, was to implement variables as negative integers. Of course, this means that the user cannot use negative integers elsewhere in patterns, but that turned out to be acceptable for the application at hand. The moral is to know which features are done well in your particular implementation and to go out of your way to use them in critical situations, but to stick with the most straightforward implementation in noncritical sections.

Lisp makes it easy to rely on lists, but one must avoid the temptation to overuse lists; to use them where another data structure is more appropriate. For example, if you need to access elements of a sequence in arbitrary order, then a vector is more appropriate than list. If the sequence can grow, use an adjustable vector. Consider the problem of maintaining information about a set of people, and searching that set. A naive implementation might look like this:

```
(defvar *people* nil "Will hold a list of people")

(defstruct person name address id-number)

(defun person-with-id (id)
  (find id *people* :key #'person-id-number))
```

In a traditional language like C, the natural solution is to include in the person structure a pointer to the next person, and to write a loop to follow these pointers. Of course, we can do that in Lisp too:

```
(defstruct person name address id-number next)

(defun person-with-id (id)
  (loop for person = *people* then (person-next person)
        until (null person)
        do (when (eql id (person-id-number person))
             (RETURN person))))
```

This solution takes less space and is probably faster, because it requires less memory accesses: one for each person rather than one for each person plus one for each cons cell. So there is a small price to pay for using lists. But Lisp programmers feel that price is worth it, because of the convenience and ease of coding and debugging afforded by general-purpose functions like find.

In any case, if there are going to be a large number of people, the list is definitely the wrong data structure. Fortunately, Lisp makes it easy to switch to more efficient data structures, for example:

```
(defun person-with-id (id)
  (gethash id *people*))
```

The Right Data Structure: Queues

A *queue* is a data structure where one can add elements at the rear and remove them from the front. This is almost like a stack, except that in a stack, elements are both added and removed at the same end.

Lists can be used to implement stacks, but there is a problem in using lists to implement queues: adding an element to the rear requires traversing the entire list. So collecting n elements would be $O(n^2)$ instead of $O(n)$.

An alternative implementation of queues is as a cons of two pointers: one to the list of elements of the queue (the contents), and one to the last cons cell in the list. Initially, both pointers would be nil. This implementation in fact existed in BBN Lisp and UCI Lisp under the function name tconc:

```
;;; A queue is a (contents . last) pair

(defun tconc (item q)
  "Insert item at the end of the queue."
  (setf (cdr q)
        (if (null (cdr q))
            (setf (car q) (cons item nil))
            (setf (rest (cdr q))
                  (cons item nil)))))
```

The tconc implementation has the disadvantage that adding the first element to
the contents is different from adding subsequent elements, so an if statement is
required to decide which action to take. The definition of queues given below avoids
this disadvantage with a clever trick. First, the order of the two fields is reversed.
The car of the cons cell is the last element, and the cdr is the contents. Second, the
empty queue is a cons cell where the cdr (the contents field) is nil, and the car (the
last field) is the cons itself. In the definitions below, we change the name tconc to
the more standard enqueue, and provide the other queue functions as well:

```
;;; A queue is a (last . contents) pair

(proclaim '(inline queue-contents make-queue enqueue dequeue
                   front empty-queue-p queue-nconc))

(defun queue-contents (q) (cdr q))

(defun make-queue ()
  "Build a new queue, with no elements."
  (let ((q (cons nil nil)))
    (setf (car q) q)))

(defun enqueue (item q)
  "Insert item at the end of the queue."
  (setf (car q)
        (setf (rest (car q))
              (cons item nil)))
  q)

(defun dequeue (q)
  "Remove an item from the front of the queue."
  (pop (cdr q))
  (if (null (cdr q)) (setf (car q) q))
  q)

(defun front (q) (first (queue-contents q)))

(defun empty-queue-p (q) (null (queue-contents q)))
```

```
(defun queue-nconc (q list)
  "Add the elements of LIST to the end of the queue."
  (setf (car q)
        (last (setf (rest (car q)) list))))
```

The Right Data Structure: Tables

A *table* is a data structure to which one can insert a key and associate it with a value, and later use the key to look up the value. Tables may have other operations, like counting the number of keys, clearing out all keys, or mapping a function over each key/value pair.

Lisp provides a wide variety of choices to implement tables. An association list is perhaps the simplest: it is just a list of key/value pairs. It is appropriate for small tables, up to a few dozen pairs. The hash table is designed to be efficient for large tables, but may have significant overhead for small ones. If the keys are symbols, property lists can be used. If the keys are integers in a narrow range (or can be mapped into them), then a vector may be the most efficient choice.

Here we implement an alternative data structure, the *trie*. A trie implements a table for keys that are composed of a finite sequence of components. For example, if we were implementing a dictionary as a trie, each key would be a word, and each letter of the word would be a component. The value of the key would be the word's definition. At the top of the dictionary trie is a multiway branch, one for each possible first letter. Each second-level node has a branch for every possible second letter, and so on. To find an n-letter word requires n reads. This kind of organization is especially good when the information is stored on secondary storage, because a single read can bring in a node with all its possible branches.

If the keys can be arbitrary list structures, rather than a simple sequence of letters, we need to regularize the keys, transforming them into a simple sequence. One way to do that makes use of the fact that any tree can be written as a linear sequence of atoms and cons operations, in prefix form. Thus, we would make the following transformation:

```
(a (b c) d) ≡
(cons a (cons (cons b (cons c nil)) (cons d nil))) ≡
(cons a  cons  cons b  cons c nil    cons d nil)
```

In the implementation of tries below, this transformation is done on the fly: The four user-level functions are make-trie to create a new trie, put-trie and get-trie to add and retrieve key/value pairs, and delete-trie to remove them.

Notice that we use a distinguished value to mark deleted elements, and that get-trie returns two values: the actual value found, and a flag saying if anything was found or not. This is consistent with the interface to gethash and find, and allows us to store null values in the trie. It is an inobtrusive choice, because the programmer who decides not to store null values can just ignore the second value, and everything will work properly.

```lisp
(defstruct trie (value nil) (arcs nil))
(defconstant trie-deleted "deleted")

(defun put-trie (key trie value)
  "Set the value of key in trie."
  (setf (trie-value (find-trie key t trie)) value))

(defun get-trie (key trie)
  "Return the value for a key in a trie, and t/nil if found."
  (let* ((key-trie (find-trie key nil trie))
         (val (if key-trie (trie-value key-trie))))
    (if (or (null key-trie) (eq val trie-deleted))
        (values nil nil)
        (values val t))))


(defun delete-trie (key trie)
  "Remove a key from a trie."
  (put-trie key trie trie-deleted))

(defun find-trie (key extend? trie)
  "Find the trie node for this key.
  If EXTEND? is true, make a new node if need be."
  (cond ((null trie) nil)
        ((atom key)
         (follow-arc key extend? trie))
        (t (find-trie
             (cdr key) extend?
             (find-trie
               (car key) extend?
               (find-trie
                 "." extend? trie))))))

(defun follow-arc (component extend? trie)
  "Find the trie node for this component of the key.
  If EXTEND? is true, make a new node if need be."
  (let ((arc (assoc component (trie-arcs trie))))
    (cond ((not (null arc)) (cdr arc))
          ((not extend?) nil)
          (t (let ((new-trie (make-trie)))
               (push (cons component new-trie)
                     (trie-arcs trie))
               new-trie)))))
```

There are a few subtleties in the implementation. First, we test for deleted entries with an eq comparison to a distinguished marker, the string `trie-deleted`. No other object will be eq to this string except `trie-deleted` itself, so this is a good test. We also use a distinguished marker, the string `"."`, to mark cons cells. Components are implicitly compared against this marker with an eql test by the assoc in `follow-arc`. Maintaining the identity of this string is crucial; if, for example, you recompiled the definition of `find-trie` (without changing the definition at all), then you could no longer find keys that were indexed in an existing trie, because the `"."` used by `find-trie` would be a different one from the `"."` in the existing trie.

Artificial Intelligence Programming (Charniak et al. 1987) discusses variations on the trie, particularly in the indexing scheme. If we always use proper lists (no non-null `cdr`s), then a more efficient encoding is possible. As usual, the best type of indexing depends on the data to be indexed. It should be noted that Charniak et al. call the trie a *discrimination net*. In general, that term refers to any tree with tests at the nodes.

A trie is, of course, a kind of tree, but there are cases where it pays to convert a trie into a *dag*—a directed acyclic graph. A dag is a tree where some of the subtrees are shared. Imagine you have a spelling corrector program with a list of some 50,000 or so words. You could put them into a trie, each word with the value t. But there would be many subtrees repeated in this trie. For example, given a word list containing *look, looks, looked,* and *looking* as well as *show, shows, showed,* and *showing*, there would be repetition of the subtree containing *-s, -ed* and *-ing*. After the trie is built, we could pass the whole trie to `unique`, and it would collapse the shared subtrees, saving storage. Of course, you can no longer add or delete keys from the dag without risking unintended side effects.

This process was carried out for a 56,000 word list. The trie took up 3.2Mbytes, while the dag was 1.1Mbytes. This was still deemed unacceptable, so a more compact encoding of the dag was created, using a .2Mbytes vector. Encoding the same word list in a hash table took twice this space, even with a special format for encoding suffixes.

Tries work best when neither the indexing key nor the retrieval key contains variables. They work reasonably well when the variables are near the end of the sequence. Consider looking up the pattern `"yello?"` in the dictionary, where the `"?"` character indicates a match of any letter. Following the branches for `"yello"` leads quickly to the only possible match, `"yellow"`. In contrast, fetching with the pattern `"??llow"` is much less efficient. The table lookup function would have to search all 26 top-level branches, and for each of those consider all possible second letters, and for each of those consider the path `"llow"`. Quite a bit of searching is required before arriving at the complete set of matches: bellow, billow, fallow, fellow, follow, hallow, hollow, mallow, mellow, pillow, sallow, tallow, wallow, willow, and yellow.

We will return to the problem of discrimination nets with variables in section 14.8, page 472.

10.6   Exercises

Exercise 10.1 [h]   Define the macro `deftable`, such that `(deftable person assoc)` will act much like a `defstruct`—it will define a set of functions for manipulating a table of people: `get-person`, `put-person`, `clear-person`, and `map-person`. The table should be implemented as an association list. Later on, you can change the representation of the table simply by changing the form to `(deftable person hash)`, without having to change anything else in your code. Other implementation options include property lists and vectors. `deftable` should also take three keyword arguments: `inline`, `size` and `test`. Here is a possible macroexpansion:

```
> (macroexpand '(deftable person hash :inline t :size 100)) ≡
(progn
  (proclaim '(inline get-person put-person map-person))
  (defparameter *person-table*
    (make-hash-table :test #'eql :size 100))
  (defun get-person (x &optional default)
    (gethash x *person-table* default))
  (defun put-person (x value)
    (setf (gethash x *person-table*) value))
  (defun clear-person () (clrhash *person-table*))
  (defun map-person (fn) (maphash fn *person-table*))
  (defsetf get-person put-person)
  'person)
```

Exercise 10.2 [m]   We can use the `:type` option to `defstruct` to define structures implemented as lists. However, often we have a two-field structure that we would like to implement as a cons cell rather than a two-element list, thereby cutting storage in half. Since `defstruct` does not allow this, define a new macro that does.

Exercise 10.3 [m]   Use `reuse-cons` to write a version of `flatten` (see page 329) that shares as much of its input with its output as possible.

Exercise 10.4 [h]   Consider the data type *set*. A set has two main operations: adjoin an element and test for membership. It is convenient to also add a map-over-elements operation. With these primitive operations it is possible to build up more complex operations like union and intersection.

As mentioned in section 3.9, Common Lisp provides several implementations of sets. The simplest uses lists as the underlying representation, and provides the functions `adjoin`, `member`, `union`, `intersection`, and `set-difference`. Another uses bit vectors, and a similar one uses integers viewed as bit sequences. Analyze the time complexity of each implementation for each operation.

Next, show how *sorted lists* can be used to implement sets, and compare the operations on sorted lists to their counterparts on unsorted lists.

10.7 Answers

Answer 10.2

```
(defmacro def-cons-struct (cons car cdr &optional inline?)
  "Define aliases for cons, car and cdr."
  `(progn (proclaim '(,(if inline? 'inline 'notinline)
                      ,car ,cdr ,cons))
          (defun ,car (x) (car x))
          (defun ,cdr (x) (cdr x))
          (defsetf ,car (x) (val) `(setf (car ,x) ,val))
          (defsetf ,cdr (x) (val) `(setf (cdr ,x) ,val))
          (defun ,cons (x y) (cons x y))))
```

Answer 10.3

```
(defun flatten (exp &optional (so-far nil) last-cons)
  "Return a flat list of the atoms in the input.
  Ex: (flatten '((a) (b (c) d))) => (a b c d)."
  (cond ((null exp) so-far)
        ((atom exp) (reuse-cons exp so-far last-cons))
        (t (flatten (first exp)
                    (flatten (rest exp) so-far exp)
                    exp))))
```

CHAPTER 11

Logic Programming

*A language that doesn't affect the way you think
about programming is not worth knowing.*

—Alan Perlis

L isp is the major language for AI work, but it is by no means the only one. The other strong contender is Prolog, whose name derives from "programming in logic."[1] The idea behind logic programming is that the programmer should state the relationships that describe a problem and its solution. These relationships act as constraints on the algorithms that can solve the problem, but the system itself, rather than the programmer, is responsible for the details of the algorithm. The tension between the "programming" and "logic" will be covered in chapter 14, but for now it is safe to say that Prolog is an approximation to the ideal goal of logic programming. Prolog has arrived at a comfortable niche between a traditional programming language and a logical specification language. It relies on three important ideas:

---

[1] Actually, *programmation en logique*, since it was invented by a French group (see page 382).

- Prolog encourages the use of a single *uniform data base*. Good compilers provide efficient access to this data base, reducing the need for vectors, hash tables, property lists, and other data structures that the Lisp programmer must deal with in detail. Because it is based on the idea of a data base, Prolog is *relational*, while Lisp (and most languages) are *functional*. In Prolog we would represent a fact like "the population of San Francisco is 750,000" as a relation. In Lisp, we would be inclined to write a function, population, which takes a city as input and returns a number. Relations are more flexible; they can be used not only to find the population of San Francisco but also, say, to find the cities with populations over 500,000.

- Prolog provides *logic variables* instead of "normal" variables. A logic variable is bound by *unification* rather than by assignment. Once bound, a logic variable can never change. Thus, they are more like the variables of mathematics. The existence of logic variables and unification allow the logic programmer to state equations that constrain the problem (as in mathematics), without having to state an order of evaluation (as with assignment statements).

- Prolog provides *automatic backtracking*. In Lisp each function call returns a single value (unless the programmer makes special arrangements to have it return multiple values, or a list of values). In Prolog, each query leads to a search for relations in the data base that satisfy the query. If there are several, they are considered one at a time. If a query involves multiple relations, as in "what city has a population over 500,000 and is a state capital?," Prolog will go through the population relation to find a city with a population over 500,000. For each one it finds, it then checks the capital relation to see if the city is a capital. If it is, Prolog prints the city; otherwise it *backtracks*, trying to find another city in the population relation. So Prolog frees the programmer from worrying about both how data is stored and how it is searched. For some problems, the naive automatic search will be too inefficient, and the programmer will have to restate the problem. But the ideal is that Prolog programs state constraints on the solution, without spelling out in detail how the solutions are achieved.

This chapter serves two purposes: it alerts the reader to the possibility of writing certain programs in Prolog rather than Lisp, and it presents implementations of the three important Prolog ideas, so that they may be used (independently or together) within Lisp programs. Prolog represents an interesting, different way of looking at the programming process. For that reason it is worth knowing. In subsequent chapters we will see several useful applications of the Prolog approach.

11.1   Idea 1: A Uniform Data Base

The first important Prolog idea should be familiar to readers of this book: manipulating a stored data base of assertions. In Prolog the assertions are called *clauses*, and they can be divided into two types: *facts*, which state a relationship that holds between some objects, and *rules*, which are used to state contingent facts. Here are representations of two facts about the population of San Francisco and the capital of California. The relations are population and capital, and the objects that participate in these relations are SF, 750000, Sacramento, and CA:

```
(population SF 750000)
(capital Sacramento CA)
```

We are using Lisp syntax, because we want a Prolog interpreter that can be imbedded in Lisp. The actual Prolog notation would be population(sf,750000). Here are some facts pertaining to the likes relation:

```
(likes Kim Robin)
(likes Sandy Lee)
(likes Sandy Kim)
(likes Robin cats)
```

These facts could be interpreted as meaning that Kim likes Robin, Sandy likes both Lee and Kim, and Robin likes cats. We need some way of telling Lisp that these are to be interpreted as Prolog facts, not a Lisp function call. We will use the macro <- to mark facts. Think of this as an assignment arrow which adds a fact to the data base:

```
(<- (likes Kim Robin))
(<- (likes Sandy Lee))
(<- (likes Sandy Kim))
(<- (likes Robin cats))
```

One of the major differences between Prolog and Lisp hinges on the difference between relations and functions. In Lisp, we would define a function likes, so that (likes 'Sandy) would return the list (Lee Kim). If we wanted to access the information the other way, we would define another function, say, likers-of, so that (likers-of 'Lee) returns (Sandy). In Prolog, we have a single likes relation instead of multiple functions. This single relation can be used as if it were multiple functions by posing different queries. For example, the query (likes Sandy ?who) succeeds with ?who bound to Lee or Kim, and the query (likes ?who Lee) succeeds with ?who bound to Sandy.

The second type of clause in a Prolog data base is the *rule*. Rules state contingent facts. For example, we can represent the rule that Sandy likes anyone who likes cats as follows:

```
(<- (likes Sandy ?x) (likes ?x cats))
```

This can be read in two ways. Viewed as a logical assertion, it is read, "For any x, Sandy likes x if x likes cats." This is a *declarative* interpretation. Viewed as a piece of a Prolog program, it is read, "If you ever want to show that Sandy likes some x, one way to do it is to show that x likes cats." This is a *procedural* interpretation. It is called a *backward-chaining* interpretation, because one reasons backward from the goal (Sandy likes x) to the premises (x likes cats). The symbol <- is appropriate for both interpretations: it is an arrow indicating logical implication, and it points backwards to indicate backward chaining.

It is possible to give more than one procedural interpretation to a declarative form. (We did that in chapter 1, where grammar rules were used to generate both strings of words and parse trees.) The rule above could have been interpreted procedurally as "If you ever find out that some x likes cats, then conclude that Sandy likes x." This would be *forward chaining*: reasoning from a premise to a conclusion. It turns out that Prolog does backward chaining exclusively. Many expert systems use forward chaining exclusively, and some systems use a mixture of the two.

The leftmost expression in a clause is called the *head*, and the remaining ones are called the *body*. In this view, a fact is just a rule that has no body; that is, a fact is true no matter what. In general, then, the form of a clause is:

```
(<- head body...)
```

A clause asserts that the head is true only if all the goals in the body are true. For example, the following clause says that Kim likes anyone who likes both Lee and Kim:

```
(<- (likes Kim ?x) (likes ?x Lee) (likes ?x Kim))
```

This can be read as:

> *For any x, deduce that* Kim likes x
> *if it can be proved that* x likes Lee *and* x likes Kim.

11.2   Idea 2: Unification of Logic Variables

Unification is a straightforward extension of the idea of pattern matching. The pattern-matching functions we have seen so far have always matched a pattern (an expression containing variables) against a constant expression (one with no variables). In unification, two patterns, each of which can contain variables, are matched against each other. Here's an example of the difference between pattern matching and unification:

```
> (pat-match '(?x + ?y) '(2 + 1)) ⇒ ((?Y . 1) (?X . 2))

> (unify '(?x + 1) '(2 + ?y)) ⇒ ((?Y . 1) (?X . 2))
```

Within the unification framework, variables (such as ?x and ?y above) are called *logic variables*. Like normal variables, a logic variable can be assigned a value, or it can be unbound. The difference is that a logic variable can never be altered. Once it is assigned a value, it keeps that value. Any attempt to unify it with a different value leads to failure. It is possible to unify a variable with the same value more than once, just as it was possible to do a pattern match of (?x + ?x) with (2 + 2).

The difference between simple pattern matching and unification is that unification allows two variables to be matched against each other. The two variables remain unbound, but they become equivalent. If either variable is subsequently bound to a value, then both variables adopt that value. The following example equates the variables ?x and ?y by binding ?x to ?y:

```
> (unify '(f ?x) '(f ?y)) ⇒ ((?X . ?Y))
```

Unification can be used to do some sophisticated reasoning. For example, if we have two equations, $a + a = 0$ and $x + y = y$, and if we know that these two equations unify, then we can conclude that a, x, and y are all 0. The version of unify we will define shows this result by binding ?y to 0, ?x to ?y, and ?a to ?x. We will also define the function unifier, which shows the structure that results from unifying two structures.

```
> (unify '(?a + ?a = 0) '(?x + ?y = ?y)) ⇒
((?Y . 0) (?X . ?Y) (?A . ?X))

> (unifier '(?a + ?a = 0) '(?x + ?y = ?y)) ⇒ (0 + 0 = 0)
```

To avoid getting carried away by the power of unification, it is a good idea to take stock of exactly what unification provides. It *does* provide a way of stating that variables are equal to other variables or expressions. It does *not* provide a way of automatically solving equations or applying constraints other than equality. The following example makes it clear that unification treats the symbol + only as an uninterpreted atom, not as the addition operator:

```
> (unifier '(?a + ?a = 2) '(?x + ?y = ?y))  ⇒ (2 + 2 = 2)
```

Before developing the code for unify, we repeat here the code taken from the pattern-matching utility (chapter 6):

```
(defconstant fail nil "Indicates pat-match failure")

(defconstant no-bindings '((t . t))
  "Indicates pat-match success, with no variables.")

(defun variable-p (x)
  "Is x a variable (a symbol beginning with '?')?"
  (and (symbolp x) (equal (char (symbol-name x) 0) #\?)))

(defun get-binding (var bindings)
  "Find a (variable . value) pair in a binding list."
  (assoc var bindings))

(defun binding-val (binding)
  "Get the value part of a single binding."
  (cdr binding))

(defun lookup (var bindings)
  "Get the value part (for var) from a binding list."
  (binding-val (get-binding var bindings)))

(defun extend-bindings (var val bindings)
  "Add a (var . value) pair to a binding list."
  (cons (cons var val)
        ;; Once we add a "real" binding,
        ;; we can get rid of the dummy no-bindings
        (if (and (eq bindings no-bindings))
            nil
            bindings)))

(defun match-variable (var input bindings)
  "Does VAR match input?  Uses (or updates) and returns bindings."
  (let ((binding (get-binding var bindings)))
    (cond ((not binding) (extend-bindings var input bindings))
          ((equal input (binding-val binding)) bindings)
          (t fail))))
```

The unify function follows; it is identical to pat-match (as defined on page 180) except for the addition of the line marked ***. The function unify-variable also follows match-variable closely:

```
(defun unify (x y &optional (bindings no-bindings))
  "See if x and y match with given bindings."
  (cond ((eq bindings fail) fail)
        ((variable-p x) (unify-variable x y bindings))
        ((variable-p y) (unify-variable y x bindings)) ;***
        ((eql x y) bindings)
        ((and (consp x) (consp y))
         (unify (rest x) (rest y)
                (unify (first x) (first y) bindings)))
        (t fail)))

(defun unify-variable (var x bindings)
  "Unify var with x, using (and maybe extending) bindings."
  ;; Warning - buggy version
  (if (get-binding var bindings)
      (unify (lookup var bindings) x bindings)
      (extend-bindings var x bindings)))
```

Unfortunately, this definition is not quite right. It handles simple examples:

```
> (unify '(?x + 1) '(2 + ?y)) ⇒ ((?Y . 1) (?X . 2))

> (unify '?x '?y) ⇒ ((?X . ?Y))

> (unify '(?x ?x) '(?y ?y)) ⇒ ((?Y . ?Y) (?X . ?Y))
```

but there are several pathological cases that it can't contend with:

```
> (unify '(?x ?x ?x) '(?y ?y ?y))
>>Trap #o43622 (PDL-OVERFLOW REGULAR)
The regular push-down list has overflowed.
While in the function GET-BINDING ⇐ UNIFY-VARIABLE ⇐ UNIFY
```

The problem here is that once ?y gets bound to itself, the call to unify inside unify-variable leads to an infinite loop. But matching ?y against itself must always succeed, so we can move the equality test in unify before the variable test. This assumes that equal variables are eql, a valid assumption for variables implemented as symbols (but be careful if you ever decide to implement variables some other way).

```
(defun unify (x y &optional (bindings no-bindings))
  "See if x and y match with given bindings."
  (cond ((eq bindings fail) fail)
        ((eql x y) bindings) ;*** moved this line
        ((variable-p x) (unify-variable x y bindings))
        ((variable-p y) (unify-variable y x bindings))
        ((and (consp x) (consp y))
         (unify (rest x) (rest y)
```

```
                        (unify (first x) (first y) bindings)))
           (t fail)))
```

Here are some test cases:

```
> (unify '(?x ?x) '(?y ?y)) ⇒ ((?X . ?Y))

> (unify '(?x ?x ?x) '(?y ?y ?y)) ⇒ ((?X . ?Y))

> (unify '(?x ?y) '(?y ?x)) ⇒ ((?Y . ?X) (?X . ?Y))

> (unify '(?x ?y a) '(?y ?x ?x))
>>Trap #o43622 (PDL-OVERFLOW REGULAR)
The regular push-down list has overflowed.
While in the function GET-BINDING ⇐ UNIFY-VARIABLE ⇐ UNIFY
```

We have pushed off the problem but not solved it. Allowing both (?Y . ?X) and
(?X . ?Y) in the same binding list is as bad as allowing (?Y . ?Y). To avoid the
problem, the policy should be never to deal with bound variables, but rather with
their values, as specified in the binding list. The function unify-variable fails to
implement this policy. It does have a check that gets the binding for var when it is a
bound variable, but it should also have a check that gets the value of x, when x is a
bound variable:

```
(defun unify-variable (var x bindings)
  "Unify var with x, using (and maybe extending) bindings."
  (cond ((get-binding var bindings)
         (unify (lookup var bindings) x bindings))
        ((and (variable-p x) (get-binding x bindings)) ;***
         (unify var (lookup x bindings) bindings))      ;***
        (t (extend-bindings var x bindings)))))
```

Here are some more test cases:

```
> (unify '(?x ?y) '(?y ?x)) ⇒ ((?X . ?Y))

> (unify '(?x ?y a) '(?y ?x ?x)) ⇒ ((?Y . A) (?X . ?Y))
```

It seems the problem is solved. Now let's try a new problem:

```
> (unify '?x '(f ?x)) ⇒ ((?X F ?X))
```

Here ((?X F ?X)) really means ((?X . ((F ?X)))), so ?X is bound to (F ?X). This
represents a circular, infinite unification. Some versions of Prolog, notably Prolog II
(Giannesini et al. 1986), provide an interpretation for such structures, but it is tricky
to define the semantics of infinite structures.

The easiest way to deal with such infinite structures is just to ban them. This ban can be realized by modifying the unifier so that it fails whenever there is an attempt to unify a variable with a structure containing that variable. This is known in unification circles as the *occurs check*. In practice the problem rarely shows up, and since it can add a lot of computational complexity, most Prolog systems have ignored the occurs check. This means that these systems can potentially produce unsound answers. In the final version of unify following, a variable is provided to allow the user to turn occurs checking on or off.

```
(defparameter *occurs-check* t "Should we do the occurs check?")

(defun unify (x y &optional (bindings no-bindings))
  "See if x and y match with given bindings."
  (cond ((eq bindings fail) fail)
        ((eql x y) bindings)
        ((variable-p x) (unify-variable x y bindings))
        ((variable-p y) (unify-variable y x bindings))
        ((and (consp x) (consp y))
         (unify (rest x) (rest y)
                (unify (first x) (first y) bindings)))
        (t fail)))

(defun unify-variable (var x bindings)
  "Unify var with x, using (and maybe extending) bindings."
  (cond ((get-binding var bindings)
         (unify (lookup var bindings) x bindings))
        ((and (variable-p x) (get-binding x bindings))
         (unify var (lookup x bindings) bindings))
        ((and *occurs-check* (occurs-check var x bindings))
         fail)
        (t (extend-bindings var x bindings))))

(defun occurs-check (var x bindings)
  "Does var occur anywhere inside x?"
  (cond ((eq var x) t)
        ((and (variable-p x) (get-binding x bindings))
         (occurs-check var (lookup x bindings) bindings))
        ((consp x) (or (occurs-check var (first x) bindings)
                       (occurs-check var (rest x) bindings)))
        (t nil)))
```

Now we consider how unify will be used. In particular, one thing we want is a function for substituting a binding list into an expression. We originally chose association lists as the implementation of bindings because of the availability of the function sublis. Ironically, sublis won't work any more, because variables can be bound to other variables, which are in turn bound to expressions. The function subst-bindings acts like sublis, except that it substitutes recursive bindings.

```
(defun subst-bindings (bindings x)
  "Substitute the value of variables in bindings into x,
  taking recursively bound variables into account."
  (cond ((eq bindings fail) fail)
        ((eq bindings no-bindings) x)
        ((and (variable-p x) (get-binding x bindings))
         (subst-bindings bindings (lookup x bindings)))
        ((atom x) x)
        (t (reuse-cons (subst-bindings bindings (car x))
                       (subst-bindings bindings (cdr x))
                       x))))
```

Now let's try unify on some examples:

```
> (unify '(?x ?y a) '(?y ?x ?x)) ⇒ ((?Y . A) (?X . ?Y))
> (unify '?x '(f ?x)) ⇒ NIL
> (unify '(?x ?y) '((f ?y) (f ?x))) ⇒ NIL
> (unify '(?x ?y ?z) '((?y ?z) (?x ?z) (?x ?y))) ⇒ NIL
> (unify 'a 'a) ⇒ ((T . T))
```

Finally, the function unifier calls unify and substitutes the resulting binding list into one of the arguments. The choice of x is arbitrary; an equal result would come from substituting the binding list into y.

```
(defun unifier (x y)
  "Return something that unifies with both x and y (or fail)."
  (subst-bindings (unify x y) x))
```

Here are some examples of unifier:

```
> (unifier '(?x ?y a) '(?y ?x ?x)) ⇒ (A A A)
> (unifier '((?a * ?x ^ 2) + (?b * ?x) + ?c)
           '(?z + (4 * 5) + 3)) ⇒
  ((?A * 5 ^ 2) + (4 * 5) + 3)
```

When *occurs-check* is false, we get the following answers:

```
> (unify '?x '(f ?x)) ⇒ ((?X F ?X))

> (unify '(?x ?y) '((f ?y) (f ?x))) ⇒
((?Y F ?X) (?X F ?Y))

> (unify '(?x ?y ?z) '((?y ?z) (?x ?z) (?x ?y))) ⇒
((?Z ?X ?Y) (?Y ?X ?Z) (?X ?Y ?Z))
```

Programming with Prolog

The amazing thing about Prolog clauses is that they can be used to express relations that we would normally think of as "programs," not "data." For example, we can define the member relation, which holds between an item and a list that contains that item. More precisely, an item is a member of a list if it is either the first element of the list or a member of the rest of the list. This definition can be translated into Prolog almost verbatim:

```
(<- (member ?item (?item . ?rest)))
(<- (member ?item (?x . ?rest)) (member ?item ?rest))
```

Of course, we can write a similar definition in Lisp. The most visible difference is that Prolog allows us to put patterns in the head of a clause, so we don't need recognizers like consp or accessors like first and rest. Otherwise, the Lisp definition is similar:[2]

```
(defun lisp-member (item list)
  (and (consp list)
       (or (eql item (first list))
           (lisp-member item (rest list)))))
```

If we wrote the Prolog code without taking advantage of the pattern feature, it would look more like the Lisp version:

```
(<- (member ?item ?list)
    (= ?list (?item . ?rest)))
```

---

[2]Actually, this is more like the Lisp find than the Lisp member. In this chapter we have adopted the traditional Prolog definition of member.

```
(<- (member ?item ?list)
    (= ?list (?x . ?rest))
    (member ?item ?rest))
```

If we define *or* in Prolog, we would write a version that is clearly just a syntactic variant of the Lisp version.

```
(<- (member ?item ?list)
    (= ?list (?first . ?rest))
    (or (= ?item ?first)
        (member ?item ?rest)))
```

Let's see how the Prolog version of member works. Imagine that we have a Prolog interpreter that can be given a query using the macro ?-, and that the definition of member has been entered. Then we would see:

```
> (?- (member 2 (1 2 3)))
Yes;

> (?- (member 2 (1 2 3 2 1)))
Yes;
Yes;
```

The answer to the first query is "yes" because 2 is a member of the rest of the list. In the second query the answer is "yes" twice, because 2 appears in the list twice. This is a little surprising to Lisp programmers, but there still seems to be a fairly close correspondence between Prolog's and Lisp's member. However, there are things that the Prolog member can do that Lisp cannot:

```
> (?- (member ?x (1 2 3)))
?X = 1;
?X = 2;
?X = 3;
```

Here member is used not as a predicate but as a generator of elements in a list. While Lisp functions always map from a specified input (or inputs) to a specified output, Prolog relations can be used in several ways. For member, we see that the first argument, ?x, can be either an input or an output, depending on the goal that is specified. This power to use a single specification as a function going in several different directions is a very flexible feature of Prolog. (Unfortunately, while it works very well for simple relations like member, in practice it does not work well for large programs. It is very difficult to, say, design a compiler and automatically have it work as a disassembler as well.)

Now we turn to the implementation of the Prolog interpreter, as summarized in figure 11.1. The first implementation choice is the representation of rules and facts. We will build a single uniform data base of clauses, without distinguishing rules from facts. The simplest representation of clauses is as a cons cell holding the head and the body. For facts, the body will be empty.

```
;; Clauses are represented as (head . body) cons cells
(defun clause-head (clause) (first clause))
(defun clause-body (clause) (rest clause))
```

The next question is how to index the clauses. Recall the procedural interpretation of a clause: when we want to prove the head, we can do it by proving the body. This suggests that clauses should be indexed in terms of their heads. Each clause will be stored on the property list of the predicate of the head of the clause. Since the data base is now distributed across the property list of various symbols, we represent the entire data base as a list of symbols stored as the value of *db-predicates*.

```
;; Clauses are stored on the predicate's plist
(defun get-clauses (pred) (get pred 'clauses))
(defun predicate (relation) (first relation))

(defvar *db-predicates* nil
  "A list of all predicates stored in the database.")
```

Now we need a way of adding a new clause. The work is split up into the macro <-, which provides the user interface, and a function, add-clause, that does the work. It is worth defining a macro to add clauses because in effect we are defining a new language: Prolog-In-Lisp. This language has only two syntactic constructs: the <- macro to add clauses, and the ?- macro to make queries.

```
(defmacro <- (&rest clause)
  "Add a clause to the data base."
  '(add-clause ',clause))

(defun add-clause (clause)
  "Add a clause to the data base, indexed by head's predicate."
  ;; The predicate must be a non-variable symbol.
  (let ((pred (predicate (clause-head clause))))
    (assert (and (symbolp pred) (not (variable-p pred))))
    (pushnew pred *db-predicates*)
    (setf (get pred 'clauses)
          (nconc (get-clauses pred) (list clause)))
    pred))
```

Now all we need is a way to remove clauses, and the data base will be complete.

	Top-Level Macros
`<-`	Add a clause to the data base.
`?-`	Prove a query and print answer(s).
	Special Variables
`*db-predicates*`	A list of all predicates.
`*occurs-check*`	Should we check for circular unifications?
	Data Types
`clause`	Consists of a head and a body.
`variable`	A symbol starting with a ?.
	Major Functions
`add-clause`	Add a clause to the data base.
`prove`	Return a list of possible solutions to goal.
`prove-all`	Return a list of solutions to the conjunction of goals.
`top-level-prove`	Prove the goals, and print variables readably.
	Auxiliary Functions
`get-clauses`	Find all the clauses for a predicate.
`predicate`	Pick out the predicate from a relation.
`clear-db`	Remove all clauses (for all predicates) from the data base.
`clear-predicate`	Remove the clauses for a single predicate.
`rename-variables`	Replace all variables in x with new ones.
`unique-find-anywhere-if`	Find all unique leaves satisfying predicate.
`show-prolog-solutions`	Print the variables in each of the solutions.
`show-prolog-vars`	Print each variable with its binding.
`variables-in`	Return a list of all the variables in an expression.
	Previously Defined Constants
`fail`	An indication that unification has failed.
`no-bindings`	A succesful unification with no variables.
	Previously Defined Functions
`unify`	Return bindings that unify two expressions (section 11.2).
`unify-variable`	Unify a variable against an expression.
`occurs-check`	See if a particular variable occurs inside an expression.
`subst-bindings`	Substitute bindings into an expression.
`get-binding`	Get the (*var* . *val*) binding for a variable.
`lookup`	Get the value for a variable.
`extend-bindings`	Add a new variable/value pair to a binding list.
`variable-p`	Is the argument a variable?
`reuse-cons`	Like `cons`, except will reuse an old value if possible.

Figure 11.1: Glossary for the Prolog Interpreter

```
(defun clear-db ()
  "Remove all clauses (for all predicates) from the data base."
  (mapc #'clear-predicate *db-predicates*))

(defun clear-predicate (predicate)
  "Remove the clauses for a single predicate."
  (setf (get predicate 'clauses) nil))
```

A data base is useless without a way of getting data out, as well as putting it in. The function prove will be used to prove that a given goal either matches a fact that is in the data base directly or can be derived from the rules. To prove a goal, first find all the candidate clauses for that goal. For each candidate, check if the goal unifies with the head of the clause. If it does, try to prove all the goals in the body of the clause. For facts, there will be no goals in the body, so success will be immediate. For rules, the goals in the body need to be proved one at a time, making sure that bindings from the previous step are maintained. The implementation is straightforward:

```
(defun prove (goal bindings)
  "Return a list of possible solutions to goal."
  (mapcan #'(lambda (clause)
              (let ((new-clause (rename-variables clause)))
                (prove-all (clause-body new-clause)
                           (unify goal (clause-head new-clause) bindings))))
          (get-clauses (predicate goal))))

(defun prove-all (goals bindings)
  "Return a list of solutions to the conjunction of goals."
  (cond ((eq bindings fail) fail)
        ((null goals) (list bindings))
        (t (mapcan #'(lambda (goal1-solution)
                       (prove-all (rest goals) goal1-solution))
                   (prove (first goals) bindings)))))
```

The tricky part is that we need some way of distinguishing a variable ?x in one clause from another variable ?x in another clause. Otherwise, a variable used in two different clauses in the course of a proof would have to take on the same value in each clause, which would be a mistake. Just as arguments to a function can have different values in different recursive calls to the function, so the variables in a clause are allowed to take on different values in different recursive uses. The easiest way to keep variables distinct is just to rename all variables in each clause before it is used. The function rename-variables does this:[3]

_____

[3]See exercise 11.12 for an alternative approach.

```
(defun rename-variables (x)
  "Replace all variables in x with new ones."
  (sublis (mapcar #'(lambda (var) (cons var (gensym (string var))))
                  (variables-in x))
          x))
```

`Rename-variables` makes use of `gensym`, a function that generates a new symbol each time it is called. The symbol is not interned in any package, which means that there is no danger of a programmer typing a symbol of the same name. The predicate `variables-in` and its auxiliary function are defined here:

```
(defun variables-in (exp)
  "Return a list of all the variables in EXP."
  (unique-find-anywhere-if #'variable-p exp))

(defun unique-find-anywhere-if (predicate tree
                                &optional found-so-far)
  "Return a list of leaves of tree satisfying predicate,
  with duplicates removed."
  (if (atom tree)
      (if (funcall predicate tree)
          (adjoin tree found-so-far)
          found-so-far)
      (unique-find-anywhere-if
        predicate
        (first tree)
        (unique-find-anywhere-if predicate (rest tree)
                                 found-so-far))))
```

Finally, we need a nice interface to the proving functions. We will use `?-` as a macro to introduce a query. The query might as well allow a conjunction of goals, so `?-` will call `prove-all`. Together, `<-` and `?-` define the complete syntax of our Prolog-In-Lisp language.

```
(defmacro ?- (&rest goals) '(prove-all ',goals no-bindings))
```

Now we can enter all the clauses given in the prior example:

```
(<- (likes Kim Robin))
(<- (likes Sandy Lee))
(<- (likes Sandy Kim))
(<- (likes Robin cats))
(<- (likes Sandy ?x) (likes ?x cats))
(<- (likes Kim ?x) (likes ?x Lee) (likes ?x Kim))
(<- (likes ?x ?x))
```

To ask whom Sandy likes, we would use:

```
> (?- (likes Sandy ?who))
((((?WHO . LEE))
 ((?WHO . KIM))
 ((?X2856 . ROBIN) (?WHO . ?X2856))
 ((?X2860 . CATS) (?X2857 . CATS) (?X2856 . SANDY) (?WHO . ?X2856))
 ((?X2865 . CATS) (?X2856 . ?X2865) (?WHO . ?X2856))
 ((?WHO . SANDY) (?X2867 . SANDY)))
```

Perhaps surprisingly, there are six answers. The first two answers are Lee and Kim, because of the facts. The next three stem from the clause that Sandy likes everyone who likes cats. First, Robin is an answer because of the fact that Robin likes cats. To see that Robin is the answer, we have to unravel the bindings: ?who is bound to ?x2856, which is in turn bound to Robin.

Now we're in for some surprises: Sandy is listed, because of the following reasoning: (1) Sandy likes anyone/thing who likes cats, (2) cats like cats because everyone likes themself, (3) therefore Sandy likes cats, and (4) therefore Sandy likes Sandy. Cats is an answer because of step (2), and finally, Sandy is an answer again, because of the clause about liking oneself. Notice that the result of the query is a list of solutions, where each solution corresponds to a different way of proving the query true. Sandy appears twice because there are two different ways of showing that Sandy likes Sandy. The order in which solutions appear is determined by the order of the search. Prolog searches for solutions in a top-down, left-to-right fashion. The clauses are searched from the top down, so the first clauses entered are the first ones tried. Within a clause, the body is searched left to right. In using the (likes Kim ?x) clause, Prolog would first try to find an x who likes Lee, and then see if x likes Kim.

The output from prove-all is not very pretty. We can fix that by defining a new function, top-level-prove, which calls prove-all as before, but then passes the list of solutions to show-prolog-solutions, which prints them in a more readable format. Note that show-prolog-solutions returns no values: (values). This means the read-eval-print loop will not print anything when (values) is the result of a top-level call.

```
(defmacro ?- (&rest goals)
  '(top-level-prove ',goals))

(defun top-level-prove (goals)
  "Prove the goals, and print variables readably."
  (show-prolog-solutions
    (variables-in goals)
    (prove-all goals no-bindings)))
```

```
(defun show-prolog-solutions (vars solutions)
  "Print the variables in each of the solutions."
  (if (null solutions)
      (format t "~&No.")
      (mapc #'(lambda (solution) (show-prolog-vars vars solution))
            solutions))
  (values))

(defun show-prolog-vars (vars bindings)
  "Print each variable with its binding."
  (if (null vars)
      (format t "~&Yes")
      (dolist (var vars)
        (format t "~&~a = ~a" var
                (subst-bindings bindings var))))
  (princ ";"))
```

Now let's try some queries:

```
> (?- (likes Sandy ?who))
?WHO = LEE;
?WHO = KIM;
?WHO = ROBIN;
?WHO = SANDY;
?WHO = CATS;
?WHO = SANDY;

> (?- (likes ?who Sandy))
?WHO = SANDY;
?WHO = KIM;
?WHO = SANDY;

> (?- (likes Robin Lee))
No.
```

The first query asks again whom Sandy likes, and the second asks who likes Sandy. The third asks for confirmation of a fact. The answer is "no," because there are no clauses or facts that say Robin likes Lee. Here's another example, a list of pairs of people who are in a mutual liking relation. The last answer has an uninstantiated variable, indicating that everyone likes themselves.

```
> (?- (likes ?x ?y) (likes ?y ?x))
?Y = KIM
?X = SANDY;
?Y = SANDY
?X = SANDY;
?Y = SANDY
?X = SANDY;
?Y = SANDY
?X = KIM;
?Y = SANDY
?X = SANDY;
?Y = ?X3251
?X = ?X3251;
```

It makes sense in Prolog to ask open-ended queries like "what lists is 2 a member of?" or even "what items are elements of what lists?"

```
(?- (member 2 ?list))
(?- (member ?item ?list))
```

These queries are valid Prolog and will return solutions, but there will be an infinite number of them. Since our interpreter collects all the solutions into a single list before showing any of them, we will never get to see the solutions. The next section shows how to write a new interpreter that fixes this problem.

Exercise 11.1 [m]   The representation of relations has been a list whose first element is a symbol. However, for relations with no arguments, some people prefer to write (<- p q r) rather than (<- (p) (q) (r)). Make changes so that either form is acceptable.

Exercise 11.2 [m]   Some people find the <- notation difficult to read. Define macros rule and fact so that we can write:

```
(fact (likes Robin cats))
(rule (likes Sandy ?x) if (likes ?x cats))
```

11.3   Idea 3: Automatic Backtracking

The Prolog interpreter implemented in the last section solves problems by returning a list of all possible solutions. We'll call this a *batch* approach, because the answers are retrieved in one uninterrupted batch of processing. Sometimes that is just what you want, but other times a single solution will do. In real Prolog, solutions are presented one at a time, as they are found. After each solution is printed, the user has the option of asking for more solutions, or stopping. This is an *incremental* approach. The incremental approach will be faster when the desired solution is one of the first out of many alternatives. The incremental approach will even work when there is an infinite number of solutions. And if that is not enough, the incremental approach can be implemented so that it searches depth-first. This means that at any point it will require less storage space than the batch approach, which must keep all solutions in memory at once.

In this section we implement an incremental Prolog interpreter. One approach would be to modify the interpreter of the last section to use pipes rather than lists. With pipes, unnecessary computation is delayed, and even infinite lists can be expressed in a finite amount of time and space. We could change to pipes simply by changing the mapcan in prove and prove-all to mappend-pipe (page 286). The books by Winston and Horn (1988) and by Abelson and Sussman (1985) take this approach. We take a different one.

The first step is a version of prove and prove-all that return a single solution rather than a list of all possible solutions. This should be reminiscent of achieve and achieve-all from gps (chapter 4). Unlike gps, recursive subgoals and clobbered sibling goals are not checked for. However, prove is required to search systematically through all solutions, so it is passed an additional parameter: a list of other goals to achieve after achieving the first goal. This is equivalent to passing a continuation to prove. The result is that if prove ever succeeds, it means the entire top-level goal has succeeded. If it fails, it just means the program is backtracking and trying another sequence of choices. Note that prove relies on the fact that fail is nil, because of the way it uses some.

```
(defun prove-all (goals bindings)
  "Find a solution to the conjunction of goals."
  (cond ((eq bindings fail) fail)
        ((null goals) bindings)
        (t (prove (first goals) bindings (rest goals)))))

(defun prove (goal bindings other-goals)
  "Return a list of possible solutions to goal."
  (some #'(lambda (clause)
            (let ((new-clause (rename-variables clause)))
              (prove-all
                (append (clause-body new-clause) other-goals)
```

```
                         (unify goal (clause-head new-clause) bindings))))
              (get-clauses (predicate goal)))))
```

If prove does succeed, it means a solution has been found. If we want more solutions, we need some way of making the process fail, so that it will backtrack and try again. One way to do that is to extend every query with a goal that will print out the variables, and ask the user if the computation should be continued. If the user says yes, then the goal *fails,* and backtracking starts. If the user says no, the goal succeeds, and since it is the final goal, the computation ends. This requires a brand new type of goal: one that is not matched against the data base, but rather causes some procedure to take action. In Prolog, such procedures are called *primitives,* because they are built-in to the language, and new ones may not be defined by the user. The user may, of course, define nonprimitive procedures that call upon the primitives.

In our implementation, primitives will be represented as Lisp functions. A predicate can be represented either as a list of clauses (as it has been so far) or as a single primitive. Here is a version of prove that calls primitives when appropriate:

```
(defun prove (goal bindings other-goals)
  "Return a list of possible solutions to goal."
  (let ((clauses (get-clauses (predicate goal))))
    (if (listp clauses)
        (some
          #'(lambda (clause)
              (let ((new-clause (rename-variables clause)))
                (prove-all
                  (append (clause-body new-clause) other-goals)
                  (unify goal (clause-head new-clause) bindings))))
          clauses)
        ;; The predicate's "clauses" can be an atom:
        ;; a primitive function to call
        (funcall clauses (rest goal) bindings
                 other-goals))))
```

Here is the version of top-level-prove that adds the primitive goal show-prolog-vars to the end of the list of goals. Note that this version need not call show-prolog-solutions itself, since the printing will be handled by the primitive for show-prolog-vars.

```
(defun top-level-prove (goals)
  (prove-all '(,@goals (show-prolog-vars ,@(variables-in goals)))
             no-bindings)
  (format t "~&No.")
  (values))
```

Here we define the primitive show-prolog-vars. All primitives must be functions of three arguments: a list of arguments to the primitive relation (here a list of variables to show), a binding list for these arguments, and a list of pending goals. A primitive should either return fail or call prove-all to continue.

```lisp
(defun show-prolog-vars (vars bindings other-goals)
  "Print each variable with its binding.
  Then ask the user if more solutions are desired."
  (if (null vars)
      (format t "~&Yes")
      (dolist (var vars)
        (format t "~&~a = ~a" var
                (subst-bindings bindings var))))
  (if (continue-p)
      fail
      (prove-all other-goals bindings)))
```

Since primitives are represented as entries on the clauses property of predicate symbols, we have to register show-prolog-vars as a primitive like this:

```lisp
(setf (get 'show-prolog-vars 'clauses) 'show-prolog-vars)
```

Finally, the Lisp predicate continue-p asks the user if he or she wants to see more solutions:

```lisp
(defun continue-p ()
  "Ask user if we should continue looking for solutions."
  (case (read-char)
    (#\; t)
    (#\. nil)
    (#\newline (continue-p))
    (otherwise
      (format t " Type ; to see more or . to stop")
      (continue-p))))
```

This version works just as well as the previous version on finite problems. The only difference is that the user, not the system, types the semicolons. The advantage is that we can now use the system on infinite problems as well. First, we'll ask what lists 2 is a member of:

```
> (?- (member 2 ?list))
?LIST = (2 . ?REST3302);
?LIST = (?X3303 2 . ?REST3307);
?LIST = (?X3303 ?X3308 2 . ?REST3312);
?LIST = (?X3303 ?X3308 ?X3313 2 . ?REST3317).
No.
```

The answers mean that 2 is a member of any list that starts with 2, or whose second element is 2, or whose third element is 2, and so on. The infinite computation was halted when the user typed a period rather than a semicolon. The "no" now means that there are no more answers to be printed; it will appear if there are no answers at all, if the user types a period, or if all the answers have been printed.

We can ask even more abstract queries. The answer to the next query says that an item is an element of a list when it is the the first element, or the second, or the third, or the fourth, and so on.

```
> (?- (member ?item ?list))
?ITEM = ?ITEM3318
?LIST = (?ITEM3318 . ?REST3319);
?ITEM = ?ITEM3323
?LIST = (?X3320 ?ITEM3323 . ?REST3324);
?ITEM = ?ITEM3328
?LIST = (?X3320 ?X3325 ?ITEM3328 . ?REST3329);
?ITEM = ?ITEM3333
?LIST = (?X3320 ?X3325 ?X3330 ?ITEM3333 . ?REST3334).
No.
```

Now let's add the definition of the relation length:

```
(<- (length () 0))
(<- (length (?x . ?y) (1+ ?n)) (length ?y ?n))
```

Here are some queries showing that length can be used to find the second argument, the first, or both:

```
> (?- (length (a b c d) ?n))
?N = (1+ (1+ (1+ (1+ 0))));
No.

> (?- (length ?list (1+ (1+ 0))))
?LIST = (?X3869 ?X3872);
No.
```

```
> (?- (length ?list ?n))
?LIST = NIL
?N = 0;
?LIST = (?X3918)
?N = (1+ 0);
?LIST = (?X3918 ?X3921)
?N = (1+ (1+ 0)).
No.
```

The next two queries show the two lists of length two with a as a member. Both queries give the correct answer, a two-element list that either starts or ends with a. However, the behavior after generating these two solutions is quite different.

```
> (?- (length ?l (1+ (1+ 0))) (member a ?l))
?L = (A ?X4057);
?L = (?Y4061 A);
No.

> (?- (member a ?l) (length ?l (1+ (1+ 0))))
?L = (A ?X4081);
?L = (?Y4085 A);[Abort]
```

In the first query, length only generates one possible solution, the list with two unbound elements. member takes this solution and instantiates either the first or the second element to a.

In the second query, member keeps generating potential solutions. The first two partial solutions, where a is the first or second member of a list of unknown length, are extended by length to yield the solutions where the list has length two. After that, member keeps generating longer and longer lists, which length keeps rejecting. It is implicit in the definition of member that subsequent solutions will be longer, but because that is not explicitly known, they are all generated anyway and then explicitly tested and rejected by length.

This example reveals the limitations of Prolog as a pure logic-programming language. It turns out the user must be concerned not only about the logic of the problem but also with the flow of control. Prolog is smart enough to backtrack and find all solutions when the search space is small enough, but when it is infinite (or even very large), the programmer still has a responsibility to guide the flow of control. It is possible to devise languages that do much more in terms of automatic flow of control.[4] Prolog is a convenient and efficient middle ground between imperative languages and pure logic.

---

[4]See the MU-Prolog and NU-Prolog languages (Naish 1986).

Approaches to Backtracking

Suppose you are asked to make a "small" change to an existing program. The problem is that some function, f, which was thought to be single-valued, is now known to return two or more valid answers in certain circumstances. In other words, f is nondeterministic. (Perhaps f is sqrt, and we now want to deal with negative numbers). What are your alternatives as a programmer? Five possibilities can be identified:

- Guess. Choose one possibility and discard the others. This requires a means of making the right guesses, or recovering from wrong guesses.

- Know. Sometimes you can provide additional information that is enough to decide what the right choice is. This means changing the calling function(s) to provide the additional information.

- Return a list. This means that the calling function(s) must be changed to expect a list of replies.

- Return a *pipe*, as defined in section 9.3. Again, the calling function(s) must be changed to expect a pipe.

- Guess and save. Choose one possibility and return it, but record enough information to allow computing the other possibilities later. This requires saving the current state of the computation as well as some information on the remaining possibilities.

The last alternative is the most desirable. It is efficient, because it doesn't require computing answers that are never used. It is unobtrusive, because it doesn't require changing the calling function (and the calling function's calling function) to expect a list or pipe of answers. Unfortunately, it does have one major difficulty: there has to be a way of packaging up the current state of the computation and saving it away so that it can be returned to when the first choice does not work. For our Prolog interpreter, the current state is succinctly represented as a list of goals. In other problems, it is not so easy to summarize the entire state.

We will see in section 22.4 that the Scheme dialect of Lisp provides a function, call-with-current-continuation, that does exactly what we want: it packages the current state of the computation into a function, which can be stored away and invoked later. Unfortunately, there is no corresponding function in Common Lisp.

Anonymous Variables

Before moving on, it is useful to introduce the notion of an *anonymous variable*. This is a variable that is distinct from all others in a clause or query, but which the programmer does not want to bother to name. In real Prolog, the underscore is used for anonymous variables, but we will use a single question mark. The definition of member that follows uses anonymous variables for positions within terms that are not needed within a clause:

```
(<- (member ?item (?item . ?)))
(<- (member ?item (? . ?rest)) (member ?item ?rest))
```

However, we also want to allow several anonymous variables in a clause but still be able to keep each anonymous variable distinct from all other variables. One way to do that is to replace each anonymous variable with a unique variable. The function replace-?-vars uses gensym to do just that. It is installed in the top-level macros <- and ?- so that all clauses and queries get the proper treatment.

```
(defmacro <- (&rest clause)
  "Add a clause to the data base."
  '(add-clause ',(replace-?-vars clause)))

(defmacro ?- (&rest goals)
  "Make a query and print answers."
  '(top-level-prove ',(replace-?-vars goals)))

(defun replace-?-vars (exp)
  "Replace any ? within exp with a var of the form ?123."
  (cond ((eq exp '?) (gensym "?"))
        ((atom exp) exp)
        (t (reuse-cons (replace-?-vars (first exp))
                       (replace-?-vars (rest exp))
                       exp))))
```

A named variable that is used only once in a clause can also be considered an anonymous variable. This is addressed in a different way in section 12.3.

11.4   The Zebra Puzzle

Here is an example of something Prolog is very good at: a logic puzzle. There are fifteen facts, or constraints, in the puzzle:

1. There are five houses in a line, each with an owner, a pet, a cigarette, a drink, and a color.

2. The Englishman lives in the red house.

3. The Spaniard owns the dog.

4. Coffee is drunk in the green house.

5. The Ukrainian drinks tea.

6. The green house is immediately to the right of the ivory house.

7. The Winston smoker owns snails.

8. Kools are smoked in the yellow house.

9. Milk is drunk in the middle house.

10. The Norwegian lives in the first house on the left.

11. The man who smokes Chesterfields lives next to the man with the fox.

12. Kools are smoked in the house next to the house with the horse.

13. The Lucky Strike smoker drinks orange juice.

14. The Japanese smokes Parliaments.

15. The Norwegian lives next to the blue house.

The questions to be answered are: who drinks water and who owns the zebra? To solve this puzzle, we first define the relations nextto (for "next to") and iright (for "immediately to the right of"). They are closely related to member, which is repeated here.

```
(<- (member ?item (?item . ?rest)))
(<- (member ?item (?x . ?rest)) (member ?item ?rest))

(<- (nextto ?x ?y ?list) (iright ?x ?y ?list))
(<- (nextto ?x ?y ?list) (iright ?y ?x ?list))

(<- (iright ?left ?right (?left ?right . ?rest)))
(<- (iright ?left ?right (?x . ?rest))
    (iright ?left ?right ?rest))

(<- (= ?x ?x))
```

We also defined the identity relation, =. It has a single clause that says that any x is equal to itself. One might think that this implements eq or equal. Actually, since Prolog uses unification to see if the two arguments of a goal each unify with ?x, this means that = is unification.

Now we are ready to define the zebra puzzle with a single (long) clause. The variable ?h represents the list of five houses, and each house is represented by a term of the form (house *nationality pet cigarette drink color*). The variable ?w is the water drinker, and ?z is the zebra owner. Each of the 15 constraints in the puzzle is listed in the body of zebra, although constraints 9 and 10 have been combined into the first one. Consider constraint 2, "The Englishman lives in the red house." This is interpreted as "there is a house whose nationality is Englishman and whose color is red, and which is a member of the list of houses": in other words, (member (house englishman ? ? ? red) ?h). The other constraints are similarly straightforward.

```
(<- (zebra ?h ?w ?z)
  ;; Each house is of the form:
  ;; (house nationality pet cigarette drink house-color)
  (= ?h ((house norwegian ? ? ? ?)              ;1,10
         ?
         (house ? ? ? milk ?) ? ?))             ; 9
  (member (house englishman ? ? ? red) ?h)      ; 2
  (member (house spaniard dog ? ? ?) ?h)        ; 3
  (member (house ? ? ? coffee green) ?h)        ; 4
  (member (house ukrainian ? ? tea ?) ?h)       ; 5
  (iright (house ? ? ? ? ivory)                 ; 6
          (house ? ? ? ? green) ?h)
  (member (house ? snails winston ? ?) ?h)      ; 7
  (member (house ? ? kools ? yellow) ?h)        ; 8
  (nextto (house ? ? chesterfield ? ?)          ;11
          (house ? fox ? ? ?) ?h)
  (nextto (house ? ? kools ? ?)                 ;12
          (house ? horse ? ? ?) ?h)
  (member (house ? ? luckystrike orange-juice ?) ?h);13
  (member (house japanese ? parliaments ? ?) ?h)    ;14
  (nextto (house norwegian ? ? ? ?)             ;15
          (house ? ? ? ? blue) ?h)
  ;; Now for the questions:
  (member (house ?w ? ? water ?) ?h)            ;Q1
  (member (house ?z zebra ? ? ?) ?h))           ;Q2
```

Here's the query and solution to the puzzle:

```
> (?- (zebra ?houses ?water-drinker ?zebra-owner))
?HOUSES = ((HOUSE NORWEGIAN FOX KOOLS WATER YELLOW)
           (HOUSE UKRAINIAN HORSE CHESTERFIELD TEA BLUE)
           (HOUSE ENGLISHMAN SNAILS WINSTON MILK RED)
           (HOUSE SPANIARD DOG LUCKYSTRIKE ORANGE-JUICE IVORY)
           (HOUSE JAPANESE ZEBRA PARLIAMENTS COFFEE GREEN))
?WATER-DRINKER = NORWEGIAN
?ZEBRA-OWNER = JAPANESE.
No.
```

This took 278 seconds, and profiling (see page 288) reveals that the function prove was called 12,825 times. A call to prove has been termed a *logical inference*, so our system is performing $12825/278 = 46$ logical inferences per second, or LIPS. Good Prolog systems perform at 10,000 to 100,000 LIPS or more, so this is barely limping along.

Small changes to the problem can greatly affect the search time. For example, the relation nextto holds when the first house is immediately right of the second, or when the second is immediately right of the first. It is arbitrary in which order these clauses are listed, and one might think it would make no difference in which order they were listed. In fact, if we reverse the order of these two clauses, the execution time is roughly cut in half.

11.5   The Synergy of Backtracking and Unification

Prolog's backward chaining with backtracking is a powerful technique for generating the possible solutions to a problem. It makes it easy to implement a *generate-and-test* strategy, where possible solutions are considered one at a time, and when a candidate solution is rejected, the next is suggested. But generate-and-test is only feasible when the space of possible solutions is small.

In the zebra puzzle, there are five attributes for each of the five houses. Thus there are $5!^5$, or over 24 billion candidate solutions, far too many to test one at a time. It is the concept of unification (with the corresponding notion of a logic variable) that makes generate-and-test feasible on this puzzle. Instead of enumerating complete candidate solutions, unification allows us to specify *partial* candidates. We start out knowing that there are five houses, with the Norwegian living on the far left and the milk drinker in the middle. Rather than generating all complete candidates that satisfy these two constraints, we leave the remaining information vague, by unifying the remaining houses and attributes with anonymous logic variables. The next constraint (number 2) places the Englishman in the red house. Because of the way member is written, this first tries to place the Englishman in the leftmost house. This is rejected, because Englishman and Norwegian fail to unify, so the next possibility is considered, and the Englishman is placed in the second house. But no other features of the second house are specified—we didn't have to make separate guesses for the Englishman's house being green, yellow, and so forth. The search continues, filling in only as much as is necessary and backing up whenever a unification fails.

For this problem, unification serves the same purpose as the delay macro (page 281). It allows us to delay deciding the value of some attribute as long as possible, but to immediately reject a solution that tries to give two different values to the same attribute. That way, we save time if we end up backtracking before the computation is made, but we are still able to fill in the value later on.

It is possible to extend unification so that it is doing more work, and backtracking is doing less work. Consider the following computation:

```
(?- (length ?l 4)
    (member d ?l) (member a ?l) (member c ?l) (member b ?l)
    (= ?l (a b c d)))
```

The first two lines generate permutations of the list (d a c b), and the third line tests for a permutation equal to (a b c d). Most of the work is done by backtracking. An alternative is to extend unification to deal with lists, as well as constants and variables. Predicates like length and member would be primitives that would have to know about the representation of lists. Then the first two lines of the above program would set ?l to something like #s(list :length 4 :members (d a c d)). The third line would be a call to the extended unification procedure, which would further specify ?l to be something like:

```
#s(list :length 4 :members (d a c d) :order (a b c d))
```

By making the unification procedure more complex, we eliminate the need for backtracking entirely.

Exercise 11.3 [s] Would a unification algorithm that delayed member tests be a good idea or a bad idea for the zebra puzzle?

11.6 Destructive Unification

As we saw in section 11.2, keeping track of a binding list of variables is a little tricky. It is also prone to inefficiency if the binding list grows large, because the list must be searched linearly, and because space must be allocated to hold the binding list. An alternative implementation is to change unify to a destructive operation. In this approach, there are no binding lists. Instead, each variable is represented as a structure that includes a field for its binding. When the variable is unified with another expression, the variable's binding field is modified to point to the expression. Such variables will be called vars to distinguish them from the implementation of variables as symbols starting with a question mark. vars are defined with the following code:

```
(defconstant unbound "Unbound")

(defstruct var name (binding unbound))

(defun bound-p (var) (not (eq (var-binding var) unbound)))
```

The macro deref gets at the binding of a variable, returning its argument when it is an unbound variable or a nonvariable expression. It includes a loop because a variable can be bound to another variable, which in turn is bound to the ultimate value.

Normally, it would be considered bad practice to implement deref as a macro, since it could be implemented as an inline function, provided the caller was willing to write (setf x (deref x)) instead of (deref x). However, deref will appear in code generated by some versions of the Prolog compiler that will be presented in the next section. Therefore, to make the generated code look neater, I have allowed myself the luxury of the deref macro.

```lisp
(defmacro deref (exp)
  "Follow pointers for bound variables."
  '(progn (loop while (and (var-p ,exp) (bound-p ,exp))
            do (setf ,exp (var-binding ,exp)))
          ,exp))
```

The function unify! below is the destructive version of unify. It is a predicate that returns true for success and false for failure, and has the side effect of altering variable bindings.

```lisp
(defun unify! (x y)
  "Destructively unify two expressions"
  (cond ((eql (deref x) (deref y)) t)
        ((var-p x) (set-binding! x y))
        ((var-p y) (set-binding! y x))
        ((and (consp x) (consp y))
         (and (unify! (first x) (first y))
              (unify! (rest x) (rest y))))
        (t nil)))

(defun set-binding! (var value)
  "Set var's binding to value.  Always succeeds (returns t)."
  (setf (var-binding var) value)
  t)
```

To make vars easier to read, we can install a :print-function:

```lisp
(defstruct (var (:print-function print-var))
    name (binding unbound))
  (defun print-var (var stream depth)
    (if (or (and (numberp *print-level*)
                 (>= depth *print-level*))
            (var-p (deref var)))
        (format stream "?~a" (var-name var))
        (write var :stream stream)))
```

This is the first example of a carefully crafted `:print-function`. There are three things to notice about it. First, it explicitly writes to the stream passed as the argument. It does not write to a default stream. Second, it checks the variable depth against `*print-level*`, and prints just the variable name when the depth is exceeded. Third, it uses `write` to print the bindings. This is because `write` pays attention to the current values of `*print-escape*`, `*print-pretty*`, and so on. Other printing functions such as `prin1` or `print` do not pay attention to these variables.

Now, for backtracking purposes, we want to make `set-binding!` keep track of the bindings that were made, so they can be undone later:

```
(defvar *trail* (make-array 200 :fill-pointer 0 :adjustable t))

(defun set-binding! (var value)
  "Set var's binding to value, after saving the variable
  in the trail.  Always returns t."
  (unless (eq var value)
    (vector-push-extend var *trail*)
    (setf (var-binding var) value))
  t)

(defun undo-bindings! (old-trail)
  "Undo all bindings back to a given point in the trail."
  (loop until (= (fill-pointer *trail*) old-trail)
     do (setf (var-binding (vector-pop *trail*)) unbound)))
```

Now we need a way of making new variables, where each one is distinct. That could be done by `gensym`-ing a new name for each variable, but a quicker solution is just to increment a counter. The constructor function `?` is defined to generate a new variable with a name that is a new integer. This is not strictly necessary; we could have just used the automatically provided constructor `make-var`. However, I thought that the operation of providing new anonymous variable was different enough from providing a named variable that it deserved its own function. Besides, `make-var` may be less efficient, because it has to process the keyword arguments. The function `?` has no arguments; it just assigns the default values specified in the slots of the `var` structure.

```
(defvar *var-counter* 0)

(defstruct (var (:constructor ? ())
                (:print-function print-var))
  (name (incf *var-counter*))
  (binding unbound))
```

A reasonable next step would be to use destructive unification to make a more efficient interpreter. This is left as an exercise, however, and instead we put the interpreter aside, and in the next chapter develop a compiler.

11.7   Prolog in Prolog

As stated at the start of this chapter, Prolog has many of the same features that make Lisp attractive for program development. Just as it is easy to write a Lisp interpreter in Lisp, it is easy to write a Prolog interpreter in Prolog. The following Prolog metainterpreter has three main relations. The relation clause is used to store clauses that make up the rules and facts that are to be interpreted. The relation prove is used to prove a goal. It calls prove-all, which attempts to prove a list of goals. prove-all succeeds in two ways: (1) if the list is empty, or (2) if there is some clause whose head matches the first goal, and if we can prove the body of that clause, followed by the remaining goals:

```
(<- (prove ?goal) (prove-all (?goal)))

(<- (prove-all nil))
(<- (prove-all (?goal . ?goals))
    (clause (<- ?goal . ?body))
    (concat ?body ?goals ?new-goals)
    (prove-all ?new-goals))
```

Now we add two clauses to the data base to define the member relation:

```
(<- (clause (<- (mem ?x (?x . ?y)))))
(<- (clause (<- (mem ?x (? . ?z)) (mem ?x ?z))))
```

Finally, we can prove a goal using our interpreter:

```
(?- (prove (mem ?x (1 2 3))))
?X = 1;
?X = 2;
?X = 3;
No.
```

11.8   Prolog Compared to Lisp

Many of the features that make Prolog a succesful language for AI (and for program development in general) are the same as Lisp's features. Let's reconsider the list of features that make Lisp different from conventional languages (see page 25) and see what Prolog has to offer:

- *Built-in Support for Lists (and other data types).* New data types can be created easily using lists or structures (structures are preferred). Support for reading, printing, and accessing components is provided automatically. Numbers, symbols, and characters are also supported. However, because logic variables cannot be altered, certain data structures and operations are not provided. For example, there is no way to update an element of a vector in Prolog.

- *Automatic Storage Management.* The programmer can allocate new objects without worrying about reclaiming them. Reclaiming is usually faster in Prolog than in Lisp, because most data can be stack-allocated instead of heap-allocated.

- *Dynamic Typing.* Declarations are not required. Indeed, there is no standard way to make type declarations, although some implementations allow for them. Some Prolog systems provide only fixnums, so that eliminates the need for a large class of declarations.

- *First-Class Functions.* Prolog has no equivalent of lambda, but the built-in predicate call allows a term—a piece of data—to be called as a goal. Although backtracking choice points are not first-class objects, they can be used in a way very similar to continuations in Lisp.

- *Uniform Syntax.* Like Lisp, Prolog has a uniform syntax for both programs and data. This makes it easy to write interpreters and compilers in Prolog. While Lisp's prefix-operator list notation is more uniform, Prolog allows infix and postfix operators, which may be more natural for some applications.

- *Interactive Environment.* Expressions can be immediately evaluated. High-quality Prolog systems offer both a compiler and interpreter, along with a host of debugging tools.

- *Extensibility.* Prolog syntax is extensible. Because programs and data share the same format, it is possible to write the equivalent of macros in Prolog and to define embedded languages. However, it can be harder to ensure that the resulting code will be compiled efficiently. The details of Prolog compilation are implementation-dependent.

To put things in perspective, consider that Lisp is at once one of the highest-level languages available and a universal assembly language. It is a high-level language because it can easily capture data, functional, and control abstractions. It is a good assembly language because it is possible to write Lisp in a style that directly reflects the operations available on modern computers.

Prolog is generally not as efficient as an assembly language, but it can be more concise as a specification language, at least for some problems. The user writes specifications: lists of axioms that describe the relationships that can hold in the problem domain. If these specifications are in the right form, Prolog's automatic backtracking can find a solution, even though the programmer does not provide an explicit algorithm. For other problems, the search space will be too large or infinite, or Prolog's simple depth-first search with backup will be too inflexible. In this case, Prolog must be used as a programming language rather than a specification language. The programmer must be aware of Prolog's search strategy, using it to implement an appropriate algorithm for the problem at hand.

Prolog, like Lisp, has suffered unfairly from some common myths. It has been thought to be an inefficient language because early implementations were interpreted, and because it has been used to write interpreters. But modern compiled Prolog can be quite efficient (see Warren et al. 1977 and Van Roy 1990). There is a temptation to see Prolog as a solution in itself rather than as a programming language. Those who take that view object that Prolog's depth-first search strategy and basis in predicate calculus is too inflexible. This objection is countered by Prolog programmers who use the facilities provided by the language to build more powerful search strategies and representations, just as one would do in Lisp or any other language.

11.9 History and References

Cordell Green (1968) was the first to articulate the view that mathematical results on theorem proving could be used to make deductions and thereby answer queries. However, the major technique in use at the time, resolution theorem proving (see Robinson 1965), did not adequately constrain search, and thus was not practical. The idea of goal-directed computing was developed in Carl Hewitt's work (1971) on the PLANNER language for robot problem solving. He suggested that the user provide explicit hints on how to control deduction.

At about the same time and independently, Alain Colmerauer was developing a system to perform natural language analysis. His approach was to weaken the logical language so that computationally complex statements (such as logical disjunctions) could not be made. Colmerauer and his group implemented the first Prolog interpreter using Algol-W in the summer of 1972 (see Roussel 1975). It was Roussel's wife, Jacqueline, who came up with the name Prolog as an abbreviation for "programmation en logique." The first large Prolog program was their natural language system, also completed that year (Colmerauer et al. 1973). For those who read English better than French, Colmerauer (1985) presents an overview of Prolog. Robert Kowalski is generally considered the coinventer of Prolog. His 1974 article outlines his approach, and his 1988 article is a historical review on the early logic programming work.

There are now dozens of text books on Prolog. In my mind, six of these stand out. Clocksin and Mellish's *Programming in Prolog* (1987) was the first and remains one of the best. Sterling and Shapiro's *The Art of Prolog* (1986) has more substantial examples but is not as complete as a reference. An excellent overview from a slightly more mathematical perspective is Pereira and Shieber's *Prolog and Natural-Language Analysis* (1987). The book is worthwhile for its coverage of Prolog alone, and it also provides a good introduction to the use of logic programming for language understanding (see part V for more on this subject). O'Keefe's *The Craft of Prolog* (1990) shows a number of advanced techinques. O'Keefe is certainly one of the most influential voices in the Prolog community. He has definite views on what makes for good and bad coding style and is not shy about sharing his opinions. The reader is warned that this book evolved from a set of notes on the Clocksin and Mellish book, and the lack of organization shows in places. However, it contains advanced material that can be found nowhere else. Another collection of notes that has been organized into a book is Coelho and Cotta's *Prolog by Example.* Published in 1988, this is an update of their 1980 book, *How to Solve it in Prolog.* The earlier book was an underground classic in the field, serving to educate a generation of Prolog programmers. Both versions include a wealth of examples, unfortunately with little documentation and many typos. Finally, Ivan Bratko's *Prolog Programming for Artificial Intelligence* (1990) covers some introductory AI material from the Prolog perspective.

Maier and Warren's *Computing with Logic* (1988) is the best reference for those interested in implementing Prolog. It starts with a simple interpreter for a variable-free version of Prolog, and then moves up to the full language, adding improvements to the interpreter along the way. (Note that the second author, David S. Warren of Stonybrook, is different from David H. D. Warren, formerly at Edinburgh and now at Bristol. Both are experts on Prolog.)

Lloyd's *Foundations of Logic Programming* (1987) provides a theoretical explanation of the formal semantics of Prolog and related languages. Lassez et al. (1988) and Knight (1989) provide overviews of unification.

There have been many attempts to extend Prolog to be closer to the ideal of Logic Programming. The language MU-Prolog and NU-Prolog (Naish 1986) and Prolog III (Colmerauer 1990) are particularly interesting. The latter includes a systematic treatment of the $\neq$ relation and an interpretation of infinite trees.

11.10 Exercises

Exercise 11.4 [m] It is somewhat confusing to see "no" printed after one or more valid answers have appeared. Modify the program to print "no" only when there are no answers at all, and "no more" in other cases.

Exercise 11.5 [h] At least six books (Abelson and Sussman 1985, Charniak and McDermott 1985, Charniak et al. 1986, Hennessey 1989, Wilensky 1986, and Winston and Horn 1988) present unification algorithms with a common error. They all have problems unifying (?x ?y a) with (?y ?x ?x). Some of these texts assume that unify will be called in a context where no variables are shared between the two arguments. However, they are still suspect to the bug, as the following example points out:

```
> (unify '(f (?x ?y a) (?y ?x ?x)) '(f ?z ?z))
((?Y . A) (?X . ?Y) (?Z ?X ?Y A))
```

Despite this subtle bug, I highly recommend each of the books to the reader. It is interesting to compare different implementations of the same algorithm. It turns out there are more similarities than differences. This indicates two things: (1) there is a generally agreed-upon style for writing these functions, and (2) good programmers sometimes take advantage of opportunities to look at other's code.

The question is: Can you give an informal proof of the correctness of the algorithm presented in this chapter? Start by making a clear statement of the specification. Apply that to the other algorithms, and show where they go wrong. Then see if you can prove that the unify function in this chapter is correct. Failing a complete proof, can you at least prove that the algorithm will always terminate? See Norvig 1991 for more on this problem.

Exercise 11.6 [h] Since logic variables are so basic to Prolog, we would like them to be efficient. In most implementations, structures are not the best choice for small objects. Note that variables only have two slots: the name and the binding. The binding is crucial, but the name is only needed for printing and is arbitrary for most variables. This suggests an alternative implementation. Each variable will be a cons cell of the variable's binding and an arbitrary marker to indicate the type. This marker would be checked by variable-p. Variable names can be stored in a hash table that is cleared before each query. Implement this representation for variables and compare it to the structure representation.

Exercise 11.7 [m] Consider the following alternative implementation for anonymous variables: Leave the macros <- and ?- alone, so that anonymous variables are allowed in assertions and queries. Instead, change unify so that it lets anything match against an anonymous variable:

```
(defun unify (x y &optional (bindings no-bindings))
  "See if x and y match with given bindings."
  (cond ((eq bindings fail) fail)
        ((eql x y) bindings)
        ((or (eq x '?) (eq y '?)) bindings)        ;***
        ((variable-p x) (unify-variable x y bindings))
        ((variable-p y) (unify-variable y x bindings))
        ((and (consp x) (consp y))
         (unify (rest x) (rest y)
```

```
                    (unify (first x) (first y) bindings)))
          (t fail)))
```

Is this alternative correct? If so, give an informal proof. If not, give a counterexample.

Exercise 11.8 [h]   Write a version of the Prolog interpreter that uses destructive unification instead of binding lists.

Exercise 11.9 [m]   Write Prolog rules to express the terms father, mother, son, daughter, and grand- versions of each of them. Also define parent, child, wife, husband, brother, sister, uncle, and aunt. You will need to decide which relations are primitive (stored in the Prolog data base) and which are derived by rules.

For example, here's a definition of grandfather that says that G is the grandfather of C if G is the father of some P, who is the parent of C:

```
(<- (grandfather ?g ?c)
    (father ?g ?p)
    (parent ?p ?c))
```

Exercise 11.10 [m]   The following problem is presented in Wirth 1976:

> *I married a widow (let's call her W) who has a grown-up daughter (call her D). My father (F), who visited us often, fell in love with my step-daughter and married her. Hence my father became my son-in-law and my step-daughter became my mother. Some months later, my wife gave birth to a son (S_1), who became the brother-in-law of my father, as well as my uncle. The wife of my father, that is, my step-daughter, also had a son (S_2).*

Represent this situation using the predicates defined in the previous exercise, verify its conclusions, and prove that the narrator of this tale is his own grandfather.

Exercise 11.11 [d]   Recall the example:

```
> (?- (length (a b c d) ?n))
?N = (1+ (1+ (1+ (1+ 0))));
```

It is possible to produce 4 instead of (1+ (1+ (1+ (1+ 0)))) by extending the notion of unification. Aït-Kaci et al. 1987 might give you some ideas how to do this.

Exercise 11.12 [h]   The function rename-variables was necessary to avoid confusion between the variables in the first argument to unify and those in the second argument. An alternative is to change the unify so that it takes two binding lists, one for each argument, and keeps them separate. Implement this alternative.

11.11   Answers

Answer 11.9   We will choose as primitives the unary predicates male and female and the binary predicates child and married. The former takes the child first; the latter takes the husband first. Given these primitives, we can make the following definitions:

```
(<- (father ?f ?c)    (male ?f) (parent ?f ?c))
(<- (mother ?m ?c)    (female ?m) (parent ?m ?c))
(<- (son ?s ?p)       (male ?s) (parent ?p ?s))
(<- (daughter ?s ?p) (male ?s) (parent ?p ?s))

(<- (grandfather ?g ?c)(father ?g ?p)(parent ?p ?c))
(<- (grandmother ?g ?c)(mother ?g ?p)(parent ?p ?c))
(<- (grandson ?gs ?gp) (son ?gs ?p) (parent ?gp ?p))
(<- (granddaughter ?gd ?gp) (daughter ?gd ?p) (parent ?gp ?p))

(<- (parent ?p ?c)    (child ?c ?p))
(<- (wife ?w ?h)      (married ?h ?w))
(<- (husband ?h ?w)   (married ?h ?w))

(<- (sibling ?x ?y)   (parent ?p ?x) (parent ?p ?y))
(<- (brother ?b ?x)   (male ?b) (sibling ?b ?x))
(<- (sister ?s ?x)    (female ?s) (sibling ?s ?x))
(<- (uncle ?u ?n)     (brother ?u ?p) (parent ?p ?n))
(<- (aunt ?a ?n)      (sister ?a ?p) (parent ?p ?n))
```

Note that there is no way in Prolog to express a *true* definition. We would like to say that "P is the parent of C if and only if C is the child of P," but Prolog makes us express the biconditional in one direction only.

Answer 11.10   Because we haven't considered step-relations in the prior definitions, we have to extend the notion of parent to include step-parents. The definitions
have to be written very carefully to avoid infinite loops. The strategy is to structure
the defined terms into a strict hierarchy: the four primitives are at the bottom, then
parent is defined in terms of the primitives, then the other terms are defined in terms
of parent and the primitives.

We also provide a definition for son-in-law:

```
(<- (parent ?p ?c)     (married ?p ?w) (child ?c ?w))
(<- (parent ?p ?c)     (married ?h ?p) (child ?c ?w))
(<- (son-in-law ?s ?p) (parent ?p ?w) (married ?s ?w))
```

Now we add the information from the story. Note that we only use the four primitives
male, female, married, and child:

```
(<- (male I))   (<- (male F))   (<- (male S1))   (<- (male S2))
(<- (female W)) (<- (female D))
(<- (married I W))
(<- (married F D))
(<- (child D W))
(<- (child I F))
(<- (child S1 I))
(<- (child S2 F))
```

Now we are ready to make the queries:

```
> (?- (son-in-law F I))
Yes.

> (?- (mother D I))
Yes.

> (?- (uncle S1 I))
Yes.

> (?- (grandfather I I))
Yes.
```

CHAPTER 12

Compiling Logic Programs

T he end of chapter 11 introduced a new, more efficient representation for logic variables. It would be reasonable to build a new version of the Prolog interpreter incorporating this representation. However, chapter 9 has taught us that compilers run faster than interpreters and are not that much harder to build. Thus, this chapter will present a Prolog compiler that translates from Prolog to Lisp.

Each Prolog predicate will be translated into a Lisp function, and we will adopt the convention that a predicate called with a different number of arguments is a different predicate. If the symbol p can be called with either one or two arguments, we will need two Lisp functions to implement the two predicates. Following Prolog tradition, these will be called p/1 and p/2.

The next step is to decide what the generated Lisp code should look like. It must unify the head of each clause against the arguments, and if the unification succeeds, it must call the predicates in the body. The difficult part is that the choice points have to be remembered. If a call to a predicate in the first clause fails, we must be able to return to the second clause and try again.

This can be done by passing in a *success continuation* as an extra argument to every predicate. This continuation represents the goals that remain unsolved, the other-goals argument of prove. For each clause in the predicate, if all the goals in a clause succeed, then we should call the success continuation. If a goal fails, we don't do anything special; we just go on to the next clause. There is one complication: after failing we have to undo any bindings made by unify!. Consider an example. The clauses

```
(<- (likes Robin cats))
(<- (likes Sandy ?x) (likes ?x cats))
(<- (likes Kim ?x) (likes ?x Lee) (likes ?x Kim))
```

could be compiled into this:

```
(defun likes/2 (?arg1 ?arg2 cont)
  ;; First clause:
  (if (and (unify! ?arg1 'Robin) (unify! ?arg2 'cats))
      (funcall cont))
  (undo-bindings)
  ;; Second clause:
  (if (unify! ?arg1 'Sandy)
      (likes/2 ?arg2 'cats cont))
  (undo-bindings)
  ;; Third clause:
  (if (unify! ?arg1 'Kim)
      (likes/2 ?arg2 'Lee
               #'(lambda () (likes/2 ?arg2 'Kim cont)))))))
```

In the first clause, we just check the two arguments and, if the unifications succeed, call the continuation directly, because the first clause has no body. In the second clause, likes/2 is called recursively, to see if ?arg2 likes cats. If this succeeds, then the original goal succeeds, and the continuation cont is called. In the third clause, we have to call likes/2 recursively again, this time requesting that it check if ?arg2 likes Lee. If this check succeeds, then the continuation will be called. In this case, the continuation involves another call to likes/2, to check if ?arg2 likes Kim. If this succeeds, then the original continuation, cont, will finally be called.

Recall that in the Prolog interpreter, we had to append the list of pending goals, other-goals, to the goals in the body of the clause. In the compiler, there is no need to do an append. Instead, the continuation cont represents the other-goals, and the body of the clause is represented by explicit calls to functions.

Note that the code for likes/2 given before has eliminated some unnecessary calls to unify!. The most obvious implementation would have one call to unify! for each argument. Thus, for the second clause, we would have the code:

```
(if (and (unify! ?arg1 'Sandy) (unify! ?arg2 ?x))
    (likes/2 ?x 'cats cont))
```

where we would need a suitable let binding for the variable ?x.

12.1   A Prolog Compiler

This section presents the compiler summarized in figure 12.1. At the top level is the function prolog-compile, which takes a symbol, looks at the clauses defined for that symbol, and groups the clauses by arity. Each symbol/arity is compiled into a separate Lisp function by compile-predicate.

```
(defun prolog-compile (symbol &optional
                              (clauses (get-clauses symbol)))
  "Compile a symbol; make a separate function for each arity."
  (unless (null clauses)
    (let ((arity (relation-arity (clause-head (first clauses)))))
      ;; Compile the clauses with this arity
      (compile-predicate
        symbol arity (clauses-with-arity clauses #'= arity))
      ;; Compile all the clauses with any other arity
      (prolog-compile
        symbol (clauses-with-arity clauses #'/= arity)))))
```

Three utility functions are included here:

```
(defun clauses-with-arity (clauses test arity)
  "Return all clauses whose head has given arity."
  (find-all arity clauses
            :key #'(lambda (clause)
                     (relation-arity (clause-head clause)))
            :test test))
(defun relation-arity (relation)
  "The number of arguments to a relation.
  Example: (relation-arity '(p a b c)) => 3"
  (length (args relation)))
(defun args (x) "The arguments of a relation" (rest x))
```

The next step is to compile the clauses for a given predicate with a fixed arity into a

	Top-Level Functions
`?-`	Make a query, but compile everything first.
	Special Variables
`*trail*`	A list of all bindings made so far.
	Data Types
`var`	A box for a variable; can be destructively modified.
	Major Functions
`top-level-prove`	New version compiles everything first.
`run-prolog`	Compile everything and call a Prolog function.
`prolog-compile-symbols`	Compile a list of Prolog symbols.
`prolog-compile`	Compile a symbol; make a separate function for each arity.
`compile-predicate`	Compile all the clauses for a given symbol/arity.
`compile-clause`	Transform away the head and compile the resulting body.
`compile-body`	Compile the body of a clause.
`compile-call`	Compile a call to a Prolog predicate.
`compile-arg`	Generate code for an argument to a goal in the body.
`compile-unify`	Return code that tests if var and term unify.
	Auxiliary Functions
`clauses-with-arity`	Return all clauses whose head has given arity.
`relation-arity`	The number of arguments to a relation.
`args`	The arguments of a relation.
`make-parameters`	Build a list of parameters.
`make-predicate`	Build a symbol of the form `name/arity`.
`make-=`	Build a unification relation.
`def-prolog-compiler-macro`	Define a compiler macro for Prolog.
`prolog-compiler-macro`	Fetch the compiler macro for a Prolog predicate.
`has-variable-p`	Is there a variable anywhere in the expression x?
`proper-listp`	Is x a proper (non-dotted) list?
`maybe-add-undo-bindings`	Undo any bindings that need undoing.
`bind-unbound-vars`	Add a `let` if needed.
`make-anonymous`	Replace variables that are only used once with ?.
`anonymous-variables-in`	A list of anonymous variables.
`compile-if`	Compile an IF form. No else-part allowed.
`compile-unify-variable`	Compile the unification of a var.
`bind-variables-in`	Bind all variables in exp to themselves.
`follow-binding`	Get the ultimate binding of var according to bindings.
`bind-new-variables`	Extend bindings to include any unbound variables.
`ignore`	Do nothing—ignore the arguments.
	Previously Defined Functions
`unify!`	Destructive unification (see section 11.6).
`undo-bindings!`	Use the trail to backtrack, undoing bindings.
`binding-val`	Pick out the value part of a var/val binding.
`symbol`	Create or find an interned symbol.
`new-symbol`	Create a new uninterned symbol.
`find-anywhere`	Does item occur anywhere in tree?

Figure 12.1: Glossary for the Prolog Compiler

Lisp function. For now, that will be done by compiling each clause indepently and wrapping them in a lambda with the right parameter list.

```
(defun compile-predicate (symbol arity clauses)
  "Compile all the clauses for a given symbol/arity
  into a single LISP function."
  (let ((predicate (make-predicate symbol arity))
        (parameters (make-parameters arity)))
    (compile
     (eval
      '(defun ,predicate (,@parameters cont)
         .,(mapcar #'(lambda (clause)
                       (compile-clause parameters clause 'cont))
                   clauses))))))

(defun make-parameters (arity)
  "Return the list (?arg1 ?arg2 ... ?arg-arity)"
  (loop for i from 1 to arity
        collect (new-symbol '?arg i)))

(defun make-predicate (symbol arity)
  "Return the symbol: symbol/arity"
  (symbol symbol '/ arity))
```

Now for the hard part: we must actually generate the code for a clause. Here again is an example of the code desired for one clause. We'll start by setting as a target the simple code:

```
(<- (likes Kim ?x) (likes ?x Lee) (likes ?x Kim))

(defun likes/2 (?arg1 ?arg2 cont)
  ...
  (if (and (unify! ?arg1 'Kim) (unify! ?arg2 ?x)
      (likes/2 ?arg2 'Lee
               #'(lambda () (likes/2 ?x 'Kim))))
  ...)
```

but we'll also consider the possibility of upgrading to the improved code:

```
(defun likes/2 (?arg1 ?arg2 cont)
  ...
  (if (unify! ?arg1 'Kim)
      (likes/2 ?arg2 'Lee
               #'(lambda () (likes/2 ?arg2 'Kim))))
  ...)
```

One approach would be to write two functions, compile-head and compile-body, and then combine them into the code (if *head body*). This approach could easily generate the prior code. However, let's allow ourselves to think ahead a little. If we eventually want to generate the improved code, we will need some communication between the head and the body. We will have to know that the head decided not to compile the unification of ?arg2 and ?x, but because of this, the body will have to substitute ?arg2 for ?x. That means that the compile-head function conceptually returns two values: the code for the head, and an indication of substitutions to perform in the body. This could be handled by explicitly manipulating multiple values, but it seems complicated.

An alternate approach is to eliminate compile-head and just write compile-body. This is possible if we in effect do a source-code transformation on the clause. Instead of treating the clause as:

```
(<- (likes Kim ?x)
    (likes ?x Lee) (likes ?x Kim))
```

we transform it to the equivalent:

```
(<- (likes ?arg1 ?arg2)
    (= ?arg1 Kim) (= ?arg2 ?x) (likes ?x Lee) (likes ?x Kim))
```

Now the arguments in the head of the clause match the arguments in the function likes/2, so there is no need to generate any code for the head. This makes things simpler by eliminating compile-head, and it is a better decomposition for another reason: instead of adding optimizations to compile-head, we will add them to the code in compile-body that handles =. That way, we can optimize calls that the user makes to =, in addition to the calls introduced by the source-code transformation.

To get an overview, the calling sequence of functions will turn out to be as follows:

```
prolog-compile
  compile-predicate
    compile-clause
      compile-body
        compile-call
        compile-arg
        compile-unify
          compile-arg
```

where each function calls the ones below it that are indented one level. We have already defined the first two functions. Here then is our first version of compile-clause:

```
(defun compile-clause (parms clause cont)
  "Transform away the head, and compile the resulting body."
  (compile-body
    (nconc
      (mapcar #'make-= parms (args (clause-head clause)))
      (clause-body clause))
    cont))

(defun make-= (x y) '(= ,x ,y))
```

The bulk of the work is in compile-body, which is a little more complicated. There are three cases. If there is no body, we just call the continuation. If the body starts with a call to =, we compile a call to unify!. Otherwise, we compile a call to a function, passing in the appropriate continuation.

However, it is worthwhile to think ahead at this point. If we want to treat = specially now, we will probably want to treat other goals specially later. So instead of explicitly checking for =, we will do a data-driven dispatch, looking for any predicate that has a prolog-compiler-macro property attached to it. Like Lisp compiler macros, the macro can decline to handle the goal. We will adopt the convention that returning :pass means the macro decided not to handle it, and thus it should be compiled as a normal goal.

```
(defun compile-body (body cont)
  "Compile the body of a clause."
  (if (null body)
      '(funcall ,cont)
      (let* ((goal (first body))
             (macro (prolog-compiler-macro (predicate goal)))
             (macro-val (if macro
                            (funcall macro goal (rest body) cont))))
        (if (and macro (not (eq macro-val :pass)))
            macro-val
            (compile-call
              (make-predicate (predicate goal)
                              (relation-arity goal))
              (mapcar #'(lambda (arg) (compile-arg arg))
                      (args goal))
              (if (null (rest body))
                  cont
                  '#'(lambda ()
                       ,(compile-body (rest body) cont)))))))))

(defun compile-call (predicate args cont)
  "Compile a call to a prolog predicate."
  '(,predicate ,@args ,cont))
```

```
(defun prolog-compiler-macro (name)
  "Fetch the compiler macro for a Prolog predicate."
  ;; Note NAME is the raw name, not the name/arity
  (get name 'prolog-compiler-macro))

(defmacro def-prolog-compiler-macro (name arglist &body body)
  "Define a compiler macro for Prolog."
  '(setf (get ',name 'prolog-compiler-macro)
         #'(lambda ,arglist .,body)))

(def-prolog-compiler-macro = (goal body cont)
  (let ((args (args goal)))
    (if (/= (length args) 2)
        :pass
        '(if ,(compile-unify (first args) (second args))
             ,(compile-body body cont)))))

(defun compile-unify (x y)
  "Return code that tests if var and term unify."
  '(unify! ,(compile-arg x) ,(compile-arg y)))
```

All that remains is compile-arg, a function to compile the arguments to goals in the body. There are three cases to consider, as shown in the compilation to the argument of q below:

```
1 (<- (p ?x) (q ?x))          (q/1 ?x cont)
2 (<- (p ?x) (q (f a b)))     (q/1 '(f a b) cont)
3 (<- (p ?x) (q (f ?x b)))    (q/1 (list 'f ?x 'b) cont)
```

In case 1, the argument is a variable, and it is compiled as is. In case 2, the argument is a constant expression (one without any variables) that compiles into a quoted expression. In case 3, the argument contains a variable, so we have to generate code that builds up the expression. Case 3 is actually split into two in the list below: one compiles into a call to list, and the other a call to cons. It is important to remember that the goal (q (f ?x b)) does *not* involve a call to the function f. Rather, it involves the term (f ?x b), which is just a list of three elements.

```
(defun compile-arg (arg)
  "Generate code for an argument to a goal in the body."
  (cond ((variable-p arg) arg)
        ((not (has-variable-p arg)) '',arg)
        ((proper-listp arg)
         '(list .,(mapcar #'compile-arg arg)))
        (t '(cons ,(compile-arg (first arg))
                  ,(compile-arg (rest arg))))))
```

```
(defun has-variable-p (x)
  "Is there a variable anywhere in the expression x?"
  (find-if-anywhere #'variable-p x))

(defun proper-listp (x)
  "Is x a proper (non-dotted) list?"
  (or (null x)
      (and (consp x) (proper-listp (rest x)))))
```

Let's see how it works. We will consider the following clauses:

```
(<- (likes Robin cats))
(<- (likes Sandy ?x) (likes ?x cats))
(<- (likes Kim ?x) (likes ?x Lee) (likes ?x Kim))

(<- (member ?item (?item . ?rest)))
(<- (member ?item (?x . ?rest)) (member ?item ?rest))
```

Here's what prolog-compile gives us:

```
(DEFUN LIKES/2 (?ARG1 ?ARG2 CONT)
  (IF (UNIFY! ?ARG1 'ROBIN)
      (IF (UNIFY! ?ARG2 'CATS)
          (FUNCALL CONT)))
  (IF (UNIFY! ?ARG1 'SANDY)
      (IF (UNIFY! ?ARG2 ?X)
          (LIKES/2 ?X 'CATS CONT)))
  (IF (UNIFY! ?ARG1 'KIM)
      (IF (UNIFY! ?ARG2 ?X)
          (LIKES/2 ?X 'LEE (LAMBDA ()
                            (LIKES/2 ?X 'KIM CONT))))))

(DEFUN MEMBER/2 (?ARG1 ?ARG2 CONT)
  (IF (UNIFY! ?ARG1 ?ITEM)
      (IF (UNIFY! ?ARG2 (CONS ?ITEM ?REST))
          (FUNCALL CONT)))
  (IF (UNIFY! ?ARG1 ?ITEM)
      (IF (UNIFY! ?ARG2 (CONS ?X ?REST))
          (MEMBER/2 ?ITEM ?REST CONT))))
```

12.2   Fixing the Errors in the Compiler

There are some problems in this version of the compiler:

- We forgot to undo the bindings after each call to `unify!`.

- The definition of `undo-bindings!` defined previously requires as an argument an index into the `*trail*` array. So we will have to save the current top of the trail when we enter each function.

- Local variables, such as `?x`, were used without being introduced. They should be bound to new variables.

Undoing the bindings is simple: we add a single line to `compile-predicate`, a call to the function `maybe-add-undo-bindings`. This function inserts a call to `undo-bindings!` after every failure. If there is only one clause, no undoing is necessary, because the predicate higher up in the calling sequence will do it when it fails. If there are multiple clauses, the function wraps the whole function body in a `let` that captures the initial value of the trail's fill pointer, so that the bindings can be undone to the right point. Similarly, we can handle the unbound-variable problem by wrapping a call to `bind-unbound-vars` around each compiled clause:

```lisp
(defun compile-predicate (symbol arity clauses)
  "Compile all the clauses for a given symbol/arity
  into a single LISP function."
  (let ((predicate (make-predicate symbol arity))
        (parameters (make-parameters arity)))
    (compile
     (eval
      '(defun ,predicate (,@parameters cont)
        .,(maybe-add-undo-bindings                        ;***
           (mapcar #'(lambda (clause)
                       (compile-clause parameters
                                       clause 'cont))
                   clauses)))))))

(defun compile-clause (parms clause cont)
  "Transform away the head, and compile the resulting body."
  (bind-unbound-vars                                      ;***
   parms                                                  ;***
   (compile-body
    (nconc
     (mapcar #'make-= parms (args (clause-head clause)))
     (clause-body clause))
    cont)))
```

```
(defun maybe-add-undo-bindings (compiled-exps)
  "Undo any bindings that need undoing.
  If there are any, bind the trail before we start."
  (if (length=1 compiled-exps)
      compiled-exps
      '((let ((old-trail (fill-pointer *trail*)))
         ,(first compiled-exps)
         ,@(loop for exp in (rest compiled-exps)
                 collect '(undo-bindings! old-trail)
                 collect exp)))))

(defun bind-unbound-vars (parameters exp)
  "If there are any variables in exp (besides the parameters)
  then bind them to new vars."
  (let ((exp-vars (set-difference (variables-in exp)
                                   parameters)))
    (if exp-vars
        '(let ,(mapcar #'(lambda (var) '(,var (?)))
                       exp-vars)
           ,exp)
        exp)))
```

With these improvements, here's the code we get for likes and member:

```
(DEFUN LIKES/2 (?ARG1 ?ARG2 CONT)
  (LET ((OLD-TRAIL (FILL-POINTER *TRAIL*)))
    (IF (UNIFY! ?ARG1 'ROBIN)
        (IF (UNIFY! ?ARG2 'CATS)
            (FUNCALL CONT)))
    (UNDO-BINDINGS! OLD-TRAIL)
    (LET ((?X (?)))
      (IF (UNIFY! ?ARG1 'SANDY)
          (IF (UNIFY! ?ARG2 ?X)
              (LIKES/2 ?X 'CATS CONT))))
    (UNDO-BINDINGS! OLD-TRAIL)
    (LET ((?X (?)))
      (IF (UNIFY! ?ARG1 'KIM)
          (IF (UNIFY! ?ARG2 ?X)
              (LIKES/2 ?X 'LEE (LAMBDA ()
                                 (LIKES/2 ?X 'KIM CONT))))))))
```

```
(DEFUN MEMBER/2 (?ARG1 ?ARG2 CONT)
  (LET ((OLD-TRAIL (FILL-POINTER *TRAIL*)))
    (LET ((?ITEM (?))
          (?REST (?)))
      (IF (UNIFY! ?ARG1 ?ITEM)
          (IF (UNIFY! ?ARG2 (CONS ?ITEM ?REST))
              (FUNCALL CONT))))
    (UNDO-BINDINGS! OLD-TRAIL)
    (LET ((?X (?))
          (?ITEM (?))
          (?REST (?)))
      (IF (UNIFY! ?ARG1 ?ITEM)
          (IF (UNIFY! ?ARG2 (CONS ?X ?REST))
              (MEMBER/2 ?ITEM ?REST CONT))))))
```

12.3   Improving the Compiler

This is fairly good, although there is still room for improvement. One minor improvement is to eliminate unneeded variables. For example, ?rest in the first clause of member and ?x in the second clause are bound to new variables—the result of the (?) call—and then only used once. The generated code could be made a little tighter by just putting (?) inline, rather than binding it to a variable and then referencing that variable. There are two parts to this change: updating compile-arg to compile an anonymous variable inline, and changing the <- macro so that it converts all variables that only appear once in a clause into anonymous variables:

```
(defmacro <- (&rest clause)
  "Add a clause to the data base."
  '(add-clause ',(make-anonymous clause)))
(defun compile-arg (arg)
  "Generate code for an argument to a goal in the body."
  (cond ((eq arg '?) '(?))                              ;***
        ((variable-p arg) arg)
        ((not (has-variable-p arg)) '',arg)
        ((proper-listp arg)
         '(list .,(mapcar #'compile-arg arg)))
        (t '(cons ,(compile-arg (first arg))
                  ,(compile-arg (rest arg))))))
(defun make-anonymous (exp &optional
                       (anon-vars (anonymous-variables-in exp)))
  "Replace variables that are only used once with ?."
  (cond ((consp exp)
         (reuse-cons (make-anonymous (first exp) anon-vars)
```

```
                              (make-anonymous (rest exp) anon-vars)
                              exp))
           ((member exp anon-vars) '?)
           (t exp)))
```

Finding anonymous variables is tricky. The following function keeps two lists: the variables that have been seen once, and the variables that have been seen twice or more. The local function walk is then used to walk over the tree, recursively considering the components of each cons cell and updating the two lists as each variable is encountered. This use of local functions should be remembered, as well as an alternative discussed in exercise 12.23 on page 428.

```
(defun anonymous-variables-in (tree)
  "Return a list of all variables that occur only once in tree."
  (let ((seen-once nil)
        (seen-more nil))
    (labels ((walk (x)
               (cond
                 ((variable-p x)
                  (cond ((member x seen-once)
                          (setf seen-once (delete x seen-once))
                          (push x seen-more))
                        ((member x seen-more) nil)
                        (t (push x seen-once))))
                 ((consp x)
                  (walk (first x))
                  (walk (rest x))))))
      (walk tree)
      seen-once)))
```

Now member compiles into this:

```
(DEFUN MEMBER/2 (?ARG1 ?ARG2 CONT)
  (LET ((OLD-TRAIL (FILL-POINTER *TRAIL*)))
    (LET ((?ITEM (?)))
      (IF (UNIFY! ?ARG1 ?ITEM)
          (IF (UNIFY! ?ARG2 (CONS ?ITEM (?)))
              (FUNCALL CONT))))
    (UNDO-BINDINGS! OLD-TRAIL)
    (LET ((?ITEM (?))
          (?REST (?)))
      (IF (UNIFY! ?ARG1 ?ITEM)
          (IF (UNIFY! ?ARG2 (CONS (?) ?REST))
              (MEMBER/2 ?ITEM ?REST CONT))))))
```

12.4   Improving the Compilation of Unification

Now we turn to the improvement of compile-unify. Recall that we want to eliminate certain calls to unify! so that, for example, the first clause of member:

```
(<- (member ?item (?item . ?rest)))
```

compiles into:

```
(LET ((?ITEM (?)))
  (IF (UNIFY! ?ARG1 ?ITEM)
      (IF (UNIFY! ?ARG2 (CONS ?ITEM (?)))
          (FUNCALL CONT))))
```

when it could compile to the more efficient:

```
(IF (UNIFY! ?ARG2 (CONS ?ARG1 (?)))
    (FUNCALL CONT))
```

Eliminating the unification in one goal has repercussions in other goals later on, so we will need to keep track of expressions that have been unified together. We have a design choice. Either compile-unify can modify a global state variable, or it can return multiple values. On the grounds that global variables are messy, we make the second choice: compile-unify will take a binding list as an extra argument and will return two values, the actual code and an updated binding list. We will expect that other related functions will have to be modified to deal with these multiple values.

When compile-unify is first called in our example clause, it is asked to unify ?arg1 and ?item. We want it to return no code (or more precisely, the trivially true test, t). For the second value, it should return a new binding list, with ?item bound to ?arg1. That binding will be used to replace ?item with ?arg1 in subsequent code.

How do we know to bind ?item to ?arg1 rather than the other way around? Because ?arg1 is already bound to something—the value passed in to member. We don't know what this value is, but we can't ignore it. Thus, the initial binding list will have to indicate that the parameters are bound to something. A simple convention is to bind the parameters to themselves. Thus, the initial binding list will be:

```
((?arg1 . ?arg1) (?arg2 . ?arg2))
```

We saw in the previous chapter (page 354) that binding a variable to itself can lead to problems; we will have to be careful.

Besides eliminating unifications of new variables against parameters, there are quite a few other improvements that can be made. For example, unifications involving only constants can be done at compile time. The call (= (f a) (f a)) always succeeds, while (= 3 4) always fails. In addition, unification of two cons cells can be broken into components at compile time: (= (f ?x) (f a)) reduces to (= ?x a) and (= f f), where the latter trivially succeeds. We can even do some occurs checking at compile time: (= ?x (f ?x)) should fail.

The following table lists these improvements, along with a breakdown for the cases of unifying a bound (?arg1) or unbound (?x) variable agains another expression. The first column is the unification call, the second is the generated code, and the third is the bindings that will be added as a result of the call:

	Unification	Code	Bindings
1	(= 3 3)	t	—
2	(= 3 4)	nil	—
3	(= (f ?x) (?p 3))	t	(?x . 3) (?p . f)
4	(= ?arg1 ?y)	t	(?y . ?arg1)
5	(= ?arg1 ?arg2)	(unify! ?arg1 ?arg2)	(?arg1 . ?arg2)
6	(= ?arg1 3)	(unify! ?arg1 3)	(?arg1 . 3)
7	(= ?arg1 (f ?y))	(unify! ?arg1 ...)	(?y . ?y)
8	(= ?x ?y)	t	(?x . ?y)
9	(= ?x 3)	t	(?x . 3)
10	(= ?x (f ?y))	(unify! ?x ...)	(?y . ?y)
11	(= ?x (f ?x))	nil	—
12	(= ?x ?)	t	—

From this table we can craft our new version of compile-unify. The first part is fairly easy. It takes care of the first three cases in this table and makes sure that compile-unify-variable is called with a variable as the first argument for the other cases.

```
(defun compile-unify (x y bindings)
  "Return 2 values: code to test if x and y unify,
  and a new binding list."
  (cond
    ;; Unify constants and conses:                    ; Case
    ((not (or (has-variable-p x) (has-variable-p y)))  ; 1,2
     (values (equal x y) bindings))
    ((and (consp x) (consp y))                        ; 3
     (multiple-value-bind (code1 bindings1)
         (compile-unify (first x) (first y) bindings)
       (multiple-value-bind (code2 bindings2)
           (compile-unify (rest x) (rest y) bindings1)
         (values (compile-if code1 code2) bindings2))))
    ;; Here x or y is a variable.  Pick the right one:
    ((variable-p x) (compile-unify-variable x y bindings))
    (t              (compile-unify-variable y x bindings))))
```

```
(defun compile-if (pred then-part)
  "Compile a Lisp IF form. No else-part allowed."
  (case pred
    ((t) then-part)
    ((nil) nil)
    (otherwise `(if ,pred ,then-part))))
```

The function compile-unify-variable following is one of the most complex we have seen. For each argument, we see if it has a binding (the local variables xb and yb), and then use the bindings to get the value of each argument (x1 and y1). Note that for either an unbound variable or one bound to itself, x will equal x1 (and the same for y and y1). If either of the pairs of values is not equal, we should use the new ones (x1 or y1), and the clause commented deref does that. After that point, we just go through the cases, one at a time. It turns out that it was easier to change the order slightly from the preceding table, but each clause is commented with the corresponding number:

```
(defun compile-unify-variable (x y bindings)
  "X is a variable, and Y may be."
  (let* ((xb (follow-binding x bindings))
         (x1 (if xb (cdr xb) x))
         (yb (if (variable-p y) (follow-binding y bindings)))
         (y1 (if yb (cdr yb) y)))
    (cond                                               ; Case:
      ((or (eq x '?) (eq y '?)) (values t bindings))    ; 12
      ((not (and (equal x x1) (equal y y1)))            ; deref
       (compile-unify x1 y1 bindings))
      ((find-anywhere x1 y1) (values nil bindings))     ; 11
      ((consp y1)                                       ; 7,10
       (values `(unify! ,x1 ,(compile-arg y1 bindings))
               (bind-variables-in y1 bindings)))
      ((not (null xb))
       ;; i.e. x is an ?arg variable
       (if (and (variable-p y1) (null yb))
           (values 't (extend-bindings y1 x1 bindings))  ; 4
           (values `(unify! ,x1 ,(compile-arg y1 bindings))
                   (extend-bindings x1 y1 bindings))))   ; 5,6
      ((not (null yb))
       (compile-unify-variable y1 x1 bindings))
      (t (values 't (extend-bindings x1 y1 bindings)))))) ; 8,9
```

Take some time to understand just how this function works. Then go on to the following auxiliary functions:

```
(defun bind-variables-in (exp bindings)
  "Bind all variables in exp to themselves, and add that to
  bindings (except for variables already bound)."
  (dolist (var (variables-in exp))
    (unless (get-binding var bindings)
      (setf bindings (extend-bindings var var bindings))))
  bindings)

(defun follow-binding (var bindings)
  "Get the ultimate binding of var according to bindings."
  (let ((b (get-binding var bindings)))
    (if (eq (car b) (cdr b))
        b
        (or (follow-binding (cdr b) bindings)
            b))))
```

Now we need to integrate the new `compile-unify` into the rest of the compiler. The problem is that the new version takes an extra argument and returns an extra value, so all the functions that call it need to be changed. Let's look again at the calling sequence:

```
prolog-compile
  compile-predicate
    compile-clause
      compile-body
        compile-call
        compile-arg
          compile-unify
            compile-arg
```

First, going downward, we see that `compile-arg` needs to take a binding list as an argument, so that it can look up and substitute in the appropriate values. But it will not alter the binding list, so it still returns one value:

```
(defun compile-arg (arg bindings)
  "Generate code for an argument to a goal in the body."
  (cond ((eq arg '?) '(?))
        ((variable-p arg)
         (let ((binding (get-binding arg bindings)))
           (if (and (not (null binding))
                    (not (eq arg (binding-val binding))))
               (compile-arg (binding-val binding) bindings)
               arg)))
        ((not (find-if-anywhere #'variable-p arg)) '',arg)
        ((proper-listp arg)
         '(list .,(mapcar #'(lambda (a) (compile-arg a bindings))
```

```
                                 arg)))
            (t '(cons ,(compile-arg (first arg) bindings)
                      ,(compile-arg (rest arg) bindings)))))
```

Now, going upward, `compile-body` needs to take a binding list and pass it on to various functions:

```
(defun compile-body (body cont bindings)
  "Compile the body of a clause."
  (cond
    ((null body)
     '(funcall ,cont))
    (t (let* ((goal (first body))
              (macro (prolog-compiler-macro (predicate goal)))
              (macro-val (if macro
                             (funcall macro goal (rest body)
                                      cont bindings))))
         (if (and macro (not (eq macro-val :pass)))
             macro-val
             (compile-call
               (make-predicate (predicate goal)
                               (relation-arity goal))
               (mapcar #'(lambda (arg)
                           (compile-arg arg bindings))
                       (args goal))
               (if (null (rest body))
                   cont
                   '#'(lambda ()
                        ,(compile-body
                           (rest body) cont
                           (bind-new-variables bindings goal)))))))))))
```

The function `bind-new-variables` takes any variables mentioned in the goal that have not been bound yet and binds these variables to themselves. This is because the goal, whatever it is, may bind its arguments.

```
(defun bind-new-variables (bindings goal)
  "Extend bindings to include any unbound variables in goal."
  (let ((variables (remove-if #'(lambda (v) (assoc v bindings))
                              (variables-in goal))))
    (nconc (mapcar #'self-cons variables) bindings)))

(defun self-cons (x) (cons x x))
```

One of the functions that needs to be changed to accept a binding list is the compiler macro for =:

```
(def-prolog-compiler-macro = (goal body cont bindings)
  "Compile a goal which is a call to =."
  (let ((args (args goal)))
    (if (/= (length args) 2)
        :pass ;; decline to handle this goal
        (multiple-value-bind (code1 bindings1)
            (compile-unify (first args) (second args) bindings)
          (compile-if
            code1
            (compile-body body cont bindings1))))))
```

The last step upward is to change compile-clause so that it starts everything off by passing in to compile-body a binding list with all the parameters bound to themselves:

```
(defun compile-clause (parms clause cont)
  "Transform away the head, and compile the resulting body."
  (bind-unbound-vars
    parms
    (compile-body
      (nconc
        (mapcar #'make-= parms (args (clause-head clause)))
        (clause-body clause))
      cont
      (mapcar #'self-cons parms))))              ;***
```

Finally, we can see the fruits of our efforts:

```
(DEFUN MEMBER/2 (?ARG1 ?ARG2 CONT)
  (LET ((OLD-TRAIL (FILL-POINTER *TRAIL*)))
    (IF (UNIFY! ?ARG2 (CONS ?ARG1 (?)))
        (FUNCALL CONT))
    (UNDO-BINDINGS! OLD-TRAIL)
    (LET ((?REST (?)))
      (IF (UNIFY! ?ARG2 (CONS (?) ?REST))
          (MEMBER/2 ?ARG1 ?REST CONT)))))

(DEFUN LIKES/2 (?ARG1 ?ARG2 CONT)
  (LET ((OLD-TRAIL (FILL-POINTER *TRAIL*)))
    (IF (UNIFY! ?ARG1 'ROBIN)
        (IF (UNIFY! ?ARG2 'CATS)
            (FUNCALL CONT)))
    (UNDO-BINDINGS! OLD-TRAIL)
    (IF (UNIFY! ?ARG1 'SANDY)
        (LIKES/2 ?ARG2 'CATS CONT))
    (UNDO-BINDINGS! OLD-TRAIL)
    (IF (UNIFY! ?ARG1 'KIM)
        (LIKES/2 ?ARG2 'LEE (LAMBDA ()
                             (LIKES/2 ?ARG2 'KIM CONT))))))
```

12.5 Further Improvements to Unification

Could `compile-unify` be improved yet again? If we insist that it call `unify!`, it seems that it can't be made much better. However, we could improve it by in effect compiling `unify!`. This is a key idea in the Warren Abstract Machine, or WAM, which is the most commonly used model for Prolog compilers.

We call `unify!` in four cases (5, 6, 7, and 10), and in each case the first argument is a variable, and we know something about the second argument. But the first thing `unify!` does is redundantly test if the first argument is a variable. We could eliminate unnecessary tests by calling more specialized functions rather than the general-purpose function `unify!`. Consider this call:

```
(unify! ?arg2 (cons ?arg1 (?)))
```

If `?arg2` is an unbound variable, this code is appropriate. But if `?arg2` is a constant atom, we should fail immediately, without allowing `cons` and `?` to generate garbage. We could change the test to:

```
(and (consp-or-variable-p ?arg2)
     (unify-first! ?arg2 ?arg1)
     (unify-rest! ?arg2 (?)))
```

with suitable definitions for the functions referenced here. This change should speed execution time and limit the amount of garbage generated. Of course, it makes the generated code longer, so that could slow things down if the program ends up spending too much time bringing the code to the processor.

Exercise 12.1 [h] Write definitions for `consp-or-variable-p`, `unify-first!`, and `unify-rest!`, and change the compiler to generate code like that outlined previously. You might want to look at the function `compile-rule` in section 9.6, starting on page 300. This function compiled a call to `pat-match` into individual tests; now we want to do the same thing to `unify!`. Run some benchmarks to compare the altered compiler to the original version.

Exercise 12.2 [h] We can gain some more efficiency by keeping track of which variables have been dereferenced and calling an appropriate unification function: either one that dereferences the argument or one that assumes the argument has already been dereferenced. Implement this approach.

Exercise 12.3 [m] What code is generated for `(= (f (g ?x) ?y) (f ?y (?p a)))`?

What more efficient code represents the same unification? How easy is it to change the compiler to get this more efficient result?

Exercise 12.4 [h] In retrospect, it seems that binding variables to themselves, as in (?arg1 . ?arg1), was not such a good idea. It complicates the meaning of bindings, and prohibits us from using existing tools. For example, I had to use find-anywhere instead of occur-check for case 11, because occur-check expects a noncircular binding list. But find-anywhere does not do as complete a job as occur-check. Write a version of compile-unify that returns three values: the code, a noncircular binding list, and a list of variables that are bound to unknown values.

Exercise 12.5 [h] An alternative to the previous exercise is not to use binding lists at all. Instead, we could pass in a list of equivalence classes—that is, a list of lists, where each sublist contains one or more elements that have been unified. In this approach, the initial equivalence class list would be ((?arg1) (?arg2)). After unifying ?arg1 with ?x, ?arg2 with ?y, and ?x with 4, the list would be ((4 ?arg1 ?x) (?arg2 ?y)). This assumes the convention that the canonical member of an equivalence class (the one that will be substituted for all others) comes first. Implement this approach. What advantages and disadvantages does it have?

12.6   The User Interface to the Compiler

The compiler can translate Prolog to Lisp, but that does us no good unless we can conveniently arrange to compile the right Prolog relations and call the right Lisp functions. In other words, we have to integrate the compiler with the <- and ? macros. Surprisingly, we don't need to change these macros at all. Rather, we will change the functions these macros call. When a new clause is entered, we will enter the clause's predicate in the list *uncompiled*. This is a one-line addition to add-clause:

```
(defvar *uncompiled* nil
        "Prolog symbols that have not been compiled.")

(defun add-clause (clause)
  "Add a clause to the data base, indexed by head's predicate."
  ;; The predicate must be a non-variable symbol.
  (let ((pred (predicate (clause-head clause))))
    (assert (and (symbolp pred) (not (variable-p pred))))
    (pushnew pred *db-predicates*)
    (pushnew pred *uncompiled*)                          ;***
    (setf (get pred 'clauses)
```

```
              (nconc (get-clauses pred) (list clause)))
      pred))
```

Now when a query is made, the ?- macro expands into a call to top-level-prove. The list of goals in the query, along with the show-prolog-vars goal, is added as the sole clause for the relation top-level-query. Next, that query, along with any others that are on the uncompiled list, are compiled. Finally, the newly compiled top-level query function is called.

```
(defun top-level-prove (goals)
  "Prove the list of goals by compiling and calling it."
  ;; First redefine top-level-query
  (clear-predicate 'top-level-query)
  (let ((vars (delete '? (variables-in goals))))
    (add-clause `((top-level-query)
                  ,@goals
                  (show-prolog-vars ,(mapcar #'symbol-name vars)
                                    ,vars))))
  ;; Now run it
  (run-prolog 'top-level-query/0 #'ignore)
  (format t "~&No.")
  (values))

(defun run-prolog (procedure cont)
  "Run a 0-ary prolog procedure with a given continuation."
  ;; First compile anything else that needs it
  (prolog-compile-symbols)
  ;; Reset the trail and the new variable counter
  (setf (fill-pointer *trail*) 0)
  (setf *var-counter* 0)
  ;; Finally, call the query
  (catch 'top-level-prove
    (funcall procedure cont)))

(defun prolog-compile-symbols (&optional (symbols *uncompiled*))
  "Compile a list of Prolog symbols.
  By default, the list is all symbols that need it."
  (mapc #'prolog-compile symbols)
  (setf *uncompiled* (set-difference *uncompiled* symbols)))

(defun ignore (&rest args)
  (declare (ignore args))
  nil)
```

Note that at the top level, we don't need the continuation to do anything. Arbitrarily, we chose to pass in the function ignore, which is defined to ignore its arguments.

This function is useful in a variety of places; some programmers will proclaim it inline and then use a call to ignore in place of an ignore declaration:

```
(defun third-arg (x y z)
  (ignore x y)
  z)
```

The compiler's calling convention is different from the interpreter, so the primitives need to be redefined. The old definition of the primitive show-prolog-vars had three parameters: the list of arguments to the goal, a binding list, and a list of pending goals. The new definition of show-prolog-vars/2 also has three parameters, but that is just a coincidence. The first two parameters are the two separate arguments to the goal: a list of variable names and a list of variable values. The last parameter is a continuation function. To continue, we call that function, but to fail, we throw to the catch point set up in top-level-prove.

```
(defun show-prolog-vars/2 (var-names vars cont)
  "Display the variables, and prompt the user to see
  if we should continue.  If not, return to the top level."
  (if (null vars)
      (format t "~&Yes")
      (loop for name in var-names
            for var in vars do
            (format t "~&~a = ~a" name (deref-exp var))))
  (if (continue-p)
      (funcall cont)
      (throw 'top-level-prove nil)))

(defun deref-exp (exp)
  "Build something equivalent to EXP with variables dereferenced."
  (if (atom (deref exp))
      exp
      (reuse-cons
        (deref-exp (first exp))
        (deref-exp (rest exp))
        exp)))
```

With these definitions in place, we can invoke the compiler automatically just by making a query with the ?- macro.

Exercise 12.6 [m] Suppose you define a predicate p, which calls q, and then define q. In some implementations of Lisp, when you make a query like (?- (p ?x)), you may get a warning message like "function q/1 undefined" before getting the correct answer. The problem is that each function is compiled separately, so warnings detected during the compilation of p/1 will be printed right away, even if the function q/1 will be defined later. In ANSI Common Lisp there is a way to delay the printing of warnings until a series of compilations are done: wrap the compilation with the macro with-compilation-unit. Even if your implementation does not provide this macro, it may provide the same functionality under a different name. Find out if with-compilation-unit is already defined in your implementation, or if it can be defined.

12.7 Benchmarking the Compiler

Our compiled Prolog code runs the zebra puzzle in 17.4 seconds, a 16-fold speed-up over the interpreted version, for a rate of 740 LIPS.

Another popular benchmark is Lisp's reverse function, which we can code as the rev relation:

```
(<- (rev () ()))
(<- (rev (?x . ?a) ?b) (rev ?a ?c) (concat ?c (?x) ?b))

(<- (concat () ?l ?l))
(<- (concat (?x . ?a) ?b (?x . ?c)) (concat ?a ?b ?c))
```

rev uses the relation concat, which stands for concatenation. (concat ?a ?b ?c) is true when ?a concatenated to ?b yields ?c. This relationlike name is preferred over more procedural names like append. But rev is very similar to the following Lisp definitions:

```
(defun rev (l)
  (if (null l)
      nil
      (app (rev (rest l))
           (list (first l)))))

(defun app (x y)
  (if (null x)
      y
      (cons (first x)
            (app (rest x) y))))
```

Both versions are inefficient. It is possible to write an iterative version of reverse that does no extra consing and is tail-recursive:

```
(<- (irev ?l ?r) (irev3 ?l () ?r))
(<- (irev3 (?x . ?l) ?so-far ?r) (irev3 ?l (?x . ?so-far) ?r))
(<- (irev3 () ?r ?r))
```

The Prolog i rev is equivalent to this Lisp program:

```
(defun irev (list) (irev2 list nil))

(defun irev2 (list so-far)
  (if (consp list)
      (irev2 (rest list) (cons (first list) so-far))
      so-far))
```

The following table shows times in seconds to execute these routines on lists of length 20 and 100, for both Prolog and Lisp, both interpreted and compiled. (Only compiled Lisp could execute rev on a 100-element list without running out of stack space.) Times for the zebra puzzle are also included, although there is no Lisp version of this program.

Problem	Interp. Prolog	Comp. Prolog	Speed-up	Interp. Lisp	Comp. Lisp
zebra	278.000	17.241	16	—	—
rev 20	4.24	.208	20	.241	.0023
rev 100	—	—	—	—	.0614
irev 20	.22	.010	22	.028	.0005
irev 100	9.81	.054	181	.139	.0014

This benchmark is too small to be conclusive, but on these examples the Prolog compiler is 16 to 181 times faster than the Prolog interpreter, slightly faster than interpreted Lisp, but still 17 to 90 times slower than compiled Lisp. This suggests that the Prolog interpreter cannot be used as a practical programming tool, but the Prolog compiler can.

Before moving on, it is interesting to note that Prolog provides for optional arguments automatically. Although there is no special syntax for optional arguments, an often-used convention is to have two versions of a relation, one with n arguments and one with $n - 1$. A single clause for the $n - 1$ case provides the missing, and therefore "optional," argument. In the following example, i rev/2 can be considered as a version of i rev/3 where the missing optional argument is ( ).

```
(<- (irev ?l ?r) (irev ?l () ?r))
(<- (irev (?x . ?l) ?so-far ?r) (irev ?l (?x . ?so-far) ?r))
(<- (irev () ?r ?r))
```

This is roughly equivalent to the following Lisp verison:

```
(defun irev (list &optional (so-far nil))
  (if (consp list)
      (irev (rest list) (cons (first list) so-far))
      so-far))
```

12.8   Adding More Primitives

Just as a Lisp compiler needs machine instructions to do input/output, arithmetic, and the like, so our Prolog system needs to be able to perform certain primitive actions. For the Prolog interpreter, primitives were implemented by function symbols. When the interpreter went to fetch a list of clauses, if it got a function instead, it called that function, passing it the arguments to the current relation, the current bindings, and a list of unsatisfied goals. For the Prolog compiler, primitives can be installed simply by writing a Lisp function that respects the convention of taking a continuation as the final argument and has a name of the form *symbol/arity*. For example, here's an easy way to handle input and output:

```
(defun read/1 (exp cont)
  (if (unify! exp (read))
      (funcall cont)))

(defun write/1 (exp cont)
  (write (deref-exp exp) :pretty t)
  (funcall cont))
```

Calling (write ?x) will always succeed, so the continuation will always be called. Similarly, one could use (read ?x) to read a value and unify it with ?x. If ?x is unbound, this is the same as assigning the value. However, it is also possible to make a call like (read (?x + ?y)), which succeeds only if the input is a three-element list with + in the middle. It is an easy extension to define read/2 and write/2 as relations that indicate what stream to use. To make this useful, one would need to define open/2 as a relation that takes a pathname as one argument and gives a stream back as the other. Other optional arguments could also be supported, if desired.

The primitive nl outputs a newline:

```
(defun nl/0 (cont) (terpri) (funcall cont))
```

We provided special support for the unification predicate, =. However, we could have simplified the compiler greatly by having a simple definition for =/2:

```
(defun =/2 (?arg1 ?arg2 cont)
  (if (unify! ?arg1 ?arg2)
      (funcall cont)))
```

In fact, if we give our compiler the single clause:

```
(<- (= ?x ?x))
```

it produces just this code for the definition of =/2. There are other equality predicates to worry about. The predicate ==/2 is more like equal in Lisp. It does no unification, but instead tests if two structures are equal with regard to their elements. A variable is considered equal only to itself. Here's an implementation:

```
(defun ==/2 (?arg1 ?arg2 cont)
  "Are the two arguments EQUAL with no unification,
  but with dereferencing?  If so, succeed."
  (if (deref-equal ?arg1 ?arg2)
      (funcall cont)))

(defun deref-equal (x y)
  "Are the two arguments EQUAL with no unification,
  but with dereferencing?"
  (or (eql (deref x) (deref y))
      (and (consp x)
           (consp y)
           (deref-equal (first x) (first y))
           (deref-equal (rest x) (rest y)))))
```

One of the most important primitives is call. Like funcall in Lisp, call allows us to build up a goal and then try to prove it.

```
(defun call/1 (goal cont)
  "Try to prove goal by calling it."
  (deref goal)
  (apply (make-predicate (first goal)
                         (length (args goal)))
         (append (args goal) (list cont))))
```

This version of call will give a run-time error if the goal is not instantiated to a list whose first element is a properly defined predicate; one might want to check for that, and fail silently if there is no defined predicate. Here's an example of call where the goal is legal:

```
> (?- (= ?p member) (call (?p ?x (a b c))))
?P = MEMBER
?X = A;
?P = MEMBER
?X = B;
?P = MEMBER
?X = C;
No.
```

Now that we have call, a lot of new things can be implemented. Here are the logical connectives and and or:

```
(<- (or ?a ?b) (call ?a))
(<- (or ?a ?b) (call ?b))

(<- (and ?a ?b) (call ?a) (call ?b))
```

Note that these are only binary connectives, not the *n*-ary special forms used in Lisp. Also, this definition negates most of the advantage of compilation. The goals inside an and or or will be interpreted by call, rather than being compiled.

We can also define not, or at least the normal Prolog not, which is quite distinct from the logical not. In fact, in some dialects, not is written \+, which is supposed to be reminiscent of the logical symbol ⊬, that is, "can not be derived." The interpretation is that if goal G can not be proved, then (not G) is true. Logically, there is a difference between (not G) being true and being unknown, but ignoring that difference makes Prolog a more practical programming language. See Lloyd 1987 for more on the formal semantics of negation in Prolog.

Here's an implementation of not/1. Since it has to manipulate the trail, and we may have other predicates that will want to do the same, we'll package up what was done in maybe-add-undo-bindings into the macro with-undo-bindings:

```
(defmacro with-undo-bindings (&body body)
  "Undo bindings after each expression in body except the last."
  (if (length=1 body)
      (first body)
      '(let ((old-trail (fill-pointer *trail*)))
         ,(first body)
         ,@(loop for exp in (rest body)
                 collect '(undo-bindings! old-trail)
                 collect exp))))
(defun not/1 (relation cont)
  "Negation by failure: If you can't prove G, then (not G) true."
  ;; Either way, undo the bindings.
  (with-undo-bindings
    (call/1 relation #'(lambda () (return-from not/1 nil)))
    (funcall cont)))
```

Here's an example where not works fine:

```
> (?- (member ?x (a b c)) (not (= ?x b)))
?X = A;
?X = C;
No.
```

Now see what happens when we simply reverse the order of the two goals:

```
> (?- (not (= ?x b)) (member ?x (a b c)))
No.
```

The first example succeeds unless ?x is bound to b. In the second example, ?x is unbound at the start, so (= ?x b) succeeds, the not fails, and the member goal is never reached. So our implementation of not has a consistent procedural interpretation, but it is not equivalent to the declarative interpretation usually given to logical negation. Normally, one would expect that a and c would be valid solutions to the query, regardless of the order of the goals.

One of the fundamental differences between Prolog and Lisp is that Prolog is relational: you can easily express individual relations. Lisp, on the other hand, is good at expressing collections of things as lists. So far we don't have any way of forming a collection of objects that satisfy a relation in Prolog. We can easily iterate over the objects; we just can't gather them together. The primitive bagof is one way of doing the collection. In general, (bagof ?x (p ?x) ?bag) unifies ?bag with a list of all ?x's that satisfy (p ?x). If there are no such ?x's, then the call to bagof fails. A *bag* is an unordered collection with duplicates allowed. For example, the bag $\{a, b, a\}$ is the same as the bag $\{a, a, b\}$, but different from $\{a, b\}$. Bags stands in contrast to *sets*, which are unordered collections with no duplicates. The set $\{a, b\}$ is the same as the set $\{b, a\}$. Here is an implementation of bagof:

```
(defun bagof/3 (exp goal result cont)
  "Find all solutions to GOAL, and for each solution,
  collect the value of EXP into the list RESULT."
  ;; Ex: Assume (p 1) (p 2) (p 3).  Then:
  ;;     (bagof ?x (p ?x) ?l)  ==> ?l = (1 2 3)
  (let ((answers nil))
    (call/1 goal #'(lambda ()
                     (push (deref-copy exp) answers)))
    (if (and (not (null answers))
             (unify! result (nreverse answers)))
        (funcall cont))))
```

```
(defun deref-copy (exp)
  "Copy the expression, replacing variables with new ones.
  The part without variables can be returned as is."
  (sublis (mapcar #'(lambda (var) (cons (deref var) (?)))
                  (unique-find-anywhere-if #'var-p exp))
          exp))
```

Below we use bagof to collect a list of everyone Sandy likes. Note that the result is a bag, not a set: Sandy appears more than once.

```
> (?- (bagof ?who (likes Sandy ?who) ?bag))
?WHO = SANDY
?BAG = (LEE KIM ROBIN SANDY CATS SANDY);
No.
```

In the next example, we form the bag of every list of length three that has A and B as members:

```
> (?- (bagof ?l (and (length ?l (1+ (1+ (1+ 0))))
                     (and (member a ?l) (member b ?l)))
             ?bag))
?L = (?5 ?8 ?11 ?68 ?66)
?BAG = ((A B ?17) (A ?21 B) (B A ?31) (?38 A B) (B ?48 A) (?52 B A))
No.
```

Those who are disappointed with a bag containing multiple versions of the same answer may prefer the primitive setof, which does the same computation as bagof but then discards the duplicates.

```
(defun setof/3 (exp goal result cont)
  "Find all unique solutions to GOAL, and for each solution,
  collect the value of EXP into the list RESULT."
  ;; Ex: Assume (p 1) (p 2) (p 3).  Then:
  ;;     (setof ?x (p ?x) ?l) ==> ?l = (1 2 3)
  (let ((answers nil))
    (call/1 goal #'(lambda ()
                     (push (deref-copy exp) answers)))
    (if (and (not (null answers))
             (unify! result (delete-duplicates
                              answers
                              :test #'deref-equal)))
        (funcall cont))))
```

Prolog supports arithmetic with the operator is. For example, (is ?x (+ ?y 1)) unifies ?x with the value of ?y plus one. This expression fails if ?y is unbound, and it gives a run-time error if ?y is not a number. For our version of Prolog, we can support not just arithmetic but any Lisp expression:

```
(defun is/2 (var exp cont)
  ;; Example: (is ?x (+ 3 (* ?y (+ ?z 4))))
  ;; Or even: (is (?x ?y ?x) (cons (first ?z) ?1))
  (if (and (not (find-if-anywhere #'unbound-var-p exp))
           (unify! var (eval (deref-exp exp))))
      (funcall cont)))
(defun unbound-var-p (exp)
  "Is EXP an unbound var?"
  (and (var-p exp) (not (bound-p exp))))
```

As an aside, we might as well give the Prolog programmer access to the function unbound-var-p. The standard name for this predicate is var/1:

```
(defun var/1 (?arg1 cont)
  "Succeeds if ?arg1 is an uninstantiated variable."
  (if (unbound-var-p ?arg1)
      (funcall cont)))
```

The is primitive fails if any part of the second argument is unbound. However, there are expressions with variables that can be solved, although not with a direct call to eval. For example, the following goal could be solved by binding ?x to 2:

```
(solve (= 12 (* (+ ?x 1) 4)))
```

We might want to have more direct access to Lisp from Prolog. The problem with is is that it requires a check for unbound variables, and it calls eval to evaluate arguments recursively. In some cases, we just want to get at Lisp's apply, without going through the safety net provided by is. The primitive lisp does that. Needless to say, lisp is not a part of standard Prolog.

```
(defun lisp/2 (?result exp cont)
  "Apply (first exp) to (rest exp), and return the result."
  (if (and (consp (deref exp))
           (unify! ?result (apply (first exp) (rest exp))))
      (funcall cont)))
```

Exercise 12.7 [m] Define the primitive solve/1, which works like the function solve used in student (page 225). Decide if it should take a single equation as argument or a list of equations.

Exercise 12.8 [h]   Assume we had a goal of the form (solve (= 12 (* (+ ?x 1) 4))). Rather than manipulate the equation when solve/1 is called at run time, we might prefer to do part of the work at compile time, treating the call as if it were (solve (= ?x 2)). Write a Prolog compiler macro for solve. Notice that even when you have defined a compiler macro, you still need the underlying primitive, because the predicate might be invoked through a call/1. The same thing happens in Lisp: even when you supply a compiler macro, you still need the actual function, in case of a funcall or apply.

Exercise 12.9 [h]   Which of the predicates call, and, or, not, or repeat could benefit from compiler macros? Write compiler macros for those predicates that could use one.

Exercise 12.10 [m]   You might have noticed that call/1 is inefficient in two important ways. First, it calls make-predicate, which must build a symbol by appending strings and then look the string up in the Lisp symbol table. Alter make-predicate to store the predicate symbol the first time it is created, so it can do a faster lookup on subsequent calls. The second inefficiency is the call to append. Change the whole compiler so that the continuation argument comes first, not last, thus eliminating the need for append in call.

Exercise 12.11 [s]   The primitive true/0 always succeeds, and fail/0 always fails. Define these primitives. Hint: the first corresponds to a Common Lisp function, and the second is a function already defined in this chapter.

Exercise 12.12 [s]   Would it be possible to write ==/2 as a list of clauses rather than as a primitive?

Exercise 12.13 [m]   Write a version of deref-copy that traverses the argument expression only once.

12.9   The Cut

In Lisp, it is possible to write programs that backtrack explicitly, although it can be awkward when there are more than one or two backtrack points. In Prolog, backtracking is automatic and implicit, but we don't yet know of any way to *avoid* backtracking. There are two reasons why a Prolog programmer might want to disable backtracking. First, keeping track of the backtrack points takes up time and space. A programmer who knows that a certain problem has only one solution should be able to speed up the computation by telling the program not to consider the other possible branches. Second, sometimes a simple logical specification of a problem will yield redundant solutions, or even some unintended solutions. It may be that simply pruning the search space to eliminate some backtracking will yield only the desired answers, while restructuring the program to give all and only the right answers would be more difficult. Here's an example. Suppose we wanted to define a predicate, max/3, which holds when the third argument is the maximum of the first two arguments, where the first two arguments will always be instantiated to numbers. The straightforward definition is:

```
(<- (max ?x ?y ?x) (>= ?x ?y))
(<- (max ?x ?y ?y) (< ?x ?y))
```

Declaratively, this is correct, but procedurally it is a waste of time to compute the < relation if the >= has succeeded: in that case the < can never succeed. The cut symbol, written !, can be used to stop the wasteful computation. We could write:

```
(<- (max ?x ?y ?x) (>= ?x ?y) !)
(<- (max ?x ?y ?y))
```

The cut in the first clause says that if the first clause succeeds, then no other clauses will be considered. So now the second clause can not be interpreted on its own. Rather, it is interpreted as "if the first clause fails, then the max of two numbers is the second one."

In general, a cut can occur anywhere in the body of a clause, not just at the end. There is no good declarative interpretation of a cut, but the procedural interpretation is two-fold. First, when a cut is "executed" as a goal, it always succeeds. But in addition to succeeding, it sets up a fence that cannot be crossed by subsequent backtracking. The cut serves to cut off backtracking both from goals to the right of the cut (in the same clause) and from clauses below the cut (in the same predicate). Let's look at a more abstract example:

```
(<- (p) (q) (r) ! (s) (t))
(<- (p) (s))
```

In processing the first clause of p, backtracking can occur freely while attempting to solve q and r. Once r is solved, the cut is encountered. From that point on, backtracking can occur freely while solving s and t, but Prolog will never backtrack past the cut into r, nor will the second clause be considered. On the other hand, if q or r failed (before the cut is encountered), then Prolog would go on to the second clause.

Now that the intent of the cut is clear, let's think of how it should be implemented. We'll look at a slightly more complex predicate, one with variables and multiple cuts:

```
(<- (p ?x a) ! (q ?x))
(<- (p ?x b) (r ?x) ! (s ?x))
```

We have to arrange it so that as soon as we backtrack into a cut, no more goals are considered. In the first clause, when q/1 fails, we want to return from p/2 immediately, rather than considering the second clause. Similarly, the first time s/1 fails, we want to return from p/2, rather than going on to consider other solutions to r/1. Thus, we want code that looks something like this:

```
(defun p/2 (arg1 arg2 cont)
  (let ((old-trail (fill-pointer *trail*)))
    (if (unify! arg2 'a)
        (progn (q/1 arg1 cont)
               (return-from p/2 nil)))
    (undo-bindings! old-trail)
    (if (unify! arg2 'b)
        (r/1 arg1 #'(lambda ()
                      (progn (s/1 arg1 cont)
                             (return-from p/2 nil)))))))
```

We can get this code by making a single change to compile-body: when the first goal in a body (or what remains of the body) is the cut symbol, then we should generate a progn that contains the code for the rest of the body, followed by a return-from the predicate being compiled. Unfortunately, the name of the predicate is not available to compile-body. We could change compile-clause and compile-body to take the predicate name as an extra argument, or we could bind the predicate as a special variable in compile-predicate. I choose the latter:

```
(defvar *predicate* nil
  "The Prolog predicate currently being compiled")
```

```
(defun compile-predicate (symbol arity clauses)
  "Compile all the clauses for a given symbol/arity
  into a single LISP function."
  (let ((*predicate* (make-predicate symbol arity))     ;***
        (parameters (make-parameters arity)))
    (compile
      (eval
        '(defun ,*predicate* (,@parameters cont)          ;***
          .,(maybe-add-undo-bindings
              (mapcar #'(lambda (clause)
                          (compile-clause parameters
                                          clause 'cont))
                      clauses)))))))

(defun compile-body (body cont bindings)
  "Compile the body of a clause."
  (cond
    ((null body)
     '(funcall ,cont))
    ((eq (first body) '!)                                 ;***
     '(progn ,(compile-body (rest body) cont bindings)    ;***
             (return-from ,*predicate* nil)))             ;***
    (t (let* ((goal (first body))
              (macro (prolog-compiler-macro (predicate goal)))
              (macro-val (if macro
                             (funcall macro goal (rest body)
                                      cont bindings))))
         (if (and macro (not (eq macro-val :pass)))
             macro-val
             '(,(make-predicate (predicate goal)
                                (relation-arity goal))
               ,@(mapcar #'(lambda (arg)
                             (compile-arg arg bindings))
                         (args goal))
               ,(if (null (rest body))
                    cont
                    '#'(lambda ()
                         ,(compile-body
                            (rest body) cont
                            (bind-new-variables bindings goal)))))))))))
```

Exercise 12.14 [m] Given the definitions below, figure out what a call to `test-cut` will do, and what it will write:

```
(<- (test-cut) (p a) (p b) ! (p c) (p d))
(<- (test-cut) (p e))
```

```
(<- (p ?x) (write (?x 1)))
(<- (p ?x) (write (?x 2)))
```

Another way to use the cut is in a *repeat/fail* loop. The predicate `repeat` is defined with the following two clauses:

```
(<- (repeat))
(<- (repeat) (repeat))
```

An alternate definition as a primitive is:

```
(defun repeat/0 (cont)
  (loop (funcall cont)))
```

Unfortunately, `repeat` is one of the most abused predicates. Several Prolog books present programs like this:

```
(<- (main)
    (write "Hello.")
    (repeat)
    (write "Command: ")
    (read ?command)
    (process ?command)
    (= ?command exit)
    (write "Good bye."))
```

The intent is that commands are read one at a time, and then processed. For each command except `exit`, `process` takes the appropriate action and then fails. This causes a backtrack to the `repeat` goal, and a new command is read and processed. When the command is `exit`, the procedure returns.

There are two reasons why this is a poor program. First, it violates the principle of referential transparency. Things that look alike are supposed to be alike, regardless of the context in which they are used. But here there is no way to tell that four of the six goals in the body comprise a loop, and the other goals are outside the loop. Second, it violates the principle of abstraction. A predicate should be understandable as a separate unit. But here the predicate `process` can only be understood by considering the context in which it is called: a context that requires it to fail after processing each command. As Richard O'Keefe 1990 points out, the correct way to write this clause is as follows:

```
(<- (main)
    (write "Hello.")
    (repeat)
       (write "Command: ")
       (read ?command)
       (process ?command)
       (or (= ?command exit) (fail))
    !
    (write "Good bye."))
```

The indentation clearly indicates the limits of the repeat loop. The loop is terminated by an explicit test and is followed by a cut, so that a calling program won't accidently backtrack into the loop after it has exited. Personally, I prefer a language like Lisp, where the parentheses make constructs like loops explicit and indentation can be done automatically. But O'Keefe shows that well-structured readable programs can be written in Prolog.

The if-then and if-then-else constructions can easily be written as clauses. Note that the if-then-else uses a cut to commit to the then part if the test is satisfied.

```
(<- (if ?test ?then) (if ?then ?else (fail)))
(<- (if ?test ?then ?else)
    (call ?test)
    !
    (call ?then))
(<- (if ?test ?then ?else)
    (call ?else))
```

The cut can be used to implement the nonlogical not. The following two clauses are often given before as the definition of not. Our compiler succesfully turns these two clauses into exactly the same code as was given before for the primitive not/1:

```
(<- (not ?p) (call ?p) ! (fail))
(<- (not ?p))
```

12.10   "Real" Prolog

The Prolog-In-Lisp system developed in this chapter uses Lisp syntax because it is intended to be embedded in a Lisp system. Other Prolog implementations using Lisp syntax include micro-Prolog, Symbolics Prolog, and LMI Prolog.

However, the majority of Prolog systems use a syntax closer to traditional mathematical notation. The following table compares the syntax of "standard" Prolog to the syntax of Prolog-In-Lisp. While there is currently an international committee working on standardizing Prolog, the final report has not yet been released, so different dialects may have slightly different syntax. However, most implementations follow the notation summarized here. They derive from the Prolog developed at the University of Edinburgh for the DEC-10 by David H. D. Warren and his colleagues. The names for the primitives in the last section are also taken from Edinburgh Prolog.

	Prolog	Prolog-In-Lisp
atom	`lower`	`const`
variable	`Upper`	`?var`
anonymous	`_`	`?`
goal	`p(Var,const)`	`(p ?var const)`
rule	`p(X) :- q(X).`	`(<- (p ?x) (q ?x))`
fact	`p(a).`	`(<- (p a))`
query	`?- p(X).`	`(?- (p ?x))`
list	`[a,b,c]`	`(a b c)`
cons	`[a|Rest]`	`(a . ?rest)`
nil	`[]`	`()`
and	`p(X), q(X)`	`(and (p ?x) (q ?x))`
or	`p(X); q(X)`	`(or (p ?x) (q ?x))`
not	`\+ p(X)`	`(not (p ?x))`

We have adopted Lisp's bias toward lists; terms are built out of atoms, variables, and conses of other terms. In real Prolog cons cells are provided, but terms are usually built out of *structures*, not lists. The Prolog term p(a,b) corresponds to the Lisp vector #(p/2 a b), not the list (p a b). A minority of Prolog implementations use *structure sharing*. In this approach, every non-atomic term is represented by a skeleton that contains place holders for variables and a header that points to the skeleton and also contains the variables that will fill the place holders. With structure sharing, making a copy is easy: just copy the header, regardless of the size of the skeleton. However, manipulating terms is complicated by the need to keep track of both skeleton and header. See Boyer and Moore 1972 for more on structure sharing.

Another major difference is that real Prolog uses the equivalent of failure continuations, not success continuations. No actual continuation, in the sense of a closure, is built. Instead, when a choice is made, the address of the code for the next choice is pushed on a stack. Upon failure, the next choice is popped off the stack. This is reminiscent of the backtracking approach using Scheme's call/cc facility outlined on page 772.

Exercise 12.15 [m] Assuming an approach using a stack of failure continuations instead of success continuations, show what the code for p and member would look like. Note that you need not pass failure continuations around; you can just push them onto a stack that top-level-prove will invoke. How would the cut be implemented? Did we make the right choice in implementing our compiler with success continuations, or would failure continuations have been better?

12.11   History and References

As described in chapter 11, the idea of logic programming was fairly well understood by the mid-1970s. But because the implementations of that time were slow, logic programming did not catch on. It was the Prolog compiler for the DEC-10 that made logic programming a serious alternative to Lisp and other general-purpose languages. The compiler was developed in 1977 by David H. D. Warren with Fernando Pereira and Luís Pereira. See the paper by Warren (1979) and by all three (1977).

Unfortunately, David H. D. Warren's pioneering work on compiling Prolog has never been published in a widely accessible form. His main contribution was the description of the Warren Abstract Machine (WAM), an instruction set for compiled Prolog. Most existing compilers use this instruction set, or a slight modification of it. This can be done either through byte-code interpretation or through macro-expansion to native machine instructions. Aït-Kaci 1991 provides a good tutorial on the WAM, much less terse than the original (Warren 1983). The compiler presented in this chapter does not use the WAM. Instead, it is modeled after Mark Stickel's (1988) theorem prover. A similar compiler is briefly sketched by Jacques Cohen 1985.

12.12   Exercises

Exercise 12.16 [m] Change the Prolog compiler to allow implicit calls. That is, if a goal is not a cons cell headed by a predicate, compile it as if it were a call. The clause:

```
(<- (p ?x ?y) (?x c) ?y)
```

should be compiled as if it were:

```
(<- (p ?x ?y) (call (?x c)) (call ?y))
```

Exercise 12.17 [h] Here are some standard Prolog primitives:

- get/1 Read a single character and unify it with the argument.

- put/1 Print a single character.

- nonvar/1, /=, /== The opposites of var, = and ==, respectively.

- integer/1 True if the argument is an integer.

- atom/1 True if the argument is a symbol (like Lisp's symbolp).

- atomic/1 True if the argument is a number or symbol (like Lisp's atom).

- <, >, =<, >= Arithmetic comparison; succeeds when the arguments are both instantiated to numbers and the comparison is true.

- listing/0 Print out the clauses for all defined predicates.

- listing/1 Print out the clauses for the argument predicate.

Implement these predicates. In each case, decide if the predicate should be implemented as a primitive or a list of clauses, and if it should have a compiler macro.

There are some naming conflicts that need to be resolved. Terms like atom have one meaning in Prolog and another in Lisp. Also, in Prolog the normal notation is \= and \==, not /= and /==. For Prolog-In-Lisp, you need to decide which notations to use: Prolog's or Lisp's.

Exercise 12.18 [s] In Lisp, we are used to writing n-ary calls like (< 1 n 10) or (= x y z). Write compiler macros that expand n-ary calls into a series of binary calls. For example, (< 1 n 10) should expand into (and (< 1 n) (< n 10)).

Exercise 12.19 [m] One feature of Lisp that is absent in Prolog is the quote mechanism. Is there a use for quote? If so, implement it; if not, explain why it is not needed.

Exercise 12.20 [h] Write a tracing mechanism for Prolog. Add procedures p-trace and p-untrace to trace and untrace Prolog predicates. Add code to the compiler to generate calls to a printing procedure for goals that are traced. In Lisp, we have to trace procedures when they are called and when they return. In Prolog, there are four cases to consider: the call, successful completion, backtrack into subsequent clauses, and failure with no more clauses. We will call these four cases call, exit, redo, and fail, respectively. If we traced member, we would expect tracing output to look something like this:

```
> (?- (member ?x (a b c d)) (fail))
  CALL MEMBER: ?1 (A B C D)
  EXIT MEMBER: A (A B C D)
  REDO MEMBER: ?1 (A B C D)
    CALL MEMBER: ?1 (B C D)
    EXIT MEMBER: B (B C D)
    REDO MEMBER: ?1 (B C D)
      CALL MEMBER: ?1 (C D)
      EXIT MEMBER: C (C D)
      REDO MEMBER: ?1 (C D)
        CALL MEMBER: ?1 (D)
        EXIT MEMBER: D (D)
        REDO MEMBER: ?1 (D)
          CALL MEMBER: ?1 NIL
          REDO MEMBER: ?1 NIL
          FAIL MEMBER: ?1 NIL
        FAIL MEMBER: ?1 (D)
      FAIL MEMBER: ?1 (C D)
    FAIL MEMBER: ?1 (B C D)
  FAIL MEMBER: ?1 (A B C D)
No.
```

Exercise 12.21 [m] Some Lisp systems are very slow at compiling functions. KCL is an example; it compiles by translating to C and then calling the C compiler and assembler. In KCL it is best to compile only code that is completely debugged, and run interpreted while developing a program.

Alter the Prolog compiler so that calling the Lisp compiler is optional. In all cases, Prolog functions are translated into Lisp, but they are only compiled to machine language when a variable is set.

Exercise 12.22 [d] Some Prolog systems provide the predicate freeze to "freeze" a goal until its variables are instantiated. For example, the goal (freeze x (> x 0)) is interpreted as follows: if x is instantiated, then just evaluate the goal (> x 0), and succeed or fail depending on the result. However, if x is unbound, then succeed and continue the computation, but remember the goal (> x 0) and evaluate it as soon as x becomes instantiated. Implement freeze.

Exercise 12.23 [m] Write a recursive version of anonymous-variables-in that does not use a local function.

12.13 Answers

Answer 12.6 Here's a version that works for Texas Instruments and Lucid implementations:

```
(defmacro with-compilation-unit (options &body body)
  "Do the body, but delay compiler warnings until the end."
  ;; This is defined in Common Lisp the Language, 2nd ed.
  '(,(read-time-case
       #+TI    'compiler:compiler-warnings-context-bind
       #+Lucid 'with-deferred-warnings
               'progn)
    .,body))

(defun prolog-compile-symbols (&optional (symbols *uncompiled*))
  "Compile a list of Prolog symbols.
  By default, the list is all symbols that need it."
  (with-compilation-unit ()
    (mapc #'prolog-compile symbols)
    (setf *uncompiled* (set-difference *uncompiled* symbols))))
```

Answer 12.9 Macros for and and or are very important, since these are commonly used. The macro for and is trivial:

```
(def-prolog-compiler-macro and (goal body cont bindings)
  (compile-body (append (args goal) body) cont bindings))
```

The macro for or is trickier:

```
(def-prolog-compiler-macro or (goal body cont bindings)
  (let ((disjuncts (args goal)))
    (case (length disjuncts)
      (0 fail)
      (1 (compile-body (cons (first disjuncts) body) cont bindings))
      (t (let ((fn (gensym "F")))
           '(flet ((,fn () ,(compile-body body cont bindings)))
             .,(maybe-add-undo-bindings
                 (loop for g in disjuncts collect
                   (compile-body (list g) '#',fn
                                 bindings)))))))))
```

Answer 12.11 true/0 is funcall: when a goal succeeds, we call the continuation. fail/0 is ignore: when a goal fails, we ignore the continuation. We could also define compiler macros for these primitives:

```
(def-prolog-compiler-macro true (goal body cont bindings)
  (compile-body body cont bindings))

(def-prolog-compiler-macro fail (goal body cont bindings)
  (declare (ignore goal body cont bindings))
  nil)
```

Answer 12.13

```
(defun deref-copy (exp)
  "Build a copy of the expression, which may have variables.
  The part without variables can be returned as is."
  (let ((var-alist nil))
    (labels
      ((walk (exp)
        (deref exp)
        (cond ((consp exp)
                (reuse-cons (walk (first exp))
                            (walk (rest exp))
                            exp))
              ((var-p exp)
               (let ((entry (assoc exp var-alist)))
                 (if (not (null entry))
                     (cdr entry)
                     (let ((var-copy (?)))
                       (push (cons exp var-copy) var-alist)
                       var-copy))))
              (t exp))))
      (walk exp))))
```

Answer 12.14 In the first clause of test-cut, all four calls to p will succeed via the first clause of p. Then backtracking will occur over the calls to (p c) and (p d). All four combinations of 1 and 2 succeed. After that, backtracking would normally go back to the call to (p b). But the cut prevents this, and the whole (test-cut) goal fails, without ever considering the second clause. Here's the actual output:

```
(?- (test-cut))
(A 1)(B 1)(C 1)(D 1)
Yes;
(D 2)
Yes;
(C 2)(D 1)
Yes;
(D 2)
Yes;
No.
```

Answer 12.17 For example:

```
(defun >/2 (x y cont)
  (if (and (numberp (deref x)) (numberp (deref y)) (> x y))
      (funcall cont)))

(defun numberp/1 (x cont)
  (if (numberp (deref x))
      (funcall cont)))
```

Answer 12.19 Lisp uses quote in two ways: to distinguish a symbol from the value of the variable represented by that symbol, and to distinguish a literal list from the value that would be returned by evaluating a function call. The first distinction Prolog makes by a lexical convention: variables begin with a question mark in our Prolog, and they are capitalized in real Prolog. The second distinction is not necessary because Prolog is relational rather than functional. An expression is a goal if it is a member of the body of a clause, and is a literal if it is an argument to a goal.

Answer 12.20 Hint: Here's how member could be augmented with calls to a procedure, prolog-trace, which will print information about the four kinds of tracing events:

```
(defun member/2 (?arg1 ?arg2 cont)
  (let ((old-trail (fill-pointer *trail*))
        (exit-cont #'(lambda ()
                        (prolog-trace 'exit 'member ?arg1 ?arg2 )
                        (funcall cont))))
    (prolog-trace 'call 'member ?arg1 ?arg2)
    (if (unify! ?arg2 (cons ?arg1 (?)))
        (funcall exit-cont))
    (undo-bindings! old-trail)
    (prolog-trace 'redo 'member ?arg1 ?arg2)
    (let ((?rest (?)))
      (if (unify! ?arg2 (cons (?) ?rest))
          (member/2 ?arg1 ?rest exit-cont)))
    (prolog-trace 'fail 'member ?arg1 ?arg2)))
```

The definition of prolog-trace is:

```
(defvar *prolog-trace-indent* 0)

(defun prolog-trace (kind predicate &rest args)
  (if (member kind '(call redo))
    (incf *prolog-trace-indent* 3))
  (format t "~&~VT~a ~a:~{ ~a~}"
          *prolog-trace-indent* kind predicate args)
  (if (member kind '(fail exit))
    (decf *prolog-trace-indent* 3)))
```

Answer 12.23

```lisp
(defun anonymous-variables-in (tree)
  "Return a list of all variables that occur only once in tree."
  (values (anon-vars-in tree nil nil)))

(defun anon-vars-in (tree seen-once seen-more)
  "Walk the data structure TREE, returning a list of variables
  seen once, and a list of variables seen more than once."
  (cond
    ((consp tree)
     (multiple-value-bind (new-seen-once new-seen-more)
         (anon-vars-in (first tree) seen-once seen-more)
       (anon-vars-in (rest tree) new-seen-once new-seen-more)))
    ((not (variable-p tree)) (values seen-once seen-more))
    ((member tree seen-once)
     (values (delete tree seen-once) (cons tree seen-more)))
    ((member tree seen-more)
     (values seen-once seen-more))
    (t (values (cons tree seen-once) seen-more))))
```

CHAPTER 13

Object-Oriented Programming

T he programs in this book cover a wide range of problems. It is only natural that a wide range of programming styles have been introduced to attack these problems. One style not yet covered that has gained popularity in recent years is called *object-oriented programming*. To understand what object-oriented programming entails, we need to place it in the context of other styles.

Historically, the first computer programs were written in an *imperative programming* style. A program was construed as a series of instructions, where each instruction performs some action: changing the value of a memory location, printing a result, and so forth. Assembly language is an example of an imperative language.

As experience (and ambition) grew, programmers looked for ways of controlling the complexity of programs. The invention of subroutines marked the *algorithmic* or *procedural programming* style, a subclass of the imperative style. Subroutines are helpful for two reasons: breaking up the problem into small pieces makes each piece easier to understand, and it also makes it possible to reuse pieces. Examples of procedural languages are FORTRAN, C, Pascal, and Lisp with setf.

Subroutines are still dependent on global state, so they are not completely separate pieces. The use of a large number of global variables has been criticized as a factor that makes it difficult to develop and maintain large programs. To eliminate this problem, the *functional programming* style insists that functions access only the parameters that are passed to them, and always return the same result for the same inputs. Functional programs have the advantage of being mathematically clean—it is easy to prove properties about them. However, some applications are more naturally seen as taking action rather than calculating functional values, and are therefore unnatural to program in a functional style. Examples of functional languages are FP and Lisp without `setf`.

In contrast to imperative languages are *declarative* languages, which attempt to express "what to do" rather than "how to do it." One type of declarative programming is *rule-based* programming, where a set of rules states how to transform a problem into a solution. Examples of rule-based systems are ELIZA and STUDENT.

An important kind of declarative programming is *logic programming*, where axioms are used to describe constraints, and computation is done by a constructive proof of a goal. An example of logic language is Prolog.

Object-oriented programming is another way to tame the problem of global state. Instead of prohibiting global state (as functional programming does), object-oriented programming breaks up the unruly mass of global state and encapsulates it into small, manageable pieces, or objects. This chapter covers the object-oriented approach.

13.1   Object-Oriented Programming

Object-oriented programming turns the world of computing on its side: instead of viewing a program primarily as a set of actions which manipulate objects, it is viewed as a set of objects that are manipulated by actions. The state of each object and the actions that manipulate that state are defined once and for all when the object is created. This can lead to modular, robust systems that are easy to use and extend. It also can make systems correspond more closely to the "real world," which we humans perceive more easily as being made up of objects rather than actions. Examples of object-oriented languages are Simula, C++, and CLOS, the Common Lisp Object System. This chapter will first introduce object-oriented programming in general, and then concentrate on the Common Lisp Object System.

Many people are promoting object-oriented programming as the solution to the software development problem, but it is hard to get people to agree on just what object-orientation means. Peter Wegner 1987 proposes the following formula as a definition:

Object-orientation = Objects + Classes + Inheritance

Briefly, *objects* are modules that encapsulate some data and operations on that data. The idea of *information hiding*—insulating the representation of that data from operations outside of the object—is an important part of this concept. *Classes* are groups of similar objects with identical behavior. Objects are said to be instances of classes. *Inheritance* is a means of defining new classes as variants of existing classes. The new class inherits the behavior of the parent class, and the programmer need only specify how the new class is different.

The object-oriented style brings with it a new vocabulary, which is summarized in the following glossary. Each term will be explained in more detail when it comes up.

> *class:* A group of similar objects with identical behavior.
> *class variable:* A variable shared by all members of a class.
> *delegation:* Passing a message from an object to one of its components.
> *generic function:* A function that accepts different types or classes of arguments.
> *inheritance:* A means of defining new classes as variants of existing classes.
> *instance:* An instance of a class is an object.
> *instance variable:* A variable encapsulated within an object.
> *message:* A name for an action. Equivalent to generic function.
> *method:* A means of handling a message for a particular class.
> *multimethod:* A method that depends on more than one argument.
> *multiple inheritance:* Inheritance from more than one parent class.
> *object:* An encapsulation of local state and behavior.

13.2   Objects

Object-oriented programming, by definition, is concerned with *objects*. Any datum that can be stored in computer memory can be thought of as an object. Thus, the number 3, the atom x, and the string "hello" are all objects. Usually, however, the term *object* is used to denote a more complex object, as we shall see.

Of course, all programming is concerned with objects, and with procedures operating on those objects. Writing a program to solve a particular problem will necessarily involve writing definitions for both objects and procedures. What distinguishes object-oriented programming is that the primary way of decomposing the problem into modules is based on the objects rather than on the procedures. The difference can best be seen with an example. Here is a simple program to create bank accounts and keep track of withdrawals, deposits, and accumulation of interest. First, the program is written in traditional procedural style:

```
(defstruct account
  (name "") (balance 0.00) (interest-rate .06))
```

```
(defun account-withdraw (account amt)
  "Make a withdrawal from this account."
  (if (<= amt (account-balance account))
      (decf (account-balance account) amt)
      'insufficient-funds))

(defun account-deposit (account amt)
  "Make a deposit to this account."
  (incf (account-balance account) amt))

(defun account-interest (account)
  "Accumulate interest in this account."
  (incf (account-balance account)
        (* (account-interest-rate account)
           (account-balance account))))
```

We can create new bank accounts with make-account and modify them with account-withdraw, account-deposit, and account-interest. This is a simple problem, and this simple solution suffices. Problems appear when we change the specification of the problem, or when we envision ways that this implementation could be inadvertently used in error. For example, suppose a programmer looks at the account structure and decides to use (decf (account-balance account)) directly instead of going through the account-withdraw function. This could lead to negative account balances, which were not intended. Or suppose that we want to create a new kind of account, where only a certain maximum amount can be withdrawn at one time. There would be no way to ensure that account-withdraw would not be applied to this new, limited account.

The problem is that once we have created an account, we have no control over what actions are applied to it. The object-oriented style is designed to provide that control. Here is the same program written in object-oriented style (using plain Lisp):

```
(defun new-account (name &optional (balance 0.00)
                              (interest-rate .06))
  "Create a new account that knows the following messages:"
  #'(lambda (message)
      (case message
        (withdraw #'(lambda (amt)
                      (if (<= amt balance)
                          (decf balance amt)
                          'insufficient-funds)))
        (deposit  #'(lambda (amt) (incf balance amt)))
        (balance  #'(lambda () balance))
        (name     #'(lambda () name))
        (interest #'(lambda ()
                      (incf balance
                            (* interest-rate balance)))))))
```

The function new-account creates account objects, which are implemented as closures that encapsulate three variables: the name, balance, and interest rate of the account. An account object also encapsulates functions to handle the five messages to which the object can respond. An account object can do only one thing: receive a message and return the appropriate function to execute that message. For example, if you pass the message withdraw to an account object, it will return a function that, when applied to a single argument (the amount to withdraw), will perform the withdrawal action. This function is called the *method* that implements the message. The advantage of this approach is that account objects are completely encapsulated; the information corresponding to the name, balance, and interest rate is only accessible through the five messages. We have a guarantee that no other code can manipulate the information in the account in any other way.[1]

The function get-method finds the method that implements a message for a given object. The function send gets the method and applies it to a list of arguments. The name send comes from the Flavors object-oriented system, which is discussed in the history section (page 456).

```
(defun get-method (object message)
  "Return the method that implements message for this object."
  (funcall object message))

(defun send (object message &rest args)
  "Get the function to implement the message,
  and apply the function to the args."
  (apply (get-method object message) args))
```

Here is an example of the use of new-account and send:

```
> (setf acct (new-account "J. Random Customer" 1000.00)) ⇒
#<CLOSURE 23652465>

> (send acct 'withdraw 500.00) ⇒ 500.0

> (send acct 'deposit 123.45) ⇒ 623.45

> (send acct 'name) ⇒ "J. Random Customer"

> (send acct 'balance) ⇒ 623.45
```

---

[1]More accurately, we have a guarantee that there is no way to get at the inside of a closure using portable Common Lisp code. Particular implementations may provide debugging tools for getting at this hidden information, such as inspect. So closures are not perfect at hiding information from these tools. Of course, no information-hiding method will be guaranteed against such covert channels—even with the most sophisticated software security measures, it is always possible to, say, wipe a magnet over the computer's disks and alter sensitive data.

13.3 Generic Functions

The send syntax is awkward, as it is different from the normal Lisp function-calling syntax, and it doesn't fit in with the other Lisp tools. For example, we might like to say (mapcar 'balance accounts), but with messages we would have to write that as:

```
(mapcar #'(lambda (acct) (send acct 'balance)) accounts)
```

We can fix this problem by defining *generic* functions that find the right method to execute a message. For example, we could define:

```
(defun withdraw (object &rest args)
  "Define withdraw as a generic function on objects."
  (apply (get-method object 'withdraw) args))
```

and then write (withdraw acct x) instead of (send acct 'withdraw x). The function withdraw is generic because it not only works on account objects but also works on any other class of object that handles the withdraw message. For example, we might have a totally unrelated class, army, which also implements a withdraw method. Then we could say (send 5th-army 'withdraw) or (withdraw 5th-army) and have the correct method executed. So object-oriented programming eliminates many problems with name clashes that arise in conventional programs.

Many of the built-in Common Lisp functions can be considered generic functions, in that they operate on different types of data. For example, sqrt does one thing when passed an integer and quite another when passed an imaginary number. The sequence functions (like find or delete) operate on lists, vectors, or strings. These functions are not implemented like withdraw, but they still act like generic functions.[2]

13.4 Classes

It is possible to write macros to make the object-oriented style easier to read and write. The macro define-class defines a class with its associated message-handling methods. It also defines a generic function for each message. Finally, it allows the programmer to make a distinction between variables that are associated with each object and those that are associated with a class and are shared by all members of the class. For example, you might want to have all instances of the class account share the same interest rate, but you wouldn't want them to share the same balance.

---

[2]There is a technical sense of "generic function" that is used within CLOS. These functions are not generic according to this technical sense.

```
(defmacro define-class (class inst-vars class-vars &body methods)
  "Define a class for object-oriented programming."
  ;; Define constructor and generic functions for methods
  '(let ,class-vars
     (mapcar #'ensure-generic-fn ',(mapcar #'first methods))
     (defun ,class ,inst-vars
       #'(lambda (message)
           (case message
             ,@(mapcar #'make-clause methods))))))

(defun make-clause (clause)
  "Translate a message from define-class into a case clause."
  '(,(first clause) #'(lambda ,(second clause) .,(rest2 clause))))

(defun ensure-generic-fn (message)
  "Define an object-oriented dispatch function for a message,
  unless it has already been defined as one."
  (unless (generic-fn-p message)
    (let ((fn #'(lambda (object &rest args)
                  (apply (get-method object message) args))))
      (setf (symbol-function message) fn)
      (setf (get message 'generic-fn) fn))))

(defun generic-fn-p (fn-name)
  "Is this a generic function?"
  (and (fboundp fn-name)
       (eq (get fn-name 'generic-fn) (symbol-function fn-name))))
```

Now we define the class account with this macro. We make interest-rate a class variable, one that is shared by all accounts:

```
(define-class account (name &optional (balance 0.00))
              ((interest-rate .06))
  (withdraw (amt) (if (<= amt balance)
                      (decf balance amt)
                      'insufficient-funds))
  (deposit  (amt) (incf balance amt))
  (balance  ()    balance)
  (name     ()    name)
  (interest ()    (incf balance (* interest-rate balance))))
```

Here we use the generic functions defined by this macro:

```
> (setf acct2 (account "A. User" 2000.00)) ⇒ #<CLOSURE 24003064>

> (deposit acct2 42.00) ⇒ 2042.0

> (interest acct2) ⇒ 2164.52
```

```
> (balance acct2) ⇒ 2164.52
> (balance acct) ⇒ 623.45
```

In this last line, the generic function balance is applied to acct, an object that was created before we even defined the account class and the function balance. But balance still works properly on this object, because it obeys the message-passing protocol.

13.5 Delegation

Suppose we want to create a new kind of account, one that requires a password for each action. We can define a new class, password-account, that has two message clauses. The first clause allows for changing the password (if you have the original password), and the second is an otherwise clause, which checks the password given and, if it is correct, passes the rest of the arguments on to the account that is being protected by the password.

The definition of password-account takes advantage of the internal details of define-class in two ways: it makes use of the fact that otherwise can be used as a catch-all clause in a case form, and it makes use of the fact that the dispatch variable is called message. Usually, it is not a good idea to rely on details about the implementation of a macro, and soon we will see cleaner ways of defining classes. But for now, this simple approach works:

```
(define-class password-account (password acct) ()
  (change-password (pass new-pass)
                   (if (equal pass password)
                       (setf password new-pass)
                       'wrong-password))
  (otherwise (pass &rest args)
             (if (equal pass password)
                 (apply message acct args)
                 'wrong-password)))
```

Now we see how the class password-account can be used to provide protection for an existing account:

```
(setf acct3 (password-account "secret" acct2)) ⇒ #<CLOSURE 33427277>
> (balance acct3 "secret") ⇒ 2164.52
> (withdraw acct3 "guess" 2000.00) ⇒ WRONG-PASSWORD
> (withdraw acct3 "secret" 2000.00) ⇒ 164.52
```

Now let's try one more example. Suppose we want to have a new class of account where only a limited amount of money can be withdrawn at any time. We could define the class limited-account:

```
(define-class limited-account (limit acct) ()
  (withdraw (amt)
              (if (> amt limit)
                  'over-limit
                  (withdraw acct amt)))
  (otherwise (&rest args)
              (apply message acct args)))
```

This definition redefines the withdraw message to check if the limit is exceeded before passing on the message, and it uses the otherwise clause simply to pass on all other messages unchanged. In the following example, we set up an account with both a password and a limit:

```
> (setf acct4 (password-account "pass"
                  (limited-account 100.00
                    (account "A. Thrifty Spender" 500.00)))) ⇒
#<CLOSURE 34136775>

> (withdraw acct4 "pass" 200.00) ⇒ OVER-LIMIT

> (withdraw acct4 "pass" 20.00) ⇒ 480.0

> (withdraw acct4 "guess" 20.00) ⇒ WRONG-PASSWORD
```

Note that functions like withdraw are still simple generic functions that just find the right method and apply it to the arguments. The trick is that each class defines a different way to handle the withdraw message. Calling withdraw with acct4 as argument results in the following flow of control. First, the method in the password-account class checks that the password is correct. If it is, it calls the method from the limited-account class. If the limit is not exceeded, we finally call the method from the account class, which decrements the balance. Passing control to the method of a component is called *delegation*.

The advantage of the object-oriented style is that we can introduce a new class by writing one definition that is localized and does not require changing any existing code. If we had written this in traditional procedural style, we would end up with functions like the following:

```
(defun withdraw (acct amt &optional pass)
  (cond ((and (typep acct 'password-account)
              (not (equal pass (account-password acct))))
          'wrong-password)
        ((and (typep acct 'limited-account)
```

```
          (> amt (account-limit account)))
        'over-limit)
      ((> amt balance)
       'insufficient-funds)
      (t (decf balance amt))))
```

There is nothing wrong with this, as an individual function. The problem is that when the bank decides to offer a new kind of account, we will have to change this function, along with all the other functions that implement actions. The "definition" of the new account is scattered rather than localized, and altering a bunch of existing functions is usually more error prone than writing a new class definition.

13.6   Inheritance

In the following table, data types (classes) are listed across the horizontal axis, and functions (messages) are listed up and down the vertical axis. A complete program needs to fill in all the boxes, but the question is how to organize the process of filling them in. In the traditional procedural style, we write function definitions that fill in a row at a time. In the object-oriented style, we write class definitions that fill in a column at a time. A third style, the *data-driven* or *generic* style, fills in only one box at a time.

	account	limited-account	password-account	...
name			*object*	
deposit			*oriented*	
withdraw	*function*	*oriented*		
balance				
interest	*generic*			
...				

In this table there is no particular organization to either axis; both messages and classes are listed in random order. This ignores the fact that classes are organized hierarchically: both limited-account and password-account are subclasses of account. This was implicit in the definition of the classes, because both limited-account and password-account contain accounts as components and delegate messages to those components. But it would be cleaner to make this relationship explicit.

The defstruct mechanism does allow for just this kind of explicit inheritance. If we had defined account as a structure, then we could define limited-account with:

```
(defstruct (limited-account (:include account)) limit)
```

Two things are needed to provide an inheritance facility for classes. First, we should modify define-class so that it takes the name of the class to inherit from as the second argument. This will signal that the new class will inherit all the instance variables, class variables, and methods from the parent class. The new class can, of course, define new variables and methods, or it can shadow the parent's variables and methods. In the form below, we define limited-account to be a subclass of account that adds a new instance variable, limit, and redefines the withdraw method so that it checks for amounts that are over the limit. If the amount is acceptable, then it uses the function call-next-method (not yet defined) to get at the withdraw method for the parent class, account.

```
(define-class limited-account account (limit) ()
  (withdraw (amt)
            (if (> amt limit)
                'over-limit
                (call-next-method)))))
```

If inheritance is a good thing, then multiple inheritance is an even better thing. For example, assuming we have defined the classes limited-account and password-account, it is very convenient to define the following class, which inherits from both of them:

```
(define-class limited-account-with-password
              (password-account limited-account))
```

Notice that this new class adds no new variables or methods. All it does is combine the functionality of two parent classes into one.

Exercise 13.1 [d]   Define a version of define-class that handles inheritance and call-next-method.

Exercise 13.2 [d]   Define a version of define-class that handles multiple inheritance.

13.7   CLOS: The Common Lisp Object System

So far, we have developed an object-oriented programming system using a macro, define-class, and a protocol for implementing objects as closures. There have been many proposals for adding object-oriented features to Lisp, some similar to our approach, some quite different. Recently, one approach has been approved to become an official part of Common Lisp, so we will abandon our ad hoc approach and devote the rest of this chapter to CLOS, the Common Lisp Object System. The correspondence between our system and CLOS is summarized here:

our system	CLOS
define-class	defclass
methods defined in class	defmethod
class-name	make-instance
call-next-method	call-next-method
ensure-generic-fn	ensure-generic-function

Like most object-oriented systems, CLOS is primarily concerned with defining classes and methods for them, and in creating instances of the classes. In CLOS the macro defclass defines a class, defmethod defines a method, and make-instance creates an instance of a class—an object. The general form of the macro defclass is:

(defclass *class-name* (*superclass...*) (*slot-specifier...*) *optional-class-option...*)

The class-options are rarely used. defclass can be used to define the class account:

```
(defclass account ()
  ((name :initarg :name :reader name)
   (balance :initarg :balance :initform 0.00 :accessor balance)
   (interest-rate :allocation :class :initform .06
               :reader interest-rate)))
```

In the definition of account, we see that the list of superclasses is empty, because account does not inherit from any classes. There are three slot specifiers, for the name, balance, and interest-rate slots. Each slot name can be followed by optional keyword/value pairs defining how the slot is used. The name slot has an :initarg option, which says that the name can be specified when a new account is created with make-instance. The :reader slot creates a method called name to get at the current value of the slot.

The balance slot has three options: another :initarg, saying that the balance can be specified when a new account is made; an :initform, which says that if the balance is not specified, it defaults to 0.00, and an :accessor, which creates a method for getting at the slot's value just as :reader does, and also creates a method for updating the slot with setf.

The interest-rate slot has an :initform option to give it a default value and an :allocation option to say that this slot is part of the class, not of each instance of the class.

Here we see the creation of an object, and the application of the automatically defined methods to it.

```
> (setf a1 (make-instance 'account :balance 5000.00
                          :name "Fred")) ⇒ #<ACCOUNT 26726272>

> (name a1) ⇒ "Fred"

> (balance a1) ⇒ 5000.0

> (interest-rate a1) ⇒ 0.06
```

CLOS differs from most object-oriented systems in that methods are defined separately from classes. To define a method (besides the ones defined automatically by :reader, :writer, or :accessor options) we use the defmethod macro. It is similar to defun in form:

(defmethod *method-name* (*parameter...*) *body...*)

Required parameters to a defmethod can be of the form (*var class*), meaning that this is a method that applies only to arguments of that class. Here is the method for withdrawing from an account. Note that CLOS does not have a notion of instance variable, only instance slot. So we have to use the method (balance acct) rather than the instance variable balance:

```
(defmethod withdraw ((acct account) amt)
  (if (< amt (balance acct))
      (decf (balance acct) amt)
      'insufficient-funds))
```

With CLOS it is easy to define a limited-account as a subclass of account, and to define the withdraw method for limited-accounts:

```
(defclass limited-account (account)
  ((limit :initarg :limit :reader limit)))

(defmethod withdraw ((acct limited-account) amt)
  (if (> amt (limit acct))
      'over-limit
      (call-next-method)))
```

Note the use of call-next-method to invoke the withdraw method for the account class. Also note that all the other methods for accounts automatically work on instances of the class limited-account, because it is defined to inherit from account. In the following example, we show that the name method is inherited, that the withdraw method for limited-account is invoked first, and that the withdraw method for account is invoked by the call-next-method function:

```
> (setf a2 (make-instance 'limited-account
                          :name "A. Thrifty Spender"
                          :balance 500.00 :limit 100.00)) ⇒
#<LIMITED-ACCOUNT 24155343>

> (name a2) ⇒ "A. Thrifty Spender"

> (withdraw a2 200.00) ⇒ OVER-LIMIT

> (withdraw a2 20.00) ⇒ 480.0
```

In general, there may be several methods appropriate to a given message. In that case, all the appropriate methods are gathered together and sorted, most specific first. The most specific method is then called. That is why the method for limited-account is called first rather than the method for account. The function call-next-method can be used within the body of a method to call the next most specific method.

The complete story is actually even more complicated than this. As one example of the complication, consider the class audited-account, which prints and keeps a trail of all deposits and withdrawals. It could be defined as follows using a new feature of CLOS, :before and :after methods:

```
(defclass audited-account (account)
  ((audit-trail :initform nil :accessor audit-trail)))

(defmethod withdraw :before ((acct audited-account) amt)
  (push (print '(withdrawing ,amt))
        (audit-trail acct)))

(defmethod withdraw :after ((acct audited-account) amt)
  (push (print '(withdrawal (,amt) done))
        (audit-trail acct)))
```

Now a call to withdraw with a audited-account as the first argument yields three applicable methods: the primary method from account and the :before and :after methods. In general, there might be several of each kind of method. In that case, all the :before methods are called in order, most specific first. Then the most specific primary method is called. It may choose to invoke call-next-method to get at the other methods. (It is an error for a :before or :after method to use call-next-method.) Finally, all the :after methods are called, least specific first.

The values from the :before and :after methods are ignored, and the value from the primary method is returned. Here is an example:

```
> (setf a3 (make-instance 'audited-account :balance 1000.00))
#<AUDITED-ACCOUNT 33555607>

> (withdraw a3 100.00)
(WITHDRAWING 100.0)
(WITHDRAWAL (100.0) DONE)
900.0

> (audit-trail a3)
((WITHDRAWAL (100.0) DONE) (WITHDRAWING 100.0))

> (setf (audit-trail a3) nil)
NIL
```

The last interaction shows the biggest flaw in CLOS: it fails to encapsulate information. In order to make the audit-trail accessible to the withdraw methods, we had to give it accessor methods. We would like to encapsulate the writer function for audit-trail so that it can only be used with deposit and withdraw. But once the writer function is defined it can be used anywhere, so an unscrupulous outsider can destroy the audit trail, setting it to nil or anything else.

13.8   A CLOS Example: Searching Tools

CLOS is most appropriate whenever there are several types that share related behavior. A good example of an application that fits this description is the set of searching tools defined in section 6.4. There we defined functions for breadth-first, depth-first, and best-first search, as well as tree- and graph-based search. We also defined functions to search in particular domains, such as planning a route between cities.

If we had written the tools in a straightforward procedural style, we would have ended up with dozens of similar functions. Instead, we used higher-order functions to control the complexity. In this section, we see how CLOS can be used to break up the complexity in a slightly different fashion.

We begin by defining the class of search problems. Problems will be classified according to their domain (route planning, etc.), their topology (tree or graph) and their search strategy (breadth-first or depth-first, etc.). Each combination of these features results in a new class of problem. This makes it easy for the user to add a new class to represent a new domain, or a new search strategy. The basic class, problem, contains a single-instance variable to hold the unexplored states of the problem.

```
(defclass problem ()
  ((states :initarg :states :accessor problem-states)))
```

The function `searcher` is similar to the function `tree-search` of section 6.4. The main difference is that `searcher` uses generic functions instead of passing around functional arguments.

```
(defmethod searcher ((prob problem))
  "Find a state that solves the search problem."
  (cond ((no-states-p prob) fail)
        ((goal-p prob) (current-state prob))
        (t (let ((current (pop-state prob)))
             (setf (problem-states prob)
                   (problem-combiner
                     prob
                     (problem-successors prob current)
                     (problem-states prob))))
           (searcher prob))))
```

`searcher` does not assume that the problem states are organized in a list; rather, it uses the generic function `no-states-p` to test if there are any states, `pop-state` to remove and return the first state, and `current-state` to access the first state. For the basic `problem` class, we will in fact implement the states as a list, but another class of problem is free to use another representation.

```
(defmethod current-state ((prob problem))
  "The current state is the first of the possible states."
  (first (problem-states prob)))
```

```
(defmethod pop-state ((prob problem))
  "Remove and return the current state."
  (pop (problem-states prob)))
```

```
(defmethod no-states-p ((prob problem))
  "Are there any more unexplored states?"
  (null (problem-states prob)))
```

In `tree-search`, we included a statement to print debugging information. We can do that here, too, but we can hide it in a separate method so as not to clutter up the main definition of `searcher`. It is a `:before` method because we want to see the output before carrying out the operation.

```
(defmethod searcher :before ((prob problem))
  (dbg 'search "~&;; Search: ~a" (problem-states prob)))
```

The generic functions that remain to be defined are goal-p, problem-combiner, and problem-successors. We will address goal-p first, by recognizing that for many problems we will be searching for a state that is eql to a specified goal state. We define the class eql-problem to refer to such problems, and specify goal-p for that class. Note that we make it possible to specify the goal when a problem is created, but not to change the goal:

```
(defclass eql-problem (problem)
  ((goal :initarg :goal :reader problem-goal)))

(defmethod goal-p ((prob eql-problem))
  (eql (current-state prob) (problem-goal prob)))
```

Now we are ready to specify two search strategies: depth-first search and breadth-first search. We define problem classes for each strategy and specify the problem-combiner function:

```
(defclass dfs-problem (problem) ()
  (:documentation "Depth-first search problem."))

(defclass bfs-problem (problem) ()
  (:documentation "Breadth-first search problem."))

(defmethod problem-combiner ((prob dfs-problem) new old)
  "Depth-first search looks at new states first."
  (append new old))

(defmethod problem-combiner ((prob bfs-problem) new old)
  "Depth-first search looks at old states first."
  (append old new))
```

While this code will be sufficient for our purposes, it is less than ideal, because it breaks an information-hiding barrier. It treats the set of old states as a list, which is the default for the problem class but is not necessarily the implementation that every class will use. It would have been cleaner to define generic functions add-states-to-end and add-states-to-front and then define them with append in the default class. But Lisp provides such nice list-manipulation primitives that it is difficult to avoid the temptation of using them directly.

Of course, the user who defines a new implementation for problem-states could just redefine problem-combiner for the offending classes, but this is precisely what object-oriented programming is designed to avoid: specializing one abstraction (states) should not force us to change anything in another abstraction (search strategy).

The last step is to define a class that represents a particular domain, and define problem-successors for that domain. As the first example, consider the simple binary tree search from section 6.4. Naturally, this gets represented as a class:

```
(defclass binary-tree-problem (problem) ())

(defmethod problem-successors ((prob binary-tree-problem) state)
  (let ((n (* 2 state)))
    (list n (+ n 1))))
```

Now suppose we want to solve a binary-tree problem with breadth-first search, searching for a particular goal. Simply create a class that mixes in binary-tree-problem, eql-problem and bfs-problem, create an instance of that class, and call searcher on that instance:

```
(defclass binary-tree-eql-bfs-problem
          (binary-tree-problem eql-problem bfs-problem) ())

> (setf p1 (make-instance 'binary-tree-eql-bfs-problem
                          :states '(1) :goal 12))
#<BINARY-TREE-EQL-BFS-PROBLEM 26725536>

> (searcher p1)
;; Search: (1)
;; Search: (2 3)
;; Search: (3 4 5)
;; Search: (4 5 6 7)
;; Search: (5 6 7 8 9)
;; Search: (6 7 8 9 10 11)
;; Search: (7 8 9 10 11 12 13)
;; Search: (8 9 10 11 12 13 14 15)
;; Search: (9 10 11 12 13 14 15 16 17)
;; Search: (10 11 12 13 14 15 16 17 18 19)
;; Search: (11 12 13 14 15 16 17 18 19 20 21)
;; Search: (12 13 14 15 16 17 18 19 20 21 22 23)
12
```

Best-First Search

It should be clear how to proceed to define best-first search: define a class to represent best-first search problems, and then define the necessary methods for that class. Since the search strategy only affects the order in which states are explored, the only method necessary will be for problem-combiner.

```
(defclass best-problem (problem) ()
  (:documentation "A Best-first search problem."))

(defmethod problem-combiner ((prob best-problem) new old)
  "Best-first search sorts new and old according to cost-fn."
  (sort (append new old) #'<
        :key #'(lambda (state) (cost-fn prob state)))))
```

This introduces the new function cost-fn; naturally it will be a generic function. The following is a cost-fn that is reasonable for any eql-problem dealing with numbers, but it is expected that most domains will specialize this function.

```
(defmethod cost-fn ((prob eql-problem) state)
  (abs (- state (problem-goal prob))))
```

Beam search is a modification of best-first search where all but the best b states are thrown away on each iteration. A beam search problem is represented by a class where the instance variable beam-width holds the parameter b. If this nil, then full best-first search is done. Beam search is implemented by an :around method on problem-combiner. It calls the next method to get the list of states produced by best-first search, and then extracts the first b elements.

```
(defclass beam-problem (problem)
  ((beam-width :initarg :beam-width :initform nil
               :reader problem-beam-width)))

(defmethod problem-combiner :around ((prob beam-problem) new old)
  (let ((combined (call-next-method)))
    (subseq combined 0 (min (problem-beam-width prob)
                            (length combined))))))
```

Now we apply beam search to the binary-tree problem. As usual, we have to make up another class to represent this type of problem:

```
(defclass binary-tree-eql-best-beam-problem
  (binary-tree-problem eql-problem best-problem beam-problem)
  ())

> (setf p3 (make-instance 'binary-tree-eql-best-beam-problem
                          :states '(1) :goal 12 :beam-width 3))
#<BINARY-TREE-EQL-BEST-BEAM-PROBLEM 27523251>

> (searcher p3)
;; Search: (1)
;; Search: (3 2)
;; Search: (7 6 2)
;; Search: (14 15 6)
;; Search: (15 6 28)
```

```
;; Search: (6 28 30)
;; Search: (12 13 28)
12
```

So far the case for CLOS has not been compelling. The code in this section duplicates the functionality of code in section 6.4, but the CLOS code tends to be more verbose, and it is somewhat disturbing that we had to make up so many long class names. However, this verbosity leads to flexibility, and it is easier to extend the CLOS code by adding new specialized classes. It is useful to make a distinction between the systems programmer and the applications programmer. The systems programmer would supply a library of classes like dfs-problem and generic functions like searcher. The applications programmer then just picks what is needed from the library. From the following we see that it is not too difficult to pick out the right code to define a trip-planning searcher. Compare this with the definition of trip on page 198 to see if you prefer CLOS in this case. The main difference is that here we say that the cost function is air-distance and the successors are the neighbors by defining methods; in trip we did it by passing parameters. The latter is a little more succint, but the former may be more clear, especially as the number of parameters grows.

```
(defclass trip-problem (binary-tree-eql-best-beam-problem)
  ((beam-width :initform 1)))

(defmethod cost-fn ((prob trip-problem) city)
  (air-distance (problem-goal prob) city))

(defmethod problem-successors ((prob trip-problem) city)
  (neighbors city))
```

With the definitions in place, it is easy to use the searching tool:

```
> (setf p4 (make-instance 'trip-problem
                          :states (list (city 'new-york))
                          :goal (city 'san-francisco)))
#<TRIP-PROBLEM 31572426>

> (searcher p4)
;; Search: ((NEW-YORK 73.58 40.47))
;; Search: ((PITTSBURG 79.57 40.27))
;; Search: ((CHICAGO 87.37 41.5))
;; Search: ((KANSAS-CITY 94.35 39.06))
;; Search: ((DENVER 105.0 39.45))
;; Search: ((FLAGSTAFF 111.41 35.13))
;; Search: ((RENO 119.49 39.3))
;; Search: ((SAN-FRANCISCO 122.26 37.47))
(SAN-FRANCISCO 122.26 37.47)
```

13.9   Is CLOS Object-Oriented?

There is some argument whether CLOS is really object-oriented at all. The arguments are:

CLOS *is* an object-oriented system because it provides all three of the main criteria for object-orientation: objects with internal state, classes of objects with specialized behavior for each class, and inheritance between classes.

CLOS is *not* an object-oriented system because it does not provide modular objects with information-hiding. In the audited-account example, we would like to encapsulate the audit-trail instance variable so that only the withdraw methods can change it. But because methods are written separately from class definitions, we could not do that. Instead, we had to define an accessor for audit-trail. That enabled us to write the withdraw methods, but it also made it possible for anyone else to alter the audit trail as well.

CLOS is *more general than* an object-oriented system because it allows for methods that specialize on more than one argument. In true object-oriented systems, methods are associated with objects of a particular class. This association is lexically obvious (and the message-passing metaphor is clear) when we write the methods inside the definition of the class, as in our define-class macro. The message-passing metaphor is still apparent when we write generic functions that dispatch on the class of their first argument, which is how we've been using CLOS so far.

But CLOS methods can dispatch on the class of any required argument, or any combination of them. Consider the following definition of conc, which is like append except that it works for vectors as well as lists. Rather than writing conc using conditional statements, we can use the multimethod dispatch capabilities of CLOS to define the four cases: (1) the first argument is nil, (2) the second argument is nil, (3) both arguments are lists, and (4) both arguments are vectors. Notice that if one of the arguments is nil there will be two applicable methods, but the method for null will be used because the class null is more specific than the class list.

```
(defmethod conc ((x null) y) y)

(defmethod conc (x (y null)) x)

(defmethod conc ((x list) (y list))
  (cons (first x) (conc (rest x) y)))

(defmethod conc ((x vector) (y vector))
  (let ((vect (make-array (+ (length x) (length y)))))
    (replace vect x)
    (replace vect y :start1 (length x))))
```

Here we see that this definition works:

```
> (conc nil '(a b c)) ⇒ (A B C)

> (conc '(a b c) nil) ⇒ (A B C)

> (conc '(a b c) '(d e f)) ⇒ (A B C D E F)

> (conc '#(a b c) '#(d e f)) ⇒ #(A B C D E F)
```

It works, but one might well ask: where are the objects? The metaphor of passing a message to an object does not apply here, unless we consider the object to be the list of arguments, rather than a single privileged argument.

It is striking that this style of method definition is very similar to the style used in Prolog. As another example, compare the following two definitions of len, a relation/function to compute the length of a list:

```
;; CLOS                          %% Prolog
(defmethod len ((x null)) 0)     len([],0).

(defmethod len ((x cons))        len([X|L],N1) :-
  (+ 1 (len (rest x))))            len(L,N), N1 is N+1.
```

13.10   Advantages of Object-Oriented Programming

Bertrand Meyer, in his book on the object-oriented language Eiffel (1988), lists five qualities that contribute to software quality:

- *Correctness.* Clearly, a correct program is of the upmost importance.

- *Robustness.* Programs should continue to function in a reasonable manner even for input that is beyond the original specifications.

- *Extendability.* Programs should be easy to modify when the specifications change.

- *Reusability.* Program components should be easy to transport to new programs, thus amortizing the cost of software development over several projects.

- *Compatibility.* Programs should interface well with other programs. For example, a spreadsheet program should not only manipulate numbers correctly but also be compatible with word processing programs, so that spreadsheets can easily be included in documents.

Here we list how the object-oriented approach in general and CLOS in particular can effect these measures of quality:

- *Correctness.* Correctness is usually achieved in two stages: correctness of individual modules and correctness of the whole system. The object-oriented approach makes it easier to prove correctness for modules, since they are clearly defined, and it may make it easier to analyze interactions between modules, since the interface is strictly limited. CLOS does not provide for information-hiding the way other systems do.

- *Robustness.* Generic functions make it possible for a function to accept, at run time, a class of argument that the programmer did not anticipate at compile time. This is particularly true in CLOS, because multiple inheritance makes it feasible to write default methods that can be used by a wide range of classes.

- *Extendability.* Object-oriented systems with inheritance make it easy to define new classes that are slight variants on existing ones. Again, CLOS's multiple inheritance makes extensions even easier than in single-inheritance systems.

- *Reusability.* This is the area where the object-oriented style makes the biggest contribution. Instead of writing each new program from scratch, object-oriented programmers can look over a library of classes, and either reuse existing classes as is, or specialize an existing class through inheritance. Large libraries of CLOS classes have not emerged yet. Perhaps they will when the language is more established.

- *Compatibility.* The more programs use standard components, the more they will be able to communicate with each other. Thus, an object-oriented program will probably be compatible with other programs developed from the same library of classes.

13.11   History and References

The first object-oriented language was Simula, which was designed by Ole-Johan Dahl and Krysten Nygaard (1966, Nygaard and Dahl 1981) as an extension of Algol 60. It is still in use today, mostly in Norway and Sweden. Simula provides the ability to define classes with single inheritance. Methods can be inherited from a superclass or overridden by a subclass. It also provides *coroutines*, class instances that execute continuously, saving local state in instance variables but periodically pausing to let other coroutines run. Although Simula is a general-purpose language, it provides special support for simulation, as the name implies. The built-in class `simulation` allows a programmer to keep track of simulated time while running a set of processes as coroutines.

In 1969 Alan Kay was a graduate student at the University of Utah. He became aware of Simula and realized that the object-oriented style was well suited to his research in graphics (Kay 1969). A few years later, at Xerox, he joined with Adele Goldberg and Daniel Ingalls to develop the Smalltalk language (see Goldberg and Robinson 1983). While Simula can be viewed as an attempt to add object-oriented features to strongly typed Algol 60, Smalltalk can be seen as an attempt to use the dynamic, loosely typed features of Lisp, but with methods and objects replacing functions and s-expressions. In Simula, objects existed alongside traditional data types like numbers and strings; in Smalltalk, every datum is an object. This gave Smalltalk the feel of an integrated Lisp environment, where the user can inspect, copy, or edit any part of the environment. In fact, it was not the object-oriented features of Smalltalk per se that have made a lasting impression but rather the then-innovative idea that every user would have a large graphical display and could interact with the system using a mouse and menus rather than by typing commands.

Guy Steele's *LAMBDA: The Ultimate Declarative* (1976a and b) was perhaps the first paper to demonstrate how object-oriented programming can be done in Lisp. As the title suggests, it was all done using lambda, in a similar way to our define-class example. Steele summarized the approach with the equation "Actors = Closures (mod Syntax)," refering to Carl Hewitt's "Actors" object-oriented formalism.

In 1979, the MIT Lisp Machine group developed the Flavors system based on this approach but offering considerable extensions (Cannon 1980, Weinreb 1980, Moon et al. 1983). "Flavor" was a popular jargon word for "type" or "kind" at MIT, so it was natural that it became the term for what we call classes.

The Flavor system was the first to support multiple inheritance. Other languages shunned multiple inheritance because it was too dynamic. With single inheritance, each instance variable and method could be assigned a unique offset number, and looking up a variable or method was therefore trivial. But with multiple inheritance, these computations had to be done at run time. The Lisp tradition enabled programmers to accept this dynamic computation, when other languages would not. Once it was accepted, the MIT group soon came to embrace it. They developed complex protocols for combining different flavors into new ones. The concept of *mix-ins* was developed by programmers who frequented Steve's Ice Cream parlor in nearby Davis Square. Steve's offered a list of ice cream flavors every day but also offered to create new flavors—dynamically—by mixing in various cookies, candies, or fruit, at the request of the individual customer. For example, Steve's did not have chocolate-chip ice cream on the menu, but you could always order vanilla ice cream with chocolate chips mixed in.[3]

This kind of "flavor hacking" appealed to the MIT Lisp Machine group, who

---

[3]Flavor fans will be happy to know that Steve's Ice Cream is now sold nationally in the United States. Alas, it is not possible to create flavors dynamically. Also, be warned that Steve's was bought out by his Teal Square rival, Joey's. The original Steve retired from the business for years, then came back with a new line of stores under his last name, Harrell.

adopted the metaphor for their object-oriented programming system. All flavors inherited from the top-most flavor in the hierarchy: vanilla. In the window system, for example, the flavor `basic-window` was defined to support the minimal functionality of all windows, and then new flavors of window were defined by combining mix-in flavors such as `scroll-bar-mixin`, `label-mixin`, and `border-mixin`. These mix-in flavors were used only to define other flavors. Just as you couldn't go into Steve's and order "crushed Heath bars, hold the ice cream," there was a mechanism to prohibit instantiation of mix-ins.

A complicated repetoire of *method combinations* was developed. The default method combination on Flavors was similar to CLOS: first do all the `:before` methods, then the most specific primary method, then the `:after` methods. But it was possible to combine methods in other ways as well. For example, consider the `inside-width` method, which returns the width in pixels of the usuable portion of a window. A programmer could specify that the combined method for `inside-width` was to be computed by calling all applicable methods and summing them. Then an `inside-width` method for the `basic-window` flavor would be defined to return the width of the full window, and each mix-in would have a simple method to say how much of the width it consumed. For example, if borders are 8 pixels wide and scroll bars are 12 pixels wide, then the `inside-width` method for `border-mixin` returns `-8` and `scroll-bar-mixin` returns `-12`. Then any window, no matter how many mix-ins it is composed of, automatically computes the proper inside width.

In 1981, Symbolics came out with a more efficient implementation of Flavors. Objects were no longer just closures. They were still funcallable, but there was additional hardware support that distinguished them from other functions. After a few years Symbolics abandoned the (send *object message*) syntax in favor of a new syntax based on generic functions. This system was known as New Flavors. It had a strong influence on the eventual CLOS design.

The other strong influence on CLOS was the CommonLoops system developed at Xerox PARC. (See Bobrow 1982, Bobrow et al. 1986, Stefik and Bobrow 1986.) CommonLoops continued the New Flavors trend away from message passing by introducing *multimethods:* methods that specialize on more than one argument.

As of summer 1991, CLOS itself is in a state of limbo. It was legitimitized by its appearance in *Common Lisp the Language,* 2d edition, but it is not yet official, and an important part, the metaobject protocol, is not yet complete. A tutorial on CLOS is Keene 1989.

We have seen how easy it is to build an object-oriented system on top of Lisp, using `lambda` as the primary tool. An interesting alternative is to build Lisp on top of an object-oriented system. That is the approach taken in the Oaklisp system of Lang and Perlmutter (1988). Instead of defining methods using `lambda` as the primitive, Oaklisp has `add-method` as a primitive and defines `lambda` as a macro that adds a method to an anonymous, empty operation.

Of course, object-oriented systems are thriving outside the Lisp world. With the success of UNIX-based workstations, C has become one of the most widely available programming languages. C is a fairly low-level language, so there have been several attempts to use it as a kind of portable assembly language. The most succesful of these attempts is C++, a language developed by Bjarne Stroustrup of AT&T Bell Labs (Stroustrup 1986). C++ provides a number of extensions, including the ability to define classes. However, as an add-on to an existing language, it does not provide as many features as the other languages discussed here. Crucially, it does not provide garbage collection, nor does it support fully generic functions.

Eiffel (Meyer 1988) is an attempt to define an object-oriented system from the ground up rather than tacking it on to an existing language. Eiffel supports multiple inheritance and garbage collection and a limited amount of dynamic dispatching.

So-called modern languages like Ada and Modula support information-hiding through generic functions and classes, but they do not provide inheritance, and thus can not be classified as true object-oriented languages.

Despite these other languages, the Lisp-based object-oriented systems are the only ones since Smalltalk to introduce important new concepts: multiple inheritance and method combination from Flavors, and multimethods from CommonLoops.

13.12 Exercises

Exercise 13.3 [m] Implement deposit and interest methods for the account class using CLOS.

Exercise 13.4 [m] Implement the password-account class using CLOS. Can it be done as cleanly with inheritance as it was done with delegation? Or should you use delegation within CLOS?

Exercise 13.5 [h] Implement graph searching, search paths, and A* searching as classes in CLOS.

Exercise 13.6 [h] Implement a priority queue to hold the states of a problem. Instead of a list, the problem-states will be a vector of lists, each initially null. Each new state will have a priority (determined by the generic function priority) which must be an integer between zero and the length of the vector, where zero indicates the highest priority. A new state with priority p is pushed onto element p of the vector, and the state to be explored next is the first state in the first nonempty position. As stated in the text, some of the previously defined methods made the unwarranted assumption that problem-states would always hold a list. Change these methods.

CHAPTER 14

Knowledge Representation and Reasoning

Knowledge itself is power.
—Francis Bacon (1561–1626)

The power resides in the knowledge.
—Edward Feigenbaum
Stanford University Heuristic Programming Project

Knowledge is Knowledge, and vice versa.
—Tee shirt
Stanford University Heuristic Programming Project

In the 1960s, much of AI concentrated on search techniques. In particular, a lot of work was concerned with *theorem proving:* stating a problem as a small set of axioms and searching for a proof of the problem. The implicit assumption was that the power resided in the inference mechanism—if we could just find the right search technique, then all our problems would be solved, and all our theorems would be proved.

Starting in the 1970s, this began to change. The theorem-proving approach failed to live up to its promise. AI workers slowly began to realize that they were not going to solve NP-hard problems by coming up with a clever inference algorithm. The general inferencing mechanisms that worked on toy examples just did not scale up when the problem size went into the thousands (or sometimes even into the dozens).

The *expert-system* approach offered an alternative. The key to solving hard problems was seen to be the acquisition of special-case rules to break the problem into easier problems. According to Feigenbaum, the lesson learned from expert systems like MYCIN (which we will see in chapter 16) is that the choice of inferencing mechanism is not as important as having the right knowledge. In this view it doesn't matter very much if MYCIN uses forward- or backward-chaining, or if it uses certainty factors, probabilities, or fuzzy set theory. What matters crucially is that we know pseudomonas is a gram-negative, rod-shaped organism that can infect patients with compromised immune systems. In other words, the key problem is acquiring and representing knowledge.

While the expert system approach had some successes, it also had failures, and researchers were interested in learning the limits of this new technology and understanding exactly how it works. Many found it troublesome that the meaning of the knowledge used in some systems was never clearly defined. For example, does the assertion (color apple red) mean that a particular apple is red, that all apples are red, or that some/most apples are red? The field of *knowledge representation* concentrated on providing clear semantics for such representations, as well as providing algorithms for manipulating the knowledge. Much of the emphasis was on finding a good trade-off between *expressiveness* and *efficiency*. An efficient language is one for which all queries (or at least the average query) can be answered quickly. If we want to guarantee that queries will be answered quickly, then we have to limit what can be expressed in the language.

In the late 1980s, a series of results shed doubt on the hopes of finding an efficient language with any reasonable degree of expressiveness at all. Using mathematical techniques based on worst-case analysis, it was shown that even seemingly trivial languages were *intractable*—in the worst case, it would take an exponential amount of time to answer a simple query.

Thus, in the 1990s the emphasis has shifted to *knowledge representation and reasoning*, a field that encompasses both the expressiveness and efficiency of languages but recognizes that the average case is more important than the worst case. No amount of knowledge can help solve an intractable problem in the worse case, but in practice the worst case rarely occurs.

14.1   A Taxonomy of Representation Languages

AI researchers have investigated hundreds of knowledge representation languages, trying to find languages that are convenient, expressive, and efficient. The languages can be classified into four groups, depending on what the basic unit of representation is. Here are the four categories, with some examples:

- *Logical Formulae* (Prolog)

- *Networks* (semantic nets, conceptual graphs)

- *Objects* (scripts, frames)

- *Procedures* (Lisp, production systems)

We have already dealt with *logic-based* languages like Prolog.

Network-based languages can be seen as a syntactic variation on logical languages. A link L between nodes A and B is just another way of expressing the logical relation $L(A, B)$. The difference is that network-based languages take their links more seriously: they are intended to be implemented directly by pointers in the computer, and inference is done by traversing these pointers. So placing a link L between A and B not only asserts that $L(A, B)$ is true, but it also says something about how the knowledge base is to be searched.

Object-oriented languages can also be seen as syntactic variants of predicate calculus. Here is a statement in a typical slot-filler frame language:

```
(a person
    (name = Jan)
    (age =  32))
```

This is equivalent to the logical formula:

$$\exists\, p\colon person(p) \wedge name(p, Jan) \wedge age(p, 32)$$

The frame notation has the advantage of being easier to read, in some people's opinion. However, the frame notation is less expressive. There is no way to say that the person's name is either Jan or John, or that the person's age is not 34. In predicate calculus, of course, such statements can be easily made.

Finally, *procedural* languages are to be contrasted with representation languages: procedural languages compute answers without explicit representation of knowledge.

There are also hybrid representation languages that use different methods to encode different kinds of knowledge. The KL-ONE family of languages uses both logical formulae and objects arranged into a network, for example. Many frame languages allow *procedural attachment*, a technique that uses arbitrary procedures to compute values for expressions that are inconvenient or impossible to express in the frame language itself.

14.2 Predicate Calculus and its Problems

So far, many of our representations have been based on predicate calculus, a notation with a distinguished position in AI: it serves as the universal standard by which other representations are defined and evaluated. The previous section gave an example expression from a frame language. The frame language may have many merits in terms of the ease of use of its syntax or the efficiency of its internal representation of data. However, to understand what expressions in the language mean, there must be a clear definition. More often than not, that definition is given in terms of predicate calculus.

A predicate calculus representation assumes a universe of individuals, with relations and functions on those individuals, and sentences formed by combining relations with the logical connectives and, or, and not. Philosophers and psychologists will argue the question of how appropriate predicate calculus is as a model of human thought, but one point stands clear: predicate calculus is sufficient to represent anything that can be represented in a digital computer. This is easy to show: assuming the computer's memory has n bits, and the equation $b_i = 1$ means that bit i is on, then the entire state of the computer is represented by a conjunction such as:

$$(b_0 = 0) \wedge (b_1 = 0) \wedge (b_2 = 1) \wedge \cdots \wedge (b_n = 0)$$

Once we can represent a state of the computer, it becomes possible to represent any computer program in predicate calculus as a set of axioms that map one state onto another. Thus, predicate calculus is shown to be a *sufficient* language for representing anything that goes on inside a computer—it can be used as a tool for analyzing any program from the outside.

This does not prove that predicate calculus is an *appropriate* tool for all applications. There are good reasons why we may want to represent knowledge in a form that is quite different from predicate calculus, and manipulate the knowledge with procedures that are quite different from logical inference. But we should still be able to describe our system in terms of predicate calculus axioms, and prove theorems about it. To do any less is to be sloppy. For example, we may want to manipulate numbers inside the computer by using the arithmetic instructions that are built into the CPU rather than by manipulating predicate calculus axioms, but when we write a square-root routine, it had better satisfy the axiom:

$$\sqrt{x} = y \Rightarrow y \times y = x$$

Predicate calculus also serves another purpose: as a tool that can be used *by* a program rather than *on* a program. All programs need to manipulate data, and some programs will manipulate data that is considered to be in predicate calculus notation. It is this use that we will be concerned with.

Predicate calculus makes it easy to start writing down facts about a domain. But the most straightforward version of predicate calculus suffers from a number of serious limitations:

- *Decidability*—given a set of axioms and a goal, it may be that neither the goal nor its negation can be derived from the axioms.

- *Tractability*—even when a goal is provable, it may take too long to find the proof using the available inferencing mechanisms.

- *Uncertainty*—it can be inconvenient to deal with relations that are probable to a degree but not known to be definitely true or false.

- *Monotonicity*—in pure predicate calculus, once a theorem is proved, it is true forever. But we would like a way to derive tentative theorems that rely on assumptions, and be able to retract them when the assumptions prove false.

- *Consistency*—pure predicate calculus admits no contradictions. If by accident both P and $\neg P$ are derived, then *any* theorem can be proved. In effect, a single contradiction corrupts the entire data base.

- *Omniscience*—it can be difficult to distinguish what is provable from what should be proved. This can lead to the unfounded assumption that an agent believes all the consequences of the facts it knows.

- *Expressiveness*—the first-order predicate calculus makes it awkward to talk about certain things, such as the relations and propositions of the language itself.

The view held predominantly today is that it is best to approach these problems with a dual attack that is both within and outside of predicate calculus. It is considered a good idea to invent new notations to address the problems—both for convenience and to facilitate special-purpose reasoners that are more efficient than a general-purpose theorem prover. However, it is also important to define scrupulously the meaning of the new notation in terms of familiar predicate-calculus notation. As Drew McDermott put it, "No notation without denotation!" (1978).

In this chapter we show how new notations (and their corresponding meanings) can be used to extend an existing representation and reasoning system. Prolog is chosen as the language to extend. This is not meant as an endorsement for Prolog as the ultimate knowledge representation language. Rather, it is meant solely to give us a clear and familiar foundation from which to build.

14.3   A Logical Language: Prolog

Prolog has been proposed as the answer to the problem of programming in logic. Why isn't it accepted as the universal representation language? Probably because Prolog is a compromise between a representation language and a programming language. Given two specifications that are logically equivalent, one can be an efficient Prolog program, while the other is not. Kowalski's famous equation "*algorithm* = *logic* + *control*" expresses the limits of logic alone: *logic* = *algorithm* − *control*. Many problems (especially in AI) have large or infinite search spaces, and if Prolog is not given some advice on how to search that space, it will not come up with the answer in any reasonable length of time.

Prolog's problems fall into three classes. First, in order to make the language efficient, its expressiveness was restricted. It is not possible to assert that a person's name is either Jan or John in Prolog (although it is possible to *ask* if the person's name is one of those). Similarly, it is not possible to assert that a fact is false; Prolog does not distinguish between false and unknown. Second, Prolog's inference mechanism is neither sound nor complete. Because it does not check for circular unification, it can give incorrect answers, and because it searches depth-first it can miss correct answers. Third, Prolog has no good way of adding control information to the underlying logic, making it inefficient on certain problems.

14.4   Problems with Prolog's Expressiveness

If Prolog is programming in logic, it is not the full predicate logic we are familiar with. The main problem is that Prolog can't express certain kinds of indefinite facts. It can represent definite facts: the capital of Rhode Island is Providence. It can represent conjunctions of facts: the capital of Rhode Island is Providence and the capital of California is Sacramento. But it can not represent disjunctions or negations: that the capital of California is *not* Los Angeles, or that the capital of New York is *either* New York City *or* Albany. We could try this:

```
(<- (not (capital LA CA)))
(<- (or (capital Albany NY) (capital NYC NY)))
```

but note that these last two facts concern the relation not and or, not the relation capital. Thus, they will not be considered when we ask a query about capital. Fortunately, the assertion "Either NYC or Albany is the capital of NY" can be rephrased as two assertions: "Albany is the capital of NY if NYC is not" and "NYC is the capital of NY if Albany is not:"

```
(<- (capital Albany NY) (not (capital NYC NY)))
(<- (capital NYC NY) (not (capital Albany NY)))
```

Unfortunately, Prolog's not is different from logic's not. When Prolog answers "no" to a query, it means the query cannot be proven from the known facts. If everything is known, then the query must be false, but if there are facts that are not known, the query may in fact be true. This is hardly surprising; we can't expect a program to come up with answers using knowledge it doesn't have. But in this case, it causes problems. Given the previous two clauses and the query (capital ?c NY), Prolog will go into an infinite loop. If we remove the first clause, Prolog would fail to prove that Albany is the capital, and hence conclude that NYC is. If we remove the second clause, the opposite conclusion would be drawn.

The problem is that Prolog equates "not proven" with "false." Prolog makes what is called the *closed world assumption*—it assumes that it knows everything that is true. The closed world assumption is reasonable for most programs, because the programmer does know all the relevant information. But for knowledge representation in general, we would like a system that does not make the closed world assumption and has three ways to answer a query: "yes," "no," or "unknown." In this example, we would not be able to conclude that the capital of NY is or is not NYC, hence we would not be able to conclude anything about Albany.

As another example, consider the clauses:

```
(<- (damned) (do))
(<- (damned) (not (do)))
```

With these rules, the query (? (damned)) should logically be answered "yes." Furthermore, it should be possible to conclude (damned) without even investigating if (do) is provable or not. What Prolog does is first try to prove (do). If this succeeds, then (damned) is proved. Either way, Prolog then tries again to prove (do), and this time if the proof fails, then (damned) is proved. So Prolog is doing the same proof twice, when it is unnecessary to do the proof at all. Introducing negation wrecks havoc on the simple Prolog evaluation scheme. It is no longer sufficient to consider a single clause at a time. Rather, multiple clauses must be considered together if we want to derive all the right answers.

Robert Moore 1982 gives a good example of the power of disjunctive reasoning. His problem concerned three colored blocks, but we will update it to deal with three countries. Suppose that a certain Eastern European country, E, has just decided if it will remain under communist rule or become a democracy, but we do not know the outcome of the decision. E is situated between the democracy D and the communist country C:

D	E	C

The question is: Is there a communist country next to a democracy? Moore points out that the answer is "yes," but discovering this requires reasoning by cases. If E is a democracy then it is next to C and the answer is yes. But if E is communist then it is next to D and the answer is still yes. Since those are the only two possibilities, the answer must be yes in any case. Logical reasoning gives us the right answer, but Prolog can not. We can describe the problem with the following seven assertions and one query, but Prolog can not deal with the or in the final assertion.

```
(<- (next-to D E))    (<- (next-to E D))
(<- (next-to E C))    (<- (next-to C E))
(<- (democracy D))    (<- (communist C))
(<- (or (democracy E) (communist E)))

(?- (next-to ?A ?B) (democracy ?A) (communist ?B))
```

We have seen that Prolog is not very good at representing disjunctions and negations. It also has difficulty representing existentials. Consider the following statement in English, logic, and Prolog:

Jan likes everyone.
$\forall x \, \text{person}(x) \Rightarrow \text{likes}(\text{Jan},x)$
```
(<- (likes Jan ?x) (person ?x))
```

The Prolog translation is faithful. But there is no good translation for "Jan likes someone." The closest we can get is:

Jan likes someone.
$\exists x \, \text{person}(x) \Rightarrow \text{likes}(\text{Jan},x)$
```
(<- (likes Jan p1))
(<- (person p1))
```

Here we have invented a new symbol, p1, to represent the unknown person that Jan likes, and have asserted that p1 is a person. Notice that p1 is a constant, not a variable. This use of a constant to represent a specific but unknown entity is called a *Skolem constant*, after the logician Thoralf Skolem (1887–1963). The intent is that p1 may be equal to some other person that we know about. If we find out that Adrian is the person Jan likes, then in logic we can just add the assertion p1 = Adrian. But that does not work in Prolog, because Prolog implicitly uses the *unique name assumption*—all atoms represent distinct individuals.

A Skolem constant is really just a special case of a *Skolem function*—an unknown entity that depends on one or more variable. For example, to represent "Everyone likes someone" we could use:

Everyone likes someone.
$\forall\, y\, \exists\, x\, \text{person}(x) \Rightarrow \text{likes}(y, x)$
```
(<- (likes ?y (p2 ?y)))
(<- (person (p2 ?y)))
```

Here p2 is a Skolem function that depends on the variable ?y. In other words, everyone likes some person, but not necessarily the same person.

14.5   Problems with Predicate Calculus's Expressiveness

In the previous section we saw that Prolog has traded some expressiveness for efficiency. This section explores the limits of predicate calculus's expressiveness.

Suppose we want to assert that lions, tigers, and bears are kinds of animals. In predicate calculus or in Prolog we could write an implication for each case:

```
(<- (animal ?x) (lion ?x))
(<- (animal ?x) (tiger ?x))
(<- (animal ?x) (bear ?x))
```

These implications allow us to prove that any known lion, tiger, or bear is in fact an animal. However, they do not allow us to answer the question "What kinds of animals are there?" It is not hard to imagine extending Prolog so that the query

```
(?- (<- (animal ?x) ?proposition))
```

would be legal. However, this happens not to be valid Prolog, and it is not even valid first-order predicate calculus (or FOPC). In FOPC the variables must range over constants in the language, not over relations or propositions. Higher-order predicate calculus removes this limitation, but it has a more complicated proof theory.

It is not even clear what the values of ?proposition should be in the query above. Surely (lion ?x) would be a valid answer, but so would (animal ?x), (or (tiger ?x) (bear ?x)), and an infinite number of other propositions. Perhaps we should have two types of queries, one that asks about "kinds," and another that asks about propositions.

There are other questions that we might want to ask about relations. Just as it is useful to declare the types of parameters to a Lisp function, it can be useful to declare the types of the parameters of a relation, and later query those types. For example, we might say that the likes relation holds between a person and an object.

In general, a sentence in the predicate calculus that uses a relation or sentence as a term is called a higher-order sentence. There are some quite subtle problems that come into play when we start to allow higher-order expressions. Allowing sentences in the calculus to talk about the truth of other sentences can lead to a paradox: is the sentence "This sentence is false" true or false?

Predicate calculus is defined in terms of a universe of individuals and their properties and relations. Thus it is well suited for a model of the world that picks out individuals and categorizes them—a person here, a building there, a sidewalk between them. But how well does predicate calculus fare in a world of continuous substances? Consider a body of water consisting of an indefinite number of subconstituents that are all water, with some of the water evaporating into the air and rising to form clouds. It is not at all obvious how to define the individuals here. However, Patrick Hayes has shown that when the proper choices are made, predicate calculus can describe this kind of situation quite well. The details are in Hayes 1985.

The need to define categories is a more difficult problem. Predicate calculus works very well for crisp, mathematical categories: x is a triangle if and only if x is a polygon with three sides. Unfortunately, most categories that humans deal with in everyday life are not defined so rigorously. The category *friend* refers to someone you have mostly positive feelings for, whom you can usually trust, and so on. This "definition" is not a set of necessary and sufficient conditions but rather is an open-ended list of ill-defined qualities that are highly correlated with the category *friend*. We have a prototype for what an ideal friend should be, but no clear-cut boundaries that separate *friend* from, say, *acquaintance*. Furthermore, the boundaries seem to vary from one situation to another: a person you describe as a good friend in your work place might be only an acquaintance in the context of your home life.

There are versions of predicate calculus that admit quantifiers like "most" in addition to "for all" and "there exists," and there have been attempts to define prototypes and measure distances from them. However, there is no consensus on the way to approach this problem.

14.6   Problems with Completeness

Because Prolog searches depth-first, it can get caught in one branch of the search space and never examine the other branches. This problem can show up, for example, in trying to define a commutative relation, like sibling:

```
(<- (sibling lee kim))
(<- (sibling ?x ?y) (sibling ?y ?x))
```

With these clauses, we expect to be able to conclude that Lee is Kim's sibling, and Kim is Lee's. Let's see what happens:

```
> (?- (sibling ?x ?y))
?X = LEE
?Y = KIM;
?X = KIM
?Y = LEE;
?X = LEE
?Y = KIM;
?X = KIM
?Y = LEE.
No.
```

We get the expected conclusions, but they are deduced repeatedly, because the commutative clause for siblings is applied over and over again. This is annoying, but not critical. Far worse is when we ask (?- (sibling fred ?x)). This query loops forever. Happily, this particular type of example has an easy fix: just introduce two predicates, one for data-base level facts, and one at the level of axioms and queries:

```
(<- (sibling-fact lee kim))
(<- (sibling ?x ?y) (sibling-fact ?x ?y))
(<- (sibling ?x ?y) (sibling-fact ?y ?x))
```

Another fix would be to change the interpreter to fail when a repeated goal was detected. This was the approach taken in GPS. However, even if we eliminated repeated goals, Prolog can still get stuck in one branch of a depth-first search. Consider the example:

```
(<- (natural 0))
(<- (natural (1+ ?n)) (natural ?n))
```

These rules define the natural numbers (the non-negative integers). We can use the rules either to confirm queries like (natural (1+ (1+ (1+ 0)))) or to generate the natural numbers, as in the query (natural ?n). So far, everything is fine. But suppose we wanted to define all the integers. One approach would be this:

```
(<- (integer 0))
(<- (integer ?n) (integer (1+ ?n)))
(<- (integer (1+ ?n)) (integer ?n))
```

These rules say that 0 is an integer, and any n is an integer if $n + 1$ is, and $n + 1$ is if n is. While these rules are correct in a logical sense, they don't work as a Prolog program. Asking (integer x) will result in an endless series of ever-increasing queries: (integer (1+ x)), (integer (1+ (1+ x))), and so on. Each goal is different, so no check can stop the recursion.

The occurs check may or may not introduce problems into Prolog, depending on your interpretation of infinite trees. Most Prolog systems do not do the occurs check. The reasoning is that unifying a variable with some value is the Prolog equivalent of assigning a value to a variable, and programmers expect such a basic operation to be fast. With the occurs check turned off, it will in fact be fast. With checking on, it takes time proportional to the size of the value, which is deemed unacceptable.

With occurs checking off, the programmer gets the benefit of fast unification but can run into problems with circular structures. Consider the following clauses:

```
(<- (parent ?x (mother-of ?x)))
(<- (parent ?x (father-of ?x)))
```

These clauses say that, for any person, the mother of that person and the father of that person are parents of that person. Now let us ask if there is a person who is his or her own parent:

```
> (? (parent ?y ?y))
?Y = [Abort]
```

The system has found an answer, where ?y = (mother-of ?y). The answer can't be printed, though, because deref (or subst-bindings in the interpreter) goes into an infinite loop trying to figure out what ?y is. Without the printing, there would be no infinite loop:

```
(<- (self-parent) (parent ?y ?y))

> (? (self-parent))
Yes;
Yes;
No.
```

The self-parent query succeeds twice, once with the mother clause and once with the father clause. Has Prolog done the right thing here? It depends on your interpretation of infinite circular trees. If you accept them as valid objects, then the answer is consistent. If you don't, then leaving out the occurs check makes Prolog *unsound:* it can come up with incorrect answers.

The same problem comes up if we ask if there are any sets that include themselves as members. The query (member ?set ?set) will succeed, but we will not be able to print the value of ?set.

14.7   Problems with Efficiency: Indexing

Our Prolog compiler is designed to handle "programlike" predicates—predicates with a small number of rules, perhaps with complex bodies. The compiler does much worse on "tablelike" predicates—predicates with a large number of simple facts. Consider the predicate pb, which encodes phone-book facts in the form:

```
(pb (name Jan Doe) (num 415 555 1212))
```

Suppose we have a few thousand entries of this kind. A typical query for this data base would be:

```
(pb (name Jan Doe) ?num)
```

It would be inefficient to search through the facts linearly, matching each one against the query. It would also be inefficient to recompile the whole pb/2 predicate every time a new entry is added. But that is just what our compiler does.

The solutions to the three problems—expressiveness, completeness, and indexing—will be considered in reverse order, so that the most difficult one, expressiveness, will come last.

14.8   A Solution to the Indexing Problem

A better solution to the phone-book problem is to index each phone-book entry in some kind of table that makes it easy to add, delete, and retrieve entries. That is what we will do in this section. We will develop an extension of the trie or discrimination tree data structure built in section 10.5 (page 344).

Making a discrimination tree for Prolog facts is complicated by the presence of variables in both the facts and the query. Either facts with variables in them will have to be indexed in several places, or queries with variables will have to look in several places, or both. We also have to decide if the discrimination tree itself will handle variable binding, or if it will just return candidate matches which are then checked by some other process. It is not clear what to store in the discrimination tree: copies of the fact, functions that can be passed continuations, or something else. More design choices will come up as we proceed.

It is difficult to make design choices when we don't know exactly how the system will be used. We don't know what typical facts will look like, nor typical queries. Therefore, we will design a fairly abstract tool, forgetting for the moment that it will be used to index Prolog facts.

We will address the problem of a discrimination tree where both the keys and queries are predicate structures with wild cards. A wild card is a variable, but with the understanding that there is no variable binding; each instance of a variable can match anything. A predicate structure is a list whose first element is a nonvariable symbol. The discrimination tree supports three operations:

- index—add a key/value pair to the tree

- fetch—find all values that potentially match a given key

- unindex—remove all key/value pairs that match a given key

To appreciate the problems, we need an example. Suppose we have the following six keys to index. For simplicity, the value of each key will be the key itself:

```
1 (p a b)
2 (p a c)
3 (p a ?x)
4 (p b c)
5 (p b (f c))
6 (p a (f . ?x))
```

Now assume the query (p ?y c). This should match keys 2, 3, and 4. How could we efficiently arrive at this set? One idea is to list the key/value pairs under every atom that they contain. Thus, all six would be listed under the atom p, while 2, 4, and 5 would be listed under the atom c. A unification check could eliminate 5, but we still would be missing 3. Key 3 (and every key with a variable in it) could potentially contain the atom c. So to get the right answers under this approach, we will need to index every key that contains a variable under every atom—not an appealing situation.

An alternative is to create indices based on both atoms and their position. So now we would be retrieving all the keys that have a c in the second argument position: 2 and 4, plus the keys that have a variable as the second argument: 3. This approach seems to work much better, at least for the example shown. To create the index, we essentially superimpose the list structure of all the keys on top of each other, to arrive at one big discrimination tree. At each position in the tree, we create an index of the keys that have either an atom or a variable at that position. Figure 14.1 shows the discrimination tree for the six keys.

Consider the query (p ?y c). Either the p or the c could be used as an index. The p in the predicate position retrieves all six keys. But the c in the second argument position retrieves only three keys: 2 and 4, which are indexed under c itself, and 3, which is indexed under the variable in that position.

Now consider the query (p ?y (f ?z)). Again, the p serves as an index to all six keys. The f serves as an index to only three keys: the 5 and 6, which are indexed

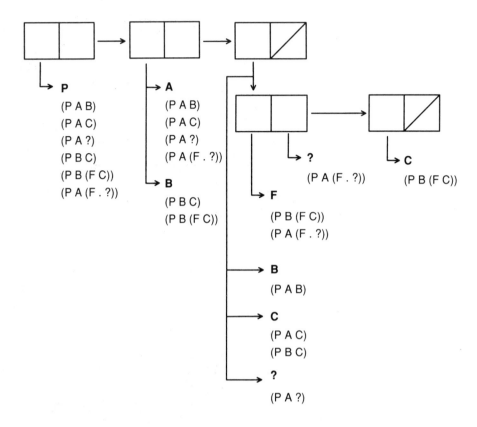

Figure 14.1: Discrimination Tree with Six Keys

directly under f in that position, and 3, which is indexed under the variable in a position along the path that lead to f. In general, all the keys indexed under variables along the path must be considered.

The retrieval mechanism can overretrieve. Given the query (p a (f ?x)), the atom p will again retrieve all six keys, the atom a retrieves 1, 2, 3, and 6, and f again retrieves 5, 6, and 3. So f retrieves the shortest list, and hence it will be used to determine the final result. But key 5 is (p b (f c)), which does not match the query (p a (f ?x)).

We could eliminate this problem by intersecting all the lists instead of just taking the shortest list. It is perhaps feasible to do the intersection using bit vectors, but probably too slow and wasteful of space to do it using lists. Even if we did intersect keys, we would still overretrieve, for two reasons. First, we don't use nil as an index, so we are ignoring the difference between (f ?x) and (f . ?x). Second, we are using wild-card semantics, so the query (p ?x ?x) would retrieve all six keys, when it should only retrieve three. Because of these problems, we make a design choice: we will first build a data base retrieval function that retrieves potential matches, and later worry about the unification process that will eliminate mismatches.

We are ready for a more complete specification of the indexing strategy:

- The value will be indexed under each non-nil nonvariable atom in the key, with a separate index for each position. For example, given the preceding data base, the atom a in the first argument position would index values 1, 2, 3, and 6, while the atom b in the second argument position would index value 4 and 5. The atom p in the predicate position would index all six values.

- In addition, we will maintain a separate index for variables at each position. For example, value 3 would be stored under the index "variable in second argument position."

- "Position" does not refer solely to the linear position in the top-level list. For example, value 5 would be indexed under atom f in the caaddr position.

- It follows that a key with n atoms will be indexed in n different ways.

For retrieval, the strategy is:

- For each non-nil nonvariable atom in the retrieval key, generate a list of possible matches. Choose the shortest such list.

- Each list of possible matches will have to be augmented with the values indexed under a variable at every position "above." For example, f in the caaddr position retrieves value 5, but it also must retrieve value 3, because the third key has a variable in the caddr position, and caddr is "above" caaddr.

- The discrimination tree may return values that are not valid matches. The purpose of the discrimination tree is to reduce the number of values we will have to unify against, not to determine the exact set of matches.

It is important that the retrieval function execute quickly. If it is slow, we might just as well match against every key in the table linearly. Therefore, we will take care to implement each part efficiently. Note that we will have to compare the length of lists to choose the shortest possibility. Of course, it is trivial to compare lengths using length, but length requires traversing the whole list. We can do better if we store the length of the list explicitly. A list with its length will be called an nlist. It will be implemented as a cons cell containing the number of elements and a list of the elements themselves. An alternative would be to use extensible vectors with fill pointers.

```
;; An nlist is implemented as a (count . elements) pair:
(defun make-empty-nlist ()
  "Create a new, empty nlist."
  (cons 0 nil))

(defun nlist-n (x) "The number of elements in an nlist." (car x))
(defun nlist-list (x) "The elements in an nlist." (cdr x))

(defun nlist-push (item nlist)
  "Add a new element to an nlist."
  (incf (car nlist))
  (push item (cdr nlist))
  nlist)
```

Now we need a place to store these nlists. We will build the data base out of discrimination tree nodes called dtree nodes. Each dtree node has a field to hold the variable index, the atom indices, and pointers to two subnodes, one for the first and one for the rest. We implement dtrees as vectors for efficiency, and because we will never need a dtree-p predicate.

```
(defstruct (dtree (:type vector))
  (first nil) (rest nil) (atoms nil) (var (make-empty-nlist)))
```

A separate dtree will be stored for each predicate. Since the predicates must be symbols, it is possible to store the dtrees on the predicate's property list. In most implementations, this will be faster than alternatives such as hash tables.

```
(let ((predicates nil))

  (defun get-dtree (predicate)
    "Fetch (or make) the dtree for this predicate."
    (cond ((get predicate 'dtree))
          (t (push predicate predicates)
             (setf (get predicate 'dtree) (make-dtree)))))

  (defun clear-dtrees ()
    "Remove all the dtrees for all the predicates."
    (dolist (predicate predicates)
      (setf (get predicate 'dtree) nil))
    (setf predicates nil)))
```

The function index takes a relation as key and stores it in the dtree for the predicate of the relation. It calls dtree-index to do all the work of storing a value under the proper indices for the key in the proper dtree node.

The atom indices are stored in an association list. Property lists would not work, because they are searched using eq and atoms can be numbers, which are not necessarily eq. Association lists are searched using eql by default. An alternative would be to use hash tables for the index, or even to use a scheme that starts with association lists and switches to a hash table when the number of entries gets large. I use lookup to look up the value of a key in a property list. This function, and its setf method, are defined on page 896.

```lisp
(defun index (key)
  "Store key in a dtree node.  Key must be (predicate . args);
  it is stored in the predicate's dtree."
  (dtree-index key key (get-dtree (predicate key))))

(defun dtree-index (key value dtree)
  "Index value under all atoms of key in dtree."
  (cond
    ((consp key)                  ; index on both first and rest
     (dtree-index (first key) value
                  (or (dtree-first dtree)
                      (setf (dtree-first dtree) (make-dtree))))
     (dtree-index (rest key) value
                  (or (dtree-rest dtree)
                      (setf (dtree-rest dtree) (make-dtree)))))
    ((null key))                  ; don't index on nil
    ((variable-p key)             ; index a variable
     (nlist-push value (dtree-var dtree)))
    (t ;; Make sure there is an nlist for this atom, and add to it
     (nlist-push value (lookup-atom key dtree)))))

(defun lookup-atom (atom dtree)
  "Return (or create) the nlist for this atom in dtree."
  (or (lookup atom (dtree-atoms dtree))
      (let ((new (make-empty-nlist)))
        (push (cons atom new) (dtree-atoms dtree))
        new)))
```

Now we define a function to test the indexing routine. Compare the output with figure 14.1.

```lisp
(defun test-index ()
  (let ((props '((p a b) (p a c) (p a ?x) (p b c)
                 (p b (f c)) (p a (f . ?x)))))
    (clear-dtrees)
    (mapc #'index props)
    (write (list props (get-dtree 'p))
           :circle t :array t :pretty t)
    (values)))
```

```
> (test-index)
((#1=(P A B)
  #2=(P A C)
  #3=(P A ?X)
  #4=(P B C)
  #5=(P B (F C))
  #6=(P A (F . ?X)))
 #(#(NIL NIL (P (6 #6# #5# #4# #3# #2# #1#)) (0))
   #(#(NIL NIL (B (2 #5# #4#) A (4 #6# #3# #2# #1#)) (0))
     #(#(#(NIL NIL (F (2 #6# #5#)) (0))
         #(#(NIL NIL (C (1 #5#)) (0))
           #(NIL NIL NIL (0)) NIL (1 #6#))
         (C (2 #4# #2#) B (1 #1#))
         (1 #3#))
       #(NIL NIL NIL (0))
       NIL (0))
     NIL (0))
   NIL (0)))
```

The next step is to fetch matches from the dtree data base. The function fetch takes a query, which must be a valid relation, as its argument, and returns a list of possible matches. It calls dtree-fetch to do the work:

```
(defun fetch (query)
  "Return a list of buckets potentially matching the query,
  which must be a relation of form (predicate . args)."
  (dtree-fetch query (get-dtree (predicate query))
               nil 0 nil most-positive-fixnum))
```

dtree-fetch must be passed the query and the dtree, of course, but it is also passed four additional arguments. First, we have to accumulate matches indexed under variables as we are searching through the dtree. So two arguments are used to pass the actual matches and a count of their total number. Second, we want dtree-fetch to return the shortest possible index, so we pass it the shortest answer found so far, and the size of the shortest answer. That way, as it is making its way down the tree, accumulating values indexed under variables, it can be continually comparing the size of the evolving answer with the best answer found so far.

We could use nlists to pass around count/values pairs, but nlists only support a push operation, where one new item is added. We need to append together lists of values coming from the variable indices with values indexed under an atom. Append is expensive, so instead we make a list-of-lists and keep the count in a separate variable. When we are done, dtree-fetch and hence fetch does a multiple-value return, yielding the list-of-lists and the total count.

There are four cases to consider in dtree-fetch. If the dtree is null or the query pattern is either null or a variable, then nothing will be indexed, so we should just return the best answer found so far. Otherwise, we bind var-n and var-list to the count and list-of-lists of variable matches found so far, including at the current node. If the count var-n is greater than the best count so far, then there is no sense continuing, and we return the best answer found. Otherwise we look at the query pattern. If it is an atom, we use dtree-atom-fetch to return either the current index (along with the accumulated variable index) or the accumulated best answer, whichever is shorter. If the query is a cons, then we use dtree-fetch on the first part of the cons, yielding a new best answer, which is passed along to the call of dtree-fetch on the rest of the cons.

```
(defun dtree-fetch (pat dtree var-list-in var-n-in best-list best-n)
  "Return two values: a list-of-lists of possible matches to pat,
  and the number of elements in the list-of-lists."
  (if (or (null dtree) (null pat) (variable-p pat))
      (values best-list best-n)
      (let* ((var-nlist (dtree-var dtree))
             (var-n (+ var-n-in (nlist-n var-nlist)))
             (var-list (if (null (nlist-list var-nlist))
                           var-list-in
                           (cons (nlist-list var-nlist)
                                 var-list-in))))
        (cond
          ((>= var-n best-n) (values best-list best-n))
          ((atom pat) (dtree-atom-fetch pat dtree var-list var-n
                                        best-list best-n))
          (t (multiple-value-bind (list1 n1)
                 (dtree-fetch (first pat) (dtree-first dtree)
                              var-list var-n best-list best-n)
               (dtree-fetch (rest pat) (dtree-rest dtree)
                            var-list var-n list1 n1)))))))

(defun dtree-atom-fetch (atom dtree var-list var-n best-list best-n)
  "Return the answers indexed at this atom (along with the vars),
  or return the previous best answer, if it is better."
  (let ((atom-nlist (lookup atom (dtree-atoms dtree))))
    (cond
      ((or (null atom-nlist) (null (nlist-list atom-nlist)))
       (values var-list var-n))
      ((and atom-nlist (< (incf var-n (nlist-n atom-nlist)) best-n))
       (values (cons (nlist-list atom-nlist) var-list) var-n))
      (t (values best-list best-n)))))
```

Here we see a call to fetch on the data base created by test-index. It returns two values: a list-of-lists of facts, and the total number of facts, three.

```
> (fetch '(p ? c))
(((P B C) (P A C))
 ((P A ?X)))
3
```

Now let's stop and see what we have accomplished. The functions `fetch` and `dtree-fetch` fulfill their contract of returning potential matches. However, we still need to integrate the dtree facility with Prolog. We need to go through the potential matches and determine which candidates are actual matches. For simplicity we will use the version of `unify` with binding lists defined in section 11.2. (It is also possible to construct a more efficient version that uses the compiler and the destructive function `unify!`.)

The function `mapc-retrieve` calls `fetch` to get a list-of-lists of potential matches and then calls `unify` to see if the match is a true one. If the match is true, it calls the supplied function with the binding list that represents the unification as the argument. `mapc-retrieve` is proclaimed `inline` so that functions passed to it can also be compiled in place.

```
(proclaim '(inline mapc-retrieve))

(defun mapc-retrieve (fn query)
  "For every fact that matches the query,
  apply the function to the binding list."
  (dolist (bucket (fetch query))
    (dolist (answer bucket)
      (let ((bindings (unify query answer)))
        (unless (eq bindings fail)
          (funcall fn bindings))))))
```

There are many ways to use this retriever. The function `retrieve` returns a list of the matching binding lists, and `retrieve-matches` substitutes each binding list into the original query so that the result is a list of expressions that unify with the query.

```
(defun retrieve (query)
  "Find all facts that match query.  Return a list of bindings."
  (let ((answers nil))
    (mapc-retrieve #'(lambda (bindings) (push bindings answers))
                   query)
    answers))

(defun retrieve-matches (query)
  "Find all facts that match query.
  Return a list of expressions that match the query."
  (mapcar #'(lambda (bindings) (subst-bindings bindings query))
          (retrieve query)))
```

There is one further complication to consider. Recall that in our original Prolog interpreter, the function prove had to rename the variables in each clause as it retrieved it from the data base. This was to insure that there was no conflict between the variables in the query and the variables in the clause. We could do that in retrieve. However, if we assume that the expressions indexed in discrimination trees are tablelike rather than rulelike and thus are not recursive, then we can get away with renaming the variables only once, when they are entered into the data base. This is done by changing index:

```
(defun index (key)
  "Store key in a dtree node.  Key must be (predicate . args);
  it is stored in the predicate's dtree."
  (dtree-index key (rename-variables key)    ; store unique vars
              (get-dtree (predicate key))))
```

With the new index in place, and after calling test-index to rebuild the data base, we are now ready to test the retrieval mechanism:

```
> (fetch '(p ?x c))
(((P B C) (P A C))
 ((P A ?X3408)))
3

> (retrieve '(p ?x c))
(((?X3408 . C) (?X . A))
 ((?X . A))
 ((?X . B)))

> (retrieve-matches '(p ?x c))
((P A C) (P A C) (P B C))

> (retrieve-matches '(p ?x (?fn c)))
((P A (?FN C)) (P A (F C)) (P B (F C)))
```

Actually, it is better to use mapc-retrieve when possible, since it doesn't cons up answers the way retrieve and retrieve-matches do. The macro query-bind is provided as a nice interface to mapc-retrieve. The macro takes as arguments a list of variables to bind, a query, and one or more forms to apply to each retrieved answer. Within this list of forms, the variables will be bound to the values that satisfy the query. The syntax was chosen to be the same as multiple-value-bind. Here we see a typical use of query-bind, its result, and its macro-expansion:

```
> (query-bind (?x ?fn) '(p ?x (?fn c))
    (format t "~&P holds between ~a and ~a of c." ?x ?fn)) ⇒
P holds between B and F of c.
P holds between A and F of c.
P holds between A and ?FN of c.
NIL

≡ (mapc-retrieve
    #'(lambda (#:bindings6369)
        (let ((?x (subst-bindings #:bindings6369 '?x))
              (?fn (subst-bindings #:bindings6369 '?fn)))
          (format t "~&P holds between ~a and ~a of c." ?x ?fn)))
    '(p ?x (?fn c)))
```

Here is the implementation:

```
(defmacro query-bind (variables query &body body)
  "Execute the body for each match to the query.
  Within the body, bind each variable."
  (let* ((bindings (gensym "BINDINGS"))
         (vars-and-vals
           (mapcar
             #'(lambda (var)
                 (list var '(subst-bindings ,bindings ',var)))
             variables)))
    '(mapc-retrieve
      #'(lambda (,bindings)
          (let ,vars-and-vals
            ,@body))
      ,query)))
```

14.9   A Solution to the Completeness Problem

We saw in chapter 6 that iterative deepening is an efficient way to cover a search space without falling into an infinite loop. Iterative deepening can also be used to guide the search in Prolog. It will insure that all valid answers are found eventually, but it won't turn an infinite search space into a finite one.

In the interpreter, iterative deepening is implemented by passing an extra argument to prove and prove-all to indicate the depth remaining to be searched. When that argument is zero, the search is cut off, and the proof fails. On the next iteration the bounds will be increased and the proof may succeed. If the search is never cut off by a depth bound, then there is no reason to go on to the next iteration, because all proofs have already been found. The special variable *search-cut-off* keeps track of this.

```
(defvar *search-cut-off* nil "Has the search been stopped?")

(defun prove-all (goals bindings depth)
  "Find a solution to the conjunction of goals."
  ;; This version just passes the depth on to PROVE.
  (cond ((eq bindings fail) fail)
        ((null goals) bindings)
        (t (prove (first goals) bindings (rest goals) depth))))

(defun prove (goal bindings other-goals depth)
  "Return a list of possible solutions to goal."
  ;; Check if the depth bound has been exceeded
  (if (= depth 0)                              ;***
      (progn (setf *search-cut-off* t)         ;***
             fail)                             ;***
      (let ((clauses (get-clauses (predicate goal))))
        (if (listp clauses)
            (some
              #'(lambda (clause)
                  (let ((new-clause (rename-variables clause)))
                    (prove-all
                      (append (clause-body new-clause) other-goals)
                      (unify goal (clause-head new-clause) bindings)
                      (- depth 1))))          ;***
              clauses)
            ;; The predicate's "clauses" can be an atom:
            ;; a primitive function to call
            (funcall clauses (rest goal) bindings
                     other-goals depth)))))    ;***
```

prove and prove-all now implement search cutoff, but we need something to control the iterative deepening of the search. First we define parameters to control the iteration: one for the initial depth, one for the maximum depth, and one for the increment between iterations. Setting the initial and increment values to one will make the results come out in strict breadth-first order, but will duplicate more effort than a slightly larger value.

```
(defparameter *depth-start* 5
  "The depth of the first round of iterative search.")
(defparameter *depth-incr* 5
  "Increase each iteration of the search by this amount.")
(defparameter *depth-max* most-positive-fixnum
  "The deepest we will ever search.")
```

A new version of top-level-prove will be used to control the iteration. It calls
prove-all for all depths from the starting depth to the maximum depth, increasing
by the increment. However, it only proceeds to the next iteration if the search was
cut off at some point in the previous iteration.

```
(defun top-level-prove (goals)
  (let ((all-goals
          '(,@goals (show-prolog-vars ,@(variables-in goals)))))
    (loop for depth from *depth-start* to *depth-max* by *depth-incr*
          while (let ((*search-cut-off* nil))
                  (prove-all all-goals no-bindings depth)
                  *search-cut-off*)))
  (format t "~&No.")
  (values))
```

There is one final complication. When we increase the depth of search, we may
find some new proofs, but we will also find all the old proofs that were found on the
previous iteration. We can modify show-prolog-vars to only print proofs that are
found with a depth less than the increment—that is, those that were not found on the
previous iteration.

```
(defun show-prolog-vars (vars bindings other-goals depth)
  "Print each variable with its binding.
  Then ask the user if more solutions are desired."
  (if (> depth *depth-incr*)
      fail
      (progn
        (if (null vars)
            (format t "~&Yes")
            (dolist (var vars)
              (format t "~&~a = ~a" var
                      (subst-bindings bindings var))))
        (if (continue-p)
            fail
            (prove-all other-goals bindings depth)))))
```

To test that this works, try setting *depth-max* to 5 and running the following
assertions and query. The infinite loop is avoided, and the first four solutions
are found.

```
(<- (natural 0))
(<- (natural (1+ ?n)) (natural ?n))

> (?- (natural ?n))
?N = 0;
?N = (1+ 0);
?N = (1+ (1+ 0));
?N = (1+ (1+ (1+ 0)));
No.
```

14.10   Solutions to the Expressiveness Problems

In this section we present solutions to three of the limitations described above:

- Treatment of (limited) higher-order predications.

- Introduction of a frame-based syntax.

- Support for possible worlds, negation, and disjunction.

We also introduce a way to attach functions to predicates to do forward-chaining and error detection, and we discuss ways to extend unification to handle Skolem constants and other problems.

Higher-Order Predications

First we will tackle the problem of answering questions like "What kinds of animals are there?" Paradoxically, the key to allowing more expressiveness in this case is to invent a new, more limited language and insist that all assertions and queries are made in that language. That way, queries that would have been higher-order in the original language become first-order in the restricted language.

The language admits three types of objects: *categories, relations,* and *individuals.* A category corresponds to a one-place predicate, a relation to a two-place predicate, and an individual to constant, or zero-place predicate. Statements in the language must have one of five primitive operators: sub, rel, ind, val, and and. They have the following form:

```
(sub subcategory supercategory)
(rel relation domain-category range-category)
(ind individual category)
(val relation individual value)
(and assertion ...)
```

The following table gives some examples, along with English translations:

```
(sub dog animal)          Dog is a kind of animal.
(rel birthday animal date) The birthday relation holds between each animal
                               and some date.
(ind fido dog)            The individual Fido is categorized as a dog.
(val birthday fido july-1) The birthday of Fido is July-1.
(and A B)                 Both A and B are true.
```

For those who feel more comfortable with predicate calculus, the following table gives the formal definition of each primitive. The most complicated definition is for rel. The form (rel $R\ A\ B$) means that every R holds between an individual of A and an individual of B, and furthermore that every individual of A participates in at least one R relation.

$$
\begin{array}{ll}
\text{(sub } A\ B) & \forall x : A(x) \supset B(x) \\
\text{(rel } R\ A\ B) & \forall x, y : R(x,y) \supset A(x) \wedge B(y) \\
& \wedge \forall x A(x) \supset \exists y : R(x,y) \\
\text{(ind } I\ C) & C(I) \\
\text{(val } R\ I\ V) & R(I,V) \\
\text{(and } P\ Q...) & P \wedge Q...
\end{array}
$$

Queries in the language, not surprisingly, have the same form as assertions, except that they may contain variables as well as constants. Thus, to find out what kinds of animals there are, use the query (sub ?kind animal). To find out what individual animals there are, use the query (ind ?x animal). To find out what individual animals of what kinds there are, use:

```
(and (sub ?kind animal) (ind ?x ?kind))
```

The implemention of this new language can be based directly on the previous implementation of dtrees. Each assertion is stored as a fact in a dtree, except that the components of an and assertion are stored separately. The function add-fact does this:

```
(defun add-fact (fact)
  "Add the fact to the data base."
  (if (eq (predicate fact) 'and)
      (mapc #'add-fact (args fact))
      (index fact)))
```

Querying this new data base consists of querying the dtree just as before, but with a special case for conjunctive (and) queries. Conceptually, the function to do this, retrieve-fact, should be as simple as the following:

```
(defun retrieve-fact (query)
  "Find all facts that match query. Return a list of bindings.
  Warning!! this version is incomplete."
  (if (eq (predicate query) 'and)
      (retrieve-conjunction (args query))
      (retrieve query bindings)))
```

Unfortunately, there are some complications. Think about what must be done in `retrieve-conjunction`. It is passed a list of conjuncts and must return a list of binding lists, where each binding list satisfies the query. For example, to find out what people were born on July 1st, we could use the query:

```
(and (val birthday ?p july-1) (ind ?p person))
```

`retrieve-conjunction` could solve this problem by first calling `retrieve-fact` on `(val birthday ?p july-1)`. Once that is done, there is only one conjunct remaining, but in general there could be several, so we need to call `retrieve-conjunction` recursively with two arguments: the remaining conjuncts, and the result that `retrieve-fact` gave for the first solution. Since `retrieve-fact` returns a list of binding lists, it will be easiest if `retrieve-conjunction` accepts such a list as its second argument. Furthermore, when it comes time to call `retrieve-fact` on the second conjunct, we will want to respect the bindings set up by the first conjunct. So `retrieve-fact` must accept a binding list as its second argument. Thus we have:

```
(defun retrieve-fact (query &optional (bindings no-bindings))
  "Find all facts that match query.  Return a list of bindings."
  (if (eq (predicate query) 'and)
      (retrieve-conjunction (args query) (list bindings))
      (retrieve query bindings)))

(defun retrieve-conjunction (conjuncts bindings-lists)
  "Return a list of binding lists satisfying the conjuncts."
  (mapcan
    #'(lambda (bindings)
        (cond ((eq bindings fail) nil)
              ((null conjuncts) (list bindings))
              (t (retrieve-conjunction
                   (rest conjuncts)
                   (retrieve-fact
                     (subst-bindings bindings (first conjuncts))
                     bindings)))))
    bindings-lists))
```

Notice that `retrieve` and therefore `mapc-retrieve` now also must accept a binding list. The changes to them are shown in the following. In each case the extra argument is made optional so that previously written functions that call these functions without passing in the extra argument will still work.

```
(defun mapc-retrieve (fn query &optional (bindings no-bindings))
  "For every fact that matches the query,
   apply the function to the binding list."
  (dolist (bucket (fetch query))
    (dolist (answer bucket)
      (let ((new-bindings (unify query answer bindings)))
        (unless (eq new-bindings fail)
          (funcall fn new-bindings))))))

(defun retrieve (query &optional (bindings no-bindings))
  "Find all facts that match query.  Return a list of bindings."
  (let ((answers nil))
    (mapc-retrieve #'(lambda (bindings) (push bindings answers))
                   query bindings)
    answers))
```

Now add-fact and retrieve-fact comprise all we need to implement the language. Here is a short example where add-fact is used to add facts about bears and dogs, both as individuals and as species:

```
> (add-fact '(sub dog animal)) ⇒ T
> (add-fact '(sub bear animal)) ⇒ T
> (add-fact '(ind Fido dog)) ⇒ T
> (add-fact '(ind Yogi bear)) ⇒ T
> (add-fact '(val color Yogi brown)) ⇒ T
> (add-fact '(val color Fido golden)) ⇒ T
> (add-fact '(val latin-name bear ursidae)) ⇒ T
> (add-fact '(val latin-name dog canis-familiaris)) ⇒ T
```

Now retrieve-fact is used to answer three questions: What kinds of animals are there? What are the Latin names of each kind of animal? and What are the colors of each individual bear?

```
> (retrieve-fact '(sub ?kind animal))
((((?KIND . DOG))
 ((?KIND . BEAR)))

> (retrieve-fact '(and (sub ?kind animal)
                       (val latin-name ?kind ?latin)))
((((?LATIN . CANIS-FAMILIARIS) (?KIND . DOG))
 ((?LATIN . URSIDAE) (?KIND . BEAR)))
```

```
> (retrieve-fact '(and (ind ?x bear) (val color ?x ?c)))
((((?C . BROWN) (?X . YOGI)))
```

Improvements

There are quite a few improvements that can be made to this system. One direction is to provide different kinds of answers to queries. The following two functions are similar to retrieve-matches in that they return lists of solutions that match the query, rather than lists of possible bindings:

```
(defun retrieve-bagof (query)
  "Find all facts that match query.
  Return a list of queries with bindings filled in."
  (mapcar #'(lambda (bindings) (subst-bindings bindings query))
          (retrieve-fact query)))

(defun retrieve-setof (query)
  "Find all facts that match query.
  Return a list of unique queries with bindings filled in."
  (remove-duplicates (retrieve-bagof query) :test #'equal))
```

Another direction to take is to provide better error checking. The current system does not complain if a fact or query is ill-formed. It also relies on the user to input all facts, even those that could be derived automatically from the semantics of existing facts. For example, the semantics of sub imply that if (sub bear animal) and (sub polar-bear bear) are true, then (sub polar-bear animal) must also be true. This kind of implication can be handled in two ways. The typical Prolog approach would be to write rules that derive the additional sub facts by backward-chaining. Then every query would have to check if there were rules to run. The alternative is to use a *forward-chaining* approach, which caches each new sub fact by adding it to the data base. This latter alternative takes more storage, but because it avoids rederiving the same facts over and over again, it tends to be faster.

The following version of add-fact does error checking, and it automatically caches facts that can be derived from existing facts. Both of these things are done by a set of functions that are attached to the primitive operators. It is done in a data-driven style to make it easier to add new primitives, should that become necessary.

The function add-fact checks that each argument to a primitive relation is a nonvariable atom, and it also calls fact-present-p to check if the fact is already present in the data base. If not, it indexes the fact and calls run-attached-fn to do additional checking and caching:

```
(defparameter *primitives* '(and sub ind rel val))
```

```
(defun add-fact (fact)
  "Add the fact to the data base."
  (cond ((eq (predicate fact) 'and)
         (mapc #'add-fact (args fact)))
        ((or (not (every #'atom (args fact)))
             (some #'variable-p (args fact))
             (not (member (predicate fact) *primitives*)))
         (error "Ill-formed fact: ~a" fact))
        ((not (fact-present-p fact))
         (index fact)
         (run-attached-fn fact)))
  t)

(defun fact-present-p (fact)
  "Is this fact present in the data base?"
  (retrieve fact))
```

The attached functions are stored on the operator's property list under the indicator attached-fn:

```
(defun run-attached-fn (fact)
  "Run the function associated with the predicate of this fact."
  (apply (get (predicate fact) 'attached-fn) (args fact)))

(defmacro def-attached-fn (pred args &body body)
  "Define the attached function for a primitive."
  '(setf (get ',pred 'attached-fn)
         #'(lambda ,args .,body)))
```

The attached functions for ind and val are fairly simple. If we know (sub bear animal), then when (ind Yogi bear) is asserted, we have to also assert (ind Yogi animal). Similarly, the values in a val assertion must be individuals of the categories in the relation's rel assertion. That is, if (rel birthday animal date) is a fact and (val birthday Lee july-1) is added, then we can conclude (ind Lee animal) and (ind july-1 date). The following functions add the appropriate facts:

```
(def-attached-fn ind (individual category)
  ;; Cache facts about inherited categories
  (query-bind (?super) '(sub ,category ?super)
    (add-fact '(ind ,individual ,?super))))
```

```
(def-attached-fn val (relation ind1 ind2)
  ;; Make sure the individuals are the right kinds
  (query-bind (?cat1 ?cat2) '(rel ,relation ?cat1 ?cat2)
    (add-fact '(ind ,ind1 ,?cat1))
    (add-fact '(ind ,ind2 ,?cat2))))
```

The attached function for rel simply runs the attached function for any individual of the given relation. Normally one would make all rel assertions before ind assertions, so this will have no effect at all. But we want to be sure the data base stays consistent even if facts are asserted in an unusual order.

```
(def-attached-fn rel (relation cat1 cat2)
  ;; Run attached function for any IND's of this relation
  (query-bind (?a ?b) '(ind ,relation ?a ?b)
    (run-attached-fn '(ind ,relation ,?a ,?b))))
```

The most complicated attached function is for sub. Adding a fact such as (sub bear animal) causes the following to happen:

- All of animal's supercategories (such as living-thing) become supercategories of all of bear's subcategories (such as polar-bear).

- animal itself becomes a supercategory all of bear's subcategories.

- bear itself becomes a subcategory of all of animal's supercategories.

- All of the individuals of bear become individuals of animal and its supercategories.

The following accomplishes these four tasks. It does it with four calls to index-new-fact, which is used instead of add-fact because we don't need to run the attached function on the new facts. We do, however, need to make sure that we aren't indexing the same fact twice.

```
(def-attached-fn sub (subcat supercat)
  ;; Cache SUB facts
  (query-bind (?super-super) '(sub ,supercat ?super-super)
    (index-new-fact '(sub ,subcat ,?super-super))
    (query-bind (?sub-sub) '(sub ?sub-sub ,subcat)
      (index-new-fact '(sub ,?sub-sub ,?super-super))))
  (query-bind (?sub-sub) '(sub ?sub-sub ,subcat)
    (index-new-fact '(sub ,?sub-sub ,supercat)))
  ;; Cache IND facts
  (query-bind (?super-super) '(sub ,subcat ?super-super)
    (query-bind (?sub-sub) '(sub ?sub-sub ,supercat)
      (query-bind (?ind) '(ind ?ind ,?sub-sub)
        (index-new-fact '(ind ,?ind ,?super-super))))))
```

```
(defun index-new-fact (fact)
  "Index the fact in the data base unless it is already there."
  (unless (fact-present-p fact)
    (index fact)))
```

The following function tests the attached functions. It shows that adding the single fact (sub bear animal) to the given data base causes 18 new facts to be added.

```
(defun test-bears ()
  (clear-dtrees)
  (mapc #'add-fact
        '((sub animal living-thing)
          (sub living-thing thing) (sub polar-bear bear)
          (sub grizzly bear) (ind Yogi bear) (ind Lars polar-bear)
          (ind Helga grizzly)))
  (trace index)
  (add-fact '(sub bear animal))
  (untrace index))

> (test-bears)
(1 ENTER INDEX: (SUB BEAR ANIMAL))
(1 EXIT INDEX: T)
(1 ENTER INDEX: (SUB BEAR THING))
(1 EXIT INDEX: T)
(1 ENTER INDEX: (SUB GRIZZLY THING))
(1 EXIT INDEX: T)
(1 ENTER INDEX: (SUB POLAR-BEAR THING))
(1 EXIT INDEX: T)
(1 ENTER INDEX: (SUB BEAR LIVING-THING))
(1 EXIT INDEX: T)
(1 ENTER INDEX: (SUB GRIZZLY LIVING-THING))
(1 EXIT INDEX: T)
(1 ENTER INDEX: (SUB POLAR-BEAR LIVING-THING))
(1 EXIT INDEX: T)
(1 ENTER INDEX: (SUB GRIZZLY ANIMAL))
(1 EXIT INDEX: T)
(1 ENTER INDEX: (SUB POLAR-BEAR ANIMAL))
(1 EXIT INDEX: T)
(1 ENTER INDEX: (IND LARS LIVING-THING))
(1 EXIT INDEX: T)
(1 ENTER INDEX: (IND HELGA LIVING-THING))
(1 EXIT INDEX: T)
(1 ENTER INDEX: (IND YOGI LIVING-THING))
(1 EXIT INDEX: T)
(1 ENTER INDEX: (IND LARS THING))
(1 EXIT INDEX: T)
(1 ENTER INDEX: (IND HELGA THING))
```

```
(1 EXIT INDEX: T)
(1 ENTER INDEX: (IND YOGI THING))
(1 EXIT INDEX: T)
(1 ENTER INDEX: (IND LARS ANIMAL))
(1 EXIT INDEX: T)
(1 ENTER INDEX: (IND HELGA ANIMAL))
(1 EXIT INDEX: T)
(1 ENTER INDEX: (IND YOGI ANIMAL))
(1 EXIT INDEX: T)
(INDEX)
```

A Frame Language

Another direction we can take is to provide an alternative syntax that will be easier to read and write. Many representation languages are based on the idea of *frames*, and their syntax reflects this. A frame is an object with slots. We will continue to use the same data base in the same format, but we will provide an alternative syntax that considers the individuals and categories as frames, and the relations as slots.

Here is an example of the frame syntax for individuals, which uses the operator a. Note that it is more compact than the equivalent notation using the primitives.

```
(a person (name Joe) (age 27)) ≡

(and (ind person1 person)
     (val name person1 Joe)
     (val age person1 27))
```

The syntax also allows for nested expressions to appear as the values of slots. Notice that the Skolem constant person1 was generated automatically; an alternative is to supply a constant for the individual after the category name. For example, the following says that Joe is a person of age 27 whose best friend is a person named Fran who is 28 and whose best friend is Joe:

```
(a person p1 (name Joe) (age 27)
   (best-friend (a person (name Fran) (age 28)
                  (best-friend p1)))) ≡

(and (ind p1 person) (val name p1 joe) (val age p1 27)
     (ind person2 person) (val name person2 fran)
     (val age person2 28) (val best-friend person2 p1)
     (val best-friend p1 person2))
```

The frame syntax for categories uses the operator each. For example:

```
(each person (isa animal) (name person-name) (age integer)) ≡

(and (sub person animal)
     (rel name person person-name)
     (rel age person integer))
```

The syntax for queries is the same as for assertions, except that variables are used instead of the Skolem constants. This is true even when the Skolem constants are automatically generated, as in the following query:

```
(a person (age 27)) ≡ (AND (IND ?3 PERSON) (VAL AGE ?3 27))
```

To support the frame notation, we define the macros a and each to make assertions and ?? to make queries.

```
(defmacro a (&rest args)
  "Define a new individual and assert facts about it in the data base."
  '(add-fact ',(translate-exp (cons 'a args))))

(defmacro each (&rest args)
  "Define a new category and assert facts about it in the data base."
  '(add-fact ',(translate-exp (cons 'each args))))

(defmacro ?? (&rest queries)
  "Return a list of answers satisfying the query or queries."
  '(retrieve-setof
     ',(translate-exp (maybe-add 'and (replace-?-vars queries))
                      :query)))
```

All three of these macros call on translate-exp to translate from the frame syntax to the primitive syntax. Note that an a or each expression is computing a conjunction of primitive relations, but it is also computing a *term* when it is used as the nested value of a slot. It would be possible to do this by returning multiple values, but it is easier to build translate-exp as a set of local functions that construct facts and push them on the local variable conjuncts. At the end, the list of conjuncts is returned as the value of the translation. The local functions translate-a and translate-each return the atom that represents the term they are translating. The local function translate translates any kind of expression, translate-slot handles a slot, and collect-fact is responsible for pushing a fact onto the list of conjuncts. The optional argument query-mode-p tells what to do if the individual is not provided in an a expression. If query-mode-p is true, the individual will be represented by a variable; otherwise it will be a Skolem constant.

```lisp
(defun translate-exp (exp &optional query-mode-p)
  "Translate exp into a conjunction of the four primitives."
  (let ((conjuncts nil))
    (labels
        ((collect-fact (&rest terms) (push terms conjuncts))

         (translate (exp)
           ;; Figure out what kind of expression this is
           (cond
             ((atom exp) exp)
             ((eq (first exp) 'a) (translate-a (rest exp)))
             ((eq (first exp) 'each) (translate-each (rest exp)))
             (t (apply #'collect-fact exp) exp)))

         (translate-a (args)
           ;; translate (A category [ind] (rel filler)*)
           (let* ((category (pop args))
                  (self (cond ((and args (atom (first args)))
                               (pop args))
                              (query-mode-p (gentemp "?"))
                              (t (gentemp (string category))))))
             (collect-fact 'ind self category)
             (dolist (slot args)
               (translate-slot 'val self slot))
             self))

         (translate-each (args)
           ;; translate (EACH category [(isa cat*)] (slot cat)*)
           (let* ((category (pop args)))
             (when (eq (predicate (first args)) 'isa)
               (dolist (super (rest (pop args)))
                 (collect-fact 'sub category super)))
             (dolist (slot args)
               (translate-slot 'rel category slot))
             category))

         (translate-slot (primitive self slot)
           ;; translate (relation value) into a REL or SUB
           (assert (= (length slot) 2))
           (collect-fact primitive (first slot) self
                         (translate (second slot)))))

      ;; Body of translate-exp:
      (translate exp) ;; Build up the list of conjuncts
      (maybe-add 'and (nreverse conjuncts)))))
```

The auxiliary functions `maybe-add` and `replace-?-vars` are shown in the following:

```lisp
(defun maybe-add (op exps &optional if-nil)
  "For example, (maybe-add 'and exps t) returns
  t if exps is nil, (first exps) if there is only one,
  and (and exp1 exp2...) if there are several exps."
  (cond ((null exps) if-nil)
        ((length=1 exps) (first exps))
        (t (cons op exps))))

(defun length=1 (x)
  "Is x a list of length 1?"
  (and (consp x) (null (cdr x))))

(defun replace-?-vars (exp)
  "Replace each ? in exp with a temporary var: ?123"
  (cond ((eq exp '?) (gentemp "?"))
        ((atom exp) exp)
        (t (reuse-cons (replace-?-vars (first exp))
                       (replace-?-vars (rest exp))
                       exp))))
```

Possible Worlds: Truth, Negation, and Disjunction

In this section we address four problems: distinguishing unknown from `false`, representing negations, representing disjunctions, and representing multiple possible states of affairs. It turns out that all four problems can be solved by introducing two new techniques: possible worlds and negated predicates. The solution is not completely general, but it is practical in a wide variety of applications.

There are two basic ways to distinguish unknown from false. The first possibility is to store a truth value—`true` or `false`—along with each proposition. The second possibility is to include the truth value as part of the proposition. There are several syntactic variations on this theme. The following table shows the possibilities for the propositions "Jan likes Dean is true" and "Jan likes Ian is false:"

Approach	True Prop.	False Prop.
(1)	`(likes Jan Dean) -- true`	`(likes Jan Ian) -- false`
(2a)	`(likes true Jan Dean)`	`(likes false Jan Ian)`
(2b)	`(likes Jan Dean)`	`(not (likes Jan Dean))`
(2c)	`(likes Jan Dean)`	`(~likes Jan Dean)`

The difference between (1) and (2) shows up when we want to make a query. With (1), we make the single query `(likes Jan Dean)` (or perhaps `(likes Jan ?x)`), and the answers will tell us who Jan does and does not like. With (2), we make one query to find out what liking relationships are true, and another to find out which ones are false. In either approach, if there are no responses then the answer is truly unknown.

Approach (1) is better for applications where most queries are of the form "Is this sentence true or false?" But applications that include backward-chaining rules are not like this. The typical backward-chaining rule says "Conclude X is true if Y is true." Thus, most queries will be of the type "Is Y true?" Therefore, some version of approach (2) is preferred.

Representing true and false opens the door to a host of possible extensions. First, we could add multiple truth values beyond the simple "true" and "false." These could be symbolic values like "probably-true" or "false-by-default" or they could be numeric values representing probabilities or certainty factors.

Second, we could introduce the idea of *possible worlds*. That is, the truth of a proposition could be unknown in the current world, but true if we assume p, and false if we assume q. In the possible world approach, this is handled by calling the current world W, and then creating a new world W_1, which is just like W except that p is true, and W_2, which is just like W except that q is true. By doing reasoning in different worlds we can make predictions about the future, resolve ambiguitites about the current state, and do reasoning by cases.

For example, possible worlds allow us to solve Moore's communism/democracy problem (page 466). We create two new possible worlds, one where E is a democracy and one where it is communist. In each world it is easy to derive that there is a democracy next to a communist country. The trick is to realize then that the two worlds form a partition, and that therefore the assertion holds in the original "real" world as well. This requires an interaction between the Prolog-based tactical reasoning going on within a world and the planning-based strategic reasoning that decides which worlds to consider.

We could also add a *truth maintenance system* (or TMS) to keep track of the assumptions or justifications that lead to each fact being considered true. A truth maintenance system can lessen the need to backtrack in a search for a global solution. Although truth maintenance systems are an important part of AI programming, they will not be covered in this book.

In this section we extend the dtree facility (section 14.8) to handle truth values and possible worlds. With so many options, it is difficult to make design choices. We will choose a fairly simple system, one that remains close to the simplicity and speed of Prolog but offers additional functionality when needed. We will adopt approach (2c) to truth values, using negated predicates. For example, the negated predicate of `likes` is `~likes`, which is pronounced "not likes."

We will also provide minimal support for possible worlds. Assume that there is always a current world, W, and that there is a way to create alternative worlds and change the current world to an alternative one. Assertions and queries will always be made with respect to the current world. Each fact is indexed by the atoms it contains, just as before. The difference is that the facts are also indexed by the current world. To support this, we need to modify the notion of the numbered list, or `nlist`, to include a numbered association list, or `nalist`. The following is an `nalist` showing six facts indexed under three different worlds: W0, W1, and W2:

```
(6 (W0 #1# #2# #3#) (W1 #4#) (W2 #5# #6#))
```

The fetching routine will remain unchanged, but the postfetch processing will have to sort through the nalists to find only the facts in the current world. It would also be possible for `fetch` to do this work, but the reasoning is that most facts will be indexed under the "real world," and only a few facts will exist in alternative, hypothetical worlds. Therefore, we should delay the effort of sorting through the answers to eliminate those answers in the wrong world—it may be that the first answer fetched will suffice, and then it would have been a waste to go through and eliminate other answers. The following changes to `index` and `dtree-index` add support for worlds:

```lisp
(defvar *world* 'W0 "The current world used by index and fetch.")

(defun index (key &optional (world *world*))
  "Store key in a dtree node.  Key must be (predicate . args);
  it is stored in the dtree, indexed by the world."
  (dtree-index key key world (get-dtree (predicate key))))

(defun dtree-index (key value world dtree)
  "Index value under all atoms of key in dtree."
  (cond
    ((consp key)               ; index on both first and rest
     (dtree-index (first key) value world
                  (or (dtree-first dtree)
                      (setf (dtree-first dtree) (make-dtree))))
     (dtree-index (rest key) value world
                  (or (dtree-rest dtree)
                      (setf (dtree-rest dtree) (make-dtree)))))
    ((null key))               ; don't index on nil

    ((variable-p key)          ; index a variable
     (nalist-push world value (dtree-var dtree)))
    (t ;; Make sure there is an nlist for this atom, and add to it
     (nalist-push world value (lookup-atom key dtree)))))
```

The new function `nalist-push` adds a value to an nalist, either by inserting the value in an existing key's list or by adding a new key/value list:

```
(defun nalist-push (key val nalist)
  "Index val under key in a numbered alist."
  ;; An nalist is of the form (count (key val*)*)
  ;; Ex: (6 (nums 1 2 3) (letters a b c))
  (incf (car nalist))
  (let ((pair (assoc key (cdr nalist))))
    (if pair
        (push val (cdr pair))
        (push (list key val) (cdr nalist)))))
```

In the following, `fetch` is used on the same data base created by `test-index`, indexed under the world `W0`. This time the result is a list-of-lists of world/values a-lists. The count, 3, is the same as before.

```
> (fetch '(p ?x c))
(((W0 (P B C) (P A C)))
 ((W0 (P A ?X))))
3
```

So far, worlds have been represented as symbols, with the implication that different symbols represent completely distinct worlds. That doesn't make worlds very easy to use. We would like to be able to use worlds to explore alternatives—create a new hypothetical world, make some assumptions (by asserting them as facts in the hypothetical world), and see what can be derived in that world. It would be tedious to have to copy all the facts from the real world into each hypothetical world.

An alternative is to establish an inheritance hierarchy among worlds. Then a fact is considered true if it is indexed in the current world or in any world that the current world inherits from.

To support inheritance, we will implement worlds as structures with a name field and a field for the list of parents the world inherits from. Searching through the inheritance lattice could become costly, so we will do it only once each time the user changes worlds, and mark all the current worlds by setting the `current` field on or off. Here is the definition for the world structure:

```
(defstruct (world (:print-function print-world))
  name parents current)
```

We will need a way to get from the name of a world to the world structure. Assuming names are symbols, we can store the structure on the name's property list. The function `get-world` gets the structure for a name, or builds a new one and stores it. `get-world` can also be passed a world instead of a name, in which case it just returns the world. We also include a definition of the default initial world.

```lisp
(defun get-world (name &optional current (parents (list *world*)))
  "Look up or create the world with this name.
  If the world is new, give it the list of parents."
  (cond ((world-p name) name) ; ok if it already is a world
        ((get name 'world))
        (t (setf (get name 'world)
                 (make-world :name name :parents parents
                             :current current)))))

(defvar *world* (get-world 'W0 nil nil)
  "The current world used by index and fetch.")
```

The function use-world is used to switch to a new world. It first makes the current world and all its parents no longer current, and then makes the new chosen world and all its parents current. The function use-new-world is more efficient in the common case where you want to create a new world that inherits from the current world. It doesn't have to turn any worlds off; it just creates the new world and makes it current.

```lisp
(defun use-world (world)
  "Make this world current."
  ;; If passed a name, look up the world it names
  (setf world (get-world world))
  (unless (eq world *world*)
    ;; Turn the old world(s) off and the new one(s) on,
    ;; unless we are already using the new world
    (set-world-current *world* nil)
    (set-world-current world t)
    (setf *world* world)))

(defun use-new-world ()
  "Make up a new world and use it.
  The world inherits from the current world."
  (setf *world* (get-world (gensym "W")))
  (setf (world-current *world*) t)
  *world*)

(defun set-world-current (world on/off)
  "Set the current field of world and its parents on or off."
  ;; nil is off, anything else is on.
  (setf (world-current world) on/off)
  (dolist (parent (world-parents world))
    (set-world-current parent on/off)))
```

We also add a print function for worlds, which just prints the world's name.

```lisp
(defun print-world (world &optional (stream t) depth)
  (declare (ignore depth))
  (prin1 (world-name world) stream))
```

The format of the dtree data base has changed to include worlds, so we need new retrieval functions to search through this new format. Here the functions `mapc-retrieve`, `retrieve`, and `retrieve-bagof` are modified to give new versions that treat worlds. To reflect this change, the new functions all have names ending in `-in-world`:

```lisp
(defun mapc-retrieve-in-world (fn query)
  "For every fact in the current world that matches the query,
  apply the function to the binding list."
  (dolist (bucket (fetch query))
    (dolist (world/entries bucket)
      (when (world-current (first world/entries))
        (dolist (answer (rest world/entries))
          (let ((bindings (unify query answer)))
            (unless (eq bindings fail)
              (funcall fn bindings))))))))

(defun retrieve-in-world (query)
  "Find all facts that match query.  Return a list of bindings."
  (let ((answers nil))
    (mapc-retrieve-in-world
      #'(lambda (bindings) (push bindings answers))
      query)
    answers))

(defun retrieve-bagof-in-world (query)
  "Find all facts in the current world that match query.
  Return a list of queries with bindings filled in."
  (mapcar #'(lambda (bindings) (subst-bindings bindings query))
          (retrieve-in-world query)))
```

Now let's see how these worlds work. First, in W0 we see that the facts from `test-index` are still in the data base:

```lisp
> *world* ⇒ W0

> (retrieve-bagof-in-world '(p ?z c)) ⇒
((P A C) (P A C) (P B C))
```

Now we create and use a new world that inherits from W0. Two new facts are added to this new world:

```
> (use-new-world) ⇒ W7031
> (index '(p new c)) ⇒ T
> (index '(~p b b)) ⇒ T
```

We see that the two new facts are accessible in this world:

```
> (retrieve-bagof-in-world '(p ?z c)) ⇒
((P A C) (P A C) (P B C) (P NEW C))
> (retrieve-bagof-in-world '(~p ?x ?y)) ⇒
((~P B B))
```

Now we create another world as an alternative to the current one by first switching back to the original W0, then creating the new world, and then adding some facts:

```
> (use-world 'W0) ⇒ W0
> (use-new-world) ⇒ W7173
> (index '(p newest c)) ⇒ T
> (index '(~p c newest)) ⇒ T
```

Here we see that the facts entered in W7031 are not accessible, but the facts in the new world and in W0 are:

```
> (retrieve-bagof-in-world '(p ?z c)) ⇒
((P A C) (P A C) (P B C) (P NEWEST C))
> (retrieve-bagof-in-world '(~p ?x ?y)) ⇒
((~P C NEWEST))
```

Unification, Equality, Types, and Skolem Constants

The lesson of the zebra puzzle in section 11.4 was that unification can be used to lessen the need for backtracking, because an uninstantiated logic variable or partially instantiated term can stand for a whole range of possible solutions. However, this advantage can quickly disappear when the representation forces the problem solver to enumerate possible solutions rather than treating a whole range of solutions as one. For example, consider the following query in the frame language and its expansion into primitives:

```
(a person (name Fran))
≡ (and (ind ?p person) (val name ?p fran))
```

The way to answer this query is to enumerate all individuals ?p of type person and then check the name slot of each such person. It would be more efficient if (ind ?p person) did not act as an enumeration, but rather as a constraint on the possible values of ?p. This would be possible if we changed the definition of variables (and of the unification function) so that each variable had a type associated with it. In fact, there are at least three sources of information that have been implemented as constraints on variables terms:

- The type or category of the term.

- The members or size of a term considered as a set or list.

- Other terms this term is equal or not equal to.

Note that with a good solution to the problem of equality, we can solve the problem of Skolem constants. The idea is that a regular constant unifies with itself but no other regular constant. On the other hand, a Skolem constant can potentially unify with any other constant (regular or Skolem). The equality mechanism is used to keep track of each Skolem variable's possible bindings.

14.11   History and References

Brachman and Levesque (1985) collect thirty of the key papers in knowledge representation. Included are some early approaches to semantic network based (Quillian 1967) and logic-based (McCarthy 1968) representation. Two thoughtful critiques of the ad hoc use of representations without defining their meaning are by Woods (1975) and McDermott (1978). It is interesting to contrast the latter with McDermott 1987, which argues that logic by itself is not sufficient to solve the problems of AI. This argument should not be surprising to those who remember the slogan *logic = algorithm − control*.

Genesereth and Nilsson's textbook (1987) cover the predicate-calculus-based approach to knowledge representation and AI in general. Ernest Davis (1990) presents a good overview of the field that includes specialized representations for time, space, qualitative physics, propositional attitudes, and the interaction between agents.

Many representation languages focus on the problem of defining descriptions for categories of objects. These have come to be known as *term-subsumption languages*. Examples include KL-ONE (Schmolze and Lipkis 1983) and KRYPTON (Brachman, Fikes, and Levesque 1983). See Lakoff 1987 for much more on the problem of categories and prototypes.

Hector Levesque (1986) points out that the areas Prolog has difficulty with—disjunction, negation, and existentials—all involve a degree of vagueness. In his term, they lack *vividness*. A vivid proposition is one that could be represented directly in a picture: the car is blue; she has a martini in her left hand; Albany is the capital of New York. Nonvivid propositions cannot be so represented: the car is not blue; she has a martini in one hand; either Albany or New York City is the capital of New York. There is interest in separating vivid from nonvivid reasoning, but no current systems are actually built this way.

The possible world approach of section 14.10 was used in the MRS system (Russell 1985). More recent knowledge representation systems tend to use truth maintenance systems instead of possible worlds. This approach was pioneered by Doyle (1979) and McAllester (1982). Doyle tried to change the name to "reason maintenance," in (1983), but it was too late. The version in widest used today is the assumption-based truth maintenance system, or ATMS, developed by de Kleer (1986a,b,c). Charniak et al. (1987) present a complete Common Lisp implementation of a McAllester-style TMS.

There is little communication between the logic programming and knowledge representation communities, even though they cover overlapping territory. Colmerauer (1990) and Cohen (1990) describe Logic Programming languages that address some of the issues covered in this chapter. Key papers in equality reasoning include Galler and Fisher 1974, Kornfeld 1983,[1] Jaffar, Lassez, and Maher 1984, and van Emden and Yukawa 1987. Hölldobler's book (1987) includes an overview of the area. Papers on extending unification in ways other than equality include Aït-Kaci et al. 1987 and Staples and Robinson 1988. Finally, papers on extending Prolog to cover disjunction and negation (i.e., non-Horn clauses) include Loveland 1987, Plaisted 1988, and Stickel 1988.

14.12   Exercises

Exercise 14.1 [m]   Arrange to store dtrees in a hash table rather than on the property list of predicates.

Exercise 14.2 [m]   Arrange to store the `dtree-atoms` in a hash table rather than in an association list.

Exercise 14.3 [m]   Change the `dtree` code so that `nil` is used as an atom index. Time the performance on an application and see if the change helps or hurts.

---

[1]A commentary on this paper appears in Elcock and Hoddinott 1986.

Exercise 14.4 [m] Consider the query (p a b c d e f g). If the index under a returns only one or two keys, then it is probably a waste of time for dtree-fetch to consider the other keys in the hope of finding a smaller bucket. It is certainly a waste if there are no keys at all indexed under a. Make appropriate changes to dtree-fetch.

Exercise 14.5 [h] Arrange to delete elements from a dtree.

Exercise 14.6 [h] Implement iterative-deepening search in the Prolog compiler. You will have to change each function to accept the depth as an extra argument, and compile in checks for reaching the maximum depth.

Exercise 14.7 [d] Integrate the Prolog compiler with the dtree data base. Use the dtrees for predicates with a large number of clauses, and make sure that each predicate that is implemented as a dtree has a Prolog primitive accessing the dtree.

Exercise 14.8 [d] Add support for possible worlds to the Prolog compiler with dtrees. This support has already been provided for dtrees, but you will have to provide it for ordinary Prolog rules.

Exercise 14.9 [h] Integrate the language described in section 14.10 and the frame syntax from section 14.10 with the extended Prolog compiler from the previous exercise.

Exercise 14.10 [d] Build a strategic reasoner that decides when to create a possible world and does reasoning by cases over these worlds. Use it to solve Moore's problem (page 466).

14.13   Answers

Answer 14.1

```lisp
(let ((dtrees (make-hash-table :test #'eq)))

  (defun get-dtree (predicate)
    "Fetch (or make) the dtree for this predicate."
    (setf (gethash predicate dtrees)
          (or (gethash predicate dtrees)
              (make-dtree))))

  (defun clear-dtrees ()
    "Remove all the dtrees for all the predicates."
    (clrhash dtrees)))
```

Answer 14.5   Hint: here is the code for nlist-delete. Now figure out how to find all the nlists that an item is indexed under.

```lisp
(defun nlist-delete (item nlist)
  "Remove an element from an nlist.
  Assumes that item is present exactly once."
  (decf (car nlist))
  (setf (cdr nlist) (delete item (cdr nlist) :count 1))
  nlist)
```

PART IV

ADVANCED AI PROGRAMS

CHAPTER 15

Symbolic Mathematics with Canonical Forms

Anything simple always interests me.

—David Hockney

C hapter 8 started with high hopes: to take an existing pattern matcher, copy down some mathematical identities out of a reference book, and come up with a usable symbolic algebra system. The resulting system *was* usable for some purposes, and it showed that the technique of rule-based translation is a powerful one. However, the problems of section 8.5 show that not everything can be done easily and efficiently within the rule-based pattern matching framework.

There are important mathematical transformations that are difficult to express in the rule-based approach. For example, dividing two polynomials to obtain a quotient and remainder is a task that is easier to express as an algorithm—a program—than as a rule or set of rules.

In addition, there is a problem with efficiency. Pieces of the input expressions are simplified over and over again, and much time is spent interpreting rules that do not apply. Section 9.6 showed some techniques for speeding up the program by a factor of 100 on inputs of a dozen or so symbols, but for expressions with a hundred or so symbols, the speed-up is not enough. We can do better by designing a specialized representation from the ground up.

Serious algebraic manipulation programs generally enforce a notion of *canonical simplification*. That is, expressions are converted into a canonical internal format that may be far removed from the input form. They are then manipulated, and translated back to external form for output. Of course, the simplifier we have already does this kind of translation, to some degree. It translates (3 + x + -3 + y) into (+ x y) internally, and then outputs it as (x + y). But a *canonical* representation must have the property that any two expressions that are equal have identical canonical forms. In our system the expression (5 + y + x + -5) is translated to the internal form (+ y x), which is not identical to (+ x y), even though the two expressions are equal. Thus, our system is not canonical. Most of the problems of the previous section stem from the lack of a canonical form.

Adhering to canonical form imposes grave restrictions on the representation. For example, $x^2 - 1$ and $(x-1)(x+1)$ are equal, so they must be represented identically. One way to insure this is to multiply out all factors and collect similar terms. So $(x-1)(x+1)$ is $x^2 - x + x - 1$, which simplifies to $x^2 - 1$, in whatever the canonical internal form is. This approach works fine for $x^2 - 1$, but for an expression like $(x-1)^{1000}$, multiplying out all factors would be quite time- (and space-) consuming. It is hard to find a canonical form that is ideal for all problems. The best we can do is choose one that works well for the problems we are most likely to encounter.

15.1   A Canonical Form for Polynomials

This section will concentrate on a canonical form for *polynomials*. Mathematically speaking, a polynomial is a function (of one or more variables) that can be computed using only addition and multiplication. We will speak of a polynomial's *main variable, coefficents,* and *degree.* In the polynomial:

$$5 \times x^3 + b \times x^2 + c \times x + 1$$

the main variable is x, the degree is 3 (the highest power of x), and the coefficients are $5, b, c$ and 1. We can define an input format for polynomials as follows:

1. Any Lisp number is a polynomial.

2. Any Lisp symbol is a polynomial.

3. If p and q are polynomials, so are $(p + q)$ and $(p * q)$.

4. If p is a polynomial and n is a positive integer, then $(p \char`^ n)$ is a polynomial.

However, the input format cannot be used as the canonical form, because it would admit both $(x + y)$ and $(y + x)$, and both 4 and $(2 + 2)$.

Before considering a canonical form for polynomials, let us see why polynomials were chosen as the target domain. First, the volume of programming needed to support canonical forms for a larger class of expressions grows substantially. To make things easier, we have eliminated complications like log and trig functions. Polynomials are a good choice because they are closed under addition and multiplication: the sum or product of any two polynomials is a polynomial. If we had allowed division, the result would not be closed, because the quotient of two polynomials need not be a polynomial. As a bonus, polynomials are also closed under differentiation and integration, so we can include those operators as well.

Second, for sufficiently large classes of expressions it becomes not just difficult but impossible to define a canonical form. This may be surprising, and we don't have space here to explain exactly why it is so, but here is an argument: Consider what would happen if we added enough functionality to duplicate all of Lisp. Then "converting to canonical form" would be the same as "running a program." But it is an elementary result of computability theory that it is in general impossible to determine the result of running an arbitrary program (this is known as the halting problem). Thus, it is not surprising that it is impossible to canonicalize complex expressions.

Our task is to convert a polynomial as previously defined into some canonical form.[1] Much of the code and some of the commentary on this format and the routines to manipulate it was written by Richard Fateman, with some enhancements made by Peter Klier.

The first design decision is to assume that we will be dealing mostly with *dense* polynomials, rather than *sparse* ones. That is, we expect most of the polynomials to be like $ax^3 + bx^2 + cx + d$, not like $ax^{100} + bx^{50} + c$. For dense polynomials, we can save space by representing the main variable (x in these examples) and the individual coefficients ($a, b, c,$ and d in these examples) explicitly, but representing the exponents only implicitly, by position. Vectors will be used instead of lists, to save space and to allow fast access to any element. Thus, the representation of $5x^3 + 10x^2 + 20x + 30$ will be the vector:

```
#(x 30 20 10 5)
```

---

[1] In fact, the algebraic properties of polynomial arithmetic and its generalizations fit so well with ideas in data abstraction that an extended example (in Scheme) on this topic is provided in *Structure and Interpretation of Computer Programs* by Abelson and Sussman (see section 2.4.3, pages 153–166). We'll pursue a slightly different approach here.

The main variable, x, is in the 0th element of the vector, and the coefficient of the ith power of x is in element $i + 1$ of the vector. A single variable is represented as a vector whose first coefficient is 1, and a number is represented as itself:

```
#(x 30 20 10 5)  represents 5x³ + 10x² + 20x + 30
#(x 0 1)         represents x
5                represents 5
```

The fact that a number is represented as itself is a possible source of confusion. The number 5, for example, is a polynomial by our mathematical definition of polynomials. But it is represented as 5, not as a vector, so (typep 5 'polynomial) will be false. The word "polynomial" is used ambiguously to refer to both the mathematical concept and the Lisp type, but it should be clear from context which is meant.

A glossary for the canonical simplifier program is given in figure 15.1.

The functions defining the type polynomial follow. Because we are concerned with efficiency, we proclaim certain short functions to be compiled inline, use the specific function svref (simple-vector reference) rather than the more general aref, and provide declarations for the polynomials using the special form the. More details on efficiency issues are given in Chapter 9.

```
(proclaim '(inline main-var degree coef
                   var= var> poly make-poly))

(deftype polynomial () 'simple-vector)

(defun main-var (p) (svref (the polynomial p) 0))
(defun coef (p i)   (svref (the polynomial p) (+ i 1)))
(defun degree (p)    (- (length (the polynomial p)) 2))
```

We had to make another design decision in defining coef, the function to extract a coefficient from a polynomial. As stated above, the ith coefficient of a polynomial is in element $i + 1$ of the vector. If we required the caller of coef to pass in $i + 1$ to get i, we might be able to save a few addition operations. The design decision was that this would be too confusing and error prone. Thus, coef expects to be passed i and does the addition itself.

For our format, we will insist that main variables be symbols, while coefficients can be numbers or other polynomials. A "production" version of the program might have to account for main variables like (sin x), as well as other complications like + and * with more than two arguments, and noninteger powers.

Now we can extract information from a polynomial, but we also need to build and modify polynomials. The function poly takes a variable and some coefficients and builds a vector representing the polynomial. make-poly takes a variable and a degree and produces a polynomial with all zero coefficients.

	Top-Level Functions
`canon-simplifier`	A read-canonicalize-print loop.
`canon`	Canonicalize argument and convert it back to infix.
	Data Types
`polynomial`	A vector of main variable and coefficients.
	Major Functions
`prefix->canon`	Convert a prefix expression to canonical polynomial.
`canon->prefix`	Convert a canonical polynomial to a prefix expression.
`poly+poly`	Add two polynomials.
`poly*poly`	Multiply two polynomials.
`poly^n`	Raise polynomial p to the nth power, n>=0.
`deriv-poly`	Return the derivative, dp/dx, of the polynomial p.
	Auxiliary Functions
`poly`	Construct a polynomial with given coefficients.
`make-poly`	Construct a polynomial of given degree.
`coef`	Pick out the ith coefficient of a polynomial.
`main-var`	The main variable of a polynomial.
`degree`	The degree of a polynomial; (degree x^2) = 2.
`var=`	Are two variables identical?
`var>`	Is one variable ordered before another?
`poly+`	Unary or binary polynomial addition.
`poly-`	Unary or binary polynomial subtraction.
`k+poly`	Add a constant k to a polynomial p.
`k*poly`	Multiply a polynomial p by a constant k.
`poly+same`	Add two polynomials with the same main variable.
`poly*same`	Multiply two polynomials with the same main variable.
`normalize-poly`	Alter a polynomial by dropping trailing zeros.
`exponent->prefix`	Used to convert to prefix.
`args->prefix`	Used to convert to prefix.
`rat-numerator`	Select the numerator of a rational.
`rat-denominator`	Select the denominator of a rational.
`rat*rat`	Multiply two rationals.
`rat+rat`	Add two rationals.
`rat/rat`	Divide two rationals.

Figure 15.1: Glossary for the Symbolic Manipulation Program

```
(defun poly (x &rest coefs)
  "Make a polynomial with main variable x
  and coefficients in increasing order."
  (apply #'vector x coefs))

(defun make-poly (x degree)
  "Make the polynomial 0 + 0*x + 0*x^2 + ... 0*x^degree"
  (let ((p (make-array (+ degree 2) :initial-element 0)))
    (setf (main-var p) x)
    p))
```

A polynomial can be altered by setting its main variable or any one of its coefficients using the following defsetf forms.

```
(defsetf main-var (p) (val)
  '(setf (svref (the polynomial ,p) 0) ,val))

(defsetf coef (p i) (val)
  '(setf (svref (the polynomial ,p) (+ ,i 1)) ,val))
```

The function poly constructs polynomials in a fashion similar to list or vector: with an explicit list of the contents. make-poly, on the other hand, is like make-array: it makes a polynomial of a specified size.

We provide setf methods for modifying the main variable and coefficients. Since this is the first use of defsetf, it deserves some explanation. A defsetf form takes a function (or macro) name, an argument list, and a second argument list that must consist of a single argument, the value to be assigned. The body of the form is an expression that stores the value in the proper place. So the defsetf for main-var says that (setf (main-var p) val) is equivalent to (setf (svref (the polynomial p) 0) val). A defsetf is much like a defmacro, but there is a little less burden placed on the writer of defsetf. Instead of passing p and val directly to the setf method, Common Lisp binds local variables to these expressions, and passes those variables to the setf method. That way, the writer does not have to worry about evaluating the expressions in the wrong order or the wrong number of times. It is also possible to gain finer control over the whole process with define-setf-method, as explained on page 884.

The functions poly+poly, poly*poly and poly^n perform addition, multiplication, and exponentiation of polynomials, respectively. They are defined with several helping functions. k*poly multiplies a polynomial by a constant, k, which may be a number or another polynomial that is free of polynomial p's main variable. poly*same is used to multiply two polynomials with the same main variable. For addition, the functions k+poly and poly+same serve analogous purposes. With that in mind, here's the function to convert from prefix to canonical form:

```
(defun prefix->canon (x)
  "Convert a prefix Lisp expression to canonical form.
  Exs: (+ (^ x 2) (* 3 x)) => #(x 0 3 1)
       (- (* (- x 1) (+ x 1)) (- (^ x 2) 1)) => 0"
  (cond ((numberp x) x)
        ((symbolp x) (poly x 0 1))
        ((and (exp-p x) (get (exp-op x) 'prefix->canon))
         (apply (get (exp-op x) 'prefix->canon)
                (mapcar #'prefix->canon (exp-args x))))
        (t (error "Not a polynomial: ~a" x))))
```

It is data-driven, based on the `prefix->canon` property of each operator. In the following we install the appropriate functions. The existing functions `poly*poly` and `poly^n` can be used directly. But other operators need interface functions. The operators + and - need interface functions that handle both unary and binary.

```
(dolist (item '((+ poly+) (- poly-) (* poly*poly)
                (^ poly^n) (D deriv-poly)))
  (setf (get (first item) 'prefix->canon) (second item)))

(defun poly+ (&rest args)
  "Unary or binary polynomial addition."
  (ecase (length args)
    (1 (first args))
    (2 (poly+poly (first args) (second args)))))

(defun poly- (&rest args)
  "Unary or binary polynomial subtraction."
  (ecase (length args)
    (1 (poly*poly -1 (first args)))
    (2 (poly+poly (first args) (poly*poly -1 (second args))))))
```

The function `prefix->canon` accepts inputs that were not part of our definition of polynomials: unary positive and negation operators and binary subtraction and differentiation operators. These are permissible because they can all be reduced to the elementary + and * operations.

Remember that our problems with canonical form all began with the inability to decide which was simpler: (+ x y) or (+ y x). In this system, we define a canonical form by imposing an ordering on variables (we use alphabetic ordering as defined by `string>`). The rule is that a polynomial p can have coefficients that are polynomials in a variable later in the alphabet than p's main variable, but no coefficients that are polynomials in variables earlier than p's main variable. Here's how to compare variables:

```
(defun var= (x y) (eq x y))
(defun var> (x y) (string> x y))
```

The canonical form of the variable x will be #(x 0 1), which is $0 \times x^0 + 1 \times x^1$. The canonical form of (+ x y) is #(x #(y 0 1) 1). It couldn't be #(y #(x 0 1) 1), because then the resulting polynomial would have a coefficient with a lesser main variable. The policy of ordering variables assures canonicality, by properly grouping like variables together and by imposing a particular ordering on expressions that would otherwise be commutative.

Here, then, is the code for adding two polynomials:

```
(defun poly+poly (p q)
  "Add two polynomials."
  (normalize-poly
    (cond
      ((numberp p)                          (k+poly p q))
      ((numberp q)                          (k+poly q p))
      ((var= (main-var p) (main-var q)) (poly+same p q))
      ((var> (main-var q) (main-var p)) (k+poly q p))
      (t                                    (k+poly p q)))))

(defun k+poly (k p)
  "Add a constant k to a polynomial p."
  (cond ((eql k 0) p)                       ;; 0 + p = p
        ((and (numberp k)(numberp p))
         (+ k p))                           ;; Add numbers
        (t (let ((r (copy-poly p)))   ;; Add k to x^0 term of p
             (setf (coef r 0) (poly+poly (coef r 0) k))
             r))))

(defun poly+same (p q)
  "Add two polynomials with the same main variable."
  ;; First assure that q is the higher degree polynomial
  (if (> (degree p) (degree q))
      (poly+same q p)
      ;; Add each element of p into r (which is a copy of q).
      (let ((r (copy-poly q)))
        (loop for i from 0 to (degree p) do
              (setf (coef r i) (poly+poly (coef r i) (coef p i))))
        r)))

(defun copy-poly (p)
  "Make a copy a polynomial."
  (copy-seq p))
```

and the code for multiplying polynomials:

```
(defun poly*poly (p q)
  "Multiply two polynomials."
  (normalize-poly
    (cond
      ((numberp p)                       (k*poly p q))
      ((numberp q)                       (k*poly q p))
      ((var= (main-var p) (main-var q)) (poly*same p q))
      ((var> (main-var q) (main-var p)) (k*poly q p))
      (t                                 (k*poly p q)))))

(defun k*poly (k p)
  "Multiply a polynomial p by a constant factor k."
  (cond
    ((eql k 0)        0)         ;; 0 * p = 0
    ((eql k 1)        p)         ;; 1 * p = p
    ((and (numberp k)
          (numberp p)) (* k p))  ;; Multiply numbers
    (t ;; Multiply each coefficient
     (let ((r (make-poly (main-var p) (degree p))))
       ;; Accumulate result in r;  r[i] = k*p[i]
       (loop for i from 0 to (degree p) do
             (setf (coef r i) (poly*poly k (coef p i))))
       r))))
```

The hard part is multiplying two polynomials with the same main variable. This is done by creating a new polynomial, r, whose degree is the sum of the two input polynomials p and q. Initially, all of r's coefficients are zero. A doubly nested loop multiplies each coefficient of p and q and adds the result into the appropriate coefficient of r.

```
(defun poly*same (p q)
  "Multiply two polynomials with the same variable."
  ;; r[i] = p[0]*q[i] + p[1]*q[i-1] + ...
  (let* ((r-degree (+ (degree p) (degree q)))
         (r (make-poly (main-var p) r-degree)))
    (loop for i from 0 to (degree p) do
          (unless (eql (coef p i) 0)
            (loop for j from 0 to (degree q) do
                  (setf (coef r (+ i j))
                        (poly+poly (coef r (+ i j))
                                   (poly*poly (coef p i)
                                              (coef q j)))))))
    r))
```

Both poly+poly and poly*poly make use of the function normalize-poly to "normalize" the result. The idea is that (- (^ x 5) (^ x 5)) should return 0, not #(x 0 0 0 0 0). Note that normalize-poly is a destructive operation: it calls delete, which can actually alter its argument. Normally this is a dangerous thing, but since normalize-poly is replacing something with its conceptual equal, no harm is done.

```
(defun normalize-poly (p)
  "Alter a polynomial by dropping trailing zeros."
  (if (numberp p)
      p
      (let ((p-degree (- (position 0 p :test (complement #'eql)
                                   :from-end t)
                         1)))
        (cond ((<= p-degree 0) (normalize-poly (coef p 0)))
              ((< p-degree (degree p))
               (delete 0 p :start p-degree))
              (t p)))))
```

There are a few loose ends to clean up. First, the exponentiation function:

```
(defun poly^n (p n)
  "Raise polynomial p to the nth power, n>=0."
  (check-type n (integer 0 *))
  (cond ((= n 0) (assert (not (eql p 0))) 1)
        ((integerp p) (expt p n))
        (t (poly*poly p (poly^n p (- n 1))))))
```

15.2   Differentiating Polynomials

The differentiation routine is easy, mainly because there are only two operators (+ and *) to deal with:

```
(defun deriv-poly (p x)
  "Return the derivative, dp/dx, of the polynomial p."
  ;; If p is a number or a polynomial with main-var > x,
  ;; then p is free of x, and the derivative is zero;
  ;; otherwise do real work.
  ;; But first, make sure X is a simple variable,
  ;; of the form #(X 0 1).
  (assert (and (typep x 'polynomial) (= (degree x) 1)
               (eql (coef x 0) 0) (eql (coef x 1) 1)))
```

```
(cond
  ((numberp p) 0)
  ((var> (main-var p) (main-var x)) 0)
  ((var= (main-var p) (main-var x))
   ;; d(a + bx + cx^2 + dx^3)/dx = b + 2cx + 3dx^2
   ;; So, shift the sequence p over by 1, then
   ;; put x back in, and multiply by the exponents
   (let ((r (subseq p 1)))
     (setf (main-var r) (main-var x))
     (loop for i from 1 to (degree r) do
           (setf (coef r i) (poly*poly (+ i 1) (coef r i))))
     (normalize-poly r)))
  (t ;; Otherwise some coefficient may contain x. Ex:
   ;; d(z + 3x + 3zx^2 + z^2x^3)/dz
   ;; = 1 +  0 +  3x^2 +  2zx^3
   ;; So copy p, and differentiate the coefficients.
   (let ((r (copy-poly p)))
     (loop for i from 0 to (degree p) do
           (setf (coef r i) (deriv-poly (coef r i) x)))
     (normalize-poly r)))))
```

Exercise 15.1 [h]   Integrating polynomials is not much harder than differentiating them. For example:

$$\int ax^2 + bx \, dx = \frac{ax^3}{3} + \frac{bx^2}{2} + c.$$

Write a function to integrate polynomials and install it in prefix->canon.

Exercise 15.2 [m]   Add support for *definite* integrals, such as $\int_a^b y \, dx$. You will need to make up a suitable notation and properly install it in both infix->prefix and prefix->canon. A full implementation of this feature would have to consider infinity as a bound, as well as the problem of integrating over singularities. You need not address these problems.

15.3   Converting between Infix and Prefix

All that remains is converting from canonical form back to prefix form, and from there back to infix form. This is a good point to extend the prefix form to allow expressions with more than two arguments. First we show an updated version of prefix->infix that handles multiple arguments:

```lisp
(defun prefix->infix (exp)
  "Translate prefix to infix expressions.
  Handles operators with any number of args."
  (if (atom exp)
      exp
      (intersperse
        (exp-op exp)
        (mapcar #'prefix->infix (exp-args exp)))))

(defun intersperse (op args)
  "Place op between each element of args.
  Ex: (intersperse '+ '(a b c)) => '(a + b + c)"
  (if (length=1 args)
      (first args)
      (rest (loop for arg in args
              collect op
              collect arg))))
```

Now we need only convert from canonical form to prefix:

```lisp
(defun canon->prefix (p)
  "Convert a canonical polynomial to a lisp expression."
  (if (numberp p)
      p
      (args->prefix
        '+ 0
        (loop for i from (degree p) downto 0
              collect (args->prefix
                        '* 1
                        (list (canon->prefix (coef p i))
                              (exponent->prefix
                                (main-var p) i)))))))

(defun exponent->prefix (base exponent)
  "Convert canonical base^exponent to prefix form."
  (case exponent
    (0 1)
    (1 base)
    (t '(^ ,base ,exponent))))

(defun args->prefix (op identity args)
  "Convert arg1 op arg2 op ... to prefix form."
  (let ((useful-args (remove identity args)))
    (cond ((null useful-args) identity)
          ((and (eq op '*) (member 0 args)) 0)
          ((length=1 args) (first useful-args))
          (t (cons op (mappend
                        #'(lambda (exp)
```

```
                              (if (starts-with exp op)
                                  (exp-args exp)
                                  (list exp)))
                          useful-args))))))
```

Finally, here's a top level to make use of all this:

```
(defun canon (infix-exp)
  "Canonicalize argument and convert it back to infix"
  (prefix->infix
    (canon->prefix
      (prefix->canon
        (infix->prefix infix-exp)))))

(defun canon-simplifier ()
  "Read an expression, canonicalize it, and print the result."
  (loop
    (print 'canon>)
    (print (canon (read)))))
```

and an example of it in use:

```
> (canon-simplifier)
CANON> (3 + x + 4 - x)
7
CANON> (x + y + y + x)
((2 * X) + (2 * Y))
CANON> (3 * x + 4 * x)
(7 * X)
CANON> (3 * x + y + x + 4 * x)
((8 * X) + Y)
CANON> (3 * x + y + z + x + 4 * x)
((8 * X) + (Y + Z))
CANON> ((x + 1) ^ 10)
((X ^ 10) + (10 * (X ^ 9)) + (45 * (X ^ 8)) + (120 * (X ^ 7))
 + (210 * (X ^ 6)) + (252 * (X ^ 5)) + (210 * (X ^ 4))
 + (120 * (X ^ 3)) + (45 * (X ^ 2)) + (10 * X) + 1)
CANON> ((x + 1) ^ 10 + (x - 1) ^ 10)
((2 * (X ^ 10)) + (90 * (X ^ 8)) + (420 * (X ^ 6))
 + (420 * (X ^ 4)) + (90 * (X ^ 2)) + 2)
CANON> ((x + 1) ^ 10 - (x - 1) ^ 10)
((20 * (X ^ 8)) + (240 * (X ^ 7)) + (504 * (X ^ 5))
 + (240 * (X ^ 3)) + (20 * X))
CANON> (3 * x ^ 3 + 4 * x * y * (x - 1) + x ^ 2 * (x + y))
((4 * (X ^ 3)) + ((5 * Y) * (X ^ 2)) + ((-4 * Y) * X))
CANON> (3 * x ^ 3 + 4 * x * w * (x - 1) + x ^ 2 * (x + w))
((((5 * (X ^ 2)) + (-4 * X)) * W) + (4 * (X ^ 3)))
```

```
CANON> (d (3 * x ^ 2 + 2 * x + 1) / d x)
((6 * X) + 2)
CANON> (d(z + 3 * x + 3 * z * x ^ 2 + z ^ 2 * x ^ 3) / d z)
(((2 * Z) * (X ^ 3)) + (3 * (X ^ 2)) + 1)
CANON> [Abort]
```

15.4   Benchmarking the Polynomial Simplifier

Unlike the rule-based program, this version gets all the answers right. Not only is the program correct (at least as far as these examples go), it is also fast. We can compare it to the canonical simplifier originally written for MACSYMA by William Martin (circa 1968), and modified by Richard Fateman. The modified version was used by Richard Gabriel in his suite of Common Lisp benchmarks (1985). The benchmark program is called frpoly, because it deals with polynomials and was originally written in the dialect Franz Lisp. The frpoly benchmark encodes polynomials as lists rather than vectors, and goes to great lengths to be efficient. Otherwise, it is similar to the algorithms used here (although the code itself is quite different, using progs and gos and other features that have fallen into disfavor in the intervening decades). The particular benchmark we will use here is raising $1 + x + y + z$ to the 15th power:

```
(defun r15-test ()
  (let ((r (prefix->canon '(+ 1 (+ x (+ y z))))))
    (time (poly^n r 15))
    nil))
```

This takes .97 seconds on our system. The equivalent test with the original frpoly code takes about the same time: .98 seconds. Thus, our program is as fast as production-quality code. In terms of storage space, vectors use about half as much storage as lists, because half of each cons cell is a pointer, while vectors are all useful data.[2]

How much faster is the polynomial-based code than the rule-based version? Unfortunately, we can't answer that question directly. We can time (simp '((1 + x + y + z) ^ 15))). This takes only a tenth of a second, but that is because it is doing no work at all—the answer is the same as the input! Alternately, we can take the expression computed by (poly^n r 15), convert it to prefix, and pass that to simplify. simplify takes 27.8 seconds on this, so the rule-based version is

---

[2]Note: systems that use "cdr-coding" take about the same space for lists that are allocated all at once as for vectors. But cdr-coding is losing favor as RISC chips replace microcoded processors.

much slower. Section 9.6 describes ways to speed up the rule-based program, and a comparison of timing data appears on page 525.

There are always surprises when it comes down to measuring timing data. For example, the alert reader may have noticed that the version of poly^n defined above requires n multiplications. Usually, exponentiation is done by squaring a value when the exponent is even. Such an algorithm takes only $\log n$ multiplications instead of n. We can add a line to the definition of poly^n to get an $O(\log n)$ algorithm:

```
(defun poly^n (p n)
  "Raise polynomial p to the nth power, n>=0."
  (check-type n (integer 0 *))
  (cond ((= n 0) (assert (not (eql p 0))) 1)
        ((integerp p) (expt p n))
        ((evenp n) (poly^2 (poly^n p (/ n 2))))     ;***
        (t (poly*poly p (poly^n p (- n 1))))))))

(defun poly^2 (p) (poly*poly p p))
```

The surprise is that this takes *longer* to raise *r* to the 15th power. Even though it does fewer poly*poly operations, it is doing them on more complex arguments, and there is more work altogether. If we use this version of poly^n, then r15-test takes 1.6 seconds instead of .98 seconds.

By the way, this is a perfect example of the conceptual power of recursive functions. We took an existing function, poly^n, added a single cond clause, and changed it from an $O(n)$ to $O(\log n)$ algorithm. (This turned out to be a bad idea, but that's beside the point. It would be a good idea for raising integers to powers.) The reasoning that allows the change is simple: First, p^n is certainly equal to $(p^{n/2})^2$ when n is even, so the change can't introduce any wrong answers. Second, the change continues the policy of decrementing n on every recursive call, so the function must eventually terminate (when $n = 0$). If it gives no wrong answers, and it terminates, then it must give the right answer.

In contrast, making the change for an iterative algorithm is more complex. The initial algorithm is simple:

```
(defun poly^n (p n)
  (let ((result 1))
    (loop repeat n do (setf result (poly*poly p result)))
    result))
```

But to change it, we have to change the repeat loop to a while loop, explicitly put in the decrement of n, and insert a test for the even case:

```lisp
(defun poly^n (p n)
  (let ((result 1))
    (loop while (> n 0)
       do (if (evenp n)
              (setf p (poly^2 p)
                    n (/ n 2))
              (setf result (poly*poly p result)
                    n (- n 1))))
    result))
```

For this problem, it is clear that thinking recursively leads to a simpler function that is easier to modify.

It turns out that this is not the final word. Exponentiation of polynomials can be done even faster, with a little more mathematical sophistication. Richard Fateman's 1974 paper on Polynomial Multiplication analyzes the complexity of a variety of exponentiation algorithms. Instead of the usual asymptotic analysis (e.g. $O(n)$ or $O(n^2)$), he uses a fine-grained analysis that computes the constant factors (e.g. $1000 \times n$ or $2 \times n^2$). Such analysis is crucial for small values of n. It turns out that for a variety of polynomials, an exponentiation algorithm based on the binomial theorem is best. The binomial theorem states that

$$(a + b)^n = \sum_{i=0}^{n} \frac{n!}{i!(n - i)!} a^i b^{n-i}$$

for example,

$$(a + b)^3 = b^3 + 3ab^2 + 3a^2b + a^3$$

We can use this theorem to compute a power of a polynomial all at once, instead of computing it by repeated multiplication or squaring. Of course, a polynomial will in general be a sum of more than two components, so we have to decide how to split it into the a and b pieces. There are two obvious ways: either cut the polynomial in half, so that a and b will be of equal size, or split off one component at a time. Fateman shows that the latter method is more efficient in most cases. In other words, a polynomial $k_1 x^n + k_2 x^{n-1} + k_3 x^{n-2} + \cdots$ will be treated as the sum $a + b$ where $a = k_1 x^n$ and b is the rest of the polynomial.

Following is the code for binomial exponentiation. It is somewhat messy, because the emphasis is on efficiency. This means reusing some data and using p-add-into! instead of the more general poly+poly.

```lisp
(defun poly^n (p n)
  "Raise polynomial p to the nth power, n>=0."
  ;; Uses the binomial theorem
  (check-type n (integer 0 *))
  (cond
    ((= n 0) 1)
```

```
((integerp p) (expt p n))
(t ;; First: split the polynomial p = a + b, where
 ;; a = k*x^d and b is the rest of p
 (let ((a (make-poly (main-var p) (degree p)))
       (b (normalize-poly (subseq p 0 (- (length p) 1))))
       ;; Allocate arrays of powers of a and b:
       (a^n (make-array (+ n 1)))
       (b^n (make-array (+ n 1)))
       ;; Initialize the result:
       (result (make-poly (main-var p) (* (degree p) n))))
   (setf (coef a (degree p)) (coef p (degree p)))
   ;; Second: Compute powers of a^i and b^i for i up to n
   (setf (aref a^n 0) 1)
   (setf (aref b^n 0) 1)
   (loop for i from 1 to n do
        (setf (aref a^n i) (poly*poly a (aref a^n (- i 1))))
        (setf (aref b^n i) (poly*poly b (aref b^n (- i 1)))))
   ;; Third: add the products into the result,
   ;; so that result[i] = (n choose i) * a^i * b^(n-i)
   (let ((c 1)) ;; c helps compute (n choose i) incrementally
     (loop for i from 0 to n do
          (p-add-into! result c
                        (poly*poly (aref a^n i)
                                   (aref b^n (- n i))))
          (setf c (/ (* c (- n i)) (+ i 1)))))
   (normalize-poly result)))))

(defun p-add-into! (result c p)
  "Destructively add c*p into result."
  (if (or (numberp p)
          (not (var= (main-var p) (main-var result))))
      (setf (coef result 0)
            (poly+poly (coef result 0) (poly*poly c p)))
      (loop for i from 0 to (degree p) do
           (setf (coef result i)
                 (poly+poly (coef result i) (poly*poly c (coef p i))))))
  result)
```

Using this version of poly^n, r15-test takes only .23 seconds, four times faster than the previous version. The following table compares the times for r15-test with the three versions of poly^n, along with the times for applying simply to the r15 polynomial, for various versions of simplify:

	program	secs	speed-up
	rule-based versions		
1	original	27.8	–
2	memoization	7.7	4
3	memo+index	4.0	7
4	compilation only	2.5	11
5	memo+compilation	1.9	15
	canonical versions		
6	squaring poly^n	1.6	17
7	iterative poly^n	.98	28
8	binomial poly^n	.23	120

As we remarked earlier, the general techniques of memoization, indexing, and compilation provide for dramatic speed-ups. However, in the end, they do not lead to the fastest program. Instead, the fastest version was achieved by throwing out the original rule-based program, replacing it with a canonical-form-based program, and fine-tuning the algorithms within that program, using mathematical analysis.

Now that we have achieved a sufficiently fast system, the next two sections concentrate on making it more powerful.

15.5   A Canonical Form for Rational Expressions

A *rational* number is defined as a fraction: the quotient of two integers. A *rational expression* is hereby defined as the quotient of two polynomials. This section presents a canonical form for rational expressions.

First, a number or polynomial will continue to be represented as before. The quotient of two polynomials will be represented as a cons cells of numerator and denominator pairs. However, just as Lisp automatically reduces rational numbers to simplest form (6/8 is represented as 3/4), we must reduce rational expressions. So, for example, $(x^2 - 1)/(x - 1)$ must be reduced to $x + 1$, not left as a quotient of two polynomials.

The following functions build and access rational expressions but do not reduce to simplest form, except in the case where the denominator is a number. Building up the rest of the functionality for full rational expressions is left to a series of exercises:

```
(defun make-rat (numerator denominator)
   "Build a rational: a quotient of two polynomials."
   (if (numberp denominator)
       (k*poly (/ 1 denominator) numerator)
       (cons numerator denominator)))
```

```
(defun rat-numerator (rat)
  "The numerator of a rational expression."
  (typecase rat
    (cons (car rat))
    (number (numerator rat))
    (t rat)))

(defun rat-denominator (rat)
  "The denominator of a rational expression."
  (typecase rat
    (cons (cdr rat))
    (number (denominator rat))
    (t 1)))
```

Exercise 15.3 [s] Modify prefix->canon to accept input of the form x / y and to return rational expressions instead of polynomials. Also allow for input of the form x ^ - n.

Exercise 15.4 [m] Add arithmetic routines for multiplication, addition, and division of rational expressions. Call them rat*rat, rat+rat, and rat/rat respectively. They will call upon poly*poly, poly+poly and a new function, poly/poly, which is defined in the next exercise.

Exercise 15.5 [h] Define poly-gcd, which computes the greatest common divisor of two polynomials.

Exercise 15.6 [h] Using poly-gcd, define the function poly/poly, which will implement division for polynomials. Polynomials are closed under addition and multiplication, so poly+poly and poly*poly both returned polynomials. Polynomials are not closed under division, so poly/poly will return a rational expression.

15.6   Extending Rational Expressions

Now that we can divide polynomials, the final step is to reinstate the logarithmic, exponential, and trigonometric functions. The problem is that if we allow all these functions, we get into problems with canonical form again. For example, the following three expressions are all equivalent:

$$\sin(x)$$

$$\cos(x - \frac{\pi}{2})$$

$$\frac{e^{ix} - e^{-ix}}{2i}$$

If we are interested in assuring we have a canonical form, the safest thing is to allow only e^x and $\log(x)$. All the other functions can be defined in terms of these two. With this extension, the set of expressions we can form is closed under differentiation, and it is possible to canonicalize expressions. The result is a mathematically sound construction known as a *differentiable field*. This is precisely the construct that is assumed by the Risch integration algorithm (Risch 1969, 1979).

The disadvantage of this minimal extension is that answers may be expressed in unfamiliar terms. The user asks for $d\sin(x^2)/dx$, expecting a simple answer in terms of cos, and is surprised to see a complex answer involving e^{ix}. Because of this problem, most computer algebra systems have made more radical extensions, allowing sin, cos, and other functions. These systems are treading on thin mathematical ice. Algorithms that would be guaranteed to work over a simple differentiable field may fail when the domain is extended this way. In general, the result will not be a wrong answer but rather the failure to find an answer at all.

15.7   History and References

A brief history of symbolic algebra systems is given in chapter 8. Fateman (1979), Martin and Fateman (1971), and Davenport et al. (1988) give more details on the MAC-SYMA system, on which this chapter is loosely based. Fateman (1991) discusses the `frpoly` benchmark and introduces the vector implementation used in this chapter.

15.8   Exercises

Exercise 15.7 [h]   Implement an extension of the rationals to include logarithmic, exponential, and trigonometric functions.

Exercise 15.8 [m]   Modify `deriv` to handle the extended rational expressions.

Exercise 15.9 [d]   Adapt the integration routine from section 8.6 (page 252) to the rational expression representation. Davenport et al. 1988 may be useful.

Exercise 15.10 [s]   Give several reasons why constant polynomials, like 3, are represented as integers rather than as vectors.

15.9   Answers

Answer 15.4

```lisp
(defun rat*rat (x y)
  "Multiply rationals: a/b * c/d = a*c/b*d"
  (poly/poly (poly*poly (rat-numerator x)
                        (rat-numerator y))
             (poly*poly (rat-denominator x)
                        (rat-denominator y))))

(defun rat+rat (x y)
  "Add rationals: a/b + c/d = (a*d + c*b)/b*d"
  (let ((a (rat-numerator x))
        (b (rat-denominator x))
        (c (rat-numerator y))
        (d (rat-denominator y)))
    (poly/poly (poly+poly (poly*poly a d) (poly*poly c b))
               (poly*poly b d))))

(defun rat/rat (x y)
  "Divide rationals: a/b / c/d = a*d/b*c"
  (rat*rat x (make-rat (rat-denominator y) (rat-numerator y))))
```

Answer 15.6

```lisp
(defun poly/poly (p q)
  "Divide p by q: if d is the greatest common divisor of p and q
  then p/q = (p/d) / (q/d).  Note if q=1, then p/q = p."
  (if (eql q 1)
      p
      (let ((d (poly-gcd p q)))
        (make-rat (poly/poly p d)
                  (poly/poly q d)))))
```

Answer 15.10   (1) An integer takes less time and space to process. (2) Representing
numbers as a polynomial would cause an infinite regress, because the coefficients
would be numbers. (3) Unless a policy was decided upon, the representation would
not be canonical, since #(x 3) and #(y 3) both represent 3.

CHAPTER *16*

Expert Systems

An expert is one who knows more and more about less and less.

—Nicholas Murray Butler (1862–1947)

In the 1970s there was terrific interest in the area of *knowledge-based expert systems*. An expert system or knowledge-based system is one that solves problems by applying knowledge that has been garnered from one or more experts in a field. Since these experts will not in general be programmers, they will very probably express their expertise in terms that cannot immediately be translated into a program. It is the goal of expert-system research to come up with a representation that is flexible enough to handle expert knowledge, but still capable of being manipulated by a computer program to come up with solutions.

A plausible candidate for this representation is as logical facts and rules, as in Prolog. However, there are three areas where Prolog provides poor support for a general knowledge-based system:

- Reasoning with uncertainty. Prolog only deals with the black-and-white world of facts that are clearly true or false (and it doesn't even handle false very well). Often experts will express rules of thumb that are "likely" or "90% certain."

- Explanation. Prolog gives solutions to queries but no indication of how those solutions were derived. A system that can explain its solutions to the user in understandable terms will be trusted more.

- Flexible flow of control. Prolog works by backward-chaining from the goal. In some cases, we may need more varied control strategy. For example, in medical diagnosis, there is a prescribed order for acquiring certain information about the patient. A medical system must follow this order, even if it doesn't fit in with the backward-chaining strategy.

The early expert systems used a wide variety of techniques to attack these problems. Eventually, it became clear that certain techniques were being used frequently, and they were captured in *expert-system shells:* specialized programming environments that helped acquire knowledge from the expert and use it to solve problems and provide explanations. The idea was that these shells would provide a higher level of abstraction than just Lisp or Prolog and would make it easy to write new expert systems.

The MYCIN expert system was one of the earliest and remains one of the best known. It was written by Dr. Edward Shortliffe in 1974 as an experiment in medical diagnosis. MYCIN was designed to prescribe antibiotic therapy for bacterial blood infections, and when completed it was judged to perform this task as well as experts in the field. Its name comes from the common suffix in drugs it prescribes: erythromycin, clindamycin, and so on. The following is a slightly modified version of one of MYCIN's rules, along with an English paraphrase generated by the system:

```
(defrule 52
  if (site culture is blood)
     (gram organism is neg)
     (morphology organism is rod)
     (burn patient is serious)
  then .4
     (identity organism is pseudomonas))
```

```
Rule 52:
  If
    1) THE SITE OF THE CULTURE IS BLOOD
    2) THE GRAM OF THE ORGANISM IS NEG
    3) THE MORPHOLOGY OF THE ORGANISM IS ROD
    4) THE BURN OF THE PATIENT IS SERIOUS
  Then there is weakly suggestive evidence (0.4) that
    1) THE IDENTITY OF THE ORGANISM IS PSEUDOMONAS
```

MYCIN lead to the development of the EMYCIN expert-system shell. EMYCIN stands for "essential MYCIN," although it is often mispresented as "empty MYCIN." Either way, the name refers to the shell for acquiring knowledge, reasoning with it, and explaining the results, without the specific medical knowledge.

EMYCIN is a backward-chaining rule interpreter that has much in common with Prolog. However, there are four important differences. First, and most importantly, EMYCIN deals with uncertainty. Instead of insisting that all predications be true or false, EMYCIN associates a *certainty factor* with each predication. Second, EMYCIN caches the results of its computations so that they need not be duplicated. Third, EMYCIN provides an easy way for the system to ask the user for information. Fourth, it provides explanations of its behavior. This can be summed up in the equation:

EMYCIN = Prolog + uncertainty + caching + questions + explanations

We will first cover the ways EMYCIN is different from Prolog. After that we will return to the main core of EMYCIN, the backward-chaining rule interpreter. Finally, we will show how to add some medical knowledge to EMYCIN to reconstruct MYCIN. A glossary of the program is in figure 16.1.

16.1   Dealing with Uncertainty

EMYCIN deals with uncertainty by replacing the two boolean values, true and false, with a range of values called *certainty factors*. These are numbers from −1 (false) to +1 (true), with 0 representing a complete unknown. In Lisp:

```
(defconstant true    +1.0)
(defconstant false   -1.0)
(defconstant unknown  0.0)
```

To define the logic of certainty factors, we need to define the logical operations, such as and, or, and not. The first operation to consider is the combination of two distinct pieces of evidence expressed as certainty factors. Suppose we are trying to

	Top-Level Functions for the Client
emycin	Run the shell on a list of contexts representing a problem.
mycin	Run the shell on the microbial infection domain.
	Top-Level Functions for the Expert
defcontext	Define a context.
defparm	Define a parameter.
defrule	Define a rule.
	Constants
true	A certainty factor of +1.
false	A certainty factor of -1.
unknown	A certainty factor of 0.
cf-cut-off	Below this certainty we cut off search.
	Data Types
context	A subdomain concerning a particular problem.
parm	A parameter.
rule	A backward-chaining rule with certainty factors.
yes/no	The type with members yes and no.
	Major Functions within Emycin
get-context-data	Collect data and draw conclusions.
find-out	Determine values by knowing, asking, or using rules.
get-db	Retrieve a fact from the data base.
use-rules	Apply all rules relevent to a parameter.
use-rule	Apply one rule.
new-instance	Create a new instance of a context.
report-findings	Print the results.
	Auxiliary Functions
cf-or	Combine certainty factors (CFs) with OR.
cf-and	Combine certainty factors (CFs) with AND.
true-p	Is this CF true for purposes of search?
false-p	Is this CF false for purposes of search?
cf-p	Is this a certainty factor?
put-db	Place a fact in the data base.
clear-db	Clear all facts from the data base.
get-vals	Get value and CF for a parameter/instance.
get-cf	Get CF for a parameter/instance/value triplet.
update-cf	Change CF for a parameter/instance/value triplet.
ask-vals	Ask the user for value/CF for a parameter/instance.
prompt-and-read-vals	Print a prompt and read a reply.
inst-name	The name of an instance.
check-reply	See if reply is valid list of CF/values.
parse-reply	Convert reply into list of CF/values.
parm-type	Values of this parameter must be of this type.
get-parm	Find or make a parameter structure for this name.
put-rule	Add a new rule, indexed under each conclusion.
get-rules	Retrieve rules that help determine a parameter.
clear-rules	Remove all rules.
satisfy-premises	Calculate the combined CF for the premises.
eval-condition	Determine the CF for a condition.
reject-premise	Rule out a premise if it is clearly false.
conclude	Add a parameter/instance/value/CF to the data base.
is	An alias for equal.
check-conditions	Make sure a rule is valid.
print-rule	Print a rule.
print-conditions	Print a list of conditions.
print-condition	Print a single condition.
cf->english	Convert .7 to "suggestive evidence," etc.
print-why	Say why a rule is being used.

Figure 16.1: Glossary for the EMYCIN Program

determine the chances of a patient having disease X. Assume we have a population of prior patients that have been given two lab tests. One test says that 60% of the patients have the disease and the other says that 40% have it. How should we combine these two pieces of evidence into one? Unfortunately, there is no way to answer that question correctly without knowing more about the *dependence* of the two sources on each other. Suppose the first test says that 60% of the patients (who all happen to be male) have the disease, and the second says that 40% (who all happen to be female) have it. Then we should conclude that 100% have it, because the two tests cover the entire population. On the other hand, if the first test is positive only for patients that are 70 years old or older, and the second is positive only for patients that are 80 or older, then the second is just a subset of the first. This adds no new information, so the correct answer is 60% in this case.

In section 16.9 we will consider ways to take this kind of reasoning into account. For now, we will present the combination method actually used in EMYCIN. It is defined by the formula:

combine (A, B) =

$$
\begin{aligned}
&A + B - AB; \quad A, B > 0 \\
&A + B + AB; \quad A, B < 0 \\
&\frac{A + B}{1 - \min(|A|, |B|)}; \text{ otherwise}
\end{aligned}
$$

According to this formula, combine(.60,.40) = .76, which is a compromise between the extremes of .60 and 1.00. It is the same as the probability p(A or B), assuming that A and B are independent.

However, it should be clear that certainty factors are not the same thing as probabilities. Certainty factors attempt to deal with disbelief as well as belief, but they do not deal with dependence and independence. The EMYCIN combination function has a number of desirable properties:

- It always computes a number between −1 and +1.

- Combining unknown (zero) with anything leaves it unchanged.

- Combining true with anything (except false) gives true.

- Combining true and false is an error.

- Combining two opposites gives unknown.

- Combining two positives (except true) gives a larger positive.

- Combining a positive and a negative gives something in between.

So far we have seen how to combine two separate pieces of evidence for the same hypothesis. In other words, if we have the two rules:

$A \Rightarrow C$
$B \Rightarrow C$

and we know A with certainty factor (cf) .6 and B with cf .4, then we can conclude C with cf .76. But consider a rule with a conjunction in the premise:

A and $B \Rightarrow C$

Combining A and B in this case is quite different from combining them when they are in separate rules. EMYCIN chooses to combine conjunctions by taking the minimum of each conjunct's certainty factor. If certainty factors were probabilities, this would be equivalent to assuming dependence between conjuncts in a rule. (If the conjuncts were independent, then the product of the probabilities would be the correct answer.) So EMYCIN is making the quite reasonable (but sometimes incorrect) assumption that conditions that are tied together in a single rule will be dependent on one another, while conditions in separate rules are independent.

The final complication is that rules themselves may be uncertain. That is, MYCIN accommodates rules that look like:

A and $B \Rightarrow .9 C$

to say that A and B imply C with .9 certainty. EMYCIN simply multiplies the rule's cf by the combined cf of the premise. So if A has cf .6 and B has cf .4, then the premise as a whole has cf .4 (the minimum of A and B), which is multiplied by .9 to get .36. The .36 is then combined with any exisiting cf for C. If C is previously unknown, then combining .36 with 0 will give .36. If C had a prior cf of .76, then the new cf would be $.36 + .76 - (.36 \times .76) = .8464$.

Here are the EMYCIN certainty factor combination functions in Lisp:

```lisp
(defun cf-or (a b)
  "Combine the certainty factors for the formula (A or B).
  This is used when two rules support the same conclusion."
  (cond ((and (> a 0) (> b 0))
         (+ a b (* -1 a b)))
        ((and (< a 0) (< b 0))
         (+ a b (* a b)))
        (t (/ (+ a b)
              (- 1 (min (abs a) (abs b)))))))

(defun cf-and (a b)
  "Combine the certainty factors for the formula (A and B)."
  (min a b))
```

Certainty factors can be seen as a generalization of truth values. EMYCIN is a backward-chaining rule system that combines certainty factors according to the functions laid out above. But if we only used the certainty factors `true` and `false`, then EMYCIN would behave exactly like Prolog, returning only answers that are definitely true. It is only when we provide fractional certainty factors that the additional EMYCIN mechanism makes a difference.

Truth values actually serve two purposes in Prolog. They determine the final answer, yes, but they also determine when to cut off search: if any one of the premises of a rule is false, then there is no sense looking at the other premises. If in EMYCIN we only cut off the search when one of the premises was absolutely false, then we might have to search through a lot of rules, only to yield answers with very low certainty factors. Instead, EMYCIN arbitrarily cuts off the search and considers a premise false when it has a certainty factor below .2. The following functions support this arbitrary cutoff point:

```lisp
(defconstant cf-cut-off 0.2
  "Below this certainty we cut off search.")

(defun true-p (cf)
  "Is this certainty factor considered true?"
  (and (cf-p cf) (> cf cf-cut-off)))

(defun false-p (cf)
  "Is this certainty factor considered false?"
  (and (cf-p cf) (< cf (- cf-cut-off 1.0))))

(defun cf-p (x)
  "Is X a valid numeric certainty factor?"
  (and (numberp x) (<= false x true)))
```

Exercise 16.1 [m] Suppose you read the headline "Elvis Alive in Kalamazoo" in a tabloid newspaper to which you attribute a certainty factor of .01. If you combine certainties using EMYCIN's combination rule, how many more copies of the newspaper would you need to see before you were .95 certain Elvis is alive?

16.2   Caching Derived Facts

The second thing that makes EMYCIN different from Prolog is that EMYCIN *caches* all the facts it derives in a data base. When Prolog is asked to prove the same goal twice, it performs the same computation twice, no matter how laborious. EMYCIN performs the computation the first time and just fetches it the second time.

We can implement a simple data base by providing three functions: put-db to add an association between a key and a value, get-db to retrieve a value, and clear-db to empty the data base and start over:

```
(let ((db (make-hash-table :test #'equal)))
  (defun get-db (key) (gethash key db))
  (defun put-db (key val) (setf (gethash key db) val))
  (defun clear-db () (clrhash db)))
```

This data base is general enough to hold any association between key and value. However, most of the information we will want to store is more specific. EMYCIN is designed to deal with objects (or *instances*) and attributes (or *parameters*) of those objects. For example, each patient has a name parameter. Presumably, the value of this parameter will be known exactly. On the other hand, each microscopic organism has an identity parameter that is normally not known at the start of the consultation. Applying the rules will lead to several possible values for this parameter, each with its own certainty factor. In general, then, the data base will have keys of the form (*parameter instance*) with values of the form ((val_1 cf_1) (val_2 cf_2)...). In the following code, get-vals returns the list of value/cf pairs for a given parameter and instance, get-cf returns the certainty factor for a parameter/instance/value triplet, and update-cf changes the certainty factor by combining the old one with a new one. Note that the first time update-cf is called on a given parameter/instance/value triplet, get-cf will return unknown (zero). Combining that with the given cf yields cf itself. Also note that the data base has to be an equal hash table, because the keys may include freshly consed lists.

```
(defun get-vals (parm inst)
  "Return a list of (val cf) pairs for this (parm inst)."
  (get-db (list parm inst)))

(defun get-cf (parm inst val)
  "Look up the certainty factor or return unknown."
  (or (second (assoc val (get-vals parm inst)))
      unknown))

(defun update-cf (parm inst val cf)
  "Change the certainty factor for (parm inst is val),
  by combining the given cf with the old."
  (let ((new-cf (cf-or cf (get-cf parm inst val))))
    (put-db (list parm inst)
            (cons (list val new-cf)
                  (remove val (get-db (list parm inst))
                          :key #'first)))))
```

The data base holds all information related to an instance of a problem. For example, in the medical domain, the data base would hold all information about the current patient. When we want to consider a new patient, the data base is cleared.

There are three other sources of information that cannot be stored in this data base, because they have to be maintained from one problem to the next. First, the *rule base* holds all the rules defined by the expert. Second, there is a structure to define each parameter; these are indexed under the name of each parameter. Third, we shall see that the flow of control is managed in part by a list of *contexts* to consider. These are structures that will be passed to the mycin function.

16.3   Asking Questions

The third way that EMYCIN differs from Prolog is in providing an automatic means of asking the user questions when answers cannot be derived from the rules. This is not a fundamental difference; after all, it is not too hard to write Prolog rules that print a query and read a reply. EMYCIN lets the knowledge-base designer write a simple declaration instead of a rule, and will even assume a default declaration if none is provided. The system also makes sure that the same question is never asked twice.

The following function ask-vals prints a query that asks for the parameter of an instance, and reads from the user the value or a list of values with associated certainty factors. The function first looks at the data base to make sure the question has not been asked before. It then checks each value and certainty factor to see if each is of the correct type, and it also allows the user to ask certain questions. A ? reply will show what type answer is expected. Rule will show the current rule that the system is working on. Why also shows the current rule, but it explains in more detail what the system knows and is trying to find out. Finally, help prints the following summary:

```
(defconstant help-string
  "~&Type one of the following:
?     - to see possible answers for this parameter
rule  - to show the current rule
why   - to see why this question is asked
help  - to see this list
xxx   - (for some specific xxx) if there is a definite answer
(xxx .5 yyy .4) - If there are several answers with
                  different certainty factors.")
```

Here is ask-vals. Note that the why and rule options assume that the current rule has been stored in the data base. The functions print-why, parm-type, and check-reply will be defined shortly.

```
(defun ask-vals (parm inst)
  "Ask the user for the value(s) of inst's parm parameter,
  unless this has already been asked.  Keep asking until the
  user types UNKNOWN (return nil) or a valid reply (return t)."
  (unless (get-db '(asked ,parm ,inst))
    (put-db '(asked ,parm ,inst) t)
    (loop
      (let ((ans (prompt-and-read-vals parm inst)))
        (case ans
          (help (format t help-string))
          (why  (print-why (get-db 'current-rule) parm))
          (rule (princ (get-db 'current-rule)))
          ((unk unknown) (RETURN nil))
          (?    (format t "~&A ~a must be of type ~a"
                        parm (parm-type parm)) nil)
          (t    (if (check-reply ans parm inst)
                    (RETURN t)
                    (format t "~&Illegal reply.  ~
                            Type ? to see legal ones."))))))))
```

The following is prompt-and-read-vals, the function that actually asks the query and reads the reply. It basically calls format to print a prompt and read to get the reply, but there are a few subtleties. First, it calls finish-output. Some Lisp implementations buffer output on a line-by-line basis. Since the prompt may not end in a newline, finish-output makes sure the output is printed before the reply is read.

So far, all the code that refers to a parm is really referring to the name of a parameter—a symbol. The actual parameters themselves will be implemented as structures. We use get-parm to look up the structure associated with a symbol, and the selector functions parm-prompt to pick out the prompt for each parameter and parm-reader to pick out the reader function. Normally this will be the function read, but read-line is appropriate for reading string-valued parameters.

The macro defparm (shown here) provides a way to define prompts and readers for parameters.

```
(defun prompt-and-read-vals (parm inst)
  "Print the prompt for this parameter (or make one up) and
  read the reply."
  (fresh-line)
  (format t (parm-prompt (get-parm parm)) (inst-name inst) parm)
  (princ " ")
  (finish-output)
  (funcall (parm-reader (get-parm parm))))
```

```
(defun inst-name (inst)
  "The name of this instance."
  ;; The stored name is either like (("Jan Doe" 1.0)) or nil
  (or (first (first (get-vals 'name inst)))
      inst))
```

The function check-reply uses parse-reply to convert the user's reply into a canonical form, and then checks that each value is of the right type, and that each certainty factor is valid. If so, the data base is updated to reflect the new certainty factors.

```
(defun check-reply (reply parm inst)
  "If reply is valid for this parm, update the DB.
  Reply should be a val or (val1 cf1 val2 cf2 ...).
  Each val must be of the right type for this parm."
  (let ((answers (parse-reply reply)))
    (when (every #'(lambda (pair)
                     (and (typep (first pair) (parm-type parm))
                          (cf-p (second pair))))
                 answers)
      ;; Add replies to the data base
      (dolist (pair answers)
        (update-cf parm inst (first pair) (second pair)))
      answers)))

(defun parse-reply (reply)
  "Convert the reply into a list of (value cf) pairs."
  (cond ((null reply) nil)
        ((atom reply) '((,reply ,true)))
        (t (cons (list (first reply) (second reply))
                 (parse-reply (rest2 reply))))))
```

Parameters are implemented as structures with six slots: the name (a symbol), the context the parameter is for, the prompt used to ask for the parameter's value, a Boolean that tells if we should ask the user before or after using rules, a type restriction describing the legal values, and finally, the function used to read the value of the parameter.

Parameters are stored on the property list of their names under the parm property, so getting the parm-type of a name requires first getting the parm structure, and then selecting the type restriction field. By default, a parameter is given type t, meaning that any value is valid for that type. We also define the type yes/no, which comes in handy for Boolean parameters.

We want the default prompt to be "What is the PARM of the INST?" But most user-defined prompts will want to print the inst, and not the parm. To make it easy to write user-defined prompts, prompt-and-read-vals makes the instance be the first argument to the format string, with the parm second. Therefore, in the default prompt we need to use the format directive "~*" to skip the instance argument, and "~2:*" to back up two arguments to get back to the instance. (These directives are common in cerror calls, where one list of arguments is passed to two format strings.)

defparm is a macro that calls new-parm, the constructor function defined in the parm structure, and stores the resulting structure under the parm property of the parameter's name.

```
(defstruct (parm (:constructor
                   new-parm (name &optional context type-restriction
                              prompt ask-first reader)))
  name (context nil) (prompt "~&What is the ~*~a of ~2:*~a?")
  (ask-first nil) (type-restriction t) (reader 'read))

(defmacro defparm (parm &rest args)
  "Define a parameter."
  '(setf (get ',parm 'parm) (apply #'new-parm ',parm ',args)))

(defun parm-type (parm-name)
  "What type is expected for a value of this parameter?"
  (parm-type-restriction (get-parm parm-name)))

(defun get-parm (parm-name)
  "Look up the parameter structure with this name."
  ;; If there is none, make one
  (or (get parm-name 'parm)
      (setf (get parm-name 'parm) (new-parm parm-name))))

(deftype yes/no () '(member yes no))
```

16.4   Contexts Instead of Variables

Earlier we gave an equation relating EMYCIN to Prolog. That equation was not quite correct, because EMYCIN lacks one of Prolog's most important features: the logic variable. Instead, EMYCIN uses *contexts*. So the complete equation is:

EMYCIN = Prolog + uncertainty + caching + questions + explanations
   + contexts − variables

A context is defined by the designers of MYCIN as a situation within which the program reasons. But it makes more sense to think of a context simply as a data type. So the list of contexts supplied to the program will determine what types of objects can be reasoned about. The program keeps track of the most recent instance of each type, and the rules can refer to those instances only, using the name of the type. In our version of MYCIN, there are three types or contexts: patients, cultures, and organisms. Here is an example of a rule that references all three contexts:

```
(defrule 52
  if (site culture is blood)
     (gram organism is neg)
     (morphology organism is rod)
     (burn patient is serious)
  then .4
     (identity organism is pseudomonas))
```

Ignoring certainty factors for the moment, this MYCIN rule is equivalent to a Prolog rule of the form:

```
(<- (identity ?o ?pseudomonas)
    (and (culture ?c) (site ?c blood)
         (organism ?o) (gram ?o neg) (morphology ?o rod)
         (patient ?p) (burn ?p serious)))
```

The context mechanism provides sufficient flexibility to handle many of the cases that would otherwise be handled by variables. One important thing that cannot be done is to refer to more than one instance of the same context. Only the most recent instance can be referred to. Contexts are implemented as structures with the following definition:

```
(defstruct context
  "A context is a sub-domain, a type."
  name (number 0) initial-data goals)

(defmacro defcontext (name &optional initial-data goals)
  "Define a context."
  '(make-context :name ',name :initial-data ',initial-data
                 :goals ',goals))
```

The name field is something like patient or organism. Instances of contexts are numbered; the number field holds the number of the most recent instance. Each context also has two lists of parameters. The initial-data parameters are asked for when each instance is created. Initial data parameters are normally known by the user. For example, a doctor will normally know the patient's name, age, and sex, and as a matter of training expects to be asked these questions first, even if they don't factor into every case. The goal parameters, on the other hand, are usually unknown to the user. They are determined through the backward-chaining process.

The following function creates a new instance of a context, writes a message, and stores the instance in two places in the data base: under the key current-instance, and also under the name of the context. The contexts form a tree. In our example, the patient context is the root of the tree, and the current patient is stored in the data base under the key patient. The next level of the tree is for cultures taken from the patient; the current culture is stored under the culture key. Finally, there is a level for organisms found in each culture. The current organism is stored under both the organism and current-instance keys. The context tree is shown in figure 16.2.

```lisp
(defun new-instance (context)
  "Create a new instance of this context."
  (let ((instance (format nil "~a-~d"
                          (context-name context)
                          (incf (context-number context)))))
    (format t "~&------ ~a ------~&" instance)
    (put-db (context-name context) instance)
    (put-db 'current-instance instance)))
```

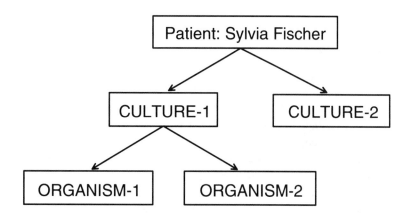

Figure 16.2: A Context Tree

16.5   Backward-Chaining Revisited

Now that we have seen how EMYCIN is different from Prolog, we are ready to tackle the way in which it is the same: the backward-chaining rule interpreter. Like Prolog, EMYCIN is given a goal and applies rules that are appropriate to the goal. Applying a rule means treating each premise of the rule as a goal and recursively applying rules that are appropriate to each premise.

There are still some remaining differences. In Prolog, a goal can be any expression, and appropriate rules are those whose heads unify with the goal. If any appropriate rule succeeds, then the goal is known to be true. In EMYCIN, a rule might give a goal a certainty of .99, but we still have to consider all the other rules that are appropriate to the goal, because they might bring the certainty down below the cutoff threshold. Thus, EMYCIN always gathers all evidence relating to a parameter/instance pair first, and only evaluates the goal after all the evidence is in. For example, if the goal was (`temp patient` > `98.6`), EMYCIN would first evaluate all rules with conclusions about the current patient's temperature, and only then compare the temperature to 98.6.

Another way of looking at it is that Prolog has the luxury of searching depth-first, because the semantics of Prolog rules is such that if any rule says a goal is true, then it is true. EMYCIN must search breadth-first, because a goal with certainty of .99 might turn out to be false when more evidence is considered.

We are now ready to sketch out the design of the EMYCIN rule interpreter: To find-out a parameter of an instance: If the value is already stored in the data base, use the known value. Otherwise, the two choices are using the rules or asking the user. Do these in the order specified for this parameter, and if the first one succeeds, don't bother with the second. Note that `ask-vals` (defined above) will not ask the same question twice.

To `use-rules`, find all the rules that concern the given parameter and evaluate them with `use-rule`. After each rule has been tried, if any of them evaluate to true, then succeed.

To `use-rule` a rule, first check if any of the premises can be rejected outright. If we did not have this check, then the system could start asking the user questions that were obviously irrelevant. So we waste some of the program's time (checking each premise twice) to save the more valuable user time. (The function `eval-condition` takes an optional argument specifying if we should recursively ask questions in trying to accept or reject a condition.)

If no premise can be rejected, then evaluate each premise in turn with `evaluate-condition`, keeping track of the accumulated certainty factor with `cf-and` (which is currently just `min`), and cutting off evaluation when the certainty factor drops below threshold. If the premises evaluate true, then add the conclusions to the data base. The calling sequence looks like this. Note that the recursive call to `find-out` is what enables chaining to occur:

```
find-out              ; To find out a parameter for an instance:
  get-db              ;   See if it is cached in the data base
  ask-vals            ;   See if the user knows the answer
  use-rules           ;   See if there is a rule for it:
    reject-premise     ;     See if the rule is outright false
    satisfy-premises   ;     Or see if each condition is true:
      eval-condition   ;       Evaluate each condition
        find-out       ;         By finding the parameter's values
```

Before showing the interpreter, here is the structure definition for rules, along with the functions to maintain a data base of rules:

```
(defstruct (rule (:print-function print-rule))
  number premises conclusions cf)

(let ((rules (make-hash-table)))

  (defun put-rule (rule)
    "Put the rule in a table, indexed under each
    parm in the conclusion."
    (dolist (concl (rule-conclusions rule))
      (push rule (gethash (first concl) rules)))
    rule)

  (defun get-rules (parm)
    "A list of rules that help determine this parameter."
    (gethash parm rules))

  (defun clear-rules () (clrhash rules)))
```

Here, then, is the interpreter, find-out. It can find out the value(s) of a parameter three ways. First, it looks to see if the value is already stored in the data base. Next, it tries asking the user or using the rules. The order in which these two options are tried depends on the parm-ask-first property of the parameter. Either way, if an answer is determined, it is stored in the data base.

```
(defun find-out (parm &optional (inst (get-db 'current-instance)))
  "Find the value(s) of this parameter for this instance,
  unless the values are already known.
  Some parameters we ask first; others we use rules first."
  (or (get-db '(known ,parm ,inst))
      (put-db '(known ,parm ,inst)
              (if (parm-ask-first (get-parm parm))
                  (or (ask-vals parm inst) (use-rules parm))
                  (or (use-rules parm) (ask-vals parm inst))))))

(defun use-rules (parm)
  "Try every rule associated with this parameter.
  Return true if one of the rules returns true."
  (some #'true-p (mapcar #'use-rule (get-rules parm))))
```

```
(defun use-rule (rule)
  "Apply a rule to the current situation."
  ;; Keep track of the rule for the explanation system:
  (put-db 'current-rule rule)
  ;; If any premise is known false, give up.
  ;; If every premise can be proved true,  then
  ;; draw conclusions (weighted with the certainty factor).
  (unless (some #'reject-premise (rule-premises rule))
    (let ((cf (satisfy-premises (rule-premises rule) true)))
      (when (true-p cf)
        (dolist (conclusion (rule-conclusions rule))
          (conclude conclusion (* cf (rule-cf rule))))
        cf)))))

(defun satisfy-premises (premises cf-so-far)
  "A list of premises is satisfied if they are all true.
  A combined cf is returned."
  ;; cf-so-far is an accumulator of certainty factors
  (cond ((null premises) cf-so-far)
        ((not (true-p cf-so-far)) false)
        (t (satisfy-premises
             (rest premises)
             (cf-and cf-so-far
                     (eval-condition (first premises)))))))
```

The function eval-condition evaluates a single condition, returning its certainty factor. If find-out-p is true, it first calls find-out, which may either query the user or apply appropriate rules. If find-out-p is false, it evaluates the condition using the current state of the data base. It does this by looking at each stored value for the parameter/instance pair and evaluating the operator on it. For example, if the condition is (temp patient > 98.6) and the values for temp for the current patient are ((98 .3) (99 .6) (100 .1)), then eval-condition will test each of the values 98, 99, and 100 against 98.6 using the > operator. This test will succeed twice, so the resulting certainty factor is $.6 + .1 = .7$.

The function reject-premise is designed as a quick test to eliminate a rule. As such, it calls eval-condition with find-out-p nil, so it will reject a premise only if it is clearly false without seeking additional information.

If a rule's premises are true, then the conclusions are added to the data base by conclude. Note that is is the only operator allowed in conclusions. is is just an alias for equal.

```
(defun eval-condition (condition &optional (find-out-p t))
  "See if this condition is true, optionally using FIND-OUT
  to determine unknown parameters."
  (multiple-value-bind (parm inst op val)
      (parse-condition condition)
```

```
(when find-out-p
  (find-out parm inst))
;; Add up all the (val cf) pairs that satisfy the test
(loop for pair in (get-vals parm inst)
      when (funcall op (first pair) val)
      sum (second pair))))


(defun reject-premise (premise)
  "A premise is rejected if it is known false, without
  needing to call find-out recursively."
  (false-p (eval-condition premise nil)))

(defun conclude (conclusion cf)
  "Add a conclusion (with specified certainty factor) to DB."
  (multiple-value-bind (parm inst op val)
      (parse-condition conclusion)
    (update-cf parm inst val cf)))

(defun is (a b) (equal a b))
```

All conditions are of the form: (*parameter instance operator value*). For example: (morphology organism is rod). The function parse-condition turns a list of this form into four values. The trick is that it uses the data base to return the current instance of the context, rather than the context name itself:

```
(defun parse-condition (condition)
  "A condition is of the form (parm inst op val).
  So for (age patient is 21), we would return 4 values:
  (age patient-1 is 21), where patient-1 is the current patient."
  (values (first condition)
          (get-db (second condition))
          (third condition)
          (fourth condition)))
```

At this point a call like (find-out 'identity 'organism-1) would do the right thing only if we had somehow entered the proper information on the current patient, culture, and organism. The function get-context-data makes sure that each context is treated in order. First an instance is created, then find-out is used to determine both the initial data parameters and the goals. The findings for each goal are printed, and the program asks if there is another instance of this context. Finally, we also need a top-level function, emycin, which just clears the data base before calling get-context-data.

```
(defun emycin (contexts)
  "An Expert-System Shell.  Accumulate data for instances of each
  context, and solve for goals.  Then report the findings."
  (clear-db)
  (get-context-data contexts))

(defun get-context-data (contexts)
  "For each context, create an instance and try to find out
  required data.  Then go on to other contexts, depth first,
  and finally ask if there are other instances of this context."
  (unless (null contexts)
    (let* ((context (first contexts))
           (inst (new-instance context)))
      (put-db 'current-rule 'initial)
      (mapc #'find-out (context-initial-data context))
      (put-db 'current-rule 'goal)
      (mapc #'find-out (context-goals context))
      (report-findings context inst)
      (get-context-data (rest contexts))
      (when (y-or-n-p "Is there another ~a?"
                      (context-name context))
        (get-context-data contexts)))))
```

16.6   Interacting with the Expert

At this point all the serious computational work is done: we have defined a backward-chaining rule mechanism that deals with uncertainty, caching, questions, and contexts. But there is still quite a bit of work to do in terms of input/output interaction. A programming language needs only to interface with programmers, so it is acceptable to make the programmer do all the work. But an expert-system shell is supposed to alleviate (if not abolish) the need for programmers. Expert-system shells really have two classes of users: the experts use the shell when they are developing the system, and the end users or clients use the resulting expert system when it is completed. Sometimes the expert can enter knowledge directly into the shell, but more often it is assumed the expert will have the help of a *knowledge engineer*—someone who is trained in the use of the shell and in eliciting knowledge, but who need not be either an expert in the domain or an expert programmer.

In our version of EMYCIN, we provide only the simplest tools for making the expert's job easier. The macros defcontext and defparm, defined above, are a little easier than calling make-context and make-parm explicitly, but not much. The macro defrule defines a rule and checks for some obvious errors:

```
(defmacro defrule (number &body body)
  "Define a rule with conditions, a certainty factor, and
  conclusions.  Example: (defrule R001 if ... then .9 ...)"
  (assert (eq (first body) 'if))
  (let* ((then-part (member 'then body))
         (premises (ldiff (rest body) then-part))
         (conclusions (rest2 then-part))
         (cf (second then-part)))
    ;; Do some error checking:
    (check-conditions number premises 'premise)
    (check-conditions number conclusions 'conclusion)
    (when (not (cf-p cf))
      (warn "Rule ~a: Illegal certainty factor: ~a" number cf))
    ;; Now build the rule:
    '(put-rule
       (make-rule :number ',number :cf ,cf :premises ',premises
                  :conclusions ',conclusions))))
```

The function check-conditions makes sure that each rule has at least one premise
and conclusion, that each condition is of the right form, and that the value of the
condition is of the right type for the parameter. It also checks that conclusions use
only the operator is:

```
(defun check-conditions (rule-num conditions kind)
  "Warn if any conditions are invalid."
  (when (null conditions)
    (warn "Rule ~a: Missing ~a" rule-num kind))
  (dolist (condition conditions)
    (when (not (consp condition))
      (warn "Rule ~a: Illegal ~a: ~a" rule-num kind condition))
    (multiple-value-bind (parm inst op val)
        (parse-condition condition)
      (declare (ignore inst))
      (when (and (eq kind 'conclusion) (not (eq op 'is)))
        (warn "Rule ~a: Illegal operator (~a) in conclusion: ~a"
              rule-num op condition))
      (when (not (typep val (parm-type parm)))
        (warn "Rule ~a: Illegal value (~a) in ~a: ~a"
              rule-num val kind condition)))))
```

The real EMYCIN had an interactive environment that prompted the expert for each
context, parameter, and rule. Randall Davis (1977, 1979, Davis and Lenat 1982)
describes the TEIRESIAS program, which helped experts enter and debug rules.

16.7   Interacting with the Client

Once the knowledge is in, we need some way to get it out. The client wants to run the system on his or her own problem and see two things: a solution to the problem, and an explanation of why the solution is reasonable. EMYCIN provides primitive facilities for both of these. The function `report-findings` prints information on all the goal parameters for a given instance:

```
(defun report-findings (context inst)
  "Print findings on each goal for this instance."
  (when (context-goals context)
    (format t "~&Findings for ~a:" (inst-name inst))
    (dolist (goal (context-goals context))
      (let ((values (get-vals goal inst)))
        ;; If there are any values for this goal,
        ;; print them sorted by certainty factor.
        (if values
            (format t "~& ~a:~{~{ ~a (~,3f)  ~}~}" goal
                    (sort (copy-list values) #'> :key #'second))
            (format t "~& ~a: unknown" goal))))))
```

The only explanation facility our version of EMYCIN offers is a way to see the current rule. If the user types `rule` in response to a query, a pseudo-English translation of the current rule is printed. Here is a sample rule and its translation:

```
(defrule 52
  if (site culture is blood)
     (gram organism is neg)
     (morphology organism is rod)
     (burn patient is serious)
  then .4
     (identity organism is pseudomonas))

Rule 52:
  If
    1) THE SITE OF THE CULTURE IS BLOOD
    2) THE GRAM OF THE ORGANISM IS NEG
    3) THE MORPHOLOGY OF THE ORGANISM IS ROD
    4) THE BURN OF THE PATIENT IS SERIOUS
  Then there is weakly suggestive evidence (0.4) that
    1) THE IDENTITY OF THE ORGANISM IS PSEUDOMONAS
```

The function `print-rule` generates this translation:

```
(defun print-rule (rule &optional (stream t) depth)
  (declare (ignore depth))
  (format stream "~&Rule ~a:~& If" (rule-number rule))
  (print-conditions (rule-premises rule) stream)
  (format stream "~&  Then ~a (~a) that"
          (cf->english (rule-cf rule)) (rule-cf rule))
  (print-conditions (rule-conclusions rule) stream))

(defun print-conditions (conditions &optional
                                    (stream t) (num 1))
  "Print a list of numbered conditions."
  (dolist (condition conditions)
    (print-condition condition stream num)))

(defun print-condition (condition stream number)
  "Print a single condition in pseudo-English."
  (format stream "~&    ~d)~{ ~a~}" number
          (let ((parm (first condition))
                (inst (second condition))
                (op (third condition))
                (val (fourth condition)))
            (case val
              (YES '(the ,inst ,op ,parm))
              (NO  '(the ,inst ,op not ,parm))
              (T   '(the ,parm of the ,inst ,op ,val))))))

(defun cf->english (cf)
  "Convert a certainy factor to an English phrase."
  (cond ((= cf  1.0) "there is certain evidence")
        ((> cf   .8) "there is strongly suggestive evidence")
        ((> cf   .5) "there is suggestive evidence")
        ((> cf  0.0) "there is weakly suggestive evidence")
        ((= cf  0.0) "there is NO evidence either way")
        ((< cf  0.0) (concatenate 'string (cf->english (- cf))
                                  " AGAINST the conclusion"))))
```

If the user types why in response to a query, a more detailed account of the same rule is printed. First, the premises that are already known are displayed, followed by the remainder of the rule. The parameter being asked for will always be the first premise in the remainder of the rule. The current-rule is stored in the data base by use-rule whenever a rule is applied, but it is also set by get-context-data to the atom initial or goal when the system is prompting for parameters. print-why checks for this case as well. Note the use of the partition-if function from page 256.

```
(defun print-why (rule parm)
  "Tell why this rule is being used.  Print what is known,
what we are trying to find out, and what we can conclude."
  (format t "~&[Why is the value of ~a being asked for?]" parm)
  (if (member rule '(initial goal))
      (format t "~&~a is one of the ~a parameters."
              parm rule)
      (multiple-value-bind (knowns unknowns)
          (partition-if #'(lambda (premise)
                            (true-p (eval-condition premise nil)))
                        (rule-premises rule))
        (when knowns
          (format t "~&It is known that:")
          (print-conditions knowns)
          (format t "~&Therefore,"))
        (let ((new-rule (copy-rule rule)))
          (setf (rule-premises new-rule) unknowns)
          (print new-rule)))))
```

That completes the definition of emycin. We are now ready to apply the shell to a specific domain, yielding the beginnings of an expert system.

16.8 MYCIN, A Medical Expert System

This section applies emycin to MYCIN's original domain: infectious blood disease. In our version of MYCIN, there are three contexts: first we consider a patient, then any cultures that have been grown from samples taken from the patient, and finally any infectious organisms in the cultures. The goal is to determine the identity of each organism. The real MYCIN was more complex, taking into account any drugs or operations the patient may previously have had. It also went on to decide the real question: what therapy to prescribe. However, much of this was done by special-purpose procedures to compute optimal dosages and the like, so it is not included here. The original MYCIN also made a distinction between current versus prior cultures, organisms, and drugs. All together, it had ten contexts to consider, while our version only has three:

```
(defun mycin ()
  "Determine what organism is infecting a patient."
  (emycin
    (list (defcontext patient  (name sex age)  ())
          (defcontext culture  (site days-old) ())
          (defcontext organism ()              (identity)))))
```

These contexts declare that we will first ask each patient's name, sex, and age, and each culture's site and the number of days ago it was isolated. Organisms have no initial questions, but they do have a goal: to determine the identity of the organism.

The next step is to declare parameters for the contexts. Each parameter is given a type, and most are given prompts to improve the naturalness of the dialogue:

```
;;; Parameters for patient:
(defparm name patient t "Patient's name: " t read-line)
(defparm sex patient (member male female) "Sex:" t)
(defparm age patient number "Age:" t)
(defparm burn patient (member no mild serious)
  "Is ~a a burn patient?  If so, mild or serious?" t)
(defparm compromised-host patient yes/no
  "Is ~a a compromised host?")

;;; Parameters for culture:
(defparm site culture (member blood)
  "From what site was the specimen for ~a taken?" t)
(defparm days-old culture number
  "How many days ago was this culture (~a) obtained?" t)

;;; Parameters for organism:
(defparm identity organism
  (member pseudomonas klebsiella enterobacteriaceae
          staphylococcus bacteroides streptococcus)
  "Enter the identity (genus) of ~a:" t)
(defparm gram organism (member acid-fast pos neg)
  "The gram stain of ~a:" t)
(defparm morphology organism (member rod coccus)
  "Is ~a a rod or coccus (etc.):")
(defparm aerobicity organism (member aerobic anaerobic))
(defparm growth-conformation organism
  (member chains pairs clumps))
```

Now we need some rules to help determine the identity of the organisms. The following rules are taken from Shortliffe 1976. The rule numbers refer to the pages on which they are listed. The real MYCIN had about 400 rules, dealing with a much wider variety of premises and conclusions.

```
(clear-rules)

(defrule 52
  if (site culture is blood)
     (gram organism is neg)
     (morphology organism is rod)
     (burn patient is serious)
  then .4
     (identity organism is pseudomonas))
```

```
(defrule 71
  if (gram organism is pos)
     (morphology organism is coccus)
     (growth-conformation organism is clumps)
  then .7
     (identity organism is staphylococcus))

(defrule 73
  if (site culture is blood)
     (gram organism is neg)
     (morphology organism is rod)
     (aerobicity organism is anaerobic)
  then .9
     (identity organism is bacteroides))

(defrule 75
  if (gram organism is neg)
     (morphology organism is rod)
     (compromised-host patient is yes)
  then .6
     (identity organism is pseudomonas))

(defrule 107
  if (gram organism is neg)
     (morphology organism is rod)
     (aerobicity organism is aerobic)
  then .8
     (identity organism is enterobacteriaceae))

(defrule 165
  if (gram organism is pos)
     (morphology organism is coccus)
     (growth-conformation organism is chains)
  then .7
     (identity organism is streptococcus))
```

Here is an example of the program in use:

```
> (mycin)
------ PATIENT-1 ------
Patient's name: Sylvia Fischer
Sex: female
Age: 27
------ CULTURE-1 ------
From what site was the specimen for CULTURE-1 taken? blood
How many days ago was this culture (CULTURE-1) obtained? 3
------ ORGANISM-1 ------
Enter the identity (genus) of ORGANISM-1: unknown
The gram stain of ORGANISM-1: ?
```

```
A GRAM must be of type (MEMBER ACID-FAST POS NEG)
The gram stain of ORGANISM-1: neg
```

The user typed ? to see the list of valid responses. The dialog continues:

```
Is ORGANISM-1 a rod or coccus (etc.): rod
What is the AEROBICITY of ORGANISM-1? why
[Why is the value of AEROBICITY being asked for?]
It is known that:
    1) THE GRAM OF THE ORGANISM IS NEG
    2) THE MORPHOLOGY OF THE ORGANISM IS ROD
Therefore,
Rule 107:
  If
    1) THE AEROBICITY OF THE ORGANISM IS AEROBIC
  Then there is suggestive evidence (0.8) that
    1) THE IDENTITY OF THE ORGANISM IS ENTEROBACTERIACEAE
```

The user wants to know why the system is asking about the organism's aerobicity. The reply shows the current rule, what is already known about the rule, and the fact that if the organism is aerobic, then we can conclude something about its identity. In this hypothetical case, the organism is in fact aerobic:

```
What is the AEROBICITY of ORGANISM-1? aerobic
Is Sylvia Fischer a compromised host? yes
Is Sylvia Fischer a burn patient? If so, mild or serious? why
[Why is the value of BURN being asked for?]
It is known that:
    1) THE SITE OF THE CULTURE IS BLOOD
    2) THE GRAM OF THE ORGANISM IS NEG
    3) THE MORPHOLOGY OF THE ORGANISM IS ROD
Therefore,
Rule 52:
  If
    1) THE BURN OF THE PATIENT IS SERIOUS
  Then there is weakly suggestive evidence (0.4) that
    1) THE IDENTITY OF THE ORGANISM IS PSEUDOMONAS
Is Sylvia Fischer a burn patient? If so, mild or serious? serious
Findings for ORGANISM-1:
 IDENTITY: ENTEROBACTERIACEAE (0.800)    PSEUDOMONAS (0.760)
```

The system used rule 107 to conclude the identity might be enterobacteriaceae. The certainty is .8, the certainty for the rule itself, because all the conditions were known to be true with certainty. Rules 52 and 75 both support the hypothesis of pseudomonas. The certainty factors of the two rules, .6 and .4, are combined by the formula $.6 + .4 - (.6 \times .4) = .76$. After printing the findings for the first organism, the system asks if another organism was obtained from this culture:

```
Is there another ORGANISM? (Y or N) Y
------ ORGANISM-2 ------
Enter the identity (genus) of ORGANISM-2: unknown
The gram stain of ORGANISM-2: (neg .8 pos .2)
Is ORGANISM-2 a rod or coccus (etc.): rod
What is the AEROBICITY of ORGANISM-2?  anaerobic
```

For the second organism, the lab test was inconclusive, so the user entered a qualified answer indicating that it is probably gram-negative, but perhaps gram-positive. This organism was also a rod but was anaerobic. Note that the system does not repeat questions that it already knows the answers to. In considering rules 75 and 52 it already knows that the culture came from the blood, and that the patient is a compromised host and a serious burn patient. In the end, rule 73 contributes to the bacteroides conclusion, and rules 75 and 52 again combine to suggest pseudomonas, although with a lower certainty factor, because the neg finding had a lower certainty factor:

```
Findings for ORGANISM-2:
  IDENTITY: BACTEROIDES (0.720)   PSEUDOMONAS (0.646)
```

Finally, the program gives the user the opportunity to extend the context tree with new organisms, cultures, or patients:

```
Is there another ORGANISM? (Y or N) N
Is there another CULTURE? (Y or N) N
Is there another PATIENT? (Y or N) N
```

The set of rules listed above do not demonstrate two important features of the system: the ability to backward-chain, and the ability to use operators other than `is` in premises.

If we add the following three rules and repeat the case shown above, then evaluating rule 75 will back-chain to rule 1, 2, and finally 3 trying to determine if the patient is a compromised host. Note that the question asked will be "What is Sylvia Fischer's white blood cell count?" and not "Is the white blood cell count of Sylvia Fischer < 2.5?" The latter question would suffice for the premise at hand, but it would not be as useful for other rules that might refer to the WBC.

```
(defparm wbc patient number
  "What is ~a's white blood cell count?")
```

```
(defrule 1
  if (immunosuppressed patient is yes)
  then 1.0 (compromised-host patient is yes))

(defrule 2
  if (leukopenia patient is yes)
  then 1.0 (immunosuppressed patient is yes))

(defrule 3
  if (wbc patient < 2.5)
  then .9 (leukopenia patient is yes))
```

16.9 Alternatives to Certainty Factors

Certainty factors are a compromise. The good news is that a system based on rules with certainty factors requires the expert to come up with only a small set of numbers (one for each rule) and will allow fast computation of answers. The bad news is that the answer computed may lead to irrational decisions.

Certainty factors have been justified by their performance (MYCIN performed as well or better than expert doctors) and by intuitive appeal (they satisfy the criteria listed on page 534). However, they are subject to paradoxes where they compute bizarre results (as in Exercise 16.1, page 536). If the rules that make up the knowledge base are designed in a modular fashion, then problems usually do not arise, but it is certainly worrisome that the answers may be untrustworthy.

Before MYCIN, most reasoning with uncertainty was done using probability theory. The laws of probability—in particular, Bayes's law—provide a well-founded mathematical formalism that is not subject to the inconsistencies of certainty factors. Indeed, probability theory can be shown to be the only formalism that leads to rational behavior, in the sense that if you have to make a series of bets on some uncertain events, combining information with probability theory will give you the highest expected value for your bets. Despite this, probability theory was largely set aside in the mid-1970s. The argument made by Shortliffe and Buchanan (1975) was that probability theory required too many conditional probabilities, and that people were not good at estimating these. They argued that certainty factors were intuitively easier to deal with. Other researchers of the time shared this view. Shafer, with later refinements by Dempster, created a theory of belief functions that, like certainty factors, represented a combination of the belief for and against an event. Instead of representing an event by a single probability or certainty, Dempster-Shafer theory maintains two numbers, which are analogous to the lower and upper bound on the probability. Instead of a single number like .5, Dempster-Shafer theory would have an interval like [.4,.6] to represent a range of probabilities. A complete lack of knowledge would be represented by the range [0,1]. A great deal of effort in the late 1970s and early 1980s was invested in these and other nonprobabilistic theories. Another example is Zadeh's fuzzy set theory, which is also based on intervals.

There is ample evidence that people have difficulty with problems involving probability. In a very entertaining and thought-provoking series of articles, Tversky and Kahneman (1974, 1983, 1986) show how people make irrational choices when faced with problems that are quite simple from a mathematical viewpoint. They liken these errors in choice to errors in visual perception caused by optical illusions. Even trained doctors and statisticians are subject to these errors.

As an example, consider the following scenario. Adrian and Dominique are to be married. Adrian goes for a routine blood test and is told that the results are positive for a rare genetic disorder, one that strikes only 1 in 10,000 people. The doctor says that the test is 99% accurate—it gives a false positive reading in only 1 in 100 cases. Adrian is despondent, being convinced that the probability of actually having the disease is 99%. Fortunately, Dominique happens to be a Bayesian, and quickly reassures Adrian that the chance is more like 1%. The reasoning is as follows: Take 10,001 people at random. Of these, only 1 is expected to have the disease. That person could certainly expect to test positive for the disease. But if the other 10,000 people all took the blood test, then 1% of them, or 100 people would also test positive. Thus, the chance of actually having the disease given that one tests positive is 1/101. Doctors are trained in this kind of analysis, but unfortunately many of them continue to reason more like Adrian than Dominique.

In the late 1980s, the tide started to turn back to subjective Bayesian probability theory. Cheeseman (1985) showed that, while Dempster-Shafer theory looks like it can, in fact it cannot help you make better decisions than probability theory. Heckerman (1986) re-examined MYCIN's certainty factors, showing how they could be interpreted as probabilities. Judea Pearl's 1988 book is an eloquent defense of probability theory. He shows that there are efficient algorithms for combining and propagating probabilities, as long as the network of interdependencies does not contain loops. It seems likely that uncertain reasoning in the 1990s will be based increasingly on Bayesian probability theory.

16.10   History and References

The MYCIN project is well documented in Buchanan and Shortliffe 1984. An earlier book, Shortliffe 1976, is interesting mainly for historical purposes. Good introductions to expert systems in general include Weiss and Kulikowski 1984, Waterman 1986, Luger and Stubblefield 1989, and Jackson 1990.

Dempster-Shafer evidence theory is presented enthusiastically in Gordon and Shortliffe 1984 and in a critical light in Pearl 1989/1978. Fuzzy set theory is presented in Zadeh 1979 and Dubois and Prade 1988.

Pearl (1988) captures most of the important points that lead to the renaissance of probability theory. Shafer and Pearl 1990 is a balanced collection of papers on all kinds of uncertain reasoning.

16.11   Exercises

Exercise 16.2 [s]   Suppose the rule writer wanted to be able to use symbolic certainty factors instead of numbers. What would you need to change to support rules like this:

```
(defrule 100 if ... then true ...)
(defrule 101 if ... then probably ...)
```

Exercise 16.3 [m]   Change `prompt-and-read-vals` so that it gives a better prompt for parameters of type yes/no.

Exercise 16.4 [m]   Currently, the rule writer can introduce a new parameter without defining it first. That is handy for rapid testing, but it means that the user of the system won't be able to see a nice English prompt, nor ask for the type of the parameter. In addition, if the rule writer simply misspells a parameter, it will be treated as a new one. Make a simple change to fix these problems.

Exercise 16.5 [d]   Write rules in a domain you are an expert in, or find and interview an expert in some domain, and write down rules coaxed from the expert. Evaluate your resulting system. Was it easier to develop your system with EMYCIN than it would have been without it?

Exercise 16.6 [s]   It is said that an early version of MYCIN asked if the patient was pregnant, even though the patient was male. Write a rule that would fix this problem.

Exercise 16.7 [m]   To a yes/no question, what is the difference between yes and (no -1)? What does this suggest?

Exercise 16.8 [m]   What happens if the user types why to the prompt about the patient's name? What happens if the expert wants to have more than one context with a name parameter? If there is a problem, fix it.

The remaining exercises discuss extensions that were in the original EMYCIN, but were not implemented in our version. Implementing all the extensions will result in a system that is very close to the full power of EMYCIN. These extensions are discussed in chapter 3 of Buchanan and Shortliffe 1984.

Exercise 16.9 [h] Add a spelling corrector to ask-vals. If the user enters an invalid reply, and the parameter type is a member expression, check if the reply is "close" in spelling to one of the valid values, and if so, use that value. That way, the user can type just entero instead of enterobacteriaceae. You may experiment with the definition of "close," but you should certainly allow for prefixes and at least one instance of a changed, missing, inserted, or transposed letter.

Exercise 16.10 [m] Indent the output for each new branch in the context tree. In other words, have the prompts and findings printed like this:

```
------ PATIENT-1 ------
Patient's name: Sylvia Fischer
Sex: female
Age: 27
    ------ CULTURE-1 ------
    From what site was the specimen for CULTURE-1 taken? blood
    How many days ago was this culture (CULTURE-1) obtained? 3
        ------ ORGANISM-1 ------
        Enter the identity (genus) of ORGANISM-1: unknown
        The gram stain of ORGANISM-1: neg
        ...
        Findings for ORGANISM-1:
         IDENTITY: ENTEROBACTERIACEAE (0.800) PSEUDOMONAS (0.760)
        Is there another ORGANISM? (Y or N) N
    Is there another CULTURE? (Y or N) N
Is there another PATIENT? (Y or N) N
```

Exercise 16.11 [h] We said that our emycin looks at all possible rules for each parameter, because there is no telling how a later rule may affect the certainty factor. Actually, that is not quite true. If there is a rule that leads to a conclusion with certainty 1, then no other rules need be considered. This was called a *unity path*. Modify the program to look for unity paths first.

Exercise 16.12 [m] Depending on whether a parameter is in initial-data or not, all the relevant rules are run either before or after asking the user for the value of the parameter. But there are some cases when not all initial data parameters should be asked for. As an example, suppose that identity and gram were initial data parameters of organism. If the user gave a positive answer for identity, then it would be wasteful to ask for the gram parameter, since it could be determined directly from rules. After receiving complaints about this problem, a system of *antecedent rules* was developed. These rules were always run first, before asking questions. Implement antecedent rules.

Exercise 16.13 [h] It is useful to be able to write *default rules* that fill in a value after all other rules have failed to determine one. A default rule looks like this:

```
(defrule n if (parm inst unknown) then (parm inst is default))
```

It may also have other conjuncts in the premise. Beside details like writing the unknown operator, the difficult part is in making sure that these rules get run at the right time (after other rules have had a chance to fill in the parameter), and that infinite loops are avoided.

Exercise 16.14 [h] The context tree proved to be a limitation. Eventually, the need arose for a rule that said, "If any of the organisms in a culture has property X, then the culture has property Y." Implement a means of checking for some or every instance of a context.

Exercise 16.15 [m] As the rule base grew, it became increasingly hard to remember the justification for previous rules. Implement a mechanism that keeps track of the author and date of creation of each rule, and allows the author to add documentation explaining the rationale for the rule.

Exercise 16.16 [m] It is difficult to come up with the perfect prompt for each parameter. One solution is not to insist that one prompt fits all users, but rather to allow the expert to supply three different prompts: a normal prompt, a verbose prompt (or reprompt) for when the user replies with a ?, and a terse prompt for the experienced user. Modify defparm to accommodate this concept, add a command for the user to ask for the terse prompts, and change ask-vals to use the proper prompt.

The remaining exercises cover three additional replies the user can make: how, stop, and change.

Exercise 16.17 [d] In addition to why replies, EMYCIN also allowed for how questions. The user can ask how the value of a particular parameter/instance pair was determined, and the system will reply with a list of rules and the evidence they supplied for or against each value. Implement this mechanism. It will require storing additional information in the data base.

Exercise 16.18 [m]   There was also a stop command that immediately halted the session. Implement it.

Exercise 16.19 [d]   The original EMYCIN also had a change command to allow the user to change the answer to certain questions without starting all over. Each question was assigned a number, which was printed before the prompt. The command change, followed by a list of numbers, causes the system to look up the questions associated with each number and delete the answer to these questions. The system also throws away the entire context tree and all derived parameter values. At that point the entire consultation is restarted, using only the data obtained from the unchanged questions. Although it may seem wasteful to start over from the beginning, it will not be wasteful of the user's time, since correct answers will not be asked again.

Identify what needs to be altered to implement change and make the alterations.

Exercise 16.20 [h]   Change the definition of cf-and and cf-or to use fuzzy set theory instead of certainty factors. Do the same for Dempster-Shafer theory.

16.12   Answers

Answer 16.1   Because EMYCIN assumes independence, each reading of the same headline would increase the certainty factor. The following computation shows that 298 more copies would be needed to reach .95 certainty. A more sophisticated reasoner would realize that multiple copies of a newspaper are completely dependent on one another, and would not change the certainty with each new copy.

```
> (loop for cf = .01 then (cf-or .01 cf)
        until (> cf .95)
        count t)
298
```

Answer 16.2   The defrule expands to (make-rule :number '101 :cf true ...); that is, the certainty factor is unquoted, so it is already legal to use true as a certainty factor! To support probably and other hedges, just define new constants.

Answer 16.4 Just make the default parameter type be nil (by changing t to nil in parm-type). Then any rule that uses an undefined parameter will automatically generate a warning.

Answer 16.6

```
(defrule 4
  if (sex patient is male)
  then -1 (pregnant patient is yes))
```

Answer 16.7 Logically, there should be no difference, but to EMYCIN there is a big difference. EMYCIN would not complain if you answered (yes 1 no 1). This suggests that the system should have some way of dealing with mutually exclusive answers. One way would be to accept only yes responses for Boolean parameters, but have the input routine translate no to (yes -1) and (no *cf*) to (yes 1−*cf*). Another possibility would be to have update-cf check to see if any certainty factor on a mutually exclusive value is 1, and if so, change the other values to -1.

Answer 16.18 Add the clause (stop (throw 'stop nil)) to the case statement in ask-vals and wrap a (catch 'stop ...) around the code in emycin.

CHAPTER 17

Line-Diagram Labeling by Constraint Satisfaction

*It is wrong to think of Waltz's work only as a
statement of the epistemology of line drawings of
polyhedra. Instead I think it is an elegant case study
of a paradigm we can expect to see again and again.*

—Patrick Winston
The Psychology of Computer Vision (1975)

This book touches only the areas of AI that deal with abstract reasoning. There is another side of AI, the field of *robotics*, that deals with interfacing abstract reasoning with the real world through sensors and motors. A robot receives input from cameras, microphones, sonar, and touch-sensitive devices, and produces "ouput" by moving its appendages or generating sounds. The real world is a messier place than the abstract worlds we have been covering. A robot must deal with noisy data, faulty components, and other agents and events in the world that can affect changes in the environment.

Computer vision is the subfield of robotics that deals with interpreting visual information. Low-level vision takes its input directly from a camera and detects lines, regions and textures. We will not be concerned with this. High-level vision uses the findings of the low-level component to build a three-dimensional model of the objects depicted in the scene. This chapter covers one small aspect of high-level vision.

17.1   The Line-Labeling Problem

In this chapter we look at the line-diagram labeling problem: Given a list of lines and the vertexes at which they intersect, how can we determine what the lines represent? For example, given the nine lines in figure 17.1, how can we interpret the diagram as a cube?

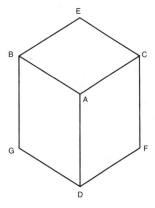

Figure 17.1: A Cube

Before we can arrive at an interpretation, we have to agree on what the candidates are. After all, figure 17.1 could be just a hexagon with three lines in the middle. For the purposes of this chapter, we will consider only diagrams that depict one or more *polyhedra*—three-dimensional solid figures whose surfaces are flat faces bounded by straight lines. In addition, we will only allow *trihedral* vertexes. That is, each vertex must be formed by the intersection of three faces, as in the corner of a cube, where the top, front, and side of the cube come together. A third restriction on diagrams is that no so-called *accidental* vertexes are allowed. For example, figure 17.1 might be a picture of three different cubes hanging in space, which just happen to line up so that the edge of one is aligned with the edge of another from our viewpoint. We will assume that this is not the case.

Given a diagram that fits these three restrictions, our goal is to identify each line, placing it in one of three classes:

1. A convex line separates two visible faces of a polyhedron such that a line from one face to the other would lie inside the polyhedron. It will be marked with a plus sign: +.

2. A concave line separates two faces of two polyhedra such that a line between the two spaces would pass through empty space. It will be marked with a minus sign: −.

3. A boundary line denotes the same physical situation as a convex line, but the diagram is oriented in such a way that only one of the two faces of the polyhedron is visible. Thus, the line marks the boundary between the polyhedron and the background. It will be marked with an arrow: →. Traveling along the line from the tail to the point of the arrow, the polyhedron is on the right, and the background is on the left.

Figure 17.2 shows a labeling of the cube using these conventions. Vertex A is the near corner of the cube, and the three lines coming out of it are all convex lines. Lines GD and DF are concave lines, indicating the junction between the cube and the surface on which it is resting. The remaining lines are boundary lines, indicating that there is no physical connection between the cube and the background there, but that there are other sides of the cube that cannot be seen.

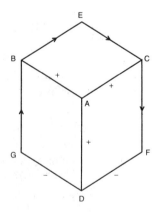

Figure 17.2: A Line-labeled Cube

The line-labeling technique developed in this chapter is based on a simple idea. First we enumerate all the possible vertexes, and all the possible labelings for each vertex. It turns out there are only four different vertex types in the trihedral polygon world. We call them L, Y, W, and T vertexes, because of their shape. The Y and W vertexes are also known as forks and arrows, respectively. The vertexes are listed in figure 17.3. Each vertex imposes some constraints on the lines that compose it. For example, in a W vertex, the middle line can be labeled with a + or −, but not with an arrow.

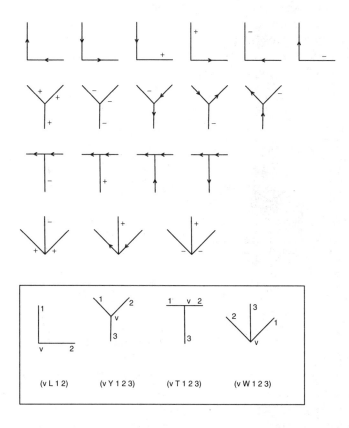

Figure 17.3: The Possible Vertexes and Labels

Each line connects two vertexes, so it must satisfy both constraints. This suggests a simple algorithm for labeling a diagram based on constraint propagation: First, label each vertex with all the possible labelings for the vertex type. An L vertex has six possibilities, Y has five, T has four, and W has three. Next, pick a vertex, V. Consider a neighboring vertex, N (that is, N and V are connected by a line). N will also have a set of possible labelings. If N and V agree on the possible labelings for the line between them, then we have gained nothing. But if the intersection of the two possibility sets is smaller than V's possibility set, then we have found a constraint on the diagram. We adjust N and V's possible labelings accordingly. Every time we add a constraint at a vertex, we repeat the whole process for all the neighboring vertexes, to give the constraint a chance to propagate as far as possible. When every vertex has been visited at least once and there are no more constraints to propagate, then we are done.

Figure 17.4 illustrates this process. On the left we start with a cube. All vertexes have all possible labelings, except that we know line GD is concave (-), indicating that the cube is resting on a surface. This constrains vertex D in such a way that line DA must be convex (+). In the middle picture the constraint on vertex D has propagated to vertex A, and in the right-hand picture it propagates to vertex B. Soon, the whole cube will be uniquely labeled.

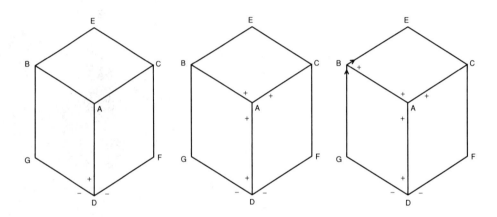

Figure 17.4: Propagating Constraints

Many diagrams will be labeled uniquely by this constraint propagation process. Some diagrams, however, are ambiguous. They will still have multiple labelings after constraint propagation has finished. In this case, we can search for a solution. Simply choose an ambiguous vertex, choose one of the possible labelings for that vertex, and repeat the constraint propagation/search process. Keep going until the diagram is either unambiguous or inconsistent.

That completes the sketch of the line-labeling algorithm. We are now ready to implement a labeling program. It's glossary is in figure 17.5.

The two main data structures are the diagram and the vertex. It would have been possible to implement a data type for lines, but it is not necessary: lines are defined implicitly by the two vertexes at their end points.

A diagram is completely specified by its list of vertexes, so the structure diagram needs only one slot. A vertex, on the other hand, is a more complex structure. Each vertex has an identifying name (usually a single letter), a vertex type (L, Y, W, or T), a

	Top-Level Functions
print-labelings	Label the diagram by propagating constraints and then searching.
	Data Types
diagram	A diagram is a list of vertexes.
vertex	A vertex has a name, type, and list of neighbors and labelings.
	Major Functions
find-labelings	Do the same constraint propagation, but don't print anything.
propagate-constraints	Reduce the number of labelings on vertex by considering neighbors.
consistent-labelings	Return the set of labelings that are consistent with neighbors.
search-solutions	Try all labelings for one ambiguous vertex, and propagate.
defdiagram	(macro) Define a diagram.
diagram	Retrieve a diagram stored by name.
ground	Attach the line between the two vertexes to the ground.
	Auxiliary Functions
labels-for	Return all the labels for the line going to vertex.
reverse-label	Reverse left and right on arrow labels.
ambiguous-vertex-p	A vertex is ambiguous if it has more than one labeling.
number-of-labelings	Number of labels on a vertex.
find-vertex	Find the vertex with the given name.
matrix-transpose	Turn a matrix on its side.
possible-labelings	The list of possible labelings for a given vertex type.
print-vertex	Print a vertex in the short form.
show-vertex	Print a vertex in a long form, on a new line.
show-diagram	Print a diagram in a long form. Include a title.
construct-diagram	Build a new diagram from a set of vertex descriptions.
construct-vertex	Build a new vertex from a vertex description.
make-copy-diagram	Make a copy of a diagram, preserving connectivity.
check-diagram	Check if the description appears consistent.

Figure 17.5: Glossary for the Line-Labeling Program

list of neighboring vertexes, and a list of possible labelings. A labeling is a list of line labels. For example, a Y vertex will initially have a list of five possible labelings. If it is discovered that the vertex is the interior of a concave corner, then it will have the single labeling (- - -). We give type information on the slots of vertex because it is a complicated data type. The syntax of defstruct is such that you cannot specify a :type without first specifying a default value. We chose L as the default value for the type slot at random, but note that it would have been an error to give nil as the default value, because nil is not of the right type.

```
(defstruct diagram "A diagram is a list of vertexes." vertexes)
(defstruct (vertex (:print-function print-vertex))
    (name      nil :type atom)
    (type      'L  :type (member L Y W T))
    (neighbors nil :type list)  ; of vertex
    (labelings nil :type list)) ; of lists of (member + - L R)))))
```

An ambiguous vertex will have several labelings, while an unambiguous vertex has exactly one, and a vertex with no labelings indicates an impossible diagram. Initially we don't know which vertexes are what, so they all start with several possible labelings. Note that a labeling is a list, not a set: the order of the labels is significant and matches the order of the neighboring vertexes. The function possible-labelings gives a list of all possible labelings for each vertex type. We use R and L instead of arrows as labels, because the orientation of the arrows is significant. An R means that as you travel from the vertex to its neighbor, the polyhedron is on the right and the background object is on the left. Thus, an R is equivalent to an arrow pointing away from the vertex. The L is just the reverse.

```lisp
(defun ambiguous-vertex-p (vertex)
  "A vertex is ambiguous if it has more than one labeling."
  (> (number-of-labelings vertex) 1))

(defun number-of-labelings (vertex)
  (length (vertex-labelings vertex)))

(defun impossible-vertex-p (vertex)
  "A vertex is impossible if it has no labeling."
  (null (vertex-labelings vertex)))

(defun impossible-diagram-p (diagram)
  "An impossible diagram is one with an impossible vertex."
  (some #'impossible-vertex-p (diagram-vertexes diagram)))

(defun possible-labelings (vertex-type)
  "The list of possible labelings for a given vertex type."
  ;; In these labelings, R means an arrow pointing away from
  ;; the vertex, L means an arrow pointing towards it.
  (case vertex-type
    ((L) '((R L)   (L R)   (+ R)   (L +)   (- L)   (R -)))
    ((Y) '((+ + +) (- - -) (L R -) (- L R) (R - L)))
    ((T) '((R L +) (R L -) (R L L) (R L R)))
    ((W) '((L R +) (- - +) (+ + -)))))
```

17.2   Combining Constraints and Searching

The main function print-labelings takes a diagram as input, reduces the number of labelings on each vertex by constraint propagation, and then searches for all consistent interpretations. Output is printed before and after each step.

```lisp
(defun print-labelings (diagram)
  "Label the diagram by propagating constraints and then
  searching for solutions if necessary.  Print results."
  (show-diagram diagram "~&The initial diagram is:")
  (every #'propagate-constraints (diagram-vertexes diagram))
  (show-diagram diagram
             "~2&After constraint propagation the diagram is:")
  (let* ((solutions (if (impossible-diagram-p diagram)
                        nil
                        (search-solutions diagram)))
         (n (length solutions)))
    (unless (= n 1)
      (format t "~2&There are ~r solution~:p:" n)
      (mapc #'show-diagram solutions)))
  (values))
```

The function `propagate-constraints` takes a vertex and considers the constraints imposed by neighboring vertexes to get a list of all the `consistent-labelings` for the vertex. If the number of consistent labelings is less than the number before we started, then the neighbors' constraints have had an effect on this vertex, so we propagate the new-found constraints on this vertex back to each neighbor. The function returns nil and thus immediately stops the propagation if there is an impossible vertex. Otherwise, propagation continues until there are no more changes to the labelings.

The whole propagation algorithm is started by a call to every in `print-labelings`, which propagates constraints from each vertex in the diagram. But it is not obvious that this is all that is required. After propagating from each vertex once, couldn't there be another vertex that needs relabeling? The only vertex that could possibly need relabeling would be one that had a neighbor changed since its last update. But any such vertex would have been visited by `propagate-constraint`, since we propagate to all neighbors. Thus, a single pass through the vertexes, compounded with recursive calls, will find and apply all possible constraints.

The next question worth asking is if the algorithm is guaranteed to terminate. Clearly, it is, because `propagate-constraints` can only produce recursive calls when it removes a labeling. But since there are a finite number of labelings initially (no more than six per vertex), there must be a finite number of calls to `propagate-constraints`.

```lisp
(defun propagate-constraints (vertex)
  "Reduce the labelings on vertex by considering neighbors.
  If we can reduce, propagate the constraints to each neighbor."
  ;; Return nil only when the constraints lead to an impossibility
  (let ((old-num (number-of-labelings vertex)))
    (setf (vertex-labelings vertex) (consistent-labelings vertex))
    (unless (impossible-vertex-p vertex)
      (when (< (number-of-labelings vertex) old-num)
        (every #'propagate-constraints (vertex-neighbors vertex)))
      t)))
```

The function `consistent-labelings` is passed a vertex. It gets all the labels for this vertex from the neighboring vertexes, collecting them in `neighbor-labels`. It then checks all the labels on the current vertex, keeping only the ones that are consistent with all the neighbors' constraints. The auxiliary function `labels-for` finds the labels for a particular neighbor at a vertex, and `reverse-label` accounts for the fact that L and R labels are interpreted with respect to the vertex they point at.

```
(defun consistent-labelings (vertex)
  "Return the set of labelings that are consistent with neighbors."
  (let ((neighbor-labels
          (mapcar #'(lambda (neighbor) (labels-for neighbor vertex))
                  (vertex-neighbors vertex))))
    ;; Eliminate labelings that don't have all lines consistent
    ;; with the corresponding line's label from the neighbor.
    ;; Account for the L-R mismatch with reverse-label.
    (find-all-if
      #'(lambda (labeling)
          (every #'member (mapcar #'reverse-label labeling)
                 neighbor-labels))
      (vertex-labelings vertex))))
```

Constraint propagation is often sufficient to yield a unique interpretation. But sometimes the diagram is still underconstrained, and we will have to search for solutions. The function `search-solutions` first checks to see if the diagram is ambiguous, by seeing if it has an ambiguous vertex, v. If the diagram is unambiguous, then it is a solution, and we return it (in a list, since `search-solutions` is designed to return a list of all solutions). Otherwise, for each of the possible labelings for the ambiguous vertex, we create a brand new copy of the diagram and set v's labeling in the copy to one of the possible labelings. In effect, we are guessing that a labeling is a correct one. We call `propagate-constraints`; if it fails, then we have guessed wrong, so there are no solutions with this labeling. But if it succeeds, then we call `search-solutions` recursively to give us the list of solutions generated by this labeling.

```
(defun search-solutions (diagram)
  "Try all labelings for one ambiguous vertex, and propagate."
  ;; If there is no ambiguous vertex, return the diagram.
  ;; If there is one, make copies of the diagram trying each of
  ;; the possible labelings.  Propagate constraints and append
  ;; all the solutions together.
  (let ((v (find-if #'ambiguous-vertex-p
                    (diagram-vertexes diagram))))
    (if (null v)
        (list diagram)
        (mapcan
          #'(lambda (v-labeling)
```

```
            (let* ((diagram2 (make-copy-diagram diagram))
                   (v2 (find-vertex (vertex-name v) diagram2)))
              (setf (vertex-labelings v2) (list v-labeling))
              (if (propagate-constraints v2)
                  (search-solutions diagram2)
                  nil)))
          (vertex-labelings v)))))
```

That's all there is to the algorithm; all that remains are some auxiliary functions.
Here are three of them:

```
(defun labels-for (vertex from)
  "Return all the labels for the line going to vertex."
  (let ((pos (position from (vertex-neighbors vertex))))
    (mapcar #'(lambda (labeling) (nth pos labeling))
            (vertex-labelings vertex))))

(defun reverse-label (label)
  "Account for the fact that one vertex's right is another's left."
  (case label (L 'R) (R 'L) (otherwise label)))

(defun find-vertex (name diagram)
  "Find the vertex in the given diagram with the given name."
  (find name (diagram-vertexes diagram) :key #'vertex-name))
```

Here are the printing functions. print-vertex prints a vertex in short form. It obeys
the print convention of returning the first argument. The functions show-vertex and
show-diagram print more detailed forms. They obey the convention for describe-like
functions of returning no values at all.

```
(defun print-vertex (vertex stream depth)
  "Print a vertex in the short form."
  (declare (ignore depth))
  (format stream "~a/~d" (vertex-name vertex)
          (number-of-labelings vertex))
  vertex)

(defun show-vertex (vertex &optional (stream t))
  "Print a vertex in a long form, on a new line."
  (format stream "~&   ~a ~d:" vertex (vertex-type vertex))
  (mapc #'(lambda (neighbor labels)
            (format stream " ~a~a=[~{~a~}]" (vertex-name vertex)
                    (vertex-name neighbor) labels))
        (vertex-neighbors vertex)
        (matrix-transpose (vertex-labelings vertex)))
  (values))
```

```lisp
(defun show-diagram (diagram &optional (title "~2&Diagram:")
                                       (stream t))
  "Print a diagram in a long form.  Include a title."
  (format stream title)
  (mapc #'show-vertex (diagram-vertexes diagram))
  (let ((n (reduce #'* (mapcar #'number-of-labelings
                               (diagram-vertexes diagram)))))
  (when (> n 1)
    (format stream "~&For ~:d interpretation~:p." n))
  (values)))
```

Note that matrix-transpose is called by show-vertex to turn the matrix of labelings on its side. It works like this:

```lisp
> (possible-labelings 'Y)
((+ + +)
 (- - -)
 (L R -)
 (- L R)
 (R - L))

> (matrix-transpose (possible-labelings 'Y))
((+ - L - R)
 (+ - R L -)
 (+ - - R L))
```

The implementation of matrix-transpose is surprisingly concise. It is an old Lisp trick, and well worth understanding:

```lisp
(defun matrix-transpose (matrix)
  "Turn a matrix on its side."
  (if matrix (apply #'mapcar #'list matrix)))
```

The remaining code has to do with creating diagrams. We need some handy way of specifying diagrams. One way would be with a line-recognizing program operating on digitized input from a camera or bitmap display. Another possibility is an interactive drawing program using a mouse and bitmap display. But since there is not yet a Common Lisp standard for interacting with such devices, we will have to settle for a textual description. The macro defdiagram defines and names a diagram. The name is followed by a list of vertex descriptions. Each description is a list consisting of the name of a vertex, the vertex type (Y, A, L, or T), and the names of the neighboring vertexes. Here again is the defdiagram description for the cube shown in figure 17.6.

```
(defdiagram cube
  (a Y b c d)
  (b W g e a)
  (c W e f a)
  (d W f g a)
  (e L c b)
  (f L d c)
  (g L b d))
```

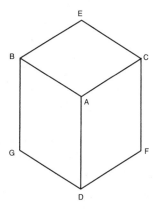

Figure 17.6: A Cube

The macro `defdiagram` calls `construct-diagram` to do the real work. It would be feasible to have `defdiagram` expand into a `defvar`, making the names be special variables. But then it would be the user's responsibility to make copies of such a variable before passing it to a destructive function. Instead, I use `put-diagram` and `diagram` to put and get diagrams in a table. `diagram` retrieves the named diagram and makes a copy of it. Thus, the user cannot corrupt the original diagrams stored in the table. Another possibility would be to have `defdiagram` expand into a function definition for name that returns a copy of the diagram. I chose to keep the diagram name space separate from the function name space, since names like cube make sense in both spaces.

```
(defmacro defdiagram (name &rest vertex-descriptors)
  "Define a diagram.  A copy can be gotten by (diagram name)."
  '(put-diagram ',name (construct-diagram ',vertex-descriptors)))

(let ((diagrams (make-hash-table)))
```

```
(defun diagram (name)
  "Get a fresh copy of the diagram with this name."
  (make-copy-diagram (gethash name diagrams)))

(defun put-diagram (name diagram)
  "Store a diagram under a name."
  (setf (gethash name diagrams) diagram)
  name))
```

The function construct-diagram translates each vertex description, using construct-vertex, and then fills in the neighbors of each vertex.

```
(defun construct-diagram (vertex-descriptors)
  "Build a new diagram from a set of vertex descriptor."
  (let ((diagram (make-diagram)))
    ;; Put in the vertexes
    (setf (diagram-vertexes diagram)
          (mapcar #'construct-vertex vertex-descriptors))
    ;; Put in the neighbors for each vertex
    (dolist (v-d vertex-descriptors)
      (setf (vertex-neighbors (find-vertex (first v-d) diagram))
            (mapcar #'(lambda (neighbor)
                        (find-vertex neighbor diagram))
                    (v-d-neighbors v-d))))
    diagram))

(defun construct-vertex (vertex-descriptor)
  "Build the vertex corresponding to the descriptor."
  ;; Descriptors are like: (x L y z)
  (make-vertex
    :name (first vertex-descriptor)
    :type (second vertex-descriptor)
    :labelings (possible-labelings (second vertex-descriptor))))

(defun v-d-neighbors (vertex-descriptor)
  "The neighboring vertex names in a vertex descriptor."
  (rest (rest vertex-descriptor)))
```

The defstruct for diagram automatically creates the function copy-diagram, but it just copies each field, without copying the contents of each field. Thus we need make-copy-diagram to create a copy that shares no structure with the original.

```
(defun make-copy-diagram (diagram)
  "Make a copy of a diagram, preserving connectivity."
  (let* ((new (make-diagram
                :vertexes (mapcar #'copy-vertex
                                   (diagram-vertexes diagram)))))
    ;; Put in the neighbors for each vertex
    (dolist (v (diagram-vertexes new))
      (setf (vertex-neighbors v)
            (mapcar #'(lambda (neighbor)
                        (find-vertex (vertex-name neighbor) new))
                    (vertex-neighbors v))))
    new))
```

17.3 Labeling Diagrams

We are now ready to try labeling diagrams. First the cube:

```
> (print-labelings (diagram 'cube))
The initial diagram is:
    A/5 Y: AB=[+-L-R] AC=[+-RL-] AD=[+--RL]
    B/3 W: BG=[L-+] BE=[R-+] BA=[++-]
    C/3 W: CE=[L-+] CF=[R-+] CA=[++-]
    D/3 W: DF=[L-+] DG=[R-+] DA=[++-]
    E/6 L: EC=[RL+L-R] EB=[LRR+L-]
    F/6 L: FD=[RL+L-R] FC=[LRR+L-]
    G/6 L: GB=[RL+L-R] GD=[LRR+L-]
For 29,160 interpretations.

After constraint propagation the diagram is:
    A/1 Y: AB=[+] AC=[+] AD=[+]
    B/2 W: BG=[L-] BE=[R-] BA=[++]
    C/2 W: CE=[L-] CF=[R-] CA=[++]
    D/2 W: DF=[L-] DG=[R-] DA=[++]
    E/3 L: EC=[R-R] EB=[LL-]
    F/3 L: FD=[R-R] FC=[LL-]
    G/3 L: GB=[R-R] GD=[LL-]
For 216 interpretations.

There are four solutions:
```

```
Diagram:
   A/1 Y: AB=[+] AC=[+] AD=[+]
   B/1 W: BG=[L] BE=[R] BA=[+]
   C/1 W: CE=[L] CF=[R] CA=[+]
   D/1 W: DF=[L] DG=[R] DA=[+]
   E/1 L: EC=[R] EB=[L]
   F/1 L: FD=[R] FC=[L]
   G/1 L: GB=[R] GD=[L]

Diagram:
   A/1 Y: AB=[+] AC=[+] AD=[+]
   B/1 W: BG=[L] BE=[R] BA=[+]
   C/1 W: CE=[L] CF=[R] CA=[+]
   D/1 W: DF=[-] DG=[-] DA=[+]
   E/1 L: EC=[R] EB=[L]
   F/1 L: FD=[-] FC=[L]
   G/1 L: GB=[R] GD=[-]

Diagram:
   A/1 Y: AB=[+] AC=[+] AD=[+]
   B/1 W: BG=[L] BE=[R] BA=[+]
   C/1 W: CE=[-] CF=[-] CA=[+]
   D/1 W: DF=[L] DG=[R] DA=[+]
   E/1 L: EC=[-] EB=[L]
   F/1 L: FD=[R] FC=[-]
   G/1 L: GB=[R] GD=[L]

Diagram:
   A/1 Y: AB=[+] AC=[+] AD=[+]
   B/1 W: BG=[-] BE=[-] BA=[+]
   C/1 W: CE=[L] CF=[R] CA=[+]
   D/1 W: DF=[L] DG=[R] DA=[+]
   E/1 L: EC=[R] EB=[-]
   F/1 L: FD=[R] FC=[L]
   G/1 L: GB=[-] GD=[L]
```

The four interpretations correspond, respectively, to the cases where the cube is free floating, attached to the floor (GD and DF = -), attached to a wall on the right (EC and CF = -), or attached to a wall on the left (BG and BE = -). These are shown in figure 17.7. It would be nice if we could supply information about where the cube is attached, and see if we can get a unique interpretation. The function ground takes a diagram and modifies it by making one or more lines be grounded lines—lines that have a concave (-) label, corresponding to a junction with the ground.

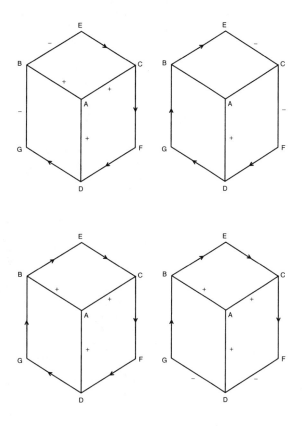

Figure 17.7: Four Interpretations of the Cube

```
(defun ground (diagram vertex-a vertex-b)
  "Attach the line between the two vertexes to the ground.
  That is, label the line with a -"
  (let* ((A (find-vertex vertex-a diagram))
         (B (find-vertex vertex-b diagram))
         (i (position B (vertex-neighbors A))))
    (assert (not (null i)))
    (setf (vertex-labelings A)
          (find-all-if #'(lambda (l) (eq (nth i l) '-))
                       (vertex-labelings A)))
    diagram))
```

We can see how this works on the cube:

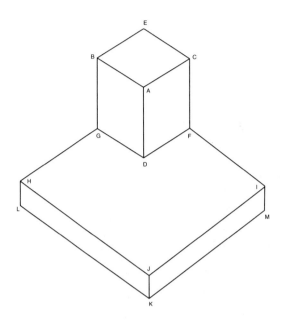

Figure 17.8: Cube on a Plate

```
> (print-labelings (ground (diagram 'cube) 'g 'd))
The initial diagram is:
    A/5 Y: AB=[+-L-R] AC=[+-RL-] AD=[+--RL]
    B/3 W: BG=[L-+] BE=[R-+] BA=[++-]
    C/3 W: CE=[L-+] CF=[R-+] CA=[++-]
    D/3 W: DF=[L-+] DG=[R-+] DA=[++-]
    E/6 L: EC=[RL+L-R] EB=[LRR+L-]
    F/6 L: FD=[RL+L-R] FC=[LRR+L-]
    G/1 L: GB=[R] GD=[-]
For 4,960 interpretations.

After constraint propagation the diagram is:
    A/1 Y: AB=[+] AC=[+] AD=[+]
    B/1 W: BG=[L] BE=[R] BA=[+]
    C/1 W: CE=[L] CF=[R] CA=[+]
    D/1 W: DF=[-] DG=[-] DA=[+]
    E/1 L: EC=[R] EB=[L]
    F/1 L: FD=[-] FC=[L]
    G/1 L: GB=[R] GD=[-]
```

Note that the user only had to specify one of the two ground lines, GD. The program found that DF is also grounded. Similarly, in programming ground-line, we only had to update one of the vertexes. The rest is done by constraint propagation.

The next example yields the same four interpretations, in the same order (free floating, attached at bottom, attached at right, and attached at left) when interpreted ungrounded. The grounded version yields the unique solution shown in the following output and in figure 17.9.

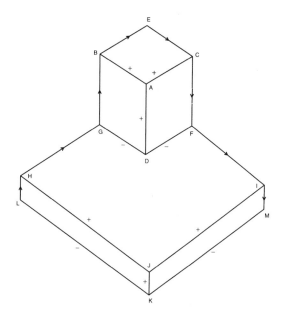

Figure 17.9: Labeled Cube on a Plate

```
(defdiagram cube-on-plate
  (a Y b c d)
  (b W g e a)
  (c W e f a)
  (d W f g a)
  (e L c b)
  (f Y d c i)
  (g Y b d h)
  (h W l g j)
  (i W f m j)
  (j Y h i k)
  (k W m l j)
  (l L h k)
```

```
    (m L k i))

> (print-labelings (ground (diagram 'cube-on-plate) 'k 'm))
The initial diagram is:
    A/5 Y: AB=[+-L-R] AC=[+-RL-] AD=[+--RL]
    B/3 W: BG=[L-+] BE=[R-+] BA=[++-]
    C/3 W: CE=[L-+] CF=[R-+] CA=[++-]
    D/3 W: DF=[L-+] DG=[R-+] DA=[++-]
    E/6 L: EC=[RL+L-R] EB=[LRR+L-]
    F/5 Y: FD=[+-L-R] FC=[+-RL-] FI=[+--RL]
    G/5 Y: GB=[+-L-R] GD=[+-RL-] GH=[+--RL]
    H/3 W: HL=[L-+] HG=[R-+] HJ=[++-]
    I/3 W: IF=[L-+] IM=[R-+] IJ=[++-]
    J/5 Y: JH=[+-L-R] JI=[+-RL-] JK=[+--RL]
    K/1 W: KM=[-] KL=[-] KJ=[+]
    L/6 L: LH=[RL+L-R] LK=[LRR+L-]
    M/6 L: MK=[RL+L-R] MI=[LRR+L-]
For 32,805,000 interpretations.

After constraint propagation the diagram is:
    A/1 Y: AB=[+] AC=[+] AD=[+]
    B/1 W: BG=[L] BE=[R] BA=[+]
    C/1 W: CE=[L] CF=[R] CA=[+]
    D/1 W: DF=[-] DG=[-] DA=[+]
    E/1 L: EC=[R] EB=[L]
    F/1 Y: FD=[-] FC=[L] FI=[R]
    G/1 Y: GB=[R] GD=[-] GH=[L]
    H/1 W: HL=[L] HG=[R] HJ=[+]
    I/1 W: IF=[L] IM=[R] IJ=[+]
    J/1 Y: JH=[+] JI=[+] JK=[+]
    K/1 W: KM=[-] KL=[-] KJ=[+]
    L/1 L: LH=[R] LK=[-]
    M/1 L: MK=[-] MI=[L]
```

It is interesting to try the algorithm on an "impossible" diagram. It turns out the algorithm correctly finds no interpretation for this well-known illusion:

```
(defdiagram poiuyt
  (a L b g)
  (b L j a)
  (c L d l)
  (d L h c)
  (e L f i)
  (f L k e)
  (g L a l)
  (h L l d)
  (i L e k)
  (j L k b)
```

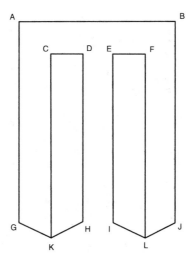

Figure 17.10: An Impossible Figure (A Poiuyt)

```
(k W j i f)
(l W h g c))

> (print-labelings (diagram 'poiuyt))
The initial diagram is:
    A/6 L: AB=[RL+L-R] AG=[LRR+L-]
    B/6 L: BJ=[RL+L-R] BA=[LRR+L-]
    C/6 L: CD=[RL+L-R] CL=[LRR+L-]
    D/6 L: DH=[RL+L-R] DC=[LRR+L-]
    E/6 L: EF=[RL+L-R] EI=[LRR+L-]
    F/6 L: FK=[RL+L-R] FE=[LRR+L-]
    G/6 L: GA=[RL+L-R] GL=[LRR+L-]
    H/6 L: HL=[RL+L-R] HD=[LRR+L-]
    I/6 L: IE=[RL+L-R] IK=[LRR+L-]
    J/6 L: JK=[RL+L-R] JB=[LRR+L-]
    K/3 W: KJ=[L-+] KI=[R-+] KF=[++-]
    L/3 W: LH=[L-+] LG=[R-+] LC=[++-]
For 544,195,584 interpretations.

After constraint propagation the diagram is:
    A/5 L: AB=[RL+-R] AG=[LRRL-]
    B/5 L: BJ=[RLL-R] BA=[LR+L-]
    C/2 L: CD=[LR] CL=[+-]
    D/3 L: DH=[RL-] DC=[LRL]
    E/3 L: EF=[RLR] EI=[LR-]
    F/2 L: FK=[+-] FE=[RL]
```

```
  G/4 L: GA=[RL-R] GL=[L+L-]
  H/4 L: HL=[R+-R] HD=[LRL-]
  I/4 L: IE=[RL-R] IK=[L+L-]
  J/4 L: JK=[R+-R] JB=[LRL-]
  K/3 W: KJ=[L-+] KI=[R-+] KF=[++-]
  L/3 W: LH=[L-+] LG=[R-+] LC=[++-]
For 2,073,600 interpretations.

There are zero solutions:
```

Now we try a more complex diagram:

```
(defdiagram tower
  (a Y b c d)    (n L q o)
  (b W g e a)    (o W y j n)
  (c W e f a)    (p L r i)
  (d W f g a)    (q W n s w)
  (e L c b)      (r W s p x)
  (f Y d c i)    (s L r q)
  (g Y b d h)    (t W w x z)
  (h W l g j)    (u W x y z)
  (i W f m p)    (v W y w z)
  (j Y h o k)    (w Y t v q)
  (k W m l j)    (x Y r u t)
  (l L h k)      (y Y v u o)
  (m L k i)      (z Y t u v)))

> (print-labelings (ground (diagram 'tower) 'l 'k))
The initial diagram is:
  A/5 Y: AB=[+-L-R] AC=[+-RL-] AD=[+--RL]
  B/3 W: BG=[L-+] BE=[R-+] BA=[++-]
  C/3 W: CE=[L-+] CF=[R-+] CA=[++-]
  D/3 W: DF=[L-+] DG=[R-+] DA=[++-]
  E/6 L: EC=[RL+L-R] EB=[LRR+L-]
  F/5 Y: FD=[+-L-R] FC=[+-RL-] FI=[+--RL]
  G/5 Y: GB=[+-L-R] GD=[+-RL-] GH=[+--RL]
  H/3 W: HL=[L-+] HG=[R-+] HJ=[++-]
  I/3 W: IF=[L-+] IM=[R-+] IP=[++-]
  J/5 Y: JH=[+-L-R] JO=[+-RL-] JK=[+--RL]
  K/3 W: KM=[L-+] KL=[R-+] KJ=[++-]
  L/1 L: LH=[R] LK=[-]
  M/6 L: MK=[RL+L-R] MI=[LRR+L-]
  N/6 L: NQ=[RL+L-R] NO=[LRR+L-]
  O/3 W: OY=[L-+] OJ=[R-+] ON=[++-]
  P/6 L: PR=[RL+L-R] PI=[LRR+L-]
  Q/3 W: QN=[L-+] QS=[R-+] QW=[++-]
  R/3 W: RS=[L-+] RP=[R-+] RX=[++-]
  S/6 L: SR=[RL+L-R] SQ=[LRR+L-]
```

```
T/3 W: TW=[L-+] TX=[R-+] TZ=[++-]
U/3 W: UX=[L-+] UY=[R-+] UZ=[++-]
V/3 W: VY=[L-+] VW=[R-+] VZ=[++-]
W/5 Y: WT=[+-L-R] WV=[+-RL-] WQ=[+--RL]
X/5 Y: XR=[+-L-R] XU=[+-RL-] XT=[+--RL]
Y/5 Y: YV=[+-L-R] YU=[+-RL-] YO=[+--RL]
Z/5 Y: ZT=[+-L-R] ZU=[+-RL-] ZV=[+--RL]
```
For 1,614,252,037,500,000 interpretations.

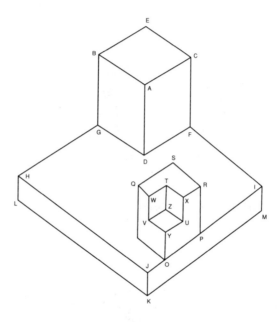

Figure 17.11: A Tower

After constraint propagation the diagram is:
A/1 Y: AB=[+] AC=[+] AD=[+]
B/1 W: BG=[L] BE=[R] BA=[+]
C/1 W: CE=[L] CF=[R] CA=[+]
D/1 W: DF=[-] DG=[-] DA=[+]
E/1 L: EC=[R] EB=[L]
F/1 Y: FD=[-] FC=[L] FI=[R]
G/1 Y: GB=[R] GD=[-] GH=[L]
H/1 W: HL=[L] HG=[R] HJ=[+]
I/1 W: IF=[L] IM=[R] IP=[+]
J/1 Y: JH=[+] JO=[+] JK=[+]

```
K/1 W: KM=[-] KL=[-] KJ=[+]
L/1 L: LH=[R] LK=[-]
M/1 L: MK=[-] MI=[L]
N/1 L: NQ=[R] NO=[-]
O/1 W: OY=[+] OJ=[+] ON=[-]
P/1 L: PR=[L] PI=[+]
Q/1 W: QN=[L] QS=[R] QW=[+]
R/1 W: RS=[L] RP=[R] RX=[+]
S/1 L: SR=[R] SQ=[L]
T/1 W: TW=[+] TX=[+] TZ=[-]
U/1 W: UX=[+] UY=[+] UZ=[-]
V/1 W: VY=[+] VW=[+] VZ=[-]
W/1 Y: WT=[+] WV=[+] WQ=[+]
X/1 Y: XR=[+] XU=[+] XT=[+]
Y/1 Y: YV=[+] YU=[+] YO=[+]
Z/1 Y: ZT=[-] ZU=[-] ZV=[-]
```

We see that the algorithm was able to arrive at a single interpretation. Moreover, even though there were a large number of possibilities—over a quadrillion—the computation is quite fast. Most of the time is spent printing, so to get a good measurement, we define a function to find solutions without printing anything:

```
(defun find-labelings (diagram)
  "Return a list of all consistent labelings of the diagram."
  (every #'propagate-constraints (diagram-vertexes diagram))
  (search-solutions diagram))
```

When we time the application of find-labelings to the grounded tower and the poiuyt, we find the tower takes 0.11 seconds, and the poiuyt 21 seconds. This is over 180 times longer, even though the poiuyt has only half as many vertexes and only about half a million interpretations, compared to the tower's quadrillion. The poiuyt takes a long time to process because there are few local constraints, so violations are discovered only by considering several widely separated parts of the figure all at the same time. It is interesting that the same fact that makes the processing of the poiuyt take longer is also responsible for its interest as an illusion.

17.4   Checking Diagrams for Errors

This section considers one more example, and considers what to do when there are apparent errors in the input. The example is taken from Charniak and McDermott's *Introduction to Artificial Intelligence*, page 138, and shown in figure 17.12.

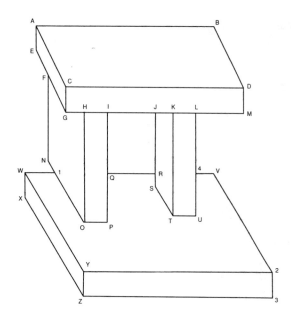

Figure 17.12: Diagram of an arch

```
(defdiagram arch
   (a W e b c)   (p L o q)
   (b L d a)     (q T p i r)
   (c Y a d g)   (r T j s q)
   (d Y c b m)   (s L r t)
   (e L a f)     (t W v s k)
   (f T e g n)   (u L t l)
   (g W h f c)   (v L 2 4)
   (h T g i o)   (w W x 1 y)
   (i T h j q)   (x L w z)
   (j T i k r)   (y Y w 2 z)
   (k T j l t)   (z W 3 x y)
   (l T k m v)   (1 T n o w)
   (m L l d)     (2 W v 3 y)
   (n L f 1)     (3 L z 2)
   (o W p 1 h)   (4 T u l v))
```

Unfortunately, running this example results in no consistent interpretations after
constraint propagation. This seems wrong. Worse, when we try to ground the
diagram on the line XZ and call print-labelings on that, we get the following error:

```
>>>ERROR: The first argument to NTH was of the wrong type.
The function expected a fixnum >= zero.
While in the function LABELS-FOR ⇐ CONSISTENT-LABELINGS

Debugger entered while in the following function:

LABELS-FOR (P.C. = 23)
   Arg 0 (VERTEX): U/6
   Arg 1 (FROM): 4/4
```

What has gone wrong? A good guess is that the diagram is somehow inconsistent—somewhere an error was made in transcribing the diagram. It could be that the diagram is in fact impossible, like the poiuyt. But that is unlikely, as it is easy for us to provide an intuitive interpretation. We need to debug the diagram, and it would also be a good idea to handle the error more gracefully.

One property of the diagram that is easy to check for is that every line should be mentioned twice. If there is a line between vertexes A and B, there should be two entries in the vertex descriptors of the following form:

```
(A ? ... B ...)
(B ? ... A ...)
```

Here the symbol "?" means we aren't concerned about the type of the vertexes, only with the presence of the line in two places. The following code makes this check when a diagram is defined. It also checks that each vertex is one of the four legal types, and has the right number of neighbors.

```
(defmacro defdiagram (name &rest vertex-descriptors)
  "Define a diagram.  A copy can be gotten by (diagram name)."
  '(put-diagram ',name (construct-diagram
                         (check-diagram ',vertex-descriptors))))

(defun check-diagram (vertex-descriptors)
  "Check if the diagram description appears consistent."
  (let ((errors 0))
    (dolist (v-d vertex-descriptors)
      ;; v-d is like: (a Y b c d)
      (let ((A (first v-d))
            (v-type (second v-d)))
        ;; Check that the number of neighbors is right for
        ;; the vertex type (and that the vertex type is legal)
        (when (/= (length (v-d-neighbors v-d))
                  (case v-type ((W Y T) 3) ((L) 2) (t -1)))
          (warn "Illegal type/neighbor combo: ~a" v-d)
          (incf errors))
        ;; Check that each neighbor B is connected to
```

```
          ;; this vertex, A, exactly once
          (dolist (B (v-d-neighbors v-d))
            (when (/= 1 (count-if
                          #'(lambda (v-d2)
                              (and (eql (first v-d2) B)
                                   (member A (v-d-neighbors v-d2)))))
                       vertex-descriptors))
              (warn "Inconsistent vertex: ~a-~a" A B)
              (incf errors)))))
      (when (> errors 0)
        (error "Inconsistent diagram.  ~d total error~:p."
               errors)))
    vertex-descriptors)
```

Now let's try the arch again:

```
(defdiagram arch
  (a W e b c)   (p L o q)
  (b L d a)     (q T p i r)
  (c Y a d g)   (r T j s q)
  (d Y c b m)   (s L r t)
  (e L a f)     (t W v s k)
  (f T e g n)   (u L t l)
  (g W h f c)   (v L 2 4)
  (h T g i o)   (w W x 1 y)
  (i T h j q)   (x L w z)
  (j T i k r)   (y Y w 2 z)
  (k T j l t)   (z W 3 x y)
  (l T k m v)   (1 T n o w)
  (m L l d)     (2 W v 3 y)
  (n L f 1)     (3 L z 2)
  (o W p 1 h)   (4 T u l v))
Warning: Inconsistent vertex: T-V
Warning: Inconsistent vertex: U-T
Warning: Inconsistent vertex: U-L
Warning: Inconsistent vertex: L-V
Warning: Inconsistent vertex: 4-U
Warning: Inconsistent vertex: 4-L

>>ERROR: Inconsistent diagram.  6 total errors.
```

The defdiagram was transcribed from a hand-labeled diagram, and it appears that the transcription has fallen prey to one of the oldest problems in mathematical notation: confusing a "u" with a "v." The other problem was in seeing the line U-L as a single line, when in fact it is broken up into two segments, U-4 and 4-L. Repairing these bugs gives the diagram:

```
(defdiagram arch
  (a W e b c)  (p L o q)
  (b L d a)    (q T p i r)
  (c Y a d g)  (r T j s q)
  (d Y c b m)  (s L r t)
  (e L a f)    (t W u s k)    ; t-u not t-v
  (f T e g n)  (u L t 4)      ; u-4 not u-l
  (g W h f c)  (v L 2 4)
  (h T g i o)  (w W x 1 y)
  (i T h j q)  (x L w z)
  (j T i k r)  (y Y w 2 z)
  (k T j l t)  (z W 3 x y)
  (l T k m 4)  (1 T n o w)    ; l-4 not l-v
  (m L l d)    (2 W v 3 y)
  (n L f 1)    (3 L z 2)
  (o W p 1 h)  (4 T u l v))
```

This time there are no errors detected by check-diagram, but running print-labelings again still does not give a solution. To get more information about which constraints are applied, I modified propagate-constraints to print out some information:

```
(defun propagate-constraints (vertex)
  "Reduce the number of labelings on vertex by considering neighbors.
  If we can reduce, propagate the new constraint to each neighbor."
  ;; Return nil only when the constraints lead to an impossibility
  (let ((old-num (number-of-labelings vertex)))
    (setf (vertex-labelings vertex) (consistent-labelings vertex))
    (unless (impossible-vertex-p vertex)
      (when (< (number-of-labelings vertex) old-num)
        (format t "~&; ~a: ~14a ~a" vertex              ;***
                (vertex-neighbors vertex)                ;***
                (vertex-labelings vertex))               ;***
        (every #'propagate-constraints (vertex-neighbors vertex)))
      vertex)))
```

Running the problem again gives the following trace:

```
> (print-labelings (ground (diagram 'arch) 'x 'z))
The initial diagram is:
  A/3 W: AE=[L-+] AB=[R-+] AC=[++-]
  P/6 L: PO=[RL+L-R] PQ=[LRR+L-]
  B/6 L: BD=[RL+L-R] BA=[LRR+L-]
  Q/4 T: QP=[RRRR] QI=[LLLL] QR=[+-LR]
  C/5 Y: CA=[+-L-R] CD=[+-RL-] CG=[+--RL]
  R/4 T: RJ=[RRRR] RS=[LLLL] RQ=[+-LR]
  D/5 Y: DC=[+-L-R] DB=[+-RL-] DM=[+--RL]
```

```
     S/6 L: SR=[RL+L-R] ST=[LRR+L-]
     E/6 L: EA=[RL+L-R] EF=[LRR+L-]
     T/3 W: TU=[L-+] TS=[R-+] TK=[++-]
     F/4 T: FE=[RRRR] FG=[LLLL] FN=[+-LR]
     U/6 L: UT=[RL+L-R] U4=[LRR+L-]
     G/3 W: GH=[L-+] GF=[R-+] GC=[++-]
     V/6 L: V2=[RL+L-R] V4=[LRR+L-]
     H/4 T: HG=[RRRR] HI=[LLLL] HO=[+-LR]
     W/3 W: WX=[L-+] W1=[R-+] WY=[++-]
     I/4 T: IH=[RRRR] IJ=[LLLL] IQ=[+-LR]
     X/1 L: XW=[R] XZ=[-]
     J/4 T: JI=[RRRR] JK=[LLLL] JR=[+-LR]
     Y/5 Y: YW=[+-L-R] Y2=[+-RL-] YZ=[+--RL]
     K/4 T: KJ=[RRRR] KL=[LLLL] KT=[+-LR]
     Z/3 W: Z3=[L-+] ZX=[R-+] ZY=[++-]
     L/4 T: LK=[RRRR] LM=[LLLL] L4=[+-LR]
     1/4 T: 1N=[RRRR] 10=[LLLL] 1W=[+-LR]
     M/6 L: ML=[RL+L-R] MD=[LRR+L-]
     2/3 W: 2V=[L-+] 23=[R-+] 2Y=[++-]
     N/6 L: NF=[RL+L-R] N1=[LRR+L-]
     3/6 L: 3Z=[RL+L-R] 32=[LRR+L-]
     O/3 W: OP=[L-+] O1=[R-+] OH=[++-]
     4/4 T: 4U=[RRRR] 4L=[LLLL] 4V=[+-LR]
For 2,888,816,545,234,944,000 interpretations.
; P/2: (O/3 Q/4)        ((R L) (- L))
; O/1: (P/2 1/4 H/4)    ((R L +))
; P/1: (O/1 Q/4)        ((R L))
; 1/3: (N/6 O/1 W/3)    ((R L +) (R L -) (R L L))
; N/2: (F/4 1/3)        ((R L) (- L))
; F/2: (E/6 G/3 N/2)    ((R L -) (R L L))
; E/2: (A/3 F/2)        ((R L) (- L))
; A/2: (E/2 B/6 C/5)    ((L R +) (- - +))
; B/3: (D/5 A/2)        ((R L) (- L) (R -))
; D/3: (C/5 B/3 M/6)    ((- - -) (- L R) (R - L))
; W/1: (X/1 1/3 Y/5)    ((L R +))
; 1/1: (N/2 O/1 W/1)    ((R L L))
; Y/1: (W/1 2/3 Z/3)    ((+ + +))
; 2/2: (V/6 3/6 Y/1)    ((L R +) (- - +))
; V/3: (2/2 4/4)        ((R L) (- L) (R -))
; 4/2: (U/6 L/4 V/3)    ((R L -) (R L R))
; U/2: (T/3 4/2)        ((R L) (- L))
; T/2: (U/2 S/6 K/4)    ((L R +) (- - +))
; S/2: (R/4 T/2)        ((R L) (R -))
; K/1: (J/4 L/4 T/2)    ((R L +))
; J/1: (I/4 K/1 R/4)    ((R L L))
; I/1: (H/4 J/1 Q/4)    ((R L R))
; L/1: (K/1 M/6 4/2)    ((R L R))
; M/2: (L/1 D/3)        ((R L) (R -))
```

```
; 3/3: (Z/3 2/2)       ((R L) (- L) (R -))
; Z/1: (3/3 X/1 Y/1)   ((- - +))
; 3/1: (Z/1 2/2)       ((- L))
; 2/1: (V/3 3/1 Y/1)   ((L R +))
; V/2: (2/1 4/2)       ((R L) (R -))
```

After constraint propagation the diagram is:

```
A/0 W:
P/1 L: PO=[R] PQ=[L]
B/0 L:
Q/4 T: QP=[RRRR] QI=[LLLL] QR=[+-LR]
C/0 Y:
R/4 T: RJ=[RRRR] RS=[LLLL] RQ=[+-LR]
D/0 Y:
S/2 L: SR=[RR] ST=[L-]
E/2 L: EA=[R-] EF=[LL]
T/2 W: TU=[L-] TS=[R-] TK=[++]
F/2 T: FE=[RR] FG=[LL] FN=[-L]
U/2 L: UT=[R-] U4=[LL]
G/0 W:
V/2 L: V2=[RR] V4=[L-]
H/0 T:
W/1 W: WX=[L] W1=[R] WY=[+]
I/1 T: IH=[R] IJ=[L] IQ=[R]
X/1 L: XW=[R] XZ=[-]
J/1 T: JI=[R] JK=[L] JR=[L]
Y/1 Y: YW=[+] Y2=[+] YZ=[+]
K/1 T: KJ=[R] KL=[L] KT=[+]
Z/1 W: Z3=[-] ZX=[-] ZY=[+]
L/1 T: LK=[R] LM=[L] L4=[R]
1/1 T: 1N=[R] 1O=[L] 1W=[L]
M/2 L: ML=[RR] MD=[L-]
2/1 W: 2V=[L] 23=[R] 2Y=[+]
N/2 L: NF=[R-] N1=[LL]
3/1 L: 3Z=[-] 32=[L]
O/1 W: OP=[L] O1=[R] OH=[+]
4/2 T: 4U=[RR] 4L=[LL] 4V=[-R]
```

From the diagram after constraint propagation we can see that the vertexes A, B, C, D, G, and H have no interpretations, so they are a good place to look first for an error. From the trace generated by propagate-constraints (the lines beginning with a semi-colon), we see that constraint propagation started at P and after seven propagations reached some of the suspect vertexes:

```
; A/2: (E/2 B/6 C/5)  ((L R +) (- - +))
; B/3: (D/5 A/2)      ((R L) (- L) (R -))
; D/3: (C/5 B/3 M/6)  ((- - -) (- L R) (R - L))
```

A and B look acceptable, but look at the entry for vertex D. It shows three interpretations, and it shows that the neighbors are C, B, and M. Note that line DC, the first entry in each of the interpretations, must be either -, - or R. But this is an error, because the "correct" interpretation has DC as a + line. Looking more closely, we notice that D is in fact a W-type vertex, not a Y vertex as written in the definition. We should have:

```
(defdiagram arch
  (a W e b c)  (p L o q)
  (b L d a)    (q T p i r)
  (c Y a d g)  (r T j s q)
  (d W b m c)  (s L r t)      ; d is a W, not Y
  (e L a f)    (t W u s k)
  (f T e g n)  (u L t 4)
  (g W h f c)  (v L 2 4)
  (h T g i o)  (w W x 1 y)
  (i T h j q)  (x L w z)
  (j T i k r)  (y Y w 2 z)
  (k T j l t)  (z W 3 x y)
  (l T k m 4)  (1 T n o w)
  (m L l d)    (2 W v 3 y)
  (n L f 1)    (3 L z 2)
  (o W p 1 h)  (4 T u l v))
```

By running the problem again and inspecting the trace output, we soon discover the real root of the problem: the most natural interpretation of the diagram is beyond the scope of the program! There are many interpretations that involve blocks floating in air, but if we ground lines OP, TU and XZ, we run into trouble. Remember, we said that we were considering trihedral vertexes only. But vertex 1 would be a quad-hedral vertex, formed by the intersection of four planes: the top and back of the base, and the bottom and left-hand side of the left pillar. The intuitively correct labeling for the diagram would have O1 be a concave (-) line and A1 be an occluding line, but our repertoire of labelings for T vertexes does not allow this. Hence, the diagram cannot be labeled consistently.

Let's go back and consider the error that came up in the first version of the diagram. Even though the error no longer occurs on this diagram, we want to make sure that it won't show up in another case. Here's the error:

```
>>>ERROR: The first argument to NTH was of the wrong type.
The function expected a fixnum >= zero.
While in the function LABELS-FOR ⇐ CONSISTENT-LABELINGS

Debugger entered while in the following function:

LABELS-FOR (P.C. = 23)
    Arg 0 (VERTEX): U/6
    Arg 1 (FROM): 4/4
```

Looking at the definition of labels-for, we see that it is looking for the from vertex, which in this case is 4, among the neighbors of U. It was not found, so pos became nil, and the function nth complained that it was not given an integer as an argument. So this error, if we had pursued it earlier, would have pointed out that 4 was not listed as a neighbor of U, when it should have been. Of course, we found that out by other means. In any case, there is no bug here to fix—as long as a diagram is guaranteed to be consistent, the labels-for bug will not appear again.

This section has made two points: First, write code that checks the input as thoroughly as possible. Second, even when input checking is done, it is still up to the user to understand the limitations of the program.

17.5   History and References

Guzman (1968) was one of the first to consider the problem of interpreting line diagrams. He classified vertexes, and defined some heuristics for combining information from adjacent vertexes. Huffman (1971) and Clowes (1971) independently came up with more formal and complete analyses, and David Waltz (1975) extended the analysis to handle shadows, and introduced the constraint propagation algorithm to cut down on the need for search. The algorithm is sometimes called "Waltz filtering" in his honor. With shadows and nontrihedral angles, there are thousands of vertex labelings instead of 18, but there are also more constraints, so the constraint propagation actually does better than it does in our limited world. Waltz's approach and the Huffman-Clowes labels are covered in most introductory AI books, including Rich and Knight 1990, Charniak and McDermott 1985, and Winston 1984. Waltz's original paper appears in *The Psychology of Computer Vision* (Winston 1975), an influential volume collecting early work done at MIT. He also contributed a summary article on Waltz filtering (Waltz 1990).

Many introductory AI texts give vision short coverage, but Charniak and McDermott (1985) and Tanimoto (1990) provide good overviews of the field. Zucker (1990) provides an overview of low-level vision.

Ramsey and Barrett (1987) give an implementation of a line-recognition program. It would make a good project to connect their program to the one presented in this chapter, and thereby go all the way from pixels to 3-D descriptions.

17.6 Exercises

This chapter has solved the problem of line-labeling for polyhedra made of trihedral vertexes. The following exercises extend this solution.

Exercise 17.1 [h] Use the line-labeling to produce a face labeling. Write a function that takes a labeled diagram as input and produces a list of the faces (planes) that comprise the diagram.

Exercise 17.2 [h] Use the face labeling to produce a polyhedron labeling. Write a function that takes a list of faces and a diagram and produces a list of polyhedra (blocks) that comprise the diagram.

Exercise 17.3 [d] Extend the system to include quad-hedral vertexes and/or shadows. There is no conceptual difficulty in this, but it is a very demanding task to find all the possible vertex types and labelings for them. Consult Waltz 1975.

Exercise 17.4 [d] Implement a program to recognize lines from pixels.

Exercise 17.5 [d] If you have access to a workstation with a graphical interface, implement a program to allow a user to draw diagrams with a mouse. Have the program generate output in the form expected by construct-diagram.

CHAPTER 18

Search and the Game of Othello

*In the beginner's mind there are
endless possibilities;
in the expert's there are few.*

—Suzuki Roshi, Zen Master

G ame playing has been the target of much early work in AI for three reasons. First, the rules of most games are formalized, and they can be implemented in a computer program rather easily. Second, in many games the interface requirements are trivial. The computer need only print out its moves and read in the opponent's moves. This is true for games like chess and checkers, but not for ping-pong and basketball, where vision and motor skills are crucial. Third, playing a good game of chess is considered by many an intellectual achievement. Newell, Shaw, and Simon say, "Chess is the intellectual game *par excellence*," and Donald Michie called chess the "*Drosophila melanogaster* of machine intelligence," meaning that chess is a relatively simple yet interesting domain that can lead to advances in AI, just as study of the fruit fly served to advance biology.

Today there is less emphasis on game playing in AI. It has been realized that techniques that work well in the limited domain of a board game do not necessarily lead to intelligent behavior in other domains. Also, as it turns out, the techniques that allow computers to play well are not the same as the techniques that good human players use. Humans are capable of recognizing abstract patterns learned from previous games, and formulating plans of attack and defense. While some computer programs try to emulate this approach, the more succesful programs work by rapidly searching thousands of possible sequences of moves, making fairly superficial evaluations of the worth of each sequence.

While much previous work on game playing has concentrated on chess and checkers, this chapter demonstrates a program to play the game of Othello.[1] Othello is a variation on the nineteenth-century game Reversi. It is an easy game to program because the rules are simpler than chess. Othello is also a rewarding game to program, because a simple search technique can yield an excellent player. There are two reasons for this. First, the number of legal moves per turn is low, so the search is not too explosive. Second, a single Othello move can flip a dozen or more opponent pieces. This makes it difficult for human players to visualize the long-range consequences of a move. Search-based programs are not confused, and thus do well relative to humans.

The very name "Othello" derives from the fact that the game is so unpredictable, like the Moor of Venice. The name may also be an allusion to the line, "Your daughter and the Moor are now making the beast with two backs,"[2] since the game pieces do indeed have two backs, one white and one black. In any case, the association between the game and the play carries over to the name of several programs: Cassio, Iago, and Bill. The last two will be discussed in this chapter. They are equal to or better than even champion human players. We will be able to develop a simplified version that is not quite a champion but is much better than beginning players.

18.1 The Rules of the Game

Othello is played on a 8-by-8 board, which is initially set up with four pieces in the center, as shown in figure 18.1. The two players, black and white, alternate turns, with black playing first. On each turn, a player places a single piece of his own color on the board. No piece can be moved once it is placed, but subsequent moves may flip a piece from one color to another. Each piece must be placed so that it *brackets* one or more opponent pieces. That is, when black plays a piece there must be a line (horizontal, vertical, or diagonal) that goes through the piece just played, then through one or more white pieces, and then to another black piece. The intervening

---

[1] Othello is a registered trademark of CBS Inc. Gameboard design © 1974 CBS Inc.

[2] *Othello,* [I. i. 117] William Shakespeare.

white pieces are flipped over to black. If there are bracketed white pieces in more than one direction, they are all flipped. Figure 18.2 (a) indicates the legal moves for black with small dots. Figure 18.2 (b) shows the position after black moves to square b4. Players alternate turns, except that a player who has no legal moves must pass. When neither player has any moves, the game is over, and the player with the most pieces on the board wins. This usually happens because there are no empty squares left, but it occasionally happens earlier in the game.

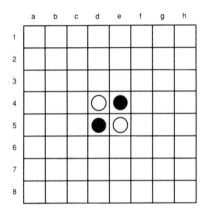

Figure 18.1: The Othello Board

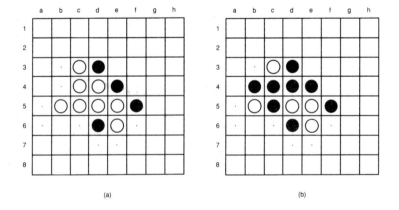

Figure 18.2: Legal Othello Moves

18.2   Representation Choices

In developing an Othello program, we will want to test out various strategies, playing those strategies against each other and against human players. We may also want our program to allow two humans to play a game. Therefore, our main function, othello, will be a monitoring function that takes as arguments two strategies. It uses these strategies to get each player's moves, and then applies these moves to a representation of the game board, perhaps printing out the board as it goes.

The first choice to make is how to represent the board and the pieces on it. The board is an 8-by-8 square, and each square can be filled by a black or white piece or can be empty. Thus, an obvious representation choice is to make the board an 8-by-8 array, where each element of the array is the symbol black, white, or nil.

Notice what is happening here: we are following the usual Lisp convention of implementing an *enumerated type* (the type of pieces that can fill a square) as a set of symbols. This is an appropriate representation because it supports the primary operation on elements of an enumerated type: test for equality using eq. It also supports input and output quite handily.

In many other languages (such as C or Pascal), enumerated types are implemented as integers. In Pascal one could declare:

```
type piece = (black, white, empty);
```

to define piece as a set of three elements that is treated as a subtype of the integers. The language does not allow for direct input and output of such types, but equality can be checked. An advantage of this approach is that an element can be packed into a small space. In the Othello domain, we anticipate that efficiency will be important, because one way to pick a good move is to look at a large number of possible sequences of moves, and choose a sequence that leads toward a favorable result. Thus, we are willing to look hard at alternative representations to find an efficient one. It takes only two bits to represent one of the three possible types, while it takes many more (perhaps 32) to represent a symbol. Thus, we may save space by representing pieces as small integers rather than symbols.

Next, we consider the board. The two-dimensional array seems like such an obvious choice that it is hard to imagine a better representation. We could consider an 8-element list of 8-element lists, but this would just waste space (for the cons cells) and time (in accessing the later elements of the lists). However, we will have to implement two other abstract data types that we have not yet considered: the square and the direction. We will need, for example, to represent the square that a player chooses to move into. This will be a pair of integers, such as 4,5. We could represent this as a two-element list, or more compactly as a cons cell, but this still means that we may have to generate garbage (create a cons cell) every time we want to refer to a new square. Similarly, we need to be able to scan in a given direction from a square, looking for pieces to flip. Directions will be represented as a pair of integers, such as +1,-1. One clever possibility is to use complex numbers for both squares and directions, with the real component mapped to the horizontal axis and the imaginary component mapped to the vertical axis. Then moving in a given direction from a square is accomplished by simply adding the direction to the square. But in most implementations, creating new complex numbers will also generate garbage.

Another possibility is to represent squares (and directions) as two distinct integers, and have the routines that manipulate them accept two arguments instead of one. This would be efficient, but it is losing an important abstraction: that squares (and directions) are conceptually single objects.

A way out of this dilemma is to represent the board as a one-dimensional vector. Squares are represented as integers in the range 0 to 63. In most implementations, small integers (fixnums) are represented as immediate data that can be manipulated without generating garbage. Directions can also be implemented as integers, representing the numerical difference between adjacent squares along that direction. To get a feel for this, take a look at the board:

```
 0  1  2  3  4  5  6  7
 8  9 10 11 12 13 14 15
16 17 18 19 20 21 22 23
24 25 26 27 28 29 30 31
32 33 34 35 36 37 38 39
40 41 42 43 44 45 46 47
48 49 50 51 52 53 54 55
56 57 58 59 60 61 62 63
```

You can see that the direction +1 corresponds to movement to the right, +7 corresponds to diagonal movement downward and to the left, +8 is downward, and +9 is diagonally downward and to the right. The negations of these numbers (-1, -7, -8, -9) represent the opposite directions.

There is one complication with this scheme: we need to know when we hit the edge of the board. Starting at square 0, we can move in direction +1 seven times to arrive at the right edge of the board, but we aren't allowed to move in that direction yet again to arrive at square 8. It is possible to check for the edge of the board by considering quotients and remainders modulo 8, but it is somewhat complicated and expensive to do so.

A simpler solution is to represent the edge of the board explicitly, by using a 100-element vector instead of a 64-element vector. The outlying elements are filled with a marker indicating that they are outside the board proper. This representation wastes some space but makes edge detection much simpler. It also has the minor advantage that legal squares are represented by numbers in the range 11-88, which makes them easier to understand while debugging. Here's the new 100-element board:

```
 0  1  2  3  4  5  6  7  8  9
10 11 12 13 14 15 16 17 18 19
20 21 22 23 24 25 26 27 28 29
30 31 32 33 34 35 36 37 38 39
40 41 42 43 44 45 46 47 48 49
50 51 52 53 54 55 56 57 58 59
60 61 62 63 64 65 66 67 68 69
70 71 72 73 74 75 76 77 78 79
80 81 82 83 84 85 86 87 88 89
90 91 92 93 94 95 96 97 98 99
```

The horizontal direction is now ± 1, vertical is ± 10, and the diagonals are ± 9 and ± 11. We'll tentatively adopt this latest representation, but leave open the possibility of changing to another format. With this much decided, we are ready to begin. Figure 18.3 is the glossary for the complete program. A glossary for a second version of the program is on page 623.

What follows is the code for directions and pieces. We explicitly define the type piece to be a number from empty to outer (0 to 3), and define the function name-of to map from a piece number to a character: a dot for empty, @ for black, 0 for white, and a question mark (which should never be printed) for outer.

```lisp
(defconstant all-directions '(-11 -10 -9 -1 1 9 10 11))

(defconstant empty 0 "An empty square")
(defconstant black 1 "A black piece")
(defconstant white 2 "A white piece")
(defconstant outer 3 "Marks squares outside the 8x8 board")

(deftype piece () '(integer ,empty ,outer))

(defun name-of (piece) (char ".@0?" piece))

(defun opponent (player) (if (eql player black) white black))
```

And here is the code for the board. Note that we introduce the function bref, for "board reference" rather than using the built-in function aref. This facilitates possible changes to the representation of boards. Also, even though there is no contiguous range of numbers that represents the legal squares, we can define the constant all-squares to be a list of the 64 legal squares, computed as those numbers from 11 to 88 whose value mod 10 is between 1 and 8.

```lisp
(deftype board () '(simple-array piece (100)))

(defun bref (board square) (aref board square))
(defsetf bref (board square) (val)
  '(setf (aref ,board ,square) ,val))
```

	Top-Level Function
othello	Play a game of Othello. Return the score.
	Constants
empty	0 represents an empty square.
black	1 represents a black piece.
white	2 represents a white piece.
outer	3 represents a piece outside the 8 × 8 board.
all-directions	A list of integers representing the eight directions.
all-squares	A list of all legal squares.
winning-value	The best possible evaluation.
losing-value	The worst possible evaluation.
	Data Types
piece	An integer from empty to outer.
board	A vector of 100 pieces.
	Major Functions
get-move	Call the player's strategy function to get a move.
make-move	Update board to reflect move by player.
human	A strategy that prompts a human player.
random-strategy	Make any legal move.
maximize-difference	A strategy that maximizes the difference in pieces.
maximizer	Return a strategy that maximizes some measure.
weighted-squares	Sum of the weights of player's squares minus opponent's.
modified-weighted-squares	Like above, but treating corners better.
minimax	Find the best move according to EVAL-FN, searching PLY levels.
minimax-searcher	Return a strategy that uses minimax to search.
alpha-beta	Find the best move according to EVAL-FN, searching PLY levels.
alpha-beta-searcher	Return a strategy that uses alpha-beta to search.
	Auxiliary Functions
bref	Reference to a position on the board.
copy-board	Make a new board.
initial-board	Return a board, empty except for four pieces in the middle.
print-board	Print a board, along with some statistics.
count-difference	Count player's pieces minus opponent's pieces.
name-of	A character used to print a piece.
opponent	The opponent of black is white, and vice-versa.
valid-p	A syntactically valid square.
legal-p	A legal move on the board.
make-flips	Make any flips in the given direction.
would-flip?	Would this move result in any flips in this direction?
find-bracketing-piece	Return the square number of the bracketing piece.
any-legal-move?	Does player have any legal moves in this position?
next-to-play	Compute the player to move next, or NIL if nobody can move.
legal-moves	Returns a list of legal moves for player.
final-value	Is this a win, loss, or draw for player?
neighbors	Return a list of all squares adjacent to a square.
switch-strategies	Play one strategy for a while, then switch.
	Previously Defined Functions
random-elt	Choose a random element from a sequence. (pg. 36)

Figure 18.3: Glossary for the Othello Program

```lisp
(defun copy-board (board)
  (copy-seq board))

(defconstant all-squares
  (loop for i from 11 to 88 when (<= 1 (mod i 10) 8) collect i))

(defun initial-board ()
  "Return a board, empty except for four pieces in the middle."
  ;; Boards are 100-element vectors, with elements 11-88 used,
  ;; and the others marked with the sentinel OUTER.  Initially
  ;; the 4 center squares are taken, the others empty.
  (let ((board (make-array 100 :element-type 'piece
                               :initial-element outer)))
    (dolist (square all-squares)
      (setf (bref board square) empty))
    (setf (bref board 44) white    (bref board 45) black
          (bref board 54) black    (bref board 55) white)
    board))

(defun print-board (board)
  "Print a board, along with some statistics."
  (format t "~2&    1 2 3 4 5 6 7 8   [~c=~2a ~c=~2a (~@d)]"
          (name-of black) (count black board)
          (name-of white) (count white board)
          (count-difference black board))
  (loop for row from 1 to 8 do
        (format t "~&  ~d " (* 10 row))
        (loop for col from 1 to 8
              for piece = (bref board (+ col (* 10 row)))
              do (format t "~c " (name-of piece))))
  (format t "~2&"))

(defun count-difference (player board)
  "Count player's pieces minus opponent's pieces."
  (- (count player board)
     (count (opponent player) board)))
```

Now let's take a look at the initial board, as it is printed by print-board, and by a raw write (I added the line breaks to make it easier to read):

```
> (write (initial-board)      > (print-board (initial-board))
        :array t)
#(3 3 3 3 3 3 3 3 3 3            1 2 3 4 5 6 7 8 [@=2 0=2 (+0)]
  3 0 0 0 0 0 0 0 0 3         10 . . . . . . . .
  3 0 0 0 0 0 0 0 0 3         20 . . . . . . . .
  3 0 0 0 0 0 0 0 0 3         30 . . . . . . . .
  3 0 0 0 2 1 0 0 0 3         40 . . . 0 @ . . .
  3 0 0 0 1 2 0 0 0 3         50 . . . @ 0 . . .
  3 0 0 0 0 0 0 0 0 3         60 . . . . . . . .
  3 0 0 0 0 0 0 0 0 3         70 . . . . . . . .
  3 0 0 0 0 0 0 0 0 3         80 . . . . . . . .
  3 3 3 3 3 3 3 3 3 3)
#<ART-2B-100 -72570734>        NIL
```

Notice that print-board provides some additional information: the number of pieces that each player controls, and the difference between these two counts.

The next step is to handle moves properly: given a board and a square to move to, update the board to reflect the effects of the player moving to that square. This means flipping some of the opponent's pieces. One design decision is whether the procedure that makes moves, make-move, will be responsible for checking for error conditions. My choice is that make-move assumes it will be passed a legal move. That way, a strategy can use the function to explore sequences of moves that are known to be valid without slowing make-move down. Of course, separate procedures will have to insure that a move is legal. Here we introduce two terms: a *valid* move is one that is syntactically correct: an integer from 11 to 88 that is not off the board. A *legal* move is a valid move into an empty square that will flip at least one opponent. Here's the code:

```
(defun valid-p (move)
  "Valid moves are numbers in the range 11-88 that end in 1-8."
  (and (integerp move) (<= 11 move 88) (<= 1 (mod move 10) 8)))

(defun legal-p (move player board)
  "A Legal move must be into an empty square, and it must
  flip at least one opponent piece."
  (and (eql (bref board move) empty)
       (some #'(lambda (dir) (would-flip? move player board dir))
             all-directions)))

(defun make-move (move player board)
  "Update board to reflect move by player"
  ;; First make the move, then make any flips
  (setf (bref board move) player)
  (dolist (dir all-directions)
    (make-flips move player board dir))
  board)
```

Now all we need is to make-flips. To do that, we search in all directions for a *bracketing* piece: a piece belonging to the player who is making the move, which sandwiches a string of opponent pieces. If there are no opponent pieces in that direction, or if an empty or outer piece is hit before the player's piece, then no flips are made. Note that would-flip? is a semipredicate that returns false if no flips would be made in the given direction, and returns the square of the bracketing piece if there is one.

```lisp
(defun make-flips (move player board dir)
  "Make any flips in the given direction."
  (let ((bracketer (would-flip? move player board dir)))
    (when bracketer
      (loop for c from (+ move dir) by dir until (eql c bracketer)
            do (setf (bref board c) player)))))

(defun would-flip? (move player board dir)
  "Would this move result in any flips in this direction?
  If so, return the square number of the bracketing piece."
  ;; A flip occurs if, starting at the adjacent square, c, there
  ;; is a string of at least one opponent pieces, bracketed by
  ;; one of player's pieces
  (let ((c (+ move dir)))
    (and (eql (bref board c) (opponent player))
         (find-bracketing-piece (+ c dir) player board dir))))

(defun find-bracketing-piece (square player board dir)
  "Return the square number of the bracketing piece."
  (cond ((eql (bref board square) player) square)
        ((eql (bref board square) (opponent player))
         (find-bracketing-piece (+ square dir) player board dir))
        (t nil)))
```

Finally we can write the function that actually monitors a game. But first we are faced with one more important choice: how will we represent a player? We have already distinguished between black and white's pieces, but we have not decided how to ask black or white for their moves. I choose to represent player's strategies as functions. Each function takes two arguments: the color to move (black or white) and the current board. The function should return a legal move number.

```lisp
(defun othello (bl-strategy wh-strategy &optional (print t))
  "Play a game of Othello.  Return the score, where a positive
  difference means black (the first player) wins."
  (let ((board (initial-board)))
    (loop for player = black
            then (next-to-play board player print)
          for strategy = (if (eql player black)
```

```
                        bl-strategy
                        wh-strategy)
            until (null player)
            do (get-move strategy player board print))
      (when print
        (format t "~&The game is over.  Final result:")
        (print-board board))
      (count-difference black board)))
```

We need to be able to determine who plays next at any point. The rules say that players alternate turns, but if one player has no legal moves, the other can move again. When neither has a legal move, the game is over. This usually happens because there are no empty squares left, but it sometimes happens earlier in the game. The player with more pieces at the end of the game wins. If neither player has more, the game is a draw.

```
(defun next-to-play (board previous-player print)
  "Compute the player to move next, or NIL if nobody can move."
  (let ((opp (opponent previous-player)))
    (cond ((any-legal-move? opp board) opp)
          ((any-legal-move? previous-player board)
           (when print
             (format t "~&~c has no moves and must pass."
                     (name-of opp)))
           previous-player)
          (t nil))))

(defun any-legal-move? (player board)
  "Does player have any legal moves in this position?"
  (some #'(lambda (move) (legal-p move player board))
        all-squares))
```

Note that the argument `print` (of `othello`, `next-to-play`, and below, `get-move`) determines if information about the progress of the game will be printed. For an interactive game, `print` should be true, but it is also possible to play a "batch" game with `print` set to false.

In `get-move` below, the player's strategy function is called to determine his move. Illegal moves are detected, and proper moves are reported when `print` is true. The strategy function is passed a number representing the player to move (black or white) and a copy of the board. If we passed the *real* game board, the function could cheat by changing the pieces on the board!

```
(defun get-move (strategy player board print)
  "Call the player's strategy function to get a move.
  Keep calling until a legal move is made."
  (when print (print-board board))
  (let ((move (funcall strategy player (copy-board board))))
    (cond
      ((and (valid-p move) (legal-p move player board))
       (when print
         (format t "~&~c moves to ~d." (name-of player) move))
       (make-move move player board))
      (t (warn "Illegal move: ~d" move)
         (get-move strategy player board print)))))
```

Here we define two simple strategies:

```
(defun human (player board)
  "A human player for the game of Othello"
  (declare (ignore board))
  (format t "~&~c to move: " (name-of player))
  (read))

(defun random-strategy (player board)
  "Make any legal move."
  (random-elt (legal-moves player board)))

(defun legal-moves (player board)
  "Returns a list of legal moves for player"
  (loop for move in all-squares
    when (legal-p move player board) collect move))
```

We are now in a position to play the game. The expression
(othello #'human #'human) will let two people play against each other. Alternately,
(othello #'random-strategy #'human) will allow us to match our wits against a
particularly poor strategy. The rest of this chapter shows how to develop a better
strategy.

18.3   Evaluating Positions

The random-move strategy is, of course, a poor one. We would like to make a good
move rather than a random move, but so far we don't know what makes a good
move. The only positions we are able to evaluate for sure are final positions: when
the game is over, we know that the player with the most pieces wins. This suggests a
strategy: choose the move that maximizes count-difference, the piece differential.

The function `maximize-difference` does just that. It calls `maximizer`, a higher-order function that chooses the best move according to an arbitrary evaluation function.

```
(defun maximize-difference (player board)
  "A strategy that maximizes the difference in pieces."
  (funcall (maximizer #'count-difference) player board))

(defun maximizer (eval-fn)
  "Return a strategy that will consider every legal move,
  apply EVAL-FN to each resulting board, and choose
  the move for which EVAL-FN returns the best score.
  FN takes two arguments: the player-to-move and board"
  #'(lambda (player board)
      (let* ((moves (legal-moves player board))
             (scores (mapcar #'(lambda (move)
                                 (funcall
                                   eval-fn
                                   player
                                   (make-move move player
                                     (copy-board board))))
                             moves))
             (best (apply #'max scores)))
        (elt moves (position best scores)))))
```

Exercise 18.1 Play some games with `maximize-difference` against `random-strategy` and `human`. How good is `maximize-difference`?

Those who complete the exercise will quickly see that the `maximize-difference` player does better than random, and may even beat human players in their first game or two. But most humans are able to improve, learning to take advantage of the overly greedy play of `maximize-difference`. Humans learn that the edge squares, for example, are valuable because the player dominating the edges can surround the opponent, while it is difficult to recapture an edge. This is especially true of corner squares, which can never be recaptured.

Using this knowledge, a clever player can temporarily sacrifice pieces to obtain edge and corner squares in the short run, and win back pieces in the long run. We can approximate some of this reasoning with the `weighted-squares` evaluation function. Like `count-difference`, it adds up all the player's pieces and subtracts the opponents, but each piece is weighted according to the square it occupies. Edge squares are weighted highly, corner squares higher still, and squares adjacent to the corners and edges have negative weights, because occupying these squares often gives the opponent a means of capturing the desirable square. Figure 18.4 shows the standard nomenclature for edge squares: X, A, B, and C. In general, X and C squares are to be avoided, because taking them gives the opponent a chance to take the corner. The `weighted-squares` evaluation function reflects this.

	a	b	c	d	e	f	g	h
1		C	A	B	B	A	C	
2	C	X					X	C
3	A							A
4	B							B
5	B							B
6	A							A
7	C	X					X	C
8		C	A	B	B	A	C	

Figure 18.4: Names for Edge Squares

```
(defparameter *weights*
  '#(0   0   0  0  0  0  0   0   0 0
     0 120 -20 20  5  5 20 -20 120 0
     0 -20 -40 -5 -5 -5 -5 -40 -20 0
     0  20  -5 15  3  3 15  -5  20 0
     0   5  -5  3  3  3  3  -5   5 0
     0   5  -5  3  3  3  3  -5   5 0
     0  20  -5 15  3  3 15  -5  20 0
     0 -20 -40 -5 -5 -5 -5 -40 -20 0
     0 120 -20 20  5  5 20 -20 120 0
     0   0   0  0  0  0  0   0   0 0))

(defun weighted-squares (player board)
  "Sum of the weights of player's squares minus opponent's."
  (let ((opp (opponent player)))
    (loop for i in all-squares
          when (eql (bref board i) player)
          sum (aref *weights* i)
          when (eql (bref board i) opp)
          sum (- (aref *weights* i)))))
```

Exercise 18.2 Compare strategies by evaluating the two forms below. What happens? Is this a good test to determine which strategy is better?

```
(othello (maximizer #'weighted-squares)
         (maximizer #'count-difference) nil)

(othello (maximizer #'count-difference)
         (maximizer #'weighted-squares) nil)
```

18.4   Searching Ahead: Minimax

Even the weighted-squares strategy is no match for an experienced player. There are two ways we could improve the strategy. First, we could modify the evaluation function to take more information into account. But even without changing the evaluation function, we can improve the strategy by searching ahead. Instead of choosing the move that leads immediately to the highest score, we can also consider the opponent's possible replies, our replies to those replies, and so on. By searching through several levels of moves, we can steer away from potential disaster and find good moves that were not immediately apparent.

Another way to look at the maximizer function is as a search function that searches only one level, or *ply*, deep:

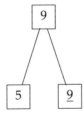

The top of the tree is the current board position, and the squares below that indicate possible moves. The maximizer function evaluates each of these and picks the best move, which is underlined in the diagram.

Now let's see how a 3-ply search might go. The first step is to apply maximizer to the positions just above the bottom of the tree. Suppose we get the following values:

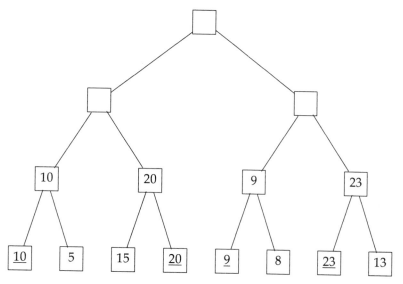

Each position is shown as having two possible legal moves, which is unrealistic but makes the diagram fit on the page. In a real game, five to ten legal moves per position is typical. The values at the leaves of the tree were computed by applying the evaluation function, while the values one level up were computed by maximizer. The result is that we know what our best move is for any of the four positions just above the bottom of the tree.

Going up a level, it is the opponent's turn to move. We can assume the opponent will choose the move that results in the minimal value to us, which would be the maximal value to the opponent. Thus, the opponent's choices would be the 10- and 9-valued positions, avoiding the 20- and 23-valued positions.

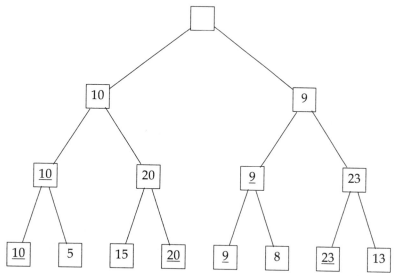

Now it is our turn to move again, so we apply `maximizer` once again to get the final value of the top-level position:

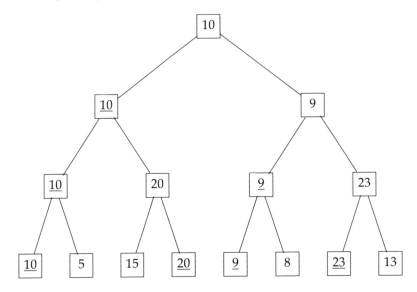

If the opponent plays as expected, we will always follow the left branch of the tree and end up at the position with value 10. If the opponent plays otherwise, we will end up at a position with a better value.

This kind of search is traditionally called a *minimax* search, because of the alternate application of the `maximizer` and a hypothetical `minimizer` function. Notice that only the leaf positions in the tree are looked at by the evaluation function. The value of all other positions is determined by minimizing and maximizing.

We are almost ready to code the minimax algorithm, but first we have to make a few design decisions. First, we could write two functions, `minimax` and `maximin`, which correspond to the two players' analyses. However, it is easier to write a single function that maximizes the value of a position for a particular player. In other words, by adding the player as a parameter, we avoid having to write two otherwise identical functions.

Second, we have to decide if we are going to write a general minimax searcher or an Othello-specific searcher. I decided on the latter for efficiency reasons, and because there are some Othello-specific complications that need to be accounted for. First, it is possible that a player will not have any legal moves. In that case, we want to continue the search with the opponent to move. If the opponent has no moves either, then the game is over, and the value of the position can be determined with finality by counting the pieces.

Third, we need to decide the interaction between the normal evaluation function and this final evaluation that occurs when the game is over. We could insist that each evaluation function determine when the game is over and do the proper computation. But that overburdens the evaluation functions and may lead to wasteful checking for the end of game. Instead, I implemented a separate final-value evaluation function, which returns 0 for a draw, a large positive number for a win, and a large negative number for a loss. Because fixnum arithmetic is most efficient, the constants most-positive-fixnum and most-negative-fixnum are used. The evaluation functions must be careful to return numbers that are within this range. All the evaluation functions in this chapter will be within range if fixnums are 20 bits or more.

In a tournament, it is not only important who wins and loses, but also by how much. If we were trying to maximize the margin of victory, then final-value would be changed to include a small factor for the final difference.

```lisp
(defconstant winning-value most-positive-fixnum)
(defconstant losing-value  most-negative-fixnum)

(defun final-value (player board)
  "Is this a win, loss, or draw for player?"
  (case (signum (count-difference player board))
    (-1 losing-value)
    ( 0 0)
    (+1 winning-value)))
```

Fourth, and finally, we need to decide on the parameters for the minimax function. Like the other evaluation functions, it needs the player to move and the current board as parameters. It also needs an indication of how many ply to search, and the static evaluation function to apply to the leaf positions. Thus, minimax will be a function of four arguments. What will it return? It needs to return the best move, but it also needs to return the value of that move, according to the static evaluation function. We use multiple values for this.

```lisp
(defun minimax (player board ply eval-fn)
  "Find the best move, for PLAYER, according to EVAL-FN,
  searching PLY levels deep and backing up values."
  (if (= ply 0)
      (funcall eval-fn player board)
      (let ((moves (legal-moves player board)))
        (if (null moves)
            (if (any-legal-move? (opponent player) board)
                (- (minimax (opponent player) board
                            (- ply 1) eval-fn))
                (final-value player board))
            (let ((best-move nil)
                  (best-val nil))
              (dolist (move moves)
```

```
(let* ((board2 (make-move move player
                          (copy-board board)))
       (val (- (minimax
                 (opponent player) board2
                 (- ply 1) eval-fn))))
  (when (or (null best-val)
            (> val best-val))
    (setf best-val val)
    (setf best-move move))))
(values best-val best-move)))))))
```

The minimax function cannot be used as a strategy function as is, because it takes too many arguments and returns too many values. The functional minimax-searcher returns an appropriate strategy. Remember that a strategy is a function of two arguments: the player and the board. get-move is responsible for passing the right arguments to the function, so the strategy need not worry about where the arguments come from.

```
(defun minimax-searcher (ply eval-fn)
  "A strategy that searches PLY levels and then uses EVAL-FN."
  #'(lambda (player board)
      (multiple-value-bind (value move)
          (minimax player board ply eval-fn)
        (declare (ignore value))
        move)))
```

We can test the minimax strategy, and see that searching ahead 3 ply is indeed better than looking at only 1 ply. I show only the final result, which demonstrates that it is indeed an advantage to be able to look ahead:

```
> (othello (minimax-searcher 3 #'count-difference)
           (maximizer #'count-difference))
...

The game is over.  Final result:

    1 2 3 4 5 6 7 8   [@=53 0=0  (+53)]
10 @ @ @ @ @ @ @ @
20 @ @ @ @ @ @ @ @
30 @ @ @ @ @ @ @ @
40 @ @ @ @ @ @ @ @
50 @ @ @ @ @ @ @ @
60 . . @ @ @ @ @ @
70 . . . @ @ @ @ @
80 . . . . @ @ . .
```

18.5   Smarter Searching: Alpha-Beta Search

The problem with a full minimax search is that it considers too many positions. It looks at every line of play, including many improbable ones. Fortunately, there is a way to find the optimal line of play without looking at every possible position. Let's go back to our familiar search tree:

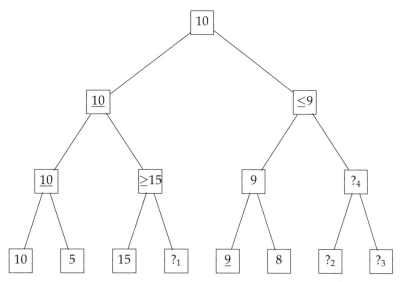

Here we have marked certain positions with question marks. The idea is that the whole search tree evaluates to 10 regardless of the value of the positions labeled $?_i$. Consider the position labeled $?_1$. It does not matter what this position evaluates to, because the opponent will always choose to play toward the 10-position, to avoid the possibility of the 15. Thus, we can cut off the search at this point and not consider the ?-position. This kind of cutoff has historically been called a *beta* cutoff.

Now consider the position labeled $?_4$. It does not matter what this position evaluates to, because we will always prefer to choose the 10 position at the left branch, rather than giving the opponent a chance to play to the 9-position. This is an *alpha* cutoff. Notice that it cuts off a whole subtree of positions below it (labeled $?_2$ and $?_3$).

In general, we keep track of two parameters that bound the true value of the current position. The lower bound is a value we know we can achieve by choosing a certain line of play. The idea is that we need not even consider moves that will lead to a value lower than this. The lower bound has traditionally been called *alpha*, but we will name it `achievable`. The upper bound represents a value the opponent can achieve by choosing a certain line of play. It has been called *beta*, but we will call it `cutoff`. Again, the idea is that we need not consider moves with a higher value than this (because then the opponent would avoid the move that is so good for us). The alpha-beta algorithm is just minimax, but with some needless evaluations pruned by these two parameters.

In deeper trees with higher branching factors, many more evaluations can be pruned. In general, a tree of depth d and branching factor b requires b^d evaluations for full minimax, and as few as $b^{d/2}$ evaluations with alpha-beta minimax.

To implement alpha-beta search, we add two more parameters to the function `minimax` and rename it `alpha-beta`. `achievable` is the best score the player can achieve; it is what we want to maximize. The `cutoff` is a value that, when exceeded, will make the opponent choose another branch of the tree, thus making the rest of the current level of the tree irrelevant. The test `until` (`>= achievable cutoff`) in the penultimate line of `minimax` does the cutoff; all the other changes just involve passing the parameters around properly.

```lisp
(defun alpha-beta (player board achievable cutoff ply eval-fn)
  "Find the best move, for PLAYER, according to EVAL-FN,
  searching PLY levels deep and backing up values,
  using cutoffs whenever possible."
  (if (= ply 0)
      (funcall eval-fn player board)
      (let ((moves (legal-moves player board)))
        (if (null moves)
            (if (any-legal-move? (opponent player) board)
                (- (alpha-beta (opponent player) board
                               (- cutoff) (- achievable)
                               (- ply 1) eval-fn))
                (final-value player board))
            (let ((best-move (first moves)))
              (loop for move in moves do
                (let* ((board2 (make-move move player
                                          (copy-board board)))
                       (val (- (alpha-beta
                                (opponent player) board2
                                (- cutoff) (- achievable)
                                (- ply 1) eval-fn))))
                  (when (> val achievable)
                    (setf achievable val)
                    (setf best-move move)))
                until (>= achievable cutoff))
              (values achievable best-move))))))

(defun alpha-beta-searcher (depth eval-fn)
  "A strategy that searches to DEPTH and then uses EVAL-FN."
  #'(lambda (player board)
      (multiple-value-bind (value move)
          (alpha-beta player board losing-value winning-value
                      depth eval-fn)
```

```
(declare (ignore value))
move)))
```

It must be stressed that alpha-beta computes the exact same result as the full-search version of minimax. The only advantage of the cutoffs is making the search go faster by considering fewer positions.

18.6   An Analysis of Some Games

Now is a good time to stop and analyze where we have gone. We've demonstrated a program that can play a *legal* game of Othello, and some strategies that may or may not play a *good* game. First, we'll look at some individual games to see the mistakes made by some strategies, and then we'll generate some statistics for series of games.

Is the weighted-squares measure a good one? We can compare it to a strategy of maximizing the number of pieces. Such a strategy would of course be perfect if it could look ahead to the end of the game, but the speed of our computers limits us to searching only a few ply, even with cutoffs. Consider the following game, where black is maximizing the difference in the number of pieces, and white is maximizing the weighted sum of squares. Both search to a depth of 4 ply:

```
> (othello (alpha-beta-searcher 4 #'count-difference)
           (alpha-beta-searcher 4 #'weighted-squares))
```

Black is able to increase the piece difference dramatically as the game progresses. After 17 moves, white is down to only one piece:

```
   1 2 3 4 5 6 7 8   [@=20 0=1  (+19)]
10 0 @ . . . . . .
20 . @ . . . @ @ .
30 @ @ @ @ @ @ . .
40 . @ . @ @ . . .
50 @ @ @ @ @ @ . .
60 . @ . . . . . .
70 . . . . . . . .
80 . . . . . . . .
```

Although behind by 19 points, white is actually in a good position, because the piece in the corner is safe and threatens many of black's pieces. White is able to maintain good position while being numerically far behind black, as shown in these positions later in the game:

```
    1 2 3 4 5 6 7 8   [@=32 0=15 (+17)]
10  0 0 0 0 @ @ 0 0
20  @ @ 0 @ @ @ @ @
30  @ @ 0 0 @ 0 @ @
40  0 0 @ @ @ @ @ @
50  @ 0 @ @ @ @ . .
60  @ @ 0 @ @ 0 . .
70  @ . . @ @ . . .
80  . . . . . . . .

    1 2 3 4 5 6 7 8   [@=34 0=19 (+15)]
10  0 0 0 0 @ @ 0 0
20  @ @ 0 @ @ @ @ @
30  @ @ 0 0 @ 0 @ @
40  0 @ 0 @ @ @ @ @
50  0 @ 0 @ @ @ @ .
60  0 @ 0 @ @ @ . .
70  0 @ @ @ @ . . .
80  0 @ 0 . . . . .
```

After some give-and-take, white gains the advantage for good by capturing eight pieces on a move to square 85 on the third-to-last move of the game:

```
    1 2 3 4 5 6 7 8   [@=31 0=30 (+1)]
10  0 0 0 0 @ @ 0 0
20  @ @ 0 0 @ @ @ 0
30  @ @ 0 0 0 @ @ 0
40  0 @ 0 0 0 @ @ 0
50  0 @ 0 @ 0 @ @ 0
60  0 @ 0 @ @ @ @ 0
70  0 @ @ @ @ @ 0 0
80  0 @ @ @ . . . 0
```

0 moves to 85.

```
    1 2 3 4 5 6 7 8   [@=23 0=39 (-16)]
10  0 0 0 0 @ @ 0 0
20  @ @ 0 0 @ @ @ 0
30  @ @ 0 0 0 @ @ 0
40  0 @ 0 0 0 @ @ 0
50  0 @ 0 @ 0 @ @ 0
60  0 @ 0 @ 0 @ 0 0
70  0 @ @ 0 0 0 0 0
80  0 0 0 0 0 . . 0
```

@ moves to 86.

```
       1 2 3 4 5 6 7 8    [@=26 0=37 (-11)]
    10 0 0 0 0 0 @ @ 0 0
    20 @ @ 0 0 @ @ @ 0
    30 @ @ 0 0 0 @ @ 0
    40 0 @ 0 0 0 @ @ 0
    50 0 @ 0 @ 0 @ @ 0
    60 0 @ 0 @ 0 @ 0 0
    70 0 @ @ 0 @ @ 0 0
    80 0 0 0 0 0 @ . 0
```

0 moves to 87.
The game is over. Final result:

```
       1 2 3 4 5 6 7 8    [@=24 0=40 (-16)]
    10 0 0 0 0 0 @ @ 0 0
    20 @ @ 0 0 @ @ @ 0
    30 @ @ 0 0 0 @ @ 0
    40 0 @ 0 0 0 @ @ 0
    50 0 @ 0 @ 0 @ @ 0
    60 0 @ 0 @ 0 @ 0 0
    70 0 @ @ 0 @ 0 0 0
    80 0 0 0 0 0 0 0 0
-16
```

White ends up winning by 16 pieces. Black's strategy was too greedy: black was willing to give up position (all four corners and all but four of the edge squares) for temporary gains in material.

Increasing the depth of search does not compensate for a faulty evaluation function. In the following game, black's search depth is increased to 6 ply, while white's is kept at 4. The same things happen, although black's doom takes a bit longer to unfold.

```
> (othello (alpha-beta-searcher 6 #'count-difference)
           (alpha-beta-searcher 4 #'weighted-squares))
```

Black slowly builds up an advantage:

```
       1 2 3 4 5 6 7 8    [@=21 0=8  (+13)]
    10 . . @ @ @ @ @ .
    20 . @ . @ 0 @ . .
    30 0 @ @ 0 @ 0 0 .
    40 . @ . @ 0 @ 0 .
    50 . @ @ @ @ . . .
    60 . @ . @ . 0 . .
    70 . . . . . . . .
    80 . . . . . . . .
```

But at this point white has clear access to the upper left corner, and through that corner threatens to take the whole top edge. Still, black maintains a material edge as the game goes on:

```
     1 2 3 4 5 6 7 8   [@=34 O=11 (+23)]
10 0 . @ @ @ @ @ .
20 . 0 0 @ @ @ . .
30 0 @ 0 0 @ @ @ @
40 @ @ @ @ 0 @ @ .
50 @ @ @ @ @ 0 @ .
60 @ @ @ @ @ @ 0 0
70 @ . . @ . . @ 0
80 . . . . . . . .
```

But eventually white's weighted-squares strategy takes the lead:

```
     1 2 3 4 5 6 7 8   [@=23 O=27 (-4)]
10 0 0 0 0 0 0 0 0
20 @ @ 0 @ @ @ . .
30 0 @ 0 0 @ @ @ @
40 0 @ 0 @ 0 @ @ .
50 0 @ 0 @ @ 0 @ .
60 0 0 0 @ @ @ 0 0
70 0 . 0 @ . . @ 0
80 0 . . . . . . .
```

and is able to hold on to win:

```
     1 2 3 4 5 6 7 8   [@=24 O=40 (-16)]
10 0 0 0 0 0 0 0 0
20 @ @ 0 @ 0 0 @ @
30 0 @ 0 0 @ @ @ @
40 0 @ 0 0 @ @ @ 0
50 0 0 @ @ 0 @ 0 0
60 0 0 0 @ 0 @ @ 0
70 0 0 0 0 @ @ 0 0
80 0 0 0 0 0 @ @ 0
  -16
```

This shows that brute-force searching is not a panacea. While it is helpful to be able to search deeper, greater gains can be made by making the evaluation function more accurate. There are many problems with the weighted-squares evaluation function. Consider again this position from the first game above:

```
     1 2 3 4 5 6 7 8   [@=20 0=1  (+19)]
10 0 @ . . . . . .
20 . @ . . . @ @ .
30 @ @ @ @ @ @ . .
40 . @ . @ @ . . .
50 @ @ @ @ @ @ . .
60 . @ . . . . . .
70 . . . . . . . .
80 . . . . . . . .
```

Here white, playing the weighted-squares strategy, chose to play 66. This is probably a mistake, as 13 would extend white's dominance of the top edge, and allow white to play again (since black would have no legal moves). Unfortunately, white rejects this move, primarily because square 12 is weighted as -20. Thus, there is a disincentive to taking this square. But 12 is weighted -20 because it is a bad idea to take such a square when the corner is empty—the opponent will then have a chance to capture the corner, regaining the 12 square as well. Thus, we want squares like 12 to have a negative score when the corner is empty, but not when it is already occupied. The modified-weighted-squares evaluation function does just that.

```lisp
(defun modified-weighted-squares (player board)
  "Like WEIGHTED-SQUARES, but don't take off for moving
  near an occupied corner."
  (let ((w (weighted-squares player board)))
    (dolist (corner '(11 18 81 88))
      (when (not (eql (bref board corner) empty))
        (dolist (c (neighbors corner))
          (when (not (eql (bref board c) empty))
            (incf w (* (- 5 (aref *weights* c))
                       (if (eql (bref board c) player)
                           +1 -1)))))))
    w))

(let ((neighbor-table (make-array 100 :initial-element nil)))
  ;; Initialize the neighbor table
  (dolist (square all-squares)
    (dolist (dir all-directions)
      (if (valid-p (+ square dir))
          (push (+ square dir)
                (aref neighbor-table square)))))

(defun neighbors (square)
  "Return a list of all squares adjacent to a square."
  (aref neighbor-table square)))
```

18.7   The Tournament Version of Othello

While the othello function serves as a perfectly good moderator for casual play, there are two points that need to be fixed for tournament-level play. First, tournament games are played under a strict time limit: a player who takes over 30 minutes total to make all the moves forfeits the game. Second, the standard notation for Othello games uses square names in the range a1 to h8, rather than in the 11 to 88 range that we have used so far. a1 is the upper left corner, a8 is the lower left corner, and h8 is the lower right corner. We can write routines to translate between this notation and the one we were using by creating a table of square names.

```lisp
(let ((square-names
        (cross-product #'symbol
                       '(? a b c d e f g h ?)
                       '(? 1 2 3 4 5 6 7 8 ?))))

  (defun h8->88 (str)
    "Convert from alphanumeric to numeric square notation."
    (or (position (string str) square-names :test #'string-equal)
        str))

  (defun 88->h8 (num)
    "Convert from numeric to alphanumeric square notation."
    (if (valid-p num)
        (elt square-names num)
        num)))

(defun cross-product (fn xlist ylist)
  "Return a list of all (fn x y) values."
  (mappend #'(lambda (y)
               (mapcar #'(lambda (x) (funcall fn x y))
                       xlist))
           ylist))
```

Note that these routines return their input unchanged when it is not one of the expected values. This is to allow commands other than moving to a particular square. For example, we will add a feature that recognizes resign as a move.

The human player needs to be changed slightly to read moves in this format. While we're at it, we'll also print the list of possible moves:

```lisp
(defun human (player board)
  "A human player for the game of Othello"
  (format t "~&~c to move ~a: " (name-of player)
          (mapcar #'88->h8 (legal-moves player board)))
  (h8->88 (read)))
```

Top-Level Functions	
`othello-series`	Play a series of N games.
`random-othello-series`	Play a series of games, starting from a random position.
`round-robin`	Play a tournament among strategies.
Special Variables	
`*clock*`	A copy of the game clock (tournament version only).
`*board*`	A copy of the game board (tournament version only).
`*move-number*`	Number of moves made (tournament version only).
`*ply-boards*`	A vector of boards; used as a resource to avoid consing.
Data Structures	
`node`	Holds a board and its evaluation.
Main Functions	
`alpha-beta2`	Sorts moves by static evaluation.
`alpha-beta-searcher2`	Strategy using `alpha-beta2`.
`alpha-beta3`	Uses the killer heuristic.
`alpha-beta-searcher3`	Strategy using `alpha-beta3`.
`Iago-eval`	Evaluation function based on Rosenbloom's program.
`Iago`	Strategy using `Iago-eval`.
Auxiliary Functions	
`h8->88`	Convert from alphanumeric to numeric square notation.
`88->h8`	Convert from numeric to alphanumeric square notation.
`time-string`	Convert internal time units to a mm:ss string.
`switch-strategies`	Play one strategy for a while, then another.
`mobility`	A strategy that counts the number of legal moves.
`legal-nodes`	A list of legal moves sorted by their evaluation.
`negate-node`	Set the value of a node to its negative.
`put-first`	Put the killer move first, if it is legal.
Previously Defined Functions	
`cross-product`	Apply fn to all pairs of arguments. (pg. 47)
`symbol`	Build a symbol by concatenating components.

Figure 18.5: Glossary for the Tournament Version of Othello

The `othello` function needn't worry about notation, but it does need to monitor the time. We make up a new data structure, the clock, which is an array of integers saying how much time (in internal units) each player has left. For example, `(aref clock black)` is the amount of time black has left to make all his moves. In Pascal, we would declare the clock array as `array[black..white]`, but in Common Lisp all arrays are zero-based, so we need an array of three elements to allow the subscript `black`, which is 2.

The clock is passed to `get-move` and `print-board` but is otherwise unused. I could have complicated the main game loop by adding tests for forfeits because of expired time and, as we shall see later, resignation by either player. However, I felt that would add a great deal of complexity for rarely used options. Instead, I wrap the whole game loop, along with the computation of the final score, in a `catch` special form. Then, if get-move encounters a forfeit or resignation, it can throw an appropriate final score: 64 or -64, depending on which player forfeits.

```
(defvar *move-number* 1 "The number of the move to be played")

(defun othello (bl-strategy wh-strategy
                 &optional (print t) (minutes 30))
  "Play a game of othello.  Return the score, where a positive
  difference means black, the first player, wins."
  (let ((board (initial-board))
        (clock (make-array (+ 1 (max black white))
                           :initial-element
                           (* minutes 60
                              internal-time-units-per-second))))
    (catch 'game-over
      (loop for *move-number* from 1
            for player = black then (next-to-play board player print)
            for strategy = (if (eql player black)
                               bl-strategy
                               wh-strategy)
            until (null player)
            do (get-move strategy player board print clock))
      (when print
        (format t "~&The game is over.  Final result:")
        (print-board board clock))
      (count-difference black board))))
```

Strategies now have to comply with the time-limit rule, so they may want to look at the time remaining. Rather than passing the clock in as an argument to the strategy, I decided to store the clock in the special variable *clock*. The new version of othello also keeps track of the *move-number*. This also could have been passed to the strategy functions as a parameter. But adding these extra arguments would require changes to all the strategies we have developed so far. By storing the information in special variables, strategies that want to can look at the clock or the move number, but other strategies don't have to know about them.

We still have the security problem—we don't want a strategy to be able to set the opponent's remaining time to zero and thereby win the game. Thus, we use *clock* only as a copy of the "real" game clock. The function replace copies the real clock into *clock*, and also copies the real board into *board*.

```
(defvar *clock* (make-array 3) "A copy of the game clock")
(defvar *board* (initial-board) "A copy of the game board")
```

```
(defun get-move (strategy player board print clock)
  "Call the player's strategy function to get a move.
  Keep calling until a legal move is made."
  ;; Note we don't pass the strategy function the REAL board.
  ;; If we did, it could cheat by changing the pieces on the board.
  (when print (print-board board clock))
  (replace *clock* clock)
  (let* ((t0 (get-internal-real-time))
         (move (funcall strategy player (replace *board* board)))
         (t1 (get-internal-real-time)))
    (decf (elt clock player) (- t1 t0))
    (cond
      ((< (elt clock player) 0)
       (format t "~&~c has no time left and forfeits."
               (name-of player))
       (THROW 'game-over (if (eql player black) -64 64)))
      ((eq move 'resign)
       (THROW 'game-over (if (eql player black) -64 64)))
      ((and (valid-p move) (legal-p move player board))
       (when print
         (format t "~&~c moves to ~a."
                 (name-of player) (88->h8 move)))
       (make-move move player board))
      (t (warn "Illegal move: ~a" (88->h8 move))
         (get-move strategy player board print clock)))))
```

Finally, the function print-board needs to print the time remaining for each player; this requires an auxiliary function to get the number of minutes and seconds from an internal-format time interval. Note that we make the arguments optional, so that in debugging one can say just (print-board) to see the current situation. Also note the esoteric format option: "~2,'0d" prints a decimal number using at least two places, padding on the left with zeros.

```
(defun print-board (&optional (board *board*) clock)
  "Print a board, along with some statistics."
  ;; First print the header and the current score
  (format t "~2&    a b c d e f g h   [~c=~2a ~c=~2a (~@d)]"
          (name-of black) (count black board)
          (name-of white) (count white board)
          (count-difference black board))
  ;; Print the board itself
  (loop for row from 1 to 8 do
        (format t "~&  ~d " row)
        (loop for col from 1 to 8
              for piece = (bref board (+ col (* 10 row)))
              do (format t "~c " (name-of piece)))))
```

```
;; Finally print the time remaining for each player
(when clock
  (format t "  [~c=~a  ~c=~a]~2&"
          (name-of black) (time-string (elt clock black))
          (name-of white) (time-string (elt clock white)))))

(defun time-string (time)
  "Return a string representing this internal time in min:secs."
  (multiple-value-bind (min sec)
      (floor (round time internal-time-units-per-second) 60)
    (format nil "~2d:~2,'0d" min sec)))
```

18.8   Playing a Series of Games

A single game is not enough to establish that one strategy is better than another. The following function allows two strategies to compete in a series of games:

```
(defun othello-series (strategy1 strategy2 n-pairs)
  "Play a series of 2*n-pairs games, swapping sides."
  (let ((scores (loop repeat n-pairs
                   collect (othello strategy1 strategy2 nil)
                   collect (- (othello strategy2 strategy1 nil)))))
    ;; Return the number of wins, (1/2 for a tie),
    ;; the total of the point differences, and the
    ;; scores themselves, all from strategy1's point of view.
    (values (+ (count-if #'plusp scores)
               (/ (count-if #'zerop scores) 2))
            (apply #'+ scores)
            scores)))
```

Let's see what happens when we use it to pit the two weighted-squares functions against each other in a series of ten games:

```
> (othello-series
    (alpha-beta-searcher 2 #'modified-weighted-squares)
    (alpha-beta-searcher 2 #'weighted-squares) 5)
0
60
(-28 40 -28 40 -28 40 -28 40 -28 40)
```

Something is suspicious here—the same scores are being repeated. A little thought reveals why: neither strategy has a random component, so the exact same game was played five times with one strategy going first, and another game was played five times when the other strategy goes first! A more accurate appraisal of the two strategies' relative worth would be gained by starting each game from some random position and playing from there.

Think for a minute how you would design to run a series of games starting from a random position. One possibility would be to change the function othello to accept an optional argument indicating the initial state of the board. Then othello-series could be changed to somehow generate a random board and pass it to othello. While this approach is feasible, it means changing two existing working functions, as well as writing another function, generate-random-board. But we couldn't generate just any random board: it would have to be a legal board, so it would have to call othello and somehow get it to stop before the game was over.

An alternative is to leave both othello and othello-series alone and build another function on top of it, one that works by passing in two new strategies: strategies that make a random move for the first few moves and then revert to the normal specified behavior. This is a better solution because it uses existing functions rather than modifying them, and because it requires no new functions besides switch-strategies, which could prove useful for other purposes, and random-othello-series, which does nothing more than call othello-series with the proper arguments.

```
(defun random-othello-series (strategy1 strategy2
                                n-pairs &optional (n-random 10))
  "Play a series of 2*n games, starting from a random position."
  (othello-series
    (switch-strategies #'random-strategy n-random strategy1)
    (switch-strategies #'random-strategy n-random strategy2)
    n-pairs))

(defun switch-strategies (strategy1 m strategy2)
  "Make a new strategy that plays strategy1 for m moves,
  then plays according to strategy2."
  #'(lambda (player board)
      (funcall (if (<= *move-number* m) strategy1 strategy2)
               player board)))
```

There is a problem with this kind of series: it may be that one of the strategies just happens to get better random positions. A fairer test would be to play two games from each random position, one with the each strategy playing first. One way to do that is to alter othello-series so that it saves the random state before playing the first game of a pair, and then restores the saved random state before playing the second game. That way the same random position will be duplicated.

```
(defun othello-series (strategy1 strategy2 n-pairs)
  "Play a series of 2*n-pairs games, swapping sides."
  (let ((scores
          (loop repeat n-pairs
              for random-state = (make-random-state)
              collect (othello strategy1 strategy2 nil)
              do (setf *random-state* random-state)
              collect (- (othello strategy2 strategy1 nil)))))
    ;; Return the number of wins (1/2 for a tie),
    ;; the total of the point differences, and the
    ;; scores themselves, all from strategy1's point of view.
    (values (+ (count-if #'plusp scores)
               (/ (count-if #'zerop scores) 2))
            (apply #'+ scores)
            scores)))
```

Now we are in a position to do a more meaningful test. In the following, the weighted-squares strategy wins 4 out of 10 games against the modified strategy, losing by a total of 76 pieces, with the actual scores indicated.

```
> (random-othello-series
    (alpha-beta-searcher 2 #'weighted-squares)
    (alpha-beta-searcher 2 #'modified-weighted-squares)
    5)
4
-76
(-8 -40 22 -30 10 -10 12 -18 4 -18)
```

The random-othello-series function is useful for comparing two strategies. When there are more than two strategies to be compared at the same time, the following function can be useful:

```
(defun round-robin (strategies n-pairs &optional
                            (n-random 10) (names strategies))
  "Play a tournament among the strategies.
  N-PAIRS = games each strategy plays as each color against
  each opponent.  So with N strategies, a total of
  N*(N-1)*N-PAIRS games are played."
  (let* ((N (length strategies))
         (totals (make-array N :initial-element 0))
         (scores (make-array (list N N)
                             :initial-element 0)))
    ;; Play the games
    (dotimes (i N)
      (loop for j from (+ i 1) to (- N 1) do
        (let* ((wins (random-othello-series
```

```
                        (elt strategies i)
                        (elt strategies j)
                        n-pairs n-random))
                (losses (- (* 2 n-pairs) wins)))
           (incf (aref scores i j) wins)
           (incf (aref scores j i) losses)
           (incf (aref totals i) wins)
           (incf (aref totals j) losses))))
    ;; Print the results
    (dotimes (i N)
      (format t "~&~a~20T ~4f: " (elt names i) (elt totals i))
      (dotimes (j N)
        (format t "~4f " (if (= i j) '---
                             (aref scores i j)))))))
```

Here is a comparison of five strategies that search only 1 ply:

```
(defun mobility (player board)
  "The number of moves a player has."
  (length (legal-moves player board)))

> (round-robin
    (list (maximizer #'count-difference)
          (maximizer #'mobility)
          (maximizer #'weighted-squares)
          (maximizer #'modified-weighted-squares)
          #'random-strategy)
    5 10
    '(count-difference mobility weighted modified-weighted random))

COUNT-DIFFERENCE    12.5:  ---  3.0 2.5 0.0 7.0
MOBILITY            20.5:  7.0  --- 1.5 5.0 7.0
WEIGHTED            28.0:  7.5  8.5 --- 3.0 9.0
MODIFIED-WEIGHTED   31.5: 10.0  5.0 7.0 --- 9.5
RANDOM               7.5:  3.0  3.0 1.0 0.5 ---
```

The parameter n-pairs is 5, meaning that each strategy plays five games as black and five as white against each of the other four strategies, for a total of 40 games for each strategy and 100 games overall. The first line of output says that the count-difference strategy won 12.5 of its 40 games, including 3 against the mobility strategy, 2.5 against the weighted strategy, none against the modified weighted, and 7 against the random strategy. The fact that the random strategy manages to win 7.5 out of 40 games indicates that the other strategies are not amazingly strong. Now we see what happens when the search depth is increased to 4 ply (this will take a while to run):

```
> (round-robin
    (list (alpha-beta-searcher 4 #'count-difference)
          (alpha-beta-searcher 4 #'weighted-squares)
          (alpha-beta-searcher 4 #'modified-weighted-squares)
          #'random-strategy)
     5 10
    '(count-difference weighted modified-weighted random))
```

COUNT-DIFFERENCE	12.0:	---	2.0	0.0	10.0
WEIGHTED	23.5:	8.0	---	5.5	10.0
MODIFIED-WEIGHTED	24.5:	10.0	4.5	---	10.0
RANDOM	0.0:	0.0	0.0	0.0	---

Here the random strategy does not win any games—an indication that the other strategies are doing something right. Notice that the modified weighted-squares has only a slight advantage over the weighted-squares, and in fact it lost their head-to-head series, four games to five, with one draw. So it is not clear which strategy is better.

The output does not break down wins by black or white, nor does it report the numerical scores. I felt that that would clutter up the output too much, but you're welcome to add this information. It turns out that white wins 23 (and draws 1) of the 40 games played between 4-ply searching strategies. Usually, Othello is a fairly balanced game, because black has the advantage of moving first but white usually gets to play last. It is clear that these strategies do not play well in the opening game, but for the last four ply they play perfectly. This may explain white's slight edge, or it may be a statistical aberration.

18.9   More Efficient Searching

The alpha-beta cutoffs work when we have established a good move and another move proves to be not as good. Thus, we will be able to make cutoffs earlier if we ensure that good moves are considered first. Our current algorithm loops through the list of legal-moves, but legal-moves makes no attempt to order the moves in any way. We will call this the *random-ordering* strategy (even though the ordering is not random at all—square 11 is always considered first, then 12, etc.).

One way to try to generate good moves first is to search highly weighted squares first. Since legal-moves considers squares in the order defined by all-squares, all we have to do is redefine the list all-squares[3]:

---

[3]Remember, when a constant is redefined, it may be necessary to recompile any functions that use the constant.

```
(defconstant all-squares
  (sort (loop for i from 11 to 88
              when (<= 1 (mod i 10) 8) collect i)
        #'> :key #'(lambda (sq) (elt *weights* sq)))))
```

Now the corner squares will automatically be considered first, followed by the other highly weighted squares. We call this the *static-ordering* strategy, because the ordering is not random, but it does not change depending on the situation.

A more informed way to try to generate good moves first is to sort the moves according to the evaluation function. This means making more evaluations. Previously, only the boards at the leaves of the search tree were evaluated. Now we need to evaluate every board. In order to avoid evaluating a board more than once, we make up a structure called a node, which holds a board, the square that was taken to result in that board, and the evaluation value of that board. The search is the same except that nodes are passed around instead of boards, and the nodes are sorted by their value.

```
(defstruct (node) square board value)

(defun alpha-beta-searcher2 (depth eval-fn)
  "Return a strategy that does A-B search with sorted moves."
  #'(lambda (player board)
      (multiple-value-bind (value node)
          (alpha-beta2
            player (make-node :board board
                              :value (funcall eval-fn player board))
            losing-value winning-value depth eval-fn)
        (declare (ignore value))
        (node-square node)))))

(defun alpha-beta2 (player node achievable cutoff ply eval-fn)
  "A-B search, sorting moves by eval-fn"
  ;; Returns two values: achievable-value and move-to-make
  (if (= ply 0)
      (values (node-value node) node)
      (let* ((board (node-board node))
             (nodes (legal-nodes player board eval-fn)))
        (if (null nodes)
            (if (any-legal-move? (opponent player) board)
                (values (- (alpha-beta2 (opponent player)
                                        (negate-value node)
                                        (- cutoff) (- achievable)
                                        (- ply 1) eval-fn))
                        nil)
                (values (final-value player board) nil))
            (let ((best-node (first nodes)))
              (loop for move in nodes
```

```
                              for val = (- (alpha-beta2
                                             (opponent player)
                                             (negate-value move)
                                             (- cutoff) (- achievable)
                                             (- ply 1) eval-fn))
                          do (when (> val achievable)
                               (setf achievable val)
                               (setf best-node move))
                          until (>= achievable cutoff))
                  (values achievable best-node))))))

(defun negate-value (node)
  "Set the value of a node to its negative."
  (setf (node-value node) (- (node-value node)))
  node)

(defun legal-nodes (player board eval-fn)
  "Return a list of legal moves, each one packed into a node."
  (let ((moves (legal-moves player board)))
    (sort (map-into
            moves
            #'(lambda (move)
                (let ((new-board (make-move move player
                                             (copy-board board))))
                  (make-node
                    :square move :board new-board
                    :value (funcall eval-fn player new-board))))
            moves)
          #'> :key #'node-value)))
```

(Note the use of the function map-into. This is part of ANSI Common Lisp, but if it is not a part of your implementation, a definition is provided on page 857.)

The following table compares the performance of the random-ordering strategy, the sorted-ordering strategy and the static-ordering strategy in the course of a single game. All strategies search 6 ply deep. The table measures the number of boards investigated, the number of those boards that were evaluated (in all cases the evaluation function was modified-weighted-squares) and the time in seconds to compute a move.

random order			sorted order			static order		
boards	evals	secs	boards	evals	secs	boards	evals	secs
13912	10269	69	5556	5557	22	2365	1599	19
9015	6751	56	6571	6572	25	3081	2188	18
9820	7191	46	11556	11557	45	5797	3990	31
4195	3213	20	5302	5303	17	2708	2019	15
10890	7336	60	10709	10710	38	3743	2401	23
13325	9679	63	6431	6432	24	4222	2802	24
13163	9968	58	9014	9015	32	6657	4922	31
16642	12588	70	9742	9743	33	10421	7488	51
18016	13366	80	11002	11003	37	9508	7136	41
23295	17908	104	15290	15291	48	26435	20282	111
34120	25895	143	22994	22995	75	20775	16280	78
56117	43230	224	46883	46884	150	48415	36229	203
53573	41266	209	62252	62253	191	37803	28902	148
43943	33184	175	31039	31040	97	33180	24753	133
51124	39806	193	45709	45710	135	19297	15064	69
24743	18777	105	20003	20004	65	15627	11737	66
1.0	1.0	1.0	.81	1.07	.62	.63	.63	.63

The last two lines of the table give the averages and the averages normalized to the random-ordering strategy's performance. The sorted-ordering strategy takes only 62% of the time of the random-ordering strategy, and the static-ordering takes 63%. These times are not to be trusted too much, because a large-scale garbage collection was taking place during the latter part of the game, and it may have thrown off the times. The board and evaluation count may be better indicators, and they both show the static-ordering strategy doing the best.

We have to be careful how we evaluate these results. Earlier I said that alpha-beta search makes more cutoffs when it is presented first with better moves. The actual truth is that it makes more cutoffs when presented first with moves that *the evaluation function thinks* are better. In this case the evaluation function and the static-ordering strategy are in strong agreement on what are the best moves, so it is not surprising that static ordering does so well. As we develop evaluation functions that vary from the weighted-squares approach, we will have to run experiments again to see if the static-ordering is still the best.

18.10   It Pays to Precycle

The progressive city of Berkeley, California, has a strong recycling program to reclaim glass, paper, and aluminum that would otherwise be discarded as garbage. In 1989,

Berkeley instituted a novel program of *precycling*: consumers are encouraged to avoid buying products that come in environmentally wasteful packages.

Your Lisp system also has a recycling program: the Lisp garbage collector automatically recycles any unused storage. However, there is a cost to this program, and you the consumer can get better performance by precycling your data. Don't buy wasteful data structures when simpler ones can be used or reused. You, the Lisp programmer, may not be able to save the rain forests or the ozone layer, but you can save valuable processor time.

We saw before that the search routines look at tens of thousands of boards per move. Currently, each board position is created anew by copy-board and discarded soon thereafter. We could avoid generating all this garbage by reusing the same board at each ply. We'd still need to keep the board from the previous ply for use when the search backs up. Thus, a vector of boards is needed. In the following we assume that we will never search deeper than 40 ply. This is a safe assumption, as even the fastest Othello programs can only search about 15 ply before running out of time.

```
(defvar *ply-boards*
  (apply #'vector (loop repeat 40 collect (initial-board))))
```

Now that we have sharply limited the number of boards needed, we may want to reevaluate the implementation of boards. Instead of having the board as a vector of pieces (to save space), we may want to implement boards as vectors of bytes or full words. In some implementations, accessing elements of such vectors is faster. (In other implementations, there is no difference.)

An implementation using the vector of boards will be done in the next section. Note that there is another alternative: use only one board, and update it by making and retracting moves. This is a good alternative in a game like chess, where a move only alters two squares. In Othello, many squares can be altered by a move, so copying the whole board over and making the move is not so bad.

It should be mentioned that it is worth looking into the problem of copying a position from one board to another. The function replace copies one sequence (or part of it) into another, but it is a generic function that may be slow. In particular, if each element of a board is only 2 bits, then it may be much faster to use displaced arrays to copy 32 bits at a time. The advisability of this approach depends on the implementation, and so it is not explored further here.

18.11   Killer Moves

In section 18.9, we considered the possibility of searching moves in a different order, in an attempt to search the better moves first, thereby getting more alpha-beta pruning. In this section, we consider the *killer heuristic*, which states that a move that has proven to be a good one in one line of play is also likely to be a good one in another line of play. To use chess as perhaps a more familiar example, suppose I consider one move, and it leads to the opponent replying by capturing my queen. This is a killer move, one that I would like to avoid. Therefore, when I consider other possible moves, I want to immediately consider the possibility of the opponent making that queen-capturing move.

The function `alpha-beta3` adds the parameter `killer`, which is the best move found so far at the current level. After we determine the `legal-moves`, we use `put-first` to put the killer move first, if it is in fact a legal move. When it comes time to search the next level, we keep track of the best move in `killer2`. This requires keeping track of the value of the best move in `killer2-val`. Everything else is unchanged, except that we get a new board by recycling the `*ply-boards*` vector rather than by allocating fresh ones.

```
(defun alpha-beta3 (player board achievable cutoff ply eval-fn
                    killer)
  "A-B search, putting killer move first."
  (if (= ply 0)
      (funcall eval-fn player board)
      (let ((moves (put-first killer (legal-moves player board))))
        (if (null moves)
            (if (any-legal-move? (opponent player) board)
                (- (alpha-beta3 (opponent player) board
                                (- cutoff) (- achievable)
                                (- ply 1) eval-fn nil))
                (final-value player board))
            (let ((best-move (first moves))
                  (new-board (aref *ply-boards* ply))
                  (killer2 nil)
                  (killer2-val winning-value))
              (loop for move in moves
                    do (multiple-value-bind (val reply)
                           (alpha-beta3
                             (opponent player)
                             (make-move move player
                                        (replace new-board board))
                             (- cutoff) (- achievable)
                             (- ply 1) eval-fn killer2)
                         (setf val (- val))
                         (when (> val achievable)
                           (setf achievable val)
                           (setf best-move move))
                         (when (and reply (< val killer2-val))
                           (setf killer2 reply)
                           (setf killer2-val val)))
                    until (>= achievable cutoff))
```

```
                  (values achievable best-move))))))

(defun alpha-beta-searcher3 (depth eval-fn)
  "Return a strategy that does A-B search with killer moves."
  #'(lambda (player board)
      (multiple-value-bind (value move)
          (alpha-beta3 player board losing-value winning-value
                       depth eval-fn nil)
        (declare (ignore value))
        move)))

(defun put-first (killer moves)
  "Move the killer move to the front of moves,
  if the killer move is in fact a legal move."
  (if (member killer moves)
      (cons killer (delete killer moves))
      moves))
```

Another experiment on a single game reveals that adding the killer heuristic to static-ordering search (again at 6-ply) cuts the number of boards and evaluations, and the total time, all by about 20%. To summarize, alpha-beta search at 6 ply with random ordering takes 105 seconds per move (in our experiment), adding static-ordering cuts it to 66 seconds, and adding killer moves to that cuts it again to 52 seconds. This doesn't include the savings that alpha-beta cutoffs give over full minimax search. At 6 ply with a branching factor of 7, full minimax would take about nine times longer than static ordering with killers. The savings increase with increased depth. At 7 ply and a branching factor of 10, a small experiment shows that static-ordering with killers looks at only 28,000 boards in about 150 seconds. Full minimax would evaluate 10 million boards and take 350 times longer. The times for full minimax are estimates based on the number of boards per second, not on an actual experiment.

The algorithm in this section just keeps track of one killer move. It is of course possible to keep track of more than one. The Othello program Bill (Lee and Mahajan 1990b) merges the idea of killer moves with legal move generation: it keeps a list of possible moves at each level, sorted by their value. The legal move generator then goes down this list in sorted order.

It should be stressed once again that all this work on alpha-beta cutoffs, ordering, and killer moves has not made any change at all in the moves that are selected. We still end up choosing the same move that would be made by a full minimax search to the given depth, we are just doing it faster, without looking at possibilities that we can prove are not as good.

18.12   Championship Programs: Iago and Bill

As mentioned in the introduction, the unpredictability of Othello makes it a difficult game for humans to master, and thus programs that search deeply can do comparatively well. In fact, in 1981 the reigning champion, Jonathan Cerf, proclaimed "In my opinion the top programs ... are now equal (if not superior) to the best human players." In discussing Rosenbloom's Iago program (1982), Cerf went on to say "I understand Paul Rosenbloom is interested in arranging a match against me. Unfortunately my schedule is very full, and I'm going to see that it remains that way for the foreseeable future."

In 1989, another program, Bill (Lee and Mahajan 1990) beat the highest rated American Othello player, Brian Rose, by a score of 56-8. Bill's evaluation function is fast enough to search 6–8 ply under tournament conditions, yet it is so accurate that it beats its creator, Kai-Fu Lee, searching only 1 ply. (However, Lee is only a novice Othello player; his real interest is in speech recognition; see Waibel and Lee 1991.) There are other programs that also play at a high level, but they have not been written up in the AI literature as Iago and Bill have.

In this section we present an evaluation function based on Iago's, although it also contains elements of Bill, and of an evaluation function written by Eric Wefald in 1989. The evaluation function makes use of two main features: *mobility* and *edge stability*.

Mobility

Both Iago and Bill make heavy use of the concept of *mobility*. Mobility is a measure of the ability to make moves; basically, the more moves one can make, the better. This is not quite true, because there is no advantage in being able to make bad moves, but it is a useful heuristic. We define *current mobility* as the number of legal moves available to a player, and *potential mobility* as the number of blank squares that are adjacent to opponent's pieces. These include the legal moves. A better measure of mobility would try to count only good moves. The following function computes both current and potential mobility for a player:

```lisp
(defun mobility (player board)
  "Current mobility is the number of legal moves.
  Potential mobility is the number of blank squares
  adjacent to an opponent that are not legal moves.
  Returns current and potential mobility for player."
  (let ((opp (opponent player))
        (current 0)    ; player's current mobility
        (potential 0)) ; player's potential mobility
    (dolist (square all-squares)
      (when (eql (bref board square) empty)
        (cond ((legal-p square player board)
```

```
                (incf current))
            ((some #'(lambda (sq) (eql (bref board sq) opp))
                   (neighbors square))
             (incf potential)))))
      (values current (+ current potential)))))
```

Edge Stability

Success at Othello often hinges around edge play, and both Iago and Bill evaluate
the edges carefully. Edge analysis is made easier by the fact that the edges are fairly
independent of the interior of the board: once a piece is placed on the edge, no
interior moves can flip it. This independence allows a simplifying assumption: to
evaluate a position's edge strength, evaluate each of the four edges independently,
without consideration of the interior of the board. The evaluation can be made more
accurate by considering the X-squares to be part of the edge.

Even evaluating a single edge is a time-consuming task, so Bill and Iago compile
away the evaluation by building a table of all possible edge positions. An "edge"
according to Bill is ten squares: the eight actual edge squares and the two X-squares.
Since each square can be black, white, or empty, there are 3^{10} or 59,049 possible edge
positions—a large but manageable number.

The value of each edge position is determined by a process of succesive approximation. Just as in a minimax search, we will need a static edge evaluation function
to determine the value of a edge position without search. This static edge evaluation
function is applied to every possible edge position, and the results are stored in a
59,049 element vector. The static evaluation is just a weighted sum of the occupied
squares, with different weights given depending on if the piece is stable or unstable.

Each edge position's evaluation can be improved by a process of search. Iago
uses a single ply search: given a position, consider all moves that could be made
(including no move at all). Some moves will be clearly legal, because they flip pieces
on the edge, but other moves will only be legal if there are pieces in the interior of
the board to flip. Since we are only considering the edge, we don't know for sure if
these moves are legal. They will be assigned probabilities of legality. The updated
evaluation of a position is determined by the values and probabilities of each move.
This is done by sorting the moves by value and then summing the product of the
value times the probability that the move can be made. This process of iterative
approximation is repeated five times for each position. At that point, Rosenbloom
reports, the values have nearly converged.

In effect, this extends the depth of the normal alpha-beta search by including an
edge-only search in the evaluation function. Since each edge position with n pieces
is evaluated as a function of the positions with $n + 1$ pieces, the search is complete—it
is an implicit 10-ply search.

Calculating edge stability is a bit more complicated than the other features. The first step is to define a variable, *edge-table*, which will hold the evaluation of each edge position, and a constant, edge-and-x-lists, which is a list of the squares on each of the four edges. Each edge has ten squares because the X-squares are included.

```
(defvar *edge-table* (make-array (expt 3 10))
  "Array of values to player-to-move for edge positions.")

(defconstant edge-and-x-lists
  '((22 11 12 13 14 15 16 17 18 27)
    (72 81 82 83 84 85 86 87 88 77)
    (22 11 21 31 41 51 61 71 81 72)
    (27 18 28 38 48 58 68 78 88 77))
  "The four edges (with their X-squares).")
```

Now for each edge we can compute an index into the edge table by building a 10-digit base-3 number, where each digit is 1 if the corresponding edge square is occupied by the player, 2 if by the opponent, and 0 if empty. The function edge-index computes this, and edge-stability sums the values of the four edge indexes.

```
(defun edge-index (player board squares)
  "The index counts 1 for player; 2 for opponent,
  on each square---summed as a base 3 number."
  (let ((index 0))
    (dolist (sq squares)
      (setq index (+ (* index 3)
                     (cond ((eql (bref board sq) empty) 0)
                           ((eql (bref board sq) player) 1)
                           (t 2)))))
    index))

(defun edge-stability (player board)
  "Total edge evaluation for player to move on board."
  (loop for edge-list in edge-and-x-lists
        sum (aref *edge-table*
                  (edge-index player board edge-list))))
```

The function edge-stability is all we will need in Iago's evaluation function, but we still need to generate the edge table. Since this needs to be done only once, we don't have to worry about efficiency. In particular, rather than invent a new data structure to represent edges, we will continue to use complete boards, even though they will be mostly empty. The computations for the edge table will be made on the top edge, from the point of view of black, with black to play. But the same table can be used for white, or for one of the other edges, because of the way the edge index is computed.

Each position in the table is first initialized to a static value computed by a kind of weighted-squares metric, but with different weights depending on if a piece is in danger of being captured. After that, each position is updated by considering the possible moves that can be made from the position, and the values of each of these moves.

```
(defconstant top-edge (first edge-and-x-lists))

(defun init-edge-table ()
  "Initialize *edge-table*, starting from the empty board."
  ;; Initialize the static values
  (loop for n-pieces from 0 to 10 do
        (map-edge-n-pieces
          #'(lambda (board index)
              (setf (aref *edge-table* index)
                    (static-edge-stability black board)))
          black (initial-board) n-pieces top-edge 0))
  ;; Now iterate five times trying to improve:
  (dotimes (i 5)
    ;; Do the indexes with most pieces first
    (loop for n-pieces from 9 downto 1 do
          (map-edge-n-pieces
            #'(lambda (board index)
                (setf (aref *edge-table* index)
                      (possible-edge-moves-value
                        black board index)))
            black (initial-board) n-pieces top-edge 0))))
```

The function map-edge-n-pieces iterates through all edge positions with a total of n pieces (of either color), applying a function to each such position. It also keeps a running count of the edge index as it goes. The function should accept two arguments: the board and the index. Note that a single board can be used for all the positions because squares are reset after they are used. The function has three cases: if the number of squares remaining is less than n, then it will be impossible to place n pieces on those squares, so we give up. If there are no more squares then n must also be zero, so this is a valid position, and the function fn is called. Otherwise we first try leaving the current square blank, then try filling it with player's piece, and then with the opponent's piece, in each case calling map-edge-n-pieces recursively.

```
(defun map-edge-n-pieces (fn player board n squares index)
  "Call fn on all edges with n pieces."
  ;; Index counts 1 for player; 2 for opponent
  (cond
    ((< (length squares) n) nil)
    ((null squares) (funcall fn board index))
    (t (let ((index3 (* 3 index))
             (sq (first squares)))
         (map-edge-n-pieces fn player board n (rest squares) index3)
```

```
(when (and (> n 0) (eql (bref board sq) empty))
  (setf (bref board sq) player)
  (map-edge-n-pieces fn player board (- n 1) (rest squares)
                     (+ 1 index3))
  (setf (bref board sq) (opponent player))
  (map-edge-n-pieces fn player board (- n 1) (rest squares)
                     (+ 2 index3))
  (setf (bref board sq) empty))))))
```

The function `possible-edge-moves-value` searches through all possible moves to determine an edge value that is more accurate than a static evaluation. It loops through every empty square on the edge, calling `possible-edge-move` to return a (*probability value*) pair. Since it is also possible for a player not to make any move at all on an edge, the pair (1.0 *current-value*) is also included.

```
(defun possible-edge-moves-value (player board index)
  "Consider all possible edge moves.
  Combine their values into a single number."
  (combine-edge-moves
    (cons
      (list 1.0 (aref *edge-table* index)) ;; no move
      (loop for sq in top-edge              ;; possible moves
            when (eql (bref board sq) empty)
            collect (possible-edge-move player board sq)))
    player))
```

The value of each position is determined by making the move on the board, then looking up in the table the value of the resulting position for the opponent, and negating it (since we are interested in the value to us, not to our opponent).

```
(defun possible-edge-move (player board sq)
  "Return a (prob val) pair for a possible edge move."
  (let ((new-board (replace (aref *ply-boards* player) board)))
    (make-move sq player new-board)
    (list (edge-move-probability player board sq)
          (- (aref *edge-table*
                   (edge-index (opponent player)
                               new-board top-edge))))))
```

The possible moves are combined with `combine-edge-moves`, which sorts the moves best-first. (Since `init-edge-table` started from black's perspective, black tries to maximize and white tries to minimize scores.) We then go down the moves, increasing the total value by the value of each move times the probability of the move, and decreasing the remaining probability by the probability of the move. Since there will always be a least one move (pass) with probability 1.0, this is guaranteed to converge. In the end we round off the total value, so that we can do the run-time calculations with fixnums.

```lisp
(defun combine-edge-moves (possibilities player)
  "Combine the best moves."
  (let ((prob 1.0)
        (val 0.0)
        (fn (if (eql player black) #'> #'<)))
    (loop for pair in (sort possibilities fn :key #'second)
          while (>= prob 0.0)
          do (incf val (* prob (first pair) (second pair)))
             (decf prob (* prob (first pair))))
    (round val)))
```

We still need to compute the probability that each possible edge move is legal. These probabilities should reflect things such as the fact that it is easy to capture a corner if the opponent is in the adjacent X-square, and very difficult otherwise. First we define some functions to recognize corner and X-squares and relate them to their neighbors:

```lisp
(let ((corner/xsqs '((11 . 22) (18 . 27) (81. 72) (88 . 77))))
  (defun corner-p (sq) (assoc sq corner/xsqs))
  (defun x-square-p (sq) (rassoc sq corner/xsqs))
  (defun x-square-for (corner) (cdr (assoc corner corner/xsqs)))
  (defun corner-for (xsq) (car (rassoc xsq corner/xsqs))))
```

Now we consider the probabilities. There are four cases. First, since we don't know anything about the interior of the board, we assume each player has a 50% chance of being able to play in an X-square. Second, if we can show that a move is legal (because it flips opponent pieces on the edge) then it has 100% probability. Third, for the corner squares, we assign a 90% chance if the opponent occupies the X-square, 10% if it is empty, and only .1% if we occupy it. Otherwise, the probability is determined by the two neighboring squares: if a square is next to one or more opponents it is more likely we can move there; if it is next to our pieces it is less likely. If it is legal for the opponent to move into the square, then the chances are cut in half (although we may still be able to move there, since we move first).

```lisp
(defun edge-move-probability (player board square)
  "What's the probability that player can move to this square?"
  (cond
    ((x-square-p square) .5) ;; X-squares
    ((legal-p square player board) 1.0) ;; immediate capture
    ((corner-p square) ;; move to corner depends on X-square
```

```
    (let ((x-sq (x-square-for square)))
      (cond
        ((eql (bref board x-sq) empty) .1)
        ((eql (bref board x-sq) player) 0.001)
        (t .9))))
    (t (/ (aref
            '#2A((.1  .4 .7)
                 (.05 .3  *)
                 (.01  *  *))
            (count-edge-neighbors player board square)
            (count-edge-neighbors (opponent player) board square))
        (if (legal-p square (opponent player) board) 2 1)))))

(defun count-edge-neighbors (player board square)
  "Count the neighbors of this square occupied by player."
  (count-if #'(lambda (inc)
                (eql (bref board (+ square inc)) player))
            '(+1 -1)))
```

Now we return to the problem of determining the static value of an edge position. This is computed by a weighted-squares metric, but the weights depend on the *stability* of each piece. A piece is called stable if it cannot be captured, unstable if it is in immediate danger of being captured, and semistable otherwise. A table of weights follows for each edge square and stability. Note that corner squares are always stable, and X-squares we will call semistable if the adjacent corner is taken, and unstable otherwise.

```
(defparameter *static-edge-table*
  '#2A(;stab  semi    un
       (  *     0 -2000) ; X
       ( 700     *    *) ; corner
       (1200   200   -25) ; C
       (1000   200    75) ; A
       (1000   200    50) ; B
       (1000   200    50) ; B
       (1000   200    75) ; A
       (1200   200   -25) ; C
       ( 700     *    *) ; corner
       (  *     0 -2000) ; X
       ))
```

The static evaluation then just sums each piece's value according to this table:

```
(defun static-edge-stability (player board)
  "Compute this edge's static stability"
  (loop for sq in top-edge
        for i from 0
        sum (cond
              ((eql (bref board sq) empty) 0)
              ((eql (bref board sq) player)
               (aref *static-edge-table* i
                     (piece-stability board sq)))
              (t (- (aref *static-edge-table* i
                          (piece-stability board sq)))))))
```

The computation of stability is fairly complex. It centers around finding the two "pieces," p1 and p2, which lay on either side of the piece in question and which are not of the same color as the piece. These "pieces" may be empty, or they may be off the board. A piece is unstable if one of the two is empty and the other is the opponent; it is semistable if there are opponents on both sides and at least one empty square to play on, or if it is surrounded by empty pieces. Finally, if either p1 or p2 is nil then the piece is stable, since it must be connected by a solid wall of pieces to the corner.

```
(let ((stable 0) (semi-stable 1) (unstable 2))


(defun piece-stability (board sq)
  (cond
    ((corner-p sq) stable)
    ((x-square-p sq)
     (if (eql (bref board (corner-for sq)) empty)
         unstable semi-stable))
    (t (let* ((player (bref board sq))
              (opp (opponent player))
              (p1 (find player board :test-not #'eql
                        :start sq :end 19))
              (p2 (find player board :test-not #'eql
                        :start 11 :end sq
                        :from-end t)))
         (cond
           ;; unstable pieces can be captured immediately
           ;; by playing in the empty square
           ((or (and (eql p1 empty) (eql p2 opp))
                (and (eql p2 empty) (eql p1 opp)))
            unstable)
           ;; semi-stable pieces might be captured
           ((and (eql p1 opp) (eql p2 opp))
```

```
                              (find empty board :start 11 :end 19))
                            semi-stable)
                           ((and (eql p1 empty) (eql p2 empty))
                            semi-stable)
                           ;; Stable pieces can never be captured
                           (t stable)))))))
```

The edge table can now be built by a call to `init-edge-table`. After the table is built once, it is a good idea to save it so that we won't need to repeat the initialization. We could write simple routines to dump the table into a file and read it back in, but it is faster and easier to use existing tools that already do this job quite well: `compile-file` and `load`. All we have to do is create and compile a file containing the single line:

```
(setf *edge-table* '#.*edge-table*)
```

The `#.` read macro evaluates the following expression at read time. Thus, the compiler will see and compile the current edge table. It will be able to store this more compactly and load it back in more quickly than if we printed the contents of the vector in decimal (or any other base).

Combining the Factors

Now we have a measure of the three factors: current mobility, potential mobility, and edge stability. All that remains is to find a good way to combine them into a single evaluation metric. The combination function used by Rosenbloom (1982) is a linear combination of the three factors, but each factor's coefficient is dependent on the move number. Rosenbloom's features are normalized to the range [-1000, 1000]; we normalize to the range [-1, 1] by doing a division after multiplying by the coefficient. That allows us to use fixnuums for the coefficients. Since our three factors are not calculated in quite the same way as Rosenbloom's, it is not surprising that his coefficients are not the best for our program. The edge coefficient was doubled and the potential coefficient cut by a factor of five.

```
(defun Iago-eval (player board)
  "Combine edge-stability, current mobility and
  potential mobility to arrive at an evaluation."
  ;; The three factors are multiplied by coefficients
  ;; that vary by move number:
  (let ((c-edg (+ 312000 (* 6240 *move-number*)))
        (c-cur (if (< *move-number* 25)
                   (+ 50000 (* 2000 *move-number*))
                   (+ 75000 (* 1000 *move-number*))))
        (c-pot 20000))
```

```
(multiple-value-bind (p-cur p-pot)
    (mobility player board)
  (multiple-value-bind (o-cur o-pot)
      (mobility (opponent player) board)
    ;; Combine the three factors into one sum:
    (+ (round (* c-edg (edge-stability player board)) 32000)
       (round (* c-cur (- p-cur o-cur)) (+ p-cur o-cur 2))
       (round (* c-pot  (- p-pot o-pot)) (+ p-pot o-pot 2)))))))
```

Finally, we are ready to code the Iago function. Given a search depth, Iago returns a strategy that will do alpha-beta search to that depth using the Iago-eval evaluation function. This version of Iago was able to defeat the modified weighted-squares strategy in 8 of 10 games at 3 ply, and 9 of 10 at 4 ply. On an Explorer II, 4-ply search takes about 20 seconds per move. At 5 ply, many moves take over a minute, so the program runs the risk of forfeiting. At 3 ply, the program takes only a few seconds per move, but it still was able to defeat the author in five straight games, by scores of 50-14, 64-0, 51-13, 49-15 and 36-28. Despite these successes, it is likely that the evaluation function could be improved greatly with a little tuning of the parameters.

```
(defun Iago (depth)
  "Use an approximation of Iago's evaluation function."
  (alpha-beta-searcher3 depth #'iago-eval))
```

18.13   Other Techniques

There are many other variations that can be tried to speed up the search and improve play. Unfortunately, choosing among the techniques is a bit of a black art. You will have to experiment to find the combination that is best for each domain and each evaluation function. Most of the following techniques were incorporated, or at least considered and rejected, in Bill.

Iterative Deepening

We have seen that the average branching factor for Othello is about 10. This means that searching to depth $n + 1$ takes roughly 10 times longer than search to depth n. Thus, we should be willing to go to a lot of overhead before we search one level deeper, to assure two things: that search will be done efficiently, and that we won't forfeit due to running out of time. A by-now familiar technique, iterative deepening (see chapters 6 and 14), serves both these goals.

Iterative deepening is used as follows. The strategy determines how much of the remaining time to allocate to each move. A simple strategy could allocate a constant amount of time for each move, and a more sophisticated strategy could allocate more time for moves at crucial points in the game. Once the time allocation is determined for a move, the strategy starts an iterative deepening alpha-beta search. There are two complications: First, the search at n ply keeps track of the best moves, so that the search at $n + 1$ ply will have better ordering information. In many cases it will be faster to do both the n and $n + 1$ ply searches with the ordering information than to do only the $n + 1$ ply search without it. Second, we can monitor how much time has been taken searching each ply, and cut off the search when searching one more ply would exceed the allocated time limit. Thus, iterative-deepening search degrades gracefully as time limits are imposed. It will give a reasonable answer even with a short time allotment, and it will rarely exceed the allotted time.

Forward Pruning

One way to cut the number of positions searched is to replace the legal move generator with a *plausible* move generator: in other words, only consider good moves, and never even look at moves that seem clearly bad. This technique is called *forward pruning*. It has fallen on disfavor because of the difficulty in determining which moves are plausible. For most games, the factors that would go into a plausible move generator would be duplicated in the static evaluation function anyway, so forward pruning would require more effort without much gain. Worse, forward pruning could rule out a brilliant sacrifice—a move that looks bad initially but eventually leads to a gain.

For some games, forward pruning is a necessity. The game of Go, for example, is played on a 19 by 19 board, so the first player has 361 legal moves, and a 6-ply search would involve over 2 quadrillion positions. However, many good Go programs can be viewed as not doing forward pruning but doing abstraction. There might be 30 empty squares in one portion of the board, and the program would treat a move to any of these squares equivalently.

Bill uses forward pruning in a limited way to rule out certain moves adjacent to the corners. It does this not to save time but because the evaluation function might lead to such a move being selected, even though it is in fact a poor move. In other words, forward pruning is used to correct a bug in the evaluation function cheaply.

Nonspeculative Forward Pruning

This technique makes use of the observation that there are limits in the amount the evaluation function can change from one position to the next. For example, if we are using the count difference as the evaluation function, then the most a move can change the evaluation is +37 (one for placing a piece in the corner, and six captures in each of the three directions). The smallest change is 0 (if the player is forced to pass). Thus, if there are 2 ply left in the search, and the backed-up value of position A has been established as 38 points better than the static value of position B, then it is useless to expand position B. This assumes that we are evaluating every position, perhaps to do sorted ordering or iterative deepening. It also assumes that no position in the search tree is a final position, because then the evaluation could change by more than 37 points. In conclusion, it seems that nonspeculative forward pruning is not very useful for Othello, although it may play a role in other games.

Aspiration Search

Alpha-beta search is initated with the `achievable` and `cutoff` boundaries set to `losing-value` and `winning-value`, respectively. In other words, the search assumes nothing: the final position may be anything from a loss to a win. But suppose we are in a situation somewhere in the mid-game where we are winning by a small margin (say the static evaluation for the current position is 50). In most cases, a single move will not change the evaluation by very much. Therefore, if we invoked the alpha-beta search with a window defined by boundaries of, say, 0 and 100, two things can happen: if the actual backed-up evaluation for this position is in fact in the range 0 to 100, then the search will find it, and it will be found quickly, because the reduced window will cause more pruning. If the actual value is not in the range, then the value returned will reflect that, and we can search again using a larger window. This is called aspiration search, because we aspire to find a value within a given window. If the window is chosen well, then often we will succeed and will have saved some search time.

Pearl (1984) suggests an alternative called zero-window search. At each level, the first possible move, which we'll call m, is searched using a reasonably wide window to determine its exact value, which we'll call v. Then the remaining possible moves are searched using v as both the lower and upper bounds of the window. Thus, the result of the search will tell if each subsequent move is better or worse than m, but won't tell how much better or worse. There are three outcomes for zero-window search. If no move turns out to be better than m, then stick with m. If a single move is better, then use it. If several moves are better than m, then they have to be searched again using a wider window to determine which is best.

There is always a trade-off between time spent searching and information gained. Zero-window search makes an attractive trade-off: we gain some search time by losing information about the value of the best move. We are still guaranteed of finding the best move, we just don't know its exact value.

Bill's zero-window search takes only 63% of the time taken by full alpha-beta search. It is effective because Bill's move-ordering techniques ensure that the first move is often best. With random move ordering, zero-window search would not be effective.

Think-Ahead

A program that makes its move and then waits for the opponent's reply is wasting half the time available to it. A better use of time is to compute, or *think-ahead* while the opponent is moving. Think-ahead is one factor that helps Bill defeat Iago. While many programs have done think-ahead by choosing the most likely move by the opponent and then starting an iterative-deepening search assuming that move, Bill's algorithm is somewhat more complex. It can consider more than one move by the opponent, depending on how much time is available.

Hashing and Opening Book Moves

We have been treating the search space as a tree, but in general it is a directed acyclic graph (dag): there may be more than one way to reach a particular position, but there won't be any loops, because every move adds a new piece. This raises the question we explored briefly in section 6.4: should we treat the search space as a tree or a graph? By treating it as a graph we eliminate duplicate evaluations, but we have the overhead of storing all the previous positions, and of checking to see if a new position has been seen before. The decision must be based on the proportion of duplicate positions that are actually encountered in play. One compromise solution is to store in a hash table a partial encoding of each position, encoded as, say, a single fixnum (one word) instead of the seven or so words needed to represent a full board. Along with the encoding of each position, store the move to try first. Then, for each new position, look in the hash table, and if there is a hit, try the corresponding move first. The move may not even be legal, if there is an accidental hash collision, but there is a good chance that the move will be the right one, and the overhead is low.

One place where it is clearly worthwhile to store information about previous positions is in the opening game. Since there are fewer choices in the opening, it is a good idea to compile an opening "book" of moves and to play by it as long as possible, until the opponent makes a move that departs from the book. Book moves can be gleaned from the literature, although not very much has been written about Othello (as compared to openings in chess). However, there is a danger in following expert advice: the positions that an expert thinks are advantageous may not be the same as the positions from which our program can play well. It may be better to compile the book by playing the program against itself and determining which positions work out best.

The End Game

It is also a good idea to try to save up time in the midgame and then make an all-out effort to search the complete game tree to completion as soon as feasible. Bill can search to completion from about 14 ply out. Once the search is done, of course, the most promising lines of play should be saved so that it won't be necessary to solve the game tree again.

Metareasoning

If it weren't for the clock, Othello would be a trivial game: just search the complete game tree all the way to the end, and then choose the best move. The clock imposes a complication: we have to make all our moves before we run out of time. The algorithms we have seen so far manage the clock by allocating a certain amount of time to each move, such that the total time is guaranteed (or at least very likely) to be less than the allotted time. This is a very crude policy. A finer-grained way of managing time is to consider computation itself as a possible move. That is, at every tick of the clock, we need to decide if it is better to stop and play the best move we have computed so far or to continue and try to compute a better move. It will be better to compute more only in the case where we eventually choose a better move; it will be better to stop and play only in the case where we would otherwise forfeit due to time constraints, or be forced to make poor choices later in the game. An algorithm that includes computation as a possible move is called a metareasoning system, because it reasons about how much to reason.

Russell and Wefald (1989) present an approach based on this view. In addition to an evaluation function, they assume a variance function, which gives an estimate of how much a given position's true value is likely to vary from its static value. At each step, their algorithm compares the value and variance of the best move computed so far and the second best move. If the best move is clearly better than the second best (taking variance into account), then there is no point computing any more. Also, if the top two moves have similar values but both have very low variance, then computing will not help much; we can just choose one of the two at random.

For example, if the board is in a symmetric position, then there may be two symmetric moves that will have identical value. By searching each move's subtree more carefully, we soon arrive at a low variance for both moves, and then we can choose either one, without searching further. Of course, we could also add special-case code to check for symmetry, but the metareasoning approach will work for nonsymmetric cases as well as symmetric ones. If there is a situation where two moves both lead to a clear win, it won't waste time choosing between them.

The only situation where it makes sense to continue computing is when there are two moves with high variance, so that it is uncertain if the true value of one exceeds the other. The metareasoning algorithm is predicated on devoting time to just this case.

Learning

From the earliest days of computer game playing, it was realized that a championship program would need to learn to improve itself. Samuel (1959) describes a program that plays checkers and learns to improve its evaluation function. The evaluation function is a linear combination of features, such as the number of pieces for each player, the number of kings, the number of possible forks, and so on. Learning is done by a hill-climbing search procedure: change one of the coefficients for one of the features at random, and then see if the changed evaluation function is better than the original one.

Without some guidance, this hill-climbing search would be very slow. First, the space is very large—Samuel used 38 different features, and although he restricted the coefficients to be a power of two between 0 and 20, that still leaves 21^{38} possible evaluation functions. Second, the obvious way of determining the relative worth of two evaluation functions—playing a series of games between them and seeing which wins more often—is quite time-consuming.

Fortunately, there is a faster way of evaluating an evaluation function. We can apply the evaluation function to a position and compare this static value with the backed-up value determined by an alpha-beta search. If the evaluation function is accurate, the static value should correlate well with the backed-up value. If it does not correlate well, the evaluation function should be changed in such a way that it does. This approach still requires the trial-and-error of hill-climbing, but it will converge much faster if we can gain information from every position, rather than just from every game.

In the past few years there has been increased interest in learning by a process of guided search. *Neural nets* are one example of this. They have been discussed elsewhere. Another example is *genetic learning* algorithms. These algorithms start with several candidate solutions. In our case, each candidate would consist of a set of coefficients for an evaluation function. On each generation, the genetic algorithm sees how well each candidate does. The worst candidates are eliminated, and the best ones "mate" and "reproduce"—two candidates are combined in some way to yield a new one. If the new offspring has inherited both its parents' good points, then it will prosper; if it has inherited both its parents' bad points, then it will quickly die out. Either way, the idea is that natural selection will eventually yield a high-quality solution. To increase the chances of this, it is a good idea to allow for mutations: random changes in the genetic makeup of one of the candidates.

18.14   History and References

Lee and Mahajan (1986, 1990) present the current top Othello program, Bill. Their description outlines all the techniques used but does not go into enough detail to allow the reader to reconstruct the program. Bill is based in large part on Rosenbloom's Iago program. Rosenbloom's article (1982) is more thorough. The presentation in this chapter is based largely on this article, although it also contains some ideas from Bill and from other sources.

The journal *Othello Quarterly* is the definitive source for reports on both human and computer Othello games and strategies.

The most popular game for computer implementation is chess. Shannon (1950a,b) speculated that a computer might play chess. In a way, this was one of the boldest steps in the history of AI. Today, writing a chess program is a challenging but feasible project for an undergraduate. But in 1950, even suggesting that such a program might be possible was a revolutionary step that changed the way people viewed these arithmetic calculating devices. Shannon introduced the ideas of a game tree search, minimaxing, and evaluation functions—ideas that remain intact to this day. Marsland (1990) provides a good short introduction to computer chess, and David Levy has two books on the subject (1976, 1988). It was Levy, an international chess master, who in 1968 accepted a bet from John McCarthy, Donald Michie, and others that a computer chess program would not beat him in the next ten years. Levy won the bet. Levy's *Heuristic Programming* (1990) and *Computer Games* (1988) cover a variety of computer game playing programs. The studies by DeGroot (1965, 1966) give a fascinating insight into the psychology of chess masters.

Knuth and Moore (1975) analyze the alpha-beta algorithm, and Pearl's book *Heuristics* (1984) covers all kinds of heuristic search, games included.

Samuel (1959) is the classic work on learning evaluation function parameters. It is based on the game of checkers. Lee and Mahajan (1990) present an alternative learning mechanism, using Bayesian classification to learn an evaluation function that optimally distinguishes winning positions from losing positions. Genetic algorithms are discussed by L. Davis (1987, 1991) and Goldberg (1989).

18.15   Exercises

Exercise 18.3 [s]   How many different Othello positions are there? Would it be feasible to store the complete game tree and thus have a perfect player?

Exercise 18.4 [m]   At the beginning of this chapter, we implemented pieces as an enumerated type. There is no built-in facility in Common Lisp for doing this, so we had to introduce a series of defconstant forms. Define a macro for defining enumerated types. What else should be provided besides the constants?

Exercise 18.5 [h]   Add fixnum and speed declarations to the Iago evaluation function and the alpha-beta code. How much does this speed up Iago? What other efficiency measures can you take?

Exercise 18.6 [h] Implement an iterative deepening search that allocates time for each move and checks between each iteration if the time is exceeded.

Exercise 18.7 [h] Implement zero-window search, as described in section 18.13.

Exercise 18.8 [d] Read the references on Bill (Lee and Mahajan 1990, and 1986 if you can get it), and reimplement Bill's evaluation function as best you can, using the table-based approach. It will also be helpful to read Rosenbloom 1982.

Exercise 18.9 [d] Improve the evaluation function by tuning the parameters, using one of the techniques described in section 18.13.

Exercise 18.10 [h] Write move-generation and evaluation functions for another game, such as chess or checkers.

18.16   Answers

Answer 18.2 The weighted-squares strategy wins the first game by 20 pieces, but when count-difference plays first, it captures all the pieces on its fifth move. These two games alone are not enough to determine the best strategy; the function othello-series on page 626 shows a better comparison.

Answer 18.3 $3^{64} = 3,433,683,820,292,512,484,657,849,089,281$. No.

Answer 18.4 Besides the constants, we provide a `deftype` for the type itself, and conversion routines between integers and symbols:

```
(defmacro define-enumerated-type (type &rest elements)
  "Represent an enumerated type with integers 0-n."
  '(progn
     (deftype ,type () '(integer 0 ,(- (length elements) 1)))
     (defun ,(symbol type '->symbol) (,type)
       (elt ',elements ,type))
     (defun ,(symbol 'symbol-> type) (symbol)
       (position symbol ',elements))
     ,@(loop for element in elements
             for i from 0
             collect '(defconstant ,element ,i))))
```

Here's how the macro would be used to define the `piece` data type, and the code produced:

```
> (macroexpand
    '(define-enumerated-type piece
       empty black white outer))
(PROGN
  (DEFTYPE PIECE () '(INTEGER 0 3))
  (DEFUN PIECE->SYMBOL (PIECE)
    (ELT '(EMPTY BLACK WHITE OUTER) PIECE))
  (DEFUN SYMBOL->PIECE (SYMBOL)
    (POSITION SYMBOL '(EMPTY BLACK WHITE OUTER)))
  (DEFCONSTANT EMPTY 0)
  (DEFCONSTANT BLACK 1)
  (DEFCONSTANT WHITE 2)
  (DEFCONSTANT OUTER 3))
```

A more general facility would, like `defstruct`, provide for several options. For example, it might allow for a documentation string for the type and each constant, and for a `:conc-name`, so the constants could have names like `piece-empty` instead of `empty`. This would avoid conflicts with other types that wanted to use the same names. The user might also want the ability to start the values at some number other than zero, or to assign specific values to some of the symbols.

CHAPTER 19

Introduction to
Natural Language

Language is everywhere. It permeates our thoughts,
mediates our relations with others, and even creeps
into our dreams. The overwhelming bulk of human
knowledge is stored and transmitted in language.
Language is so ubiquitous that we take it for granted,
but without it, society as we know it would
be impossible.

—Ronand Langacker
Language and its Structure (1967)

A natural language is a language spoken by people, such as English, German, or Tagalog. This is in opposition to artificial languages like Lisp, FORTRAN, or Morse code. Natural language processing is an important part of AI because language is intimately connected to thought. One measure of this is the number of important books that mention language and thought in the title: in AI, Schank and Colby's *Computer Models of Thought and Language;* in linguistics, Whorf's *Language, Thought, and Reality* (and Chomsky's *Language and Mind;*) in philosophy, Fodor's *The Language of Thought;* and in psychology, Vygotsky's *Thought and Language* and John Anderson's *Language, Memory, and Thought.* Indeed, language is the trait many think of as being the most characteristic of humans. Much controversy has been generated over the question of whether animals, especially primates and dolphins, can use and "understand" language. Similar controversy surrounds the same question asked of computers.

The study of language has been traditionally separated into two broad classes: syntax, or grammar, and semantics, or meaning. Historically, syntax has achieved the most attention, largely because on the surface it is more amenable to formal and semiformal methods. Although there is evidence that the boundary between the two is at best fuzzy, we still maintain the distinction for the purposes of these notes. We will cover the "easier" part, syntax, first, and then move on to semantics.

A good artificial language, like Lisp or C, is unambiguous. There is only one interpretation for a valid Lisp expression. Of course, the interpretation may depend on the state of the current state of the Lisp world, such as the value of global variables. But these dependencies can be explicitly enumerated, and once they are spelled out, then there can only be one meaning for the expression.[1]

Natural language does not work like this. Natural expressions are inherently ambiguous, depending on any number of factors that can never be quite spelled out completely. It is perfectly reasonable for two people to disagree on what some other person meant by a natural language expression. (Lawyers and judges make their living largely by interpreting natural language expressions—laws—that are meant to be unambiguous but are not.)

This chapter is a brief introduction to natural language processing. The next chapter gives a more thorough treatment from the point of view of logic grammars, and the chapter after that puts it all together into a full-fledged system.

19.1   Parsing with a Phrase-Structure Grammar

To parse a sentence means to recover the constituent structure of the sentence—to discover what sequence of generation rules could have been applied to come up with the sentence. In general, there may be several possible derivations, in which case we say the sentence is grammatically ambiguous. In certain circles, the term "parse" means to arrive at an understanding of a sentence's meaning, not just its grammatical form. We will attack that more difficult question later.

---

[1]Some erroneous expressions are underspecified and may return different results in different implementations, but we will ignore that problem.

We start with the grammar defined on page 39 for the generate program:

```
(defvar *grammar* "The grammar used by GENERATE.")

(defparameter *grammar1*
  '((Sentence -> (NP VP))
    (NP -> (Art Noun))
    (VP -> (Verb NP))
    (Art -> the a)
    (Noun -> man ball woman table)
    (Verb -> hit took saw liked)))
```

Our parser takes as input a list of words and returns a structure containing the parse tree and the unparsed words, if any. That way, we can parse the remaining words under the next category to get compound rules. For example, in parsing "the man saw the table," we would first parse "the man," returning a structure representing the noun phrase, with the remaining words "saw the table." This remainder would then be parsed as a verb phrase, returning no remainder, and the two phrases could then be joined to form a parse that is a complete sentence with no remainder.

Before proceeding, I want to make a change in the representation of grammar rules. Currently, rules have a left-hand side and a list of alternative right-hand sides. But each of these alternatives is really a separate rule, so it would be more modular to write them separately. For the generate program it was fine to have them all together, because that made processing choices easier, but now I want a more flexible representation. Later on we will want to add more information to each rule, like the semantics of the assembled left-hand side, and constraints between constituents on the right-hand side, so the rules would become quite large indeed if we didn't split up the alternatives. I also take this opportunity to clear up the confusion between words and category symbols. The convention is that a right-hand side can be either an atom, in which case it is a word, or a list of symbols, which are then all interpreted as categories. To emphasize this, I include "noun" and "verb" as nouns in the grammar *grammar3*, which is otherwise equivalent to the previous *grammar1*.

```
(defparameter *grammar3*
  '((Sentence -> (NP VP))
    (NP -> (Art Noun))
    (VP -> (Verb NP))
    (Art -> the) (Art -> a)
    (Noun -> man) (Noun -> ball) (Noun -> woman) (Noun -> table)
    (Noun -> noun) (Noun -> verb)
    (Verb -> hit) (Verb -> took) (Verb -> saw) (Verb -> liked)))

(setf *grammar* *grammar3*)
```

I also define the data types rule, parse, and tree, and some functions for getting at the rules. Rules are defined as structures of type list with three slots: the left-hand side, the arrow (which should always be represented as the literal ->) and the right-hand side. Compare this to the treatment on page 40.

```lisp
(defstruct (rule (:type list)) lhs -> rhs)

(defstruct (parse) "A parse tree and a remainder." tree rem)

;; Trees are of the form: (lhs . rhs)
(defun new-tree (cat rhs) (cons cat rhs))
(defun tree-lhs (tree) (first tree))
(defun tree-rhs (tree) (rest tree))

(defun parse-lhs (parse) (tree-lhs (parse-tree parse)))

(defun lexical-rules (word)
  "Return a list of rules with word on the right-hand side."
  (find-all word *grammar* :key #'rule-rhs :test #'equal))

(defun rules-starting-with (cat)
  "Return a list of rules where cat starts the rhs."
  (find-all cat *grammar*
            :key #'(lambda (rule) (first-or-nil (rule-rhs rule)))))

(defun first-or-nil (x)
  "The first element of x if it is a list; else nil."
  (if (consp x) (first x) nil))
```

Now we're ready to define the parser. The main function parser takes a list of words to parse. It calls parse, which returns a list of all parses that parse some subsequence of the words, starting at the beginning. parser keeps only the parses with no remainder—that is, the parses that span all the words.

```lisp
(defun parser (words)
  "Return all complete parses of a list of words."
  (mapcar #'parse-tree (complete-parses (parse words))))

(defun complete-parses (parses)
  "Those parses that are complete (have no remainder)."
  (find-all-if #'null parses :key #'parse-rem))
```

The function parse looks at the first word and considers each category it could be. It makes a parse of the first word under each category, and calls extend-parse to try to continue to a complete parse. parse uses mapcan to append together all the resulting parses. As an example, suppose we are trying to parse "the man took the ball." parse would find the single lexical rule for "the" and call extend-parse with a parse with tree (Art the) and remainder "man took the ball," with no more categories needed.

extend-parse has two cases. If the partial parse needs no more categories to be complete, then it returns the parse itself, along with any parses that can be formed by extending parses starting with the partial parse. In our example, there is one rule starting with Art, namely (NP -> (Art Noun)), so the function would try to extend the parse tree (NP (Art the)) with remainder "man took the ball," with the category Noun needed. That call to extend-parse represents the second case. We first parse "man took the ball," and for every parse that is of category Noun (there will be only one), we combine with the partial parse. In this case we get (NP (Art the) (Noun man)). This gets extended as a sentence with a VP needed, and eventually we get a parse of the complete list of words.

```lisp
(defun parse (words)
  "Bottom-up parse, returning all parses of any prefix of words."
  (unless (null words)
    (mapcan #'(lambda (rule)
                (extend-parse (rule-lhs rule) (list (first words))
                              (rest words) nil))
            (lexical-rules (first words)))))

(defun extend-parse (lhs rhs rem needed)
  "Look for the categories needed to complete the parse."
  (if (null needed)
      ;; If nothing needed, return parse and upward extensions
      (let ((parse (make-parse :tree (new-tree lhs rhs) :rem rem)))
        (cons parse
              (mapcan
                #'(lambda (rule)
                    (extend-parse (rule-lhs rule)
                                  (list (parse-tree parse))
                                  rem (rest (rule-rhs rule))))
                (rules-starting-with lhs))))
      ;; otherwise try to extend rightward
      (mapcan
        #'(lambda (p)
            (if (eq (parse-lhs p) (first needed))
                (extend-parse lhs (append1 rhs (parse-tree p))
                              (parse-rem p) (rest needed))))
        (parse rem))))
```

This makes use of the auxiliary function append1:

```lisp
(defun append1 (items item)
  "Add item to end of list of items."
  (append items (list item)))
```

Some examples of the parser in action are shown here:

```
> (parser '(the table))
((NP (ART THE) (NOUN TABLE)))

> (parser '(the ball hit the table))
((SENTENCE (NP (ART THE) (NOUN BALL))
          (VP (VERB HIT)
              (NP (ART THE) (NOUN TABLE)))))

> (parser '(the noun took the verb))
((SENTENCE (NP (ART THE) (NOUN NOUN))
          (VP (VERB TOOK)
              (NP (ART THE) (NOUN VERB)))))
```

19.2   Extending the Grammar and Recognizing Ambiguity

Overall, the parser seems to work fine, but the range of sentences we can parse is quite limited with the current grammar. The following grammar includes a wider variety of linguistic phenomena: adjectives, prepositional phrases, pronouns, and proper names. It also uses the usual linguistic conventions for category names, summarized in the table below:

	Category	Examples
S	Sentence	*John likes Mary*
NP	Noun Phrase	*John; a blue table*
VP	Verb Phrase	*likes Mary; hit the ball*
PP	Prepositional Phrase	*to Mary; with the man*
A	Adjective	*little; blue*
A+	A list of one or more adjectives	*little blue*
D	Determiner	*the; a*
N	Noun	*ball; table*
Name	Proper Name	*John; Mary*
P	Preposition	*to; with*
Pro	Pronoun	*you; me*
V	Verb	*liked; hit*

Here is the grammar:

```
(defparameter *grammar4*
  '((S -> (NP VP))
    (NP -> (D N))
    (NP -> (D A+ N))
    (NP -> (NP PP))
    (NP -> (Pro))
    (NP -> (Name))
    (VP -> (V NP))
    (VP -> (V))
    (VP -> (VP PP))
    (PP -> (P NP))
    (A+ -> (A))
    (A+ -> (A A+))
    (Pro -> I) (Pro -> you) (Pro -> he) (Pro -> she)
    (Pro -> it) (Pro -> me) (Pro -> him) (Pro -> her)
    (Name -> John) (Name -> Mary)
    (A -> big) (A -> little) (A -> old) (A -> young)
    (A -> blue) (A -> green) (A -> orange) (A -> perspicuous)
    (D -> the) (D -> a) (D -> an)
    (N -> man) (N -> ball) (N -> woman) (N -> table) (N -> orange)
    (N -> saw) (N -> saws) (N -> noun) (N -> verb)
    (P -> with) (P -> for) (P -> at) (P -> on) (P -> by) (P -> of) (P -> in)
    (V -> hit) (V -> took) (V -> saw) (V -> liked) (V -> saws)))

(setf *grammar* *grammar4*)
```

Now we can parse more interesting sentences, and we can see a phenomenon that was not present in the previous examples: ambiguous sentences. The sentence "The man hit the table with the ball" has two parses, one where the ball is the thing that hits the table, and the other where the ball is on or near the table. parser finds both of these parses (although of course it assigns no meaning to either parse):

```
> (parser '(The man hit the table with the ball))
((S (NP (D THE) (N MAN))
    (VP (VP (V HIT) (NP (D THE) (N TABLE)))
        (PP (P WITH) (NP (D THE) (N BALL))))))
 (S (NP (D THE) (N MAN))
    (VP (V HIT)
        (NP (NP (D THE) (N TABLE))
            (PP (P WITH) (NP (D THE) (N BALL)))))))
```

Sentences are not the only category that can be ambiguous, and not all ambiguities have to be between parses in the same category. Here we see a phrase that is ambiguous between a sentence and a noun phrase:

```
> (parser '(the orange saw))
((S (NP (D THE) (N ORANGE)) (VP (V SAW)))
 (NP (D THE) (A+ (A ORANGE)) (N SAW)))
```

19.3   More Efficient Parsing

With more complex grammars and longer sentences, the parser starts to slow down. The main problem is that it keeps repeating work. For example, in parsing "The man hit the table with the ball," it has to reparse "with the ball" for both of the resulting parses, even though in both cases it receives the same analysis, a PP. We have seen this problem before and have already produced an answer: memoization (see section 9.6). To see how much memoization will help, we need a benchmark:

```
> (setf s (generate 's))
(THE PERSPICUOUS BIG GREEN BALL BY A BLUE WOMAN WITH A BIG MAN
 HIT A TABLE BY THE SAW BY THE GREEN ORANGE)

> (time (length (parser s)))
Evaluation of (LENGTH (PARSER S)) took 33.11 Seconds of elapsed time.
10
```

The sentence S has 10 parses, since there are two ways to parse the subject NP and five ways to parse the VP. It took 33 seconds to discover these 10 parses with the parse function as it was written.

We can improve this dramatically by memoizing parse (along with the table-lookup functions). Besides memoizing, the only change is to clear the memoization table within parser.

```
(memoize 'lexical-rules)
(memoize 'rules-starting-with)
(memoize 'parse :test #'eq)

(defun parser (words)
  "Return all complete parses of a list of words."
  (clear-memoize 'parse) ;***
  (mapcar #'parse-tree (complete-parses (parse words))))
```

In normal human language use, memoization would not work very well, since the interpretation of a phrase depends on the context in which the phrase was uttered. But with context-free grammars we have a guarantee that the context cannot affect the interpretation. The call (parse words) must return all possible parses for the words. We are free to choose between the possibilities based on contextual information, but context can never supply a new interpretation that is not in the context-free list of parses.

The function use is introduced to tell the table-lookup functions that they are out of date whenever the grammar changes:

```
(defun use (grammar)
  "Switch to a new grammar."
  (clear-memoize 'rules-starting-with)
  (clear-memoize 'lexical-rules)
  (length (setf *grammar* grammar)))
```

Now we run the benchmark again with the memoized version of parse:

```
> (time (length (parser s)))
Evaluation of (LENGTH (PARSER S 'S)) took .13 Seconds of elapsed time.
10
```

By memoizing parse we reduce the parse time from 33 to .13 seconds, a 250-fold speed-up. We can get a more systematic comparison by looking at a range of examples. For example, consider sentences of the form "The man hit the table [with the ball]*" for zero or more repetitions of the PP "with the ball." In the following table we record N, the number of repetitions of the PP, along with the number of resulting parses[2], and for both memoized and unmemoized versions of parse, the number of seconds to produce the parse, the number of parses per second (PPS), and the number of recursive calls to parse. The performance of the memoized version is quite acceptable; for N=5, a 20-word sentence is parsed into 132 possibilities in .68 seconds, as opposed to the 20 seconds it takes in the unmemoized version.

---

[2]The number of parses of sentences of this kind is the same as the number of bracketings of a arithmetic expression, or the number of binary trees with a given number of leaves. The resulting sequence (1,2,5,14,42,...) is known as the Catalan Numbers. This kind of ambiguity is discussed by Church and Patil (1982) in their article *Coping with Syntactic Ambiguity, or How to Put the Block in the Box on the Table.*

		Memoized			Unmemoized		
N	**Parses**	**Secs**	**PPS**	**Calls**	**Secs**	**PPS**	**Calls**
0	1	0.02	60	4	0.02	60	17
1	2	0.02	120	11	0.07	30	96
2	5	0.05	100	21	0.23	21	381
3	14	0.10	140	34	0.85	16	1388
4	42	0.23	180	50	3.17	13	4999
5	132	0.68	193	69	20.77	6	18174
6	429	1.92	224	91	—		
7	1430	5.80	247	116	—		
8	4862	20.47	238	144	—		

Exercise 19.1 [h]   It seems that we could be more efficient still by memoizing with a table consisting of a vector whose length is the number of words in the input (plus one). Implement this approach and see if it entails less overhead than the more general hash table approach.

19.4   The Unknown-Word Problem

As it stands, the parser cannot deal with unknown words. Any sentence containing a word that is not in the grammar will be rejected, even if the program can parse all the rest of the words perfectly. One way of treating unknown words is to allow them to be any of the "open-class" categories—nouns, verbs, adjectives, and names, in our grammar. An unknown word will not be considered as one of the "closed-class" categories—prepositions, determiners, or pronouns. This can be programmed very simply by having lexical-rules return a list of these open-class rules for every word that is not already known.

```
(defparameter *open-categories* '(N V A Name)
  "Categories to consider for unknown words")

(defun lexical-rules (word)
  "Return a list of rules with word on the right-hand side."
  (or (find-all word *grammar* :key #'rule-rhs :test #'equal)
      (mapcar #'(lambda (cat) '(,cat -> ,word)) *open-categories*)))
```

With memoization of lexical-rules, this means that the lexicon is expanded every time an unknown word is encountered. Let's try this out:

```
> (parser '(John liked Mary))
((S (NP (NAME JOHN))
    (VP (V LIKED) (NP (NAME MARY)))))
```

```
> (parser '(Dana liked Dale))
((S (NP (NAME DANA))
    (VP (V LIKED) (NP (NAME DALE)))))

> (parser '(the rab zaggled the woogly quax))
((S (NP (D THE) (N RAB))
    (VP (V ZAGGLED) (NP (D THE) (A+ (A WOOGLY)) (N QUAX)))))
```

We see the parser works as well with words it knows (John and Mary) as with new words (Dana and Dale), which it can recognize as names because of their position in the sentence. In the last sentence in the example, it recognizes each unknown word unambiguously. Things are not always so straightforward, unfortunately, as the following examples show:

```
> (parser '(the slithy toves gymbled))
((S (NP (D THE) (N SLITHY)) (VP (V TOVES) (NP (NAME GYMBLED))))
 (S (NP (D THE) (A+ (A SLITHY)) (N TOVES)) (VP (V GYMBLED)))
 (NP (D THE) (A+ (A SLITHY) (A+ (A TOVES))) (N GYMBLED)))

> (parser '(the slithy toves gymbled on the wabe))
((S (NP (D THE) (N SLITHY))
    (VP (VP (V TOVES) (NP (NAME GYMBLED)))
        (PP (P ON) (NP (D THE) (N WABE)))))
 (S (NP (D THE) (N SLITHY))
    (VP (V TOVES) (NP (NP (NAME GYMBLED))
                      (PP (P ON) (NP (D THE) (N WABE))))))
 (S (NP (D THE) (A+ (A SLITHY)) (N TOVES))
    (VP (VP (V GYMBLED)) (PP (P ON) (NP (D THE) (N WABE)))))
 (NP (NP (D THE) (A+ (A SLITHY) (A+ (A TOVES))) (N GYMBLED))
     (PP (P ON) (NP (D THE) (N WABE)))))
```

If the program knew morphology—that a y at the end of a word often signals an adjective, an s a plural noun, and an *ed* a past-tense verb—then it could do much better.

19.5 Parsing into a Semantic Representation

Syntactic parse trees of a sentence may be interesting, but by themselves they're not very useful. We use sentences to communicate ideas, not to display grammatical structures. To explore the idea of the semantics, or meaning, of a phrase, we need a domain to talk about. Imagine the scenario of a compact disc player capable of playing back selected songs based on their track number. Imagine further that this machine has buttons on the front panel indicating numbers, as well as words such as "play," "to," "and," and "without." If you then punch in the sequence of buttons "play

1 to 5 without 3," you could reasonably expect the machine to respond by playing tracks 1, 2, 4, and 5. After a few such successful interactions, you might say that the machine "understands" a limited language. The important point is that the utility of this machine would not be enhanced much if it happened to display a parse tree of the input. On the other hand, you would be justifiably annoyed if it responded to "play 1 to 5 without 3" by playing 3 or skipping 4.

Now let's stretch the imagination one more time by assuming that this CD player comes equipped with a full Common Lisp compiler, and that we are now in charge of writing the parser for its input language. Let's first consider the relevant data structures. We need to add a component for the semantics to both the rule and tree structures. Once we've done that, it is clear that trees are nothing more than instances of rules, so their definitions should reflect that. Thus, I use an `:include` defstruct to define trees, and I specify no copier function, because `copy-tree` is already a Common Lisp function, and I don't want to redefine it. To maintain consistency with the old `new-tree` function (and to avoid having to put in all those keywords) I define the constructor `new-tree`. This option to `defstruct` makes `(new-tree a b c)` equivalent to `(make-tree :lhs a :sem b :rhs c)`.

```
(defstruct (rule (:type list))
  lhs -> rhs sem)

(defstruct (tree (:type list) (:include rule) (:copier nil)
              (:constructor new-tree (lhs sem rhs))))
```

We will adopt the convention that the semantics of a word can be any Lisp object. For example, the semantics of the word "1" could be the object 1, and the semantics of "without" could be the function `set-difference`. The semantics of a tree is formed by taking the semantics of the rule that generated the tree and applying it (as a function) to the semantics of the constituents of the tree. Thus, the grammar writer must insure that the semantic component of rules are functions that expect the right number of arguments. For example, given the rule

```
(NP -> (NP CONJ NP) infix-funcall)
```

then the semantics of the phrase "1 to 5 without 3" could be determined by first determining the semantics of "1 to 5" to be (1 2 3 4 5), of "without" to be `set-difference`, and of "3" to be (3). After these sub-constituents are determined, the rule is applied by calling the function `infix-funcall` with the three arguments (1 2 3 4 5), `set-difference`, and (3). Assuming that `infix-funcall` is defined to apply its second argument to the other two arguments, the result will be (1 2 4 5).

This may make more sense if we look at a complete grammar for the CD player problem:

```
(use
  '((NP -> (NP CONJ NP) infix-funcall)
    (NP -> (N)           list)
    (NP -> (N P N)       infix-funcall)
    (N -> (DIGIT)        identity)
    (P -> to             integers)
    (CONJ -> and         union)
    (CONJ -> without     set-difference)
    (N -> 1 1) (N -> 2 2) (N -> 3 3) (N -> 4 4) (N -> 5 5)
    (N -> 6 6) (N -> 7 7) (N -> 8 8) (N -> 9 9) (N -> 0 0)))

(defun integers (start end)
  "A list of all the integers in the range [start...end] inclusive."
  (if (> start end) nil
      (cons start (integers (+ start 1) end))))

(defun infix-funcall (arg1 function arg2)
  "Apply the function to the two arguments"
  (funcall function arg1 arg2))
```

Consider the first three grammar rules, which are the only nonlexical rules. The first says that when two NPs are joined by a conjunction, we assume the translation of the conjunction will be a function, and the translation of the phrase as a whole is derived by calling that function with the translations of the two NPs as arguments. The second rule says that a single noun (whose translation should be a number) translates into the singleton list consisting of that number. The third rule is similar to the first, but concerns joining Ns rather than NPs. The overall intent is that the translation of an NP will always be a list of integers, representing the songs to play.

As for the lexical rules, the conjunction "and" translates to the union function, "without" translates to the function that subtracts one set from another, and "to" translates to the function that generates a list of integers between two end points. The numbers "0" to "9" translate to themselves. Note that both lexical rules like "CONJ -> and" and nonlexical rules like "NP -> (N P N)" can have functions as their semantic translations; in the first case, the function will just be returned as the semantic translation, whereas in the second case the function will be applied to the list of constituents.

Only minor changes are needed to parse to support this kind of semantic processing. As we see in the following, we add a sem argument to extend-parse and arrange to pass the semantic components around properly. When we have gathered all the right-hand-side components, we actually do the function application. All changes are marked with ***. We adopt the convention that the semantic value nil indicates failure, and we discard all such parses.

```
(defun parse (words)
  "Bottom-up parse, returning all parses of any prefix of words.
  This version has semantics."
  (unless (null words)
    (mapcan #'(lambda (rule)
                (extend-parse (rule-lhs rule) (rule-sem rule) ;***
                              (list (first words)) (rest words) nil))
            (lexical-rules (first words)))))

(defun extend-parse (lhs sem rhs rem needed) ;***
  "Look for the categories needed to complete the parse.
  This version has semantics."
  (if (null needed)
      ;; If nothing is needed, return this parse and upward extensions,
      ;; unless the semantics fails
      (let ((parse (make-parse :tree (new-tree lhs sem rhs) :rem rem)))
        (unless (null (apply-semantics (parse-tree parse))) ;***
          (cons parse
                (mapcan
                  #'(lambda (rule)
                      (extend-parse (rule-lhs rule) (rule-sem rule) ;***
                                    (list (parse-tree parse)) rem
                                    (rest (rule-rhs rule))))
                  (rules-starting-with lhs)))))
      ;; otherwise try to extend rightward
      (mapcan
        #'(lambda (p)
            (if (eq (parse-lhs p) (first needed))
                (extend-parse lhs sem (append1 rhs (parse-tree p)) ;***
                              (parse-rem p) (rest needed))))
        (parse rem))))
```

We need to add some new functions to support this:

```
(defun apply-semantics (tree)
  "For terminal nodes, just fetch the semantics.
  Otherwise, apply the sem function to its constituents."
  (if (terminal-tree-p tree)
      (tree-sem tree)
      (setf (tree-sem tree)
            (apply (tree-sem tree)
                   (mapcar #'tree-sem (tree-rhs tree))))))

(defun terminal-tree-p (tree)
  "Does this tree have a single word on the rhs?"
  (and (length=1 (tree-rhs tree))
       (atom (first (tree-rhs tree)))))
```

```
(defun meanings (words)
  "Return all possible meanings of a phrase.  Throw away the syntactic part."
  (remove-duplicates (mapcar #'tree-sem (parser words)) :test #'equal))
```

Here are some examples of the meanings that the parser can extract:

```
> (meanings '(1 to 5 without 3))
((1 2 4 5))

> (meanings '(1 to 4 and 7 to 9))
((1 2 3 4 7 8 9))

> (meanings '(1 to 6 without 3 and 4))
((1 2 4 5 6)
 (1 2 5 6))
```

The example "(1 to 6 without 3 and 4)" is ambiguous. The first reading corresponds to "((1 to 6) without 3) and 4," while the second corresponds to "(1 to 6) without (3 and 4)." The syntactic ambiguity leads to a semantic ambiguity—the two meanings have different lists of numbers in them. However, it seems that the second reading is somehow better, in that it doesn't make a lot of sense to talk of adding 4 to a set that already includes it, which is what the first translation does.

We can upgrade the lexicon to account for this. The following lexicon insists that "and" conjoins disjoint sets and that "without" removes only elements that were already in the first argument. If these conditions do not hold, then the translation will return nil, and the parse will fail. Note that this also means that an empty list, such as "3 to 2," will also fail.

The previous grammar only allowed for the numbers 0 to 9. We can allow larger numbers by stringing together digits. So now we have two rules for numbers: a number is either a single digit, in which case the value is the digit itself (the identity function), or it is a number followed by another digit, in which case the value is 10 times the number plus the digit. We could alternately have specified a number to be a digit followed by a number, or even a number followed by a number, but either of those formulations would require a more complex semantic interpretation.

```
(use
  '((NP -> (NP CONJ NP)  infix-funcall)
    (NP -> (N)           list)
    (NP -> (N P N)       infix-funcall)
    (N  -> (DIGIT)       identity)
    (N  -> (N DIGIT)     10*N+D)
    (P  -> to            integers)
    (CONJ -> and         union*)
    (CONJ -> without     set-diff)
    (DIGIT -> 1 1) (DIGIT -> 2 2) (DIGIT -> 3 3)
```

```
        (DIGIT -> 4 4) (DIGIT -> 5 5) (DIGIT -> 6 6)
        (DIGIT -> 7 7) (DIGIT -> 8 8) (DIGIT -> 9 9)
        (DIGIT -> 0 0)))
(defun union* (x y) (if (null (intersection x y)) (append x y)))
(defun set-diff (x y) (if (subsetp y x) (set-difference x y)))
(defun 10*N+D (N D) (+ (* 10 N) D))
```

With this new grammar, we can get single interpretations out of most reasonable inputs:

```
> (meanings '(1 to 6 without 3 and 4))
((1 2 5 6))

> (meanings '(1 and 3 to 7 and 9 without 5 and 6))
((1 3 4 7 9))

> (meanings '(1 and 3 to 7 and 9 without 5 and 2))
((1 3 4 6 7 9 2))

> (meanings '(1 9 8 to 2 0 1))
((198 199 200 201))

> (meanings '(1 2 3))
(123 (123))
```

The example "1 2 3" shows an ambiguity between the number 123 and the list (123), but all the others are unambiguous.

19.6   Parsing with Preferences

One reason we have unambiguous interpretations is that we have a very limited domain of interpretation: we are dealing with sets of numbers, not lists. This is perhaps typical of the requests faced by a CD player, but it does not account for all desired input. For example, if you had a favorite song, you couldn't hear it three times with the request "1 and 1 and 1" under this grammar. We need some compromise between the permissive grammar, which generated all possible parses, and the restrictive grammar, which eliminates too many parses. To get the "best" interpretation out of an arbitrary input, we will not only need a new grammar, we will also need to modify the program to compare the relative worth of candidate interpretations. In other words, we will assign each interpretation a numeric score, and then pick the interpretation with the highest score.

We start by once again modifying the rule and tree data types to include a score component. As with the sem component, this will be used to hold first a function to compute a score and then eventually the score itself.

```
(defstruct (rule (:type list)
                 (:constructor
                  rule (lhs -> rhs &optional sem score)))
  lhs -> rhs sem score)

(defstruct (tree (:type list) (:include rule) (:copier nil)
                 (:constructor new-tree (lhs sem score rhs))))
```

Note that we have added the constructor function `rule`. The intent is that the `sem` and `score` component of grammar rules should be optional. The user does not have to supply them, but the function `use` will make sure that the function `rule` is called to fill in the missing `sem` and `score` values with `nil`.

```
(defun use (grammar)
  "Switch to a new grammar."
  (clear-memoize 'rules-starting-with)
  (clear-memoize 'lexical-rules)
  (length (setf *grammar*
               (mapcar #'(lambda (r) (apply #'rule r))
                       grammar))))
```

Now we modify the parser to keep track of the score. The changes are again minor, and mirror the changes needed to add semantics. There are two places where we put the score into trees as we create them, and one place where we apply the scoring function to its arguments.

```
(defun parse (words)
  "Bottom-up parse, returning all parses of any prefix of words.
  This version has semantics and preference scores."
  (unless (null words)
    (mapcan #'(lambda (rule)
                (extend-parse
                  (rule-lhs rule) (rule-sem rule)
                  (rule-score rule) (list (first words)) ;***
                  (rest words) nil))
            (lexical-rules (first words)))))

(defun extend-parse (lhs sem score rhs rem needed) ;***
  "Look for the categories needed to complete the parse.
  This version has semantics and preference scores."
  (if (null needed)
      ;; If nothing is needed, return this parse and upward extensions,
      ;; unless the semantics fails
      (let ((parse (make-parse :tree (new-tree lhs sem score rhs) ;***
                               :rem rem)))
        (unless (null (apply-semantics (parse-tree parse)))
```

```
            (apply-scorer (parse-tree parse)) ;***
            (cons parse
                  (mapcan
                    #'(lambda (rule)
                        (extend-parse
                          (rule-lhs rule) (rule-sem rule)
                          (rule-score rule) (list (parse-tree parse)) ;***
                          rem (rest (rule-rhs rule))))
                      (rules-starting-with lhs)))))
     ;; otherwise try to extend rightward
     (mapcan
       #'(lambda (p)
           (if (eq (parse-lhs p) (first needed))
               (extend-parse lhs sem score
                             (append1 rhs (parse-tree p)) ;***
                             (parse-rem p) (rest needed))))
       (parse rem))))
```

Again we need some new functions to support this. Most important is `apply-scorer`, which computes the score for a tree. If the tree is a terminal (a word), then the function just looks up the score associated with that word. In this grammar all words have a score of 0, but in a grammar with ambiguous words it would be a good idea to give lower scores for infrequently used senses of ambiguous words. If the tree is a nonterminal, then the score is computed in two steps. First, all the scores of the constituents of the tree are added up. Then, this is added to a measure for the tree as a whole. The rule associated with each tree will have either a number attached to it, which is added to the sum, or a function. In the latter case, the function is applied to the tree, and the result is added to obtain the final score. As a final special case, if the function returns nil, then we assume it meant to return zero. This will simplify the definition of some of the scoring functions.

```
(defun apply-scorer (tree)
  "Compute the score for this tree."
  (let ((score (or (tree-score tree) 0)))
    (setf (tree-score tree)
          (if (terminal-tree-p tree)
              score
              ;; Add up the constituent's scores,
              ;; along with the tree's score
              (+ (sum (tree-rhs tree) #'tree-score-or-0)
                 (if (numberp score)
                     score
                     (or (apply score (tree-rhs tree)) 0)))))))
```

Here is an accessor function to pick out the score from a tree:

```
(defun tree-score-or-0 (tree)
   (if (numberp (tree-score tree))
       (tree-score tree)
       0))
```

Here is the updated grammar. First, I couldn't resist the chance to add more features to the grammar. I added the postnominal adjectives "shuffled," which randomly permutes the list of songs, and "reversed," which reverses the order of play. I also added the operator "repeat," as in "1 to 3 repeat 5," which repeats a list a certain number of times. I also added brackets to allow input that says explicitly how it should be parsed.

```
(use
  '((NP -> (NP CONJ NP) infix-funcall  infix-scorer)
    (NP -> (N P N)      infix-funcall  infix-scorer)
    (NP -> (N)          list)
    (NP -> ([ NP ])     arg2)
    (NP -> (NP ADJ)     rev-funcall    rev-scorer)
    (NP -> (NP OP N)    infix-funcall)
    (N  -> (D)          identity)
    (N  -> (N D)        10*N+D)
    (P  -> to           integers       prefer<)
    ([  -> [            [)
    (]  -> ]            ])
    (OP -> repeat       repeat)
    (CONJ -> and        append         prefer-disjoint)
    (CONJ -> without    set-difference prefer-subset)
    (ADJ -> reversed    reverse        inv-span)
    (ADJ -> shuffled    permute        prefer-not-singleton)
    (D -> 1 1) (D -> 2 2) (D -> 3 3) (D -> 4 4) (D -> 5 5)
    (D -> 6 6) (D -> 7 7) (D -> 8 8) (D -> 9 9) (D -> 0 0)))
```

The following scoring functions take trees as inputs and compute bonuses or penalties for those trees. The scoring function prefer<, used for the word "to," gives a one-point penalty for reversed ranges: "5 to 1" gets a score of -1, while "1 to 5" gets a score of 0. The scorer for "and," prefer-disjoint, gives a one-point penalty for intersecting lists: "1 to 3 and 7 to 9" gets a score of 0, while "1 to 4 and 2 to 5" gets -1. The "x without y" scorer, prefer-subset, gives a three-point penalty when the y list has elements that aren't in the x list. It also awards points in inverse proportion to the length (in words) of the x phrase. The idea is that we should prefer to bind "without" tightly to some small expression on the left. If the final scores come out as positive or as nonintegers, then this scoring component is responsible, since all the other components are negative intgers. The "x shuffled" scorer, prefer-not-singleton, is similar, except that there the penalty is for shuffling a list of less than two songs.

```lisp
(defun prefer< (x y)
  (if (>= (sem x) (sem y)) -1))
(defun prefer-disjoint (x y)
  (if (intersection (sem x) (sem y)) -1))
(defun prefer-subset (x y)
  (+ (inv-span x) (if (subsetp (sem y) (sem x)) 0 -3)))
(defun prefer-not-singleton (x)
  (+ (inv-span x) (if (< (length (sem x)) 2) -4 0)))
```

The infix-scorer and rev-scorer functions don't add anything new, they just assure that the previously mentioned scoring functions will get applied in the right place.

```lisp
(defun infix-scorer (arg1 scorer arg2)
  (funcall (tree-score scorer) arg1 arg2))

(defun rev-scorer (arg scorer) (funcall (tree-score scorer) arg))
```

Here are the functions mentioned in the grammar, along with some useful utilities:

```lisp
(defun arg2 (a1 a2 &rest a-n) (declare (ignore a1 a-n)) a2)

(defun rev-funcall (arg function) (funcall function arg))

(defun repeat (list n)
  "Append list n times."
  (if (= n 0)
      nil
      (append list (repeat list (- n 1)))))

(defun span-length (tree)
  "How many words are in tree?"
  (if (terminal-tree-p tree) 1
      (sum (tree-rhs tree) #'span-length)))

(defun inv-span (tree) (/ 1 (span-length tree)))

(defun sem (tree) (tree-sem tree))

(defun integers (start end)
  "A list of all the integers in the range [start...end] inclusive.
   This version allows start > end."
  (cond ((< start end) (cons start (integers (+ start 1) end)))
        ((> start end) (cons start (integers (- start 1) end)))
        (t (list start))))

(defun sum (numbers &optional fn)
  "Sum the numbers, or sum (mapcar fn numbers)."
  (if fn
      (loop for x in numbers sum (funcall fn x))
      (loop for x in numbers sum x)))
```

```
(defun permute (bag)
  "Return a random permutation of the given input list."
  (if (null bag)
      nil
      (let ((e (random-elt bag)))
        (cons e (permute (remove e bag :count 1 :test #'eq))))))
```

We will need a way to show off the preference rankings:

```
(defun all-parses (words)
  (format t "~%Score  Semantics~25T~a" words)
  (format t "~%=====  =========~25T===========================~%")
  (loop for tree in (sort (parser words) #'> :key #'tree-score)
    do (format t "~5,1f  ~9a~25T~a~%" (tree-score tree) (tree-sem tree)
              (bracketing tree)))
  (values))

(defun bracketing (tree)
  "Extract the terminals, bracketed with parens."
  (cond ((atom tree) tree)
        ((length=1 (tree-rhs tree))
         (bracketing (first (tree-rhs tree))))
        (t (mapcar #'bracketing (tree-rhs tree)))))
```

Now we can try some examples:

```
> (all-parses '(1 to 6 without 3 and 4))
Score  Semantics          (1 TO 6 WITHOUT 3 AND 4)
=====  =========          ===========================
  0.3  (1 2 5 6)          ((1 TO 6) WITHOUT (3 AND 4))
 -0.7  (1 2 4 5 6 4)      (((1 TO 6) WITHOUT 3) AND 4)
> (all-parses '(1 and 3 to 7 and 9 without 5 and 6))
Score  Semantics          (1 AND 3 TO 7 AND 9 WITHOUT 5 AND 6)
=====  =========          ===========================
  0.2  (1 3 4 7 9)        (1 AND (((3 TO 7) AND 9) WITHOUT (5 AND 6)))
  0.1  (1 3 4 7 9)        (((1 AND (3 TO 7)) AND 9) WITHOUT (5 AND 6))
  0.1  (1 3 4 7 9)        ((1 AND ((3 TO 7) AND 9)) WITHOUT (5 AND 6))
 -0.8  (1 3 4 6 7 9 6)    ((1 AND (((3 TO 7) AND 9) WITHOUT 5)) AND 6)
 -0.8  (1 3 4 6 7 9 6)    (1 AND ((((3 TO 7) AND 9) WITHOUT 5) AND 6))
 -0.9  (1 3 4 6 7 9 6)    ((((1 AND (3 TO 7)) AND 9) WITHOUT 5) AND 6)
 -0.9  (1 3 4 6 7 9 6)    (((1 AND ((3 TO 7) AND 9)) WITHOUT 5) AND 6)
 -2.0  (1 3 4 5 6 7 9)    ((1 AND (3 TO 7)) AND (9 WITHOUT (5 AND 6)))
 -2.0  (1 3 4 5 6 7 9)    (1 AND ((3 TO 7) AND (9 WITHOUT (5 AND 6))))
 -3.0  (1 3 4 5 6 7 9 6)  (((1 AND (3 TO 7)) AND (9 WITHOUT 5)) AND 6)
 -3.0  (1 3 4 5 6 7 9 6)  ((1 AND (3 TO 7)) AND ((9 WITHOUT 5) AND 6))
 -3.0  (1 3 4 5 6 7 9 6)  ((1 AND ((3 TO 7) AND (9 WITHOUT 5))) AND 6)
```

```
-3.0  (1 3 4 5 6 7 9 6) (1 AND (((3 TO 7) AND (9 WITHOUT 5)) AND 6))
-3.0  (1 3 4 5 6 7 9 6) (1 AND ((3 TO 7) AND ((9 WITHOUT 5) AND 6)))

> (all-parses '(1 and 3 to 7 and 9 without 5 and 2))
Score  Semantics        (1 AND 3 TO 7 AND 9 WITHOUT 5 AND 2)
=====  =========        ===================================
 0.2   (1 3 4 6 7 9 2)  ((1 AND (((3 TO 7) AND 9) WITHOUT 5)) AND 2)
 0.2   (1 3 4 6 7 9 2)  (1 AND ((((3 TO 7) AND 9) WITHOUT 5) AND 2))
 0.1   (1 3 4 6 7 9 2)  ((((1 AND (3 TO 7)) AND 9) WITHOUT 5) AND 2)
 0.1   (1 3 4 6 7 9 2)  (((1 AND ((3 TO 7) AND 9)) WITHOUT 5) AND 2)
-2.0   (1 3 4 5 6 7 9 2)  (((1 AND (3 TO 7)) AND (9 WITHOUT 5)) AND 2)
-2.0   (1 3 4 5 6 7 9 2)  ((1 AND (3 TO 7)) AND ((9 WITHOUT 5) AND 2))
-2.0   (1 3 4 5 6 7 9)  ((1 AND (3 TO 7)) AND (9 WITHOUT (5 AND 2)))
-2.0   (1 3 4 5 6 7 9 2)  ((1 AND ((3 TO 7) AND (9 WITHOUT 5))) AND 2)
-2.0   (1 3 4 5 6 7 9 2)  (1 AND (((3 TO 7) AND (9 WITHOUT 5)) AND 2))
-2.0   (1 3 4 5 6 7 9 2)  (1 AND ((3 TO 7) AND ((9 WITHOUT 5) AND 2)))
-2.0   (1 3 4 5 6 7 9)  (1 AND ((3 TO 7) AND (9 WITHOUT (5 AND 2))))
-2.8   (1 3 4 6 7 9)  (1 AND (((3 TO 7) AND 9) WITHOUT (5 AND 2)))
-2.9   (1 3 4 6 7 9)  (((1 AND (3 TO 7)) AND 9) WITHOUT (5 AND 2))
-2.9   (1 3 4 6 7 9)  ((1 AND ((3 TO 7) AND 9)) WITHOUT (5 AND 2))
```

In each case, the preference rules are able to assign higher scores to more reasonable interpretations. It turns out that, in each case, all the interpretations with positive scores represent the same set of numbers, while interpretations with negative scores seem worse. Seeing all the scores in gory detail may be of academic interest, but what we really want is something to pick out the best interpretation. The following code is appropriate for many situations. It picks the top scorer, if there is a unique one, or queries the user if several interpretations tie for the best score, and it complains if there are no valid parses at all. The query-user function may be useful in many applications, but note that meaning uses it only as a default; a program that had some automatic way of deciding could supply another tie-breaker function to meaning.

```lisp
(defun meaning (words &optional (tie-breaker #'query-user))
  "Choose the single top-ranking meaning for the words."
  (let* ((trees (sort (parser words) #'> :key #'tree-score))
         (best-score (if trees (tree-score (first trees)) 0))
         (best-trees (delete best-score trees
                        :key #'tree-score :test-not #'eql))
         (best-sems (delete-duplicates (mapcar #'tree-sem best-trees)
                                 :test #'equal)))
    (case (length best-sems)
      (0 (format t "~&Sorry, I didn't understand that.") nil)
      (1 (first best-sems))
      (t (funcall tie-breaker best-sems)))))
```

```
(defun query-user (choices &optional
                         (header-str "~&Please pick one:")
                         (footer-str "~&Your choice? "))
  "Ask user to make a choice."
  (format *query-io* header-str)
  (loop for choice in choices for i from 1 do
        (format *query-io* "~&~3d: ~a" i choice))
  (format *query-io* footer-str)
  (nth (- (read) 1) choices))
```

Here we see some final examples:

```
> (meaning '(1 to 5 without 3 and 4))
(1 2 5)

> (meaning '(1 to 5 without 3 and 6))
(1 2 4 5 6)

> (meaning '(1 to 5 without 3 and 6 shuffled))
(6 4 1 2 5)

> (meaning '([ 1 to 5 without [ 3 and 6 ] ] reversed))
(5 4 2 1)

> (meaning '(1 to 5 to 9))
Sorry, I didn't understand that.
NIL

> (meaning '(1 to 5 without 3 and 7 repeat 2))
Please pick one:
  1: (1 2 4 5 7 1 2 4 5 7)
  2: (1 2 4 5 7 7)
Your choice? 1
(1 2 4 5 7 1 2 4 5 7)

> (all-parses '(1 to 5 without 3 and 7 repeat 2))
Score  Semantics              (1 TO 5 WITHOUT 3 AND 7 REPEAT 2)
=====  =========              ================================
 0.3   (1 2 4 5 7 1 2 4 5 7)  ((((1 TO 5) WITHOUT 3) AND 7) REPEAT 2)
 0.3   (1 2 4 5 7 7)          (((1 TO 5) WITHOUT 3) AND (7 REPEAT 2))
-2.7   (1 2 4 5 1 2 4 5)      (((1 TO 5) WITHOUT (3 AND 7)) REPEAT 2)
-2.7   (1 2 4 5)              ((1 TO 5) WITHOUT ((3 AND 7) REPEAT 2))
-2.7   (1 2 4 5)              ((1 TO 5) WITHOUT (3 AND (7 REPEAT 2)))
```

This last example points out a potential problem: I wasn't sure what was a good scoring function for "repeat," so I left it blank, it defaulted to 0, and we end up with two parses with the same score. This example suggests that "repeat" should probably involve inv-span like the other modifiers, but perhaps other factors should be involved as well. There can be a complicated interplay between phrases, and it is not always clear where to assign the score. For example, it doesn't make much sense to repeat a "without" phrase; that is, the bracketing (x without (y repeat n)) is probably a bad one. But the scorer for "without" nearly handles that already. It assigns a penalty if its right argument is not a subset of its left. Unfortunately, repeated elements are not counted in sets, so for example, the list (1 2 3 1 2 3) is a subset of (1 2 3 4). However, we could change the scorer for "without" to test for sub-bag-p (not a built-in Common Lisp function) instead, and then "repeat" would not have to be concerned with that case.

19.7   The Problem with Context-Free Phrase-Structure Rules

The fragment of English grammar we specified in section 19.2 admits a variety of ungrammatical phrases. For example, it is equally happy with both "I liked her" and "me liked she." Only the first of these should be accepted; the second should be ruled out. Similarly, our grammar does not state that verbs have to agree with their subjects in person and number. And, since the grammar has no notion of meaning, it will accept sentences that are semantically anomalous (or at least unusual), such as "the table liked the man."

There are also some technical problems with context-free grammars. For example, it can be shown that no context-free grammar can be written to account for the language consisting of just the strings ABC, AABBCC, AAABBBCCC, and so forth, where each string has an equal number of As, Bs, and Cs. Yet sentences roughly of that form show up (admittedly rarely) in natural languages. An example is "Robin and Sandy loved and hated Pat and Kim, respectively." While there is still disagreement over whether it is possible to generate natural languages with a context-free grammar, clearly it is much easier to use a more powerful grammatical formalism. For example, consider solving the subject-predicate agreement problem. It is possible to do this with a context-free language including categories like singular-NP, plural-NP, singular-VP, and plural-VP, but it is far easier to augment the grammatical formalism to allow passing features between constituents.

It should be noted that context-free phrase-structure rules turned out to be very useful for describing programming languages. Starting with Algol 60, the formalism has been used under the name *Backus-Naur Form* (BNF) by computer scientists. In this book we are more interested in natural languages, so in the next chapter we will see a more powerful formalism known as *unification grammar* that can handle the problem of agreement, as well as other difficulties. Furthermore, *unification grammars* allow a natural way of attaching semantics to a parse.

19.8   History and References

There is a class of parsing algorithms known as *chart parsers* that explicitly cache partial parses and reuse them in constructing larger parses. Earley's algorithm (1970) is the first example, and Martin Kay (1980) gives a good overview of the field and introduces a data structure, the *chart*, for storing substrings of a parse. Winograd (1983) gives a complex (five-page) specification of a chart parser. None of these authors have noticed that one can achieve the same results by augmenting a simple (one-page) parser with memoization. In fact, it is possible to write a top-down parser that is even more succinct. (See exercise 19.3 below.)

For a general overview of natural language processing, my preferences (in order) are Allen 1987, Winograd 1983 or Gazdar and Mellish 1989.

19.9   Exercises

Exercise 19.2 [m-h]   Experiment with the grammar and the parser. Find sentences it cannot parse correctly, and try to add new syntactic rules to account for them.

Exercise 19.3 [m-h]   The parser works in a bottom-up fashion. Write a top-down parser, and compare it to the bottom-up version. Can both parsers work with the same grammar? If not, what constraints on the grammar does each parsing strategy impose?

Exercise 19.4 [h]   Imagine an interface to a dual cassette deck. Whereas the CD player had one assumed verb, "play," this unit has three explicit verb forms: "record," "play," and "erase." There should also be modifiers "from" and "to," where the object of a "to" is either 1 or 2, indicating which cassette to use, and the object of a "from" is either 1 or 2, or one of the symbols PHONO, CD, or AUX. It's up to you to design the grammar, but you should allow input something like the following, where I have chosen to generate actual Lisp code as the meaning:

```
> (meaning '(play 1 to 5 from CD shuffled and
             record 1 to 5 from CD and 1 and 3 and 7 from 1))
(PROGN (PLAY '(1 5 2 3 4) :FROM 'CD)
       (RECORD '(1 2 3 4 5) :FROM 'CD)
       (RECORD '(1 3 7) :FROM '1))
```

This assumes that the functions play and record take keyword arguments (with defaults) for :from and :to. You could also extend the grammar to accommodate an automatic timer, with phrases like "at 3:00."

Exercise 19.5 [m] In the definition of permute, repeated here, why is the :test #'eq needed?

```lisp
(defun permute (bag)
  "Return a random permutation of the given input list."
  (if (null bag)
      nil
      (let ((e (random-elt bag)))
        (cons e (permute (remove e bag :count 1 :test #'eq))))))
```

Exercise 19.6 [m] The definition of permute takes $O(n^2)$. Replace it by an $O(n)$ algorithm.

19.10   Answers

Answer 19.1

```lisp
(defun parser (words)
  "Return all complete parses of a list of words."
  (let* ((table (make-array (+ (length words) 1) :initial-element 0))
         (parses (parse words (length words) table)))
    (mapcar #'parse-tree (complete-parses parses))))

(defun parse (words num-words table)
  "Bottom-up parse, returning all parses of any prefix of words."
  (unless (null words)
    (let ((ans (aref table num-words)))
      (if (not (eq ans 0))
          ans
          (setf (aref table num-words)
                (mapcan #'(lambda (rule)
                            (extend-parse (rule-lhs rule)
                                          (list (first words))
                                          (rest words) nil
                                          (- num-words 1) table))
                        (lexical-rules (first words))))))))
```

```
(defun extend-parse (lhs rhs rem needed num-words table)
  "Look for the categories needed to complete the parse."
  (if (null needed)
      ;; If nothing is needed, return this parse and upward extensions
      (let ((parse (make-parse :tree (new-tree lhs rhs) :rem rem)))
        (cons parse
              (mapcan
                #'(lambda (rule)
                    (extend-parse (rule-lhs rule)
                                  (list (parse-tree parse))
                                  rem (rest (rule-rhs rule))
                                  num-words table))
                (rules-starting-with lhs))))
      ;; otherwise try to extend rightward
      (mapcan
        #'(lambda (p)
            (if (eq (parse-lhs p) (first needed))
                (extend-parse lhs (append1 rhs (parse-tree p))
                              (parse-rem p) (rest needed)
                              (length (parse-rem p)) table)))
        (parse rem num-words table))))
```

It turns out that, for the Lisp system used in the timings above, this version is no faster than normal memoization.

Answer 19.3 Actually, the top-down parser is a little easier (shorter) than the bottom-up version. The problem is that the most straightforward way of implementing a top-down parser does not handle so-called *left recursive* rules—rules of the form (X -> (X ...)). This includes rules we've used, like (NP -> (NP and NP)). The problem is that the parser will postulate an NP, and then postulate that it is of the form (NP and NP), and that the first NP of that expression is of the form (NP and NP), and so on. An infinite structure of NPs is explored before even the first word is considered.

Bottom-up parsers are stymied by rules with null right-hand sides: (X -> ()). Note that I was careful to exclude such rules in my grammars earlier.

```
(defun parser (words &optional (cat 'S))
  "Parse a list of words; return only parses with no remainder."
  (mapcar #'parse-tree (complete-parses (parse words cat))))

(defun parse (tokens start-symbol)
  "Parse a list of tokens, return parse trees and remainders."
  (if (eq (first tokens) start-symbol)
      (list (make-parse :tree (first tokens) :rem (rest tokens)))
      (mapcan #'(lambda (rule)
                  (extend-parse (lhs rule) nil tokens (rhs rule)))
              (rules-for start-symbol))))
```

```
(defun extend-parse (lhs rhs rem needed)
  "Parse the remaining needed symbols."
  (if (null needed)
      (list (make-parse :tree (cons lhs rhs) :rem rem))
      (mapcan
        #'(lambda (p)
            (extend-parse lhs (append rhs (list (parse-tree p)))
                          (parse-rem p) (rest needed)))
        (parse rem (first needed)))))

(defun rules-for (cat)
  "Return all the rules with category on lhs"
  (find-all cat *grammar* :key #'rule-lhs))
```

Answer 19.5 If it were omitted, then :test would default to #'eql, and it would be possible to remove the "wrong" element from the list. Consider the list (1.0 1.0) in an implementation where floating-point numbers are eql but not eq. if random-elt chooses the first 1.0 first, then everything is satisfactory—the result list is the same as the input list. However, if random-elt chooses the second 1.0, then the second 1.0 will be the first element of the answer, but remove will remove the wrong 1.0! It will remove the first 1.0, and the final answer will be a list with two pointers to the second 1.0 and none to the first. In other words, we could have:

```
> (member (first x) (permute x) :test #'eq)
NIL
```

Answer 19.6

```
(defun permute (bag)
  "Return a random permutation of the bag."
  ;; It is done by converting the bag to a vector, but the
  ;; result is always the same type as the input bag.
  (let ((bag-copy (replace (make-array (length bag)) bag))
        (bag-type (if (listp bag) 'list (type-of bag))))
    (coerce (permute-vector! bag-copy) bag-type)))

(defun permute-vector! (vector)
  "Destructively permute (shuffle) the vector."
  (loop for i from (length vector) downto 2 do
        (rotatef (aref vector (- i 1))
                 (aref vector (random i))))
  vector)
```

The answer uses rotatef, a relative of setf that swaps 2 or more values. That is, (rotatef a b) is like:

```
(let ((temp a))
  (setf a b)
  (setf b temp)
  nil)
```

Rarely, rotatef is used with more than two arguments. (rotatef a b c) is like:

```
(let ((temp a))
  (setf a b)
  (setf b c)
  (setf c temp)
  nil)
```

CHAPTER **20**

Unification Grammars

Prolog was invented because Alain Colmerauer wanted a formalism to describe the grammar of French. His intuition was that the combination of Horn clauses and unification resulted in a language that was just powerful enough to express the kinds of constraints that show up in natural languages, while not as powerful as, for example, full predicate calculus. This lack of power is important, because it enables efficient implementation of Prolog, and hence of the language-analysis programs built on top of it.

Of course, Prolog has evolved and is now used for many applications besides natural language, but Colmerauer's underlying intuition remains a good one. This chapter shows how to view a grammar as a set of logic programming clauses. The clauses define what is a legal sentence and what isn't, without any explicit reference to the process of parsing or generation. The amazing thing is that the clauses can be defined in a way that leads to a very efficient parser. Furthermore, the same grammar can be used for both parsing and generation (at least in some cases).

20.1 Parsing as Deduction

Here's how we could express the grammar rule "A sentence can be composed of a noun phrase followed by a verb phrase" in Prolog:

```
(<- (S ?s)
    (NP ?np)
    (VP ?vp)
    (concat ?np ?vp ?s))
```

The variables represent strings of words. As usual, they will be implemented as lists of symbols. The rule says that a given string of words ?s is a sentence if there is a string that is noun phrase and one that is a verb phrase, and if they can be concatenated to form ?s. Logically, this is fine, and it would work as a program to generate random sentences. However, it is a very inefficient program for parsing sentences. It will consider all possible noun phrases and verb phrases, without regard to the input words. Only when it gets to the concat goal (defined on page 411) will it test to see if the two constituents can be concatenated together to make up the input string. Thus, a better order of evaluation for parsing is:

```
(<- (S ?s)
    (concat ?np ?vp ?s)
    (NP ?np)
    (VP ?vp))
```

The first version had NP and VP guessing strings to be verified by concat. In most grammars, there will be a very large or infinite number of NPs and VPs. This second version has concat guessing strings to be verified by NP and VP. If there are n words in the sentence, then concat can only make $n + 1$ guesses, quite an improvement. However, it would be better still if we could in effect have concat and NP work together to make a more constrained guess, which would then be verified by VP.

We have seen this type of problem before. In Lisp, the answer is to return multiple values. NP would be a function that takes a string as input and returns two values: an indication of success or failure, and a remainder string of words that have not yet been parsed. When the first value indicates success, then VP would be called with the remaining string as input. In Prolog, return values are just extra arguments. So each predicate will have two parameters: an input string and a remainder string. Following the usual Prolog convention, the output parameter comes after the input. In this approach, no calls to concat are necessary, no wild guesses are made, and Prolog's backtracking takes care of the necessary guessing:

```
(<- (S ?s0 ?s2)
    (NP ?s0 ?s1)
    (VP ?s1 ?s2))
```

This rule can be read as "The string from s_0 to s_2 is a sentence if there is an s_1 such that the string from s_0 to s_1 is a noun phrase and the string from s_1 to s_2 is a verb phrase."

A sample query would be (?- (S (The boy ate the apple) ())). With suitable definitions of NP and VP, this would succeed, with the following bindings holding within S:

```
?s0 = (The boy ate the apple)
?s1 =         (ate the apple)
?s2 =                      ()
```

Another way of reading the goal (NP ?s0 ?s1), for example, is as "IS the list ?s0 minus the list ?s1 a noun phrase?" In this case, ?s0 minus ?s1 is the list (The boy). The combination of two arguments, an input list and an output list, is often called a *difference list*, to emphasize this interpretation. More generally, the combination of an input parameter and output parameter is called an *accumulator*. Accumulators, particularly difference lists, are an important technique throughout logic programming and are also used in functional programming, as we saw on page 63.

In our rule for S, the concatenation of difference lists was implicit. If we prefer, we could define a version of concat for difference lists and call it explicitly:

```
(<- (S ?s-in ?s-rem)
    (NP ?np-in ?np-rem)
    (VP ?vp-in ?vp-rem)
    (concat ?np-in ?np-rem ?vp-in ?vp-rem ?s-in ?s-rem))

(<- (concat ?a ?b  ?b ?c  ?a ?c))
```

Because this version of concat has a different arity than the old version, they can safely coexist. It states the difference list equation $(a - b) + (b - c) = (a - c)$.

In the last chapter we stated that context-free phrase-structure grammar is inconvenient for expressing things like agreement between the subject and predicate of a sentence. With the Horn-clause-based grammar formalism we are developing here, we can add an argument to the predicates NP and VP to represent agreement. In English, the agreement rule does not have a big impact. For all verbs except *be*, the difference only shows up in the third-person singular of the present tense:

	Singular	Plural
first person	I sleep	we sleep
second person	you sleep	you sleep
third person	he/she sleeps	they sleep

Thus, the agreement argument will take on one of the two values 3sg or ~3sg to indicate third-person-singular or not-third-person-singular. We could write:

```
(<- (S ?s0 ?s2)
    (NP ?agr ?s0 ?s1)
    (VP ?agr ?s1 ?s2))

(<- (NP 3sg (he . ?s) ?s))
(<- (NP ~3sg (they . ?s) ?s))

(<- (VP 3sg (sleeps . ?s) ?s))
(<- (VP ~3sg (sleep . ?s) ?s))
```

This grammar parses just the right sentences:

```
> (?- (S (He sleeps) ()))
Yes.
> (?- (S (He sleep) ()))
No.
```

Let's extend the grammar to allow common nouns as well as pronouns:

```
(<- (NP ?agr ?s0 ?s2)
    (Det ?agr ?s0 ?s1)
    (N ?agr ?s1 ?s2))

(<- (Det ?any (the . ?s) ?s))
(<- (N 3sg (boy . ?s) ?s))
(<- (N 3sg (girl . ?s) ?s))
```

The same grammar rules can be used to generate sentences as well as parse. Here are all possible sentences in this trivial grammar:

```
> (?- (S ?words ()))
?WORDS = (HE SLEEPS);
?WORDS = (THEY SLEEP);
?WORDS = (THE BOY SLEEPS);
?WORDS = (THE GIRL SLEEPS);
No.
```

So far all we have is a recognizer: a predicate that can separate sentences from nonsentences. But we can add another argument to each predicate to build up the semantics. The result is not just a recognizer but a true parser:

```
(<- (S (?pred ?subj) ?s0 ?s2)
    (NP ?agr ?subj ?s0 ?s1)
    (VP ?agr ?pred ?s1 ?s2))

(<- (NP 3sg (the male) (he . ?s) ?s))
(<- (NP ~3sg (some objects) (they . ?s) ?s))

(<- (NP ?agr (?det ?n) ?s0 ?s2)
    (Det ?agr ?det ?s0 ?s1)
    (N ?agr ?n ?s1 ?s2))

(<- (VP 3sg sleep (sleeps . ?s) ?s))
(<- (VP ~3sg sleep (sleep . ?s) ?s))

(<- (Det ?any the (the . ?s) ?s))
(<- (N 3sg (young male human) (boy . ?s) ?s))
(<- (N 3sg (young female human) (girl . ?s) ?s))
```

The semantic translations of individual words is a bit capricious. In fact, it is not too important at this point if the translation of *boy* is (young male human) or just boy. There are two properties of a semantic representation that are important. First, it should be unambiguous. The representation of *orange* the fruit should be different from *orange* the color (although the representation of the fruit might well refer to the color, or vice versa). Second, it should express generalities, or allow them to be expressed elsewhere. So either *sleep* and *sleeps* should have the same or similar representation, or there should be an inference rule relating them. Similarly, if the representation of *boy* does not say so explicitly, there should be some other rule saying that a boy is a male and a human.

Once the semantics of individual words is decided, the semantics of higher-level categories (sentences and noun phrases) is easy. In this grammar, the semantics of a sentence is the application of the predicate (the verb phrase) to the subject (the noun phrase). The semantics of a compound noun phrase is the application of the determiner to the noun.

This grammar returns the semantic interpretation but does not build a syntactic tree. The syntactic structure is implicit in the sequence of goals: S calls NP and VP, and NP can call Det and N. If we want to make this explicit, we can provide yet another argument to each nonterminal:

```
(<- (S (?pred ?subj) (s ?np ?vp) ?s0 ?s2)
    (NP ?agr ?subj ?np ?s0 ?s1)
    (VP ?agr ?pred ?vp ?s1 ?s2))

(<- (NP 3sg (the male) (np he) (he . ?s) ?s))
(<- (NP ~3sg (some objects) (np they) (they . ?s) ?s))
```

```
(<- (NP ?agr (?det ?n) (np ?det-syn ?n-syn) ?s0 ?s2)
    (Det ?agr ?det ?det-syn ?s0 ?s1)
    (N ?agr ?n ?n-syn ?s1 ?s2))

(<- (VP 3sg sleep (vp sleeps)(sleeps . ?s) ?s))
(<- (VP ~3sg sleep (vp sleep)(sleep . ?s) ?s))

(<- (Det ?any the (det the)(the . ?s) ?s))
(<- (N 3sg (young male human) (n boy)(boy . ?s) ?s))
(<- (N 3sg (young female human) (n girl)(girl . ?s) ?s))
```

This grammar can still be used to parse or generate sentences, or even to enumerate all syntax/semantics/sentence triplets:

```
;; Parsing:
> (?- (S ?sem ?syn (He sleeps) ()))
?SEM = (SLEEP (THE MALE))
?SYN = (S (NP HE) (VP SLEEPS)).

;; Generating:
> (?- (S (sleep (the male)) ? ?words ()))
?WORDS = (HE SLEEPS)

;; Enumerating:
> (?- (S ?sem ?syn ?words ()))
?SEM = (SLEEP (THE MALE))
?SYN = (S (NP HE) (VP SLEEPS))
?WORDS = (HE SLEEPS);

?SEM = (SLEEP (SOME OBJECTS))
?SYN = (S (NP THEY) (VP SLEEP))
?WORDS = (THEY SLEEP);

?SEM = (SLEEP (THE (YOUNG MALE HUMAN)))
?SYN = (S (NP (DET THE) (N BOY)) (VP SLEEPS))
?WORDS = (THE BOY SLEEPS);

?SEM = (SLEEP (THE (YOUNG FEMALE HUMAN)))
?SYN = (S (NP (DET THE) (N GIRL)) (VP SLEEPS))
?WORDS = (THE GIRL SLEEPS);

No.
```

20.2   Definite Clause Grammars

We now have a powerful and efficient tool for parsing sentences. However, it is getting to be a very messy tool—there are too many arguments to each goal, and it is hard to tell which arguments represent syntax, which represent semantics, which represent in/out strings, and which represent other features, like agreement. So, we will take the usual step when our bare programming language becomes messy: define a new language.

Edinburgh Prolog recognizes assertions called *definite clause grammar* (DCG) rules. The term *definite clause* is just another name for a Prolog clause, so DCGs are also called "logic grammars." They could have been called "Horn clause grammars" or "Prolog grammars" as well.

DCG rules are clauses whose main functor is an arrow, usually written `-->`. They compile into regular Prolog clauses with extra arguments. In normal DCG rules, only the string arguments are automatically added. But we will see later how this can be extended to add other arguments automatically as well.

We will implement DCG rules with the macro `rule` and an infix arrow. Thus, we want the expression:

```
(rule (S) --> (NP) (VP))
```

to expand into the clause:

```
(<- (S ?s0 ?s2)
    (NP ?s0 ?s1)
    (VP ?s1 ?s2))
```

While we're at it, we may as well give `rule` the ability to deal with different types of rules, each one represented by a different type of arrow. Here's the `rule` macro:

```
(defmacro rule (head &optional (arrow ':-) &body body)
  "Expand one of several types of logic rules into pure Prolog."
  ;; This is data-driven, dispatching on the arrow
  (funcall (get arrow 'rule-function) head body))
```

As an example of a rule function, the arrow `:-` will be used to represent normal Prolog clauses. That is, the form (rule *head* `:-` *body*) will be equivalent to (<- *head body*).

```
(setf (get ':- 'rule-function)
      #'(lambda (head body) `(<- ,head .,body)))
```

Before writing the rule function for DCG rules, there are two further features of the DCG formalism to consider. First, some goals in the body of a rule may be normal Prolog goals, and thus do not require the extra pair of arguments. In Edinburgh Prolog, such goals are surrounded in braces. One would write:

```
s(Sem) --> np(Subj), vp(Pred),
          {combine(Subj,Pred,Sem)}.
```

where the idea is that combine is not a grammatical constituent, but rather a Prolog predicate that could do some calculations on Subj and Pred to arrive at the proper semantics, Sem. We will mark such a test predicate not by brackets but by a list headed by the keyword :test, as in:

```
(rule (S ?sem) --> (NP ?subj) (VP ?pred)
  (:test (combine ?subj ?pred ?sem)))
```

Second, we need some way of introducing individual words on the right-hand side, as opposed to categories of words. In Prolog, brackets are used to represent a word or list of words on the right-hand side:

```
verb --> [sleeps].
```

We will use a list headed by the keyword :word:

```
(rule (NP (the male) 3sg) --> (:word he))
(rule (VP sleeps 3sg) --> (:word sleeps))
```

The following predicates test for these two special cases. Note that the cut is also allowed as a normal goal.

```
(defun dcg-normal-goal-p (x) (or (starts-with x :test) (eq x '!)))

(defun dcg-word-list-p (x) (starts-with x ':word))
```

At last we are in a position to present the rule function for DCG rules. The function make-dcg inserts variables to keep track of the strings that are being parsed.

```
(setf (get '--> 'rule-function) 'make-dcg)

(defun make-dcg (head body)
  (let ((n (count-if (complement #'dcg-normal-goal-p) body)))
    '(<- (,@head ?s0 ,(symbol '?s n))
       .,(make-dcg-body body 0))))
```

```
(defun make-dcg-body (body n)
  "Make the body of a Definite Clause Grammar (DCG) clause.
  Add ?string-in and -out variables to each constituent.
  Goals like (:test goal) are ordinary Prolog goals,
  and goals like (:word hello) are literal words to be parsed."
  (if (null body)
      nil
      (let ((goal (first body)))
        (cond
          ((eq goal '!) (cons '! (make-dcg-body (rest body) n)))
          ((dcg-normal-goal-p goal)
           (append (rest goal)
                   (make-dcg-body (rest body) n)))
          ((dcg-word-list-p goal)
           (cons
             `(= ,(symbol '?s n)
                 (,@(rest goal) .,(symbol '?s (+ n 1))))
             (make-dcg-body (rest body) (+ n 1))))
          (t (cons
               (append goal
                       (list (symbol '?s n)
                             (symbol '?s (+ n 1))))
               (make-dcg-body (rest body) (+ n 1)))))))))
```

> ⌨ **Exercise 20.1 [m]**   make-dcg violates one of the cardinal rules of macros. What does it do wrong? How would you fix it?

20.3   A Simple Grammar in DCG Format

Here is the trivial grammar from page 688 in DCG format.

```
(rule (S (?pred ?subj)) -->
  (NP ?agr ?subj)
  (VP ?agr ?pred))

(rule (NP ?agr (?det ?n)) -->
  (Det ?agr ?det)
  (N ?agr ?n))
```

```
(rule (NP 3sg (the male))          --> (:word he))
(rule (NP ~3sg (some objects))     --> (:word they))
(rule (VP 3sg sleep)               --> (:word sleeps))
(rule (VP ~3sg sleep)              --> (:word sleep))
(rule (Det ?any the)               --> (:word the))
(rule (N 3sg (young male human))   --> (:word boy))
(rule (N 3sg (young female human)) --> (:word girl))
```

This grammar is quite limited, generating only four sentences. The first way we will extend it is to allow verbs with objects: in addition to "The boy sleeps," we will allow "The boy meets the girl." To avoid generating ungrammatical sentences like "* The boy meets,"[1] we will separate the category of verb into two *subcategories*: transitive verbs, which take an object, and intransitive verbs, which don't.

Transitive verbs complicate the semantic interpretation of sentences. We would like the interpretation of "Terry kisses Jean" to be (kiss Terry Jean). The interpretation of the noun phrase "Terry" is just Terry, but then what should the interpretation of the verb phrase "kisses Jean" be? To fit our predicate application model, it must be something equivalent to (lambda (x) (kiss x Jean)). When applied to the subject, we want to get the simplification:

$$((lambda\ (x)\ (kiss\ x\ Jean))\ Terry) \Rightarrow (kiss\ Terry\ Jean)$$

Such simplification is not done automatically by Prolog, but we can write a predicate to do it. We will call it funcall, because it is similar to the Lisp function of that name, although it only handles replacement of the argument, not full evaluation of the body. (Technically, this is the lambda-calculus operation known as *beta-reduction*.) The predicate funcall is normally used with two input arguments, a function and its argument, and one output argument, the resulting reduction:

```
(<- (funcall (lambda (?x) ?body) ?x ?body))
```

With this we could write our rule for sentences as:

```
(rule (S ?sem) -->
  (NP ?agr ?subj)
  (VP ?agr ?pred)
  (:test (funcall ?pred ?subj ?sem)))
```

An alternative is to, in effect, compile away the call to funcall. Instead of having the semantic representation of VP be a single lambda expression, we can represent it as

---

[1] The asterisk at the start of a sentence is the standard linguistic notation for an utterance that is ungrammatical or otherwise ill-formed.

two arguments: an input argument, ?subj, which acts as a parameter to the output argument, ?pred, which takes the place of the body of the lambda expression. By explicitly manipulating the parameter and body, we can eliminate the call to funcall. The trick is to make the parameter and the subject one and the same:

```
(rule (S ?pred) -->
  (NP ?agr ?subj)
  (VP ?agr ?subj ?pred))
```

One way of reading this rule is "To parse a sentence, parse a noun phrase followed by a verb phrase. If they have different agreement features then fail, but otherwise insert the interpretation of the noun phrase, ?subj, into the proper spot in the interpretation of the verb phrase, ?pred, and return ?pred as the final interpretation of the sentence."

The next step is to write rules for verb phrases and verbs. Transitive verbs are listed under the predicate Verb/tr, and intransitive verbs are listed as Verb/intr. The semantics of tenses (past and present) has been ignored.

```
(rule (VP ?agr ?subj ?pred) -->
  (Verb/tr ?agr ?subj ?pred ?obj)
  (NP ?any-agr ?obj))

(rule (VP ?agr ?subj ?pred) -->
  (Verb/intr ?agr ?subj ?pred))

(rule (Verb/tr ~3sg ?x (kiss ?x ?y) ?y) --> (:word kiss))
(rule (Verb/tr 3sg ?x (kiss ?x ?y) ?y) --> (:word kisses))
(rule (Verb/tr ?any  ?x (kiss ?x ?y) ?y) --> (:word kissed))

(rule (Verb/intr ~3sg ?x (sleep ?x)) --> (:word sleep))
(rule (Verb/intr 3sg ?x (sleep ?x)) --> (:word sleeps))
(rule (Verb/intr ?any  ?x (sleep ?x)) --> (:word slept))
```

Here are the rules for noun phrases and nouns:

```
(rule (NP ?agr ?sem) -->
  (Name ?agr ?sem))

(rule (NP ?agr (?det-sem ?noun-sem)) -->
  (Det ?agr ?det-sem)
  (Noun ?agr ?noun-sem))

(rule (Name 3sg Terry) --> (:word Terry))
(rule (Name 3sg Jean)  --> (:word Jean))
```

```
(rule (Noun 3sg (young male human))          --> (:word boy))
(rule (Noun 3sg (young female human))        --> (:word girl))
(rule (Noun ~3sg (group (young male human)))   --> (:word boys))
(rule (Noun ~3sg (group (young female human))) --> (:word girls))

(rule (Det ?any the)  --> (:word the))
(rule (Det 3sg a) --> (:word a))
```

This grammar and lexicon generates more sentences, although it is still rather limited. Here are some examples:

```
> (?- (S ?sem (The boys kiss a girl) ()))
?SEM = (KISS (THE (GROUP (YOUNG MALE HUMAN)))
            (A (YOUNG FEMALE HUMAN))).

> (?- (S ?sem (The girls kissed the girls) ()))
?SEM = (KISS (THE (GROUP (YOUNG FEMALE HUMAN)))
            (THE (GROUP (YOUNG FEMALE HUMAN)))).

> (?- (S ?sem (Terry kissed the girl) ()))
?SEM = (KISS TERRY (THE (YOUNG FEMALE HUMAN))).

> (?- (S ?sem (The girls kisses the boys) ()))
No.

> (?- (S ?sem (Terry kissed a girls) ()))
No.

> (?- (S ?sem (Terry sleeps Jean) ()))
No.
```

The first three examples are parsed correctly, while the final three are correctly rejected. The inquisitive reader may wonder just what is going on in the interpretation of a sentence like "The girls kissed the girls." Do the subject and object represent the same group of girls, or different groups? Does everyone kiss everyone, or are there fewer kissings going on? Until we define our representation more carefully, there is no way to tell. Indeed, it seems that there is a potential problem in the representation, in that the predicate kiss sometimes has individuals as its arguments, and sometimes groups. More careful representations of "The girls kissed the girls" include the following candidates, using predicate calculus:

$$\forall x \forall y \; x \epsilon girls \wedge y \epsilon girls \Rightarrow kiss(x,y)$$
$$\forall x \forall y \; x \epsilon girls \wedge y \epsilon girls \wedge x \neq y \Rightarrow kiss(x,y)$$
$$\forall x \exists y,z \; x \epsilon girls \wedge y \epsilon girls \wedge z \epsilon girls \Rightarrow kiss(x,y) \wedge kiss(z,x)$$
$$\forall x \exists y \; x \epsilon girls \wedge y \epsilon girls \Rightarrow kiss(x,y) \vee kiss(y,x)$$

The first of these says that every girl kisses every other girl. The second says the same thing, except that a girl need not kiss herself. The third says that every girl kisses and is kissed by at least one other girl, but not necessarily all of them, and the fourth says that everbody is in on at least one kissing. None of these interpretations says anything about who "the girls" are.

Clearly, the predicate calculus representations are less ambiguous than the representation produced by the current system. On the other hand, it would be wrong to choose one of the representations arbitrarily, since in different contexts, "The girls kissed the girls" can mean different things. Maintaining ambiguity in a concise form is useful, as long as there is some way eventually to recover the proper meaning.

20.4   A DCG Grammar with Quantifiers

The problem in the representation we have been using becomes more acute when we consider other determiners, such as "every." Consider the sentence "Every picture paints a story." The preceding DCG, if given the right vocabulary, would produce the interpretation:

```
(paints (every picture) (a story))
```

This can be considered ambiguous between the following two meanings, in predicate calculus form:

$$\forall x \; picture(x) \Rightarrow \; \exists y \; story(y) \land paint(x,y)$$
$$\exists y \; story(y) \land \forall x \; picture(x) \Rightarrow \; paint(x,y)$$

The first says that for each picture, there is a story that it paints. The second says that there is a certain special story that every picture paints. The second is an unusual interpretation for this sentence, but for "Every U.S. citizen has a president," the second interpretation is perhaps the preferred one. In the next section, we will see how to produce representations that can be transformed into either interpretation. For now, it is a useful exercise to see how we could produce just the first representation above, the interpretation that is usually correct. First, we need to transcribe it into Lisp:

```
(all ?x (-> (picture ?x) (exists ?y (and (story ?y) (paint ?x ?y)))))
```

The first question is how the all and exists forms get in there. They must come from the determiners, "every" and "a." Also, it seems that all is followed by an implication arrow, ->, while exists is followed by a conjunction, and. So the determiners will have translations looking like this:

```
(rule (Det ?any ?x ?p ?q (the ?x (and ?p ?q)))     --> (:word the))
(rule (Det 3sg  ?x ?p ?q (exists ?x (and ?p ?q))) --> (:word a))
(rule (Det 3sg  ?x ?p ?q (all    ?x (-> ?p ?q)))  --> (:word every))
```

Once we have accepted these translations of the determiners, everything else follows. The formulas representing the determiners have two holes in them, ?p and ?q. The first will be filled by a predicate representing the noun, and the latter will be filled by the predicate that is being applied to the noun phrase as a whole. Notice that a curious thing is happening. Previously, translation to logical form was guided by the sentence's verb. Linguisticly, the verb expresses the main predicate, so it makes sense that the verb's logical translation should be the main part of the sentence's translation. In linguistic terms, we say that the verb is the *head* of the sentence.

With the new translations for determiners, we are in effect turning the whole process upside down. Now the subject's determiner carries the weight of the whole sentence. The determiner's interpretation is a function of two arguments; it is applied to the noun first, yielding a function of one argument, which is in turn applied to the verb phrase's interpretation. This primacy of the determiner goes against intuition, but it leads directly to the right interpretation.

The variables ?p and ?q can be considered holes to be filled in the final interpretation, but the variable ?x fills a quite different role. At the end of the parse, ?x will not be filled by anything; it will still be a variable. But it will be referred to by the expressions filling ?p and ?q. We say that ?x is a *metavariable*, because it is a variable in the representation, not a variable in the Prolog implementation. It just happens that Prolog variables can be used to implement these metavariables.

Here are the interpretations for each word in our target sentence and for each intermediate constituent:

```
Every        = (all ?x (-> ?p1 ?q1))
picture      = (picture ?x)
paints       = (paint ?x ?y)
a            = (exists ?y (and ?p2 ?q2))
story        = (story ?y)

Every picture = (all ?x (-> (picture ?x) ?q1))
a story       = (exists ?y (and (story ?y) ?q2))
paints a story = (exists ?y (and (story ?y) (paint ?x ?y)))
```

The semantics of a noun has to fill the ?p hole of a determiner, possibly using the metavariable ?x. The three arguments to the Noun predicate are the agreement, the metavariable ?x, and the assertion that the noun phrase makes about ?x:

```
(rule (Noun 3sg ?x (picture ?x)) --> (:word picture))
(rule (Noun 3sg ?x (story ?x)) --> (:word story))
(rule (Noun 3sg ?x (and (young ?x) (male ?x) (human ?x))) -->
  (:word boy))
```

The NP predicate is changed to take four arguments. First is the agreement, then the metavariable ?x. Third is a predicate that will be supplied externally, by the verb phrase. The final argument returns the interpretation of the NP as a whole. As we have stated, this comes from the determiner:

```
(rule (NP ?agr ?x ?pred ?pred) -->
  (Name ?agr ?name))
;(rule (NP ?agr ?x ?pred ?np) -->
;  (Det ?agr ?x ?noun ?pred ?np)
;  (Noun ?agr ?x ?noun))
```

The rule for an NP with determiner is commented out because it is convenient to introduce an extended rule to replace it at this point. The new rule accounts for certain relative clauses, such as "the boy that paints a picture":

```
(rule (NP ?agr ?x ?pred ?np) -->
  (Det ?agr ?x ?noun&rel ?pred ?np)
  (Noun ?agr ?x ?noun)
  (rel-clause ?agr ?x ?noun ?noun&rel))
(rule (rel-clause ?agr ?x ?np ?np) --> )
(rule (rel-clause ?agr ?x ?np (and ?np ?rel)) -->
  (:word that)
  (VP ?agr ?x ?rel))
```

The new rule does not account for relative clauses where the object is missing, such as "the picture that the boy paints." Nevertheless, the addition of relative clauses means we can now generate an infinite language, since we can always introduce a relative clause, which introduces a new noun phrase, which in turn can introduce yet another relative clause.

The rules for relative clauses are not complicated, but they can be difficult to understand. Of the four arguments to rel-clause, the first two hold the agreement features of the head noun and the metavariable representing the head noun. The last two arguments are used together as an accumulator for predications about the metavariable: the third argument holds the predications made so far, and the fourth will hold the predications including the relative clause. So, the first rule for rel-clause says that if there is no relative clause, then what goes in to the accumulator is the same as what goes out. The second rule says that what goes out is the conjunction of what comes in and what is predicated in the relative clause itself.

Verbs apply to either one or two metavariables, just as they did before. So we can use the definitions of Verb/tr and Verb/intr unchanged. For variety, I've added a few more verbs:

```
(rule (Verb/tr ~3sg ?x ?y (paint ?x ?y)) --> (:word paint))
(rule (Verb/tr 3sg  ?x ?y (paint ?x ?y)) --> (:word paints))
(rule (Verb/tr ?any ?x ?y (paint ?x ?y)) --> (:word painted))

(rule (Verb/intr ~3sg ?x (sleep ?x)) --> (:word sleep))
(rule (Verb/intr 3sg  ?x (sleep ?x)) --> (:word sleeps))
(rule (Verb/intr ?any ?x (sleep ?x)) --> (:word slept))

(rule (Verb/intr 3sg  ?x (sells ?x)) --> (:word sells))
(rule (Verb/intr 3sg  ?x (stinks ?x)) --> (:word stinks))
```

Verb phrases and sentences are almost as before. The only difference is in the call to NP, which now has extra arguments:

```
(rule (VP ?agr ?x ?vp) -->
  (Verb/tr ?agr ?x ?obj ?verb)
  (NP ?any-agr ?obj ?verb ?vp))

(rule (VP ?agr ?x ?vp) -->
  (Verb/intr ?agr ?x ?vp))

(rule (S ?np) -->
  (NP ?agr ?x ?vp ?np)
  (VP ?agr ?x ?vp))
```

With this grammar, we get the following correspondence between sentences and logical forms:

```
Every picture paints a story.
(ALL ?3 (-> (PICTURE ?3)
           (EXISTS ?14 (AND (STORY ?14) (PAINT ?3 ?14))))))

Every boy that paints a picture sleeps.
(ALL ?3 (-> (AND (AND (YOUNG ?3) (MALE ?3) (HUMAN ?3))
                (EXISTS ?19 (AND (PICTURE ?19)
                                (PAINT ?3 ?19))))
           (SLEEP ?3)))

Every boy that sleeps paints a picture.
(ALL ?3 (-> (AND (AND (YOUNG ?3) (MALE ?3) (HUMAN ?3))
                (SLEEP ?3))
           (EXISTS ?22 (AND (PICTURE ?22) (PAINT ?3 ?22))))))
```

```
Every boy that paints a picture that sells
paints a picture that stinks.
(ALL ?3 (-> (AND (AND (YOUNG ?3) (MALE ?3) (HUMAN ?3))
                 (EXISTS ?19 (AND (AND (PICTURE ?19) (SELLS ?19))
                                  (PAINT ?3 ?19))))
            (EXISTS ?39 (AND (AND (PICTURE ?39) (STINKS ?39))
                             (PAINT ?3 ?39)))))
```

20.5   Preserving Quantifier Scope Ambiguity

Consider the simple sentence "Every man loves a woman." This sentence is ambiguous between the following two interpretations:

$\forall m \exists w$ man(m) $\wedge$ woman(w) $\wedge$ loves(m,w)
$\exists w \forall m$ man(m) $\wedge$ woman(w) $\wedge$ loves(m,w)

The first interpretation is that every man loves some woman—his wife, perhaps. The second interpretation is that there is a certain woman whom every man loves—Natassja Kinski, perhaps. The meaning of the sentence is ambiguous, but the structure is not; there is only one syntactic parse.

In the last section, we presented a parser that would construct one of the two interpretations. In this section, we show how to construct a single interpretation that preserves the ambiguity, but can be disambiguated by a postsyntactic process. The basic idea is to construct an intermediate logical form that leaves the scope of quantifiers unspecified. This intermediate form can then be rearranged to recover the final interpretation.

To recap, here is the interpretation we would get for "Every man loves a woman," given the grammar in the previous section:

```
(all ?m (-> (man ?m) (exists ?w (and (woman ?w) (loves ?m ?w)))))
```

We will change the grammar to produce instead the intermediate form:

```
(and (all ?m (man ?m))
     (exists ?w (wowan ?w))
     (loves ?m ?w))
```

The difference is that logical components are produced in smaller chunks, with unscoped quantifiers. The typical grammar rule will build up an interpretation by conjoining constituents with and, rather than by fitting pieces into holes in other pieces. Here is the complete grammar and a just-large-enough lexicon in the new format:

```
(rule (S (and ?np ?vp)) -->
  (NP ?agr ?x ?np)
  (VP ?agr ?x ?vp))

(rule (VP ?agr ?x (and ?verb ?obj)) -->
  (Verb/tr ?agr ?x ?o ?verb)
  (NP ?any-agr ?o ?obj))

(rule (VP ?agr ?x ?verb) -->
  (Verb/intr ?agr ?x ?verb))

(rule (NP ?agr ?name t) -->
  (Name ?agr ?name))

(rule (NP ?agr ?x ?det) -->
  (Det ?agr ?x (and ?noun ?rel) ?det)
  (Noun ?agr ?x ?noun)
  (rel-clause ?agr ?x ?rel))

(rule (rel-clause ?agr ?x t) --> )
(rule (rel-clause ?agr ?x ?rel) -->
  (:word that)
  (VP ?agr ?x ?rel))

(rule (Name 3sg Terry)                        --> (:word Terry))
(rule (Name 3sg Jean)                         --> (:word Jean))
(rule (Det 3sg  ?x ?restr (all ?x ?restr)) --> (:word every))
(rule (Noun 3sg ?x (man ?x))                  --> (:word man))
(rule (Verb/tr 3sg ?x ?y (love ?x ?y))    --> (:word loves))
(rule (Verb/intr 3sg ?x (lives ?x))       --> (:word lives))
(rule (Det 3sg  ?x ?res (exists ?x ?res))  --> (:word a))
(rule (Noun 3sg ?x (woman ?x))                --> (:word woman))
```

This gives us the following parse for "Every man loves a woman":

```
(and (all ?4 (and (man ?4) t))
     (and (love ?4 ?12) (exists ?12 (and (woman ?12) t))))
```

If we simplified this, eliminating the ts and joining ands, we would get the desired representation:

```
(and (all ?m (man ?m))
     (exists ?w (wowan ?w))
     (loves ?m ?w))
```

From there, we could use what we know about syntax, in addition to what we know about men, woman, and loving, to determine the most likely final interpretation. This will be covered in the next chapter.

20.6   Long-Distance Dependencies

So far, every syntactic phenomena we have considered has been expressible in a rule that imposes constraints only at a single level. For example, we had to impose the constraint that a subject agree with its verb, but this constraint involved two immediate constituents of a sentence, the noun phrase and verb phrase. We didn't need to express a constraint between, say, the subject and a modifier of the verb's object. However, there are linguistic phenomena that require just these kinds of constraints.

Our rule for relative clauses was a very simple one: a relative clause consists of the word "that" followed by a sentence that is missing its subject, as in "every man that loves a woman." Not all relative clauses follow this pattern. It is also possible to form a relative clause by omitting the object of the embedded sentence: "every man that a woman loves ⊔." In this sentence, the symbol ⊔ indicates a gap, which is understood as being filled by the head of the complete noun phrase, the man. This has been called a *filler-gap dependency*. It is also known as a *long-distance dependency*, because the gap can occur arbitrarily far from the filler. For example, all of the following are valid noun phrases:

> The person that Lee likes ⊔
> The person that Kim thinks Lee likes ⊔
> The person that Jan says Kim thinks Lee likes ⊔

In each case, the gap is filled by the head noun, the person. But any number of relative clauses can intervene between the head noun and the gap.

The same kind of filler-gap dependency takes place in questions that begin with "who," "what," "where," and other interrogative pronouns. For example, we can ask a question about the subject of a sentence, as in "Who likes Lee?", or about the object, as in "Who does Kim like ⊔?"

Here is a grammar that covers relative clauses with gapped subjects or objects. The rules for S, VP, and NP are augmented with a pair of arguments representing an accumulator for gaps. Like a difference list, the first argument minus the second represents the presence or absence of a gap. For example, in the first two rules for noun phrases, the two arguments are the same, ?g0 and ?g0. This means that the rule as a whole has no gap, since there can be no difference between the two arguments. In the third rule for NP, the first argument is of the form (gap ...), and the second is nogap. This means that the right-hand side of the rule, an empty constituent, can be parsed as a gap. (Note that if we had been using true difference lists, the two arguments would be ((gap ...) ?g0) and ?g0. But since we are only dealing with one gap per rule, we don't need true difference lists.)

The rule for S says that a noun phrase with gap ?g0 minus ?g1 followed by a verb phrase with gap ?g1 minus ?g2 comprise a sentence with gap ?g0 minus ?g2. The rule for relative clauses finds a sentence with a gap anywhere; either in the subject position or embedded somewhere in the verb phrase. Here's the complete grammar:

```
(rule (S ?g0 ?g2 (and ?np ?vp)) -->
  (NP ?g0 ?g1 ?agr ?x ?np)
  (VP ?g1 ?g2 ?agr ?x ?vp))

(rule (VP ?g0 ?g1 ?agr ?x (and ?obj ?verb)) -->
  (Verb/tr ?agr ?x ?o ?verb)
  (NP ?g0 ?g1 ?any-agr ?o ?obj))

(rule (VP ?g0 ?g0 ?agr ?x ?verb) -->
  (Verb/intr ?agr ?x ?verb))

(rule (NP ?g0 ?g0 ?agr ?name t) -->
  (Name ?agr ?name))

(rule (NP ?g0 ?g0 ?agr ?x ?det) -->
  (Det ?agr ?x (and ?noun ?rel) ?det)
  (Noun ?agr ?x ?noun)
  (rel-clause ?agr ?x ?rel))

(rule (NP (gap NP ?agr ?x) nogap ?agr ?x t) --> )

(rule (rel-clause ?agr ?x t) --> )

(rule (rel-clause ?agr ?x ?rel) -->
  (:word that)
  (S (gap NP ?agr ?x) nogap ?rel))
```

Here are some sentence/parse pairs covered by this grammar:

```
Every man that ⊔ loves a woman likes a person.
(AND (ALL ?28 (AND (MAN ?28)
                   (AND T (AND (LOVE ?28 ?30)
                              (EXISTS ?30 (AND (WOMAN ?30)
                                              T))))))
     (AND (EXISTS ?39 (AND (PERSON ?39) T)) (LIKE ?28 ?39)))

Every man that a woman loves ⊔ likes a person.
(AND (ALL ?37 (AND (MAN ?37)
                   (AND (EXISTS ?20 (AND (WOMAN ?20) T))
                        (AND T (LOVE ?20 ?37)))))
     (AND (EXISTS ?39 (AND (PERSON ?39) T)) (LIKE ?37 ?39)))
```

```
Every man that loves a bird that ⊔flies likes a person.
(AND (ALL ?28 (AND (MAN ?28)
                    (AND T (AND (EXISTS ?54
                                  (AND (BIRD ?54)
                                        (AND T (FLY ?54))))
                            (LOVE ?28 ?54)))))
        (AND (EXISTS ?60 (AND (PERSON ?60) T)) (LIKE ?28 ?60)))
```

Actually, there are limitations on the situations in which gaps can appear. In particular, it is rare to have a gap in the subject of a sentence, except in the case of a relative clause. In the next chapter, we will see how to impose additional constraints on gaps.

20.7   Augmenting DCG Rules

In the previous section, we saw how to build up a semantic representation of a sentence by conjoining the semantics of the components. One problem with this approach is that the semantic interpretation is often something of the form (and (and t *a*) *b*), when we would prefer (and *a b*). There are two ways to correct this problem: either we add a step that takes the final semantic interpretation and simplifies it, or we complicate each individual rule, making it generate the simplified form. The second choice would be slightly more efficient, but would be very ugly and error prone. We should be doing all we can to make the rules simpler, not more complicated; that is the whole point of the DCG formalism. This suggests a third approach: change the rule interpreter so that it automatically generates the semantic interpretation as a conjunction of the constituents, unless the rule explicitly says otherwise. This section shows how to augment the DCG rules to handle common cases like this automatically.

Consider again a rule from section 20.4:

```
(rule (S (and ?np ?vp)) -->
  (NP ?agr ?x ?np)
  (VP ?agr ?x ?vp))
```

If we were to alter this rule to produce a simplified semantic interpretation, it would look like the following, where the predicate and* simplifies a list of conjunctions into a single conjunction:

```
(rule (S ?sem) -->
 (np ?agr ?x ?np)
 (vp ?agr ?x ?vp)
 (:test (and* (?np ?vp) ?sem)))
```

Many rules will have this form, so we adopt a simple convention: if the last argument of the constituent on the left-hand side of a rule is the keyword :sem, then we will build the semantics by replacing :sem with a conjunction formed by combining all the last arguments of the constituents on the right-hand side of the rule. A ==> arrow will be used for rules that follow this convention, so the following rule is equivalent to the one above:

```
(rule (S :sem) ==>
 (NP ?agr ?x ?np)
 (VP ?agr ?x ?vp))
```

It is sometimes useful to introduce additional semantics that does not come from one of the constituents. This can be indicated with an element of the right-hand side that is a list starting with :sem. For example, the following rule adds to the semantics the fact that ?x is the topic of the sentence:

```
(rule (S :sem) ==>
 (NP ?agr ?x ?np)
 (VP ?agr ?x ?vp)
 (:sem (topic ?x)))
```

Before implementing the rule function for the ==> arrow, it is worth considering if there are other ways we could make things easier for the rule writer. One possibility is to provide a notation for describing examples. Examples make it easier to understand what a rule is designed for. For the S rule, we could add examples like this:

```
(rule (S :sem) ==>
 (:ex "John likes Mary" "He sleeps")
 (NP ?agr ?x ?np)
 (VP ?agr ?x ?vp))
```

These examples not only serve as documentation for the rule but also can be stored under S and subsequently run when we want to test if S is in fact implemented properly.

Another area where the rule writer could use help is in handling left-recursive rules. Consider the rule that says that a sentence can consist of two sentences joined by a conjunction:

```
(rule (S (?conj ?s1 ?s2)) ==>
  (:ex "John likes Mary and Mary likes John")
  (S ?s1)
  (Conj ?conj)
  (S ?s2))
```

While this rule is correct as a declarative statement, it will run into difficulty when run by the standard top-down depth-first DCG interpretation process. The top-level goal of parsing an S will lead immediately to the subgoal of parsing an S, and the result will be an infinite loop.

Fortunately, we know how to avoid this kind of infinite loop: split the offending predicate, S, into two predicates: one that supports the recursion, and one that is at a lower level. We will call the lower-level predicate S_. Thus, the following rule says that a sentence can consist of two sentences, where the first one is not conjoined and the second is possibly conjoined:

```
(rule (S (?conj ?s1 ?s2)) ==>
  (S_ ?s1)
  (Conj ?conj)
  (S ?s2))
```

We also need a rule that says that a possibly conjoined sentence can consist of a nonconjoined sentence:

```
(rule (S ?sem) ==> (S_ ?sem))
```

To make this work, we need to replace any mention of S in the left-hand side of a rule with S_. References to S in the right-hand side of rules remain unchanged.

```
(rule (S_ ?sem) ==> ...)
```

To make this all automatic, we will provide a macro, conj-rule, that declares a category to be one that can be conjoined. Such a declaration will automatically generate the recursive and nonrecursive rules for the category, and will insure that future references to the category on the left-hand side of a rule will be replaced with the corresponding lower-level predicate.

One problem with this approach is that it imposes a right-branching parse on multiple conjoined phrases. That is, we will get parses like "spaghetti and (meatballs and salad)" not "(spaghetti and meatballs) and salad." Clearly, that is the wrong interpretation for this sentence. Still, it can be argued that it is best to produce a single canonical parse, and then let the semantic interpretation functions worry about rearranging the parse in the right order. We will not attempt to resolve this debate but will provide the automatic conjunction mechanism as a tool that can be convenient but has no cost for the user who prefers a different solution.

We are now ready to implement the extended DCG rule formalism that handles :sem, :ex, and automatic conjunctions. The function make-augmented-dcg, stored under the arrow ==>, will be used to implement the formalism:

```lisp
(setf (get '==> 'rule-function) 'make-augmented-dcg)

(defun make-augmented-dcg (head body)
  "Build an augmented DCG rule that handles :sem, :ex,
  and automatic conjunctiontive constituents."
  (if (eq (last1 head) :sem)
      ;; Handle :sem
      (let* ((?sem (gensym "?SEM")))
        (make-augmented-dcg
          '(,@(butlast head) ,?sem)
          '(,@(remove :sem body :key #'first-or-nil)
            (:test ,(collect-sems body ?sem)))))
      ;; Separate out examples from body
      (multiple-value-bind (exs new-body)
          (partition-if #'(lambda (x) (starts-with x :ex)) body)
        ;; Handle conjunctions
        (let ((rule '(rule ,(handle-conj head) --> ,@new-body)))
          (if (null exs)
              rule
              '(progn (:ex ,head .,(mappend #'rest exs))
                      ,rule))))))
```

First we show the code that collects together the semantics of each constituent and conjoins them when :sem is specified. The function collect-sems picks out the semantics and handles the trivial cases where there are zero or one constituents on the right-hand side. If there are more than one, it inserts a call to the predicate and*.

```lisp
(defun collect-sems (body ?sem)
  "Get the semantics out of each constituent in body,
  and combine them together into ?sem."
  (let ((sems (loop for goal in body
                    unless (or (dcg-normal-goal-p goal)
                               (dcg-word-list-p goal)
                               (starts-with goal :ex)
                               (atom goal))
                    collect (last1 goal))))
    (case (length sems)
      (0 '(= ,?sem t))
      (1 '(= ,?sem ,(first sems)))
      (t '(and* ,sems ,?sem)))))
```

We could have implemented and* with Prolog clauses, but it is slightly more efficient to do it directly in Lisp. A call to conjuncts collects all the conjuncts, and we then add an and if necessary:

```
(defun and*/2 (in out cont)
  "IN is a list of conjuncts that are conjoined into OUT."
  ;; E.g.: (and* (t (and a b) t (and c d) t) ?x) ==>
  ;;          ?x = (and a b c d)
  (if (unify! out (maybe-add 'and (conjuncts (cons 'and in)) t))
      (funcall cont)))

(defun conjuncts (exp)
  "Get all the conjuncts from an expression."
  (deref exp)
  (cond ((eq exp t) nil)
        ((atom exp) (list exp))
        ((eq (deref (first exp)) 'nil) nil)
        ((eq (first exp) 'and)
         (mappend #'conjuncts (rest exp)))
        (t (list exp))))
```

The next step is handling example phrases. The code in make-augmented-dcg turns examples into expressions of the form:

```
(:ex (S ?sem) "John likes Mary" "He sleeps")
```

To make this work, :ex will have to be a macro:

```
(defmacro :ex ((category . args) &body examples)
  "Add some example phrases, indexed under the category."
  '(add-examples ',category ',args ',examples))
```

:ex calls add-examples to do all the work. Each example is stored in a hash table indexed under the the category. Each example is transformed into a two-element list: the example phrase string itself and a call to the proper predicate with all arguments supplied. The function add-examples does this transformation and indexing, and run-examples retrieves the examples stored under a category, prints each phrase, and calls each goal. The auxiliary functions get-examples and clear-examples are provided to manipulate the example table, and remove-punction, punctuation-p and string->list are used to map from a string to a list of words.

```
(defvar *examples* (make-hash-table :test #'eq))

(defun get-examples (category) (gethash category *examples*))

(defun clear-examples () (clrhash *examples*))
```

```
(defun add-examples (category args examples)
  "Add these example strings to this category,
  and when it comes time to run them, use the args."
  (dolist (example examples)
    (when (stringp example)
      (let ((ex '(,example
                   (,category ,@args
                    ,(string->list
                       (remove-punctuation example)) ()))))
        (unless (member ex (get-examples category)
                        :test #'equal)
          (setf (gethash category *examples*)
                (nconc (get-examples category) (list ex)))))))))

(defun run-examples (&optional category)
  "Run all the example phrases stored under a category.
  With no category, run ALL the examples."
  (prolog-compile-symbols)
  (if (null category)
      (maphash #'(lambda (cat val)
                   (declare (ignore val))
                   (format t "~2&Examples of ~a:~&" cat)
                   (run-examples cat))
               *examples*)
      (dolist (example (get-examples category))
        (format t "~2&EXAMPLE: ~{~a~&~9T~a~}" example)
        (top-level-prove (cdr example)))))

(defun remove-punctuation (string)
  "Replace punctuation with spaces in string."
  (substitute-if #\space #'punctuation-p string))

(defun string->list (string)
  "Convert a string to a list of words."
  (read-from-string (concatenate 'string "(" string ")")))

(defun punctuation-p (char) (find char "*_.,;:`!?#-()\\\"\""))
```

The final part of our augmented DCG formalism is handling conjunctive constituents automatically. We already arranged to translate category symbols on the left-hand side of rules into the corresponding conjunctive category, as specified by the function handle-conj. We also want to generate automatically (or as easily as possible) rules of the following form:

```
(rule (S (?conj ?s1 ?s2)) ==>
  (S_ ?s1)
  (Conj ?conj)
  (S ?s2))
```

```
(rule (S ?sem) ==> (S_ ?sem))
```

But before we generate these rules, let's make sure they are exactly what we want. Consider parsing a nonconjoined sentence with these two rules in place. The first rule would parse the entire sentence as a S_, and would then fail to see a Conj, and thus fail. The second rule would then duplicate the entire parsing process, thus doubling the amount of time taken. If we changed the order of the two rules we would be able to parse nonconjoined sentences quickly, but would have to backtrack on conjoined sentences.

The following shows a better approach. A single rule for S parses a sentence with S_, and then calls Conj_S, which can be read as "either a conjunction followed by a sentence, or nothing." If the first sentence is followed by nothing, then we just use the semantics of the first sentence; if there is a conjunction, we have to form a combined semantics. I have added ... to show where arguments to the predicate other than the semantic argument fit in.

```
(rule (S ... ?s-combined) ==>
  (S_ ... ?sem1)
  (Conj_S ?sem1 ?s-combined))

(rule (Conj_S ?sem1 (?conj ?sem1 ?sem2)) ==>
  (Conj ?conj)
  (S ... ?sem2))

(rule (Conj_S ?sem1 ?sem1) ==>)
```

Now all we need is a way for the user to specify that these three rules are desired. Since the exact method of building up the combined semantics and perhaps even the call to Conj may vary depending on the specifics of the grammar being defined, the rules cannot be generated entirely automatically. We will settle for a macro, conj-rule, that looks very much like the second of the three rules above but expands into all three, plus code to relate S_ to S. So the user will type:

```
(conj-rule (Conj_S ?sem1 (?conj ?sem1 ?sem2)) ==>
  (Conj ?conj)
  (S ?a ?b ?c ?sem2))
```

Here is the macro definition:

```
(defmacro conj-rule ((conj-cat sem1 combined-sem) ==>
                      conj (cat . args))
  "Define this category as an automatic conjunction."
  `(progn
    (setf (get ',cat 'conj-cat) ',(symbol cat '_))
```

```
(rule (,cat ,@(butlast args) ?combined-sem) ==>
  (,(symbol cat '_) ,@(butlast args) ,sem1)
  (,conj-cat ,sem1 ?combined-sem))
(rule (,conj-cat ,sem1 ,combined-sem) ==>
  ,conj
  (,cat ,@args))
(rule (,conj-cat ?sem1 ?sem1) ==>)))
```

and here we define handle-conj to substitute S_ for S in the left-hand side of rules:

```
(defun handle-conj (head)
  "Replace (Cat ...) with (Cat_ ...) if Cat is declared
  as a conjunctive category."
  (if (and (listp head) (conj-category (predicate head)))
    (cons (conj-category (predicate head)) (args head))
    head))

(defun conj-category (predicate)
  "If this is a conjunctive predicate, return the Cat_ symbol."
  (get predicate 'conj-category))
```

20.8   History and References

As we have mentioned, Alain Colmerauer invented Prolog to use in his grammar of French (1973). His *metamorphosis grammar* formalism was more expressive but much less efficient than the standard DCG formalism.

The grammar in section 20.4 is essentially the same as the one presented in Fernando Pereira and David H. D. Warren's 1980 paper, which introduced the Definite Clause Grammar formalism as it is known today. The two developed a much more substantial grammar and used it in a very influential question-answering system called Chat-80 (Warren and Pereira, 1982). Pereira later teamed with Stuart Shieber on an excellent book covering logic grammars in more depth: *Prolog and Natural-Language Analysis* (1987). The book has many strong points, but unfortunately it does not present a grammar anywhere near as complete as the Chat-80 grammar.

The idea of a compositional semantics based on mathematical logic owes much to the work of the late linguist Richard Montague. The introduction by Dowty, Wall, and Peters (1981) and the collection by Rich Thomason (1974) cover Montague's approach.

The grammar in section 20.5 is based loosely on Michael McCord's modular logic grammar, as presented in Walker et al. 1990.

It should be noted that logic grammars are by no means the only approach to natural language processing. Woods (1970) presents an approach based on the *augmented transition network*, or ATN. A transition network is like a context-free grammar. The *augmentation* is a way of manipulating features and semantic values. This is just like the extra arguments in DCGs, except that the basic operations are setting and testing variables rather than unification. So the choice between ATNs and DCGs is largely a matter of what programming approach you are most comfortable with: procedural for ATNs and declarative for DCGs. My feeling is that unification is a more suitable primitive than assignment, so I chose to present DCGs, even though this required bringing in Prolog's backtracking and unification mechanisms.

In either approach, the same linguistic problems must be addressed—agreement, long-distance dependencies, topicalization, quantifier-scope ambiguity, and so on. Comparing Woods's (1970) ATN grammar to Pereira and Warren's (1980) DCG grammar, the careful reader will see that the solutions have much in common. The analysis is more important than the notation, as it should be.

20.9   Exercises

Exercise 20.2 [m]   Modify the grammar (from section 20.4, 20.5, or 20.6) to allow for adjectives before a noun.

Exercise 20.3 [m]   Modify the grammar to allow for prepositional phrase modifiers on verb and noun phrases.

Exercise 20.4 [m]   Modify the grammar to allow for ditransitive verbs—verbs that take two objects, as in "give the dog a bone."

Exercise 20.5   Suppose we wanted to adopt the Prolog convention of writing DCG tests and words in brackets and braces, respectively. Write a function that will alter the readtable to work this way.

Exercise 20.6 [m]   Define a rule function for a new type of DCG rule that automatically builds up a syntactic parse of the input. For example, the two rules:

```
(rule (s) => (np) (vp))
(rule (np) => (:word he))
```

should be equivalent to:

```
(rule (s (s ?1 ?2)) --> (np ?1) (vp ?2))
(rule (np (np he)) --> (:word he))
```

Exercise 20.7 [m]   There are advantages and disadvantages to the approach that Prolog takes in dividing predicates into clauses. The advantage is that it is easy to add a new clause. The disadvantage is that it is hard to alter an existing clause. If you edit a clause and then evaluate it, the new clause will be added to the end of the clause list, when what you really wanted was for the new clause to take the place of the old one. To achieve that effect, you have to call clear-predicate, and then reload all the clauses, not just the one that has been changed.

Write a macro named-rule that is just like rule, except that it attaches names to clauses. When a named rule is reloaded, it replaces the old clause rather than adding a new one.

Exercise 20.8 [h]   Extend the DCG rule function to allow or goals in the right-hand side. To make this more useful, also allow and goals. For example:

```
(rule (A) --> (B) (or (C) (and (D) (E))) (F))
```

should compile into the equivalent of:

```
(<- (A ?S0 ?S4)
    (B ?S0 ?S1)
    (OR (AND (C ?S1 ?S2) (= ?S2 ?S3))
        (AND (D ?S1 ?S2) (E ?S2 ?S3)))
    (F ?S3 ?S4))
```

20.10   Answers

Answer 20.1   It uses local variables (?s0, ?s1 ...) that are not guaranteed to be unique. This is a problem if the grammar writer wants to use these symbols anywhere in his or her rules. The fix is to gensym symbols that are guaranteed to be unique.

Answer 20.5

```lisp
(defun setup-braces (&optional (on? t) (readtable *readtable*))
  "Make [a b] read as (:word a b) and {a b} as (:test a b c)
   if ON? is true; otherwise revert {[]} to normal."
  (if (not on?)
      (map nil #'(lambda (c)
                   (set-macro-character c (get-macro-character #\a)
                                        t readtable))
           "{[]}")
      (progn
        (set-macro-character
          #\] (get-macro-character #\)) nil readtable)
        (set-macro-character
          #\} (get-macro-character #\)) nil readtable)
        (set-macro-character
          #\[ #'(lambda (s ignore)
                  (cons :word (read-delimited-list #\] s t)))
          nil readtable)
        (set-macro-character
          #\{ #'(lambda (s ignore)
                  (cons :test (read-delimited-list #\} s t)))
          nil readtable))))
```

CHAPTER 21

A Grammar of English

Prefer geniality to grammar.
—Henry Watson Fowler
The King's English (1906)

The previous two chapters outline techniques for writing grammars and parsers based on those grammars. It is quite straightforward to apply these techniques to applications like the CD player problem where input is limited to simple sentences like "Play 1 to 8 without 3." But it is a major undertaking to write a grammar for unrestricted English input. This chapter develops a grammar that covers all the major syntactic constructions of English. It handles sentences of much greater complexity, such as "Kim would not have been persuaded by Lee to look after the dog." The grammar is not comprehensive enough to handle sentences chosen at random from a book, but when augmented by suitable vocabulary it is adequate for a wide variety of applications.

This chapter is organized as a tour through the English language. We first cover noun phrases, then verb phrases, clauses, and sentences. For each category we introduce examples, analyze them linguistically, and finally show definite clause grammar rules that correspond to the analysis.

As the last chapter should have made clear, analysis more often results in complication than in simplification. For example, starting with a simple rule like (S --> NP VP), we soon find that we have to add arguments to handle agreement, semantics, and gapping information. Figure 21.1 lists the grammatical categories and their arguments. Note that the semantic argument, sem, is always last, and the gap accumulators, gap1 and gap2, are next-to-last whenever they occur. All single-letter arguments denote metavariables; for example, each noun phrase (category NP) will have a semantic interpretation, sem, that is a conjunction of relations involving the variable x. Similarly, the h in modifiers is a variable that refers to the head—the thing that is being modified. The other arguments and categories will be explained in turn, but it is handy to have this figure to refer back to.

Category	Arguments
	Preterminals
name	agr name
verb	verb inflection slots v sem
rel-pro	case type
pronoun	agr case wh x sem
art	agr quant
adj	x sem
cardinal	number agr
ordinal	number
prep	prep sem
noun	agr slots x sem
aux	inflection needs-inflection v sem
adverb	x sem
	Nonterminals
S	s sem
aux-inv-S	subject s sem
clause	inflection x int-subj v gap1 gap2 sem
subject	agr x subj-slot int-subj gap1 gap2 sem
VP	inflection x subject-slot v gap1 gap2 vp
NP	agr case wh x gap1 gap2 np
NP2	agr case x gap1 gap2 sem
PP	prep role wh np x gap1 gap2 sem
XP	slot constituent wh x gap1 gap2 sem
Det	agr wh x restriction sem
rel-clause	agr x sem
modifiers	pre/post cat info slots h gap1 gap2 sem
complement	cat info slot h gap1 gap2 sem
adjunct	pre/post cat info h gap1 gap2 sem
advp	wh x gap1 gap2 sem

Figure 21.1: Grammatical Categories and their Arguments

21.1 Noun Phrases

The simplest noun phrases are names and pronouns, such as "Kim" and "them." The rules for these cases are simple: we build up a semantic expression from a name or pronoun, and since there can be no gap, the two gap accumulator arguments are the same (?g1). Person and number agreement is propagated in the variable ?agr, and we also keep track of the *case* of the noun phrase. English has three cases that are reflected in certain pronouns. In the first person singular, "I" is the *nominative* or *subjective* case, "me" is the *accusative* or *objective* case, and "my" is the *genitive* case. To distinguish them from the genitive, we refer to the nominative and the objective cases as the *common* cases. Accordingly, the three cases will be marked by the expressions (common nom), (common obj), and gen, respectively. Many languages of the world have suffixes that mark nouns as being one case or another, but English does not. Thus, we use the expression (common ?) to mark nouns.

We also distinguish between noun phrases that can be used in questions, like "who," and those that cannot. The ?wh variable has the value +wh for noun phrases like "who" or "which one" and -wh for nonquestion phrases. Here, then, are the rules for names and pronouns. The predicates name and pronoun are used to look up words in the lexicon.

```
(rule (NP ?agr (common ?) -wh ?x ?g1 ?g1 (the ?x (name ?name ?x))) ==>
  (name ?agr ?name))

(rule (NP ?agr ?case ?wh ?x ?g1 ?g1 ?sem) ==>
  (pronoun ?agr ?case ?wh ?x ?sem))
```

Plural nouns can stand alone as noun phrases, as in "dogs," but singular nouns need a determiner, as in "the dog" or "Kim's friend's biggest dog." Plural nouns can also take a determiner, as in "the dogs." The category Det is used for determiners, and NP2 is used for the part of a noun phrase after the determiner:

```
(rule (NP (- - - +) ?case -wh ?x ?g1 ?g2 (group ?x ?sem)) ==>
  (:ex "dogs") ; Plural nouns don't need a determiner
  (NP2 (- - - +) ?case ?x ?g1 ?g2 ?sem))

(rule (NP ?agr (common ?) ?wh ?x ?g1 ?g2 ?sem) ==>
  (:ex "Every man" "The dogs on the beach")
  (Det ?agr ?wh ?x ?restriction ?sem)
  (NP2 ?agr (common ?) ?x ?g1 ?g2 ?restriction))
```

Finally, a noun phrase may appear externally to a construction, in which case the noun phrase passed in by the first gap argument will be consumed, but no words from the input will be. An example is the ⊔ in "Whom does Kim like ⊔?"

```
(rule (NP ?agr ?case ?wh ?x (gap (NP ?agr ?case ?x)) (gap nil) t)
  ==> ;; Gapped NP
  )
```

Now we address the heart of the noun phrase, the NP2 category. The lone rule for NP2 says that it consists of a noun, optionally preceded and followed by modifiers:

```
(rule (NP2 ?agr (common ?) ?x ?g1 ?g2 :sem) ==>
  (modifiers pre noun ?agr () ?x (gap nil) (gap nil) ?pre)
  (noun ?agr ?slots ?x ?noun)
  (modifiers post noun ?agr ?slots ?x ?g1 ?g2 ?post))
```

21.2   Modifiers

Modifiers are split into type types: *Complements* are modifiers that are expected by the head category that is being modified; they cannot stand alone. *Adjuncts* are modifiers that are not required but bring additional information. The distinction is clearest with verb modifiers. In "Kim visited Lee yesterday," "visited" is the head verb, "Lee" is a complement, and "yesterday" is an adjunct. Returning to nouns, in "the former mayor of Boston," "mayor" is the head noun, "of Boston" is a complement (although an optional one) and "former" is an adjunct.

The predicate modifiers takes eight arguments, so it can be tricky to understand them all. The first two arguments tell if we are before or after the head (pre or post) and what kind of head we are modifying (noun, verb, or whatever). Next is an argument that passes along any required information—in the case of nouns, it is the agreement feature. The fourth argument is a list of expected complements, here called ?slots. Next is the metavariable used to refer to the head. The final three arguments are the two gap accumulators and the semantics, which work the same way here as we have seen before. Notice that the lexicon entry for each Noun can have a list of complements that are considered as postnoun modifiers, but there can be only adjuncts as prenoun modifiers. Also note that gaps can appear in the postmodifiers but not in the premodifiers. For example, we can have "What is Kevin the former mayor of ⊔?," where the answer might be "Boston." But even though we can construct a noun phrase like "the education president," where "education" is a prenoun modifier of "president," we cannot construct "* What is George the ⊔ president?," intending that the answer be "education."

There are four cases for modification. First, a complement is a kind of modifier. Second, if a complement is marked as optional, it can be skipped. Third, an adjunct can appear in the input. Fourth, if there are no complements expected, then there need not be any modifiers at all. The following rules implement these four cases:

```
(rule (modifiers ?pre/post ?cat ?info (?slot . ?slots) ?h
                 ?g1 ?g3 :sem) ==>
 (complement ?cat ?info ?slot ?h ?g1 ?g2 ?mod)
 (modifiers ?pre/post ?cat ?info ?slots ?h ?g2 ?g3 ?mods))

(rule (modifiers ?pre/post ?cat ?info ((? (?) ?) . ?slots) ?h
                 ?g1 ?g2 ?mods) ==>
 (modifiers ?pre/post ?cat ?info ?slots ?h ?g1 ?g2 ?mods))

(rule (modifiers ?pre/post ?cat ?info ?slots ?h ?g1 ?g3 :sem) ==>
 (adjunct ?pre/post ?cat ?info ?h ?g1 ?g2 ?adjunct)
 (modifiers ?pre/post ?cat ?info ?slots ?h ?g2 ?g3 ?mods))

(rule (modifiers ? ? ? () ? ?g1 ?g1 t) ==> )
```

We need to say more about the list of complements, or slots, that can be associated with words in the lexicon. Each slot is a list of the form (*role number form*), where the role refers to some semantic relation, the number indicates the ordering of the complements, and the form is the type of constituent expected: noun phrase, verb phrase, or whatever. The details will be covered in the following section on verb phrases, and complement will be covered in the section on XPs. For now, we give a single example. The complement list for one sense of the verb "visit" is:

```
((agt 1 (NP ?)) (obj 2 (NP ?)))
```

This means that the first complement, the subject, is a noun phrase that fills the agent role, and the second complement is also a noun phrase that fills the object role.

21.3   Noun Modifiers

There are two main types of prenoun adjuncts. Most common are adjectives, as in "big slobbery dogs." Nouns can also be adjuncts, as in "water meter" or "desk lamp." Here it is clear that the second noun is the head and the first is the modifier: a desk lamp is a lamp, not a desk. These are known as noun-noun compounds. In the following rules, note that we do not need to say that more than one adjective is allowed; this is handled by the rules for modifiers.

```
(rule (adjunct pre noun ?info ?x ?gap ?gap ?sem) ==>
 (adj ?x ?sem))

(rule (adjunct pre noun ?info ?h ?gap ?gap :sem) ==>
 (:sem (noun-noun ?h ?x))
 (noun ?agr () ?x ?sem))
```

After the noun there is a wider variety of modifiers. Some nouns have complements, which are primarily prepositional phrases, as in "mayor of Boston." These will be covered when we get to the lexical entries for nouns. Prepositional phrases can be adjuncts for nouns or verbs, as in "man in the middle" and "slept for an hour." We can write one rule to cover both cases:

```
(rule (adjunct post ?cat ?info ?x ?g1 ?g2 ?sem) ==>
  (PP ?prep ?prep ?wh ?np ?x ?g1 ?g2 ?sem))
```

Here are the rules for prepositional phrases, which can be either a preposition followed by a noun phrase or can be gapped, as in "to whom are you speaking ␣?" The object of a preposition is always in the objective case: "with him" not "*with he."

```
(rule (PP ?prep ?role ?wh ?np ?x ?g1 ?g2 :sem) ==>
  (prep ?prep t)
  (:sem (?role ?x ?np))
  (NP ?agr (common obj) ?wh ?np ?g1 ?g2 ?np-sem))

(rule (PP ?prep ?role ?wh ?np ?x
          (gap (PP ?prep ?role ?np ?x)) (gap nil) t) ==> )
```

Nouns can be modified by present participles, past participles, and relative clauses. Examples are "the man eating the snack," "the snack eaten by the man," and "the man that ate the snack," respectively. We will see that each verb in the lexicon is marked with an inflection, and that the marker -ing is used for present participles while -en is used for past participles. The details of the clause will be covered later.

```
(rule (adjunct post noun ?agr ?x ?gap ?gap ?sem) ==>
  (:ex (the man) "visiting me" (the man) "visited by me")
  (:test (member ?infl (-ing passive)))
  (clause ?infl ?x ? ?v (gap (NP ?agr ? ?x)) (gap nil) ?sem))

(rule (adjunct post noun ?agr ?x ?gap ?gap ?sem) ==>
  (rel-clause ?agr ?x ?sem))
```

It is possible to have a relative clause where it is an object, not the subject, that the head refers to: "the snack that the man ate." In this kind of relative clause the relative pronoun is optional: "The snack the man ate was delicious." The following rules say that if the relative pronoun is omitted then the noun that is being modified must be an object, and the relative clause should include a subject internally. The constant int-subj indicates this.

```
(rule (rel-clause ?agr ?x :sem) ==>
  (:ex (the man) "that she liked" "that liked her"
       "that I know Lee liked")
```

```
        (opt-rel-pronoun ?case ?x ?int-subj ?rel-sem)
        (clause (finite ? ?) ? ?int-subj ?v
                (gap (NP ?agr ?case ?x)) (gap nil) ?clause-sem))

(rule (opt-rel-pronoun ?case ?x ?int-subj (?type ?x)) ==>
   (:word ?rel-pro)
   (:test (word ?rel-pro rel-pro ?case ?type)))

(rule (opt-rel-pronoun (common obj) ?x int-subj t) ==> )
```

It should be noted that it is rare but not impossible to have names and pronouns with modifiers: "John the Baptist," "lovely Rita, meter maid," "Lucy in the sky with diamonds," "Sylvia in accounting on the 42nd floor," "she who must be obeyed." Here and throughout this chapter we will raise the possibility of such rare cases, leaving them as exercises for the reader.

21.4 Determiners

We will cover three kinds of determiners. The simplest is the article: "a dog" or "the dogs." We also allow genitive pronouns, as in "her dog," and numbers, as in "three dogs." The semantic interpretation of a determiner-phrase is of the form (*quantifier variable restriction*). For example, (a ?x (dog ?x)) or ((number 3) ?x (dog ?x)).

```
    (rule (Det ?agr ?wh ?x ?restriction (?art ?x ?restriction)) ==>
       (:ex "the" "every")
       (art ?agr ?art)
       (:test (if (= ?art wh) (= ?wh +wh) (= ?wh -wh))))

    (rule (Det ?agr ?wh ?x ?r (the ?x ?restriction)) ==>
       (:ex "his" "her")
       (pronoun ?agr gen ?wh ?y ?sem)
       (:test (and* ((genitive ?y ?x) ?sem ?r) ?restriction)))

    (rule (Det ?agr -wh ?x ?r ((number ?n) ?x ?r)) ==>
       (:ex "three")
       (cardinal ?n ?agr))
```

These are the most important determiner types, but there are others, and there are pre- and postdeterminers that combine in restricted combinations. Predeterminers include all, both, half, double, twice, and such. Postdeterminers include every, many, several, and few. Thus, we can say "all her many good ideas" or "all the King's men." But we can not say "*all much ideas" or "*the our children." The details are complicated and are omitted from this grammar.

21.5   Verb Phrases

Now that we have defined `modifiers`, verb phrases are easy. In fact, we only need two rules. The first says a verb phrase consists of a verb optionally preceded and followed by modifiers, and that the meaning of the verb phrase includes the fact that the subject fills some role:

```
(rule (VP ?infl ?x ?subject-slot ?v ?g1 ?g2 :sem) ==>
  (:ex "sleeps" "quickly give the dog a bone")
  (modifiers pre verb ? () ?v (gap nil) (gap nil) ?pre-sem)
  (:sem (?role ?v ?x)) (:test (= ?subject-slot (?role 1 ?)))
  (verb ?verb ?infl (?subject-slot . ?slots) ?v ?v-sem)
  (modifiers post verb ? ?slots ?v ?g1 ?g2 ?mod-sem))
```

The `VP` category takes seven arguments. The first is an inflection, which represents the tense of the verb. To describe the possibilities for this argument we need a quick review of some basic linguistics. A sentence must have a *finite* verb, meaning a verb in the present or past tense. Thus, we say "Kim likes Lee," not "*Kim liking Lee." Subject-predicate agreement takes effect for finite verbs but not for any other tense. The other tenses show up as complements to other verbs. For example, the complement to "want" is an infinitive: "Kim wants *to like* Lee" and the complement to the modal auxiliary verb "would" is a nonfinite verb: "Kim would *like* Lee." If this were in the present tense, it would be "likes," not "like." The inflection argument takes on one of the forms in the table here:

Expression	Type	Example
`(finite ?agr present)`	present tense	eat, eats
`(finite ?agr past)`	past tense	ate
`nonfinite`	nonfinite	eat
`infinitive`	infinitive	to eat
`-en`	past participle	eaten
`-ing`	present participle	eating

The second argument is a metavariable that refers to the subject, and the third is the subject's complement slot. We adopt the convention that the subject slot must always be the first among the verb's complements. The other slots are handled by the postverb modifiers. The fourth argument is a metavariable indicating the verb phrase itself. The final three are the familiar gap and semantics arguments. As an example, if the verb phrase is the single word "slept," then the semantics of the verb phrase will be `(and (past ?v) (sleep ?v))`. Of course, adverbs, complements, and adjuncts will also be handled by this rule.

The second rule for verb phrases handles auxiliary verbs, such as "have," "is" and "would." Each auxiliary verb (or `aux`) produces a verb phrase with a particular inflection when followed by a verb phrase with the required inflection. To repeat an example, "would" produces a finite phrase when followed by a nonfinite verb. "Have" produces a nonfinite when followed by a past participle. Thus, "would have liked" is a finite verb phrase.

We also need to account for negation. The word "not" can not modify a bare main verb but can follow an auxiliary verb. That is, we can't say "*Kim not like Lee," but we can add an auxiliary to get "Kim does not like Lee."

```
(rule (VP ?infl ?x ?subject-slot ?v ?g1 ?g2 :sem) ==>
  (:ex "is sleeping" "would have given a bone to the dog."
       "did not sleep" "was given a bone by this old man")
  ;; An aux verb, followed by a VP
  (aux ?infl ?needs-infl ?v ?aux)
  (modifiers post aux ? () ?v (gap nil) (gap nil) ?mod)
  (VP ?needs-infl ?x ?subject-slot ?v ?g1 ?g2 ?vp))

(rule (adjunct post aux ? ?v ?gap ?gap (not ?v)) ==>
  (:word not))
```

21.6 Adverbs

Adverbs can serve as adjuncts before or after a verb: "to boldly go," "to go boldly." There are some limitations on where they can occur, but it is difficult to come up with firm rules; here we allow any adverb anywhere. We define the category advp for adverbial phrase, but currently restrict it to a single adverb.

```
(rule (adjunct ?pre/post verb ?info ?v ?g1 ?g2 ?sem) ==>
  (advp ?wh ?v ?g1 ?g2 ?sem))

(rule (advp ?wh ?v ?gap ?gap ?sem) ==>
  (adverb ?wh ?v ?sem))

(rule (advp ?wh ?v (gap (advp ?v)) (gap nil) t) ==> )
```

21.7 Clauses

A clause consists of a subject followed by a predicate. However, the subject need not be realized immediately before the predicate. For example, in "Alice promised Bob to lend him her car" there is an infinitive clause that consists of the predicate "to lend him her car" and the subject "Alice." The sentence as a whole is another clause. In our analysis, then, a clause is a subject followed by a verb phrase, with the possibility that the subject will be instantiated by something from the gap arguments:

```
(rule (clause ?infl ?x ?int-subj ?v ?gap1 ?gap3 :sem) ==>
  (subject ?agr ?x ?subj-slot ?int-subj ?gap1 ?gap2 ?subj-sem)
  (VP ?infl ?x ?subj-slot ?v ?gap2 ?gap3 ?pred-sem)
  (:test (subj-pred-agree ?agr ?infl)))
```

There are now two possibilities for subject. In the first case it has already been parsed, and we pick it up from the gap list. If that is so, then we also need to find the agreement feature of the subject. If the subject was a noun phrase, the agreement will be present in the gap list. If it was not, then the agreement is third-person singular. An example of this is "*That the Red Sox won* surprises me," where the italicized phrase is a non-NP subject. The fact that we need to use "surprises" and not "surprise" indicates that it is third-person singular. We will see that the code (- - + -) is used for this.

```
(rule (subject ?agree ?x ?subj-slot ext-subj
               (gap ?subj) (gap nil) t) ==>
  ;; Externally realized subject (the normal case for S)
  (:test (slot-constituent ?subj-slot ?subj ?x ?)
         (if (= ?subj (NP ?agr ?case ?x))
             (= ?agree ?agr)
             (= ?agree (- - + -)))))) ;Non-NP subjects are 3sing
```

In the second case we just parse a noun phrase as the subject. Note that the fourth argument to subject is either ext-subj or int-subj depending on if the subject is realized internally or externally. This will be important when we cover sentences in the next section. In case it was not already clear, the second argument to both clause and subject is the metavariable representing the subject.

```
(rule (subject ?agr ?x (?role 1 (NP ?x)) int-subj ?gap ?gap ?sem)
   ==>
  (NP ?agr (common nom) ?wh ?x (gap nil) (gap nil) ?sem))
```

Finally, the rules for subject-predicate agreement say that only finite predicates need to agree with their subject:

```
(<- (subj-pred-agree ?agr (finite ?agr ?)))
(<- (subj-pred-agree ? ?infl) (atom ?infl))
```

21.8   Sentences

In the previous chapter we allowed only simple declarative sentences. The current grammar supports commands and four kinds of questions in addition to declarative sentences. It also supports *thematic fronting:* placing a nonsubject at the beginning of a sentence to emphasize its importance, as in "*Smith* he says his name is" or "*Murder,* she wrote" or "*In God* we trust." In the last example it is a prepositional phrase, not a noun phrase, that occurs first. It is also possible to have a subject that is not a noun phrase: "*That the dog didn't bark* puzzled Holmes." To support all these possibilities, we introduce a new category, XP, which stands for any kind of phrase. A declarative sentence is then just an XP followed by a clause, where the subject of the clause may or may not turn out to be the XP:

```
(rule (S ?s :sem) ==>
  (:ex "Kim likes Lee" "Lee, I like _" "In god, we trust _"
       "Who likes Lee?" "Kim likes who?")
  (XP ?kind ?constituent ?wh ?x (gap nil) (gap nil) ?topic-sem)
  (clause (finite ? ?) ?x ? ?s (gap ?constituent) (gap nil) ?sem))
```

As it turns out, this rule also serves for two types of questions. The simplest kind of question has an interrogative noun phrase as its subject: "Who likes Lee?" or "What man likes Lee?" Another kind is the so-called *echo question,* which can be used only as a reply to another statement: if I tell you Kim likes Jerry Lewis, you could reasonably reply "Kim likes *who?*" Both these question types have the same structure as declarative sentences, and thus are handled by the same rule.

The following table lists some sentences that can be parsed by this rule, showing the XP and subject of each.

Sentence	XP	Subject
Kim likes Lee	Kim	Kim
Lee, Kim likes	Lee	Kim
In god, we trust	In god	we
That Kim likes Lee amazes	That Kim likes Lee	That Kim likes Lee
Who likes Lee?	Who	Who

The most common type of command has no subject at all: "Be quiet" or "Go to your room." When the subject is missing, the meaning is that the command refers to *you,* the addressee of the command. The subject can also be mentioned explicitly, and it can be "you," as in "You be quiet," but it need not be: "Somebody shut the door" or "Everybody sing along." We provide a rule only for commands with subject omitted, since it can be difficult to distinguish a command with a subject from a declarative sentence. Note that commands are always nonfinite.

```
(rule (S ?s :sem) ==>
  ;; Commands have implied second-person subject
  (:ex "Give the dog a bone.")
  (:sem (command ?s))
  (:sem (listener ?x))
  (clause nonfinite ?x ext-subj ?s
         (gap (NP ? ? ?x)) (gap nil) ?sem))
```

Another form of command starts with "let," as in "Let me see what I can do" and "Let us all pray." The second word is better considered as the object of "let" rather than the subject of the sentence, since the subject would have to be "I" or "we." This kind of command can be handled with a lexical entry for "let" rather than with an additional rule.

We now consider questions. Questions that can be answered by yes or no have the subject and auxiliary verb inverted: "Did you see him?" or "Should I have been doing this?" The latter example shows that it is only the first auxiliary verb that comes before the subject. The category aux-inv-S is used to handle this case:

```
(rule (S ?s (yes-no ?s ?sem)) ==>
  (:ex "Does Kim like Lee?" "Is he a doctor?")
  (aux-inv-S nil ?s ?sem))
```

Questions that begin with a wh-phrase also have the auxiliary verb before the subject, as in "Who did you see?" or "Why should I have been doing this?" The first constituent can also be a prepositional phrase: "For whom am I doing this?" The following rule parses an XP that must have the +wh feature and then parses an aux-inv-S to arrive at a question:

```
(rule (S ?s :sem) ==>
  (:ex "Who does Kim like _?" "To whom did he give it _?"
       "What dog does Kim like _?")
  (XP ?slot ?constituent +wh ?x (gap nil) (gap nil) ?subj-sem)
  (aux-inv-S ?constituent ?s ?sem))
```

A question can also be signaled by rising intonation in what would otherwise be a declarative statement: "You want some?" Since we don't have intonation information, we won't include this kind of question.

The implementation for aux-inv-S is straightforward: parse an auxiliary and then a clause, pausing to look for modifiers in between. (So far, a "not" is the only modifier allowed in that position.)

```
(rule (aux-inv-S ?constituent ?v :sem) ==>
  (:ex "Does Kim like Lee?" (who) "would Kim have liked")
  (aux (finite ?agr ?tense) ?needs-infl ?v ?aux-sem)
  (modifiers post aux ? () ?v (gap nil) (gap nil) ?mod)
  (clause ?needs-infl ?x int-subj ?v (gap ?constituent) (gap nil)
          ?clause-sem))
```

There is one more case to consider. The verb "to be" is the most idiosyncratic in English. It is the only verb that has agreement differences for anything besides third-person singular. And it is also the only verb that can be used in an aux-inv-S without a main verb. An example of this is "Is he a doctor?," where "is" clearly is not an auxiliary, because there is no main verb that it could be auxiliary to. Other verb can not be used in this way: "*Seems he happy?" and "*Did they it?" are ungrammatical. The only possibility is "have," as in "Have you any wool?," but this use is rare.

The following rule parses a verb, checks to see that it is a version of "be," and then parses the subject and the modifiers for the verb.

```
(rule (aux-inv-S ?ext ?v :sem) ==>
  (:ex "Is he a doctor?")
  (verb ?be (finite ?agr ?) ((?role ?n ?xp) . ?slots) ?v ?sem)
  (:test (word ?be be))
  (subject ?agr ?x (?role ?n ?xp) int-subj
          (gap nil) (gap nil) ?subj-sem)
  (:sem (?role ?v ?x))
  (modifiers post verb ? ?slots ?v (gap ?ext) (gap nil) ?mod-sem))
```

21.9 XPs

All that remains in our grammar is the XP category. XPs are used in two ways: First, a phrase can be extraposed, as in *"In god* we trust," where "in god" will be parsed as an XP and then placed on the gap list until it can be taken off as an adjunct to "trust." Second, a phrase can be a complement, as in "He wants *to be a fireman,*" where the infinitive phrase is a complement of "wants."

As it turns out, the amount of information that needs to appear in a gap list is slightly different from the information that appears in a complement slot. For example, one sense of the verb "want" has the following complement list:

```
((agt 1 (NP ?x)) (con 3 (VP infinitive ?x)))
```

This says that the first complement (the subject) is a noun phrase that serves as the agent of the wanting, and the second is an infinitive verb phrase that is the concept of the wanting. The subject of this verb phrase is the same as the subject of the wanting, so in "She wants to go home," it is she who both wants and goes. (Contrast this to "He persuaded her to go home," where it is he that persuades, but she that goes.)

But when we put a noun phrase on a gap list, we need to include its number and case as well as the fact that it is an NP and its metavariable, but we don't need to include the fact that it is an agent. This difference means we have two choices: either we can merge the notions of slots and gap lists so that they use a common notation containing all the information that either can use, or we need some way of mapping between them. I made the second choice, on the grounds that each notation was complicated enough without bringing in additional information.

The relation slot-constituent maps between the slot notation used for complements and the constituent notation used in gap lists. There are eight types of complements, five of which can appear in gap lists: noun phrases, clauses, prepositional phrases, the word "it" (as in "it is raining"), and adverbial phrases. The three phrases that are allowed only as complements are verb phrases, particles (such as "up" in "look up the number"), and adjectives. Here is the mapping between the two notations. The *** indicates no mapping:

```
(<- (slot-constituent (?role ?n (NP ?x))
                      (NP ?agr ?case ?x) ?x ?h))
(<- (slot-constituent (?role ?n (clause ?word ?infl))
                      (clause ?word ?infl ?v) ?v ?h))
(<- (slot-constituent (?role ?n (PP ?prep ?np))
                      (PP ?prep ?role ?np ?h) ?np ?h))
(<- (slot-constituent (?role ?n it)         (it ? ? ?x) ?x ?))
(<- (slot-constituent (manner 3 (advp ?x))  (advp ?v) ? ?v))
(<- (slot-constituent (?role ?n (VP ?infl ?x)) *** ? ?))
(<- (slot-constituent (?role ?n (Adj ?x))   *** ?x ?))
(<- (slot-constituent (?role ?n (P ?particle)) *** ? ?))
```

We are now ready to define complement. It takes a slot descrption, maps it into a constituent, and then calls XP to parse that constituent:

```
(rule (complement ?cat ?info (?role ?n ?xp) ?h ?gap1 ?gap2 :sem)
   ==>
   ;; A complement is anything expected by a slot
   (:sem (?role ?h ?x))
   (:test (slot-constituent (?role ?n ?xp) ?constituent ?x ?h))
   (XP ?xp ?constituent ?wh ?x ?gap1 ?gap2 ?sem))
```

The category XP takes seven arguments. The first two are the slot we are trying to fill and the constituent we need to fill it. The third is used for any additional information, and the fourth is the metavariable for the phrase. The last three supply gap and semantic information.

Here are the first five XP categories:

```
(rule (XP (PP ?prep ?np) (PP ?prep ?role ?np ?h) ?wh ?np
          ?gap1 ?gap2 ?sem) ==>
  (PP ?prep ?role ?wh ?np ?h ?gap1 ?gap2 ?sem))

(rule (XP (NP ?x) (NP ?agr ?case ?x) ?wh ?x ?gap1 ?gap2 ?sem) ==>
  (NP ?agr ?case ?wh ?x ?gap1 ?gap2 ?sem))

(rule (XP it (it ? ? ?x) -wh ?x ?gap ?gap t) ==>
  (:word it))

(rule (XP (clause ?word ?infl) (clause ?word ?infl ?v) -wh ?v
          ?gap1 ?gap2 ?sem) ==>
  (:ex (he thinks) "that she is tall")
  (opt-word ?word)
  (clause ?infl ?x int-subj ?v ?gap1 ?gap2 ?sem))

(rule (XP (?role ?n (advp ?v)) (advp ?v) ?wh ?v ?gap1 ?gap2 ?sem)
  ==>
  (advp ?wh ?v ?gap1 ?gap2 ?sem))
```

The category opt-word parses a word, which may be optional. For example, one sense of "know" subcategorizes for a clause with an optional "that": we can say either "I know that he's here" or "I know he's here." The complement list for "know" thus contains the slot (con 2 (clause (that) (finite ? ?))). If the "that" had been obligatory, it would not have parentheses around it.

```
(rule (opt-word ?word) ==> (:word ?word))
(rule (opt-word (?word)) ==> (:word ?word))
(rule (opt-word (?word)) ==>)
```

Finally, here are the three XPs that can not be extraposed:

```
(rule (XP (VP ?infl ?x) *** -wh ?v ?gap1 ?gap2 ?sem) ==>
  (:ex (he promised her) "to sleep")
  (VP ?infl ?x ?subj-slot ?v ?gap1 ?gap2 ?sem))

(rule (XP (Adj ?x) *** -wh ?x ?gap ?gap ?sem) ==>
  (Adj ?x ?sem))

(rule (XP (P ?particle) *** -wh ?x ?gap ?gap t) ==>
  (prep ?particle t))
```

21.10   Word Categories

Each word category has a rule that looks words up in the lexicon and assigns the right features. The relation word is used for all lexicon access. We will describe the most complicated word class, verb, and just list the others.

Verbs are complex because they often are *polysemous*—they have many meanings. In addition, each meaning can have several different complement lists. Thus, an entry for a verb in the lexicon will consist of the verb form, its inflection, and a list of senses, where each sense is a semantics followed by a list of possible complement lists. Here is the entry for the verb "sees," indicating that it is a present-tense verb with three senses. The understand sense has two complement lists, which correspond to "He sees" and "He sees that you are right." The look sense has one complement list corresponding to "He sees the picture," and the dating sense, corresponding to "He sees her (only on Friday nights)," has the same complement list.

```
> (?- (word sees verb ?infl ?senses))
?INFL = (FINITE (- - + -) PRESENT)
?SENSES = ((UNDERSTAND ((AGT 1 (NP ?3)))
                       ((EXP 1 (NP ?4))
                        (CON 2 (CLAUSE (THAT) (FINITE ?5 ?6)))))
           (LOOK ((AGT 1 (NP ?7)) (OBJ 2 (NP ?8))))
           (DATING ((AGT 1 (NP ?9)) (OBJ 2 (NP ?10)))))
```

The category verb takes five arguments: the verb itself, its inflection, its complement list, its metavariable, and its semantics. The member relations are used to pick a sense from the list of senses and a complement list from the list of lists, and the semantics is built from semantic predicate for the chosen sense and the metavariable for the verb:

```
(rule (verb ?verb ?infl ?slots ?v :sem) ==>
  (:word ?verb)
  (:test (word ?verb verb ?infl ?senses)
         (member (?sem . ?subcats) ?senses)
         (member ?slots ?subcats)
         (tense-sem ?infl ?v ?tense-sem))
  (:sem ?tense-sem)
  (:sem (?sem ?v)))
```

It is difficulty to know how to translate tense information into a semantic interpretation. Different applications will have different models of time and thus will want different interpretations. The relation tense-sem gives semantics for each tense. Here is a very simple definition of tense-sem:

```
(<- (tense-sem (finite ? ?tense) ?v (?tense ?v)))
(<- (tense-sem -ing ?v (progressive ?v)))
(<- (tense-sem -en  ?v (past-participle ?v)))
(<- (tense-sem infinitive ?v t))
(<- (tense-sem nonfinite ?v t))
(<- (tense-sem passive ?v (passive ?v)))
```

Auxiliary verbs and modal verbs are listed separately:

```
(rule (aux ?infl ?needs-infl ?v ?tense-sem) ==>
  (:word ?aux)
  (:test (word ?aux aux ?infl ?needs-infl)
         (tense-sem ?infl ?v ?tense-sem)))

(rule (aux (finite ?agr ?tense) nonfinite ?v (?sem ?v)) ==>
  (:word ?modal)
  (:test (word ?modal modal ?sem ?tense)))
```

Nouns, pronouns, and names are also listed separately, although they have much in common. For pronouns we use quantifier wh or pro, depending on if it is a wh-pronoun or not.

```
(rule (noun ?agr ?slots ?x (?sem ?x)) ==>
  (:word ?noun)
  (:test (word ?noun noun ?agr ?slots ?sem)))

(rule (pronoun ?agr ?case ?wh ?x (?quant ?x (?sem ?x))) ==>
  (:word ?pro)
  (:test (word ?pro pronoun ?agr ?case ?wh ?sem)
         (if (= ?wh +wh) (= ?quant wh) (= ?quant pro))))

(rule (name ?agr ?name) ==>
  (:word ?name)
  (:test (word ?name name ?agr)))
```

Here are the rules for the remaining word classes:

```
(rule (adj ?x (?sem ?x)) ==>
  (:word ?adj)
  (:test (word ?adj adj ?sem)))

(rule (adj ?x ((nth ?n) ?x)) ==> (ordinal ?n))

(rule (art ?agr ?quant) ==>
  (:word ?art)
  (:test (word ?art art ?agr ?quant)))
```

```
(rule (prep ?prep t) ==>
  (:word ?prep)
  (:test (word ?prep prep)))

(rule (adverb ?wh ?x ?sem) ==>
  (:word ?adv)
  (:test (word ?adv adv ?wh ?pred)
         (if (= ?wh +wh)
             (= ?sem (wh ?y (?pred ?x ?y)))
             (= ?sem (?pred ?x)))))

(rule (cardinal ?n ?agr) ==>
  (:ex "five")
  (:word ?num)
  (:test (word ?num cardinal ?n ?agr)))

(rule (cardinal ?n ?agr) ==>
  (:ex "5")
  (:word ?n)
  (:test (numberp ?n)
         (if (= ?n 1)
             (= ?agr (- - + -))     ;3sing
             (= ?agr (- - - +))))))  ;3plur

(rule (ordinal ?n) ==>
  (:ex "fifth")
  (:word ?num)
  (:test (word ?num ordinal ?n)))
```

21.11   The Lexicon

The lexicon itself consists of a large number of entries in the word relation, and it would certainly be possible to ask the lexicon writer to make a long list of word facts. But to make the lexicon easier to read and write, we adopt three useful tools. First, we introduce a system of abbreviations. Common expressions can be abbreviated with a symbol that will be expanded by word. Second, we provide the macros verb and noun to cover the two most complex word classes. Third, we provide a macro word that makes entries into a hash table. This is more efficient than compiling a word relation consisting of hundreds of Prolog clauses.

The implementation of these tools is left for the next section; here we show the actual lexicon, starting with the list of abbreviations.

The first set of abbreviations defines the agreement features. The obvious way to handle agreement is with two features, one for person and one for number. So first-person singular might be represented (1 sing). A problem arises when we want to describe verbs. Every verb except "be" makes the distinction only between third-person singular and all the others. We don't want to make five separate entries in the lexicon to represent all the others. One alternative is to have the agreement feature be a set of possible values, so all the others would be a single set of five values rather than five separate values. This makes a big difference in cutting down on backtracking. The problem with this approach is keeping track of when to intersect sets. Another approach is to make the agreement feature be a list of four binary features, one each for first-person singular, first-person plural, third-person singular, and third-person plural. Then "all the others" can be represented by the list that is negative in the third feature and unknown in all the others. There is no way to distinguish second-person singular from plural in this scheme, but English does not make that distinction. Here are the necessary abbreviations:

```
(abbrev 1sing      (+ - - -))
(abbrev 1plur      (- + - -))
(abbrev 3sing      (- - + -))
(abbrev 3plur      (- - - +))
(abbrev 2pers      (- - - -))
(abbrev ~3sing     (? ? - ?))
```

The next step is to provide abbreviations for some of the common verb complement lists:

```
(abbrev v/intrans   ((agt 1 (NP ?))))
(abbrev v/trans     ((agt 1 (NP ?)) (obj 2 (NP ?))))
(abbrev v/ditrans   ((agt 1 (NP ?)) (goal 2 (NP ?)) (obj 3 (NP ?))))
(abbrev v/trans2    ((agt 1 (NP ?)) (obj 2 (NP ?)) (goal 2 (PP to ?))))
(abbrev v/trans4    ((agt 1 (NP ?)) (obj 2 (NP ?)) (ben 2 (PP for ?))))
(abbrev v/it-null   ((nil 1 it)))
(abbrev v/opt-that  ((exp 1 (NP ?)) (con 2 (clause (that) (finite ? ?)))))
(abbrev v/subj-that ((con 1 (clause that (finite ? ?))) (exp 2 (NP ?))))
(abbrev v/it-that   ((nil 1 it) (exp 2 (NP ?))
                     (con 3 (clause that (finite ? ?)))))
(abbrev v/inf       ((agt 1 (NP ?x)) (con 3 (VP infinitive ?x))))
(abbrev v/promise   ((agt 1 (NP ?x)) (goal (2) (NP ?y))
                     (con 3 (VP infinitive ?x))))
(abbrev v/persuade  ((agt 1 (NP ?x)) (goal 2 (NP ?y))
                     (con 3 (VP infinitive ?y))))
(abbrev v/want      ((agt 1 (NP ?x)) (con 3 (VP infinitive ?x))))
(abbrev v/p-up      ((agt 1 (NP ?)) (pat 2 (NP ?)) (nil 3 (P up))))
(abbrev v/pp-for    ((agt 1 (NP ?)) (pat 2 (PP for ?))))
(abbrev v/pp-after  ((agt 1 (NP ?)) (pat 2 (PP after ?))))
```

Verbs

The macro verb allows us to list verbs in the form below, where the spellings of each tense can be omitted if the verb is regular:

```
(verb (base past-tense past-participle present-participle present-plural)
      (semantics complement-list...) ...)
```

For example, in the following list "ask" is regular, so only its base-form spelling is necessary. "Do," on the other hand, is irregular, so each form is spelled out. The haphazard list includes verbs that are either useful for examples or illustrate some unusual complement list.

```
(verb (ask) (query v/ditrans))
(verb (delete) (delete v/trans))
(verb (do did done doing does) (perform v/trans))
(verb (eat ate eaten) (eat v/trans))
(verb (give gave given giving) (give-1 v/trans2 v/ditrans)
      (donate v/trans v/intrans))
(verb (go went gone going goes))
(verb (have had had having has) (possess v/trans))
(verb (know knew known) (know-that v/opt-that) (know-of v/trans))
(verb (like) (like-1 v/trans))
(verb (look) (look-up v/p-up) (search v/pp-for)
      (take-care v/pp-after) (look v/intrans))
(verb (move moved moved moving moves)
      (self-propel v/intrans) (transfer v/trans2))
(verb (persuade) (persuade v/persuade))
(verb (promise) (promise v/promise))
(verb (put put put putting))
(verb (rain) (rain v/it-null))
(verb (saw) (cut-with-saw v/trans v/intrans))
(verb (see saw seen seeing)(understand v/intrans v/opt-that)
      (look v/trans)(dating v/trans))
(verb (sleep slept) (sleep v/intrans))
(verb (surprise) (surprise v/subj-that v/it-that))
(verb (tell told) (tell v/persuade))
(verb (trust) (trust v/trans ((agt 1 (NP ?)) (obj 2 (PP in ?)))))
(verb (try tried tried trying tries) (attempt v/inf))
(verb (visit) (visit v/trans))
(verb (want) (desire v/want v/persuade))
```

Auxiliary Verbs

Auxiliary verbs are simple enough to be described directly with the word macro. Each entry lists the auxiliary itself, the tense it is used to construct, and the tense it must be followed by. The auxiliaries "have" and "do" are listed, along with "to," which is used to construct infinitive clauses and thus can be treated as if it were an auxiliary.

```
(word have    aux nonfinite -en)
(word have    aux (finite ~3sing present) -en)
(word has     aux (finite 3sing present) -en)
(word had     aux (finite ? past) -en)
(word having  aux -ing -en)

(word do      aux (finite ~3sing present) nonfinite)
(word does    aux (finite  3sing present) nonfinite)
(word did     aux (finite  ?      past)   nonfinite)

(word to      aux infinitive nonfinite)
```

The auxiliary "be" is special: in addition to its use as both an auxiliary and main verb, it also is used in passives and as the main verb in aux-inverted sentences. The function copula is used to keep track of all these uses. It will be defined in the next section, but you can see it takes two arguments, a list of senses for the main verb, and a list of entries for the auxiliary verb. The three senses correspond to the examples "He is a fool," "He is a Republican," and "He is in Indiana," respectively.

```
(copula
  '((nil      ((nil 1 (NP ?x)) (nil 2 (Adj ?x))))
    (is-a     ((exp 1 (NP ?x)) (arg2 2 (NP ?y))))
    (is-loc   ((exp 1 (NP ?x)) (?prep 2 (PP ?prep ?)))))
  '((be       nonfinite -ing)
    (been     -en -ing)
    (being    -ing -en)
    (am       (finite 1sing present) -ing)
    (is       (finite 3sing present) -ing)
    (are      (finite 2pers present) -ing)
    (were     (finite (- - ? ?) past) -ing)   ; 2nd sing or pl
    (was      (finite (? - ? -) past) -ing))) ; 1st or 3rd sing
```

Following are the modal auxiliary verbs. Again, it is difficult to specify semantics for them. The word "not" is also listed here; it is not an auxiliary, but it does modify them.

```
(word can    modal able      past)
(word could  modal able      present)
(word may    modal possible  past)
(word might  modal possible  present)
(word shall  modal mandatory past)
(word should modal mandatory present)
(word will   modal expected  past)
(word would  modal expected  present)
(word must   modal necessary present)

(word not not)
```

Nouns

No attempt has been made to treat nouns seriously. We list enough nouns here to make some of the examples work. The first noun shows a complement list that is sufficient to parse "the destruction of the city by the enemy."

```
(noun destruction * destruction
      (pat (2) (PP of ?)) (agt (2) (PP by ?)))
(noun beach)
(noun bone)
(noun box boxes)
(noun city cities)
(noun color)
(noun cube)
(noun doctor)
(noun dog dogs)
(noun enemy enemies)
(noun file)
(noun friend friends friend (friend-of (2) (PP of ?)))
(noun furniture *)
(noun hat)
(noun man men)
(noun saw)
(noun woman women)
```

Pronouns

Here we list the nominative, objective, and genitive pronouns, followed by interrogative and relative pronouns. The only thing missing are reflexive pronouns, such as "myself."

```
(word I      pronoun 1sing (common nom) -wh speaker)
(word we     pronoun 1plur (common nom) -wh speaker+other)
(word you    pronoun 2pers (common    ?) -wh listener)
(word he     pronoun 3sing (common nom) -wh male)
(word she    pronoun 3sing (common nom) -wh female)
(word it     pronoun 3sing (common    ?) -wh anything)
(word they   pronoun 3plur (common nom) -wh anything)

(word me     pronoun 1sing (common obj) -wh speaker)
(word us     pronoun 1plur (common obj) -wh speaker+other)
(word him    pronoun 3sing (common obj) -wh male)
(word her    pronoun 3sing (common obj) -wh female)
(word them   pronoun 3plur (common obj) -wh anything)

(word my     pronoun 1sing gen -wh speaker)
(word our    pronoun 1plur gen -wh speaker+other)
(word your   pronoun 2pers gen -wh listener)
(word his    pronoun 3sing gen -wh male)
(word her    pronoun 3sing gen -wh female)
(word its    pronoun 3sing gen -wh anything)
(word their  pronoun 3plur gen -wh anything)
(word whose  pronoun 3sing gen +wh anything)

(word who    pronoun ? (common ?) +wh person)
(word whom   pronoun ? (common obj) +wh person)
(word what   pronoun ? (common ?) +wh thing)
(word which  pronoun ? (common ?) +wh thing)

(word who    rel-pro ? person)
(word which  rel-pro ? thing)
(word that   rel-pro ? thing)
(word whom   rel-pro (common obj) person)
```

Names

The following names were convenient for one example or another:

```
(word God    name 3sing)   (word Lynn  name 3sing)
(word Jan    name 3sing)   (word Mary  name 3sing)
(word John   name 3sing)   (word NY    name 3sing)
(word Kim    name 3sing)   (word LA    name 3sing)
(word Lee    name 3sing)   (word SF    name 3sing)
```

Adjectives

Here are a few adjectives:

```
(word big   adj big)      (word bad   adj bad)
(word old   adj old)      (word smart adj smart)
(word green adj green)    (word red   adj red)
(word tall  adj tall)     (word fun   adj fun)
```

Adverbs

The adverbs covered here include interrogatives:

```
(word quickly adv -wh quickly)
(word slowly  adv -wh slowly)

(word where   adv +wh loc)
(word when    adv +wh time)
(word why     adv +wh reason)
(word how     adv +wh manner)
```

Articles

The common articles are listed here:

```
(word the   art 3sing the)
(word the   art 3plur group)
(word a     art 3sing a)
(word an    art 3sing a)
(word every art 3sing every)
(word each  art 3sing each)
(word all   art 3sing all)
(word some  art ?     some)

(word this  art 3sing this)
(word that  art 3sing that)
(word these art 3plur this)
(word those art 3plur that)

(word what  art ?     wh)
(word which art ?     wh)
```

Cardinal and Ordinal Numbers

We can take advantage of `format`'s capabilities to fill up the lexicon. To go beyond 20, we would need a subgrammar of numbers.

```
;; This puts in numbers up to twenty, as if by
;; (word five cardinal 5 3plur)
;; (word fifth ordinal 5)

(dotimes (i 21)
  (add-word (read-from-string (format nil "~r" i))
            'cardinal i (if (= i 1) '3sing '3plur))
  (add-word (read-from-string (format nil "~:r" i)) 'ordinal i))
```

Prepositions

Here is a fairly complete list of prepositions:

```
(word above prep)    (word about prep)    (word around prep)
(word across prep)   (word after prep)    (word against prep)
(word along prep)    (word at prep)       (word away prep)
(word before prep)   (word behind prep)   (word below prep)
(word beyond prep)   (word by prep)       (word down prep)
(word for prep)      (word from prep)     (word in prep)
(word of prep)       (word off prep)      (word on prep)
(word out prep)      (word over prep)     (word past prep)
(word since prep)    (word through prep)(word throughout prep)
(word till prep)     (word to prep)       (word under prep)
(word until prep)    (word up prep)       (word with prep)
(word without prep)
```

21.12   Supporting the Lexicon

This section describes the implementation of the macros word, verb, noun, and abbrev. Abbreviations are stored in a hash table. The macro abbrev and the functions get-abbrev and clear-abbrevs define the interface. We will see how to expand abbreviations later.

```
(defvar *abbrevs* (make-hash-table))

(defmacro abbrev (symbol definition)
  "Make symbol be an abbreviation for definition."
  '(setf (gethash ',symbol *abbrevs*) ',definition))

(defun clear-abbrevs () (clrhash *abbrevs*))
(defun get-abbrev (symbol) (gethash symbol *abbrevs*))
```

Words are also stored in a hash table. Currently, words are symbols, but it might be a better idea to use strings for words, since then we could maintain capitalization information. The macro word or the function add-word adds a word to the lexicon. When used as an index into the hash table, each word returns a list of entries, where the first element of each entry is the word's category, and the other elements depend on the category.

```
(defvar *words* (make-hash-table :size 500))

(defmacro word (word cat &rest info)
  "Put word, with category and subcat info, into lexicon."
  '(add-word ',word ',cat .,(mapcar #'kwote info)))

(defun add-word (word cat &rest info)
  "Put word, with category and other info, into lexicon."
  (push (cons cat (mapcar #'expand-abbrevs-and-variables info))
        (gethash word *words*))
  word)

(defun kwote (x) (list 'quote x))
```

The function expand-abbrevs-and-variables expands abbreviations and substitutes variable structures for symbols beginning with ?. This makes it easier to make a copy of the structure, which will be needed later.

```
(defun expand-abbrevs-and-variables (exp)
  "Replace all variables in exp with vars, and expand abbrevs."
  (let ((bindings nil))
    (labels
        ((expand (exp)
           (cond
             ((lookup exp bindings))
             ((eq exp '?) (?))
             ((variable-p exp)
              (let ((var (?)))
                (push (cons exp var) bindings)
                var))
             ((consp exp)
              (reuse-cons (expand (first exp))
```

```
                              (expand (rest exp))
                              exp))
                    (t (multiple-value-bind (expansion found?)
                          (get-abbrev exp)
                        (if found?
                            (expand-abbrevs-and-variables expansion)
                            exp))))))
          (expand exp))))
```

Now we can store words in the lexicon, but we need some way of getting them out. The function word/n takes a word (which must be instantiated to a symbol) and a category and optional additional information and finds the entries in the lexicon for that word that unify with the category and additional information. For each match, it calls the supplied continuation. This means that word/n is a replacement for a long list of word facts. There are three differences: word/n hashes, so it will be faster; it is incremental (you can add a word at a time without needing to recompile); and it can not be used when the word is unbound. (It is not difficult to change it to handle an unbound word using maphash, but there are better ways of addressing that problem.)

```
(defun word/n (word cat cont &rest info)
  "Retrieve a word from the lexicon."
  (unless (unbound-var-p (deref word))
    (let ((old-trail (fill-pointer *trail*)))
      (dolist (old-entry (gethash word *words*))
        (let ((entry (deref-copy old-entry)))
          (when (and (consp entry)
                     (unify! cat (first entry))
                     (unify! info (rest entry)))
            (funcall cont)))
        (undo-bindings! old-trail)))))
```

Note that word/n does not follow our convention of putting the continuation last. Therefore, we will need the following additional functions:

```
(defun word/2 (w cat cont) (word/n w cat cont))
(defun word/3 (w cat a cont) (word/n w cat cont a))
(defun word/4 (w cat a b cont) (word/n w cat cont a b))
(defun word/5 (w cat a b c cont) (word/n w cat cont a b c))
(defun word/6 (w cat a b c d cont) (word/n w cat cont a b c d))
```

We could create the whole lexicon with the macro word, but it is convenient to create specific macros for some classes. The macro noun is used to generate two entries, one for the singular and one for the plural. The arguments are the base noun, optionally followed by the plural (which defaults to the base plus "s"), the semantics (which defaults to the base), and a list of complements. Mass nouns, like "furniture," have only one entry, and are marked by an asterisk where the plural would otherwise be.

```lisp
(defmacro noun (base &rest args)
  "Add a noun and its plural to the lexicon."
  '(add-noun-form ',base ,@(mapcar #'kwote args)))

(defun add-noun-form (base &optional (plural (symbol base 's))
                                    (sem base) &rest slots)
  (if (eq plural '*)
      (add-word base 'noun '? slots sem)
      (progn
        (add-word base 'noun '3sing slots sem)
        (add-word plural 'noun '3plur slots sem))))
```

Verbs are more complex. Each verb has seven entries: the base or nonfinite, the present tense singular and plural, the past tense, the past-participle, the present-participle, and the passive. The macro verb automatically generates all seven entries. Verbs that do not have all of them can be handled by individual calls to word. We automatically handle the spelling for the simple cases of adding "s," "ing," and "ed," and perhaps stripping a trailing vowel. More irregular spellings have to be specified explicitly. Here are three examples of the use of verb:

```lisp
(verb (do did done doing does) (perform v/trans))
(verb (eat ate eaten) (eat v/trans))
(verb (trust) (trust v/trans ((agt 1 (NP ?)) (obj 2 (PP in ?)))))
```

And here is the macro definition:

```lisp
(defmacro verb ((base &rest forms) &body senses)
  "Enter a verb into the lexicon."
  '(add-verb ',senses ',base ,@(mapcar #'kwote (mklist forms))))

(defun add-verb (senses base &optional
                    (past (symbol (strip-vowel base) 'ed))
                    (past-part past)
                    (pres-part (symbol (strip-vowel base) 'ing))
                    (plural (symbol base 's)))
  "Enter a verb into the lexicon."
  (add-word base 'verb 'nonfinite senses)
  (add-word base 'verb '(finite ~3sing present) senses)
  (add-word past 'verb '(finite ? past) senses)
  (add-word past-part 'verb '-en senses)
  (add-word pres-part 'verb '-ing senses)
  (add-word plural 'verb '(finite 3sing present) senses)
  (add-word past-part 'verb 'passive
```

```
(mapcar #'passivize-sense
        (expand-abbrevs-and-variables senses))))
```

This uses a few auxiliary functions. First, `strip-vowel` removes a vowel if it is the last character of the given argument. The idea is that for a verb like "fire," stripping the vowel yields "fir," from which we can get "fired" and "firing" automatically.

```
(defun strip-vowel (word)
  "Strip off a trailing vowel from a string."
  (let* ((str (string word))
         (end (- (length str) 1)))
    (if (vowel-p (char str end))
        (subseq str 0 end)
        str)))

(defun vowel-p (char) (find char "aeiou" :test #'char-equal))
```

We also provide a function to generate automatically the passive sense with the proper complement list(s). The idea is that the subject slot of the active verb becomes an optional slot marked by the preposition "by," and any slot that is marked with number 2 can be promoted to become the subject:

```
(defun passivize-sense (sense)
  ;; The first element of sense is the semantics; rest are slots
  (cons (first sense) (mapcan #'passivize-subcat (rest sense))))

(defun passivize-subcat (slots)
  "Return a list of passivizations of this subcat frame."
  ;; Whenever the 1 slot is of the form (?any 1 (NP ?)),
  ;; demote the 1 to a (3), and promote any 2 to a 1.
  (when (and (eql (slot-number (first slots)) 1)
             (starts-with (third (first slots)) 'NP))
    (let ((old-1 '(,(first (first slots)) (3) (PP by ?))))
      (loop for slot in slots
            when (eql (slot-number slot) 2)
            collect '((,(first slot) 1 ,(third slot))
                      ,@(remove slot (rest slots))
                      ,old-1)))))

(defun slot-number (slot) (first-or-self (second slot)))
```

Finally, we provide a special function just to define the copula, "be."

```
(defun copula (senses entries)
  "Copula entries are both aux and main verb."
  ;; They also are used in passive verb phrases and aux-inv-S
  (dolist (entry entries)
    (add-word (first entry) 'aux (second entry) (third entry))
    (add-word (first entry) 'verb (second entry) senses)
    (add-word (first entry) 'aux (second entry) 'passive)
    (add-word (first entry) 'be)))
```

The remaining functions are used for testing, debugging, and extending the grammar. First, we need functions to clear everything so that we can start over. These functions can be placed at the top of the lexicon and grammar files, respectively:

```
(defun clear-lexicon ()
  (clrhash *words*)
  (clear-abbrevs))

(defun clear-grammar ()
  (clear-examples)
  (clear-db))
```

Testing could be done with run-examples, but it is convenient to provide another interface, the macro try (and its corresponding function, try-dcg). Both macro and function can be invoked three ways. With no argument, all the examples stored by :ex are run. When the name of a category is given, all the examples for that category alone are run. Finally, the user can supply both the name of a category and a list of words to test whether those words can be parsed as that category. This option is only available for categories that are listed in the definition:

```
(defmacro try (&optional cat &rest words)
  "Tries to parse WORDS as a constituent of category CAT.
  With no words, runs all the :ex examples for category.
  With no cat, runs all the examples."
  '(try-dcg ',cat ',words))

(defun try-dcg (&optional cat words)
  "Tries to parse WORDS as a constituent of category CAT.
  With no words, runs all the :ex examples for category.
  With no cat, runs all the examples."
  (if (null words)
      (run-examples cat)
      (let ((args '((gap nil) (gap nil) ?sem ,words ())))
        (mapc #'test-unknown-word words)
        (top-level-prove
          (ecase cat
            (np '((np ? ? ?wh ?x ,@args)))))
```

```
                    (vp '((vp ?infl ?x ?sl ?v ,@args)))
                    (pp '((pp ?prep ?role ?wh ?x ,@args)))
                    (xp '((xp ?slot ?constituent ?wh ?x ,@args)))
                    (s  '((s ? ?sem ,words ())))
                    (rel-clause '((rel-clause ? ?x ?sem ,words ())))
                    (clause '((clause ?infl ?x ?int-subj ?v ?g1 ?g2
                                      ?sem ,words ()))))))))))

(defun test-unknown-word (word)
  "Print a warning message if this is an unknown word."
  (unless (or (gethash word *words*) (numberp word))
    (warn "~&Unknown word: ~a" word)))
```

21.13   Other Primitives

To support the :test predicates made in various grammar rules we need definitions of the Prolog predicates if, member, =, numberp, and atom. They are repeated here:

```
(<- (if ?test ?then) (if ?then ?else (fail)))
(<- (if ?test ?then ?else) (call ?test) ! (call ?then))
(<- (if ?test ?then ?else) (call ?else))

(<- (member ?item (?item . ?rest)))
(<- (member ?item (?x . ?rest)) (member ?item ?rest))

(<- (= ?x ?x))

(defun numberp/1 (x cont)
  (when (numberp (deref x))
    (funcall cont)))

(defun atom/1 (x cont)
  (when (atom (deref x))
    (funcall cont)))

(defun call/1 (goal cont)
  "Try to prove goal by calling it."
  (deref goal)
  (apply (make-predicate (first goal)
                         (length (args goal)))
         (append (args goal) (list cont))))
```

21.14   Examples

Here are some examples of what the parser can handle. I have edited the output
by changing variable names like ?168 to more readable names like ?J. The first
two examples show that nested clauses are supported and that we can extract a
constituent from a nested clause:

```
> (try S John promised Kim to persuade Lee to sleep)
?SEM = (AND (THE ?J (NAME JOHN ?J)) (AGT ?P ?J)
            (PAST ?P) (PROMISE ?P)
            (GOAL ?P ?K) (THE ?K (NAME KIM ?K))
            (CON ?P ?PER) (PERSUADE ?PER) (GOAL ?PER ?L)
            (THE ?L (NAME LEE ?L)) (CON ?PER ?S) (SLEEP ?S));

> (try S Who did John promise Kim to persuade to sleep)
?SEM = (AND (WH ?W (PERSON ?W)) (PAST ?P)
            (THE ?J (NAME JOHN ?J)) (AGT ?P ?J)
            (PROMISE ?P) (GOAL ?P ?K)
            (THE ?K (NAME KIM ?K)) (CON ?P ?PER)
            (PERSUADE ?PER) (GOAL ?PER ?W)
            (CON ?PER ?S) (SLEEP ?S));
```

In the next example, the "when" can be interpreted as asking about the time of any of
the three events: the promising, the persuading, or the sleeping. The grammar finds
all three.

```
> (try S When did John promise Kim to persuade Lee to sleep)
?SEM = (AND (WH ?W (TIME ?S ?W)) (PAST ?P)
            (THE ?J (NAME JOHN ?J)) (AGT ?P ?J)
            (PROMISE ?P) (GOAL ?P ?K)
            (THE ?K (NAME KIM ?K)) (CON ?P ?PER)
            (PERSUADE ?PER) (GOAL ?PER ?L)
            (THE ?L (NAME LEE ?L)) (CON ?PER ?S)
            (SLEEP ?S));

?SEM = (AND (WH ?W (TIME ?PER ?W)) (PAST ?P)
            (THE ?J (NAME JOHN ?J)) (AGT ?P ?J)
            (PROMISE ?P) (GOAL ?P ?K)
            (THE ?K (NAME KIM ?K)) (CON ?P ?PER)
            (PERSUADE ?PER) (GOAL ?PER ?L)
            (THE ?L (NAME LEE ?L)) (CON ?PER ?S)
            (SLEEP ?S));
```

```
?SEM = (AND (WH ?W (TIME ?P ?W)) (PAST ?P)
            (THE ?J (NAME JOHN ?J)) (AGT ?P ?J)
            (PROMISE ?P) (GOAL ?P ?K)
            (THE ?K (NAME KIM ?K)) (CON ?P ?PER)
            (PERSUADE ?PER) (GOAL ?PER ?L)
            (THE ?L (NAME LEE ?L)) (CON ?PER ?S)
            (SLEEP ?S)).
```

The next example shows auxiliary verbs and negation. It is ambiguous between an interpretation where Kim is searching for Lee and one where Kim is looking at something unspecified, on Lee's behalf.

```
> (try S Kim would not have been looking for Lee)
?SEM = (AND (THE ?K (NAME KIM ?K)) (AGT ?S ?K)
            (EXPECTED ?S) (NOT ?S) (PAST-PARTICIPLE ?S)
            (PROGRESSIVE ?S) (SEARCH ?S) (PAT ?S ?L)
            (PAT ?S ?L) (THE ?L (NAME LEE ?L)));

?SEM = (AND (THE ?K (NAME KIM ?K)) (AGT ?2 ?K)
            (EXPECTED ?2) (NOT ?2) (PAST-PARTICIPLE ?LOOK)
            (PROGRESSIVE ?LOOK) (LOOK ?LOOK) (FOR ?LOOK ?L)
            (THE ?L (NAME LEE ?L)));
```

The next two examples are unambiguous:

```
> (try s It should not surprise you that Kim does not like Lee)
?SEM = (AND (MANDATORY ?2) (NOT ?2) (SURPRISE ?2) (EXP ?2 ?YOU)
            (PRO ?YOU (LISTENER ?YOU)) (CON ?2 ?LIKE)
            (THE ?K (NAME KIM ?K)) (AGT ?LIKE ?K)
            (PRESENT ?LIKE) (NOT ?LIKE) (LIKE-1 ?LIKE)
            (OBJ ?LIKE ?L) (THE ?L (NAME LEE ?L)));

> (try s Kim did not want Lee to know that the man knew her)
?SEM = (AND (THE ?K (NAME KIM ?K)) (AGT ?W ?K) (PAST ?W)
            (NOT ?W) (DESIRE ?W) (GOAL ?W ?L)
            (THE ?L (NAME LEE ?L)) (CON ?W ?KN)
            (KNOW-THAT ?KN) (CON ?KN ?KN2)
            (THE ?M (MAN ?M)) (AGT ?KN2 ?M) (PAST ?KN2)
            (KNOW-OF ?KN2) (OBJ ?KN2 ?HER)
            (PRO ?HER (FEMALE ?HER))).
```

The final example appears to be unambiguous, but the parser finds four separate parses. The first is the obvious interpretation where the looking up is done quickly, and the second has quickly modifying the surprise. The last two interpretations are the same as the first two; they are artifacts of the search process. A disambiguation procedure should be equipped to weed out such duplicates.

```
> (try s That Kim looked her up quickly surprised me)
?SEM = (AND (THE ?K (NAME KIM ?K)) (AGT ?LU1 ?K) (PAST ?LU1)
            (LOOK-UP ?LU1) (PAT ?LU1 ?H) (PRO ?H (FEMALE ?H))
            (QUICKLY ?LU1) (CON ?S ?LU1) (PAST ?S) (SURPRISE ?S)
            (EXP ?S ?ME1) (PRO ?ME1 (SPEAKER ?ME1)));

?SEM = (AND (THE ?K (NAME KIM ?K)) (AGT ?LU2 ?K) (PAST ?LU2)
            (LOOK-UP ?LU2) (PAT ?LU2 ?H) (PRO ?H (FEMALE ?H))
            (CON ?S ?LU2) (QUICKLY ?S) (PAST ?S) (SURPRISE ?S)
            (EXP ?S ?ME2) (PRO ?ME2 (SPEAKER ?ME2)));

?SEM = (AND (THE ?K (NAME KIM ?K)) (AGT ?LU3 ?K) (PAST ?LU3)
            (LOOK-UP ?LU3) (PAT ?LU3 ?H) (PRO ?H (FEMALE ?H))
            (QUICKLY ?LU3) (CON ?S ?LU3) (PAST ?S) (SURPRISE ?S)
            (EXP ?S ?ME3) (PRO ?ME3 (SPEAKER ?ME3)));

?SEM = (AND (THE ?K (NAME KIM ?K)) (AGT ?LU4 ?K) (PAST ?LU4)
            (LOOK-UP ?LU4) (PAT ?LU4 ?H) (PRO ?H (FEMALE ?H))
            (CON ?S ?LU4) (QUICKLY ?S) (PAST ?S) (SURPRISE ?S)
            (EXP ?S ?ME4) (PRO ?ME4 (SPEAKER ?ME4)));
```

21.15   History and References

Chapter 20 provides some basic references on natural language. Here we will concentrate on references that provide:

1. A comprehensive grammar of English.

2. A complete implementation.

There are a few good textbooks that partially address both issues. Both Winograd (1983) and Allen (1987) do a good job of presenting the major grammatical features of English and discuss implementation techniques, but they do not provide actual code.

There are also a few textbooks that concentrate on the second issue. Ramsey and Barrett (1987) and Walker et al. (1990) provide chapter-length implementations at about the same level of detail as this chapter. Both are recommended. Pereira and Shieber 1987 and Gazdar and Mellish 1989 are book-length treatments, but because they cover a variety of parsing techniques rather than concentrating on one in depth, they are actually less comprehensive.

Several linguists have made serious attempts at addressing the first issue. The largest is the aptly named *A Comprehensive Grammar of Contemporary English* by Quirk, Greenbaum, Leech and Svartik (1985). More manageable (although hardly concise) is their abridged edition, *A Concise Grammar of Contemporary English*. Both editions contain a gold mine of examples and facts about the English langauge, but the authors do not attempt to write rigorous rules. Harris (1982) and Huddleston (1984) offer less complete grammars with greater linguistic rigor.

Naomi Sager (1981) presents the most complete computerized grammar ever published. The grammar is separated into a simple, neat, context-free component and a rather baroque augmentation that manipulates features.

21.16 Exercises

Exercise 21.1 [m] Change the grammar to account better for *mass nouns*. The current grammar treats mass nouns by making them vague between singular and plural, which is incorrect. They should be treated separately, since there are determiners such as "much" that work only with mass nouns, and other determiners such as "these" that work only with plural count nouns.

Exercise 21.2 [m] Change the grammar to make a distinction between *attributive* and *predicative* adjectives. Most adjectives fall into both classes, but some can be used only attributively, as in "an *utter* fool" but not "*the fool is *utter*." Other adjectives can only be used predicatively, as in "the woman was *loath* to admit it" but not "*a *loath* (to admit it) woman."

Exercise 21.3 [h] Implement complement lists for adjectives, so that "loath" would take an obligatory infinitive complement, and "proud" would take an optional (PP of) complement. In connection to the previous exercise, note that it is rare if not impossible for attributive adjectives to take complements: "he is proud," "he is proud of his country" and "a proud citizen" are all acceptable, but "*a proud of his country citizen" is not.

Exercise 21.4 [m] Add rules to advp to allow for adverbs to modify other adverbs, as in "extremely likely" or "very strongly."

Exercise 21.5 [h] Allow adverbs to modify adjectives, as in "very good" or "really delicious." The syntax will be easy, but it is harder to get a reasonable semantics. While you're at it, make sure that you can handle adjectives with so-called *nonintersective* semantics. Some adjectives can be handled by intersective semantics: a red circle is something that is red and is a circle. But for other adjectives, this model does not work: a former senator is not something that is former and is a senator—a former senator is not a senator at all. Similarly, a toy elephant is not an elephant.

The semantics should be represented by something closer to ((toy elephant) ?x) rather than (and (toy ?x) (elephant ?x)).

Exercise 21.6 [m] Write a function that notices punctuation instead of ignoring it. It should work something like this:

```
> (string->words "Who asked Lee, Kim and John?")
(WHO ASKED LEE |,| KIM AND JOHN |?|)
```

Exercise 21.7 [m] Change the grammar to allow optional punctuation marks at the end of sentences and before relative clauses.

Exercise 21.8 [m] Change the grammar to allow conjunction with more than two elements, using commas. Can these rules be generated automatically by conj-rule?

Exercise 21.9 [h] Make a distinction between *restrictive* and *nonrestrictive* relative clauses. In "The truck *that has 4-wheel drive* costs $5000," the italicized relative clause is restrictive. It serves to identify the truck and thus would be part of the quantifier's restriction. The complete sentence might be interpreted as:

```
(and (the ?x (and (truck ?x) (4-wheel-drive ?x)))
     (costs ?x $5000))
```

Contrast this to "The truck, which has 4-wheel drive, costs $5000." Here the relative clause is nonrestrictive and thus belongs outside the quantifier's restriction:

```
(and (the ?x (truck ?x))
   (4-wheel-drive ?x)(costs ?x $5000))
```

PART V

THE REST OF LISP

◇   ◇   ◇

CHAPTER 22

Scheme: An Uncommon Lisp

The best laid schemes o' mice an' men
—Robert Burns (1759–1796)

This chapter presents the Scheme dialect of Lisp and an interpreter for it. While it is not likely that you would use this interpreter for any serious programming, understanding how the interpreter works can give you a better appreciation of how Lisp works, and thus make you a better programmer. A Scheme interpreter is used instead of a Common Lisp one because Scheme is simpler, and also because Scheme is an important language that is worth knowing about.

Scheme is the only dialect of Lisp besides Common Lisp that is currently flourishing. Where Common Lisp tries to standardize all the important features that are in current use by Lisp programmers, Scheme tries to give a minimal set of very powerful features that can be used to implement the others. It is interesting that among all the programming languages in the world, Scheme is one of the smallest, while Common Lisp is one of the largest. The Scheme manual is only 45 pages (only 38 if you omit the example, bibliography, and index), while *Common Lisp the Language*, 2d edition, is 1029 pages. Here is a partial list of the ways Scheme is simpler than Common Lisp:

1. Scheme has fewer built-in functions and special forms.

2. Scheme has no special variables, only lexical variables.

3. Scheme uses the same name space for functions and variables (and everything else).

4. Scheme evaluates the function part of a function call in exactly the same way as the arguments.

5. Scheme functions can not have optional and keyword parameters. However, they can have the equivalent of a &rest parameter.

6. Scheme has no `block`, `return`, `go`, or `throw`; a single function (`call/cc`) replaces all of these (and does much more).

7. Scheme has no packages. Lexical variables can be used to implement package-like structures.

8. Scheme, as a standard, has no macros, although most implementations provide macros as an extension.

9. Scheme has no special forms for looping; instead it asks the user to use recursion and promises to implement the recursion efficiently.

The five main special forms in Scheme are `quote` and `if`, which are just as in Common Lisp; `begin` and `set!`, which are just different spellings for `progn` and `setq`; and `lambda`, which is as in Common Lisp, except that it doesn't require a `#'` before it. In addition, Scheme allows variables, constants (numbers, strings, and characters), and function calls. The function call is different because the function itself is evaluated in the same way as the arguments. In Common Lisp, (`f x`) means to look up the function binding of f and apply that to the value of x. In Scheme, (`f x`) means to evaluate f (in this case by looking up the value of the variable f), evaluate x (by looking up the value of the variable in exactly the same way) and then apply the function to the argument. Any expression can be in the function position, and it is evaluated just like the arguments. Another difference is that Scheme uses `#t` and `#f` for true and false, instead of t and `nil`. The empty list is denoted by (), and it is distinct from the false value, `#f`. There are also minor lexical differences in the conventions for complex numbers and numbers in different bases, but these can be ignored for all the programs in this book. Also, in Scheme a single macro, `define`, serves to define both variables and functions.

Scheme	Common Lisp
var	*var*
constant	*constant*
(quote *x*) **or** '*x*	(quote *x*) **or** '*x*
(begin *x*...)	(progn *x*...)
(set! *var x*)	(setq *var x*)
(if *p a b*)	(if *p a b*)
(lambda *parms x*...)	#'(lambda *parms x*...)
(*fn arg*...)	(*fn arg*...) **or** (funcall *fn arg*...)
#t	t
#f	nil
()	nil
(define *var exp*)	(defparameter *var exp*)
(define (*fn parm*...) *body*)	(defun *fn* (*parm*...) *body*)

Exercise 22.1 [s] What does the following expression evaluate to in Scheme? How many errors does it have as a Common Lisp expression?

```
((if (= (+ 2 2) 4)
     (lambda (x y) (+ (* x y) 12))
     cons)
 5
 6)
```

A great many functions, such as car, cdr, cons, append, +, *, and list are the same (or nearly the same) in both dialects. However, Scheme has some spelling conventions that are different from Common Lisp. Most Scheme mutators, like set!, end in '!'. Common Lisp has no consistent convention for this; some mutators start with n (nreverse, nsubst, nintersection) while others have idiosyncratic names (delete versus remove). Scheme would use consistent names—reverse! and remove!—if these functions were defined at all (they are not defined in the standard). Most Scheme predicates end in '?', not 'p'. This makes predicates more obvious and eliminates the complicated conventions for adding a hyphen before the p.[1] The only problem with this convention is in spoken language: is equal? pronounced "equal-question-mark" or "equal-q" or perhaps equal, with rising intonation? This would make Scheme a tone language, like Chinese.

---

[1] One writes numberp because there is no hyphen in number but random-state-p because there is a hyphen in random-state. However, defstruct concatenates -p in all its predicates, regardless of the presence of a hyphen in the structure's name.

In Scheme, it is an error to apply `car` or `cdr` to the empty list. Despite the fact that Scheme has `cons`, it calls the result a `pair` rather than a cons cell, so the predicate is `pair?`, not `consp`.

Scheme recognizes not all lambda expressions will be "functions" according to the mathematical definition of function, and so it uses the term "procedure" instead. Here is a partial list of correspondences between the two dialects:

Scheme Procedure	Common Lisp Function
char-ready?	listen
char?	characterp
eq?	eq
equal?	equal
eqv?	eql
even?	evenp
for-each	mapc
integer?	integerp
list->string	coerce
list->vector	coerce
list-ref	nth
list-tail	nthcdr
map	mapcar
negative?	minusp
pair?	consp
procedure?	functionp
set!	setq
set-car!	replaca
vector-set!	setf
string-set!	setf

22.1   A Scheme Interpreter

As we have seen, an interpreter takes a program (or expression) as input and returns the value computed by that program. The Lisp function `eval` is thus an interpreter, and that is essentially the function we are trying to write in this section. We have to be careful, however, in that it is possible to confuse the notions of interpreter and compiler. A compiler takes a program as input and produces as output a translation of that program into some other language—usually a language that can be directly (or more easily) executed on some machine. So it is also possible to write `eval` by compiling the argument and then interpreting the resulting machine-level program. Most modern Lisp systems support both possibilities, although some only interpret code directly, and others compile all code before executing it. To make the distinction clear, we will not write a function called eval. Instead, we will write versions of two functions: interp, a Scheme interpreter, and, in the next chapter, comp, a Scheme compiler.

An interpreter that handles the Scheme primitives is easy to write. In the interpreter interp, the main conditional has eight cases, corresponding to the five special forms, symbols, other atoms, and procedure applications (otherwise known as function calls). For the moment we will stick with t and nil instead of #t and #f. After developing a simple interpreter, we will add support for macros, then develop a tail-recursive interpreter, and finally a continuation-passing interpreter. (These terms will be defined when the time comes.). The glossary for interp is in figure 22.1.

	Top-Level Functions
scheme	A Scheme read-interp-print loop.
interp	Interpret (evaluate) an expression in an environment.
def-scheme-macro	Define a Scheme macro.
	Special Variables
scheme-procs	Some procedures to store in the global environment.
	Auxiliary Functions
set-var!	Set a variable to a value.
get-var	Get the value of a variable in an environment.
set-global-var!	Set a global variable to a value.
get-global-var	Get the value of a variable fron the global environment.
extend-env	Add some variables and values to an environment.
init-scheme-interp	Initialize some global variables.
init-scheme-proc	Define a primitive Scheme procedure.
scheme-macro	Retrieve the Scheme macro for a symbol.
scheme-macro-expand	Macro-expand a Scheme expression.
maybe-add	Add an element to the front of a non-singleton list.
print-proc	Print a procedure.
	Data Type (tail-recursive version only)
proc	A Scheme procedure.
	Functions (continuation version only)
interp-begin	Interpret a begin expression.
interp-call	Interpret a function application.
map-interp	Map interp over a list.
call/cc	call with current continuation.
	Previously Defined Functions
last1	Select the last element of a list.
length=1	Is this a list of length 1?

Figure 22.1: Glossary for the Scheme Interpreter

The simple interpreter has eight cases to worry about: (1) If the expression is a symbol, look up its value in the environment. (2) If it is an atom that is not a symbol (such as a number), just return it. Otherwise, the expression must be a list. (3) If it starts with quote, return the quoted expression. (4) If it starts with begin, interpret each subexpression, and return the last one. (5) If it starts with set!, interpret the value and then set the variable to that value. (6) If it starts with if, then interpret the conditional, and depending on if it is true or not, interpret the then-part or the else-part. (7) If it starts with lambda, build a new procedure—a closure over the current environment. (8) Otherwise, it must be a procedure application. Interpret the procedure and all the arguments, and apply the procedure value to the argument values.

```
(defun interp (x &optional env)
  "Interpret (evaluate) the expression x in the environment env."
  (cond
    ((symbolp x) (get-var x env))
    ((atom x) x)
    ((case (first x)
       (QUOTE  (second x))
       (BEGIN  (last1 (mapcar #'(lambda (y) (interp y env))
                              (rest x))))
       (SET!   (set-var! (second x) (interp (third x) env) env))
       (IF     (if (interp (second x) env)
                   (interp (third x) env)
                   (interp (fourth x) env)))
       (LAMBDA (let ((parms (second x))
                     (code (maybe-add 'begin (rest2 x))))
                 #'(lambda (&rest args)
                     (interp code (extend-env parms args env)))))
       (t      ;; a procedure application
               (apply (interp (first x) env)
                      (mapcar #'(lambda (v) (interp v env))
                              (rest x)))))))))
```

An environment is represented as an association list of variable/value pairs, except for the global environment, which is represented by values on the global-val property of symbols. It would be simpler to represent the global environment in the same way as local environments, but it is more efficient to use property lists than one big global a-list. Furthermore, the global environment is distinct in that every symbol is implicitly defined in the global environment, while local environments only contain variables that are explicitly mentioned (in a lambda expression).

As an example, suppose we interpret the function call (f 1 2 3), and that the functions f has been defined by the Scheme expression:

```
(set! f (lambda (a b c) (+ a (g b c))))
```

Then we will interpret (f 1 2 3) by interpreting the body of f with the environment:

```
((a 1) (b 2) (c 3))
```

Scheme procedures are implemented as Common Lisp functions, and in fact all the Scheme data types are implemented by the corresponding Common Lisp types. I include the function init-scheme-interp to initialize a few global values and repeat the definitions of last1 and length=1:

```
(defun set-var! (var val env)
  "Set a variable to a value, in the given or global environment."
  (if (assoc var env)
      (setf (second (assoc var env)) val)
      (set-global-var! var val))
  val)

(defun get-var (var env)
  "Get the value of a variable, from the given or global environment."
    (if (assoc var env)
        (second (assoc var env))
        (get-global-var var)))

(defun set-global-var! (var val)
  (setf (get var 'global-val) val))

(defun get-global-var (var)
  (let* ((default "unbound")
         (val (get var 'global-val default)))
    (if (eq val default)
        (error "Unbound scheme variable: ~a" var)
        val)))

(defun extend-env (vars vals env)
  "Add some variables and values to an environment."
  (nconc (mapcar #'list vars vals) env))

(defparameter *scheme-procs*
  '(+ - * / = < > <= >= cons car cdr not append list read member
    (null? null) (eq? eq) (equal? equal) (eqv? eql)
    (write prin1) (display princ) (newline terpri)))
```

```
(defun init-scheme-interp ()
  "Initialize the scheme interpreter with some global variables."
  ;; Define Scheme procedures as CL functions:
  (mapc #'init-scheme-proc *scheme-procs*)
  ;; Define the Boolean 'constants'. Unfortunately, this won't
  ;; stop someone from saying: (set! t nil)
  (set-global-var! t t)
  (set-global-var! nil nil))

(defun init-scheme-proc (f)
  "Define a Scheme procedure as a corresponding CL function."
  (if (listp f)
      (set-global-var! (first f) (symbol-function (second f)))
      (set-global-var! f (symbol-function f))))

(defun maybe-add (op exps &optional if-nil)
  "For example, (maybe-add 'and exps t) returns
  t if exps is nil, exps if there is only one,
  and (and exp1 exp2...) if there are several exps."
  (cond ((null exps) if-nil)
        ((length=1 exps) (first exps))
        (t (cons op exps))))

(defun length=1 (x)
  "Is x a list of length 1?"
  (and (consp x) (null (cdr x))))

(defun last1 (list)
  "Return the last element (not last cons cell) of list"
  (first (last list)))
```

To test the interpreter, we add a simple read-eval-print loop:

```
(defun scheme ()
  "A Scheme read-eval-print loop (using interp)"
  (init-scheme-interp)
  (loop (format t "~&==> ")
        (print (interp (read) nil))))
```

And now we're ready to try out the interpreter. Note the Common Lisp prompt is ">," while the Scheme prompt is "==>."

```
> (scheme)
==> (+ 2 2)
4

==> ((if (= 1 2) * +) 3 4)
7
```

```
==> ((if (= 1 1) * +) 3 4)
12

==> (set! fact (lambda (n)
                  (if (= n 0) 1
                      (* n (fact (- n 1))))))
#<DTP-LEXICAL-CLOSURE 36722615>

==> (fact 5)
120

==> (set! table (lambda (f start end)
                  (if (<= start end)
                      (begin
                        (write (list start (f start)))
                        (newline)
                        (table f (+ start 1) end)))))
#<DTP-LEXICAL-CLOSURE 41072172>

==> (table fact 1 10)
(1 1)
(2 2)
(3 6)
(4 24)
(5 120)
(6 720)
(7 5040)
(8 40320)
(9 362880)
(10 3628800)
NIL

==> (table (lambda (x) (* x x x)) 5 10)
(5 125)
(6 216)
(7 343)
(8 512)
(9 729)
(10 1000)
NIL

==> [ABORT]
```

22.2   Syntactic Extension with Macros

Scheme has a number of other special forms that were not listed above. Actually, Scheme uses the term "syntax" where we have been using "special form." The remaining syntax can be defined as "derived expressions" in terms of the five primitives. The Scheme standard does not recognize a concept of macros, but it is clear that a "derived expression" is like a macro, and we will implement them using macros. The following forms are used (nearly) identically in Scheme and Common Lisp:

```
let   let*   and   or   do   cond   case
```

One difference is that Scheme is less lenient as to what counts as a binding in `let`, `let*` and do. Every binding must be (*var init*); just (*var*) or *var* is not allowed. In do, a binding can be either (*var init step*) or (*var init*). Notice there is no do*. The other difference is in case and cond. Where Common Lisp uses the symbol t or `otherwise` to mark the final case, Scheme uses `else`. The final three syntactic extensions are unique to Scheme:

```
(define var val)        or        (define (proc-name arg...) body...)
(delay expression)
(letrec ((var init)...) body...)
```

define is a combination of defun and defparameter. In its first form, it assigns a value to a variable. Since there are no special variables in Scheme, this is no different than using set!. (There is a difference when the define is nested inside another definition, but that is not yet considered.) In the second form, it defines a function. delay is used to delay evaluation, as described in section 9.3, page 281. letrec is similar to let. The difference is that all the *init* forms are evaluated in an environment that includes all the *vars*. Thus, letrec can be used to define local recursive functions, just as labels does in Common Lisp.

The first step in implementing these syntactic extensions is to change interp to allow macros. Only one clause has to be added, but we'll repeat the whole definition:

```
(defun interp (x &optional env)
  "Interpret (evaluate) the expression x in the environment env.
  This version handles macros."
  (cond
    ((symbolp x) (get-var x env))
    ((atom x) x)
    ((scheme-macro (first x))                   ;***
     (interp (scheme-macro-expand x) env)) ;***
    ((case (first x)
       (QUOTE  (second x))
```

```
(BEGIN   (last1 (mapcar #'(lambda (y) (interp y env))
                          (rest x))))
(SET!    (set-var! (second x) (interp (third x) env) env))
(IF      (if (interp (second x) env)
             (interp (third x) env)
             (interp (fourth x) env)))
(LAMBDA (let ((parms (second x))
              (code (maybe-add 'begin (rest2 x))))
           #'(lambda (&rest args)
               (interp code (extend-env parms args env)))))
(t       ;; a procedure application
         (apply (interp (first x) env)
                (mapcar #'(lambda (v) (interp v env))
                        (rest x)))))))))
```

Now we provide a mechanism for defining macros. The macro definitions can be in any convenient language; the easiest choices are Scheme itself or Common Lisp. I have chosen the latter. This makes it clear that macros are not part of Scheme itself but rather are used to implement Scheme. If we wanted to offer the macro facility to the Scheme programmer, we would make the other choice. (But then we would be sure to add the backquote notation, which is so useful in writing macros.) def-scheme-macro (which happens to be a macro itself) provides a way of adding new Scheme macros. It does that by storing a Common Lisp function on the scheme-macro property of a symbol. This function, when given a list of arguments, returns the code that the macro call should expand into. The function scheme-macro tests if a symbol has a macro attached to it, and scheme-macro-expand does the actual macro-expansion:

```
(defun scheme-macro (symbol)
  (and (symbolp symbol)  (get symbol 'scheme-macro)))

(defmacro def-scheme-macro (name parmlist &body body)
  "Define a Scheme macro."
  '(setf (get ',name 'scheme-macro)
         #'(lambda ,parmlist .,body)))

(defun scheme-macro-expand (x)
  "Macro-expand this Scheme expression."
  (if (and (listp x) (scheme-macro (first x)))
      (scheme-macro-expand
        (apply (scheme-macro (first x)) (rest x)))
      x))
```

Here are the definitions of nine important macros in Scheme:

```
(def-scheme-macro let (bindings &rest body)
  `((lambda ,(mapcar #'first bindings) . ,body)
    .,(mapcar #'second bindings)))

(def-scheme-macro let* (bindings &rest body)
  (if (null bindings)
      `(begin .,body)
      `(let (,(first bindings))
         (let* ,(rest bindings) . ,body))))

(def-scheme-macro and (&rest args)
  (cond ((null args) 'T)
        ((length=1 args) (first args))
        (t `(if ,(first args)
                (and . ,(rest args))))))

(def-scheme-macro or (&rest args)
  (cond ((null args) 'nil)
        ((length=1 args) (first args))
        (t (let ((var (gensym)))
             `(let ((,var ,(first args)))
                (if ,var ,var (or . ,(rest args))))))))

(def-scheme-macro cond (&rest clauses)
  (cond ((null clauses) nil)
        ((length=1 (first clauses))
         `(or ,(first clauses) (cond .,(rest clauses))))
        ((starts-with (first clauses) 'else)
         `(begin .,(rest (first clauses))))
        (t `(if ,(first (first clauses))
                (begin .,(rest (first clauses)))
                (cond .,(rest clauses))))))

(def-scheme-macro case (key &rest clauses)
  (let ((key-val (gensym "KEY")))
    `(let ((,key-val ,key))
       (cond ,@(mapcar
                 #'(lambda (clause)
                     (if (starts-with clause 'else)
                         clause
                         `((member ,key-val ',(first clause))
                           .,(rest clause))))
                 clauses)))))

(def-scheme-macro define (name &rest body)
  (if (atom name)
      `(begin (set! ,name . ,body) ',name)
      `(define ,(first name)
         (lambda ,(rest name) . ,body))))
```

```
(def-scheme-macro delay (computation)
  '(lambda () ,computation))

(def-scheme-macro letrec (bindings &rest body)
  '(let ,(mapcar #'(lambda (v) (list (first v) nil)) bindings)
     ,@(mapcar #'(lambda (v) '(set! .,v)) bindings)
     .,body))
```

We can test out the macro facility:

```
> (scheme-macro-expand '(and p q)) ⇒ (IF P (AND Q))

> (scheme-macro-expand '(and q)) ⇒ Q

> (scheme-macro-expand '(let ((x 1) (y 2) (+ x y))) ⇒
((LAMBDA (X Y) (+ X Y)) 1 2)

> (scheme-macro-expand
    '(letrec
        ((even? (lambda (x) (or (= x 0) (odd? (- x 1)))))
         (odd?  (lambda (x) (even? (- x 1)))))
        (even? z))) ⇒
(LET ((EVEN? NIL)
      (ODD? NIL))
  (SET! EVEN? (LAMBDA (X) (OR (= X 0) (ODD? (- X 1)))))
  (SET! ODD? (LAMBDA (X) (EVEN? (- X 1))))
  (EVEN? Z))

> (scheme)
==> (define (reverse l)
      (if (null? l) nil
          (append (reverse (cdr l)) (list (car l)))))
REVERSE

==> (reverse '(a b c d))
(D C B A)

==> (let* ((x 5) (y (+ x x)))
      (if (or (= x 0) (and (< 0 y) (< y 20)))
          (list x y)
          (+ y x)))
(5 10)
```

The macro define is just like set!, except that it returns the symbol rather than the value assigned to the symbol. In addition, define provides an optional syntax for defining functions—it serves the purposes of both defun and defvar. The syntax (define (*fn* . *args*) . *body*) is an abbreviation for (define *fn* (lambda *args* . *body*)).

In addition, Scheme provides a notation where define can be used inside a function definition in a way that makes it work like let rather than set!.

The advantage of the macro-based approach to special forms is that we don't have to change the interpreter to add new special forms. The interpreter remains simple, even while the language grows. This also holds for the compiler, as we see in the next section.

22.3   A Properly Tail-Recursive Interpreter

Unfortunately, the interpreter presented above can not lay claim to the name Scheme, because a true Scheme must be properly tail-recursive. Our interpreter is tail-recursive only when run in a Common Lisp that is tail-recursive. To see the problem, consider the following Scheme procedure:

```
(define (traverse lyst)
  (if lyst (traverse (cdr lyst))))
```

Trace the function interp and execute (interp '(traverse '(a b c d))). The nested calls to interp go 16 levels deep. In general, the level of nesting is 4 plus 3 times the length of the list. Each call to interp requires Common Lisp to allocate some storage on the stack, so for very long lists, we will eventually run out of storage. To earn the name Scheme, a language must guarantee that such a program does not run out of storage.

The problem, in this example, lies in two places. Everytime we interpret an if form or a procedure call, we descend another recursive level into interp. But that extra level is not necessary. Consider the if form. It is certainly necessary to call interp recursively to decide if the test is true or not. For the sake of argument, let's say the test is true. Then we call interp again on the *then* part. This recursive call will return a value, which will then be immediately returned as the value of the original call as well.

The alternative is to replace the recursive call to interp with a renaming of variables, followed by a goto statement. That is, instead of calling interp and thereby binding a new instance of the variable x to the *then* part, we just assign the *then* part to x, and branch to the top of the interp routine. This works because we know we have no more use for the old value of x. A similar technique is used to eliminate the recursive call for the last expression in a begin form. (Many programmers have been taught the "structured programming" party line that goto statements are harmful. In this case, the goto is necessary to implement a low-level feature efficiently.)

The final thing we need to do is explicitly manage Scheme procedures. Instead of implementing Scheme procedures as Common Lisp closures, we will define a structure, proc, to contain the code, environment, parameter list, and optionally the name of the procedure. Then when we are evaluating a procedure call, we can assign the body of the procedure to x rather than recursively calling interp.

```lisp
(defstruct (proc (:print-function print-proc))
  "Represent a Scheme procedure"
  code (env nil)(name nil) (parms nil))
```

The following is a properly tail-recursive interpreter. The macro prog sets up a tagbody within which we can use go statements to branch to labels, and it also sets up a block from which we can return a value. It can also bind variables like let, although in this usage, the variable list is empty. Any symbol within the body of a prog is considered a label. In this case, the label :INTERP is the target of the branch statements (GO :INTERP). I use uppercase to indicate that go-to statements are being used, but this convention has not been widely adopted.

```lisp
(defun interp (x &optional env)
  "Evaluate the expression x in the environment env.
  This version is properly tail-recursive."
  (prog ()
    :INTERP
    (return
      (cond
        ((symbolp x) (get-var x env))
        ((atom x) x)
        ((scheme-macro (first x))
         (setf x (scheme-macro-expand x)) (go :INTERP))
        ((case (first x)
           (QUOTE  (second x))
           (BEGIN  (pop x) ; pop off the BEGIN to get at the args
                   ;; Now interpret all but the last expression
                   (loop while (rest x) do (interp (pop x) env))
                   ;; Finally, rename the last expression as x
                   (setf x (first x))
                   (GO :INTERP))
           (SET!   (set-var! (second x) (interp (third x) env) env))
           (IF     (setf x (if (interp (second x) env)
                               (third x)
                               (fourth x)))
                   ;; That is, rename the right expression as x
                   (GO :INTERP))
           (LAMBDA (make-proc :env env :parms (second x)
                              :code (maybe-add 'begin (rest2 x))))
```

```
      (t        ;; a procedure application
          (let ((proc (interp (first x) env))
                (args (mapcar #'(lambda (v) (interp v env))
                              (rest x))))
            (if (proc-p proc)
                ;; Execute procedure with rename+goto
                (progn
                  (setf x (proc-code proc))
                  (setf env (extend-env (proc-parms proc) args
                                        (proc-env proc)))
                  (GO :INTERP))
                ;; else apply primitive procedure
                (apply proc args)))))))))))

(defun print-proc (proc &optional (stream *standard-output*) depth)
  (declare (ignore depth))
  (format stream "{~a}" (or (proc-name proc) '??)))
```

By tracing the tail-recursive version of interp, you can see that calls to traverse descend only three recursive levels of interp, regardless of the length of the list traversed.

Note that we are not claiming that this interpreter allocates no storage when it makes tail-recursive calls. Indeed, it wastes quite a bit of storage in evaluating arguments and building environments. The claim is that since the storage is allocated on the heap rather than on the stack, it can be reclaimed by the garbage collector. So even if traverse is applied to an infinitely long list (i.e., a circular list), the interpreter will never run out of space—it will always be able to garbage-collect and continue.

There are many improvements that could be made to this interpreter, but effort is better spent in improving a compiler rather than an interpreter. The next chapter does just that.

22.4 Throw, Catch, and Call/cc

Tail-recursion is crucial to Scheme. The idea is that when the language is guaranteed to optimize tail-recursive calls, then there is no need for special forms to do iteration. All loops can be written using recursion, without any worry of overflowing the run-time stack. This helps keep the language simple and rules out the goto statement, the scourge of the structured programming movement. However, there are cases where some kind of nonlocal exit is the best alternative. Suppose that some unexpected event happens deep inside your program. The best action is to print an error message and pop back up to the top level of your program. This could be done trivially with a goto-like statement. Without it, every function along the calling path would have to be altered to accept either a valid result or an indication of the exceptional condition, which just gets passed up to the next level.

In Common Lisp, the functions throw and catch are provided for this kind of nonlocal exit. Scott Zimmerman, the perennial world Frisbee champion, is also a programmer for a Southern California firm. He once told me, "I'm starting to learn Lisp, and it must be a good language because it's got throw and catch in it." Unfortunately for Scott, throw and catch don't refer to Frisbees but to transfer of control. They are both special forms, with the following syntax:

```
(catch tag body...)
(throw tag value)
```

The first argument to catch is a tag, or label. The remaining arguments are evaluated one at a time, and the last one is returned. Thus, catch is much like progn. The difference is that if any code in the dynamic extent of the body of the catch evaluates the special form throw, then control is immediately passed to the enclosing catch with the same tag.

For example, the form

```
(catch 'tag
  (print 1) (throw 'tag 2) (print 3))
```

prints 1 and returns 2, without going on to print 3. A more representative example is:

```
(defun print-table (l)
  (catch 'not-a-number (mapcar #'print-sqrt-abs l)))

(defun print-sqrt-abs (x)
  (print (sqrt (abs (must-be-number x)))))

(defun must-be-number (x)
  (if (numberp x) x
      (throw 'not-a-number "huh?")))

> (print-table '(1 4 -9 x 10 20))
1
2
3
"huh?"
```

Here print-table calls print-sqrt-abs, which calls must-be-number. The first three times all is fine and the values 1,2,3 get printed. The next time x is not a number, so the value "huh?" gets thrown to the tag not-a-number established by catch in f. The throw bypasses the pending calls to abs, sqrt, and print, as well as the rest of the call to mapcar.

This kind of control is provided in Scheme with a very general and powerful procedure, call-with-current-continuation, which is often abbreviated call/cc. call/cc is a normal procedure (not a special form like throw and catch) that takes a single argument. Let's call the argument computation. computation must be a procedure of one argument. When call/cc is invoked, it calls computation, and whatever computation returns is the value of the call to call/cc. The trick is that the procedure computation also takes an argument (which we'll call cc) that is another procedure representing the current continuation point. If cc is applied to some value, that value is returned as the value of the call to call/cc. Here are some examples:

```
> (scheme)
=> (+ 1 (call/cc (lambda (cc) (+ 20 300))))
321
```

This example ignores cc and just computes (+ 1 (+ 20 300)). More precisely, it is equivalent to:

```
((lambda (val) (+ 1 val))
 (+ 20 300))
```

The next example does make use of cc:

```
=> (+ 1 (call/cc (lambda (cc) (+ 20 (cc 300)))))
301
```

This passes 300 to cc, thus bypassing the addition of 20. It effectively throws 300 out of the computation to the catch point established by call/cc. It is equivalent to:

```
((lambda (val) (+ 1 val))
 300)
```

or to:

```
((lambda (val) (+ 1 val))
 (catch 'cc
   ((lambda (v) (+ 20 v))
    (throw 'cc 300))))
```

Here's how the throw/catch mechanism would look in Scheme:

```
(define (print-table l)
  (call/cc
    (lambda (escape)
      (set! not-a-number escape)
      (map print-sqrt-abs l))))
(define (print-sqrt-abs x)
  (write (sqrt (abs (must-be-number x)))))
(define (must-be-number x)
  (if (numberp x) x
      (not-a-number "huh?")))
(define (map fn l)
  (if (null? l)
      '()
      (cons (fn (first l))
            (map fn (rest l)))))
```

The ability to return to a pending point in the computation is useful for this kind of error and interrupt handling. However, the truly amazing, wonderful thing about call/cc is the ability to return to a continuation point more than once. Consider a slight variation:

```
=> (+ 1 (call/cc (lambda (cc)
                   (set! old-cc cc)
                   (+ 20 (cc 300)))))
301

=> (old-cc 500)
501
```

Here, we first computed 301, just as before, but along the way saved cc in the global variable old-cc. Afterward, calling (old-cc 500) returns (for the second time) to the point in the computation where 1 is added, this time returning 501. The equivalent Common Lisp code leads to an error:

```
> (+ 1 (catch 'tag (+ 20 (throw 'tag 300))))
301

> (throw 'tag 500)
```
Error: there was no pending CATCH for the tag TAG

In other words, call/cc's continuations have indefinite extent, while throw/catch tags only have dynamic extent.

We can use call/cc to implement automatic backtracking (among other things). Suppose we had a special form, amb, the "ambiguous" operator, which returns one of its arguments, chosen at random. We could write:

```
(define (integer) (amb 1 (+ 1 (integer))))
```

and a call to integer would return some random positive integer. In addition, suppose we had a function, fail, which doesn't return at all but instead causes execution to continue at a prior amb point, with the other choice taken. Then we could write succinct[2] backtracking code like the following:

```
(define (prime)
  (let ((n (integer)))
    (if (prime? n) n (fail))))
```

If prime? is a predicate that returns true only when its argument is a prime number, then prime will always return some prime number, decided by generating random integers. While this looks like a major change to the language—adding backtracking and nondeterminism—it turns out that amb and fail can be implemented quite easily with call/cc. First, we need to make amb be a macro:

```
(def-scheme-macro amb (x y)
  '(random-choice (lambda () ,x) (lambda () ,y))))
```

The rest is pure Scheme. We maintain a list of backtrack-points, which are implemented as functions of no arguments. To backtrack, we just call one of these functions. That is what fail does. The function choose-first takes two functions and pushes the second, along with the proper continuation, on backtrack-points, and then calls the first, returning that value. The function random-choice is what amb expands into: it decides which choice is first, and which is second. (Note that the convention in Scheme is to write global variables like backtrack-points without asterisks.)

```
(define backtrack-points nil)

(define (fail)
  (let ((last-choice (car backtrack-points)))
    (set! backtrack-points (cdr backtrack-points))
    (last-choice)))
```

---

[2]although inefficient

```
(define (random-choice f g)
  (if (= 1 (random 2))
      (choose-first f g)
      (choose-first g f)))

(define (choose-first f g)
  (call/cc
    (lambda (k)
      (set! backtrack-points
            (cons (lambda () (k (g))) backtrack-points))
      (f))))
```

This implements chronological backtracking, as in Prolog. However, we actually have the freedom to do other kinds of backtracking as well. Instead of having fail take the first element of backtrack-points, we could choose a random element instead. Or, we could do some more complex analysis to choose a good backtrack point.

call/cc can be used to implement a variety of control structures. As another example, many Lisp implementations provide a reset function that aborts the current computation and returns control to the top-level read-eval-print loop. reset can be defined quite easily using call/cc. The trick is to capture a continuation that is at the top level and save it away for future use. The following expression, evaluated at the top level, saves the appropriate continuation in the value of reset:

```
(call/cc (lambda (cc) (set! reset (lambda ()
                                    (cc "Back to top level")))))
```

▣ **Exercise 22.2 [m]** Can you implement call/cc in Common Lisp?

▣ **Exercise 22.3 [s]** Can you implement amb and fail in Common Lisp?

▣ **Exercise 22.4 [m]** fail could be written
(define (fail) ((pop backtrack-points))) if we had the pop macro in Scheme. Write pop.

22.5   An Interpreter Supporting Call/cc

It is interesting that the more a host language has to offer, the easier it is to write an interpreter. Perhaps the hardest part of writing a Lisp interpreter (or compiler) is garbage collection. By writing our interpreter in Lisp, we bypassed the problem all together—the host language automatically collects garbage. Similarly, if we are using a Common Lisp that is properly tail-recursive, then our interpreter will be too, without taking any special steps. If not, the interpreter must be rewritten to take care of tail-recursion, as we have seen above.

It is the same with call/cc. If our host language provides continuations with indefinite extent, then it is trivial to implement call/cc. If not, we have to rewrite the whole interpreter, so that it explicitly handles continuations. The best way to do this is to make interp a function of three arguments: an expression, an environment, and a continuation. That means the top level will have to change too. Rather than having interp return a value that gets printed, we just pass it the function print as a continuation:

```
(defun scheme ()
  "A Scheme read-eval-print loop (using interp).
  Handles call/cc by explicitly passing continuations."
  (init-scheme-interp)
  (loop (format t "~&==> ")
        (interp (read) nil #'print)))
```

Now we are ready to tackle interp. For clarity, we will base it on the non-tail-recursive version. The cases for symbols, atoms, macros, and quote are almost the same as before. The difference is that the result of each computation gets passed to the continuation, cc, rather than just being returned.

The other cases are all more complex, because they all require explicit representation of continuations. That means that calls to interp cannot be nested. Instead, we call interp with a continuation that includes another call to interp. For example, to interpret (if p x y), we first call interp on the second element of the form, the predicate p. The continuation for this call is a function that tests the value of p and interprets either x or y accordingly, using the original continuation for the recursive call to interp. The other cases are similar. One important change is that Scheme procedures are implemented as Lisp functions where the first argument is the continuation:

```
(defun interp (x env cc)
  "Evaluate the expression x in the environment env,
  and pass the result to the continuation cc."
  (cond
    ((symbolp x) (funcall cc (get-var x env)))
    ((atom x) (funcall cc x))
    ((scheme-macro (first x))
     (interp (scheme-macro-expand x) env cc))
    ((case (first x)
       (QUOTE (funcall cc (second x)))
       (BEGIN (interp-begin (rest x) env cc))
```

```
(SET!    (interp (third x) env
                 #'(lambda (val)
                     (funcall cc (set-var! (second x)
                                            val env)))))
(IF      (interp (second x) env
                 #'(lambda (pred)
                     (interp (if pred (third x) (fourth x))
                             env cc))))
(LAMBDA (let ((parms (second x))
              (code (maybe-add 'begin (rest2 x))))
           (funcall
             cc
             #'(lambda (cont &rest args)
                 (interp code
                         (extend-env parms args env)
                         cont)))))
(t       (interp-call x env cc)))))))
```

A few auxiliary functions are defined, in the same continuation-passing style:

```
(defun interp-begin (body env cc)
  "Interpret each element of BODY, passing the last to CC."
  (interp (first body) env
          #'(lambda (val)
              (if (null (rest body))
                  (funcall cc val)
                  (interp-begin (rest body) env cc)))))

(defun interp-call (call env cc)
  "Interpret the call (f x...) and pass the result to CC."
  (map-interp call env
              #'(lambda (fn-and-args)
                  (apply (first fn-and-args)
                         cc
                         (rest fn-and-args)))))

(defun map-interp (list env cc)
  "Interpret each element of LIST, and pass the list to CC."
  (if (null list)
      (funcall cc nil)
      (interp (first list) env
              #'(lambda (x)
                  (map-interp (rest list) env
                              #'(lambda (y)
                                  (funcall cc (cons x y))))))))
```

Because Scheme procedures expect a continuation as the first argument, we need to redefine init-scheme-proc to install procedures that accept and apply the continuation:

```
(defun init-scheme-proc (f)
  "Define a Scheme primitive procedure as a CL function."
  (if (listp f)
      (set-global-var! (first f)
                       #'(lambda (cont &rest args)
                           (funcall cont (apply (second f) args))))
      (init-scheme-proc (list f f))))
```

We also need to define call/cc. Think for a moment about what call/cc must do. Like all Scheme procedures, it takes the current continuation as its first argument. The second argument is a procedure—a computation to be performed. call/cc performs the computation by calling the procedure. This is just a normal call, so it uses the current continuation. The tricky part is what call/cc passes the computation as its argument. It passes an escape procedure, which can be invoked to return to the same point that the original call to call/cc would have returned to. Once the working of call/cc is understood, the implementation is obvious:

```
(defun call/cc (cc computation)
  "Make the continuation accessible to a Scheme procedure."
  (funcall computation cc
           ;; Package up CC into a Scheme function:
           #'(lambda (cont val)
               (declare (ignore cont))
               (funcall cc val))))

;; Now install call/cc in the global environment
(set-global-var! 'call/cc #'call/cc)
(set-global-var! 'call-with-current-continuation #'call/cc)
```

22.6   History and References

Lisp interpreters and AI have a long history together. MIT AI Lab Memo No. 1 (McCarthy 1958) was the first paper on Lisp. McCarthy's students were working on a Lisp compiler, had written certain routines—read, print, etc.—in assembly language, and were trying to develop a full Lisp interpreter in assembler. Sometime around the end of 1958, McCarthy wrote a theoretical paper showing that Lisp was powerful enough to write the universal function, `eval`. A programmer on the project, Steve Russell, saw the paper, and, according to McCarthy:

> *Steve Russell said, look, why don't I program this* `eval` *and—you remember the interpreter—and I said to him, ho, ho, you're confusing theory with practice, this* `eval` *is intended for reading not for computing. But he went ahead and did it. That is, he compiled the* `eval` *in my paper into 704 machine code fixing bugs and then advertised this as a Lisp interpreter, which it certainly was.*[3]

So the first Lisp interpreter was the result of a programmer ignoring his boss's advice. The first compiler was for the Lisp 1.5 system (McCarthy et al. 1962). The compiler was written in Lisp; it was probably the first compiler written in its own language.

Allen's *Anatomy of Lisp* (1978) was one of the first overviews of Lisp implementation techniques, and it remains one of the best. However, it concentrates on the dynamic-scoping Lisp dialects that were in use at the time. The more modern view of a lexically scoped Lisp was documented in an influential pair of papers by Guy Steele (1976a,b). His papers "Lambda: the ultimate goto" and "Compiler optimization based on viewing lambda as rename plus goto" describe properly tail-recursive interpreters and compilers.

The Scheme dialect was invented by Gerald Sussman and Guy Steele around 1975 (see their MIT AI Memo 349). The *Revised[4] Report on the Algorithmic Language Scheme* (Clinger et al. 1991) is the definitive reference manual for the current version of Scheme.

Abelson and Sussman (1985) is probably the best introduction to computer science ever written. It may or may not be a coincidence that it uses Scheme as the programming language. It includes a Scheme interpreter. Winston and Horn's *Lisp* (1989) also develops a Lisp interpreter.

The `amb` operator for nondeterministic choice was proposed by John McCarthy (1963) and used in SCHEMER (Zabih et al. 1987), a nondeterministic Lisp. Ruf and Weise (1990) present another implementation of backtracking in Scheme that incorporates all of logic programming.

---

[3]McCarthy's words from a talk on the history of Lisp, 1974, recorded by Stoyan (1984).

22.7   Exercises

Exercise 22.5 [m]   While Scheme does not provide full-blown support for optional and keyword arguments, it does support rest parameters. Modify the interpreter to support the Scheme syntax for rest parameters:

Scheme	**Common Lisp**
(lambda x *body*)	(lambda (&rest x) *body*)
(lambda (x y . z) *body*)	(lambda (x y &rest z) *body*)

Exercise 22.6 [h]   The representation of environments is somewhat wasteful. Currently it takes $3n$ cons cells to represent an environment with n variables. Change the representation to take less space.

Exercise 22.7 [m]   As we've implemented macros, they need to be expanded each time they are encountered. This is not so bad for the compiler—you expand the source code and compile it, and then never refer to the source code again. But for the interpreter, this treatment of macros is most unsatisfactory: the work of macro-expansion must be done again and again. How can you eliminate this duplicated effort?

Exercise 22.8 [m]   It turns out Scheme allows some additional syntax in let and cond. First, there is the "named-let" expression, which binds initial values for variables but also defines a local function that can be called within the body of the let. Second, cond recognizes the symbol => when it is the second element of a cond clause, and treats it as a directive to pass the value of the test (when it is not false) to the third element of the clause, which must be a function of one argument. Here are two examples:

```
(define (fact n)
  ;; Iterative factorial; does not grow the stack
  (let loop ((result 1) (i n))
    (if (= i 0) result (loop (* result i) (- i 1)))))

(define (lookup key alist)
  ;; Find key's value in alist
  (cond ((assoc key alist) => cdr)
        (else #f)))
```

These are equivalent to:

```
(define (fact n)
  (letrec
    ((loop (lambda (result i)
             (if (= i 0)
                 result
                 (loop (* result i) (- i 1)))))))
    (loop 1 n)))

(define (lookup key alist)
  (let ((g0030 (assoc key alist)))
    (if g0030
        (cdr g0030)
        #f)))
```

Write macro definitions for let and cond allowing these variations.

Exercise 22.9 [h] Some Scheme implementations permit define statements inside the body of a lambda (and thus of a define, let, let*, or letrec as well). Here is an example:

```
(define (length l)
  (define (len l n)
    (if (null? l) n (len (cdr l) (+ n 1))))
  (len l 0))
```

The internal definition of len is interpreted not as defining a global name but rather as defining a local name as if with letrec. The above definition is equivalent to:

```
(define (length l)
  (letrec ((len (lambda (l n)
                  (if (null? l) n (len (cdr l) (+ n 1))))))
    (len l 0)))
```

Make changes to the interpreter to allow this kind of internal definition.

Exercise 22.10 Scheme programmers are often disdainful of the function or #' notation in Common Lisp. Is it possible (without changing the compiler) to make Common Lisp accept (lambda () ...) instead of #'(lambda () ...) and fn instead of #'fn?

Exercise 22.11 [m] The top level of the continuation-passing version of scheme includes the call: (interp (read) nil #'print). Will this always result in some value being printed? Or is it possible that the expression read might call some escape function that ignores the value without printing anything?

▣ **Exercise 22.12 [h]** What would have to be added or changed to turn the Scheme interpreter into a Common Lisp interpreter?

▣ **Exercise 22.13 [h]** How would you change the interpreter to allow for multiple values? Explain how this would be done both for the first version of the interpreter and for the continuation-passing version.

22.8 Answers

Answer 22.2 There is no way to implement a full call/cc to Common Lisp, but the following works for cases where the continuation is only used with dynamic extent:

```
(defun call/cc (computation)
  "Call computation, passing it the current continuation.
  The continuation has only dynamic extent."
  (funcall computation #'(lambda (x) (return-from call/cc x))))
```

Answer 22.3 No. fail requires continuations with dynamic extent.

Answer 22.5 We need only modify extend-env to know about an atomic vars list. While we're at it, we might as well add some error checking:

```
(defun extend-env (vars vals env)
  "Add some variables and values to an environment."
  (cond ((null vars)
         (assert (null vals) () "Too many arguments supplied")
         env)
        ((atom vars)
         (cons (list vars vals) env))
        (t (assert (rest vals) () "Too few arguments supplied")
           (cons (list (first vars) (first vals))
                 (extend-env (rest vars) (rest vals) env)))))
```

Answer 22.6 Storing the environment as an association list, ((*var val*)...), makes it easy to look up variables with assoc. We could save one cons cell per variable just by changing to ((*var . val*)...). But even better is to switch to a different representation, one presented by Steele and Sussman in *The Art of the Interpreter* (1978). In this representation we switch from a single list of var/val pairs to a list of frames, where each frame is a var-list/val-list pair. It looks like this:

```
(((var...) . (val...))
 ((var...) . (val...))
 ...)
```

Now extend-env is trivial:

```
(defun extend-env (vars vals env)
  "Add some variables and values to an environment."
  (cons (cons vars vals) env))
```

The advantage of this approach is that in most cases we already have a list of variables (the procedure's parameter list) and values (from the mapcar of interp over the arguments). So it is cheaper to just cons these two lists together, rather than arranging them into pairs. Of course, get-var and set-var! become more complex.

Answer 22.7 One answer is to destructively alter the source code as it is macro-expanded, so that the next time the source code is interpreted, it will already be expanded. The following code takes care of that:

```
(defun scheme-macro-expand (x)
  (displace x (apply (scheme-macro (first x)) (rest x))))

(defun displace (old new)
  "Destructively change old cons-cell to new value."
  (if (consp new)
      (progn (setf (car old) (car new))
             (setf (cdr old) (cdr new))
             old)
      (displace old `(begin ,new))))
```

One drawback to this approach is that the user's source code is actually changed, which may make debugging confusing. An alternative is to expand into something that keeps both the original and macro-expanded code around:

```
(defun displace (old new)
  "Destructively change old to a DISPLACED structure."
  (setf (car old) 'DISPLACED)
  (setf (cdr old) (list new old))
  old)
```

This means that DISPLACED is a new special form, and we need a clause for it in the interpreter. It would look something like this:

```
(case (first x)
  ...
  (DISPLACED (interp (second x) env))
  ...
```

We'd also need to modify the printing routines to print just old whenever they see (displaced old new).

Answer 22.8

```
(def-scheme-macro let (vars &rest body)
  (if (symbolp vars)
      ;; named let
      (let ((f vars) (vars (first body)) (body (rest body)))
        `(letrec ((,f (lambda ,(mapcar #'first vars) .,body)))
           (,f .,(mapcar #'second vars))))
      ;; "regular" let
      `((lambda ,(mapcar #'first vars) . ,body)
        . ,(mapcar #'second vars)))))

(def-scheme-macro cond (&rest clauses)
  (cond ((null clauses) nil)
        ((length=1 (first clauses))
         `(or ,(first clauses) (cond .,(rest clauses))))
        ((starts-with (first clauses) 'else)
         `(begin .,(rest (first clauses))))
        ((eq (second (first clauses)) '=>)
         (assert (= (length (first clauses)) 3))
         (let ((var (gensym)))
           `(let ((,var ,(first (first clauses))))
              (if ,var (,(third (first clauses)) ,var)
                  (cond .,(rest clauses))))))
        (t `(if ,(first (first clauses))
                (begin .,(rest (first clauses)))
                (cond .,(rest clauses))))))
```

Answer 22.10 It is easy to define lambda as a macro, eliminating the need for #'(lambda ...):

```
(defmacro lambda (args &rest body)
  '(function (lambda ,args ,@body)))
```

If this were part of the Common Lisp standard, I would gladly use it. But because it is not, I have avoided it, on the grounds that it can be confusing.

It is also possible to write a new function-defining macro that would do the following type of expansion:

```
(defn double (x) (* 2 x)) ⇒
(defparameter double (defun double (x) (* 2 x)))
```

This makes double a special variable, so we can write double instead of #'double. But this approach is not recommended—it is dangerous to define special variables that violate the asterisk convention, and the Common Lisp compiler may not be able to optimize special variable references the way it can function special forms. Also, this approach would not interact properly with flet and labels.

CHAPTER 23

Compiling Lisp

Many textbooks show simple interpreters for Lisp, because they are simple to write, and because it is useful to know how an interpreter works. Unfortunately, not as many textbooks show how to write a compiler, even though the same two reasons hold. The simplest compiler need not be much more complex than an interpreter.

One thing that makes a compiler more complex is that we have to describe the output of the compiler: the instruction set of the machine we are compiling for. For the moment let's assume a stack-based machine. The calling sequence on this machine for a function call with n arguments is to push the n arguments onto the stack and then push the function to be called. A "CALL n" instruction saves the return point on the stack and goes to the first instruction of the called function. By convention, the first instruction of a function will always be "ARGS n", which pops n arguments off the stack, putting them in the new function's environment, where they can be accessed by LVAR and LSET instructions. The function should return with a RETURN instruction, which resets the program counter and the environment to the point of the original CALL instruction.

In addition, our machine has three JUMP instructions; one that branches unconditionally, and two that branch depending on if the top of the stack is nil or non-nil. There is also an instruction for popping unneeded values off the stack, and for accessing and altering global variables. The instruction set is shown in figure 23.1. A glossary for the compiler program is given in figure 23.2. A summary of a more complex version of the compiler appears on page 795.

opcode	args	description
CONST	x	push a constant on the stack
LVAR	i,j	push a local variable's value
GVAR	sym	push a global variable's value
LSET	i,j	store top-of-stack in a local variable
GSET	sym	store top-of-stack in a global variable
POP		pop the stack
TJUMP	label	go to label if top-of-stack is non-nil; pop stack
FJUMP	label	go to label if top-of-stack is nil; pop stack
JUMP	label	go to label (don't pop stack)
RETURN		go to last return point
ARGS	n	move n arguments from stack to environment
CALL	n	go to start of function, saving return point
		n is the number of arguments passed
FN	fn	create a closure from argument and current environment and push it on the stack

Figure 23.1: Instruction Set for Hypothetical Stack Machine

As an example, the procedure

```
(lambda () (if (= x y) (f (g x)) (h x y (h 1 2))))
```

should compile into the following instructions:

```
        ARGS    0
        GVAR    X
        GVAR    Y
        GVAR    =
        CALL    2
        FJUMP   L1
        GVAR    X
        GVAR    G
        CALL    1
        GVAR    F
        CALL    1
        JUMP    L2
L1:     GVAR    X
        GVAR    Y
        CONST   1
        CONST   2
        GVAR    H
        CALL    2
```

```
            GVAR    H
            CALL    3
    L2:     RETURN
```

	Top-Level Functions
comp-show	Compile an expression and show the resulting code.
compiler	Compile an expression as a parameterless function.
	Special Variables
label-num	Number for the next assembly language label.
primitive-fns	List of built-in Scheme functions.
	Data Types
fn	A Scheme function.
	Major Functions
comp	Compile an expression into a list of instructions.
comp-begin	Compile a sequence of expressions.
comp-if	Compile a conditional (if) expression.
comp-lambda	Compile a lambda expression.
	Auxiliary Functions
gen	Generate a single instruction.
seq	Generate a sequence of instructions.
gen-label	Generate an assembly language label.
gen-var	Generate an instruction to reference a variable.
gen-set	Generate an instruction to set a variable.
name!	Set the name of a function to a given value.
print-fn	Print a Scheme function (just the name).
show-fn	Print the instructions in a Scheme function.
label-p	Is the argument a label?
in-env-p	Is the symbol in the environment? If so, where?

Figure 23.2: Glossary for the Scheme Compiler

The first version of the Scheme compiler is quite simple. It mimics the structure of the Scheme evaluator. The difference is that each case generates code rather than evaluating a subexpression:

```lisp
(defun comp (x env)
  "Compile the expression x into a list of instructions."
  (cond
    ((symbolp x) (gen-var x env))
    ((atom x) (gen 'CONST x))
    ((scheme-macro (first x)) (comp (scheme-macro-expand x) env))
    ((case (first x)
```

```
(QUOTE   (gen 'CONST (second x)))
(BEGIN   (comp-begin (rest x) env))
(SET!    (seq (comp (third x) env) (gen-set (second x) env)))
(IF      (comp-if (second x) (third x) (fourth x) env))
(LAMBDA (gen 'FN (comp-lambda (second x) (rest (rest x)) env)))
;; Procedure application:
;; Compile args, then fn, then the call
(t       (seq (mappend #'(lambda (y) (comp y env)) (rest x))
             (comp (first x) env)
        (gen 'call (length (rest x)))))))))))
```

The compiler comp has the same nine cases—in fact the exact same structure—as the interpreter interp from chapter 22. Each case is slightly more complex, so the three main cases have been made into separate functions: comp-begin, comp-if, and comp-lambda. A begin expression is compiled by compiling each argument in turn but making sure to pop each value but the last off the stack after it is computed. The last element in the begin stays on the stack as the value of the whole expression. Note that the function gen generates a single instruction (actually a list of one instruction), and seq makes a sequence of instructions out of two or more subsequences.

```
(defun comp-begin (exps env)
  "Compile a sequence of expressions, popping all but the last."
  (cond ((null exps) (gen 'CONST nil))
        ((length=1 exps) (comp (first exps) env))
        (t (seq (comp (first exps) env)
                (gen 'POP)
                (comp-begin (rest exps) env)))))
```

An if expression is compiled by compiling the predicate, then part, and else part, and by inserting appropriate branch instructions.

```
(defun comp-if (pred then else env)
  "Compile a conditional expression."
  (let ((L1 (gen-label))
        (L2 (gen-label)))
    (seq (comp pred env) (gen 'FJUMP L1)
         (comp then env) (gen 'JUMP L2)
         (list L1) (comp else env)
         (list L2))))
```

Finally, a lambda expression is compiled by compiling the body, surrounding it with one instruction to set up the arguments and another to return from the function, and then storing away the resulting compiled code, along with the environment. The data type fn is implemented as a structure with slots for the body of the code, the argument list, and the name of the function (for printing purposes only).

```lisp
(defstruct (fn (:print-function print-fn))
  code (env nil)(name nil) (args nil))

(defun comp-lambda (args body env)
  "Compile a lambda form into a closure with compiled code."
  (assert (and (listp args) (every #'symbolp args)) ()
          "Lambda arglist must be a list of symbols, not ~a" args)
  ;; For now, no &rest parameters.
  ;; The next version will support Scheme's version of &rest
  (make-fn
    :env env :args args
    :code (seq (gen 'ARGS (length args))
               (comp-begin body (cons args env))
               (gen 'RETURN))))
```

The advantage of compiling over interpreting is that much can be decided at compile time. For example, the compiler can determine if a variable reference is to a global or lexical variable, and if it is to a lexical variable, exactly where that lexical variable is stored. This computation is done only once by the compiler, but it has to be done each time the expression is encountered by the interpreter. Similarly, the compiler can count up the number of arguments once and for all, while the interpreter must go through a loop, counting up the number of arguments, and testing for the end of the arguments after each one is interpreted. So it is clear that the compiler can be more efficient than the interpreter.

Another advantage is that the compiler can be more robust. For example, in comp-lambda, we check that the parameter list of a lambda expression is a list containing only symbols. It would be too expensive to make such checks in an interpreter, but in a compiler it is a worthwhile trade-off to check once at compile time for error conditions rather than checking repeatedly at run time.

Before we show the rest of the compiler, here's a useful top-level interface to comp:

```lisp
(defvar *label-num* 0)

(defun compiler (x)
  "Compile an expression as if it were in a parameterless lambda."
  (setf *label-num* 0)
  (comp-lambda '() (list x) nil))
```

```
(defun comp-show (x)
  "Compile an expression and show the resulting code"
  (show-fn (compiler x))
  (values))
```

Now here's the code to generate individual instructions and sequences of instructions. A sequence of instructions is just a list, but we provide the function seq rather than using append directly for purposes of data abstraction. A label is just an atom.

```
(defun gen (opcode &rest args)
  "Return a one-element list of the specified instruction."
  (list (cons opcode args)))

(defun seq (&rest code)
  "Return a sequence of instructions"
  (apply #'append code))

(defun gen-label (&optional (label 'L))
  "Generate a label (a symbol of the form Lnnn)"
  (intern (format nil "~a~d" label (incf *label-num*))))
```

Environments are now represented as lists of frames, where each frame is a sequence of variables. Local variables are referred to not by their name but by two integers: the index into the list of frames and the index into the individual frame. As usual, the indexes are zero-based. For example, given the code:

```
(let ((a 2.0)
      (b 2.1))
  (let ((c 1.0)
        (d 1.1))
    (let ((e 0.0)
          (f 0.1))
      (+ a b c d e f))))
```

the innermost environment is ((e f) (c d) (a b)). The function in-env-p tests if a variable appears in an environment. If this environment were called env, then (in-env-p 'f env) would return (2 1) and (in-env-p 'x env) would return nil.

```
(defun gen-var (var env)
  "Generate an instruction to reference a variable's value."
  (let ((p (in-env-p var env)))
    (if p
        (gen 'LVAR (first p) (second p) ";" var)
        (gen 'GVAR var))))

(defun gen-set (var env)
  "Generate an instruction to set a variable to top-of-stack."
  (let ((p (in-env-p var env)))
    (if p
        (gen 'LSET (first p) (second p) ";" var)
        (gen 'GSET var))))
```

Finally, we have some auxiliary functions to print out the results, to distinguish between labels and instructions, and to determine the index of a variable in an environment. Scheme functions now are implemented as structures, which must have a field for the code, and one for the environment. In addition, we provide a field for the name of the function and for the argument list; these are used only for debugging purposes, We'll adopt the convention that the define macro sets the function's name field, by calling name! (which is not part of standard Scheme).

```
(def-scheme-macro define (name &rest body)
  (if (atom name)
      `(name! (set! ,name . ,body) ',name)
      (scheme-macro-expand
        `(define ,(first name)
           (lambda ,(rest name) . ,body)))))

(defun name! (fn name)
  "Set the name field of fn, if it is an un-named fn."
  (when (and (fn-p fn) (null (fn-name fn)))
    (setf (fn-name fn) name))
  name)

;; This should also go in init-scheme-interp:
(set-global-var! 'name! #'name!)

(defun print-fn (fn &optional (stream *standard-output*) depth)
  (declare (ignore depth))
  (format stream "{~a}" (or (fn-name fn) '??)))
```

```
(defun show-fn (fn &optional (stream *standard-output*) (depth 0))
    "Print all the instructions in a function.
    If the argument is not a function, just princ it,
    but in a column at least 8 spaces wide."
    (if (not (fn-p fn))
        (format stream "~8a" fn)
        (progn
          (fresh-line)
          (incf depth 8)
          (dolist (instr (fn-code fn))
            (if (label-p instr)
                (format stream "~a:" instr)
                (progn
                  (format stream "~VT" depth)
                  (dolist (arg instr)
                    (show-fn arg stream depth))
                  (fresh-line)))))))

(defun label-p (x) "Is x a label?" (atom x))

(defun in-env-p (symbol env)
    "If symbol is in the environment, return its index numbers."
    (let ((frame (find symbol env :test #'find)))
      (if frame (list (position frame env) (position symbol frame)))))
```

Now we are ready to show the compiler at work:

```
> (comp-show '(if (= x y) (f (g x)) (h x y (h 1 2))))
        ARGS    0
        GVAR    X
        GVAR    Y
        GVAR    =
        CALL    2
        FJUMP   L1
        GVAR    X
        GVAR    G
        CALL    1
        GVAR    F
        CALL    1
        JUMP    L2
L1:     GVAR    X
        GVAR    Y
        CONST   1
        CONST   2
        GVAR    H
        CALL    2
        GVAR    H
        CALL    3
L2:     RETURN
```

This example should give the reader a feeling for the code generated by the compiler.

Another reason a compiler has an advantage over an interpreter is that the compiler can afford to spend some time trying to find a more efficient encoding of an expression, while for the interpreter, the overhead of searching for a more efficient interpretation usually offsets any advantage gained. Here are some places where a compiler could do better than an interpreter (although our compiler currently does not):

```
> (comp-show '(begin "doc" (write x) y))
        ARGS    0
        CONST   doc
        POP
        GVAR    X
        GVAR    WRITE
        CALL    1
        POP
        GVAR    Y
        RETURN
```

In this example, code is generated to push the constant "doc" on the stack and then immediately pop it off. If we have the compiler keep track of what expressions are compiled "for value"—as y is the value of the expression above—and which are only compiled "for effect," then we can avoid generating any code at all for a reference to a constant or variable for effect. Here's another example:

```
> (comp-show '(begin (+ (* a x) (f x)) x))
        ARGS    0
        GVAR    A
        GVAR    X
        GVAR    *
        CALL    2
        GVAR    X
        GVAR    F
        CALL    1
        GVAR    +
        CALL    2
        POP
        GVAR    X
        RETURN
```

In this expression, if we can be assured that + and * refer to the normal arithmetic functions, then we can compile this as if it were (begin (f x) x). Furthermore, it is reasonable to assume that + and * will be instructions in our machine that can be invoked inline, rather than having to call out to a function. Many compilers spend a significant portion of their time optimizing arithmetic operations, by taking into account associativity, commutativity, distributivity, and other properties.

Besides arithmetic, compilers often have expertise in conditional expressions. Consider the following:

```
> (comp-show '(if (and p q) x y))
        ARGS    0
        GVAR    P
        FJUMP   L3
        GVAR    Q
        JUMP    L4
L3:     GVAR    NIL
L4:     FJUMP   L1
        GVAR    X
        JUMP    L2
L1:     GVAR    Y
L2:     RETURN
```

Note that (and p q) macro-expands to (if p q nil). The resulting compiled code is correct, but inefficient. First, there is an unconditional jump to L4, which labels a conditional jump to L1. This could be replaced with a conditional jump to L1. Second, at L3 we load NIL and then jump on nil to L1. These two instructions could be replaced by an unconditional jump to L1. Third, the FJUMP to L3 could be replaced by an FJUMP to L1, since we now know that the code at L3 unconditionally goes to L1.

Finally, some compilers, particularly Lisp compilers, have expertise in function calling. Consider the following:

```
> (comp-show '(f (g x y)))
        ARGS    0
        GVAR    X
        GVAR    Y
        GVAR    G
        CALL    2
        GVAR    F
        CALL    1
        RETURN
```

Here we call g and when g returns we call f, and when f returns we return from this function. But this last return is wasteful; we push a return address on the stack, and then pop it off, and return to the next return address. An alternative function-calling protocol involves pushing the return address before calling g, but then not pushing a return address before calling f; when f returns, it returns directly to the calling function, whatever that is.

Such an optimization looks like a small gain; we basically eliminate a single instruction. In fact, the implications of this new protocol are enormous: we can now invoke a recursive function to an arbitrary depth without growing the stack at all—as long as the recursive call is the last statement in the function (or in a branch of the function when there are conditionals). A function that obeys this constraint on its recursive calls is known as a *properly tail-recursive* function. This subject was discussed in section 22.3.

All the examples so far have only dealt with global variables. Here's an example using local variables:

```
> (comp-show '((lambda (x) ((lambda (y z) (f x y z)) 3 x)) 4))
        ARGS    0
        CONST   4
        FN
                ARGS    1
                CONST   3
                LVAR    0       0       ;       X
                FN
                        ARGS    2
                        LVAR    1       0       ;       X
                        LVAR    0       0       ;       Y
                        LVAR    0       1       ;       Z
                        GVAR    F
                        CALL    3
                        RETURN
                CALL    2
                RETURN
        CALL    1
        RETURN
```

The code is indented to show nested functions. The top-level function loads the constant 4 and an anonymous function, and calls the function. This function loads the constant 3 and the local variable x, which is the first (0th) element in the top (0th) frame. It then calls the double-nested function on these two arguments. This function loads x, y, and z: x is now the 0th element in the next-to-top (1st) frame, and y and z are the 0th and 1st elements of the top frame. With all the arguments in place, the function f is finally called. Note that no continuations are stored—f can return directly to the caller of this function.

However, all this explicit manipulation of environments is inefficient; in this case we could have compiled the whole thing by simply pushing 4, 3, and 4 on the stack and calling f.

	Top-Level Functions
scheme	A read-compile-execute-print loop.
comp-go	Compile and execute an expression.
machine	Run the abstract machine.
	Data Types
prim	A Scheme primitive function.
ret-addr	A return address (function, program counter, environment).
	Auxiliary Functions
arg-count	Report an error for wrong number of arguments.
comp-list	Compile a list of expressions onto the stack.
comp-const	Compile a constant expression.
comp-var	Compile a variable reference.
comp-funcall	Compile a function application.
primitive-p	Is this function a primitive?
init-scheme-comp	Initialize primitives used by compiler.
gen-args	Generate code to load arguments to a function.
make-true-list	Convert a dotted list to a nondotted one.
new-fn	Build a new function.
is	Predicate is true if instructions opcode matches.
optimize	A peephole optimizer.
gen1	Generate a single instruction.
target	The place a branch instruction branches to,
next-instr	The next instruction in a sequence.
quasi-q	Expand a quasiquote form into append, cons, etc.
	Functions for the Abstract Machine
assemble	Turn a list of instructions into a vector.
asm-first-pass	Find labels and length of code.
asm-second-pass	Put code into the code vector.
opcode	The opcode of an instruction.
args	The arguments of an instruction.
arg$i$	For $i = 1, 2, 3$ — select ith argument of instruction.

Figure 23.3: Glossary of the Scheme Compiler, Second Version

23.1   A Properly Tail-Recursive Lisp Compiler

In this section we describe a new version of the compiler, first by showing examples of its output, and then by examining the compiler itself, which is summarized in figure 23.3. The new version of the compiler also makes use of a different function calling sequence, using two new instructions, CALLJ and SAVE. As the name implies, SAVE saves a return address on the stack. The CALLJ instruction no longer saves anything; it can be seen as an unconditional jump—hence the J in its name.

First, we see how nested function calls work:

```
> (comp-show '(f (g x)))
        ARGS    0
        SAVE    K1
        GVAR    X
        GVAR    G
        CALLJ   1
K1:     GVAR    F
        CALLJ   1
```

The continuation point K1 is saved so that g can return to it, but then no continuation is saved for f, so f returns to whatever continuation is on the stack. Thus, there is no need for an explicit RETURN instruction. The final CALL is like an unconditional branch.

The following example shows that all functions but the last (f) need a continuation point:

```
> (comp-show '(f (g (h x) (h y))))
        ARGS    0
        SAVE    K1
        SAVE    K2
        GVAR    X
        GVAR    H
        CALLJ   1
K2:     SAVE    K3
        GVAR    Y
        GVAR    H
        CALLJ   1
K3:     GVAR    G
        CALLJ   2
K1:     GVAR    F
        CALLJ   1
```

This code first computes (h x) and returns to K2. Then it computes (h y) and returns to K3. Next it calls g on these two values, and returns to K1 before transferring to f. Since whatever f returns will also be the final value of the function we are compiling, there is no need to save a continuation point for f to return to.

In the next example we see that unneeded constants and variables in begin expressions are ignored:

```
> (comp-show '(begin "doc" x (f x) y))
        ARGS    0
        SAVE    K1
        GVAR    X
        GVAR    F
        CALLJ   1
K1:     POP
        GVAR    Y
        RETURN
```

One major flaw with the first version of the compiler is that it could pass data around, but it couldn't actually *do* anything to the data objects. We fix that problem by augmenting the machine with instructions to do arithmetic and other primitive operations. Unneeded primitive operations, like variables constants, and arithmetic operations are ignored when they are in the nonfinal position within begins. Contrast the following two expressions:

```
> (comp-show '(begin (+ (* a x) (f x)) x))
        ARGS    0
        SAVE    K1
        GVAR    X
        GVAR    F
        CALLJ   1
K1:     POP
        GVAR    X
        RETURN
> (comp-show '(begin (+ (* a x) (f x))))
        ARGS    0
        GVAR    A
        GVAR    X
        *
        SAVE    K1
        GVAR    X
        GVAR    F
        CALLJ   1
K1:     +
        RETURN
```

The first version of the compiler was context-free, in that it compiled all equivalent expressions equivalently, regardless of where they appeared. A properly tail-recursive compiler needs to be context-sensitive: it must compile a call that is the final value of a function differently than a call that is used as an intermediate value, or one whose value is ignored. In the first version of the compiler, comp-lambda was responsible for generating the RETURN instruction, and all code eventually reached that instruction. To make sure the RETURN was reached, the code for the two branches of if expressions had to rejoin at the end.

In the tail-recursive compiler, each piece of code is responsible for inserting its own RETURN instruction or implicitly returning by calling another function without saving a continuation point.

We keep track of these possibilities with two flags. The parameter val? is true when the expression we are compiling returns a value that is used elsewhere. The parameter more? is false when the expression represents the final value, and it is true when there is more to compute. In summary, there are three possibilities:

val?	more?	example: the X in:
true	true	(if X y z) *or* (f X y)
true	false	(if p X z) *or* (begin y X)
false	true	(begin X y)
false	false	*impossible*

The code for the compiler employing these conventions follows:

```
(defun comp (x env val? more?)
  "Compile the expression x into a list of instructions."
  (cond
    ((member x '(t nil)) (comp-const x val? more?))
    ((symbolp x) (comp-var x env val? more?))
    ((atom x) (comp-const x val? more?))
    ((scheme-macro (first x)) (comp (scheme-macro-expand x) env val? more?))
    ((case (first x)
       (QUOTE  (arg-count x 1)
               (comp-const (second x) val? more?))
       (BEGIN  (comp-begin (rest x) env val? more?))
       (SET!   (arg-count x 2)
               (assert (symbolp (second x)) (x)
                       "Only symbols can be set!, not ~a in ~a"
                       (second x) x)
               (seq (comp (third x) env t t)
                    (gen-set (second x) env)
                    (if (not val?) (gen 'POP))
                    (unless more? (gen 'RETURN))))
```

```
(IF     (arg-count x 2 3)
        (comp-if (second x) (third x) (fourth x)
                env val? more?))
(LAMBDA (when val?
        (let ((f (comp-lambda (second x) (rest2 x) env)))
          (seq (gen 'FN f) (unless more? (gen 'RETURN))))))
(t      (comp-funcall (first x) (rest x) env val? more?))))))
```

Here we've added one more case: t and nil compile directly into primitive instructions, rather than relying on them being bound as global variables. (In real Scheme, the Boolean values are #t and #f, which need not be quoted, the empty list is ( ), which must be quoted, and t and nil are ordinary symbols with no special significance.)

I've also added some error checking for the number of arguments supplied to quote, set! and if. Note that it is reasonable to do more error checking in a compiler than in an interpreter, since the checking need be done only once, not each time through. The function to check arguments is as follows:

```
(defun arg-count (form min &optional (max min))
  "Report an error if form has wrong number of args."
  (let ((n-args (length (rest form))))
    (assert (<= min n-args max) (form)
      "Wrong number of arguments for ~a in ~a:
      ~d supplied, ~d~@[ to ~d~] expected"
      (first form) form n-args min (if (/= min max) max))))
```

@ **Exercise 23.1 [m]** Modify the compiler to check for additional compile-time errors suggested by the following erroneous expression:

```
(cdr (+ (list x y) 'y (3 x) (car 3 x)))
```

The tail-recursive compiler still has the familiar nine cases, but I have introduced comp-var, comp-const, comp-if, and comp-funcall to handle the increased complexity introduced by the var? and more? parameters.

Let's go through the comp- functions one at a time. First, comp-begin and comp-list just handle and pass on the additional parameters. comp-list will be used in comp-funcall, a new function that will be introduced to compile a procedure application.

```
(defun comp-begin (exps env val? more?)
  "Compile a sequence of expressions,
  returning the last one as the value."
  (cond ((null exps) (comp-const nil val? more?))
        ((length=1 exps) (comp (first exps) env val? more?))
        (t (seq (comp (first exps) env nil t)
                (comp-begin (rest exps) env val? more?)))))

(defun comp-list (exps env)
  "Compile a list, leaving them all on the stack."
  (if (null exps) nil
      (seq (comp (first exps) env t t)
           (comp-list (rest exps) env))))
```

Then there are two trivial functions to compile variable access and constants. If the value is not needed, these produce no instructions at all. If there is no more to be done, then these functions have to generate the return instruction. This is a change from the previous version of comp, where the caller generated the return instruction. Note I have extended the machine to include instructions for the most common constants: t, nil, and some small integers.

```
(defun comp-const (x val? more?)
  "Compile a constant expression."
  (if val? (seq (if (member x '(t nil -1 0 1 2))
                    (gen x)
                    (gen 'CONST x))
                (unless more? (gen 'RETURN)))))

(defun comp-var (x env val? more?)
  "Compile a variable reference."
  (if val? (seq (gen-var x env) (unless more? (gen 'RETURN)))))
```

The remaining two functions are more complex. First consider comp-if. Rather than blindly generating code for the predicate and both branches, we will consider some special cases. First, it is clear that (if t x y) can reduce to x and (if nil x y) can reduce to y. It is perhaps not as obvious that (if p x x) can reduce to (begin p x), or that the comparison of equality between the two branches should be done on the object code, not the source code. Once these trivial special cases have been considered, we're left with three more cases: (if p x nil), (if p nil y), and (if p x y). The pattern of labels and jumps is different for each.

```
(defun comp-if (pred then else env val? more?)
  "Compile a conditional (IF) expression."
  (cond
    ((null pred)           ; (if nil x y) ==> y
     (comp else env val? more?))
    ((constantp pred)      ; (if t x y) ==> x
     (comp then env val? more?))
    ((and (listp pred)     ; (if (not p) x y) ==> (if p y x)
          (length=1 (rest pred))
          (primitive-p (first pred) env 1)
          (eq (prim-opcode (primitive-p (first pred) env 1)) 'not))
     (comp-if (second pred) else then env val? more?))
    (t (let ((pcode (comp pred env t t))
             (tcode (comp then env val? more?))
             (ecode (comp else env val? more?)))
         (cond
           ((equal tcode ecode) ; (if p x x) ==> (begin p x)
            (seq (comp pred env nil t) ecode))
           ((null tcode)  ; (if p nil y) ==> p (TJUMP L2) y L2:
            (let ((L2 (gen-label)))
              (seq pcode (gen 'TJUMP L2) ecode (list L2)
                   (unless more? (gen 'RETURN)))))
           ((null ecode)  ; (if p x) ==> p (FJUMP L1) x L1:
            (let ((L1 (gen-label)))
              (seq pcode (gen 'FJUMP L1) tcode (list L1)
                   (unless more? (gen 'RETURN)))))
           (t             ; (if p x y) ==> p (FJUMP L1) x L1: y
                          ; or p (FJUMP L1) x (JUMP L2) L1: y L2:
            (let ((L1 (gen-label))
                  (L2 (if more? (gen-label))))
              (seq pcode (gen 'FJUMP L1) tcode
                   (if more? (gen 'JUMP L2))
                   (list L1) ecode (if more? (list L2)))))))))))
```

Here are some examples of if expressions. First, a very simple example:

```
> (comp-show '(if p (+ x y) (* x y)))
        ARGS    0
        GVAR    P
        FJUMP   L1
        GVAR    X
        GVAR    Y
        +
        RETURN
L1:     GVAR    X
        GVAR    Y
        *
        RETURN
```

Each branch has its own RETURN instruction. But note that the code generated is sensitive to its context. For example, if we put the same expression inside a begin expression, we get something quite different:

```
> (comp-show '(begin (if p (+ x y) (* x y)) z))
        ARGS    0
        GVAR    Z
        RETURN
```

What happens here is that (+ x y) and (* x y), when compiled in a context where the value is ignored, both result in no generated code. Thus, the if expression reduces to (if p nil nil), which is compiled like (begin p nil), which also generates no code when not evaluated for value, so the final code just references z. The compiler can only do this optimization because it knows that + and * are side-effect-free operations. Consider what happens when we replace + with f:

```
> (comp-show '(begin (if p (f x) (* x x)) z))
        ARGS    0
        GVAR    P
        FJUMP   L2
        SAVE    K1
        GVAR    X
        GVAR    F
        CALLJ   1
K1:     POP
L2:     GVAR    Z
        RETURN
```

Here we have to call (f x) if p is true (and then throw away the value returned), but we don't have to compute (* x x) when p is false.

These examples have inadvertently revealed some of the structure of comp-funcall, which handles five cases. First, it knows some primitive functions that have corresponding instructions and compiles these instructions inline when their values are needed. If the values are not needed, then the function can be ignored, and just the arguments can be compiled. This assumes true functions with no side effects. If there are primitive operations with side effects, they too can be compiled inline, but the operation can never be ignored. The next case is when the function is a lambda expression of no arguments. We can just compile the body of the lambda expression as if it were a begin expression. Nonprimitive functions require a function call. There are two cases: when there is more to compile we have to save a continuation point, and when we are compiling the final value of a function, we can just branch to the called function. The whole thing looks like this:

```
(defun comp-funcall (f args env val? more?)
  "Compile an application of a function to arguments."
  (let ((prim (primitive-p f env (length args))))
    (cond
      (prim  ; function compilable to a primitive instruction
       (if (and (not val?) (not (prim-side-effects prim)))
           ;; Side-effect free primitive when value unused
           (comp-begin args env nil more?)
           ;; Primitive with value or call needed
           (seq (comp-list args env)
                (gen (prim-opcode prim))
                (unless val? (gen 'POP))
                (unless more? (gen 'RETURN)))))
      ((and (starts-with f 'lambda) (null (second f)))
       ;; ((lambda () body)) => (begin body)
       (assert (null args) () "Too many arguments supplied")
       (comp-begin (rest2 f) env val? more?))
      (more? ; Need to save the continuation point
       (let ((k (gen-label 'k)))
         (seq (gen 'SAVE k)
              (comp-list args env)
              (comp f env t t)
              (gen 'CALLJ (length args))
              (list k)
              (if (not val?) (gen 'POP)))))
      (t     ; function call as rename plus goto
       (seq (comp-list args env)
            (comp f env t t)
            (gen 'CALLJ (length args)))))))
```

The support for primitives is straightforward. The prim data type has five slots. The first holds the name of a symbol that is globally bound to a primitive operation. The second, n-args, is the number of arguments that the primitive requires. We have to take into account the number of arguments to each function because we want (+ x y) to compile into a primitive addition instruction, while (+ x y z) should not. It will compile into a call to the + function instead. The opcode slot gives the opcode that is used to implement the primitive. The always field is true if the primitive always returns non-nil, false if it always returns nil, and nil otherwise. It is used in exercise 23.6. Finally, the side-effects field says if the function has any side effects, like doing I/O or changing the value of an object.

```
(defstruct (prim (:type list))
  symbol n-args opcode always side-effects)

(defparameter *primitive-fns*
  '((+ 2 + true) (- 2 - true) (* 2 * true) (/ 2 / true)
    (< 2 <) (> 2 >) (<= 2 <=) (>= 2 >=) (/= 2 /=) (= 2 =)
    (eq? 2 eq) (equal? 2 equal) (eqv? 2 eql)
    (not 1 not) (null? 1 not)
    (car 1 car) (cdr 1 cdr)  (cadr 1 cadr) (cons 2 cons true)
    (list 1 list1 true) (list 2 list2 true) (list 3 list3 true)
    (read 0 read nil t) (write 1 write nil t) (display 1 display nil t)
    (newline 0 newline nil t) (compiler 1 compiler t)
    (name! 2 name! true t) (random 1 random true nil)))

(defun primitive-p (f env n-args)
  "F is a primitive if it is in the table, and is not shadowed
  by something in the environment, and has the right number of args."
  (and (not (in-env-p f env))
       (find f *primitive-fns*
             :test #'(lambda (f prim)
                       (and (eq f (prim-symbol prim))
                            (= n-args (prim-n-args prim)))))))

(defun list1 (x) (list x))
(defun list2 (x y) (list x y))
(defun list3 (x y z) (list x y z))
(defun display (x) (princ x))
(defun newline () (terpri))
```

These optimizations only work if the symbols are permanently bound to the global values given here. We can enforce that by altering gen-set to preserve them as constants:

```
(defun gen-set (var env)
  "Generate an instruction to set a variable to top-of-stack."
  (let ((p (in-env-p var env)))
    (if p
        (gen 'LSET (first p) (second p) ";" var)
        (if (assoc var *primitive-fns*)
            (error "Can't alter the constant ~a" var)
            (gen 'GSET var)))))
```

Now an expression like (+ x 1) will be properly compiled using the + instruction rather than a subroutine call, and an expression like (set! + *) will be flagged as an error when + is a global variable, but allowed when it has been locally bound. However, we still need to be able to handle expressions like (set! add +) and then (add x y). Thus, we need some function object that + will be globally bound to, even if the compiler normally optimizes away references to that function. The function init-scheme-comp takes care of this requirement:

```
(defun init-scheme-comp ()
  "Initialize the primitive functions."
  (dolist (prim *primitive-fns*)
    (setf (get (prim-symbol prim) 'global-val)
          (new-fn :env nil :name (prim-symbol prim)
                  :code (seq (gen 'PRIM (prim-symbol prim))
                             (gen 'RETURN))))))
```

There is one more change to make—rewriting comp-lambda. We still need to get the arguments off the stack, but we no longer generate a RETURN instruction, since that is done by comp-begin, if necessary. At this point we'll provide a hook for a peephole optimizer, which will be introduced in section 23.4, and for an assembler to convert the assembly language to machine code. new-fn provides this interface, but for now, new-fn acts just like make-fn.

We also need to account for the possibility of rest arguments in a lambda list. A new function, gen-args, generates the single instruction to load the arguments of the stack. It introduces a new instruction, ARGS., into the abstract machine. This instruction works just like ARGS, except it also conses any remaining arguments on the stack into a list and stores that list as the value of the rest argument. With this innovation, the new version of comp-lambda looks like this:

```lisp
(defun comp-lambda (args body env)
  "Compile a lambda form into a closure with compiled code."
  (new-fn :env env :args args
          :code (seq (gen-args args 0)
                     (comp-begin body
                                 (cons (make-true-list args) env)
                                 t nil))))

(defun gen-args (args n-so-far)
  "Generate an instruction to load the arguments."
  (cond ((null args) (gen 'ARGS n-so-far))
        ((symbolp args) (gen 'ARGS. n-so-far))
        ((and (consp args) (symbolp (first args)))
         (gen-args (rest args) (+ n-so-far 1)))
        (t (error "Illegal argument list"))))

(defun make-true-list (dotted-list)
  "Convert a possibly dotted list into a true, non-dotted list."
  (cond ((null dotted-list) nil)
        ((atom dotted-list) (list dotted-list))
        (t (cons (first dotted-list)
                 (make-true-list (rest dotted-list))))))

(defun new-fn (&key code env name args)
  "Build a new function."
  (assemble (make-fn :env env :name name :args args
                     :code (optimize code))))
```

new-fn includes calls to an assembler and an optimizer to generate actual machine code. For the moment, both will be identity functions:

```lisp
(defun optimize (code) code)
(defun assemble (fn) fn)
```

Here are some more examples of the compiler at work:

```lisp
> (comp-show '(if (null? (car l)) (f (+ (* a x) b))
                  (g (/ x 2))))
        ARGS    0
        GVAR    L
        CAR
        FJUMP   L1
        GVAR    X
        2
        /
        GVAR    G
        CALLJ   1
L1:     GVAR    A
```

```
                     GVAR     X
                     *
                     GVAR     B
                     +
                     GVAR     F
                     CALLJ    1
```

There is no need to save any continuation points in this code, because the only calls to nonprimitive functions occur as the final values of the two branches of the function.

```
> (comp-show '(define (last1 l)
                (if (null? (cdr l)) (car l)
                    (last1 (cdr l)))))
              ARGS     0
              FN
                       ARGS     1
                       LVAR     0      0       ;       L
                       CDR
                       FJUMP    L1
                       LVAR     0      0       ;       L
                       CDR
                       GVAR     LAST1
                       CALLJ    1
      L1:              LVAR     0      0       ;       L
                       CAR
                       RETURN
              GSET     LAST1
              CONST    LAST1
              NAME!
              RETURN
```

The top-level function just assigns the nested function to the global variable last1. Since last1 is tail-recursive, it has only one return point, for the termination case, and just calls itself without saving continuations until that case is executed.

Contrast that to the non-tail-recursive definition of length below. It is not tail-recursive because before it calls length recursively, it must save a continuation point, K1, so that it will know where to return to to add 1.

```
> (comp-show '(define (length 1)
                (if (null? 1) 0 (+ 1 (length (cdr 1)))))))
        ARGS    0
        FN
                ARGS    1
                LVAR    0       0       ;       L
                FJUMP   L2
                1
                SAVE    K1
                LVAR    0       0       ;       L
                CDR
                GVAR    LENGTH
                CALLJ   1
K1:             +
                RETURN
L2:             0
                RETURN
        GSET    LENGTH
        CONST   LENGTH
        NAME!
        RETURN
```

Of course, it is possible to write length in tail-recursive fashion:

```
> (comp-show '(define (length 1)
                (letrec ((len (lambda (1 n)
                                (if (null? 1) n
                                    (len (rest 1) (+ n 1)))))))
                  (len 1 0))))
        ARGS    0
        FN
                ARGS    1
                NIL
                FN
                        ARGS    1
                        FN
                                ARGS    2
                                LVAR    0       0       ;       L
                                FJUMP   L2
                                SAVE    K1
                                LVAR    0       0       ;       L
                                GVAR    REST
                                CALLJ   1
K1:                             LVAR    0       1       ;       N
                                1
                                +
                                LVAR    1       0       ;       LEN
```

```
                              CALLJ   2
        L2:                   LVAR    0       1       ;       N
                              RETURN
                      LSET    0       0       ;       LEN
                      POP
                      LVAR    1       0       ;       L
                      0
                      LVAR    0       0       ;       LEN
                      CALLJ   2
              CALLJ   1
        GSET  LENGTH
        CONST LENGTH
        NAME!
        RETURN
```

Let's look once again at an example with nested conditionals:

```
> (comp-show '(if (not (and p q (not r))) x y))
        ARGS    0
        GVAR    P
        FJUMP   L3
        GVAR    Q
        FJUMP   L1
        GVAR    R
        NOT
        JUMP    L2
L1:     NIL
L2:     JUMP    L4
L3:     NIL
L4:     FJUMP   L5
        GVAR    Y
        RETURN
L5:     GVAR    X
        RETURN
```

Here the problem is with multiple JUMPs and with not recognizing negation. If p is false, then the and expression is false, and the whole predicate is true, so we should return x. The code does in fact return x, but it first jumps to L3, loads NIL, and then does an FJUMP that will always jump to L5. Other branches have similar inefficiencies. A sufficiently clever compiler should be able to generate the following code:

```
          ARGS   0
          GVAR   P
          FJUMP  L1
          GVAR   Q
          FJUMP  L1
          GVAR   R
          TJUMP  L1
          GVAR   Y
          RETURN
L1:       GVAR X
          RETURN
```

23.2 Introducing Call/cc

Now that the basic compiler works, we can think about how to implement call/cc in our compiler. First, remember that call/cc is a normal function, not a special form. So we could define it as a primitive, in the manner of car and cons. However, primitives as they have been defined only get to see their arguments, and call/cc will need to see the run-time stack, in order to save away the current continuation. One choice is to install call/cc as a normal Scheme nonprimitive function but to write its body in assembly code ourselves. We need to introduce one new instruction, CC, which places on the stack a function (to which we also have to write the assembly code by hand) that saves the current continuation (the stack) in its environment, and, when called, fetches that continuation and installs it, by setting the stack back to that value. This requires one more instruction, SET-CC. The details of this, and of all the other instructions, are revealed in the next section.

23.3 The Abstract Machine

So far we have defined the instruction set of a mythical abstract machine and generated assembly code for that instruction set. It's now time to actually execute the assembly code and hence have a useful compiler. There are several paths we could pursue: we could implement the machine in hardware, software, or microcode, or we could translate the assembly code for our abstract machine into the assembly code of some existing machine. Each of these approaches has been taken in the past.

Hardware. If the abstract machine is simple enough, it can be implemented directly in hardware. The Scheme-79 and Scheme-81 Chips (Steele and Sussman 1980; Batali et al. 1982) were VLSI implementations of a machine designed specifically to run Scheme.

Macro-Assembler. In the translation or macro-assembler approach, each instruction in the abstract machine language is translated into one or more instructions in the host computer's instruction set. This can be done either directly or by generating assembly code and passing it to the host computer's assembler. In general this will lead to code expansion, because the host computer probably will not provide direct support for Scheme's data types. Thus, whereas in our abstract machine we could write a single instruction for addition, with native code we might have to execute a series of instructions to check the type of the arguments, do an integer add if they are both integers, a floating-point add if they are both floating-point numbers, and so on. We might also have to check the result for overflow, and perhaps convert to bignum representation. Compilers that generate native code often include more sophisticated data-flow analysis to know when such checks are required and when they can be omitted.

Microcode. The MIT Lisp Machine project, unlike the Scheme Chip, actually resulted in working machines. One important decision was to go with microcode instead of a single chip. This made it easy to change the system as experienced was gained, and as the host language was changed from ZetaLisp to Common Lisp. The most important architectural feature of the Lisp Machine was the inclusion of tag bits on each word to specify data types. Also important was microcode to implement certain frequently used generic operations. For example, in the Symbolics 3600 Lisp Machine, the microcode for addition simultaneously did an integer add, a floating-point add, and a check of the tag bits. If both arguments turned out to be either integers or floating-point numbers, then the appropriate result was taken. Otherwise, a trap was signaled, and a converison routine was entered. This approach makes the compiler relatively simple, but the trend in architecture is away from highly microcoded processors toward simpler (RISC) processors.

Software. We can remove many of these problems with a technique known as *byte-code assembly.* Here we translate the instructions into a vector of bytes and then interpret the bytes with a byte-code interpreter. This gives us (almost) the machine we want; it solves the code expansion problem, but it may be slower than native code compilation, because the byte-code interpreter is written in software, not hardware or microcode.

Each opcode is a single byte (we have less than 256 opcodes, so this will work). The instructions with arguments take their arguments in the following bytes of the instruction stream. So, for example, a CALL instruction occupies two bytes; one for the opcode and one for the argument count. This means we have imposed a limit of 256 arguments to a function call. An LVAR instruction would take three bytes; one for the opcode, one for the frame offset, and one for the offset within the frame. Again, we have imposed 256 as the limit on nesting level and variables per frame. These limits seem high enough for any code written by a human, but remember, not only humans write code. It is possible that some complex macro may expand into something with more than 256 variables, so a full implementation would have some way of accounting for this. The GVAR and CONST instructions have to refer to an arbitrary object; either we can allocate enough bytes to fit a pointer to this object, or we can add a constants field to the fn structure, and follow the instructions with a single-byte index into this vector of constants. This latter approach is more common.

We can now handle branches by changing the program counter to an index into the code vector. (It seems severe to limit functions to 256 bytes of code; a two-byte label allows for 65536 bytes of code per function.) In summary, the code is more compact, branching is efficient, and dispatching can be fast because the opcode is a small integer, and we can use a branch table to go to the right piece of code for each instruction.

Another source of inefficiency is implementing the stack as a list, and consing up new cells every time something is added to the stack. The alternative is to implement the stack as a vector with a fill-pointer. That way a push requires no consing, only a change to the pointer (and a check for overflow). The check is worthwhile, however, because it allows us to detect infinite loops in the user's code.

Here follows an assembler that generates a sequence of instructions (as a vector). This is a compromise between byte codes and the assembly language format. First, we need some accessor functions to get at parts of an instruction:

```lisp
(defun opcode (instr) (if (label-p instr) :label (first instr)))
(defun args (instr) (if (listp instr) (rest instr)))
(defun arg1 (instr) (if (listp instr) (second instr)))
(defun arg2 (instr) (if (listp instr) (third instr)))
(defun arg3 (instr) (if (listp instr) (fourth instr)))

(defsetf arg1 (instr) (val) '(setf (second ,instr) ,val))
```

Now we write the assembler, which already is integrated into the compiler with a hook in new-fn.

```lisp
(defun assemble (fn)
  "Turn a list of instructions into a vector."
  (multiple-value-bind (length labels)
      (asm-first-pass (fn-code fn))
    (setf (fn-code fn)
          (asm-second-pass (fn-code fn)
                           length labels))
    fn))

(defun asm-first-pass (code)
  "Return the labels and the total code length."
  (let ((length 0)
        (labels nil))
    (dolist (instr code)
      (if (label-p instr)
```

```
              (push (cons instr length) labels)
              (incf length)))
        (values length labels)))

(defun asm-second-pass (code length labels)
  "Put code into code-vector, adjusting for labels."
  (let ((addr 0)
        (code-vector (make-array length)))
    (dolist (instr code)
      (unless (label-p instr)
        (if (is instr '(JUMP TJUMP FJUMP SAVE))
            (setf (arg1 instr)
                  (cdr (assoc (arg1 instr) labels))))
        (setf (aref code-vector addr) instr)
        (incf addr)))
    code-vector))
```

If we want to be able to look at assembled code, we need a new printing function:

```
(defun show-fn (fn &optional (stream *standard-output*) (indent 2))
  "Print all the instructions in a function.
  If the argument is not a function, just princ it,
  but in a column at least 8 spaces wide."
  ;; This version handles code that has been assembled into a vector
  (if (not (fn-p fn))
      (format stream "~8a" fn)
      (progn
        (fresh-line)
        (dotimes (i (length (fn-code fn)))
          (let ((instr (elt (fn-code fn) i)))
            (if (label-p instr)
                (format stream "~a:" instr)
                (progn
                  (format stream "~VT~2d: " indent i)
                  (dolist (arg instr)
                    (show-fn arg stream (+ indent 8)))
                  (fresh-line)))))))))


(defstruct ret-addr fn pc env)

(defun is (instr op)
  "True if instr's opcode is OP, or one of OP when OP is a list."
  (if (listp op)
      (member (opcode instr) op)
      (eq (opcode instr) op)))

(defun top (stack) (first stack))
```

```lisp
(defun machine (f)
  "Run the abstract machine on the code for f."
  (let* ((code (fn-code f))
         (pc 0)
         (env nil)
         (stack nil)
         (n-args 0)
         (instr))
    (loop
      (setf instr (elt code pc))
      (incf pc)
      (case (opcode instr)

        ;; Variable/stack manipulation instructions:
        (LVAR  (push (elt (elt env (arg1 instr)) (arg2 instr))
                     stack))
        (LSET  (setf (elt (elt env (arg1 instr)) (arg2 instr))
                     (top stack)))
        (GVAR  (push (get (arg1 instr) 'global-val) stack))
        (GSET  (setf (get (arg1 instr) 'global-val) (top stack)))
        (POP   (pop stack))
        (CONST (push (arg1 instr) stack))

        ;; Branching instructions:
        (JUMP  (setf pc (arg1 instr)))
        (FJUMP (if (null (pop stack)) (setf pc (arg1 instr))))
        (TJUMP (if (pop stack) (setf pc (arg1 instr))))

        ;; Function call/return instructions:
        (SAVE  (push (make-ret-addr :pc (arg1 instr)
                                    :fn f :env env)
                     stack))
        (RETURN ;; return value is top of stack; ret-addr is second
         (setf f (ret-addr-fn (second stack))
               code (fn-code f)
               env (ret-addr-env (second stack))
               pc (ret-addr-pc (second stack)))
         ;; Get rid of the ret-addr, but keep the value
         (setf stack (cons (first stack) (rest2 stack))))
        (CALLJ  (pop env)                    ; discard the top frame
                (setf f  (pop stack)
                      code (fn-code f)
                      env (fn-env f)
                      pc 0
                      n-args (arg1 instr)))
        (ARGS   (assert (= n-args (arg1 instr)) ()
```

```
                          "Wrong number of arguments:~
                          ~d expected, ~d supplied"
                          (arg1 instr) n-args)
              (push (make-array (arg1 instr)) env)
              (loop for i from (- n-args 1) downto 0 do
                    (setf (elt (first env) i) (pop stack)))))
   (ARGS.     (assert (>= n-args (arg1 instr)) ()
                          "Wrong number of arguments:~
                          ~d or more expected, ~d supplied"
                          (arg1 instr) n-args)
              (push (make-array (+ 1 (arg1 instr))) env)
              (loop repeat (- n-args (arg1 instr)) do
                    (push (pop stack) (elt (first env) (arg1 instr))))
              (loop for i from (- (arg1 instr) 1) downto 0 do
                    (setf (elt (first env) i) (pop stack)))))
   (FN        (push (make-fn :code (fn-code (arg1 instr))
                             :env env) stack))
   (PRIM      (push (apply (arg1 instr)
                           (loop with args = nil repeat n-args
                                 do (push (pop stack) args)
                                 finally (return args)))
                    stack))

   ;; Continuation instructions:
   (SET-CC (setf stack (top stack)))
   (CC        (push (make-fn
                     :env (list (vector stack))
                     :code '((ARGS 1) (LVAR 1 0 ";" stack) (SET-CC)
                             (LVAR 0 0) (RETURN)))
                    stack))

   ;; Nullary operations:
   ((SCHEME-READ NEWLINE)
    (push (funcall (opcode instr)) stack))

   ;; Unary operations:
   ((CAR CDR CADR NOT LIST1 COMPILER DISPLAY WRITE RANDOM)
    (push (funcall (opcode instr) (pop stack)) stack))

   ;; Binary operations:
   ((+ - * / < > <= >= /= = CONS LIST2 NAME! EQ EQUAL EQL)
    (setf stack (cons (funcall (opcode instr) (second stack)
                              (first stack))
                     (rest2 stack))))
```

```
                   ;; Ternary operations:
                   (LIST3
                    (setf stack (cons (funcall (opcode instr) (third stack)
                                                  (second stack) (first stack))
                                     (rest3 stack))))

                   ;; Constants:
                   ((T NIL -1 0 1 2)
                    (push (opcode instr) stack))

                   ;; Other:
                   ((HALT) (RETURN (top stack)))
                   (otherwise (error "Unknown opcode: ~a" instr))))))

(defun init-scheme-comp ()
  "Initialize values (including call/cc) for the Scheme compiler."
  (set-global-var! 'exit
    (new-fn :name 'exit :args '(val) :code '((HALT))))
  (set-global-var! 'call/cc
    (new-fn :name 'call/cc :args '(f)
         :code '((ARGS 1) (CC) (LVAR 0 0 ";" f) (CALLJ 1))))
  (dolist (prim *primitive-fns*)
    (setf (get (prim-symbol prim) 'global-val)
        (new-fn :env nil :name (prim-symbol prim)
             :code (seq (gen 'PRIM (prim-symbol prim))
                      (gen 'RETURN))))))
```

Here's the Scheme top level. Note that it is written in Scheme itself; we compile the definition of the read-eval-print loop,[1] load it into the machine, and then start executing it. There's also an interface to compile and execute a single expression, comp-go.

```
(defconstant scheme-top-level
  '(begin (define (scheme)
            (newline)
            (display "=> ")
            (write ((compiler (read))))
            (scheme))
          (scheme)))

(defun scheme ()
  "A compiled Scheme read-eval-print loop"
  (init-scheme-comp)
  (machine (compiler scheme-top-level)))
```

---

[1]Strictly speaking, this is a read-compile-funcall-write loop.

```
(defun comp-go (exp)
  "Compile and execute the expression."
  (machine (compiler '(exit ,exp))))
```

Exercise 23.2 [m] This implementation of the machine is wasteful in its representation of environments. For example, consider what happens in a tail-recursive
function. Each ARG instruction builds a new frame and pushes it on the environment.
Then each CALL pops the latest frame off the environment. So, while the stack does
not grow with tail-recursive calls, the heap certainly does. Eventually, we will have
to garbage-collect all those unused frames (and the cons cells used to make lists out
of them). How could we avoid or limit this garbage collection?

23.4   A Peephole Optimizer

In this section we investigate a simple technique that will generate slightly better
code in cases where the compiler gives inefficient sequences of instructions. The
idea is to look at short sequences of instructions for prespecified patterns and replace
them with equivalent but more efficient instructions.

In the following example, comp-if has already done some source-level optimization, such as eliminating the (f x) call.

```
> (comp-show '(begin (if (if t 1 (f x)) (set! x 2)) x))
   0: ARGS    0
   1: 1
   2: FJUMP   6
   3: 2
   4: GSET    X
   5: POP
   6: GVAR    X
   7: RETURN
```

But the generated code could be made much better. This could be done with more
source-level optimizations to transform the expression into (set! x 2). Alterna-
tively, it could also be done by looking at the preceding instruction sequence and
transforming local inefficiencies. The optimizer presented in this section is capable
of generating the following code:

```
> (comp-show '(begin (if (if t 1 (f x)) (set! x 2)) x))
   0: ARGS     0
   1: 2
   2: GSET     X
   3: RETURN
```

The function `optimize` is implemented as a data-driven function that looks at the opcode of each instruction and makes optimizations based on the following instructions. To be more specific, `optimize` takes a list of assembly language instructions and looks at each instruction in order, trying to apply an optimization. If any changes at all are made, then `optimize` will be called again on the whole instruction list, because further changes might be triggered by the first round of changes.

```
(defun optimize (code)
  "Perform peephole optimization on assembly code."
  (let ((any-change nil))
    ;; Optimize each tail
    (loop for code-tail on code do
          (setf any-change (or (optimize-1 code-tail code)
                               any-change)))
    ;; If any changes were made, call optimize again
    (if any-change
        (optimize code)
        code)))
```

The function `optimize-1` is responsible for each individual attempt to optimize. It is passed two arguments: a list of instructions starting at the current one and going to the end of the list, and a list of all the instructions. The second argument is rarely used. The whole idea of a peephole optimizer is that it should look at only a few instructions following the current one. `optimize-1` is data-driven, based on the opcode of the first instruction. Note that the optimizer functions do their work by destructively modifying the instruction sequence, *not* by consing up and returning a new sequence.

```
(defun optimize-1 (code all-code)
  "Perform peephole optimization on a tail of the assembly code.
  If a change is made, return true."
  ;; Data-driven by the opcode of the first instruction
  (let* ((instr (first code))
         (optimizer (get-optimizer (opcode instr))))
    (when optimizer
      (funcall optimizer instr code all-code))))
```

We need a table to associate the individual optimizer functions with the opcodes. Since opcodes include numbers as well as symbols, an eql hash table is an appropriate choice:

```lisp
(let ((optimizers (make-hash-table :test #'eql)))

  (defun get-optimizer (opcode)
    "Get the assembly language optimizer for this opcode."
    (gethash opcode optimizers))

  (defun put-optimizer (opcode fn)
    "Store an assembly language optimizer for this opcode."
    (setf (gethash opcode optimizers) fn)))
```

We could now build a table with put-optimizer, but it is worth defining a macro to make this a little neater:

```lisp
(defmacro def-optimizer (opcodes args &body body)
  "Define assembly language optimizers for these opcodes."
  (assert (and (listp opcodes) (listp args) (= (length args) 3)))
  '(dolist (op ',opcodes)
     (put-optimizer op #'(lambda ,args .,body))))
```

Before showing example optimizer functions, we will introduce three auxiliary functions. gen1 generates a single instruction, target finds the code sequence that a jump instruction branches to, and next-instr finds the next actual instruction in a sequence, skipping labels.

```lisp
(defun gen1 (&rest args) "Generate a single instruction" args)
(defun target (instr code) (second (member (arg1 instr) code)))
(defun next-instr (code) (find-if (complement #'label-p) code))
```

Here are six optimizer functions that implement a few important peephole optimizations.

```lisp
(def-optimizer (:LABEL) (instr code all-code)
  ;; ... L ... => ... ...     ;if no reference to L
  (when (not (find instr all-code :key #'arg1))
    (setf (first code) (second code)
          (rest code) (rest2 code))
    t))
```

```
(def-optimizer (GSET LSET) (instr code all-code)
  ;; ex: (begin (set! x y) (if x z))
  ;; (SET X) (POP) (VAR X) ==> (SET X)
  (when (and (is (second code) 'POP)
             (is (third code) '(GVAR LVAR))
             (eq (arg1 instr) (arg1 (third code))))
    (setf (rest code) (nthcdr 3 code))
    t))


(def-optimizer (JUMP CALL CALLJ RETURN) (instr code all-code)
  ;; (JUMP L1) ...dead code... L2 ==> (JUMP L1) L2
  (setf (rest code) (member-if #'label-p (rest code)))
  ;; (JUMP L1) ... L1 (JUMP L2) ==> (JUMP L2)  ... L1 (JUMP L2)
  (when (and (is instr 'JUMP)
             (is (target instr code) '(JUMP RETURN)))
    (setf (first code) (copy-list (target instr code)))
    t)))


(def-optimizer (TJUMP FJUMP) (instr code all-code)
  ;; (FJUMP L1) ... L1 (JUMP L2) ==> (FJUMP L2) ... L1 (JUMP L2)
  (when (is (target instr code) 'JUMP)
    (setf (second instr) (arg1 (target instr code)))
    t))


(def-optimizer (T -1 0 1 2) (instr code all-code)
  (case (opcode (second code))
    (NOT ;; (T) (NOT) ==> NIL
     (setf (first code) (gen1 'NIL)
           (rest code) (rest2 code))
     t)
    (FJUMP ;; (T) (FJUMP L) ... => ...
     (setf (first code) (third code)
           (rest code) (rest3 code))
     t)
    (TJUMP ;; (T) (TJUMP L) ... => (JUMP L) ...
     (setf (first code) (gen1 'JUMP (arg1 (next-instr code))))
     t)))
```

```
(def-optimizer (NIL) (instr code all-code)
  (case (opcode (second code))
    (NOT ;; (NIL) (NOT) ==> T
     (setf (first code) (gen1 'T)
           (rest code) (rest2 code))
     t)
    (TJUMP ;; (NIL) (TJUMP L) ... => ...
     (setf (first code) (third code)
           (rest code) (rest3 code))
     t)
    (FJUMP ;; (NIL) (FJUMP L) ==> (JUMP L)
     (setf (first code) (gen1 'JUMP (arg1 (next-instr code))))
     t)))
```

23.5 Languages with Different Lexical Conventions

This chapter has shown how to evaluate a language with Lisp-like syntax, by writing a read-eval-print loop where only the `eval` needs to be replaced. In this section we see how to make the `read` part slightly more general. We still read Lisp-like syntax, but the lexical conventions can be slightly different.

The Lisp function `read` is driven by an object called the *readtable*, which is stored in the special variable `*readtable*`. This table associates some action to take with each of the possible characters that can be read. The entry in the readtable for the character `#\(`, for example, would be directions to read a list. The entry for `#\;` would be directions to ignore every character up to the end of the line.

Because the readtable is stored in a special variable, it is possible to alter completely the way `read` works just by dynamically rebinding this variable.

The new function `scheme-read` temporarily changes the readtable to a new one, the Scheme readtable. It also accepts an optional argument, the stream to read from, and it returns a special marker on end of file. This can be tested for with the predicate `eof-object?`. Note that once `scheme-read` is installed as the value of the Scheme symbol `read` we need do no more—`scheme-read` will always be called when appropriate (by the top level of Scheme, and by any user Scheme program).

```
(defconstant eof "EoF")
(defun eof-object? (x) (eq x eof))
(defvar *scheme-readtable* (copy-readtable))
```

```
(defun scheme-read (&optional (stream *standard-input*))
  (let ((*readtable* *scheme-readtable*))
    (read stream nil eof)))
```

The point of having a special eof constant is that it is unforgeable. The user cannot type in a sequence of characters that will be read as something eq to eof. In Common Lisp, but not Scheme, there is an escape mechanism that makes eof forgable. The user can type #.eof to get the effect of an end of file. This is similar to the ^D convention in UNIX systems, and it can be quite handy.

So far the Scheme readtable is just a copy of the standard readtable. The next step in implementing scheme-read is to alter *scheme-readtable*, adding read macros for whatever characters are necessary. Here we define macros for #t and #f (the true and false values), for #d (decimal numbers) and for the backquote read macro (called quasiquote in Scheme). Note that the backquote and comma characters are defined as read macros, but the @ in ,@ is processed by reading the next character, not by a read macro on @.

```
(set-dispatch-macro-character #\# #\t
  #'(lambda (&rest ignore) t)
  *scheme-readtable*)

(set-dispatch-macro-character #\# #\f
  #'(lambda (&rest ignore) nil)
  *scheme-readtable*)

(set-dispatch-macro-character #\# #\d
  ;; In both Common Lisp and Scheme,
  ;; #x, #o and #b are hexidecimal, octal, and binary,
  ;; e.g. #xff = #o377 = #b11111111 = 255
  ;; In Scheme only, #d255 is decimal 255.
  #'(lambda (stream &rest ignore)
      (let ((*read-base* 10)) (scheme-read stream)))
  *scheme-readtable*)

(set-macro-character #\`
  #'(lambda (s ignore) (list 'quasiquote (scheme-read s)))
  nil *scheme-readtable*)

(set-macro-character #\,
  #'(lambda (stream ignore)
      (let ((ch (read-char stream)))
        (if (char= ch #\@)
            (list 'unquote-splicing (read stream))
            (progn (unread-char ch stream)
                   (list 'unquote (read stream))))))
  nil *scheme-readtable*)
```

Finally, we install scheme-read and eof-object? as primitives:

```
(defparameter *primitive-fns*
  '((+ 2 + true nil) (- 2 - true nil) (* 2 * true nil) (/ 2 / true nil)
    (< 2 < nil nil) (> 2 > nil nil) (<= 2 <= nil nil) (>= 2 >= nil nil)
    (/= 2 /= nil nil) (= 2 = nil nil)
    (eq? 2 eq nil nil) (equal? 2 equal nil nil) (eqv? 2 eql nil nil)
    (not 1 not nil nil) (null? 1 not nil nil) (cons 2 cons true nil)
    (car 1 car nil nil) (cdr 1 cdr nil nil) (cadr 1 cadr nil nil)
    (list 1 list1 true nil) (list 2 list2 true nil) (list 3 list3 true nil)
    (read 0 read nil t) (write 1 write nil t) (display 1 display nil t)
    (newline 0 newline nil t) (compiler 1 compiler t nil)
    (name! 2 name! true t) (random 1 random true nil)))
```

Here we test scheme-read. The characters in italics were typed as a response to the scheme-read.

```
> (scheme-read) #t
T

> (scheme-read) #f
NIL

> (scheme-read) '(a ,b ,@c d)
(QUASIQUOTE (A (UNQUOTE B) (UNQUOTE-SPLICING C) D))
```

The final step is to make quasiquote a macro that expands into the proper sequence of calls to cons, list, and append. The careful reader will keep track of the difference between the form returned by scheme-read (something starting with quasiquote), the expansion of this form with the Scheme macro quasiquote (which is implemented with the Common Lisp function quasi-q), and the eventual evaluation of the expansion. In an environment where b is bound to the number 2 and c is bound to the list (c1 c2), we might have:

Typed:	'(a ,b ,@c d)
Read:	(quasiquote (a (unquote b) (unquote-splicing c) d))
Expanded:	(cons 'a (cons b (append c '(d))))
Evaluated:	(a 2 c1 c2 d)

The implementation of the quasiquote macro is modeled closely on the one given in Charniak et al.'s *Artificial Intelligence Programming*. I added support for vectors. In combine-quasiquote I add the trick of reusing the old cons cell x rather than consing together left and right when that is possible. However, the implementation still wastes cons cells—a more efficient version would pass back multiple values rather than consing quote onto a list, only to strip it off again.

```
(setf (scheme-macro 'quasiquote) 'quasi-q)

(defun quasi-q (x)
  "Expand a quasiquote form into append, list, and cons calls."
  (cond
    ((vectorp x)
     (list 'apply 'vector (quasi-q (coerce x 'list))))
    ((atom x)
     (if (constantp x) x (list 'quote x)))
    ((starts-with x 'unquote)
     (assert (and (rest x) (null (rest2 x))))
     (second x))
    ((starts-with x 'quasiquote)
     (assert (and (rest x) (null (rest2 x))))
     (quasi-q (quasi-q (second x))))
    ((starts-with (first x) 'unquote-splicing)
     (if (null (rest x))
         (second (first x))
         (list 'append (second (first x)) (quasi-q (rest x)))))
    (t (combine-quasiquote (quasi-q (car x))
                           (quasi-q (cdr x))
                           x))))

(defun combine-quasiquote (left right x)
  "Combine left and right (car and cdr), possibly re-using x."
  (cond ((and (constantp left) (constantp right))
         (if (and (eql (eval left) (first x))
                  (eql (eval right) (rest x)))
             (list 'quote x)
             (list 'quote (cons (eval left) (eval right)))))
        ((null right) (list 'list left))
        ((starts-with right 'list)
         (list* 'list left (rest right)))
        (t (list 'cons left right))))
```

Actually, there is a major problem with the quasiquote macro, or more accurately, in the entire approach to macro-expansion based on textual substitution. Suppose we wanted a function that acted like this:

```
> (extrema '(3 1 10 5 20 2))
((max 20) (min 1))
```

We could write the Scheme function:

```
(define (extrema list)
  ;; Given a list of numbers, return an a-list
  ;; with max and min values
  '((max ,(apply max list)) (min ,(apply min list))))
```

After expansion of the quasiquote, the definition of extrema will be:

```
(define extrema
  (lambda (list)
    (list (list 'max (apply max list))
          (list 'min (apply min list)))))
```

The problem is that list is an argument to the function extrema, and the argument shadows the global definition of list as a function. Thus, the function will fail. One way around this dilemma is to have the macro-expansion use the global value of list rather than the symbol list itself. In other words, replace the 'list in quasi-q with (get-global-var 'list). Then the expansion can be used even in an environment where list is locally bound. One has to be careful, though: if this tack is taken, then comp-funcall should be changed to recognize function constants, and to do the right thing with respect to primitives.

It is problems like these that made the designers of Scheme admit that they don't know the best way to specify macros, so there is no standard macro definition mechanism in Scheme. Such problems rarely come up in Common Lisp because functions and variables have different name spaces, and because local function definitions (with flet or labels) are not widely used. Those who do define local functions tend not to use already established names like list and append.

23.6 History and References

Guy Steele's 1978 MIT master's thesis on the language Scheme, rewritten as Steele 1983, describes an innovative and influential compiler for Scheme, called RABBIT.[2] A good article on an "industrial-strength" Scheme compiler based on this approach is described in Kranz et al.'s 1986 paper on ORBIT, the compiler for the T dialect of Scheme.

Abelson and Sussman's *Structure and Interpretation of Computer Programs* (1985) contains an excellent chapter on compilation, using slightly different techniques and compiling into a somewhat more confusing machine language. Another good text

---

[2]At the time, the MacLisp compiler dealt with something called "lisp assembly code" or LAP. The function to input LAP was called lapin. Those who know French will get the pun.

is John Allen's *Anatomy of Lisp* (1978). It presents a very clear, simple compiler, although it is for an older, dynamically scoped dialect of Lisp and it does not address tail-recursion or `call/cc`.

The peephole optimizer described here is based on the one in Masinter and Deutsch 1980.

23.7   Exercises

Exercise 23.3 [h]   Scheme's syntax for numbers is slightly different from Common Lisp's. In particular, complex numbers are written like 3+4i rather than #c(3 4). How could you make `scheme-read` account for this?

Exercise 23.4 [m]   Is it possible to make the core Scheme language even smaller, by eliminating any of the five special forms (`quote`, `begin`, `set!`, `if`, `lambda`) and replacing them with macros?

Exercise 23.5 [m]   Add the ability to recognize internal defines (see page 779).

Exercise 23.6 [h]   In `comp-if` we included a special case for `(if t x y)` and `(if nil x y)`. But there are other cases where we know the value of the predicate. For example, `(if (* a b) x y)` can also reduce to x. Arrange for these optimizations to be made. Note the `prim-always` field of the `prim` structure has been provided for this purpose.

Exercise 23.7 [m]   Consider the following version of the quicksort algorithm for sorting a vector:

```
(define (sort-vector vector test)
  (define (sort lo hi)
    (if (>= lo hi)
        vector
        (let ((pivot (partition vector lo hi test)))
          (sort lo pivot)
          (sort (+ pivot 1) hi))))
  (sort 0 (- (vector-length vector 1))))
```

Here the function `partition` takes a vector, two indices into the vector, and a comparison function, `test`. It modifies the vector and returns an index, `pivot`, such that all elements of the vector below `pivot` are less than all elements at `pivot` or above.

It is well known that quicksort takes time proportional to $n \log n$ to sort a vector of n elements, if the pivots are chosen well. With poor pivot choices, it can take time proportional to n^2.

The question is, what is the space required by quicksort? Besides the vector itself, how much additional storage must be temporarily allocated to sort a vector?

Now consider the following modified version of quicksort. What time and space complexity does it have?

```
(define (sort-vector vector test)
  (define (sort lo hi)
    (if (>= lo hi)
        vector
        (let ((pivot (partition vector lo hi)))
          (if (> (- hi pivot) (- pivot lo))
              (begin (sort lo pivot)
                     (sort (+ pivot 1) hi))
              (begin (sort (+ pivot 1) hi)
                     (sort lo pivot))))))
  (sort 0 (- (vector-length vector 1))))
```

The next three exercises describe extensions that are not part of the Scheme standard.

Exercise 23.8 [h] The set! special form is defined only when its first argument is a symbol. Extend set! to work like setf when the first argument is a list. That is, (set! (car x) y) should expand into something like ((setter car) y x), where (setter car) evaluates to the primitive procedure set-car!. You will need to add some new primitive functions, and you should also provide a way for the user to define new set! procedures. One way to do that would be with a setter function for set!, for example:

```
(set! (setter third)
      (lambda (val list) (set-car! (cdr (cdr list)) val)))
```

Exercise 23.9 [m] It is a curious asymmetry of Scheme that there is a special notation for lambda expressions within define expressions, but not within let. Thus, we see the following:

```
(define square (lambda (x) (* x x)))        ; is the same as
(define (square x) (* x x))
```

```
(let ((square (lambda (x) (* x x)))) ...)   ; is not the same as
(let (((square x) (* x x))) ...)            ;  ⇐ illegal!
```

Do you think this last expression should be legal? If so, modify the macros for
let, let*, and letrec to allow the new syntax. If not, explain why it should not be
included in the language.

Exercise 23.10 [m]   Scheme does not define funcall, because the normal function-
call syntax does the work of funcall. This suggests two problems. (1) Is it possible
to define funcall in Scheme? Show a definition or explain why there can't be one.
Would you ever have reason to use funcall in a Scheme program? (2) Scheme does
define apply, as there is no syntax for an application. One might want to extend the
syntax to make (+ . numbers) equivalent to (apply + numbers). Would this be a
good idea?

Exercise 23.11 [d]   Write a compiler that translates Scheme to Common Lisp. This
will involve changing the names of some procedures and special forms, figuring out
a way to map Scheme's single name space into Common Lisp's distinct function and
variable name spaces, and dealing with Scheme's continuations. One possibility is
to translate a call/cc into a catch and throw, and disallow dynamic continuations.

23.8   Answers

Answer 23.2   We can save frames by making a resource for frames, as was done
on page 337. Unfortunately, we can't just use the defresource macro as is, because
we need a separate resource for each size frame. Thus, a two-dimensional array or
a vector of vectors is necessary. Furthermore, one must be careful in determining
when a frame is no longer needed, and when it has been saved and may be used again.
Some compilers will generate a special calling sequence for a tail-recursive call where
the environment can be used as is, without discarding and then creating a new frame
for the arguments. Some compilers have varied and advanced representations for
environments. An environment may never be represented explicitly as a list of
frames; instead it may be represented implicitly as a series of values in registers.

Answer 23.3 We could read in Scheme expressions as before, and then convert any symbols that looked like complex numbers into numbers. The following routines do this without consing.

```
(defun scheme-read (&optional (stream *standard-input*))
  (let ((*readtable* *scheme-readtable*))
    (convert-numbers (read stream nil eof))))

(defun convert-numbers (x)
  "Replace symbols that look like Scheme numbers with their values."
  ;; Don't copy structure, make changes in place.
  (typecase x
    (cons  (setf (car x) (convert-numbers (car x)))
           (setf (cdr x) (convert-numbers (cdr x)))
           x)
    (symbol (or (convert-number x) x))
    (vector (dotimes (i (length x))
              (setf (aref x i) (convert-numbers (aref x i))))
            x)
    (t x)))

(defun convert-number (symbol)
  "If str looks like a complex number, return the number."
  (let* ((str (symbol-name symbol))
         (pos (position-if #'sign-p str))
         (end (- (length str) 1)))
    (when (and pos (char-equal (char str end) #\i))
      (let ((re (read-from-string str nil nil :start 0 :end pos))
            (im (read-from-string str nil nil :start pos :end end)))
        (when (and (numberp re) (numberp im))
          (complex re im))))))

(defun sign-p (char) (find char "+-"))
```

Actually, that's not quite good enough, because a Scheme complex number can have multiple signs in it, as in 3.4e-5+6.7e+8i, and it need not have two numbers, as in 3i or 4+i or just +i. The other problem is that complex numbers can only have a lowercase i, but read does not distinguish between the symbols 3+4i and 3+4I.

Answer 23.4 Yes, it is possible to implement begin as a macro:

```
(setf (scheme-macro 'begin)
      #'(lambda (&rest exps) '((lambda () .,exps))))
```

With some work we could also eliminate quote. Instead of 'x, we could use (string->symbol "X"), and instead of '(1 2), we could use something like (list 1 2). The problem is in knowing when to reuse the same list. Consider:

```
=> (define (one-two) '(1 2))
ONE-TWO

=> (eq? (one-two) (one-two))
T

=> (eq? '(1 2) '(1 2))
NIL
```

A clever memoized macro for quote could handle this, but it would be less efficient than having quote as a special form. In short, what's the point?

It is also (nearly) possible to replace if with alternate code. The idea is to replace:

(if *test then-part else-part*)

with

(*test* (delay *then-part*) (delay *else-part*))

Now if we are assured that any *test* returns either #t or #f, then we can make the following definitions:

```
(define #t (lambda (then-part else-part) (force then-part)))
(define #f (lambda (then-part else-part) (force else-part)))
```

The only problem with this is that any value, not just #t, counts as true.

This seems to be a common phenomenon in Scheme compilers: translating everything into a few very general constructs, and then recognizing special cases of these constructs and compiling them specially. This has the disadvantage (compared to explicit use of many special forms) that compilation may be slower, because all macros have to be expanded first, and then special cases have to be recognized. It has the advantage that the optimizations will be applied even when the user did not have a special construct in mind. Common Lisp attempts to get the advantages of both by allowing implementations to play loose with what they implement as macros and as special forms.

Answer 23.6   We define the predicate always and install it in two places in comp-if:

```
(defun always (pred env)
  "Does predicate always evaluate to true or false?"
  (cond ((eq pred t) 'true)
        ((eq pred nil) 'false)
        ((symbolp pred) nil)
        ((atom pred) 'true)
        ((scheme-macro (first pred))
         (always (scheme-macro-expand pred) env))
        ((case (first pred)
           (QUOTE (if (null (second pred)) 'false 'true))
           (BEGIN (if (null (rest pred)) 'false
                      (always (last1 pred) env)))
           (SET! (always (third pred) env))
           (IF (let ((test (always (second pred)) env)
                     (then (always (third pred)) env)
                     (else (always (fourth pred)) env))
                 (cond ((eq test 'true) then)
                       ((eq test 'false) else)
                       ((eq then else) then))))
           (LAMBDA 'true)
           (t (let ((prim (primitive-p (first pred)  env
                            (length (rest pred)))))
               (if prim (prim-always prim)))))))))

(defun comp-if (pred then else env val? more?)
  (case (always pred env)
    (true            ; (if nil x y) ==> y ; ***
     (comp then env val? more?))          ; ***
    (false           ; (if t x y) ==> x   ; ***
     (comp else env val? more?))          ; ***
    (otherwise
     (let ((pcode (comp pred env t t))
           (tcode (comp then env val? more?))
           (ecode (comp else env val? more?)))
       (cond
         ((and (listp pred)   ; (if (not p) x y) ==> (if p y x)
               (length=1 (rest pred))
               (primitive-p (first pred) env 1)
               (eq (prim-opcode (primitive-p (first pred) env 1))
                   'not))
          (comp-if (second pred) else then env val? more?))
         ((equal tcode ecode) ; (if p x x) ==> (begin p x)
          (seq (comp pred env nil t) ecode))
         ((null tcode)        ; (if p nil y) ==> p (TJUMP L2) y L2:
          (let ((L2 (gen-label)))
            (seq pcode (gen 'TJUMP L2) ecode (list L2)
```

```
              (unless more? (gen 'RETURN)))))
  ((null ecode)        ; (if p x) ==> p (FJUMP L1) x L1:
   (let ((L1 (gen-label)))
     (seq pcode (gen 'FJUMP L1) tcode (list L1)
          (unless more? (gen 'RETURN)))))
  (t                    ; (if p x y) ==> p (FJUMP L1) x L1: y
                        ; or p (FJUMP L1) x (JUMP L2) L1: y L2:
   (let ((L1 (gen-label))
         (L2 (if more? (gen-label))))
     (seq pcode (gen 'FJUMP L1) tcode
          (if more? (gen 'JUMP L2))
          (list L1) ecode (if more? (list L2)))))))))))
```

Development note: originally, I had coded always as a predicate that took a Boolean value as input and returned true if the expression always had that value. Thus, you had to ask first if the predicate was always true, and then if it was always false. Then I realized this was duplicating much effort, and that the duplication was exponential, not just linear: for a triply-nested conditional I would have to do eight times the work, not twice the work. Thus I switched to the above formulation, where always is a three-valued function, returning true, false, or nil for none-of-the-above. But to demonstrate that the right solution doesn't always appear the first time, I give my original definition as well:

```
(defun always (boolean pred env)
  "Does predicate always evaluate to boolean in env?"
  (if (atom pred)
      (and (constantp pred) (equiv boolean pred))
      (case (first pred)
        (QUOTE (equiv boolean pred))
        (BEGIN (if (null (rest pred)) (equiv boolean nil)
                   (always boolean (last1 pred) env)))
        (SET! (always boolean (third pred) env))
        (IF (or (and (always t (second pred) env)
                     (always boolean (third pred) env))
                (and (always nil (second pred) env)
                     (always boolean (fourth pred) env))
                (and (always boolean (third pred) env)
                     (always boolean (fourth pred) env))))
        (LAMBDA (equiv boolean t))
        (t (let ((prim (primitive-p (first pred) env
                                    (length (rest pred)))))
             (and prim
                  (eq (prim-always prim)
                      (if boolean 'true 'false)))))))))

(defun equiv (x y) "Boolean equivalence" (eq (not x) (not y)))
```

Answer 23.7 The original version requires $O(n)$ stack space for poorly chosen pivots. Assuming a properly tail-recursive compiler, the modified version will never require more than $O(\log n)$ space, because at each step at least half of the vector is being sorted tail-recursively.

Answer 23.10 (1) `(defun (funcall fn . args) (apply fn args))`
(2) Suppose you changed the piece of code `(+ . numbers)` to `(+ . (map sqrt numbers))`. The latter is the same expression as `(+ map sqrt numbers)`, which is not the intended result at all. So there would be an arbitrary restriction: the last argument in an apply form would have to be an atom. This kind of restriction goes against the grain of Scheme.

CHAPTER 24

ANSI Common Lisp

T his chapter briefly covers some advanced features of Common Lisp that were not used in the rest of the book. The first topic, packages, is crucial in building large systems but was not covered in this book, since the programs are concise. The next four topics—error handling, pretty printing, series, and the loop macro—are covered in *Common Lisp the Language*, 2d edition, but not in the first edition of the book. Thus, they may not be applicable to your Lisp compiler. The final topic, sequence functions, shows how to write efficient functions that work for either lists or vectors.

24.1 Packages

A *package* is a symbol table that maps from strings to symbols named by those strings. When read is confronted with a sequence of characters like list, it uses the symbol table to determine that this refers to the symbol list. The important point is that every use of the symbol name list refers to the same symbol. That makes it easy to refer to predefined symbols, but it also makes it easy to introduce unintended name conflicts. For example, if I wanted to hook up the emycin expert system from chapter 16 with the parser from chapter 19, there would be a conflict because both programs use the symbol defrule to mean different things.

Common Lisp uses the package system to help resolve such conflicts. Instead of a single symbol table, Common Lisp allows any number of packages. The function read always uses the current package, which is defined to be the value of the special variable *package*. By default, Lisp starts out in the common-lisp-user package.[1] That means that if we type a new symbol, like zxv@!?+qw, it will be entered into that package. Converting a string to a symbol and placing it in a package is called *interning*. It is done automatically by read, and can be done by the function intern if necessary. Name conflicts arise when there is contention for names within the common-lisp-user package.

To avoid name conflicts, simply create your new symbols in another package, one that is specific to your program. The easiest way to implement this is to split each system into at least two files—one to define the package that the system resides in, and the others for the system itself. For example, the emycin system should start with a file that defines the emycin package. The following form defines the emycin package to use the lisp package. That means that when the current package is emycin, you can still refer to all the built-in Lisp symbols.

```lisp
(make-package "EMYCIN" :use '("LISP"))
```

The file containing the package definition should always be loaded before the rest of the system. Those files should start with the following call, which insures that all new symbols will be interned in the emycin package:

```lisp
(in-package "EMYCIN")
```

Packages are used for information-hiding purposes as well as for avoiding name clashes. A distinction is made between *internal* and *external* symbols. External symbols are those that a user of a system would want to refer to, while internal symbols are those that help implement the system but are not needed by a user of the system. The symbol rule would probably be internal to both the emycin and parser package, but defrule would be external, because a user of the emycin system uses defrule to define new rules. The designer of a system is responsible for advertising which symbols are external. The proper call is:

```lisp
(export '(emycin defrule defcontext defparm yes/no yes no is))
```

Now the user who wants to refer to symbols in the emycin package has four choices. First, he or she can use the *package prefix* notation. To refer to the symbol defrule in the emycin package, type emycin:defrule. Second, the user can make emycin be the current package with (in-package "EMYCIN"). Then, of course, we need

---

[1]Or in the user package in non-ANSI systems.

only type `defrule`. Third, if we only need part of the functionality of a system, we can import specific symbols into the current package. For example, we could call (`import 'emycin:defrule`). From then on, typing `defrule` (in the current package) will refer to `emycin:defrule`. Fourth, if we want the full functionality of the system, we call (`use-package "EMYCIN"`). This makes all the external symbols of the `emycin` package accessible in the current package.

While packages help eliminate name conflicts, `import` and `use-package` allow them to reappear. The advantage is that there will only be conflicts between external symbols. Since a carefully designed package should have far fewer external than internal symbols, the problem has at least been reduced. But if two packages both have an external `defrule` symbol, then we cannot `use-package` both these packages, nor `import` both symbols without producing a genuine name conflict. Such conflicts can be resolved by *shadowing* one symbol or the other; see *Common Lisp the Language* for details.

The careful reader may be confused by the distinction between "EMYCIN" and `emycin`. In *Common Lisp the Language*, it was not made clear what the argument to package functions must be. Thus, some implementations signal an error when given a symbol whose print name is a package. In ANSI Common Lisp, all package functions are specified to take either a package, a package name (a string), or a symbol whose print name is a package name. In addition, ANSI Common Lisp adds the convenient `defpackage` macro. It can be used as a replacement for separate calls to `make-package`, `use-package`, `import`, and `export`. Also note that ANSI renames the `lisp` package as `common-lisp`.

```
(defpackage emycin
  (:use common-lisp)
  (:export emycin defrule defcontext defparm yes/no yes no is))
```

For more on packages and building systems, see section 25.16 or *Common Lisp the Language*.

The Seven Name Spaces

One important fact to remember about packages is that they deal with symbols, and only indirectly deal with the uses those symbols might have. For example, you may think of (`export 'parse`) as exporting the function `parse`, but really it is exporting the symbol `parse`, which may happen to have a function definition associated with it. However, if the symbol is put to another use—perhaps as a variable or a data type—then those uses are made accessible by the `export` statement as well.

Common Lisp has at least seven name spaces. The two we think of most often are (1) for functions and macros and (2) for variables. We have seen that Scheme conflates these two name spaces, but Common Lisp keeps them separate, so that in a function application like (f) the function/macro name space is consulted for the value of f, but in (+ f), f is treated as a variable name. Those who understand the scope and extent rules of Common Lisp know that (3) special variables form a distinct name space from lexical variables. So the f in (+ f) is treated as either a special or lexical variable, depending on if there is an applicable special declaration. There is also a name space (4) for data types. Even if f is defined as a function and/or a variable, it can also be defined as a data type with defstruct, deftype, or defclass. It can also be defined as (5) a label for go statements within a tagbody or (6) a block name for return-from statements within a block. Finally, symbols inside a quoted expression are treated as constants, and thus form name space (7). These symbols are often used as keys in user-defined tables, and in a sense each such table defines a new name space. One example is the *tag* name space, used by catch and throw. Another is the package name space.

It is a good idea to limit each symbol to only one name space. Common Lisp will not be confused if a symbol is used in multiple ways, but the poor human reader probably will be.

In the following example f, can you identify which of the twelve uses of f refer to which name spaces?

```lisp
(defun f (f)
  (block f
    (tagbody
      f (catch 'f
          (if (typep f 'f)
              (throw 'f (go f)))
          (funcall #'f (get (symbol-value 'f) 'f)))))))
```

24.2 Conditions and Error Handling

An extraordinary feature of ANSI Common Lisp is the facility for handling errors. In most languages it is very difficult for the programmer to arrange to recover from an error. Although Ada and some implementations of C provide functions for error recovery, they are not generally part of the repertoire of most programmers. Thus, we find C programs that exit with the ungraceful message Segmentation violation: core dumped.

Common Lisp provides one of the most comprehensive and easy-to-use error-handling mechanism of any programming language, which leads to more robust programs. The process of error handling is divided into two parts: signaling an error, and handling it.

Signaling Errors

An *error* is a condition that the program does not know how to handle. Since the program does not know what to do, its only recourse is to announce the occurrence of the error, with the hope that some other program or user will know what to do. This announcement is called *signaling* an error. An error can be signaled by a Common Lisp built-in function, as when (/ 3 0) signals a divide-by-zero error. Errors can also be signaled explicitly by the programmer, as in a call to (error "Illegal value.").

Actually, it is a bit of a simplification to talk only of *signaling errors*. The precise term is *signaling a condition*. Some conditions, like end-of-file, are not considered errors, but nevertheless they are unusual conditions that must be dealt with. The condition system in Common Lisp allows for the definition of all kinds of conditions, but we will continue to talk about errors in this brief discussion, since most conditions are in fact error conditions.

Handling Errors

By default, signaling an error invokes the debugger. In the following example, the >> prompt means that the user is in the debugger rather than at the top level.

```
> (/ 3 0)
Error: An attempt was made to divide by zero.
>>
```

ANSI Common Lisp provides ways of changing this default behavior. Conceptually, this is done by setting up an *error handler* which handles the error in some way. Error handlers are bound dynamically and are used to process signaled errors. An error handler is much like a catch, and signaling an error is like a throw. In fact, in many systems catch and throw are implemented with the error-condition system.

The simplest way of handling an error is with the macro ignore-errors. If no error occurs, ignore-errors is just like progn. But if an error does occur, ignore-errors will return nil as its first value and t as its second, to indicate that an error has occurred but without doing anything else:

```
> (ignore-errors (/ 3 1)) ⇒ 3 NIL
> (ignore-errors (/ 3 0)) ⇒ NIL T
```

ignore-errors is a very coarse-grain tool. In an interactive interpreter, ignore-errors can be used to recover from any and all errors in the response to one input and get back to the read-process-print loop for the next input. If the errors that are ignored are not serious ones, this can be a very effective way of transforming a buggy program into a useful one.

But some errors are too important to ignore. If the error is running out of memory, then ignoring it will not help. Instead, we need to find some way of freeing up memory and continuing.

The condition-handling system can be used to handle only certain errors. The macro handler-case, is a convenient way to do this. Like case, its first argument is evaluated and used to determine what to do next. If no error is signaled, then the value of the expression is returned. But if an error does occur, the following clauses are searched for one that matches the type of the error. In the following example, handler-case is used to handle division by zero and other arithmetic errors (perhaps floating-point underflow), but it allows all other errors to pass unhandled.

```
(defun div (x y)
  (handler-case (/ x y)
    (division-by-zero () most-positive-fixnum)
    (arithmetic-error () 0)))
> (div 8 2) ⇒ 4
> (div 3 0) ⇒ 16777215
> (div 'xyzzy 1)
Error: The value of NUMBER, XYZZY, should be a number
```

Through judicious use of handler-case, the programmer can create robust code that reacts well to unexpected situations. For more details, see chapter 29 of *Common Lisp the Language,* 2d edition.

24.3   Pretty Printing

ANSI Common Lisp adds a facility for user-controlled pretty printing. In general, *pretty printing* refers to the process of printing complex expressions in a format that uses indentation to improve readability. The function pprint was always available, but before ANSI Common Lisp it was left unspecified, and it could not be extended by the user. Chapter 27 of *Common Lisp the Language,* 2d edition presents a pretty-printing facility that gives the user fine-grained control over the printing of all types of objects. In addition, the facility is integrated with the format function.

24.4   Series

The functional style of programming with higher-order functions is one of the attractions of Lisp. The following expression to sum the square roots of the positive numbers in the list nums is clear and concise:

```
(reduce #'+ (mapcar #'sqrt (find-all-if #'plusp nums)))
```

Unfortunately, it is inefficient: both find-all-if and mapcar cons up intermediate lists that are not needed in the final sum. The following two versions using loop and dolist are efficient but not as pretty:

```
;; Using Loop                          ;; Using dolist
(loop for num in nums                  (let ((sum 0))
      when (plusp num)                   (dolist (num nums sum)
      sum (sqrt num))                      (when (plusp num)
                                             (incf sum num)))))
```

A compromise between the two approaches is provided by the *series* facility, defined in appendix A of *Common Lisp the Language,* 2d edition. The example using series would look like:

```
(collect-sum (#Msqrt (choose-if #'plusp nums)))
```

This looks very much like the functional version: only the names have been changed. However, it compiles into efficient iterative code very much like the dolist version.

Like pipes (see section 9.3), elements of a series are only evaluated when they are needed. So we can write (scan-range :from 0) to indicate the infinite series of integers starting from 0, but if we only use, say, the first five elements of this series, then only the first five elements will be generated.

The series facility offers a convenient and efficient alternative to iterative loops and sequence functions. Although the series proposal has not yet been adopted as an official part of ANSI Common Lisp, its inclusion in the reference manual has made it increasingly popular.

24.5   The Loop Macro

The original specification of Common Lisp included a simple loop macro. The body of the loop was executed repeatedly, until a return was encountered. ANSI Common Lisp officially introduces a far more complex loop macro, one that had been used in ZetaLisp and its predecessors for some time. This book has occasionally used the complex loop in place of alternatives such as do, dotimes, dolist, and the mapping functions.

If your Lisp does not include the complex loop macro, this chapter gives a definition that will run all the examples in this book, although it does not support all the features of loop. This chapter also serves as an example of a complex macro. As with any macro, the first thing to do is to look at some macro calls and what they might expand into. Here are two examples:

```
(loop for i from 1 to n do (print (sqrt i))) ≡
(LET* ((I 1)
       (TEMP N))
  (TAGBODY
   LOOP
      (IF (> I TEMP)
          (GO END))
      (PRINT (SQRT I))
      (SETF I (+ I 1))
      (GO LOOP)
   END))
(loop for v in list do (print v)) ≡
(LET* ((IN LIST)
       (V (CAR IN)))
  (TAGBODY
   LOOP
      (IF (NULL IN)
          (GO END))
      (PRINT V)
      (SETF IN (CDR IN))
      (SETF V (CAR IN))
      (GO LOOP)
   END))
```

Each loop initializes some variables, then enters a loop with some exit tests and a body. So the template is something like:

```
(let* (variables...)
  (tagbody
   loop
      (if exit-tests
          (go end))
      body
      (go loop)
   end))
```

Actually, there's more we might need in the general case. There may be a prologue that appears before the loop but after the variable initialization, and similarly there may be an epilogue after the loop. This epilogue may involve returning a value, and since we want to be able to return from the loop in any case, we need to wrap a block around it. So the complete template is:

```
(let* (variables...)
  (block name
    prologue
    (tagbody
     loop
        body
        (go loop)
     end
        epilogue
        (return result))))
```

To generate this template from the body of a loop form, we will employ a structure with fields for each of the parts of the template:

```
(defstruct loop
  "A structure to hold parts of a loop as it is built."
  (vars nil) (prologue nil) (body nil) (steps nil)
  (epilogue nil) (result nil) (name nil))
```

Now the loop macro needs to do four things: (1) decide if this is a use of the simple, non-keyword loop or the complex ANSI loop. If it is the latter, then (2) make an instance of the loop structure, (3) process the body of the loop, filling in apprpriate fields of the structure, and (4) place the filled fields into the template. Here is the loop macro:

```
(defmacro loop (&rest exps)
  "Supports both ANSI and simple LOOP.
  Warning: Not every loop keyword is supported."
  (if (every #'listp exps)
      ;; No keywords implies simple loop:
      '(block nil (tagbody loop ,@exps (go loop)))
      ;; otherwise process loop keywords:
      (let ((l (make-loop)))
        (parse-loop-body l exps)
        (fill-loop-template l))))

(defun fill-loop-template (l)
  "Use a loop-structure instance to fill the template."
  '(let* ,(nreverse (loop-vars l))
     (block ,(loop-name l)
       ,@(nreverse (loop-prologue l))
       (tagbody
        loop
           ,@(nreverse (loop-body l))
           ,@(nreverse (loop-steps l))
           (go loop)
```

```
      end
    ,@(nreverse (loop-epilogue 1))
    (return ,(loop-result 1))))))))
```

Most of the work is in writing `parse-loop-body`, which takes a list of expressions and parses them into the proper fields of a loop structure. It will use the following auxiliary functions:

```
(defun add-body (1 exp) (push exp (loop-body 1)))

(defun add-test (1 test)
  "Put in a test for loop termination."
  (push '(if ,test (go end)) (loop-body 1)))

(defun add-var (1 var init &optional (update nil update?))
  "Add a variable, maybe including an update step."
  (unless (assoc var (loop-vars 1))
    (push (list var init) (loop-vars 1)))
  (when update?
    (push '(setq ,var ,update) (loop-steps 1))))
```

There are a number of alternative ways of implementing this kind of processing. One would be to use special variables: `*prologue*`, `*body*`, `*epilogue*`, and so on. This would mean we wouldn't have to pass around the loop structure 1, but there would be significant clutter in having seven new special variables. Another possibility is to use local variables and close the definitions of `loop`, along with the `add-` functions in that local environment:

```
(let (body prologue epilogue steps vars name result)
  (defmacro loop ...)
  (defun add-body ...)
  (defun add-test ...)
  (defun add-var ...))
```

This is somewhat cleaner style, but some early Common Lisp compilers do not support embedded `defun`s, so I chose to write in a style that I knew would work in all implementations. Another design choice would be to return multiple values for each of the components and have `parse-loop-body` put them all together. This is in fact done in one of the Lisp Machine implementations of `loop`, but I think it is a poor decision: seven components are too many to keep track of by positional notation.

Anatomy of a Loop

All this has just been to set up for the real work: parsing the expressions that make up the loop with the function `parse-loop-body`. Every loop consists of a sequence of clauses, where the syntax of each clause is determined by the first expression of the clause, which should be a known symbol. These symbols are called *loop keywords,* although they are not in the keyword package.

The loop keywords will be defined in a data-driven fashion. Every keyword has a function on its property list under the loop-fn indicator. The function takes three arguments: the loop structure being built, the very next expression in the loop body, and a list of the remaining expressions after that. The function is responsible for updating the loop structure (usually by making appropriate calls to the add- functions) and then returning the unparsed expressions. The three-argument calling convention is used because many of the keywords only look at one more expression. So those functions see that expression as their first argument, and they can conveniently return their second argument as the unparsed remainder. Other functions will want to look more carefully at the second argument, parsing some of it and returning the rest.

The macro defloop is provided to add new loop keywords. This macro enforces the three-argument calling convention. If the user supplies only two arguments, then a third argument is automatically added and returned as the remainder. Also, if the user specifies another symbol rather than a list of arguments, this is taken as an alias, and a function is constructed that calls the function for that keyword:

```
(defun parse-loop-body (l exps)
  "Parse the exps based on the first exp being a keyword.
  Continue until all the exps are parsed."
  (unless (null exps)
    (parse-loop-body
      l (call-loop-fn l (first exps) (rest exps)))))

(defun call-loop-fn (l key exps)
  "Return the loop parsing function for this keyword."
  (if (and (symbolp key) (get key 'loop-fn))
      (funcall (get key 'loop-fn) l (first exps) (rest exps))
      (error "Unknown loop key: ~a" key)))

(defmacro defloop (key args &rest body)
  "Define a new LOOP keyword."
  ;; If the args do not have a third arg, one is supplied.
  ;; Also, we can define an alias with (defloop key other-key)
  `(setf (get ',key 'loop-fn)
         ,(cond ((and (symbolp args) (null body))
                 `#'(lambda (l x y)
                      (call-loop-fn l ',args (cons x y))))
                ((and (listp args) (= (length args) 2))
                 `#'(lambda (,@args -exps-) ,@body -exps-))
                (t `#'(lambda ,args ,@body)))))
```

Now we are ready to define some loop keywords. Each of the following sections refers to (and implements the loop keywords in) a section of chapter 26 of *Common Lisp the Language,* 2d edition.

Iteration Control (26.6)

Here we define keywords for iterating over elements of a sequence and for stopping the iteration. The following cases are covered, where uppercase words represent loop keywords:

```
(LOOP REPEAT n ...)
(LOOP FOR i FROM s TO e BY inc ...)
(LOOP FOR v IN l ...)
(LOOP FOR v ON l ...)
(LOOP FOR v = expr [THEN step] ...)
```

The implementation is straightforward, although somewhat tedious for complex keywords like for. Take the simpler keyword, repeat. To handle it, we generate a new variable that will count down the number of times to repeat. We call add-var to add that variable, with its initial value, to the loop structure. We also give this variable an update expression, which decrements the variable by one each time through the loop. Then all we need to do is call add-test to insert code that will exit the loop when the variable reaches zero:

```
(defloop repeat (l times)
  "(LOOP REPEAT n ...) does loop body n times."
  (let ((i (gensym "REPEAT")))
    (add-var l i times '(- ,i 1))
    (add-test l '(<= ,i 0))))
```

The loop keyword for is more complicated, but each case can be analyzed in the same way as repeat:

```
(defloop as for)  ;; AS is the same as FOR

(defloop for (l var exps)
  "4 of the 7 cases for FOR are covered here:
  (LOOP FOR i FROM s TO e BY inc ...) does arithemtic iteration
  (LOOP FOR v IN l ...) iterates for each element of l
  (LOOP FOR v ON l ...) iterates for each tail of l
  (LOOP FOR v = expr [THEN step]) initializes and iterates v"
  (let ((key (first exps))
        (source (second exps))
        (rest (rest2 exps)))
    (ecase key
```

```
              ((from downfrom upfrom to downto upto by)
               (loop-for-arithmetic l var exps))
              (in (let ((v (gensym "IN")))
                   (add-var l v source '(cdr ,v))
                   (add-var l var '(car ,v) '(car ,v))
                   (add-test l '(null ,v))
                   rest))
              (on (add-var l var source '(cdr ,var))
                  (add-test l '(null ,var))
                 rest)
              (= (if (eq (first rest) 'then)
                     (progn
                       (pop rest)
                       (add-var l var source (pop rest)))
                     (progn
                       (add-var l var nil)
                       (add-body l '(setq ,var ,source))))
                rest)
              ;; ACROSS, BEING clauses omitted
              )))

(defun loop-for-arithmetic (l var exps)
  "Parse loop expressions of the form:
  (LOOP FOR var [FROM|DOWNFROM|UPFROM exp1] [TO|DOWNTO|UPTO exp2]
       [BY exp3]"
  ;; The prepositions BELOW and ABOVE are omitted
  (let ((exp1 0)
        (exp2 nil)
        (exp3 1)
        (down? nil))
    ;; Parse the keywords:
    (when (member (first exps) '(from downfrom upfrom))
      (setf exp1 (second exps)
            down? (eq (first exps) 'downfrom)
            exps (rest2 exps)))
    (when (member (first exps) '(to downto upto))
      (setf exp2 (second exps)
            down? (or down? (eq (first exps) 'downto))
            exps (rest2 exps)))
    (when (eq (first exps) 'by)
      (setf exp3 (second exps)
            exps (rest2 exps)))
    ;; Add variables and tests:
    (add-var l var exp1
            '(,(if down? '- '+) ,var ,(maybe-temp l exp3)))
    (when exp2
      (add-test l '(,(if down? '< '>) ,var ,(maybe-temp l exp2))))
    ;; and return the remaining expressions:
```

```
      exps))

(defun maybe-temp (l exp)
  "Generate a temporary variable, if needed."
  (if (constantp exp)
      exp
      (let ((temp (gensym "TEMP")))
        (add-var l temp exp)
        temp)))
```

End-Test Control (26.7)

In this section we cover the following clauses:

```
(LOOP UNTIL test ...)
(LOOP WHILE test ...)
(LOOP ALWAYS condition ...)
(LOOP NEVER condition ...)
(LOOP THEREIS condition ...)
(LOOP ... (LOOP-FINISH) ...)
```

Each keyword is quite simple:

```
(defloop until (l test) (add-test l test))

(defloop while (l test) (add-test l '(not ,test)))

(defloop always (l test)
  (setf (loop-result l) t)
  (add-body l '(if (not ,test) (return nil))))

(defloop never (l test)
  (setf (loop-result l) t)
  (add-body l '(if ,test (return nil))))

(defloop thereis (l test) (add-body l '(return-if ,test)))

(defmacro return-if (test)
  "Return TEST if it is non-nil."
  (once-only (test)
    '(if ,test (return ,test))))

(defmacro loop-finish () '(go end))
```

Value Accumulation (26.8)

The collect keyword poses another challenge. How do you collect a list of expressions presented one at a time? The answer is to view the expressions as a queue, one where we add items to the rear but never remove them from the front of the queue. Then we can use the queue functions defined in section 10.5.

Unlike the other clauses, value accumulation clauses can communicate with each other. There can be, say, two collect and an append clause in the same loop, and they all build onto the same list. Because of this, I use the same variable name for the accumulator, rather than gensyming a new variable for each use. The name chosen is stored in the global variable *acc*. In the official loop standard it is possible for the user to specify the variable with an into modifier, but I have not implemented that option. The clauses covered are:

```
(LOOP COLLECT item ...)
(LOOP NCONC item ...)
(LOOP APPEND item ...)
(LOOP COUNT item ...)
(LOOP SUM item ...)
(LOOP MAXIMIZE item ...)
(LOOP MINIMIZE item ...)
```

The implementation is:

```
(defconstant *acc* (gensym "ACC")
  "Variable used for value accumulation in LOOP.")

;;; INTO preposition is omitted

(defloop collect (l exp)
  (add-var l *acc* '(make-queue))
  (add-body l '(enqueue ,exp ,*acc*))
  (setf (loop-result l) '(queue-contents ,*acc*)))

(defloop nconc (l exp)
  (add-var l *acc* '(make-queue))
  (add-body l '(queue-nconc ,*acc* ,exp))
  (setf (loop-result l) '(queue-contents ,*acc*)))

(defloop append (l exp exps)
  (call-loop-fn l 'nconc '((copy-list ,exp) .,exps)))

(defloop count (l exp)
  (add-var l *acc* 0)
  (add-body l '(when ,exp (incf ,*acc*)))
  (setf (loop-result l) *acc*))
```

```
(defloop sum (1 exp)
  (add-var 1 *acc* 0)
  (add-body 1 '(incf ,*acc* ,exp))
  (setf (loop-result 1) *acc*))

(defloop maximize (1 exp)
  (add-var 1 *acc* nil)
  (add-body 1 '(setf ,*acc*
                 (if ,*acc*
                     (max ,*acc* ,exp)
                     ,exp)))
  (setf (loop-result 1) *acc*))

(defloop minimize (1 exp)
  (add-var 1 *acc* nil)
  (add-body 1 '(setf ,*acc*
                 (if ,*acc*
                     (min ,*acc* ,exp)
                     ,exp)))
  (setf (loop-result 1) *acc*))

(defloop collecting collect)
(defloop nconcing   nconc)
(defloop appending  append)
(defloop counting   count)
(defloop summing    sum)
(defloop maximizing maximize)
(defloop minimizing minimize)
```

Exercise 24.1   loop lets us build aggregates (lists, maximums, sums, etc.) over the body of the loop. Sometimes it is inconvenient to be restricted to a single-loop body. For example, we might want a list of all the nonzero elements of a two-dimensional array. One way to implement this is with a macro, with-collection, that sets up and returns a queue structure that is built by calls to the function collect. For example:

```
> (let ((A '#2a((1 0 0) (0 2 4) (0 0 3))))
    (with-collection
      (loop for i from 0 to 2 do
        (loop for j from 0 to 2 do
          (if (> (aref a i j) 0)
              (collect (aref A i j)))))))
(1 2 4 3)
```

Implement with-collection and collect.

Variable Initialization (26.9)

The with clause allows local variables—I have included it, but recommend using a let instead. I have not included the and preposition, which allows the variables to nest at different levels.

```
;;;; 26.9. Variable Initializations ("and" omitted)

(defloop with (l var exps)
  (let ((init nil))
    (when (eq (first exps) '=)
      (setf init (second exps)
            exps (rest2 exps)))
    (add-var l var init)
    exps))
```

Conditional Execution (26.10)

loop also provides forms for conditional execution. These should be avoided whenever possible, as Lisp already has a set of perfectly good conditional macros. However, sometimes you want to make, say, a collect conditional on some test. In that case, loop conditionals are acceptable. The clauses covered here are:

```
(LOOP WHEN test ... [ELSE ...])   ; IF is a synonym for WHEN
(LOOP UNLESS test ... [ELSE ...])
```

Here is an example of when:

```
> (loop for x from 1 to 10
        when (oddp x)
             collect x
        else collect (- x))
(1 -2 3 -4 5 -6 7 -8 9 -10)
```

Of course, we could have said collect (if (oddp x) x (- x)) and done without the conditional. There is one extra feature in loop's conditionals: the value of the test is stored in the variable it for subsequent use in the THEN or ELSE parts. (This is just the kind of feature that makes some people love loop and others throw up their hands in despair.) Here is an example:

```
> (loop for x from 1 to 10
        when (second (assoc x '((1 one) (3 three) (5 five))))
        collect it)
(ONE THREE FIVE)
```

The conditional clauses are a little tricky to implement, since they involve parsing other clauses. The idea is that call-loop-fn parses the THEN and ELSE parts, adding whatever is necessary to the body and to other parts of the loop structure. Then add-body is used to add labels and go statements that branch to the labels as needed. This is the same technique that is used to compile conditionals in chapter 23; see the function comp-if on page 787. Here is the code:

```
(defloop when (l test exps)
  (loop-unless l '(not ,(maybe-set-it test exps)) exps))

(defloop unless (l test exps)
  (loop-unless l (maybe-set-it test exps) exps))

(defun maybe-set-it (test exps)
  "Return value, but if the variable IT appears in exps,
  then return code that sets IT to value."
  (if (find-anywhere 'it exps)
      '(setq it ,test)
      test))

(defloop if when)

(defun loop-unless (l test exps)
  (let ((label (gensym "L")))
    (add-var l 'it nil)
    ;; Emit code for the test and the THEN part
    (add-body l '(if ,test (go ,label)))
    (setf exps (call-loop-fn l (first exps) (rest exps)))
    ;; Optionally emit code for the ELSE part
    (if (eq (first exps) 'else)
        (progn
          (let ((label2 (gensym "L")))
            (add-body l '(go ,label2))
            (add-body l label)
            (setf exps (call-loop-fn l (second exps) (rest2 exps)))
            (add-body l label2)))
        (add-body l label)))
    exps)
```

Unconditional Execution (26.11)

The unconditional execution keywords are do and return:

```
(defloop do (l exp exps)
  (add-body l exp)
  (loop (if (symbolp (first exps)) (RETURN exps))
        (add-body l (pop exps))))

(defloop return (l exp) (add-body l '(return ,exp)))
```

Miscellaneous Features (26.12)

Finally, the miscellaneous features include the keywords initially and finally, which define the loop prologue and epilogue, and the keyword named, which gives a name to the loop for use by a return-from form. I have omitted the data-type declarations and destructuring capabilities.

```
(defloop initially (l exp exps)
  (push exp (loop-prologue l))
  (loop (if (symbolp (first exps)) (RETURN exps))
        (push (pop exps) (loop-prologue l))))

(defloop finally (l exp exps)
  (push exp (loop-epilogue l))
  (loop (if (symbolp (first exps)) (RETURN exps))
        (push (pop exps) (loop-epilogue l))))

(defloop named (l exp) (setf (loop-name l) exp))
```

24.6   Sequence Functions

Common Lisp provides sequence functions to make the programmer's life easier: the same function can be used for lists, vectors, and strings. However, this ease of use comes at a cost. Sequence functions must be written very carefully to make sure they are efficient. There are three main sources of indeterminacy that can lead to inefficiency: (1) the sequences can be of different types; (2) some functions have keyword arguments; (3) some functions have a &rest argument. Careful coding can limit or eliminate these sources of inefficiency, by making as many choices as possible at compile time and making the remaining choices outside of the main loop.

In this section we see how to implement the new ANSI sequence function `map-into` and the updated function `reduce` efficiently. This is essential for those without an ANSI compiler. Even those who do have access to an ANSI compiler will benefit from seeing the efficiency techniques used here.

Before defining the sequence functions, the macro `once-only` is introduced.

Once-only: A Lesson in Macrology

The macro `once-only` has been around for a long time on various systems, although it didn't make it into the Common Lisp standard. I include it here for two reasons: first, it is used in the following `funcall-if` macro, and second, if you can understand how to write and when to use `once-only`, then you truly understand macro.

First, you have to understand the problem that `once-only` addresses. Suppose we wanted to have a macro that multiplies its input by itself:[2]

```
(defmacro square (x) '(* ,x ,x))
```

This definition works fine in the following case:

```
> (macroexpand '(square z)) ⇒ (* Z Z)
```

But it doesn't work as well here:

```
> (macroexpand '(square (print (incf i))))
(* (PRINT (INCF I)) (PRINT (INCF I)))
```

The problem is that `i` will get incremented twice, not once, and two different values will get printed, not one. We need to bind `(print (incf i))` to a local variable before doing the multiplication. On the other hand, it would be superfluous to bind `z` to a local variable in the previous example. This is where `once-only` comes in. It allows us to write macro definitions like this:

```
(defmacro square (x) (once-only (x) '(* ,x ,x)))
```

and have the generated code be just what we want:

```
> (macroexpand '(square z))
(* Z Z)
```

---

[2]As was noted before, the proper way to do this is to proclaim `square` as an inline function, not a macro, but please bear with the example.

```
> (macroexpand '(square (print (incf i))))
(LET ((G3811 (PRINT (INCF I))))
  (* G3811 G3811))
```

You have now learned lesson number one of once-only: you know how macros differ from functions when it comes to arguments with side effects, and you now know how to handle this. Lesson number two comes when you try to write (or even understand) a definition of once-only—only when you truly understand the nature of macros will you be able to write a correct version. As always, the first thing to determine is what a call to once-only should expand into. The generated code should test the variable to see if it is free of side effects, and if so, generate the body as is; otherwise it should generate code to bind a new variable, and use that variable in the body of the code. Here's roughly what we want:

```
> (macroexpand '(once-only (x) '(* ,x ,x)))
(if (side-effect-free-p x)
    '(* ,x ,x)
    '(let ((g001 ,x))
       ,(let ((x 'g001))
          '(* ,x ,x))))
```

where g001 is a new symbol, to avoid conflicts with the x or with symbols in the body. Normally, we generate macro bodies using backquotes, but if the macro body itself has a backquote, then what? It is possible to nest backquotes (and appendix C of *Common Lisp the Language*, 2d edition has a nice discussion of doubly and triply nested backquotes), but it certainly is not trivial to understand. I recommend replacing the inner backquote with its equivalent using list and quote:

```
(if (side-effect-free-p x)
    '(* ,x ,x)
    (list 'let (list (list 'g001 x))
          (let ((x 'g001))
            '(* ,x ,x))))
```

Now we can write once-only. Note that we have to account for the case where there is more than one variable and where there is more than one expression in the body.

```
(defmacro once-only (variables &rest body)
  "Returns the code built by BODY.  If any of VARIABLES
  might have side effects, they are evaluated once and stored
  in temporary variables that are then passed to BODY."
  (assert (every #'symbolp variables))
  (let ((temps (loop repeat (length variables) collect (gensym))))
    '(if (every #'side-effect-free-p (list .,variables))
```

```
                    (progn .,body)
                    (list 'let
                        ,'(list ,@(mapcar #'(lambda (tmp var)
                                            '(list ',tmp ,var))
                                        temps variables))
                        (let ,(mapcar #'(lambda (var tmp) '(,var ',tmp))
                                    variables temps)
                            .,body)))))

(defun side-effect-free-p (exp)
  "Is exp a constant, variable, or function,
  or of the form (THE type x) where x is side-effect-free?"
  (or (constantp exp) (atom exp) (starts-with exp 'function)
      (and (starts-with exp 'the)
          (side-effect-free-p (third exp)))))
```

Here we see the expansion of the call to once-only and a repeat of the expansions of two calls to square:

```
> (macroexpand '(once-only (x) '(* ,x ,x)))
(IF (EVERY #'SIDE-EFFECT-FREE-P (LIST X))
    (PROGN
      '(* ,X ,X))
    (LIST 'LET (LIST (LIST 'G3763 X))
          (LET ((X 'G3763))
            '(* ,X ,X))))

> (macroexpand '(square z))
(* Z Z)

> (macroexpand '(square (print (incf i))))
(LET ((G3811 (PRINT (INCF I))))
  (* G3811 G3811))
```

This output was produced with *print-gensym* set to nil. When this variable is non-nil, uninterned symbols are printed with a prefix #:, as in #:G3811. This insures that the symbol will not be interned by a subsequent read.

It is worth noting that Common Lisp automatically handles problems related to multiple evaluation of subforms in setf methods. See page 884 for an example.

Avoid Overusing Macros

A word to the wise: don't get carried away with macros. Use macros freely to represent your *problem*, but shy away from new macros in the implementation of your *solution*, unless absolutely necessary. So, it is good style to introduce a macro, say, `defrule`, which defines rules for your application, but adding macros to the code itself may just make things harder for others to use.

Here is a story. Before `if` was a standard part of Lisp, I defined my own version of `if`. Unlike the simple `if`, my version took any number of test/result pairs, followed by an optional `else` result. In general, the expansion was:

```
(if a b c d ... x) => (cond (a b) (c d) ... (T x))
```

My `if` also had one more feature: the symbol 'that' could be used to refer to the value of the most recent test. For example, I could write:

```
(if (assoc item a-list)
    (process (cdr that)))
```

which would expand into:

```
(LET (THAT)
  (COND
    ((SETQ THAT (ASSOC ITEM A-LIST)) (PROCESS (CDR THAT)))))
```

This was a convenient feature (compare it to the => feature of Scheme's cond, as discussed on page 778), but it backfired often enough that I eventually gave up on my version of `if`. Here's why. I would write code like this:

```
(if (total-score x)
    (print (/ that number-of-trials))
    (error "No scores"))
```

and then make a small change:

```
(if (total-score x)
    (if *print-scores* (print (/ that number-of-trials)))
    (error "No scores"))
```

The problem is that the variable that now refers to `*print-scores*`, not (`total-score` x), as it did before. My macro violates referential transparency. In general, that's the whole point of macros, and it is why macros are sometimes convenient. But in this case, violating referential transparency can lead to confusion.

MAP-INTO

The function map-into is used on page 632. This function, added for the ANSI version of Common Lisp, is like map, except that instead of building a new sequence, the first argument is changed to hold the results. This section describes how to write a fairly efficient version of map-into, using techniques that are applicable to any sequence function. We'll start with a simple version:

```
(defun map-into (result-sequence function &rest sequences)
  "Destructively set elements of RESULT-SEQUENCE to the results
  of applying FUNCTION to respective elements of SEQUENCES."
  (replace result-sequence (apply #'map 'list function sequences)))
```

This does the job, but it defeats the purpose of map-into, which is to avoid generating garbage. Here's a version that generates less garbage:

```
(defun map-into (result-sequence function &rest sequences)
  "Destructively set elements of RESULT-SEQUENCE to the results
  of applying FUNCTION to respective elements of SEQUENCES."
  (let ((n (loop for seq in (cons result-sequence sequences)
                minimize (length seq))))
    (dotimes (i n)
      (setf (elt result-sequence i)
            (apply function
                   (mapcar #'(lambda (seq) (elt seq i))
                           sequences))))))
```

There are three problems with this definition. First, it wastes space: mapcar creates a new argument list each time, only to have the list be discarded. Second, it wastes time: doing a setf of the ith element of a list makes the algorithm $O(n^2)$ instead of $O(n)$, where n is the length of the list. Third, it is subtly wrong: if result-sequence is a vector with a fill pointer, then map-into is supposed to ignore result-sequence's current length and extend the fill pointer as needed. The following version fixes those problems:

```
(defun map-into (result-sequence function &rest sequences)
  "Destructively set elements of RESULT-SEQUENCE to the results
  of applying FUNCTION to respective elements of SEQUENCES."
  (let ((arglist (make-list (length sequences)))
        (n (if (listp result-sequence)
               most-positive-fixnum
               (array-dimension result-sequence 0))))
    ;; arglist is made into a list of args for each call
    ;; n is the length of the longest vector
```

```
(when sequences
  (setf n (min n (loop for seq in sequences
                       minimize (length seq)))))
;; Define some shared functions:
(flet
  ((do-one-call (i)
     (loop for seq on sequences
           for arg on arglist
           do (if (listp (first seq))
                  (setf (first arg)
                        (pop (first seq)))
                  (setf (first arg)
                        (aref (first seq) i))))
     (apply function arglist))
   (do-result (i)
     (if (and (vectorp result-sequence)
              (array-has-fill-pointer-p result-sequence))
         (setf (fill-pointer result-sequence)
               (max i (fill-pointer result-sequence))))))
  (declare (inline do-one-call))
  ;; Decide if the result is a list or vector,
  ;; and loop through each element
  (if (listp result-sequence)
      (loop for i from 0 to (- n 1)
            for r on result-sequence
            do (setf (first r)
                     (do-one-call i)))
      (loop for i from 0 to (- n 1)
            do (setf (aref result-sequence i)
                     (do-one-call i))
            finally (do-result n))))
  result-sequence))
```

There are several things worth noticing here. First, I split the main loop into two versions, one where the result is a list, and the other where it is a vector. Rather than duplicate code, the local functions do-one-call and do-result are defined. The former is declared inline because it it called often, while the latter is not. The arguments are computed by looking at each sequence in turn, taking the ith element if it is a vector, and popping the sequence if it is a list. The arguments are stored into the list arglist, which has been preallocated to the correct size. All in all, we compute the answer fairly efficiently, without generating unnecessary garbage.

The application could be done more efficiently, however. Think what apply must do: scan down the argument list, and put each argument into the location expected by the function-calling conventions, and then branch to the function. Some implementations provide a better way of doing this. For example, the TI Lisp Machine provides two low-level primitive functions, %push and %call, that compile into single instructions to put the arguments into the right locations and branch to the function. With these primitives, the body of do-one-call would be:

```
(loop for seq on sequences
      do (if (listp (first seq))
             (%push (pop (first seq)))
             (%push (aref (first seq) i))))
(%call function length-sequences)
```

There is a remaining inefficiency, though. Each sequence is type-checked each time through the loop, even though the type remains constant once it is determined the first time. Theoretically, we could code separate loops for each combination of types, just as we coded two loops depending on the type of the result sequence. But that would mean 2^n loops for n sequences, and there is no limit on how large n can be.

It might be worth it to provide specialized functions for small values of n, and dispatch to the appropriate function. Here's a start at that approach:

```
(defun map-into (result function &rest sequences)
  (apply
    (case (length sequences)
      (0 (if (listp result) #'map-into-list-0 #'map-into-vect-0))
      (1 (if (listp result)
             (if (listp (first sequences))
                 #'map-into-list-1-list #'map-into-list-1-vect)
             (if (listp (first sequences))
                 #'map-into-vect-1-list #'map-into-vect-1-vect)))
      (2 (if (listp result)
             (if (listp (first sequences))
                 (if (listp (second sequences))
                     #'map-into-list-2-list-list
                     #'map-into-list-2-list-vect)
                 ...)))
      (t (if (listp result) #'map-into-list-n #'map-into-vect-n)))
    result function sequences))
```

The individual functions are not shown. This approach is efficient in execution time, but it takes up a lot of space, considering that map-into is a relatively obscure function. If map-into is declared inline and the compiler is reasonably good, then it will produce code that just calls the appropriate function.

REDUCE with :key

Another change in the ANSI proposal is to add a :key keyword to reduce. This is a useful addition—in fact, for years I had been using a reduce-by function that provided just this functionality. In this section we see how to add the :key keyword.

At the top level, I define reduce as an interface to the keywordless function reduce*. They are both proclaimed inline, so there will be no overhead for the keywords in normal uses of reduce.

```
(proclaim '(inline reduce reduce*))

(defun reduce* (fn seq from-end start end key init init-p)
  (funcall (if (listp seq) #'reduce-list #'reduce-vect)
           fn seq from-end (or start 0) end key init init-p))

(defun reduce (function sequence &key from-end start end key
                 (initial-value nil initial-value-p))
  (reduce* function sequence from-end start end
           key initial-value initial-value-p))
```

The easier case is when the sequence is a vector:

```
(defun reduce-vect (fn seq from-end start end key init init-p)
  (when (null end) (setf end (length seq)))
  (assert (<= 0 start end (length seq)) (start end)
          "Illegal subsequence of ~a --- :start ~d :end ~d"
          seq start end)
  (case (- end start)
    (0 (if init-p init (funcall fn)))
    (1 (if init-p
           (funcall fn init (funcall-if key (aref seq start)))
           (funcall-if key (aref seq start))))
    (t (if (not from-end)
           (let ((result
                   (if init-p
                       (funcall
                         fn init
                         (funcall-if key (aref seq start)))
                       (funcall
                         fn
                         (funcall-if key (aref seq start))
                         (funcall-if key (aref seq (+ start 1)))))))
             (loop for i from (+ start (if init-p 1 2))
                   to (- end 1)
                   do (setf result
                            (funcall
                              fn result
                              (funcall-if key (aref seq i)))))
             result)
           (let ((result
                   (if init-p
```

```
                    (funcall
                      fn
                      (funcall-if key (aref seq (- end 1)))
                      init)
                    (funcall
                      fn
                      (funcall-if key (aref seq (- end 2)))
                      (funcall-if key (aref seq (- end 1)))))))))
          (loop for i from (- end (if init-p 2 3)) downto start
                do (setf result
                      (funcall
                        fn
                        (funcall-if key (aref seq i))
                        result)))
        result)))))
```

When the sequence is a list, we go to some trouble to avoid computing the length, since that is an $O(n)$ operation on lists. The hardest decision is what to do when the list is to be traversed from the end. There are four choices:

- **recurse.** We could recursively walk the list until we hit the end, and then compute the results on the way back up from the recursions. However, some implementations may have fairly small bounds on the depths of recursive calls, and a system function like reduce should never run afoul of such limitations. In any event, the amount of stack space consumed by this approach would normally be more than the amount of heap space consumed in the next approach.

- **reverse.** We could reverse the list and then consider from-end true. The only drawback is the time and space needed to construct the reversed list.

- **nreverse.** We could destructively reverse the list in place, do the reduce computation, and then destructively reverse the list back to its original state (perhaps with an unwind-protect added). Unfortunately, this is just incorrect. The list may be bound to some variable that is accessible to the function used in the reduction. If that is so, the function will see the reversed list, not the original list.

- **coerce.** We could convert the list to a vector, and then use reduce-vect. This has an advantage over the reverse approach in that vectors generally take only half as much storage as lists. Therefore, this is the approach I adopt.

```
(defmacro funcall-if (fn arg)
  (once-only (fn)
    `(if ,fn (funcall ,fn ,arg) ,arg)))
```

```
(defun reduce-list (fn seq from-end start end key init init-p)
  (when (null end) (setf end most-positive-fixnum))
  (cond ((> start 0)
         (reduce-list fn (nthcdr start seq) from-end 0
                      (- end start) key init init-p))
        ((or (null seq) (eql start end))
         (if init-p init (funcall fn)))
        ((= (- end start) 1)
         (if init-p
             (funcall fn init (funcall-if key (first seq)))
             (funcall-if key (first seq))))
        (from-end
         (reduce-vect fn (coerce seq 'vector) t start end
                      key init init-p))
        ((null (rest seq))
         (if init-p
             (funcall fn init (funcall-if key (first seq)))
             (funcall-if key (first seq))))
        (t (let ((result
                   (if init-p
                       (funcall
                         fn init
                         (funcall-if key (pop seq)))
                       (funcall
                         fn
                         (funcall-if key (pop seq))
                         (funcall-if key (pop seq))))))
             (if end
                 (loop repeat (- end (if init-p 1 2)) while seq
                       do (setf result
                                (funcall
                                  fn result
                                  (funcall-if key (pop seq)))))
                 (loop while seq
                       do (setf result
                                (funcall
                                  fn result
                                  (funcall-if key (pop seq))))))
             result)))))
```

24.7   Exercises

Exercise 24.2 [m]   The function reduce is a very useful one, especially with the key keyword. Write nonrecursive definitions for append and length using reduce. What other common functions can be written with reduce?

Exercise 24.3   The so-called loop keywords are not symbols in the keyword package. The preceding code assumes they are all in the current package, but this is not quite right. Change the definition of loop so that any symbol with the same name as a loop keyword acts as a keyword, regardless of the symbol's package.

Exercise 24.4   Can there be a value for *exp* for which the following expressions are not equivalent? Either demonstrate such an *exp* or argue why none can exist.

```
(loop for x in list collect exp)
(mapcar #'(lambda (x) exp) list))
```

Exercise 24.5   The object-oriented language Eiffel provides two interesting loop keywords: invariant and variant. The former takes a Boolean-valued expression that must remain true on every iteration of the loop, and the latter takes a integer-valued expression that must decrease on every iteration, but never becomes negative. Errors are signaled if these conditions are violated. Use defloop to implement these two keywords. Make them generate code conditionally, based on a global flag.

24.8   Answers

Answer 24.1

```
(defvar *queue*)

(defun collect (item) (enqueue item *queue*))

(defmacro with-collection (&body body)
  '(let ((*queue* (make-queue)))
     ,@body
     (queue-contents *queue*)))
```

Here's another version that allows the collection variable to be named. That way, more than one collection can be going on at the same time.

```
(defun collect (item &optional (queue *queue*))
  (enqueue item queue))

(defmacro with-collection ((&optional (queue '*queue*))
                              &body body)
  '(let ((,queue (make-queue)))
     ,@body
     (queue-contents ,queue)))
```

Answer 24.2

```
(defun append-r (x y)
  (reduce #'cons x :initial-value y :from-end t))

(defun length-r (list)
  (reduce #'+ list :key #'(lambda (x) 1)))
```

Answer 24.4   The difference between loop and mapcar is that the former uses only one variable x, while the latter uses a different x each time. If x's extent is no bigger than its scope (as it is in most expressions) then this makes no difference. But if any x is captured, giving it a longer extent, then a difference shows up. Consider *exp* = #'(lambda () x).

```
> (mapcar #'funcall (loop for x in '(1 2 3) collect
                            #'(lambda () x)))
(3 3 3)
> (mapcar #'funcall (mapcar #'(lambda (x) #'(lambda () x))
                              '(1 2 3)))
(1 2 3)
```

Answer 24.5

```
(defvar *check-invariants* t
  "Should VARIANT and INVARIANT clauses in LOOP be checked?")

(defloop invariant (l exp)
  (when *check-invariants*
    (add-body l '(assert ,exp () "Invariant violated."))))

(defloop variant (l exp)
  (when *check-invariants*
    (let ((var (gensym "INV")))
      (add-var l var nil)
      (add-body l '(setf ,var (update-variant ,var ,exp))))))
```

```
(defun update-variant (old new)
  (assert (or (null old) (< new old)) ()
          "Variant is not monotonically decreasing")
  (assert (> new 0) () "Variant is no longer positive")
  new)
```

Here's an example:

```
(defun gcd2 (a b)
  "Greatest common divisor.  For two positive integer arguments."
  (check-type a (integer 1))
  (check-type b (integer 1))
  (loop with x = a with y = b
        invariant (and (> x 0) (> y 0)) ;; (= (gcd x y) (gcd a b))
        variant (max x y)
        until (= x y)
        do (if (> x y) (decf x y) (decf y x))
        finally (return x)))
```

Here the invariant is written semi-informally. We could include the calls to gcd, but that seems to be defeating the purpose of gcd2, so that part is left as a comment. The idea is that the comment should help the reader prove the correctness of the code, and the executable part serves to notify the lazy reader when something is demonstrably wrong at run time.

CHAPTER 25

Troubleshooting

Perhaps if we wrote programs from childhood on,
as adults we'd be able to read them.

—Alan Perlis

When you buy a new appliance such as a television, it comes with an instruction booklet that lists troubleshooting hints in the following form:

PROBLEM: Nothing works.

Diagnosis: Power is off.

Remedy: Plug in outlet and turn on power switch.

If your Lisp compiler came without such a handy instruction booklet, this chapter may be of some help. It lists some of the most common difficulties that Lisp programmers encounter.

25.1 Nothing Happens

PROBLEM: You type an expression to Lisp's read-eval-print loop and get no response—no result, no prompt.

Diagnosis: There are two likely reasons why output wasn't printed: either Lisp is still doing `read` or it is still doing `eval`. These possibilities can be broken down further into four cases:

Diagnosis: If the expression you type is incomplete, Lisp will wait for more input to complete it. An expression can be incomplete because you have left off a right parenthesis (or inserted an extra left parenthesis). Or you may have started a string, atom, or comment without finishing it. This is particularly hard to spot when the error spans multiple lines. A string begins and ends with double-quotes: `"string"`; an atom containing unusual characters can be delimited by vertical bars: `|AN ATOM|`; and a comment can be of the form `#|a comment|#`. Here are four incomplete expressions:

```
(+ (* 3 (sqrt 5) 1)
(format t "~&X=~a, Y=~a. x y)
(get '|strange-atom 'prop)
(if (= x 0) #| test if x is zero
    y
    x)
```

Remedy: Add a `)`, `"`, `|`, and `|#`, respectively. Or hit the interrupt key and type the input again.

Diagnosis: Your program may be waiting for input.

Remedy: Never do a `(read)` without first printing a prompt of some kind. If the prompt does not end with a newline, a call to `finish-output` is also in order. In fact, it is a good idea to call a function that is at a higher level than `read`. Several systems define the function `prompt-and-read`. Here is one version:

```
(defun prompt-and-read (ctl-string &rest args)
  "Print a prompt and read a reply."
  (apply #'format t ctl-string args)
  (finish-output)
  (read))
```

Diagnosis: The program may be caught in an infinite loop, either in an explicit `loop` or in a recursive function.

Remedy: Interrupt the computation, get a back trace, and see what functions are active. Check the base case and loop variant on active functions and loops.

Diagnosis: Even a simple expression like (mapc #'sqrt list) or (length list) will cause an infinite loop if list is an infinite list—that is, a list that has some tail that points back to itself.

Remedy: Be very careful any time you modify a structure with nconc, delete, setf, and so forth.

PROBLEM: You get a new prompt from the read-eval-print loop, but no output was printed.

Diagnosis: The expression you evaluated must have returned no values at all, that is, the result (values).

25.2   Change to Variable Has No Effect

PROBLEM: You redefined a variable, but the new value was ignored.

Diagnosis: Altering a variable by editing and re-evaluating a defvar form will not change the variable's value. defvar only assigns an initial value when the variable is unbound.

Remedy: Use setf to update the variable, or change the defvar to a defparameter.

Diagnosis: Updating a locally bound variable will not affect a like-named variable outside that binding. For example, consider:

```
(defun check-ops (*ops*)
  (if (null *ops*)
      (setf *ops* *default-ops*))
  (mapcar #'check-op *ops*))
```

If check-ops is called with a null argument, the *ops* that is a parameter of check-ops will be updated, but the global *ops* will not be, even if it is declared special.

Remedy: Don't shadow variables you want to update. Use a different name for the local variable. It is important to distinguish special and local variables. Stick to the naming convention for special variables: they should begin and end with asterisks. Don't forget to introduce a binding for all local variables. The following excerpt from a recent textbook is an example of this error:

```
(defun test ()
  (setq x 'test-data)        ; Warning!
  (solve-problem x))         ; Don't do this.
```

This function should have been written:

```
(defun test ()
  (let ((x 'test-data))      ; Do this instead.
    (solve-problem x)))
```

25.3   Change to Function Has No Effect

PROBLEM: You redefined a function, but the change was ignored.

Diagnosis: When you change a macro, or a function that has been declared inline, the change will not necessarily be seen by users of the changed function. (It depends on the implementation.)

Remedy: Recompile after changing a macro. Don't use inline functions until everything is debugged. (Use (declare (notinline f)) to cancel an inline declaration).

Diagnosis: If you change a normal (non-inline) function, that change *will* be seen by code that refers to the function by *name*, but not by code that refers to the old value of the function itself. Consider:

```
(defparameter *scorer* #'score-fn)
(defparameter *printer* 'print-fn)

(defun show (values)
  (funcall *printer*
           (funcall *scorer* values)
           (reduce #'better values)))
```

Now suppose that the definitions of score-fn, print-fn, and better are all changed. Does any of the prior code have to be recompiled? The variable *printer* can stay as is. When it is funcalled, the symbol print-fn will be consulted for the current functional value. Within show, the expression #'better is compiled into code that will get the current version of better, so it too is safe. However, the variable *scorer* must be changed. Its value is the old definition of score-fn.

Remedy: Re-evaluate the definition of *scorer*. It is unfortunate, but this problem encourages many programmers to use symbols where they really mean functions. Symbols will be coerced to the global function they name when passed to funcall or `apply`, but this can be the source of another error. In the following example, the symbol `local-fn` will not refer to the locally bound function. One needs to use `#'local-fn` to refer to it.

```
(flet ((local-fn (x) ...))
  (mapcar 'local-fn list))
```

Diagnosis: If you changed the name of a function, did you change the name everywhere? For example, if you decide to change the name of `print-fn` to `print-function` but forget to change the value of `*printer*`, then the old function will be called.

Remedy: Use your editor's global replace command. To be even safer, redefine obsolete functions to call `error`. The following function is handy for this purpose:

```
(defun make-obsolete (fn-name)
  "Print an error if an obsolete function is called."
  (setf (symbol-function fn-name)
        #'(lambda (&rest args)
            (declare (ignore args))
            (error "Obsolete function."))))
```

Diagnosis: Are you using `labels` and `flet` properly? Consider again the function `replace-?-vars`, which was defined in section 11.3 to replace an anonymous logic variable with a unique new variable.

```
(defun replace-?-vars (exp)
  "Replace any ? within exp with a var of the form ?123."
  (cond ((eq exp '?) (gensym "?"))
        ((atom exp) exp)
        (t (cons (replace-?-vars (first exp))
                 (replace-?-vars (rest exp))))))
```

It might occur to the reader that gensyming a different variable each time is wasteful. The variables must be unique in each clause, but they can be shared across clauses. So we could generate variables in the sequence ?1, ?2, ..., intern them, and thus reuse these variables in the next clause (provided we warn the user never to use such variable names). One way to do that is to introduce a local variable to hold the variable number, and then a local function to do the computation:

```
(defun replace-?-vars (exp)
  "Replace any ? within exp with a var of the form ?123."
  ;; *** Buggy Version ***
  (let ((n 0))
    (flet
      ((replace-?-vars (exp)
        (cond ((eq exp '?) (symbol '? (incf n)))
              ((atom exp) exp)
              (t (cons (replace-?-vars (first exp))
                       (replace-?-vars (rest exp)))))))
      (replace-?-vars exp))))
```

This version doesn't work. The problem is that flet, like let, defines a new function within the body of the flet but not within the new function's definition. So two lessons are learned here: use labels instead of flet to define recursive functions, and don't shadow a function definition with a local definition of the same name (this second lesson holds for variables as well). Let's fix the problem by changing labels to flet and naming the local function recurse:

```
(defun replace-?-vars (exp)
  "Replace any ? within exp with a var of the form ?123."
  ;; *** Buggy Version ***
  (let ((n 0))
    (labels
      ((recurse (exp)
        (cond ((eq exp '?) (symbol '? (incf n)))
              ((atom exp) exp)
              (t (cons (replace-?-vars (first exp))
                       (replace-?-vars (rest exp)))))))
      (recurse exp))))
```

Annoyingly, this version still doesn't work! This time, the problem is carelessness; we changed the replace-?-vars to recurse in two places, but not in the two calls in the body of recurse.

Remedy: In general, the lesson is to make sure you call the right function. If there are two functions with similar effects and you call the wrong one, it can be hard to see. This is especially true if they have similar names.

PROBLEM: Your closures don't seem to be working.

Diagnosis: You may be erroneously creating a lambda expression by consing up code. Here's an example from a recent textbook:

```
(defun make-specialization (c)
  (let (pred newc)
    ...
    (setf (get newc 'predicate)
          '(lambda (obj)                          ; Warning!
             (and ,(cons pred '(obj))             ; Don't do this.
                  (apply ',(get c 'predicate) (list obj)))))
    ...))
```

Strictly speaking, this is legal according to *Common Lisp the Language*, although in ANSI Common Lisp it will *not* be legal to use a list beginning with lambda as a function. But in either version, it is a bad idea to do so. A list beginning with lambda is just that: a list, not a closure. Therefore, it cannot capture lexical variables the way a closure does.

Remedy: The correct way to create a closure is to evaluate a call to the special form function, or its abbreviation, #'. Here is a replacement for the code beginning with '(lambda .... Note that it is a closure, closed over pred and c. Also note that it gets the predicate each time it is called; thus, it is safe to use even when predicates are being changed dynamically. The previous version would not work when a predicate is changed.

```
#'(lambda (obj)                                  ; Do this instead.
    (and (funcall pred obj)
         (funcall (get c 'predicate) obj)))
```

It is important to remember that function (and thus #') is a special form, and thus only returns the right value when it is evaluated. A common error is to use #' notation in positions that are not evaluated:

```
(defvar *obscure-fns* '(#'cis #'cosh #'ash #'bit-orc2)) ; wrong
```

This does not create a list of four functions. Rather, it creates a list of four sublists; the first sublist is (function cis). It is an error to funcall or apply such an object. The two correct ways to create a list of functions are shown below. The first assures that each function special form is evaluated, and the second uses function names instead of functions, thus relying on funcall or apply to coerce the names to the actual functions.

```
(defvar *obscure-fns* (list #'cis #'cosh #'ash #'bit-orc2))
(defvar *obscure-fns* '(cis cosh ash bit-orc2))
```

Another common error is to expect #'if or #'or to return a function. This is an error because special forms are just syntactic markers. There is no function named `if` or `or`; they should be thought of as directives that tell the compiler what to do with a piece of code.

By the way, the function `make-specialization` above is bad not only for its lack of `function` but also for its use of backquote. The following is a better use of backquote:

```
'(lambda (obj)
   (and (,pred obj)
        (,(get c 'predicate) obj)))
```

25.4 Values Change "by Themselves"

PROBLEM: You deleted/removed something, but it didn't take effect. For example:

```
> (setf numbers '(1 2 3 4 5)) ⇒ (1 2 3 4 5)

> (remove 4 numbers) ⇒ (1 2 3 5)

> numbers ⇒ (1 2 3 4 5)

> (delete 1 numbers) ⇒ (2 3 4 5)

> numbers ⇒ (1 2 3 4 5)
```

Remedy: Use `(setf numbers (delete 1 numbers))`. Note that `remove` is a non-destructive function, so it will never alter its arguments. `delete` is destructive, but when asked to delete the first element of a list, it returns the rest of the list, and thus does not alter the list itself. That is why `setf` is necessary. Similar remarks hold for `nconc`, `sort`, and other destructive operations.

PROBLEM: You created a hundred different structures and changed a field in one of them. Suddenly, all the other ones magically changed!

Diagnosis: Different structures may share identical subfields. For example, suppose you had:

```
(defstruct block
  (possible-colors '(red green blue))
  ...)
```

```
(setf b1 (make-block))
(setf b2 (make-block))
...
(delete 'green (block-possible-colors b1))
```

Both b1 and b2 share the initial list of possible colors. The delete function modifies this shared list, so green is deleted from b2's possible colors list just as surely as it is deleted from b1's.

Remedy: Don't share pieces of data that you want to alter individually. In this case, either use remove instead of delete, or allocate a different copy of the list to each instance:

```
(defstruct block
  (possible-colors (list 'red 'green 'blue))
  ...)
```

Remember that the initial value field of a defstruct is an expression that is evaluated anew each time make-block is called. It is incorrect to think that the initial form is evaluated once when the defstruct is defined.

25.5   Built-In Functions Don't Find Elements

PROBLEM: You tried (find item list), and you know it is there, but it wasn't found.

Diagnosis: By default, many built-in functions use eql as an equality test. find is one of them. If item is, say, a list that is equal but not eql to one of the elements of list, it will not be found.

Remedy: Use (find item list :test #'equal)

Diagnosis: If the item is nil, then nil will be returned whether it is found or not.

Remedy: Use member or position instead of find whenever the item can be nil.

25.6   Multiple Values Are Lost

PROBLEM: You only get one of the multiple values you were expecting.

Diagnosis: In certain contexts where a value must be tested by Lisp, multiple values are discarded. For example, consider:

```
(or (mv-1 x) (mv-2 x))
(and (mv-1 x) (mv-2 x))
(cond ((mv-1 x))
      (t (mv-2 x)))
```

In each case, if mv-2 returns multiple values, they will all be passed on. But if mv-1 returns multiple values, only the first value will be passed on. This is true even in the last clause of a cond. So, while the final clause (t (mv-2 x)) passes on multiple values, the final clause ((mv-2 x)) would not.

Diagnosis: Multiple values can be inadvertently lost in debugging as well. Suppose I had:

```
(multiple-value-bind (a b c)
  (mv-1 x)
  ...)
```

Now, if I become curious as to what mv-1 returns, I might change this code to:

```
(multiple-value-bind (a b c)
  (print (mv-1 x))  ;*** debugging output
  ...)
```

Unfortunately, print will see only the first value returned by mv-1, and will return only that one value to be bound to the variable a. The other values will be discarded, and b and c will be bound to nil.

25.7 Declarations Are Ignored

PROBLEM: Your program uses 1024 × 1024 arrays of floating-point numbers. But you find that it takes 15 seconds just to initialize such an array to zeros! Imagine how inefficient it is to actually do any computation! Here is your function that zeroes an array:

```
(defun zero-array (arr)
  "Set the 1024x1024 array to all zeros."
  (declare (type (array float) arr))
  (dotimes (i 1024)
    (dotimes (j 1024)
      (setf (aref arr i j) 0.0))))
```

Diagnosis: The main problem here is an ineffective declaration. The type (array float) does not help the compiler, because the array could be displaced to an array of another type, and because float encompasses both single- and double-precision floating-point numbers. Thus, the compiler is forced to allocate storage for a new copy of the number 0.0 for each of the million elements of the array. The function is slow mainly because it generates so much garbage.

Remedy: The following version uses a much more effective type declaration: a simple array of single-precision numbers. It also declares the size of the array and turns safety checks off. It runs in under a second on a SPARCstation, which is slower than optimized C, but faster than unoptimized C.

```lisp
(defun zero-array (arr)
  "Set the array to all zeros."
  (declare (type (simple-array single-float (1024 1024)) arr)
           (optimize (speed 3) (safety 0)))
  (dotimes (i 1024)
    (dotimes (j 1024)
      (setf (aref arr i j) 0.0))))
```

Another common error is to use something like (simple-vector fixnum) as a type specifier. It is a quirk of Common Lisp that the simple-vector type specifier only accepts a size, not a type, while the array, vector and simple-array specifiers all accept an optional type followed by an optional size or list of sizes. To specify a simple vector of fixnums, use (simple-array fixnum (*)).

To be precise, simple-vector means (simple-array t (*)). This means that simple-vector cannot be used in conjunction with any other type specifier. A common mistake is to think that the type (and simple-vector (vector fixnum)) is equivalent to (simple-array fixnum (*)), a simple, one-dimensional vector of fixnums. Actually, it is equivalent to (simple-array t (*)), a simple one-dimensional array of any type elements. To eliminate this problem, avoid simple-vector altogether.

25.8   My Lisp Does the Wrong Thing

When all else fails, it is tempting to shift the blame for an error away from your own code and onto the Common Lisp implementation. It is certainly true that errors are found in existing implementations. But it is also true that most of the time, Common Lisp is merely doing something the user did not expect rather than something that is in error.

For example, a common "bug report" is to complain about read-from-string. A user might write:

```
(read-from-string "a b c" :start 2)
```

expecting the expression to start reading at position 2 and thus return b. In fact, this expression returns a. The angry user thinks the implementation has erroneously ignored the :start argument and files a bug report,[1] only to get back the following explanation:

The function read-from-string takes two optional arguments, eof-errorp and eof-value, in addition to the keyword arguments. Thus, in the expression above, :start is taken as the value of eof-errorp, with 2 as the value of eof-value. The correct answer is in fact to read from the start of the string and return the very first form, a.

The functions read-from-string and parse-namestring are the only built-in functions that have this problem, because they are the only ones that have both optional and keyword arguments, with an even number of optional arguments. The functions write-line and write-string have keyword arguments and a single optional argument (the stream), so if the stream is accidently omitted, an error will be signaled. (If you type (write-line str :start 4), the system will complain either that :start is not a stream or that 4 is not a keyword.)

The moral is this: functions that have both optional and keyword arguments are confusing. Take care when using existing functions that have this problem, and abstain from using both in your own functions.

25.9 How to Find the Function You Want

Veteran Common Lisp programmers often experience a kind of software *déjà vu*: they believe that the code they are writing could be done by a built-in Common Lisp function, but they can't remember the name of the function.

Here's an example: while coding up a problem I realized I needed a function that, given the lists (a b c d) and (c d), would return (a b), that is, the part of the first list without the second list. I thought that this was the kind of function that might be in the standard, but I didn't know what it would be called. The desired function is similar to set-difference, so I looked that up in the index of *Common Lisp the Language* and was directed to page 429. I browsed through the section on "using lists as sets" but found nothing appropriate. However, I was reminded of the function butlast, which is also similar to the desired function. The index directed me to page 422 for butlast, and on the same page I found ldiff, which was exactly the desired function. It might have been easier to find (and remember) if it were called list-difference, but the methodology of browsing near similar functions paid off.

---

[1]This misunderstanding has shown up even in published articles, such as Baker 1991.

If you think you know part of the name of the desired function, then you can use apropos to find it. For example, suppose I thought there was a function to push a new element onto the front of an array. Looking under array, push-array, and array-push in the index yields nothing. But I can turn to Lisp itself and ask:

```
> (apropos "push")
PUSH                Macro    (VALUE PLACE), plist
PUSHNEW             Macro    (VALUE PLACE &KEY ...), plist
VECTOR-PUSH         function (NEW-ELEMENT VECTOR), plist
VECTOR-PUSH-EXTEND function (DATA VECTOR &OPTIONAL ...), plist
```

This should be enough to remind me that vector-push is the answer. If not, I can get more information from the manual or from the online functions documentation or describe:

```
> (documentation 'vector-push 'function)
"Add NEW-ELEMENT as an element at the end of VECTOR.
The fill pointer (leader element 0) is the index of the next
element to be added.  If the array is full, VECTOR-PUSH returns
NIL and the array is unaffected;  use VECTOR-PUSH-EXTEND instead
if you want the array to grow automatically."
```

Another possibility is to browse through existing code that performs a similar purpose. That way, you may find the exact function you want, and you may get additional ideas on how to do things differently.

25.10   Syntax of LOOP

loop by itself is a powerful programming language, one with a syntax quite different from the rest of Lisp. It is therefore important to exercise restraint in using loop, lest the reader of your program become lost. One simple rule for limiting the complexity of loops is to avoid the with and and keywords. This eliminates most problems dealing with binding and scope.

When in doubt, macro-expand the loop to see what it actually does. But if you need to macro-expand, then perhaps it would be clearer to rewrite the loop with more primitive constructs.

25.11   Syntax of COND

For many programmers, the special form cond is responsible for more syntax errors than any other, with the possible exception of loop. Because most cond-clause start with two left parentheses, beginners often come to the conclusion that every clause must. This leads to errors like the following:

```
(let ((entry (assoc item list)))
  (cond ((entry (process entry)))
        ...))
```

Here entry is a variable, but the urge to put in an extra parenthesis means that the cond-clause attempts to call entry as a function rather than testing its value as a variable.

The opposite problem, leaving out a parenthesis, is also a source of error:

```
(cond (lookup item list)
      (t nil))
```

In this case, lookup is accessed as a variable, when the intent was to call it as a function. In Common Lisp this will usually lead to an unbound variable error, but in Scheme this bug can be very difficult to pin down: the value of lookup is the function itself, and since this is not null, the test will succeed, and the expression will return list without complaining.

The moral is to be careful with cond, especially when using Scheme. Note that if is much less error prone and looks just as nice when there are no more than two branches.

25.12   Syntax of CASE

In a case special form, each clause consists of a key or list of keys, followed by the value of that case. The thing to watch out for is when the key is t, otherwise, or nil. For example:

```
(case letter
  (s ...)
  (t ...)
  (u ...))
```

Here the t is taken as the default clause; it will always succeed, and all subsequent clauses will be ignored. Similarly, using a () or nil as a key will not have the desired effect: it will be interpreted as an empty key list. If you want to be completely safe, you can use a list of keys for every clause.[2] This is a particularly good idea when you

---

[2]Scheme requires a list of keys in each clause. Now you know why.

write a macro that expands into a `case`. The following code correctly tests for `t` and `nil` keys:

```
(case letter
  ((s) ...)
  ((t) ...)
  ((u) ...)
  ((nil) ...))
```

25.13   Syntax of LET and LET*

A common error is leaving off a layer of parentheses in `let`, just like in `cond`. Another error is to refer to a variable that has not yet been bound in a `let`. To avoid this problem, use `let*` whenever a variable's initial binding refers to a previous variable.

25.14   Problems with Macros

In section 3.2 we described a four-part approach to the design of macros:

- Decide if the macro is really necessary.

- Write down the syntax of the macro.

- Figure out what the macro should expand into.

- Use `defmacro` to implement the syntax/expansion correspondence.

This section shows the problems that can arise in each part, starting with the first:

- Decide if the macro is really necessary.

Macros extend the rules for evaluating an expression, while function calls obey the rules. Therefore, it can be a mistake to define too many macros, since they can make it more difficult to understand a program. A common mistake is to define macros that *do not* violate the usual evaluation rules. One recent book on AI programming suggests the following:

```
(defmacro binding-of (binding)       ; Warning!
  '(cadr ,binding))                  ; Don't do this.
```

The only possible reason for this macro is an unfounded desire for efficiency. Always use an `inline` function instead of a macro for such cases. That way you get the efficiency gain, you have not introduced a spurious macro, and you gain the ability to `apply` or `map` the function `#'binding-of`, something you could not do with a macro:

```
(proclaim '(inline binding-of))
(defun binding-of (binding)          ; Do this instead.
  (second binding))
```

- Write down the syntax of the macro.

Try to make your macro follow conventions laid down by similar macros. For example, if your macro defines something, it should obey the conventions of `defvar`, `defstruct`, `defmacro`, and the rest: start with the letters `def`, take the name of the thing to be defined as the first argument, then a lambda-list if appropriate, then a value or body. It would be nice to allow for optional declarations and documentation strings.

If your macro binds some variables or variablelike objects, use the conventions laid down by `let`, `let*`, and `labels`: allow for a list of variable or (*variable init-val*) pairs. If you are iterating over some kind of sequence, follow `dotimes` and `dolist`. For example, here is the syntax of a macro to iterate over the leaves of a tree of conses:

```
(defmacro dotree ((var tree &optional result) &body body)
  "Perform body with var bound to every leaf of tree,
  then return result.  Return and Go can be used in body."
  ...)
```

- Figure out what the macro should expand into.

- Use `defmacro` to implement the syntax/expansion correspondence.

There are a number of things to watch out for in figuring out how to expand a macro. First, make sure you don't shadow local variables. Consider the following definition for `pop-end`, a function to pop off and return the last element of a list, while updating the list to no longer contain the last element. The definition uses `last1`, which was defined on page 305 to return the last element of a list, and the built-in function `nbutlast` returns all but the last element of a list, destructively altering the list.

```
(defmacro pop-end (place)                   ; Warning! Buggy!
  "Pop and return last element of the list in PLACE."
  '(let ((result (last1 ,place)))
    (setf ,place (nbutlast ,place))
    result))
```

This will do the wrong thing for `(pop-end result)`, or for other expressions that mention the variable `result`. The solution is to use a brand new local variable that could not possibly be used elsewhere:

```
(defmacro pop-end (place)                    ; Less buggy
  "Pop and return last element of the list in PLACE."
  (let ((result (gensym)))
    '(let ((,result (last1 ,place)))
       (setf ,place (nbutlast ,place))
       ,result)))
```

There is still the problem of shadowing local *functions*. For example, a user who writes:

```
(flet ((last1 (x) (sqrt x)))
  (pop-end list)
  ...)
```

will be in for a surprise. pop-end will expand into code that calls last1, but since last1 has been locally defined to be something else, the code won't work. Thus, the expansion of the macro violates referential transparency. To be perfectly safe, we could try:

```
(defmacro pop-end (place)                    ; Less buggy
  "Pop and return last element of the list in PLACE."
  (let ((result (gensym)))
    '(let ((,result (funcall ,#'last1 ,place)))
       (setf ,place (funcall ,#'nbutlast ,place))
       ,result)))
```

This approach is sometimes used by Scheme programmers, but Common Lisp programmers usually do not bother, since it is rarer to define local functions in Common Lisp. Indeed, in *Common Lisp the Language*, 2d edition, it was explicitly stated (page 260) that a user function cannot redefine or even bind any built-in function, variable, or macro. Even if it is not prohibited in your implementation, redefining or binding a built-in function is confusing and should be avoided.

Common Lisp programmers expect that arguments will be evaluated in left-to-right order, and that no argument is evaluated more than once. Our definition of pop-end violates the second of these expectations. Consider:

```
(pop-end (aref lists (incf i))) ≡
(LET ((#:G3096 (LAST1 (AREF LISTS (INCF I)))))
  (SETF (AREF LISTS (INCF I)) (NBUTLAST (AREF LISTS (INCF I))))
  #:G3096)
```

This increments i three times, when it should increment it only once. We could fix this by introducing more local variables into the expansion:

```
(let* ((temp1 (incf i))
       (temp2 (AREF LISTS temp1))
       (temp3 (LAST1 temp2)))
  (setf (aref lists temp1) (nbutlast temp2))
  temp3)
```

This kind of left-to-right argument processing via local variables is done automatically by the Common Lisp setf mechanism. Fortunately, the mechanism is easy to use. We can redefine pop-end to call pop directly:

```
(defmacro pop-end (place)
  "Pop and return last element of the list in PLACE."
  '(pop (last ,place)))
```

Now all we need to do is define the setf method for last. Here is a simple definition. It makes use of the function last2, which returns the last two elements of a list. In ANSI Common Lisp we could use (last list 2), but with a pre-ANSI compiler we need to define last2:

```
(defsetf last (place) (value)
  '(setf (cdr (last2 ,place)) ,value))

(defun last2 (list)
  "Return the last two elements of a list."
  (if (null (rest2 list))
      list
      (last2 (rest list))))
```

Here are some macro-expansions of calls to pop-end and to the setf method for last. Different compilers will produce different code, but they will always respect the left-to-right, one-evaluation-only semantics:

```
> (pop-end (aref (foo lists) (incf i))) ≡
(LET ((G0128 (AREF (FOO LISTS) (SETQ I (+ I 1)))))
  (PROG1
    (CAR (LAST G0128))
    (SYS:SETCDR (LAST2 G0128) (CDR (LAST G0128)))))
> (setf (last (append x y)) 'end) ≡
(SYS:SETCDR (LAST2 (APPEND X Y)) 'END)
```

Unfortunately, there is an error in the setf method for last. It assumes that the list will have at least two elements. If the list is empty, it is probably an error, but if a list has exactly one element, then (setf (last *list*) *val*) should have the same effect as (setf *list* *val*). But there is no way to do that with defsetf, because the setf method defined by defsetf never sees *list* itself. Instead, it sees a local variable that is automatically bound to the value of *list*. In other words, defsetf evaluates the *list* and *val* for you, so that you needn't worry about evaluating the arguments out of order, or more than once.

To solve the problem we need to go beyond the simple defsetf macro and delve into the complexities of define-setf-method, one of the trickiest macros in all of Common Lisp. define-setf-method defines a setf method not by writing code directly but by specifying five values that will be used by Common Lisp to write the code for a call to setf. The five values give more control over the exact order in which expressions are evaluated, variables are bound, and results are returned. The five values are: (1) a list of temporary, local variables used in the code; (2) a list of values these variables should be bound to; (3) a list of one variable to hold the value specified in the call to setf; (4) code that will store the value in the proper place; (5) code that will access the value of the place. This is necessary for variations of setf like incf and pop, which need to both access and store.

In the following setf method for last, then, we are defining the meaning of (setf (last place) value). We keep track of all the variables and values needed to evaluate place, and add to that three more local variables: last2-var will hold the last two elements of the list, last2-p will be true only if there are two or more elements in the list, and last-var will hold the form to access the last element of the list. We also make up a new variable, result, to hold the value. The code to store the value either modifies the cdr of last2-var, if the list is long enough, or it stores directly into place. The code to access the value just retrieves last-var.

```
(define-setf-method last (place)
  (multiple-value-bind (temps vals stores store-form access-form)
      (get-setf-method place)
    (let ((result (gensym))
          (last2-var (gensym))
          (last2-p (gensym))
          (last-var (gensym)))
      ;; Return 5 vals: temps vals stores store-form access-form
      (values
        '(,@temps ,last2-var ,last2-p ,last-var)
        '(,@vals (last2 ,access-form)
          (= (length ,last2-var) 2)
          (if ,last2-p (rest ,last2-var) ,access-form))
        (list result)
        '(if ,last2-p
             (setf (cdr ,last2-var) ,result)
             (let ((,(first stores) ,result))
               ,store-form))
        last-var))))
```

It should be mentioned that setf methods are very useful and powerful things. It is often better to provide a setf method for an arbitrary function, f, than to define a special setting function, say, set-f. The advantage of the setf method is that it can be used in idioms like incf and pop, in addition to setf itself. Also, in ANSI Common Lisp, it is permissible to name a function with #'(setf f), so you can also use map or apply the setf method. Most setf methods are for functions that just access data, but it is permissible to define setf methods for functions that do any computation whatsoever. As a rather fanciful example, here is a setf method for the square-root function. It makes (setf (sqrt x) 5) be almost equivalent to (setf x (* 5 5)); the difference is that the first returns 5 while the second returns 25.

```
(define-setf-method sqrt (num)
  (multiple-value-bind (temps vals stores store-form access-form)
      (get-setf-method num)
    (let ((store (gensym)))
      (values temps
              vals
              (list store)
              '(let ((,(first stores) (* ,store ,store)))
                 ,store-form
                 ,store)
              '(sqrt ,access-form)))))
```

Turning from setf methods back to macros, another hard part about writing portable macros is anticipating what compilers might warn about. Let's go back to the dotree macro. Its definition might look in part like this:

```
(defmacro dotree ((var tree &optional result) &body body)
  "Perform body with var bound to every leaf of tree,
  then return result.  Return and Go can be used in body."
  '(let ((,var))
     ...
     ,@body))
```

Now suppose a user decides to count the leaves of a tree with:

```
(let ((count 0))
  (dotree (leaf tree count)
    (incf count)))
```

The problem is that the variable leaf is not used in the body of the macro, and a compiler may well issue a warning to that effect. To make matters worse, a conscientious user might write:

```
(let ((count 0))
  (dotree (leaf tree count)
    (declare (ignore leaf))
    (incf count)))
```

The designer of a new macro must decide if declarations are allowed and must make sure that compiler warnings will not be generated unless they are warranted.

Macros have the full power of Lisp at their disposal, but the macro designer must remember the purpose of a macro is to translate macro code into primitive code, and not to do any computations. Consider the following macro, which assumes that translate-rule-body is defined elsewhere:

```
(defmacro defrule (name &body body)          ; Warning! buggy!
  "Define a new rule with the given name."
  (setf (get name 'rule)
        '#'(lambda () ,(translate-rule-body body))))
```

The idea is to store a function under the rule property of the rule's name. But this definition is incorrect because the function is stored as a side effect of expanding the macro, rather than as an effect of executing the expanded macro code. The correct definition is:

```
(defmacro defrule (name &body body)
  "Define a new rule with the given name."
  '(setf (get ',name 'rule)
         #'(lambda () ,(translate-rule-body body))))
```

Beginners sometimes fail to see the difference between these two approaches, because they both have the same result when interpreting a file that makes use of defrule. But when the file is compiled and later loaded into a different Lisp image, the difference becomes clear: the first definition erroneously stores the function in the compiler's image, while the second produces code that correctly stores the function when the code is loaded.

Beginning macro users have asked, "How can I have a macro that expands into code that does more than one thing? Can I splice in the results of a macro?"

If by this the beginner wants a macro that just *does* two things, the answer is simply to use a progn. There will be no efficiency problem, even if the progn forms are nested. That is, if macro-expansion results in code like:

```
(progn (progn (progn a b) c) (progn d e))
```

the compiler will treat it the same as (progn *a b c d e*).

On the other hand, if the beginner wants a macro that *returns* two values, the proper form is values, but it must be understood that the calling function needs to arrange specially to see both values. There is no way around this limitation. That is, there is no way to write a macro—or a function for that matter—that will "splice in" its results to an arbitrary call. For example, the function floor returns two values (the quotient and remainder), as does intern (the symbol and whether or not the symbol already existed). But we need a special form to capture these values. For example, compare:

```
> (list (floor 11 5) (intern 'x)) ⇒ (2 X)

> (multiple-value-call #'list
     (floor 11 5)(intern 'x)) ⇒ (2 1 X :INTERNAL)
```

25.15   A Style Guide to Lisp

In a sense, this whole book is a style guide to writing quality Lisp programs. But this section attempts to distill some of the lessons into a set of guidelines.

When to Define a Function

Lisp programs tend to consist of many short functions, in contrast to some languages that prefer a style using fewer, longer functions. New functions should be introduced for any of the following reasons:

1. For a specific, easily stated purpose.

2. To break up a function that is too long.

3. When the name would be useful documentation.

4. When it is used in several places.

In (2), it is interesting to consider what "too long" means. Charniak et al. (1987) suggested that 20 lines is the limit. But now that large bit-map displays have replaced 24-line terminals, function definitions have become longer. So perhaps one screenful is a better limit than 20 lines. The addition of flet and labels also contributes to longer function definitions.

When to Define a Special Variable

In general, it is a good idea to minimize the use of special variables. Lexical variables are easier to understand, precisely because their scope is limited. Try to limit special variables to one of the following uses:

1. For parameters that are used in many functions spread throughout a program.

2. For global, persistant, mutable data, such as a data base of facts.

3. For infrequent but deeply nested use.

   An example of (3) might be a variable like `*standard-output*`, which is used by low-level priniting functions. It would be confusing to have to pass this variable around among all your high-level functions just to make it available to `print`.

When to Bind a Lexical Variable

In contrast to special variables, lexical variables are encouraged. You should feel free to introduce a lexical variable (with a `let`, `lambda` or `defun`) for any of the following reasons:

1. To avoid typing in the same expression twice.

2. To avoid computing the same expression twice.

3. When the name would be useful documentation.

4. To keep the indentation manageable.

How to Choose a Name

Your choice of names for functions, variables, and other objects should be clear, meaningful, and consistent. Some of the conventions are listed here:

1. Use mostly letters and hyphens, and use full words: `delete-file`.

2. You can introduce an abbreviation if you are consistent: `get-dtree`, `dtree-fetch`. For example, this book uses `fn` consistently as the abbreviation for "function."

3. Predicates end in `-p` (or `?` in Scheme), unless the name is already a predicate: `variable-p`, `occurs-in`.

4. Destructive functions start with `n` (or end in `!` in Scheme): `nreverse`.

5. Generalized variable-setting macros end in f: `setf`, `incf`. (Push is an exception.)

6. Slot selectors created by defstruct are of the form *type-slot*. Use this for non-defstruct selectors as well: `char-bits`.

7. Many functions have the form *action-object:* `copy-list`, `delete-file`.

8. Other functions have the form *object-modifier:* `list-length`, `char-lessp`. Be consistent in your choice between these two forms. Don't have `print-edge` and `vertex-print` in the same system.

9. A function of the form *modulename-functionname* is an indication that packages are needed. Use `parser:print-tree` instead of `parser-print-tree`.

10. Special variables have asterisks: `*db*`, `*print-length*`.

11. Constants do not have asterisks: `pi`, `most-positive-fixnum`.

12. Parameters are named by type: `(defun length (sequence) ...)` or by purpose: `(defun subsetp (subset superset) ...)` or both: `(defun / (number &rest denominator-numbers) ...)`

13. Avoid ambiguity. A variable named `last-node` could have two meanings; use `previous-node` or `final-node` instead.

14. A name like `propagate-constraints-to-neighboring-vertexes` is too long, while `prp-con` is too short. In deciding on length, consider how the name will be used: `propagate-constraints` is just right, because a typical call will be `(propagate-constraints vertex)`, so it will be obvious what the constraints are propagating to.

Deciding on the Order of Parameters

Once you have decided to define a function, you must decide what parameters it will take, and in what order. In general,

1. Put important parameters first (and optional ones last).

2. Make it read like prose if possible: `(push element stack)`.

3. Group similar parameters together.

Interestingly, the choice of a parameter list for top-level functions (those that the user is expected to call) depends on the environment in which the user will function. In many systems the user can type a keystroke to get back the previous input to the top level, and can then edit that input and re-execute it. In these systems it is preferable to have the parameters that are likely to change be at the end of the parameter list, so that they can be easily edited. On systems that do not offer this kind of editing, it is better to either use keyword parameters or make the highly variable parameters first in the list (with the others optional), so that the user will not have to type as much.

Many users want to have *required* keyword parameters. It turns out that all keyword parameters are optional, but the following trick is equivalent to a required keyword parameter. First we define the function `required` to signal an error, and then we use a call to `required` as the default value for any keyword that we want to make required:

```lisp
(defun required ()
  (error "A required keyword argument was not supplied."))

(defun fn (x &key (y (required)))
  ...)
```

25.16   Dealing with Files, Packages, and Systems

While this book has covered topics that are more advanced than any other Lisp text available, it is still concerned only with programming in the small: a single project at a time, capable of being implemented by a single programmer. More challenging is the problem of programming in the large: building multiproject, multiprogrammer systems that interact well.

This section briefly outlines an approach to organizing a larger project into manageable components, and how to place those components in files.

Every system should have a separate file that defines the other files that comprise the system. I recommend defining any packages in that file, although others put package definitions in separate files.

The following is a sample file for the mythical system Project-X. Each entry in the file is discussed in turn.

1. The first line is a comment known as the *mode line*. The text editor emacs will parse the characters between `-*-` delimiters to discover that the file contains Lisp code, and thus the Lisp editing commands should be made available. The dialect of Lisp and the package are also specified. This notation is becoming widespread as other text editors emulate emacs's conventions.

2. Each file should have a description of its contents, along with information on the authors and what revisions have taken place.

3. Comments with four semicolons (;;;;) denote header lines. Many text editors supply a command to print all such lines, thus achieving an outline of the major parts of a file.

4. The first executable form in every file should be an `in-package`. Here we use the `user` package. We will soon create the `project-x` package, and it will be used in all subsequent files.

5. We want to define the Project-X system as a collection of files. Unfortunately, Common Lisp provides no way to do that, so we have to load our own system-definition functions explicitly with a call to `load`.

6. The call to `define-system` specifies the files that make up Project-X. We provide a name for the system, a directory for the source and object files, and a list of *modules* that make up the system. Each module is a list consisting of the module name (a symbol) followed by a one or more files (strings or pathnames). We have used keywords as the module names to eliminate any possible name conflicts, but any symbol could be used.

7. The call to `defpackage` defines the package `project-x`. For more on packages, see section 24.1.

8. The final form prints instructions on how to load and run the system.

```lisp
;;; -*- Mode: Lisp; Syntax: Common-Lisp; Package: User -*-

;;; (Brief description of system here.)

;;;; Define the Project-X system.

(in-package "USER")

(load "/usr/norvig/defsys.lisp") ; load define-system

(define-system  ;; Define the system Project-X
  :name :project-x
  :source-dir "/usr/norvig/project-x/*.lisp"
  :object-dir "/usr/norvig/project-x/*.bin"
  :modules '((:macros "header" "macros")
             (:main "parser" "transformer" "optimizer"
                    "commands" "database" "output")
             (:windows "xwindows" "clx" "client")))

(defpackage :project-x ;; Define the package Project-X
  (:export "DEFINE-X" "DO-X" "RUN-X")
  (:nicknames "PX")
  (:use common-lisp))
```

```
(format *debug-io* "~& To load the Project-X system, type
  (make-system :name :project-x)
To run the system, type
  (project-x:run-x)")
```

Each of the files that make up the system will start like this:

```
;;; -*- Mode: Lisp; Syntax: Common-Lisp; Package: Project-X -*-

(in-package "PROJECT-X")
```

Now we need to provide the system-definition functions, define-system
and make-system. The idea is that define-system is used to define the files that
make up a system, the modules that the system is comprised of, and the files that
make up each module. It is necessary to group files into modules because some
files may depend on others. For example, all macros, special variables, constants,
and inline functions need to be both compiled and loaded before any other files that
reference them are compiled. In Project-X, all defvar, defparameter, defconstant,
and defstruct[3] forms are put in the file header, and all defmacro forms are put in the
file macros. Together these two files form the first module, named :macros, which
will be loaded before the other two modules (:main and :windows) are compiled and
loaded.

define-system also provides a place to specify a directory where the source
and object files will reside. For larger systems spread across multiple directories,
define-system will not be adequate.

Here is the first part of the file defsys.lisp, showing the definition of
define-system and the structure sys.

```
;;; -*- Mode: Lisp; Syntax: Common-Lisp; Package: User -*-

;;;; A Facility for Defining Systems and their Components

(in-package "USER")

(defvar *systems* nil "List of all systems defined.")

(defstruct sys
  "A system containing a number of source and object files."
  name source-dir object-dir modules)
```

---

[3]defstruct forms are put here because they may create inline functions.

```lisp
(defun define-system (&key name source-dir object-dir modules)
  "Define a new system."
  ;; Delete any old system of this name, and add the new one.
  (setf *systems* (delete name *systems* :test #'string-equal
                                         :key #'sys-name))
  (push (make-sys
          :name (string name)
          :source-dir (pathname source-dir)
          :object-dir (pathname object-dir)
          :modules '((:all .,(mapcar #'first modules)) .,modules))
        *systems*)
  name)
```

The function make-system is used to compile and/or load a previously defined system. The name supplied is used to look up the definition of a system, and one of three actions is taken on the system. The keyword :cload means to compile and then load files. :load means to load files; if there is an object (compiled) file and it is newer than the source file, then it will be loaded, otherwise the source file will be loaded. Finally, :update means to compile just those source files that have been changed since their corresponding source files were last altered, and to load the new compiled version.

```lisp
(defun make-system (&key (module :all) (action :cload)
                         (name (sys-name (first *systems*))))
  "Compile and/or load a system or one of its modules."
  (let ((system (find name *systems* :key #'sys-name
                      :test #'string-equal)))
    (check-type system (not null))
    (check-type action (member :cload :update :load))
    (with-compilation-unit () (sys-action module system action))))

(defun sys-action (x system action)
  "Perform the specified action to x in this system.
  X can be a module name (symbol), file name (string)
  or a list."
  (typecase x
    (symbol (let ((files (rest (assoc x (sys-modules system)))))
              (if (null files)
                  (warn "No files for module ~a" x)
                  (sys-action files system action))))
    (list   (dolist (file x)
              (sys-action file system action)))
    ((string pathname)
            (let ((source (merge-pathnames
                            x (sys-source-dir system)))
                  (object (merge-pathnames
                            x (sys-object-dir system))))
              (case action
```

```
                        (:cload  (compile-file source) (load object))
                        (:update (unless (newer-file-p object source)
                                    (compile-file source))
                                 (load object))
                        (:load   (if (newer-file-p object source)
                                    (load object)
                                    (load source))))))
          (t       (warn "Don't know how to ~a ~a in system ~a"
                       action x system)))))
```

To support this, we need to be able to compare the write dates on files. This is not hard to do, since Common Lisp provides the function file-write-date.

```
(defun newer-file-p (file1 file2)
  "Is file1 newer than (written later than) file2?"
  (>-num (if (probe-file file1) (file-write-date file1))
         (if (probe-file file2) (file-write-date file2))))

(defun >-num (x y)
  "True if x and y are numbers, and x > y."
  (and (numberp x) (numberp y) (> x y)))
```

25.17   Portability Problems

Programming is difficult. All programmers know the frustration of trying to get a program to work according to the specification. But one thing that really defines the professional programmer is the ability to write portable programs that will work on a variety of systems. A portable program not only must work on the computer it was tested on but also must anticipate the difference between your computer and other ones. To do this, you must understand the Common Lisp specification in the abstract, not just how it is implemented on your particular machine.

There are three ways in which Common Lisp systems can vary: in the treatment of "is an error" situations, in the treatment of unspecified results, and in extensions to the language.

Common Lisp the Language specifies that it "is an error" to pass a non-number to an arithmetic function. For example, it is an error to evaluate (+ nil 1). However, it is not specified what should be done in this situation. Some implementations may signal an error, but others may not. An implementation would be within its right to return 1, or any other number or non-number as the result.

An unsuspecting programmer may code an expression that is an error but still computes reasonable results in his or her implementation. A common example is applying get to a non-symbol. This is an error, but many implementations will just return nil, so the programmer may write (get x 'prop) when (if (symbolp x) (get x 'prop) nil) is actually needed for portable code. Another common problem is with subseq and the sequence functions that take :end keywords. It is an error if the :end parameter is not an integer less than the length of the sequence, but many implementations will not complain if :end is nil or is an integer greater than the length of the sequence.

The Common Lisp specification often places constraints on the result that a function must compute, without fully specifying the result. For example, both of the following are valid results:

```
> (union '(a b c) '(b c d)) ⇒ (A B C D)
> (union '(a b c) '(b c d)) ⇒ (D A B C)
```

A program that relies on one order or the other will not be portable. The same warning applies to intersection and set-difference. Many functions do not specify how much the result shares with the input. The following computation has only one possible printed result:

```
> (remove 'x '(a b c d)) ⇒ (A B C D)
```

However, it is not specified whether the output is eq or only equal to the second input.

Input/output is particularly prone to variation, as different operating systems can have very different conceptions of how I/O and the file system works. Things to watch out for are whether read-char echoes its input or not, the need to include finish-output, and variation in where newlines are needed, particularly with respect to the top level.

Finally, many implementations provide extensions to Common Lisp, either by adding entirely new functions or by modifying existing functions. The programmer must be careful not to use such extensions in portable code.

25.18 Exercises

Exercise 25.1 [h] On your next programming project, keep a log of each bug you detect and its eventual cause and remedy. Classify each one according to the taxonomy given in this chapter. What kind of mistakes do you make most often? How could you correct that?

Exercise 25.2 [s-d] Take a Common Lisp program and get it to work with a different compiler on a different computer. Make sure you use conditional compilation read macros (#+ and #-) so that the program will work on both systems. What did you have to change?

Exercise 25.3 [m] Write a `setf` method for `if` that works like this:

```
(setf (if test (first x) y) (+ 2 3)) ≡
(let ((temp (+ 2 3)))
  (if test
      (setf (first x) temp)
      (setf y temp)))
```

You will need to use `define-setf-method`, not `defsetf`. (Why?) Make sure you handle the case where there is no else part to the `if`.

Exercise 25.4 [h] Write a `setf` method for `lookup`, a function to get the value for a key in an association list.

```
(defun lookup (key alist)
  "Get the cdr of key's entry in the association list."
  (cdr (assoc key alist)))
```

25.19 Answers

Answer 25.4 Here is the `setf` method for `lookup`. It looks for the key in the a-list, and if the key is there, it modifies the `cdr` of the pair containing the key; otherwise it adds a new key/value pair to the front of the a-list.

```
(define-setf-method lookup (key alist-place)
  (multiple-value-bind (temps vals stores store-form access-form)
      (get-setf-method alist-place)
    (let ((key-var (gensym))
          (pair-var (gensym))
          (result (gensym)))
      (values
        '(,key-var ,@temps ,pair-var)
        '(,key ,@vals (assoc ,key-var ,access-form))
        '(,result)
        '(if ,pair-var
             (setf (cdr ,pair-var) ,result)
             (let ((,(first stores)
                     (acons ,key-var ,result ,access-form)))
               ,store-form
               ,result))
        '(cdr ,pair-var)))))
```

Appendix:
Obtaining the Code
in this Book

FTP: The File Transfer Protocol

FTP is a file transfer protocol that is widely accepted by computers around the world. FTP makes it easy to transfer files between two computers on which you have accounts. But more importantly, it also allows a user on one computer to access files on a computer on which he or she does not have an account, as long as both computers are connected to the Internet. This is known as *anonymous FTP*.

All the code in this book is available for anonymous FTP from the computer mkp.com in files in the directory pub/norvig. The file README in that directory gives further instructions on using the files.

In the session below, the user smith retrieves the files from mkp.com. Smith's input is in *slanted font*. The login name must be *anonymous,* and Smith's own mail address is used as the password. The command *cd pub/norvig* changes to that directory, and the command *ls* lists all the files. The command *mget ** retrieves all files (the *m* stands for "multiple"). Normally, there would be a prompt before each file asking if you do indeed want to copy it, but the *prompt* command disabled this. The command *bye* ends the FTP session.

```
% ftp mkp.com  (or ftp 199.182.55.2)
Name (mkp.com:smith): anonymous
331 Guest login ok, send ident as password
Password: smith@cs.stateu.edu
230 Guest login ok, access restrictions apply
ftp> cd pub/norvig
```

```
250 CWD command successful.
ftp> ls
...
ftp> prompt
Interactive mode off.
ftp> mget *
...
ftp> bye
%
```

Anonymous FTP is a privilege, not a right. The site administrators at mkp.com and at other sites below have made their systems available out of a spirit of sharing, but there are real costs that must be paid for the connections, storage, and processing that makes this sharing possible. To avoid overloading these systems, do not FTP from 7:00 a.m. to 6:00 p.m. local time. This is especially true for sites not in your country. If you are using this book in a class, ask your professor for a particular piece of software before you try to FTP it; it would be wasteful if everybody in the class transferred the same thing. Use common sense and be considerate: none of us want to see sites start to close down because a few are abusing their privileges.

If you do not have FTP access to the Internet, you can still obtain the files from this book by contacting Morgan Kaufmann at the following:

Morgan Kaufmann Publishers, Inc.
340 Pine Street, Sixth Floor
San Francisco, CA 94104-3205
USA
Telephone   415/392-2665
Facsimile   415/982-2665
Internet   mkp@mkp.com
(800) 745-7323

Make sure to specify which format you want:

Macintosh diskette ISBN 1-55860-227-5
DOS 5.25 diskette   ISBN 1-55860-228-3
DOS 3.5 diskette   ISBN 1-55860-229-1

Available Software

In addition to the program from this book, a good deal of other software is available. The tables below list some of the relevant AI/Lisp programs. Each entry lists the name of the system, an address, and some comments. The address is either a computer from which you can FTP, or a mail address of a contact. Unless it is stated that distribution is by *email* or *Floppy* or requires a *license,* then you can FTP from the contact's home computer. In some cases the host computer and/or directory have been provided in italics in the comments field. However, in most cases it should be obvious what files to transfer. First do an ls command to see what files and directories are available. If there is a file called README, follow its advice: do a get README and then look at the file. If you still haven't found what you are looking for, be aware that most hosts keep their public software in the directory pub. Do a cd pub and then another ls, and you should find the desired files.

If a file ends in the suffix .Z, then you should give the FTP command binary before transferring it, and then give the UNIX command uncompress to recover the original file. Files with the suffix .tar contain several files that can be unpacked with the tar command. If you have problems, consult your local documentation or system administrator.

Knowledge Representation

System	Address	Comments
Babbler	rsfl@ra.msstate.edu	*email;* Markov chains/NLP
BACK	peltason@tubvm.cs.tu-berlin.de	*3.5″ floppy;* KL-ONE family
Belief	almond@stat.washington.edu	belief networks
Classic	dlm@research.att.com	*license;* KL-ONE family
Fol Getfol	fausto@irst.it	*tape;* Weyrauch's FOL system
Framekit	ehn+@cs.cmu.edu	*floppy;* frames
FrameWork	mkant+@cs.cmu.edu	*a.gp.cs.cmu.edu:/usr/mkant/Public;* frames
Frobs	kessler@cs.utah.edu	frames
Knowbel	kramer@ai.toronto.edu	sorted/temporal logic
MVL	ginsberg@t.stanford.edu	multivalued logics
OPS	slisp-group@b.gp.cs.cmu.edu	Forgy's OPS-5 language
PARKA	spector@cs.umd.edu	frames (designed for connection machine)
Parmenides	pshell@cs.cmu.edu	frames
Rhetorical	miller@cs.rochester.edu	planning, time logic
SB-ONE	kobsa@cs.uni-sb.de	*license;* in German; KL-ONE family
SNePS	shapiro@cs.buffalo.edu	*license;* semantic net/NLP
SPI	cs.orst.edu	Probabilistic inference
YAK	franconi@irst.it	KL-ONE family

Planning and Learning

System	Address	Comments
COBWEB/3	cobweb@ptolemy.arc.nasa.gov	*email;* concept formation
MATS	kautz@research.att.com	*license;* temporal constraints
MICRO-xxx	waander@cs.ume.edu	case-based reasoning
Nonlin	nonlin-users-request@cs.umd.edu	Tate's planner in Common Lisp
Prodigy	prodigy@cs.cmu.edu	*license;* planning and learning
PROTOS	porter@cs.utexas.edu	knowledge acquisition
SNLP	weld@cs.washington.edu	nonlinear planner
SOAR	soar-requests/@cs.cmu.edu	*license;* integrated architecture
THEO	tom.mitchell@cs.cmu.edu	frames, learning
Tileworld	pollack@ai.sri.com	planning testbed
TileWorld	tileworld@ptolemy.arc.nasa.gov	planning testbed

Mathematics

System	Address	Comments
JACAL	jaffer@altdorf.ai.mit.edu	algebraic manipulation
Maxima	rascal.ics.utexas.edu	version of Macsyma; also proof-checker, nqthm
MMA	fateman@cs.berkeley.edu	*peoplesparc.berkeley.edu:pub/mma.*;* algebra
XLispStat	umnstat.stat.umn.edu	Statistics; also S Bayes

Compilers and Utilities

System	Address	Comments
AKCL	rascal.ics.utexas.edu	Austin Koyoto Common Lisp
CLX, CLUE	export.lcs.mit.edu	Common Lisp interface to X Windows
Gambit	gambit@cs.brandeis.edu	*acorn.cs.brandeis.edu:dist/gambit*;* Scheme compiler
ISI Grapher	isi.edu	Graph displayer; also NLP word lists
PCL	arisia.xerox.com	Implementation of CLOS
Prolog	aisun1.ai.uga.edu	Prolog-based utilities and NLP programs
PYTHON	ram+@cs.cmu.edu	*a.gp.cs.cmu.edu:* Common Lisp Compiler and tools
SBProlog	arizona.edu	Stony Brook Prolog, Icon, Snobol
Scheme	altdorf.ai.mit.edu	Scheme utilities and compilers
Scheme	scheme@nexus.yorku.ca	Scheme utilities and programs
SIOD	bu.edu	*users/gjc;* small scheme interpreter
Utilities	a.gp.cs.cmu.edu	*/usr/mkant/Public;* profiling, defsystem, etc.
XLisp	cs.orst.edu	Lisp interpreter
XScheme	tut.cis.ohio-state.edu	Also mitscheme compiler; sbprolog

Bibliography

Abelson, Harold, and Gerald J. Sussman, with Julie Sussman. (1985) *Structure and Interpretation of Computer Programs*. MIT Press.

Aho, A. V., and J. D. Ullman. (1972) *The Theory of Parsing, Translation, and Compiling*. Prentice-Hall.

Aït-Kaci, Hassan. (1991) *Warren's Abstract Machine: A Tutorial Reconstruction*. MIT Press. An earlier version was published as "The WAM: A (Real) Tutorial." Digital Equipment Corporation Paris Research Lab, Report no. 5.

Aït-Kaci, Hassan, Patrick Lincoln, and Roger Nasr. (1987) "Le Fun: Logic, Equations and Functions." *Proceedings of the IEEE*, CH2472-9/87.

Allen, James. (1987) *Natural Language Understanding*. Benjamin/Cummings.

Allen, James, James Hendler, and Austin Tate. (1990) *Readings in Planning*. Morgan Kaufmann.

Allen, John. (1978) *Anatomy of Lisp*. McGraw-Hill.

Amarel, Saul. (1968) "On Representation of Problems of Reasoning about Actors." In *Machine Intelligence 3*, ed. Donald Michie. Edinburgh University Press.

Anderson, James A. D. W. (1989) *Pop-11 Comes of Age: the advancement of an AI programming language*. Ellis Horwood.

Anderson, John Robert. (1976) *Language, Memory, and Thought*. Lawrence Erlbaum.

Baker, Henry G. (1991) "Pragmatic Parsing in Common Lisp; or, Putting `defmacro` on Steroids." *Lisp Pointers 4*, no. 2.

Barr, Avron, and Edward A. Feigenbaum. (1981) *The Handbook of Artificial Intelligence*. 3 vols. Morgan Kaufmann.

Batali, John, Edmund Goodhue, Chris Hanson, Howie Shrobe, Richard M. Stallman, and Gerald Jay Sussman. (1982) "The Scheme-81 Architecture—System and Chip." In *Proceedings, Conference on Advanced Research in VLSI*, 69–77.

Bennett, James S. (1985) "Roget: A Knowledge-Based System for Acquiring the Conceptual Structure of a Diagnostic Expert System." *Journal of Automated Reasoning* 1: 49–74.

Berlekamp, E. R., J. H. Conway, and R. K. Guy. (1982) *Winning Ways*. 2 vols. Academic Press.

Berlin, Andrew, and Daniel Weise. (1990) "Compiling scientific code using partial evaluation." *IEEE Computer*, 25–37.

Bobrow, Daniel G. (1968) "Natural Language Input for a Computer Problem-Solving System." In Minsky 1968.

Bobrow, Daniel G. (1982) *LOOPS: An Object-Oriented Programming System for Interlisp*. Xerox PARC.

Bobrow, Daniel G. (1985) "If Prolog is the Answer, What is the Question? or What It Takes to Support AI Programming Paradigms." *IEEE Transactions on Software Engineering*, SE-11.

Bobrow, Daniel G., Kenneth Kahn, Gregor Kiczales, Larry Masinter, Mark Stefik, and Frank Zdybel. (1986) "Common Loops: Merging Lisp and Object-Oriented Programming." *Proceedings of the ACM Conference on Object-Oriented Systems, Languages, and Applications*.

Boyer, R. S., and J. S. Moore. (1972) "The Sharing of Structure in Theorem Proving Programs." In *Machine Intelligence 7*, ed. B. Meltzer and D. Michie. Wiley.

Brachman, Ronald J., and Hector J. Levesque. (1985) *Readings in Knowledge Representation*. Morgan Kaufmann.

Brachman, Ronald J., Richard E. Fikes, and Hector J. Levesque. (1983) "KRYPTON: A Functional Approach to Knowledge Representation," FLAIR Technical Report no. 16, Fairchild Laboratory for Artificial Intelligence. Reprinted in Brachman and Levesque 1985.

Bratko, Ivan. (1990) *Prolog Programming for Artificial Intelligence*. Addison-Wesley.

Bromley, Hank, and Richard Lamson. (1987) *A Guide to Programming the Lisp Machine*. 2d ed. Kluwer Academic.

Brooks, Rodney A. (1985) *Programming in Common Lisp*. Wiley.

Brownston, L., R. Farrell, E. Kant, and N. Martin. (1985) *Programming Expert Systems in OPS5.* Addison-Wesley.

Buchanan, Bruce G., and Edward Hance Shortliffe. (1984) *Rule-based Expert Systems: The* MYCIN *Experiments of the Stanford Heuristic Programming Project.* Addison-Wesley.

Bundy, Alan. (1984) *Catalogue of Artificial Intelligence Tools.* Springer-Verlag.

Cannon, Howard I. (1980) "Flavors." AI Lab Technical Report, MIT.

Carbonell, Jamie A. (1981) *Subjective Understanding: Computer Models of Belief Systems.* UMI Research Press.

Cardelli, Luca, and Peter Wegner. (1986) "On Understanding Types, Data Abstraction and Polymorphism." *ACM Computing Surveys* 17.

Chapman, David. (1987) "Planning for Conjunctive Goals." *Artificial Intelligence* 32:333–377. Reprinted in Allen, Hendler, and Tate 1990.

Charniak, Eugene, and Drew McDermott. (1985) *Introduction to Artificial Intelligence.* Addison-Wesley.

Charniak, Eugene, Christopher Riesbeck, Drew McDermott, and James Meehan. (1987) *Artificial Intelligence Programming.* 2d ed. Lawrence Erlbaum.

Cheeseman, Peter. (1985) "In Defense of Probability." In *Proceedings of the Ninth IJCAI* 1002–1009.

Chomsky, Noam. (1972) *Language and Mind.* Harcourt Brace Jovanovich.

Church, Alonzo. (1941) "The Calculi of Lambda-Conversion." *Annals of Mathematical Studies.* Vol. 6, Princeton University Press.

Church, Kenneth, and Ramesh Patil. (1982) "Coping with Syntactic Ambiguity, or How to Put the Block in the Box on the Table." *American Journal of Computational Linguistics* 8, nos. 3-4:139–149.

Clinger, William, and Jonathan Rees. (1991) *Revised[4] Report on the Algorithmic Language Scheme.* Unpublished document available online on cs.voregin.edu.

Clocksin, William F., and Christopher S. Mellish. (1987) *Programming in Prolog.* 3d ed. Springer-Verlag.

Clowes, Maxwell B. (1971) "On Seeing Things." *Artificial Intelligence* 2:79–116.

Coelho, Helder, and Jose C. Cotta. (1988) *Prolog by Example.* Springer-Verlag.

Cohen, Jacques. (1985) "Describing Prolog by its interpretation and compilation." *Communications of the ACM* 28, no. 12:1311–1324.

Cohen, Jacques. (1990) "Constraint Logic Programming Languages." *Communications of the ACM* 33, no. 7:52–68.

Colby, Kenneth. (1975) *Artificial Paranoia*. Pergamon.

Collins, Allan. (1978) "Fragments of a Theory of Human Plausible Reasoning. *Theoretical Issues in Natural Language Processing*. David Waltz, ed. *ACM*. Reprinted in Shafer and Pearl 1990.

Colmerauer, Alain. (1985) "Prolog in 10 figures." *Communications of the ACM* 28, no. 12:1296–1310.

Colmerauer, Alain. (1990) "An Introduction to Prolog III." *Communications of the ACM* 33, no. 7:69–90.

Colmerauer, Alain, Henri Kanoui, Robert Pasero, and Phillipe Roussel. (1973) *Un Système de Communication Homme-Machine en Français*. Rapport, Groupe d'Intelligence Artificielle, Université d'Aix-Marseille II.

Cooper, Thomas A., and Nancy Wogrin. (1988) *Rule-Based Programming with OPS5*. Morgan Kaufmann.

Dahl, Ole-Johan, and Kristen Nygaard. (1966) "SIMULA—An Algol-based Simulation Language." *Communications of the ACM* 9, no. 9:671–678.

Davenport, J. H., Y. Siret, and E. Tournier. (1988) *Computer Algebra: Systems and Algorithms for Algebraic Computation*. Academic Press.

Davis, Ernest. (1990) *Representations of Commonsense Reasoning*. Morgan Kaufmann.

Davis, Lawrence. (1987) *Genetic Algorithms and Simulated Annealing*. Morgan Kaufmann.

Davis, Lawrence. (1991) *Handbook of Genetic Algorithms*. van Nostrand Reinhold.

Davis, Randall. (1977) "Meta-Level Knowledge." *Proceedings of the Fifth IJCAI*, 920–928. Reprinted in Buchanan and Shortliffe 1984.

Davis, Randall. (1979) "Interactive Transfer of Expertise." *Artificial Intelligence* 12:121–157. Reprinted in Buchanan and Shortliffe 1984.

Davis, Randall, and Douglas B. Lenat. (1982) *Knowledge-Based Systems in Artificial Intelligence*. McGraw-Hill.

DeGroot, A. D. (1965) *Thought and Choice in Chess*. Mouton. (English translation, with additions, of the Dutch edition, 1946.)

DeGroot, A. D., (1966) "Perception and Memory versus Thought: Some Old Ideas and Recent Findings." In *Problem Solving*, ed. B. Kleinmuntz. Wiley.

de Kleer, Johan. (1986a) "An Assumption-Based Truth Maintenance System." *Artificial Intelligence* 28:127–162. Reprinted in Ginsberg 1987.

de Kleer, Johan. (1986b) "Extending the ATMS." *Artificial Intelligence* 28:163–196.

de Kleer, Johan. (1986c) "Problem-Solving with the ATMS." *Artificial Intelligence* 28:197–224.

de Kleer, Johan. (1988) "A General Labelling Algorithm for Assumption-Based Truth Maintenance." *Proceedings of the AAAI*, 188–192.

Dowty, David R., Robert E. Wall, and Stanley Peters. (1981) *Introduction to Montague Semantics*. Synthese Language Library, vol. 11. D. Reidel.

Doyle, Jon. (1979) "A Truth Maintenance System." *Artificial Intelligence* 12:231–272.

Doyle, Jon. (1983) "The Ins and Outs of Reason Maintenance." *Proceedings of the Eighth IJCAI* 349–351.

Dubois, Didier, and Henri Prade. (1988) "An Introduction to Possibilistic and Fuzzy Logics." *Non-Standard Logics for Automated Reasoning*. Academic Press. Reprinted in Shafer and Pearl 1990.

Earley, Jay. (1970) "An Efficient Context-Free Parsing Algorithm." *CACM* 6, no. 2:451–455. Reprinted in Grosz et al. 1986.

Elcock, E. W., and P. Hoddinott. (1986) "Comments on Kornfeld's 'Equality for Prolog': E-Unification as a Mechanism for Augmenting the Prolog Search Strategy." *Proceedings of the AAAI*, 766–775.

Emanuelson, P., and A. Haraldsson. (1980) "On Compiling Embedded Languages in Lisp." Lisp Conference, Stanford, Calif., 208–215.

Ernst, G. W., and Newell, Alan. (1969) *GPS: A Case Study in Generality and Problem Solving*. Academic Press.

Fateman, Richard J. (1973) "Reply to an Editorial." *ACM SIGSAM Bulletin 25* (March):9-11.

Fateman, Richard J. (1974) "Polynomial Multiplication, Powers and Asymptotic Analysis: Some Comments," *SIAM Journal of Computation* no. 3, 3:196–213.

Fateman, Richard J. (1979) "MACSYMA's general simplifier: philosophy and operation." In *Proceedings of the 1979 MACSYMA Users' Conference* (MUC-79), ed. V. E. Lewis 563–582. Lab for Computer Science, MIT.

Fateman, Richard J. (1991) "FRPOLY: A Benchmark Revisited." *Lisp and Symbolic Computation* 4:155–164.

Feigenbaum, Edward A. and Julian Feldman. (1963) *Computers and Thought*. McGraw-Hill.

Field, A.J., and P. G. Harrison. (1988) *Functional Programming*. Addison-Wesley.

Fikes, Richard E., and Nils J. Nilsson. (1971) "STRIPS: A New Approach to the Application of Theorem Proving to Problem Solving," *Artificial Intelligence* 2:189–208. Reprinted in Allen, Hendler, and Tate 1990.

Fodor, Jerry A. (1975) *The Language of Thought*. Harvard University Press.

Forgy, Charles L. (1981) "OPS5 User's Manual." Report CMU-CS-81-135, Carnegie Mellon University.

Forgy, Charles L. (1982) "RETE: A Fast Algorithm for the Many Pattern/Many Object Pattern Match Problem." *Artificial Intelligence* 19:17–37.

Franz Inc. (1988) *Common Lisp: the Reference*. Addison-Wesley.

Gabriel, Richard P. (1985) *Performance and evaluation of Lisp systems*. MIT Press.

Gabriel, Richard P. (1990) "Lisp." In *Encyclopedia of Artificial Intelligence*, ed. Stuart C. Shapiro. Wiley.

Galler, B. A., and M. J. Fisher. (1964) "An Improved Equivalence Algorithm." *Communications of the ACM* 7, no. 5:301–303.

Gazdar, Richard, and Chris Mellish. (1989) *Natural Language Processing in Lisp*. Addison-Wesley. Also published simultaneously: *Natural Language Processing in Prolog*.

Genesereth, Michael R., and Matthew L. Ginsberg. (1985) "Logic Programming." *Communications of the ACM* 28, no. 9:933–941.

Genesereth, Michael R., and Nils J. Nilsson. (1987) *Logical Foundations of Artificial Intelligence*. Morgan Kaufmann.

Giannesini, Francis, H. Kanoui, R. Pasero, and M. van Caneghem. (1986) *Prolog*. Addison-Wesley.

Ginsberg, Matthew L. (1987) *Readings in NonMonotonic Reasoning*. Morgan Kaufmann.

Ginsberg, Matthew L., and William D. Harvey. (1990) "Iterative Broadening." *Proceedings, Eighth National Conference on AI*, 216–220.

Goldberg, Adele, and David Robinson. (1983) *Smalltalk-80: The Language and its Implementation*. Addison-Wesley.

Goldberg, David E. (1989) *Genetic Algorithms in Search, Optimization and Machine Learning*. Addison-Wesley.

Gordon, Jean, and Edward H. Shortliffe. (1984) "The Dempster-Shafer Theory of Evidence." In Buchanan and Shortliffe 1984.

Green, Cordell. (1968) "Theorem-proving by resolution as a basis for question-answering systems." In *Machine Intelligence 4*, ed. Bernard Meltzer and Donald Michie. 183–205. Edinburgh University Press.

Grosz, Barbara J., Karen Sparck-Jones, and Bonnie Lynn Webber. (1986) *Readings in Natural Language Processing*. Morgan Kaufmann.

Guzman, Adolfo. (1968) "Computer Recognition of Three-Dimensional Objects in a Visual Scene." Ph.D. thesis, MAC-TR-59, Project MAC, MIT.

Hafner, Carole, and Bruce Wilcox. (1974) *LISP/MTS Programmer's Guide*. Mental Health Research Institute Communication no. 302, University of Michigan.

Harris, Zellig S. (1982) *A Grammar of English on Mathematical Principles*. Wiley.

Hasemer, Tony, and John Domingue. (1989) *Common Lisp Programming for Artificial Intelligence*. Addison-Wesley.

Hayes, Patrick. "Naive Physics I: Ontology for Liquids." In Hobbs and Moore 1985.

Heckerman, David. (1986) "Probabilistic Interpretations for Mycin's Certainty Factors." In *Uncertainty in Artificial Intelligence*, ed. L. N. Kanal and J. F. Lemmer. Elsevier (North-Holland). Reprinted in Shafer and Pearl 1990.

Hennessey, Wade L. (1989) *Common Lisp*. McGraw-Hill.

Hewitt, Carl. (1977) "Viewing Control Structures as Patterns of Passing Messages." *Artificial Intelligence* 8, no. 3:323–384.

Hobbs, Jerry R., and Robert C. Moore. (1985) *Formal Theories of the Commonsense World*. Ablex.

Hofstader, Douglas R. (1979) *Godel, Escher, Bach: An Eternal Golden Braid*. Vintage.

Hölldobler, Steffen. (1987) *Foundations of Equational Logic Programming*, Springer-Verlag Lecture Notes in Artificial Intelligence.

Huddleston, Rodney. (1984) *Introduction to the Grammar of English*. Cambridge University Press.

Huffman, David A. (1971) "Impossible Objects as Nonsense Pictures." 295–323. In *Machine Intelligence 6*, ed. B. Meltzer and D. Michie. Edinburgh University Press.

Hughes, R. J. M. (1985) "Lazy Memo Functions." In *Proceedings of the Conference on Functional Programming and Computer Architecture*, Nancy, 129–146. Springer-Verlag.

Ingerman, Peter Z. (1961) "Thunks." *Communications of the ACM* 4, no. 1:55–58.

Jaffar, Joxan, Jean-Louis Lassez, and Michael J. Maher. (1984) "A Theory of Complete Logic Programs with Equality." *Journal of Logic Programming* 3:211–223.

Jackson, Peter. (1990) *Introduction to Expert Systems*. 2d ed. Addison-Wesley.

James, Glenn, and Robert C. James. (1949) *Mathematics Dictionary*. Van Nostrand.

Kanal, L. N., and J. F. Lemmer. (1986) *Uncertainty in Artificial Intelligence*. North-Holland.

Kanal, L. N., and J. F. Lemmer. (1988) *Uncertainty in Artificial Intelligence 2*. North-Holland.

Kay, Alan. (1969) "The Reactive Engine." Ph.D. thesis, University of Utah.

Kay, Martin. (1980) *Algorithm schemata and data structures in syntactic processing*. Xerox Palo Alto Research Center Report CSL-80-12. Reprinted in Grosz et al. 1986.

Kernighan, B. W., and P. J. Plauger. (1974) *The Elements of Programming Style*. McGraw-Hill.

Kernighan, B. W., and P. J. Plauger. (1981) *Software Tools in Pascal*. Addison-Wesley.

Keene, Sonya. (1989) *Object-Oriented Programming in Common Lisp: A Programmer's Guide to CLOS*. Addison-Wesley.

Knight, K. (1989) "Unification: A Multidisciplinary Survey." *ACM Computing Surveys*, 21, no. 1:93–121.

Knuth, Donald E., and Robert W. Moore. (1975) "An Analysis of Alpha-Beta Pruning." *Artificial Intelligence*, 6, no. 4:293–326.

Kohlbecker, Eugene Edmund, Jr. (1986) "Syntactic Extensions in the Programming Language Lisp." Ph.D. thesis, Indiana University.

Korf, R. E. (1985) "Depth-first Iterative Deepening: an Optimal Admissible Tree Search." *Artificial Intelligence* 27:97–109.

Kornfeld, W. A. (1983) "Equality for Prolog." *Proceedings of the Seventh IJCAI*, 514–519.

Koschman, Timothy. (1990) *The Common Lisp Companion.* Wiley.

Kowalski, Robert. (1974) "Predicate logic as a programming language." In *Proceedings of the IFIP-74 Congress*, 569–574. North-Holland.

Kowalski, Robert. (1979) "Algorithm = Logic + Control." *Communications of the ACM* 22:424–436.

Kowalski, Robert. (1980) *Logic for Problem Solving.* North-Holland.

Kowalski, Robert. (1988) "The Early Years of Logic Programming." *Communications of the ACM* 31:38–43.

Kranz, David, Richard Kelsey, Jonathan Rees, Paul Hudak, James Philbin, and Norman Adams. (1986) "ORBIT: An optimizing compiler for Scheme." SIGPLAN Compiler Construction Conference.

Kreutzer, Wolfgang, and Bruce McKenzie. (1990) *Programming for Artificial Intelligence: Methods, Tools and Applications.* Addison-Wesley.

Lakoff, George. (1987) *Women, Fire and Dangerous Things: What Categories Reveal About the Mind.* University of Chicago Press.

Landin, Peter. (1965) "A Correspondence Between Algol 60 and Church's Lambda Notation." *Communications of the ACM* 8, no. 2:89–101.

Lang, Kevin J., and Barak A. Perlmutter. (1988) "Oaklisp: An Object-Oriented Dialect of Scheme." *Lisp and Symbolic Computing* 1:39-51.

Langacker, Ronald W. (1967) *Language and its Structure.* Harcourt, Brace & World.

Lassez, J.-L., M. J. Maher, and K. Marriott. (1988) "Unification Revisited." In *Foundations of Deductive Databases and Logic Programming,* ed. J. Minker, 587–625. Morgan Kaufmann.

Lee, Kai-Fu, and Sanjoy Mahajan. (1986) "Bill: A Table-Based, Knowledge-Intensive Othello Program." Technical Report CMU-CS-86-141, Carnegie Mellon University.

Lee, Kai-Fu, and Sanjoy Mahajan. (1990) "The Development of a World Class Othello Program." *Artificial Intelligence* 43:21–36.

Levesque, Hector. (1986) "Making Believers out of Computers." *Artificial Intelligence* 30:81–108.

Levy, David N. L. (1976) *Computer Chess*. Batsford.

Levy, David N. L. (1988) *Computer Games*. Springer-Verlag.

Levy, David N. L. (1988) *Computer Chess Compendium*. Springer-Verlag.

Levy, David N. L. (1990) *Heuristic Programming in Artificial Intelligence: the First Computer Olympiad*. Ellis Horwood.

Lloyd, J. W. (1987) *Foundations of Logic Programming*. Springer-Verlag.

Loomis, Lynn. (1974) *Calculus*. Addison-Wesley.

Loveland, D. W. (1987) "Near-Horn Prolog." *Proceedings of the Fourth International Conference on Logic Programming*, 456–469.

Luger, George F., and William A. Stubblefield, (1989) *Artificial Intelligence and the Design of Expert Systems*. Benjamin/Cummings.

Maier, David, and David S. Warren. (1988) *Computing with Logic*. Benjamin/Cummings

Marsland, T. A. (1990) "Computer Chess Methods." Entry in *Encyclopedia of Artificial Intelligence*, ed. Stuart C. Shapiro. Wiley.

Martin, William A., and Richard J. Fateman. (1971) "The MACSYMA System." *Proceedings of the Second Symposium on Symbolic and Algebraic Manipulation*, 59–75, ACM SIGSAM.

Masinter, Larry, and Peter Deutsch, (1980) "Local Optimization in a Compiler for Stack-Based Lisp Machines." *Proceedings of the Lisp and Functional Programming Conference*.

McAllester, David. (1982) "Reasoning Utility Package User's Manual." AI Memo 667, AI Lab, MIT.

McCarthy, John. (1958) "An Algebraic Language for the Manipulation of Symbolic Expressions." AI Lab Memo no. 1, MIT.

McCarthy, John. (1960) "Recursive functions of symbolic expressions and their computation by machine." *Communications of the ACM* 3, no 3:184–195.

McCarthy, John. (1963) "A basis for a mathematical theory of computation." In *Computer Programming and Formal Systems*, ed. P. Braffort and D. Hirschberg. North-Holland.

McCarthy, John. (1968) "Programs with Common Sense." In Minsky 1968. Reprinted in Brachman and Levesque 1985.

McCarthy, John. (1978) "History of Lisp." In *History of Programming Languages*, ed. Richard W. Wexelblat. Academic Press. Also in *ACM SIGPLAN Notices* 13, no. 8.

McCarthy, John, P. W. Abrahams, D. J. Edwards, P. A. Fox, T. P. Hart, and M. J. Levin. (1962) *Lisp 1.5 Programmer's Manual*. MIT Press.

McDermott, Drew. (1978) "Tarskian Semantics, or No Notation without Denotation!" *Cognitive Science*, 2:277–282. Reprinted in Grosz, Sparck-Jones and Webber 1986.

McDermott, Drew. (1987) "A Critique of Pure Reason." *Computational Intelligence* 3:151–160.

Meyer, Bertrand. (1988) *Object-oriented Software Construction*. Prentice-Hall.

Michie, Donald. (1968) "Memo Functions and Machine Learning." *Nature* 218:19–22.

Miller, Molly M., and Eric Benson. (1990) *Lisp Style & Design*. Digital Press.

Minsky, Marvin. (1968) *Semantic Information Processing*. MIT Press.

Miranker, Daniel. (1990) *TREAT: A New and Efficient Match Algorithm for AI Production Systems*. Pitman.

Moon, David. (1986) "Object-Oriented Programming with Flavors." *Proceedings of the ACM Conference on Object-Oriented Systems, Languages and Applications*.

Moon, David and Richard Stallman and Daniel Weinreb. (1983) *The Lisp Machine Manual*. AI Lab, MIT.

Moore, Robert C. (1982) "The Role of Logic in Knowledge Representation and Commonsense Reasoning." *Proceedings of the AAAI-82*. Reprinted in Brachman and Levesque 1985.

Moses, Joel. (1967) "Symbolic Integration." Report no. MAC-TR-47, Project MAC, MIT.

Moses, Joel. (1975) "A MACSYMA Primer." Mathlab Memo no. 2, Computer Science Lab, MIT.

Mueller, Robert A., and Rex L. Page. (1988) *Symbolic Computing with Lisp and Prolog*. Wiley.

Musser, David R., and Alexander A. Stepanov. (1989) *The ADA Generic Library*. Springer-Verlag.

Naish, Lee. (1986) *Negation and Control in Prolog.* Springer-Verlag Lecture Notes in Computer Science 238.

Newell, Alan, J. C. Shaw, and Herbert A. Simon. (1963) "Chess-Playing Programs and the Problem of Complexity." In Feigenbaum and Feldman 1963, 39–70.

Newell, Alan, and Herbert A. Simon. (1963) "GPS, A Program that Simulates Human Thought." In Feigenbaum and Feldman 1963, 279–293. Reprinted in Allen, Hendler, and Tate 1990.

Newell, Alan, and Herbert A. Simon, (1972) *Human Problem Solving.* Prentice-Hall.

Nilsson, Nils. (1971) *Problem-Solving Methods in Artificial Intelligence.* McGraw-Hill.

Norvig, Peter. (1991) "Correcting a Widespread Error in Unification Algorithms." *Software Practice and Experience* 21, no. 2:231–233.

Nygaard, Kristen, and Ole-Johan Dahl. (1981) "SIMULA 67." In *History of Programming Languages,* ed. Richard W. Wexelblat.

O'Keefe, Richard. (1990) *The Craft of Prolog.* MIT Press.

Pearl, Judea. (1984) *Heuristics: Intelligent Search Strategies for Computer Problem Solving.* Addison-Wesley.

Pearl, Judea. (1988) *Probabilistic Reasoning in Intelligent Systems: Networks of Plausible Inference.* Morgan Kaufmann.

Pearl, Judea. (1989) "Bayesian and Belief-Functions Formalisms for Evidential Reasoning: A Conceptual Analysis." *Proceedings, Fifth Israeli Symposium on Artificial Intelligence.* Reprinted in Shafer and Pearl 1990.

Pereira, Fernando C. N., and Stuart M. Shieber. (1987) *Prolog and Natural-Language Analysis.* Center for the Study of Language and Information, Lecture Notes no. 10.

Pereira, Fernando C. N., and David H. D. Warren. (1980) "Definite clause grammars for language analysis—a survey of the formalism and a comparison with augmented transition networks." *Artificial Intelligence* 13:231–278. Reprinted in Grosz et al. 1986.

Perlis, Alan. (1982) "Epigrams on Programming." *ACM SIGPLAN Notices* 17, no. 9.

Plaisted, David A. (1988) "Non-Horn Clause Logic Programming Without Contrapositives." *Journal of Automated Reasoning* 4:287–325.

Quillian, M. Ross. (1967) "Word Concepts: A Theory of Simulation of Some Basic Semantic Capabilities." *Behavioral Science* 12:410–430. Reprinted in Brachman and Levesque 1985.

Quirk, Randolph, Sidney Greenbaum, Geoffrey Leech, and Jan Svartik. (1985) *A Comprehensive Grammar of the English Language*. Longman.

Ramsey, Allan, and Rosalind Barrett. (1987) *AI in Practice: Examples in Pop-11*. Halstead Press.

Rich, Elaine, and Kevin Knight. (1991) *Artificial Intelligence*. McGraw-Hill.

Risch, R. H. (1969) "The Problem of Integration in Finite Terms." *Translations of the A.M.S.* 139:167–189.

Risch, R. H. (1979) "Algebraic Properties of the Elementary Functions of Analysis." *American Journal of Mathematics* 101:743–759.

Robinson, J. A. (1965) "A Machine-Oriented Logic Based on the Resolution Principle," *Journal of the ACM* 12, no. 1:23–41.

Rosenbloom, Paul S. (1982) "A World-Championship-Level Othello Program." *Artificial Intelligence* 19:279–320.

Roussel, Phillipe. (1975) *Prolog: manual de reference et d'utilization*. Groupe d'Intelligence Artificielle, Université d'Aix-Marseille.

Rowe, Neal. (1988) *Artificial Intelligence Through Prolog*. Prentice-Hall.

Ruf, Erik, and Daniel Weise. (1990) "LogScheme: Integrating Logic Programming into Scheme." *Lisp and Symbolic Computation* 3, no. 3:245–288.

Russell, Stuart. (1985) "The Compleat Guide to MRS." Computer Science Dept. Report no. STAN-CS-85-1080, Stanford University.

Russell, Stuart, and Eric Wefald. (1989) "On Optimal Game-Tree Search using Rational Meta-Reasoning." *Proceedings of the International Joint Conference on Artificial Intelligence*, 334–340.

Sacerdoti, Earl. (1974) "Planning in a Hierarchy of Abstraction Spaces." *Artificial Intelligence* 5:115–135. Reprinted in Allen, Hendler, and Tate 1990.

Sager, Naomi. (1981) *Natural Language Information Processing*. Addison-Wesley.

Samuel, A. L. (1959) "Some Studies in Machine Learning Using the Game of Checkers." *IBM Journal of Research and Development* 3:210–229. Reprinted in Feigenbaum and Feldman 1963.

Sangal, Rajeev. (1991) *Programming Paradigms in Lisp*. McGraw Hill.

Schank, Roger C., and Kenneth Mark Colby. (1973) *Computer Models of Thought and Language*. Freeman.

Schank, Roger C., and Christopher Riesbeck. (1981) *Inside Computer Understanding.* Lawrence Erlbaum.

Schmolze, J. G., and T. A. Lipkis. (1983) "Classification in the KL-ONE Knowledge Representation System." *Proceedings of the Eighth IJCAI.* 330–332.

Sedgewick, Robert. (1988) *Algorithms.* Addison-Wesley.

Shannon, Claude E. (1950a) "Programming a Digital Computer for Playing Chess." *Philosophy Magazine* 41:356–375.

Shannon, Claude E. (1950b) "Automatic Chess Player." *Scientific American*, Feb., 182.

Shebs, Stan T., and Robert R. Kessler. (1987) "Automatic Design and Implementation of Language Data Types." *SIGPLAN 87 Symposium on Interpreters and Interpretive Techniques (ACM SIGPLAN Notices* 22, no. 7:26–37.

Shapiro, Stuart C. (ed.). (1990) *Encyclopedia of Artificial Intelligence.* Wiley.

Shafer, Glenn, and Judea Pearl. (1990) *Readings in Uncertain Reasoning.* Morgan Kaufmann.

Sheil, B. A. (1983) "Power Tools for Programmers." *Datamation*, Feb., 131–144.

Shortliffe, Edward H. (1976) *Computer-Based Medical Consultation: MYCIN.* American Elsevier.

Shortliffe, Edward H., and Bruce G. Buchanan (1975) "A Model of Inexact reasoning in Medicine." *Mathematical Biosciences*, 23:351–379. Reprinted in Shafer and Pearl 1990.

Slade, Richard. (1987) *The T Programming Language: A Dialect of Lisp.* Prentice Hall.

Slagle, J. R. (1963) "A heuristic program that solves symbolic integration problems in freshman calculus." In *Computers and Thought,* ed. Feigenbaum and Feldman, 191–203. Also in *Journal of the ACM* 10:507–520.

Spiegelhalter, David J. (1986) "A Statistical View of Uncertainty in Expert Systems." In *Artificial Intelligence and Statistics,* ed. W. Gale. Addison-Wesley. Reprinted in Shafer and Pearl 1990.

Staples, John, and Peter J. Robinson. (1988) "Efficient Unification of Quantified Terms." *Journal of Logic Programming* 5:133–149.

Steele, Guy L., Jr. (1976a) "LAMBDA: The Ultimate Imperative." AI Lab Memo 353, MIT.

Steele, Guy L., Jr. (1976b) "LAMBDA: The Ultimate Declarative." AI Lab Memo 379, MIT.

Steele, Guy L., Jr. (1977) "Debunking the 'Expensive Procedure Call' Myth or, Procedure Call Implementations Considered Harmful or, LAMBDA: The Ultimate GOTO." AI Lab Memo 443, MIT.

Steele, Guy L., Jr., (1978) "Rabbit: a Compiler for Scheme (A Study in Compiler Optimization)." AI Lab Technical Report 474, MIT.

Steele, Guy L. Jr., (1983) "Compiler optimization based on viewing lambda as Rename Plus Goto." In *AI: An MIT Perspective,* vol. 2. MIT Press.

Steele, Guy L. Jr., (1984) *Common Lisp the Language.* Digital Press.

Steele, Guy L. Jr., (1990) *Common Lisp the Language,* 2d edition. Digital Press.

Steele, Guy L., Jr., and Gerald J. Sussman. (1978) "The revised report on Scheme, a dialect of Lisp." AI Lab Memo 452, MIT.

Steele, Guy L., Jr., and Gerald J. Sussman. (1978) "The art of the interpreter, or the modularity complex (parts zero, one, and two)." AI Lab Memo 453, MIT.

Steele, Guy L., Jr., and Gerald Jay Sussman. (1979) "Design of LISP-Based Processors or, SCHEME: A Dielectric LISP or, Finite Memories Considered Harmful or, LAMBDA: The Ultimate Opcode." AI Lab Memo 379, MIT.

Steele, Guy L., Jr., and Gerald J. Sussman. (1980) "Design of a Lisp-Based Processor." *Communications of the ACM* 23, no. 11:628-645.

Stefik, Mark, and Daniel G. Bobrow. (1986) "Object-Oriented Programming: Themes and Variations." *AI Magazine* 6, no. 4.

Sterling, Leon, and Ehud Shapiro. (1986) *The Art of Prolog.* MIT Press.

Sterling, L., A. Bundy, L. Byrd, R. O'Keefe and B. Silver. (1982) "Solving Symbolic Equations with PRESS." In *Computer Algebra, Lecture Notes in Computer Science No. 144,* ed. J. Calmet, 109-116. Springer-Verlag. Also in *Journal of Symbolic Computation* 7 (1989):71–84.

Stickel, Mark. (1988) "A Prolog Technology Theorem Prover: Implementation by an Extended Prolog Compiler." *Journal of Automated Reasoning* 4:353–380.

Stoyan, Herbert. (1984) "Early Lisp History." *Proceedings of the Lisp and Functional Programming Conference,* 299–310.

Stroustrup, Bjarne. (1986) *The C++ Programming Language.* Addison-Wesley.

Sussman, Gerald J. (1973) *A Computer Model of Skill Acquisition*. Elsevier.

Tanimoto, Steven. (1990) *The Elements of Artificial Intelligence using Common Lisp*. Computer Science Press.

Tate, Austin. (1977) "Generating Project Networks." IJCAI-77, Boston. Reprinted in Allen, Hendler, and Tate 1990.

Tater, Deborah G. (1987) *A Programmer's Guide to Common Lisp*. Digital Press.

Thomason, Richmond. (1974) *Formal Philosophy—Selected Papers of Richard Montague*. Yale University Press.

Touretzky, David. (1989) *Common Lisp: A Gentle Introduction to Symbolic Computation*. Benjamin/Cummings.

Tversky, Amos, and Daniel Kahneman. (1974) "Judgement Under Uncertainty: Heuristics and Biases." *Science* 185:1124–1131. Reprinted in Shafer and Pearl 1990.

Tversky, Amos, and Daniel Kahneman. (1983) "Extensional Versus Intuitive Reasoning: The Conjunction Fallacy in Probability Judgement." *Psychological Review* 90:29–315.

Tversky, Amos, and Daniel Kahneman. (1986) "Rational Choices and the Framing of Decisions." *Journal of Business* 59:S251-S278. Reprinted in Shafer and Pearl 1990.

Ungar, David. (1984) "Generation Scavenging: A Non-Disruptive High Performance Storage Reclamation Algorithm." In *Proceedings of the ACM SIGSOFT/SIGPLAN Software Engineering Symposium on Practical Software Development Environments* (Pittsburgh, Pa., April), 157–167. *ACM SIGPLAN Notices* 19, no. 5.

van Emden, Maarten H., and Keitaro Yukawa. (1987) "Logic Programming with Equations." *Journal of Logic Programming* 4:265–288.

van Melle, W. J. (1980) *System Aids in Constructing Consultation Programs*. UMI Research Press.

Van Roy, Peter L., (1990) "Can Logic Programming Execute as Fast as Imperative Programming?" Report UCB/CSD 90/600, University of California, Berkeley.

Vygotsky, Lev Semenovich. (1962) *Thought and Language*. MIT Press.

Waibel, Alex, and Kai-Fu Lee (1991) *Readings in Speech Understanding*. Morgan Kaufmann.

Waldinger, Richard. (1977) "Achieving Several Goals Simultaneously." In *Machine Intelligence 8*. Ellis Horwood Limited.

Walker, Adrian, Michael McCord, John F. Sowa, and Walter G. Wilson. (1990) *Knowledge Systems and Prolog.* Addison-Wesley.

Waltz, David I. (1975) "Understanding Line Drawings of Scenes with Shadows." In *The Psychology of Computer Vision*, ed. Patrick H. Winston. McGraw-Hill.

Waltz, David I. (1990) "Waltz Filtering." In *Encyclopedia of Artificial Intelligence,* ed. Stuart C. Shapiro. Wiley.

Wand, Mitchell. (1980) "Continuation-Based Program Transformation Strategies." *Journal of the ACM* 27, no. 1:174–180.

Warren, David H. D. (1974a) "WARPLAN: A System for Generating Plans." Department of Computational Logic Memo 76, AI, Edinburgh University.

Warren, David H. D. (1974b) "Extract from APIC Studies in Data Processing, No. 24." Reprinted in Allen, Hendler, and Tate, 1990.

Warren, David H. D. (1979) "Prolog on the DECsystem-10." In *Expert Systems in the Micro-Electronic Age*, ed. Donald Michie. Edinburgh University Press.

Warren, David H. D. (1983) *An abstract Prolog instruction set.* Technical Note 309, SRI International.

Warren, David H. D., L. M. Pereira, and Fernando C. N. Pereira. (1977) "Prolog—the Language and its Implementation Compared with Lisp." *Proceedings of the ACM SIGART-SIGPLAN Symposium on AI and Programming Languages.*

Warren, David H. D., and Fernando C. N. Pereira. (1982) "An Efficient Easily Adaptable System for Interpreting Natural Language Queries." *American Journal of Computational Linguistics*, 8, nos.3–4:110–122.

Waterman, David A. (1986) *A Guide to Expert Systems.* Addison-Wesley.

Waters, Richard C. (1991) "Supporting the Regression Testing of Lisp Programs." *Lisp Pointers* 4, no. 2:47–53.

Wegner, Peter. (1987) "Dimensions of object-based language design." *ACM SIGPLAN Notices*, 168–182.

Weinreb, Daniel, and David A. Moon (1980) "Flavors: Message Passing in the Lisp Machine." AI Memo no. 602, Project MAC, MIT.

Weiss, Sholom M., and Casimar A. Kulikowski. (1984) *A Practical Guide to Designing Expert Systems.* Rowman & Allanheld.

Weissman, Clark. (1967) *Lisp 1.5 Primer.* Dickenson.

Weizenbaum, Joseph. (1966) "ELIZA—A computer program for the study of natural language communication between men and machines." *Communications of the ACM* 9:36–45.

Weizenbaum, Joseph. (1976) *Computer Power and Human Reason.* Freeman.

Whorf, Benjamin Lee. (1956) *Language, Thought, and Reality.* MIT Press.

Wilensky, Robert. (1986) *Common LISPcraft.* Norton.

Winograd, Terry. (1983) *Language as a Cognitive Process.* Addison-Wesley.

Winston, Patrick H. (1975) *The Psychology of Computer Vision.* McGraw-Hill.

Winston, Patrick H. (1984) *Artificial Intelligence.* Addison-Wesley.

Winston, Patrick H., and Bertold K. P. Horn. (1988) *Lisp,* 3d ed. Addison-Wesley.

Wirth, N. (1976) *Algorithms + Data Structures = Programs.* Prentice Hall.

Wong, Douglas. (1981) "Language Comprehension in a Problem Solver." *Proceedings of the International Joint Conference on Artificial Intelligence,* 7–12.

Woods, William A. (1970) "Transition Network Grammars for Natural Language Analysis." *Communications of the ACM* 13:591–606. Reprinted in Grosz et al. 1986.

Woods, William A. (1975) "What's in a Link: Foundations for Semantic Networks." In *Representation and Understanding,* ed. D. G. Bobrow and A. M. Collins. Academic Press.

Woods, William A. (1977) "Lunar Rocks on Natural English: Explorations in Natural Language Question Answering." In *Linguistic Structures Processing,* ed. A. Zamponi. Elsevier-North-Holland.

Zabih, Ramin, David McAllester, and David Chapman. (1987) "Non-Deterministic Lisp with Dependency-Directed Backtracking." *Proceedings of the AAAI.*

Zadeh, Lotfi. (1978) "Fuzzy Sets as a Basis for a Theory of Possibility." *Fuzzy Sets Systems,* 1:3–28.

Zucker, S. W. (1990) "Vision, Early." In *Encyclopedia of Artificial Intelligence,* ed. Stuart C. Shapiro. Wiley.

Index